CROSSCURRENTS
Reading in the Disciplines

Eric Carl Link

University of Memphis

Steven Frye

California State University, Bakersfield

Boston • Columbus • Indianapolis • New York • San Francisco • Upper Saddle River
Amsterdam • Cape Town • Dubai • London • Madrid • Milan • Munich • Paris • Montréal • Toronto
Delhi • Mexico City • São Paulo • Sydney • Hong Kong • Seoul • Singapore • Taipei • Tokyo

Senior Acquisitions Editor: Brad Pottoff
Director of Development: Mary Ellen Curley
Senior Development Editor: Anne Brunell Ehrenworth
Senior Marketing Manager: Sandra McGuire
Senior Supplements Editor: Donna Campion
Executive Digital Producer: Stefanie Snajder
Digital Project Manager: Janell Lantana
Digital Editor: Sara Gordus
Production/Project Manager: Eric Jorgensen

Project Coordination, Editorial Services, and Text Design: Electronic Publishing Services Inc., NYC
Art Rendering and Electronic Page Makeup: Jouve
Cover Designer/Manager: Wendy Ann Fredericks
Cover Photos: Top: © Gary Crabbe/Age Fotostock; Bottom: iStockphoto
Senior Manufacturing Buyer: Dennis J. Para
Printer/Binder: LSC Communications
Cover Printer: LSC Communications

Credits and acknowledgments borrowed from other sources and reproduced, with permission, in this textbook appear on the appropriate page within text.

Library of Congress Cataloging-in-Publication Data

Link, Eric Carl.
  Crosscurrents : reading in the disciplines / Eric Carl Link, Steven Frye.
    p. cm.
  Includes index.
  ISBN-13: 978-0-205-78461-5
  ISBN-10: 0-205-78461-5
  1. English language—Rhetoric—Handbooks, manuals, etc.   2. College readers.   I. Frye, Steven.   II. Title.
  PE1408.L566 2013
  808'.0427—dc23

                                                                              2012018838

14   17

www.pearsonhighered.com

Student ISBN 10: 0-205-78461-5
ISBN 13: 978-0-205-78461-5
Exam ISBN 10: 0-205-23819-X
ISBN 13: 978-0-205-23819-4

*Eric Carl Link dedicates this volume to Laura,
Sarah, Nathaniel, Natalie, and Nolan with love.*

*Steven Frye dedicates this volume to Kristin,
Melissa, and Thomas with love.*

Contents

Chapter 3   Writing and Researching: Genres, Practices, and Processes   36

PART 2   ANTHOLOGY OF READINGS

Chapter 4   Nature, Genetics, and the Philosophy of Science   77

Introduction   77

Emily Martin, et. al., "Scientific Literacy, What It Is, Why It's Important, and Why Scientists Think We Don't Have It"   *81*
"The 'facts' of science, important as they are, can never be more than tiny pieces of the maps that people devise to guide them in life."

Foundations in the Philosophy of Science

Thomas Kuhn, "The Historical Structure of Scientific Discovery"   *88*
"Many scientific discoveries, particularly the most interesting and important, are not the sort of event about which the questions 'Where' and, more particularly, 'When' can appropriately be asked."

Paul Feyerabend, from *Against Method*   *95*
"The idea that science can, and should, be run according to fixed and universal rules, is both unrealistic and pernicious."

The Tools of Science: A World Too Small to See   *104*

Genetics and Human Identity

Barry Commoner, "Unraveling the DNA Myth"   *106*
"There is persistent public concern not only with the safety of genetically engineered foods but also with the inherent dangers in arbitrarily overriding patterns of inheritance that are embedded in the natural world through long evolutionary experience."

Francis Fukuyama, "Why We Should Worry"   *113*
"Hanging over the entire field of genetics has been the specter of eugenics—that is, the deliberate breeding of people for certain selected heritable traits."

Visions of the Posthuman   *122*

Michael J. Sandel, "The Case Against Perfection"   *124*
"When science moves faster than moral understanding, as it does today, men and women struggle to articulate their unease."

Olivia Judson, "The Selfless Gene"   *132*
"It's easy to see how evolution can account for the dark streaks in human nature—the violence, treachery, and cruelty. But how does it produce kindness, generosity, and heroism?"

Chapter 5 Business and Economics   155

Preface

Crosscurrents is a comprehensive, versatile reader that provides the readings and tools needed to support writing and to bring interdisciplinary ideas and texts into the classroom in order to make the world of ideas available and immediate for the next generation of global learners. Interdisciplinary reading and global awareness are the keys to success in the twenty-first century. The Internet, the smart phone, tablet computers, online communities, and other boundary-crossing technologies have made each of us citizens not just of a particular town or city or region or even country: in terms of the knowledge and information we access each day, we are truly global citizens. As human cultures blend and technologies make the gathering and sharing of information easier, it becomes clearer that the next generation of global citizens will need to have the ability to engage multiple disciplines, to think critically across traditional categories of knowledge, to merge science with business and the arts in increasingly creative and provocative ways.

Over the past twenty years, we have observed an increasing trend toward interdisciplinary studies at all levels and in all kinds of institutions of higher learning, from community colleges to liberal arts colleges, to state, regional, and national research universities. The trend is universal, and for good reason: our ability to read and write across multiple fields of knowledge is an essential and necessary characteristic of the educated citizen of the twenty-first century.

Writing across the curriculum recognizes that the next generation of global citizens will need to be educated in multiple disciplines and must be able to analyze and engage a marketplace of ideas in which the traditional boundaries between fields have been blurred. At the same time, students must have the reading and communication skills to be able to effectively engage with this marketplace, to bring new ideas and new ways of thinking to the vast intellectual conversation that defines the information age. It is an exciting time to be a learner in the modern college or university, and college reading and writing has become an integral part of a global, interdisciplinary education. Reading and writing across multiple disciplines—that is, reading *crosscurrently*—offers an opportunity to take another step towards global citizenship and engaged learning.

Reading and writing are the twin skills needed in all fields of knowledge for the communication of current ideas, the exchange of new ideas, and the growth of human enterprise in all respects. Reading and writing are not just a means to a certain type of communication: they are essential tools for learning itself. The act of writing and revising serves to develop cognitive skills, including the capacity to analyze, synthesize, and interpret course content. Perceived problems with writing and learning have led instructors in various disciplines to seek methods of collaboration with composition programs to enhance writing within and among academic categories. This cross disciplinary interchange has contributed to the development and success of writing across the curriculum programs nationwide. There is significant and growing need for collections of readings to support these approaches in composition classrooms.

Features

Crosscurrents contains a blend of disciplines and time frames. Each chapter in Part 2 contains foundational readings in a field of learning. These readings are drawn from the classical period through the early twentieth century and expose students to important materials emerging from a pre-modern context that inform the various disciplines today. Following these selections is a series of more contemporary readings. Within each section of recent selections are "sub-units" of grouped pieces that allow for concentrated focus around a common theme or subject and are designed for more in-depth comparison, contrast, and analysis of several themes and subjects. All of the readings are engaging in that they address the central concerns in the discipline today, but they also provide a host of different challenges for the reader, who will encounter a wide variety of styles, tones, and methods of argument and exposition. These selections are drawn from a variety of sources—books, academic journals, and general interest periodicals—and provide a wide range of choices that will engage students in an interdisciplinary conversation that is interesting, understandable, and most importantly, one that will lead to writing assignments that serve to develop both thinking and writing skills. This structure allows for a diversity of pedagogical strategies. The reader emphasizes contemporary writing. However, there are sufficient readings from the past to appeal to those who choose to explore through writing the foundations of various academic fields. In addition:

- A main table of contents linked to specific academic disciplines and departments, or a blend of related academic fields. This structure allows for ease of use in a variety of courses.

- An alternative table of contents (immediately following the appendix) organized by rhetorical strategy. Courses may be oriented in various ways, both thematically and in relation to formal genre conventions and structures.

- A comprehensive rhetoric in Part 1. This material orients readers to subjects perhaps outside their primary area of expertise. Three chapters cover the shared conventions of academic writing, the form and shape of the academic essay, differences in conventions among the disciplines, and the rhetorical strategies that emphasize research, persuasion, argumentation, analysis, and synthesis. Student sample papers in both draft and final form are included.

- Brief introductions to each chapter in Part 2. This prefatory material familiarizes readers to the particular discipline and its history, as well as its academic orientation and methods for creating knowledge and communicating that knowledge in writing. These introductions also highlight the commonalities within and among academic disciplines, and exposes readers to the evolving conventions of thought and expression in various academic areas.

- Brief headnotes before each reading in Part 2. Each writer is introduced with important biographical information, commentary on the writer's significance in the field, and a synopsis of the essential ideas contained in the selection. These segments allow readers to understand the person behind the words and provide both a human and a historical context for the material. These headnotes further provide a key to the intellectual content of the selection, allowing for greater understanding, as well as forming a basis for discussion and writing.

- Where appropriate, annotations to the primary texts. While not necessary for every selection, these carefully-crafted notes define difficult discipline-specific terminology, explain obscure references to other works, and clarify abstract concepts.

- Following each reading, a textual support section. Four question sets are included after every selection in the text. "Questions on Meaning" reinforce readers' understanding of the selection; "Questions for Discussion" provide a starting point for in-class exploration of the material in open conversation; "Looking at Rhetoric" questions ask readers to delve into the mechanics of the selections and assess the authors' writing strategies; and "Writing Assignments" present opportunities for researching and crafting writing projects. These devices enhance the text's ability to engage readers in critical reading and critical writing activities.

- A series of images in each chapter in Part 2. Photographs, posters, advertisements, fine art, cartoons, and film stills provide opportunities for students to engage in reading visuals and are accompanied by thoughtful questions designed to challenge and foster interdisciplinary engagement through visual imagery.

- End-of-chapter "Thinking Crosscurrently" questions. These thoughtful questions present opportunities for readers to capture the connections among writers, both within and outside the discipline, and in doing so, allow for cross-disciplinary interchange.

- An appendix entitled "Breaking Down Assignments." This guide provides readers with invaluable information on how to approach a writing assignment and craft a successful final product.

Focus on Technology

At a time when human knowledge is growing, technology is advancing at an ever-increasing pace. New ideas flood the intellectual landscape in waves and learning becomes both a necessary and indispensible human endeavor. *Crosscurrents* recognizes that technology is a significant part of both the reader's everyday experience—with smart phones, iPods, and tablet computers playing an increasing role in everyday engagement with the world—and a significant part of the modern educational experience, as instructors seek new methods of introducing technology-centered or technology-enhanced pedagogical strategies into the classroom. *Crosscurrents* provides numerous opportunities for readers to engage in a variety of discussions about technology:

- Chapter 4, "Nature, Genetics, and the Philosophy of Science," takes on technological advance, development, or the implications for the growth of understanding our world made possible by sophisticated scientific instruments. In addition, this chapter provides images that give readers a sense of old and new scientific instruments.

- Chapter 5, "Business and Economics," covers the business side of technological advance in Steve Denning's "Why Amazon Can't Make a Kindle in the USA." Alissa Quart examines the clash in popular culture between the educational claims of certain new media products and the hopes and desires of the modern parent in "The Baby Genius Edutainment Complex."

- Chapter 7, "Education and Society," discusses the kind of expertise often needed to develop new technologies in the modern world, as in Malcolm Gladwell's "The 10,000 Hour Rule."

- Chapter 8, "Communication and Pop Culture," contains a selection on technology with a perennial interest—television: Noel Murray and Scott Tobias' "How Has the Culture of TV (and TV-Watching) Changed?"

- Chapter 9, "Philosophy and Psychology," presents an essay by A. M. Turing ("Computing Machinery and Intelligence") that was ahead of its time and deals with the issue of creating an artificially intelligent computer. Also in this chapter, the implications of rapid technological development are explored in radical and provocative ways by Ray Kurzweil in "The Law of Accelerating Returns."

- Chapter 11, "Literature, Language, and Art," contains James Tiptree's "The Last Flight of Doctor Ain," which looks at the frightening possibilities in the development of new virus strains. In addition, a series of images on art and medicine provides ample opportunity to discuss the changes in medical technology (and its artistic representation) over the years.

New paths to human understanding and the development of the global citizen require thinking in new ways and making connections among different fields of thought. The twenty-first century learner must avoid being swept downstream in the swift current of isolated rivers of knowledge. Instead, the modern learner must break out of the confines of well-worn intellectual pathways and begin to *think crosscurrently*.

Supplements

An accompanying Instructor's Manual provides a useful resource for choosing course readings, managing class discussions, and planning class activities. The manual contains summaries of all readings, possible answers to selected discussion questions, and activities that engage students in thinking critically about the issues covered in the text.

MyCompLab (*mycomplab.com*) integrates instruction, multimedia tutorials, and exercises for writing, grammar, and research with an online composing space and assessment tools. This seamless, flexible environment comes from extensive research in partnership with composition faculty and students across the country. It provides help for writers in the context of their writing, with functions for instructors' and peers' commentary. Special features include an e-portfolio, a bibliography tool, tutoring services, an assignment builder, and a gradebook and course-management organization created specifically for writing classes.

Acknowledgements

We are grateful to our friends and peers who provided ideas about the selections we've included in this book. We owe a debt of gratitude for the assistance, collaborative consultation, and suggestions of Milissa Ackerley, David Berry, Emerson Case, Dana Centeno, Daniel Cervi, Douglas Dodd, Christy Gavin, Abbas Grammy, Kristine Holloway, Charles MacQuarrie, Nadine Nichter, Adam Smith, Andy Troup, and Kimberly Walker. For their help with proofreading and readying the manuscript, we would like to thank Emily Marshall, Lisa Sikkink, and Geoffrey Emerson. Special thanks to Susan Popham and Cynthia Marshall, who helped craft the rhetoric portion of the book, and to Susan for preparing a stellar Instructor's Manual.

This book is the product of our many years of teaching and learning, both from our students and our peers. *Crosscurrents* has also been shaped by the many instructors who reviewed the book at various stages of development. Their input has helped us immeasurably: Avis M. Adams, Green River Community College; Jaime Anderson, Wake Technical Community College; Anthony T. Atkins, University of North Carolina—Wilmington; Anne Balay, Indiana University Northwest; Candace Boeck, San Diego State University; Michael Briggs, East Tennessee State University; Gene Browning, Austin Community College; William Carney, Cameron University; Leej Copperfield, Louisburg College; Scott Earle, Tacoma Community College; David Elias, Eastern Kentucky University; Ellen Francese, Berklee College of Music; Shauna Gobble, Northampton Community College; Gary Sue Goodman, University of California at Davis; Kimberly Greenfield, Lorain County Community College; John W. Hodgson, Cameron University; Kim Jackson, Tarrant County College—Northwest Campus; Erica Jacobs, George Mason University; Selin Kalostyan, Lehman College; Christy Kinnion, Wake Technical Community College; Michelle LaFrance, University of Massachusetts—Dartmouth; Elisabeth Liebert, Louisiana State University—Shreveport; Walter Lowe, Green River Community College; Erin McCoy, Jefferson Community and Technical College; Beatrice McKinsey, Grambling State University; David M. Merchant, Louisiana Tech University; Gary A. Negin, California State University; Angelia Northrip-Rivera, Missouri State University; Penny Piva, University of Massachusetts; Heather Rodgers, St. Charles Community College; Joseph Selvaggio, Three Rivers Community College; Guinevere Shaw, Bergen Community College; Diedra M. Taylor, Southern Illinois University—Edwardsville; Andrew S. Tomko, Bergen Community College; Andrea West, Midlands Technical College.

We also want to express our deepest appreciation for the excellent and always helpful editorial team at Pearson, especially Suzanne Phelps Chambers, Anne Brunell Ehrenworth, Laney Whitt, and Erica Schweitzer.

Eric Carl Link would like to express his thanks to his wife, Laura, and his children, Sarah, Nathaniel, Natalie, and Nolan, for all of their love, encouragement, and support.

Steven Frye would like to express his appreciation to his parents, Ed and Joann Frye, as well as his sister, Laura Myers, for their unstinting support over many years. And he would especially like to thank his wife, Kristin, for her strength, faith, and patience, as well as his children, Melissa and Thomas, for their energy and imagination.

CROSSCURRENTS

1 KNOWLEDGE, READING, AND WRITING ACROSS DISCIPLINES

PREPARING A FOUNDATION FOR LEARNING

All students share many of the same goals about academic success: to become smart, to be successful, to maintain good grades, to graduate and earn a coveted degree, and perhaps even continue their studies at a professional or graduate school.

More than anything, these goals about college success depend on how much you know. Although it may seem obvious, the foundation for success is knowledge. For example, if you earn an A in a course, it means that you know the material presented to you in that course. But therein lies the conundrum: most students think that knowledge is a thing that comes to them by the end of the course. However, for successful students and smart citizens, knowledge is more of a starting point rather than an ending goal. In other words, they start by knowing something, maybe just small bits of information, and they use those small pieces as a foundation upon which to build by adding further knowledge on the same topic, trying out other pieces of knowledge about different subjects in hopes that some will fit, and balancing all these pieces of new knowledge on top of what they already had. It is not by chance that a person ends up having built a spectacular castle, nor is it by chance that a person is an expert in a given field. It takes intellectual work to achieve expertise in a field, and people who become experts rarely wait for that knowledge to be given to them. Instead, these successful thinkers—these experts—are constantly building on the knowledge they have already learned and adding to that foundation.

You already have a good bit of information, of knowledge, that you can use as a foundation for the intellectual work you will encounter in college. With any topic, ask yourself,

- "What do I already know about this?"
- "What have I heard about this?"
- "Am I sure that I know these things, or do I just have a guess?"
- "What are people around me saying about this topic?"
- "Do they know this, or are they just guessing?"
- "What else do I need to learn about this topic?"

Inquisitive questions such as these can help you lay the foundation for learning more about a topic. As you learn more about that subject, you will also learn to keep your eyes and ears open for bits of information you encounter as you build that warehouse of knowledge.

Recognize, too, that knowledge and learning come from adding newly gathered information to a foundation of already known information. If you find that you know nothing about a topic, do not despair. Remind yourself of what you know about similar subjects; ask your friends or colleagues what they know about the issue; recognize all the dimensions of the topic that you will need to learn; perhaps do some background reading on that subject before you really begin. If these strategies still leave you knowing little, then take comfort in knowing that your instructor will also help you prepare for learning by giving you some background information for a new topic. Then you can enter your studies with some preparation beforehand; your work of learning in that area, thus, will be much more successful and interesting.

UNDERSTANDING GENRES

Writing comes in many different forms, called genres. These are written structures, commonly agreed on by workplaces, communities, and readers to be effective formats and patterns of organization. You are probably already familiar with many common academic genres: book reports, essays, textbooks, short stories, poems, oral reports, and many others that exemplify the work of academia. You are also probably familiar with many genres not traditionally associated with college, like texts, letters, emails, grocery lists, novels, newspaper stories, blogs, and others related to work outside of academia, although many of these same genres (like email, letters, and blogs) also exist in the world of higher education. The point is that each of these genres has a certain task or purpose, a function that has helped to shape that genre's structure so it best meets the needs of the community in which it functions. For example, you would not expect to see a grocery list that was written in lengthy paragraph-style prose; such a list would be too bulky and awkward for use in the grocery store as you try to remember what your food needs are. Alternatively, one would be less likely to see an academic essay written in bullet-point list; while such a list may certainly be true and valid, you would likely not find it to be a very effective text for helping you learn the intricacies of philosophical concepts. Instead, academic communities, called disciplines, have agreed over time that such concepts need more lengthy explanation and examination, more suitable for a prose essay, in which a writer attempts to make clear his or her thoughts on a topic.

In different disciplines, these genres vary as the needs of the community differ. For example, if the need of the discipline were to memorize certain facts, figures, or formula, one would expect to see such information in a chart or table. If the need of the discipline were to examine and expound upon certain abstract concepts, one would expect to read such written explorations in an essay. Every discipline has certain genres, which work best for explaining, disseminating, and learning its concepts. Familiarity with these genres will help you become a more effective writer in the disciplines.

Sciences

You would be more likely to read and write laboratory reports in the scientific disciplines, like biology, chemistry, and physics, than you would in a literature class. Laboratory reports serve a specific and necessary function in science disciplines: to show that the work accomplished meets the standard of acceptable methods and that the work can be repeatable by another scientist. If a lab report were to be read in a literature class, its function would likely be very different, perhaps as a specimen of text to be analyzed according to literary theories. Other types of genres in the scientific disciplines are proposals to conduct research or to secure funding, progress or informational reports, review essays for previously examined information about the same topic, and articles written to explain one's findings to other scientists.

Social Sciences

In the Social Sciences, one might expect to read several different kinds of genres, from philosophical essays about racial justice to more scientifically focused reports on surveys and geographic data. However, these disciplines would be less likely to communicate using poetry or reports of laboratory experiments. Scholars in the social sciences would also be likely to write proposals for approval to conduct research or to secure funding, progress reports, and articles to share one's research.

Humanities

In the Humanities, genres that are primarily focused on facts and figures—like laboratory reports or periodic tables—are rare. Instead, scholars in these fields work more with genres that attempt to examine and explain concepts as they are applicable to pieces of literature, language, art, and music. These genres are much more likely to be essay-like in structure, with a statement of belief—a thesis statement or argument—as the central focus of the rest of the text. For these scholars, such a genre works well to share one's ideas and beliefs, while also providing evidence to support that thesis along with helping to prove such a thesis in the readers' minds.

Genres Used Across Fields

Some genres are common across many disciplines. Aside from the common genres of letters, memos, and emails, which most people use to function in their workplaces, other genres are likely to be used in many different disciplines, with different purposes for similar structures. For example, one could expect to write essays in several different disciplines. While essays are less common in biology and chemistry, such texts do help to show a writer's thoughts and processes better than a bulleted list of activities. Many science instructors find such essays helpful for their students, as the students attempt to show how they arrived at a specific conclusion or finding.

Narratives—a chronological accounting of events and actions—are also very common assignments in many disciplines, like the sciences, the social sciences, and to an extent, the humanities. Indeed, narratives, perhaps just one or two paragraphs, are often found within other genres such as progress reports, essays, field reports, and research articles; in such instances, they serve a function of helping the writer explain a sequence of events in a way that is easily understood by readers.

Another common genre is that of a report, which is often similar to a narrative, in that it attempts to explain in detail a sequence of events, a chronologic accounting of actions, or some other similar gathering of information that is both useful for the writer to explain information and helpful for the reader in understanding that information.

LINKING THINKING, READING, AND WRITING

Another sense in which knowledge is an important starting point is for your work as a reader and a writer: successful college-level reading and writing means that you must know something in order to read more sophisticated texts about the topic and to write skillfully about it. Too many college students believe thinking, reading, and writing are separate skills that can be accomplished in isolation from each other. However, these three skills are largely intertwined; success in any one of these tastes requires that you combine all of them.

Like the preparatory work that can help you become a better learner, there are preparatory strategies for being a good reader and writer, too. To be a successful reader, you must already know certain reading strategies, like recognizing that a title is different than a paragraph or that each paragraph has a different topic. To prepare yourself to read a document, you should ask yourself, "What do I know about this topic? How does this topic relate to other topics? What else do I need to know about it?" Acquaint yourself with the genres of readings you will likely be assigned. If you've never read the transcripts of a court trial, you might find yourself very confused about why some things are mentioned, why some are stricken or left out of the trial, and why some things, like the main argument, are so mysteriously placed. You might find it necessary to read several transcripts before you really understand why some sections are more important than others. If you've never read a scientific report, you might wonder why the lengthy section titled "Materials and Methods" comes near the beginning, while the interesting information comes at the end and may be very short. The answers to these questions may not become clear until you read several different examples of scientific reports.

Before reading a document, conduct some preliminary work. Scan the contents, the headings, the subheadings: what do these tell you about the topic, the author, and the discipline of the author? Ask yourself what you already know about this subject and if you are likely to be surprised by anything that you read in the document. Such brief but important familiarization will make your work of reading new genres much more effective.

The same strategy—preliminary familiarization—can also be used with writing, too. To be an effective writer, it is helpful to be knowledgeable about your subject before you begin and to do a lot of research about your topic while you write. If you have never written a laboratory report, you should read several first to familiarize yourself with the kinds of things that get discussed in such reports and the kinds of things that are eliminated. The same is true of many genres and forms, from memos to sonnets. If you're attempting an unfamiliar form, it would be worthwhile to read several examples before you attempt to write in the new genre. Acquaint yourself with the standards of format, acceptable topics, writing style, and vocabulary of that discipline and genre before you start to write. The point is not to copy those documents word for word, which would be considered plagiarism, but instead to become familiar with the style expected by readers of that genre. As you do this kind of preliminary reading before writing, you will likely also learn more about the topic you are investigating.

LEARNING IN THE DISCIPLINES

Many students come to college certain of their intended major and how that major leads to the career they want. Other students wait a year, two, or even more before they declare a major. Both ways are fine choices. It usually takes some time, though, for students to realize that studying in a major is not quite the same as preparing for a career. You may know that you'd like to be a doctor, but do you know which major you will choose to get you to that goal? Will you be a Biology major? A Chemistry major? A Pre-health major? Genetics?

College majors are largely based around what we call **disciplines:** areas of study in which the courses have similar topics, methods of inquiry, and units of production. Some disciplines can be grouped by similarity in topic or by similarity in research method, with some disciplines having similarities in all areas. The people who study and work in each discipline are trained to apply certain methods to certain topics to produce certain kinds of scholarship or knowledge, like articles, books, theories, and products. While different disciplines may disagree about the provability of some types of knowledge or the usefulness of certain types of knowledge, there is a general consensus among scholars that the search for knowledge is a most fundamental principle of disciplinary work.

As you study in different courses, be aware that different disciplines have different ways of knowing and of demonstrating knowledge. For example, in many disciplines, scholars use empirical research—featuring topics of the physical world, things that can be touched, heard, seen, tasted, and/or smelled—to determine the kinds of knowledge they can produce. Scholars in other disciplines prefer research that is less empirical, but more abstract or theoretical, producing knowledge that is more intangible (sometimes called qualitative research), than in the physical world. Some disciplines, like mathematics and linguistics, value both theoretical and empirical research; thus, they form a discipline based more on similarity of topic of inquiry than on research methods. Across many disciplines, scholars conduct different types of research, applying their expertise of a topic to empirical research or theoretical research. Many fields also share a contemporary tendency to blur and blend disciplinary boundaries to develop new disciplines such as Biomedical Engineering (a blend of Biology, Medicine, Mechanical Engineering, and Chemistry). In this book, the introductory section to each discipline explains more about how scholars in each discipline work, think, and write. As you read each introduction, note the kinds of thoughts that define each discipline, as well as to how those definitions might shift from different eras and cultures.

CATEGORIZING ACADEMIC DISCIPLINES

As a general stereotype, academic disciplines can be categorized as either those that focus primarily on the physical world like Natural/Physical Science, Applied Science, and Mathematics; those that focus on people and their behaviors, like Behavioral Sciences, Social Sciences, and History; and those that focus on abstract concepts, like Humanities, Performing Arts, Fine Art, and Philosophy. In general terms, however, many scholars and many disciplines do cross-disciplinary or interdisciplinary work; History, which can be a social science-like reporting of facts and social behavior, can also focus on philosophical concepts as these concepts impact societies' past behaviors, like the study of religious beliefs that influenced military decisions in the Middle Ages. As scholars in all fields and disciplines continue to conduct really interesting work, they tend to find more ways in which their insights overlap and intermingle with other disciplines. You should be aware that most disciplines and areas of academic study are not always neatly circumscribed by disciplinary boundaries; it is this interdisciplinary freedom that often gives new academic work its most interesting findings.

Natural and Applied Sciences

Disciplines of the Natural and Applied Sciences, like Engineering, Medicine, Genetics, Computer Science, and Veterinary Medicine tend to think in terms of empirical research: facts, numbers, data, and other physical evidence. They study topics related to physical objects, like the earth, outer space, or chemicals. They have certain kinds of methods called empirical research, like laboratory experiments, field work, and observations, in which they study these topics. Scientists often observe phenomena repeatedly before gathering the results into a generalized theory. They most commonly write laboratory reports, research articles, grant proposals, and other documents explaining their work to general and specialized audiences. They may also apply their knowledge about physical science to the benefit of society, such as learning about the properties of gasoline in order to produce a better engine. These are fine ways of thinking: when we climb stairs, we like to know that it was real scientific knowledge, honed after many hundreds of experiments and observations, that determined the exact density of the cement, steel, and distance needed to withhold weight and movement on those stairs.

Social Sciences

Other disciplines, like Psychology, Sociology, Political Science, and Anthropology, deal with decision making and the how's and why's of human behavior. Some fields such as Research Psychology concern themselves primarily with conducting empirical research through laboratory experiments on animals and, if ethically possible, on humans too. These scholars tend to produce work focusing on facts and theories rather than applications of that knowledge. Scholars in this area are likely to produce journal articles describing the results of their experiments, to write laboratory reports, and grant proposals. They are very likely to use charts and tables of accurate data, and to use diagrams, images, and photographs of some of their work in order to help their readers understand the results produced. When we seek rehabilitation treatments, we want to know that the treatments prescribed have been thoroughly and repeatedly researched.

Applied social science fields, such as Clinical Psychology, then determine the best ways of putting that knowledge into practice. Scholars in these social scientific disciplines tend to study systems of people's behaviors through such methods as lengthy and detailed descriptions, observed behaviors, and surveys. They tend to write deeply descriptive reports, narratives, and studies, with lengthy discussions of how they produced that knowledge or came to those conclusions. They are just as likely to rely on numbers or quantitative data as other scientists, to use graphs and charts to show some of their data in their reports, and to theorize about predictive models or theories about future behaviors. Understanding why addicts behave the way they do is as important to successful rehabilitation as thoroughly researched rehabilitation treatments.

Business and Applied/Professional Studies

Disciplines such as business, education, and law often draw from a number of other academic fields as well as rely on the experience of successful practitioners. Study in these fields is usually intended to prepare students to themselves become successful practitioners in the field upon graduation. A writer in the business world may write a number of very practical documents such as emails and memos in addition to writing reports for various audiences. Research in education often consists of using techniques common in the social sciences including field observations, interviews, and surveys. Practitioners in these applied fields are often called upon to communicate with multiple audiences and in various genres. They may engage in interdisciplinary research using methods from many other fields and produce reports, grant proposals, and even routine communication with customers, clients, and coworkers.

History, Philosophy, and Religious Studies

As mentioned earlier, scholars in these disciplines also engage in cross-disciplinary research, borrowing the methods, styles, and genres of research from other fields. Because of the diversity of research approaches, scholars in these fields are defined more by their areas of focus than by their methods of research. In other words, these scholars tend to be grouped according to the topics they like to study, rather than by the methodology they use to conduct research. Sometimes these fields are grouped with Social Sciences because they tend to focus on people's social behaviors, but scholars in these fields also tend to consider people and society in conjunction with more abstract concepts, like justice, faith, and aesthetics, that are more typically grouped with Humanities disciplines. Scholars in these areas may conduct research that is based on observations of facts and other quantitative data, or they may conduct research that is more qualitative, interpretive, conceptual, and insightful. They tend to produce narrative accounts, deeply descriptive reports, and conceptual essays. The knowledge learned from these disciplines helps guide us in our individual and social behaviors by asking us to consider deeply how our decisions affect others.

Humanities

Disciplines in the Humanities focus on more abstract concepts and the interpretation of those concepts. Scholars in these disciplines, like Literature, Languages, Classics, and others, tend to examine closely a particular work or phenomenon rather than compiling repeated facts, like in the sciences. They also focus on abstract concepts, like justice, the nature of human existence, aesthetics, humor, and other ideas that occupy our thoughts and our behaviors. When we study in these areas, we learn about ourselves and about the inner lives of others. Scholars in these disciplines are less likely to use quantitative data and instead rely on qualitative evidence to support their claims. They are more likely to analyze. For example, a language scholar might re-translate a historically significant text and reinterpret it using that updated translation; a literary critic might analyze a text through a particular theoretical perspective and, using both theory and evidence from the text itself, argue for a particular interpretation of the work. They are less likely to use charts, graphs, and tables. Instead, their data is included in essays.

Creative Arts

Sometimes Creative Arts practitioners are considered part of the Humanities, and sometimes they are considered their own separate field. These fields concern themselves with the study and critique of art and music. Although practitioners in the Creative Arts might produce works *about* other works of art or artists, the primary focus in many of these fields is on hands-on participation to become a successful sculptor, filmmaker, dancer, actor, or painter. Scholars in these fields may write journal articles like those in the humanities, comparing and contrasting works of art or viewing them through the lens of a particular philosophy or theory. They may write grants to seek support for a particular project. Practitioners in these fields may also produce creative works, like paintings, plays, or dances.

UNDERSTANDING GENRE EXPECTATIONS IN THE DISCIPLINES

Particularly in introductory courses, you may be asked to write and read types of documents that are not valued by experts in that discipline. For example, as a student in archaeology, you may be asked to write essays, reflections, narratives, and other types of documents. However, if you were to ask your instructor what kinds of things they write as an archaeologist, you might find that they tend to write field notes, reports, grant proposals, instructions, and that they rarely write essays, reflections, or narratives. Moreover, if you were to ask archaeology faculty what they tend to read, you would most likely find that they read journal articles about specific archaeological trends, but they most assuredly would not read textbooks. Sometimes this disjunction between what is valued and what is taught results in problems because your major courses may not adequately prepare you to act like an expert in that field because you may not have developed a clear sense of what is valued in that field. Of course, this problem can be resolved by asking faculty and other instructors in any discipline what kinds of reading and writing these experts do, what kinds of texts these people write, and what kinds of readings these experts find helpful for their disciplinary knowledge. Consider trying this preparatory exercise: as you enter any new discipline, ask your instructor what kinds of things he or she writes and what kinds of readings he or she values. Further, if you are asked to write and read differently than what the experts do in that discipline, those tasks are likely to help strengthen skills you can then transfer to other more expert types of texts in that discipline. Learning in a discipline will be most useful if you prepare yourself with an understanding of how these skills are likely to be useful in your future.

RESEARCHING IN THE DISCIPLINES

Conducting research is another great way to learn more about how a discipline investigates a subject. There are three main types of research: **primary, secondary,** and **tertiary.** Secondary research is most familiarly known as library research, in which one gathers knowledge that other scholars have already discovered and discussed. In tertiary research, scholars conduct meta-analyses about previous research, usually secondary research. They may summarize, synthesize, categorize, or otherwise analyze large groups of research about a topic and compile this gathering of information in a review article, an encyclopedia entry, a database, an annotated bibliography, or an epidemiological study. These two types of research will be discussed in more depth in Chapter 3. In this chapter, primary research is mentioned because it is a great way of getting to know one's chosen major or discipline.

Primary research means gathering information that has previously been unknown. Examples of primary research include field notes, laboratory experiments, surveys, and interviews. In primary research, the researcher creates the knowledge, gathers all the data, and perhaps creates the theory about what that data means. Primary researchers are the stuff of legends: Lewis and Clark's famous exploration of the North American continent; Rachel Carson's environmental work with marine biology leading to a public environmental consciousness and conscience; Louis Pasteur's discovery of the process of pasteurization; Margaret Mead's famous anthropological accounts of many native cultures. Famous primary researchers may work for decades gathering data, investigating previous ideas, rejecting hypotheses, and creating new knowledge. They should be meticulous in their work because future scholars are likely to examine their body of work carefully, perhaps in order to reject it. This attitude of carefulness and meticulousness—what we call research rigor—establishes the reputation of a primary researcher, and leads to reliable and valid arguments.

As a student, you may be asked to conduct primary research to learn more about a subject. Before you do so, you should acquaint yourself with the guidelines of research in that discipline by asking other expert faculty members the best way to conduct research. Some guidelines might include wearing protective gear when working in a lab, obtaining approval from your university's board of research ethics before you interview people, maintaining detailed notes about the situations you encounter, or seeking people's permission before you take photos or videos of them. Primary researchers must follow the safety and ethical guidelines for conducting research; otherwise, all their hard work and effort in gathering that data might be discounted by other scholars, their work might be destroyed by a research ethics council, or worse, they might be sued for libel or invasion of privacy. Thus, before you start conducting your own primary research, you should ask your instructor or other scholars the best way to learn about a subject; as you do so, you will also learn a great deal about that discipline and what they value in terms of careful, rigorous research.

REASONING

Along with learning about topics, you will also learn methods of thinking, called reasoning skills. **Deductive reasoning,** or to deduce, means to create an argument or claim by moving from the general theory to specific instances. It is the kind of reasoning that when properly followed can lead to necessary and absolute truths. Deductive reasoning forms the kind of logical argument that is irrefutable, that cannot be argued against because to do so would be to be illogical or even insane. An example of deductive reasoning is the argument that "All mammalian life forms must have water for survival; a dog is a mammal; hence, a dog must have water to survive." Deductive reasoning is typically evaluated in terms of soundness and validity; i.e. is the argument sound and is it valid? It is the kind of reasoning that lets us make decisions for specific situations, like when to water the dog, based on laws and theories that we already know to be true.

Conversely, **inductive reasoning,** or to induce, means to create an argument by moving from specific instances to a generalized claim. Inductive reasoning is the type of thinking that occurs when someone looks for patterns or categories within groups of data, often called common sense logic. It is also the type of logic used in probabilistic reasoning, causal inferences, and analogies. Inductive arguments are likely to be evaluated in terms of their strength; i.e. is this argument and its premises strong enough to believe? Inductive reasoning will almost never lead to certainty or absolute truths, but it is very useful for making practical, pragmatic decisions based on limited experience.

While many people narrowly circumscribe one type of reasoning to a discipline, it is not fair to say that all mathematic disciplines use deductive reasoning or that inductive reasoning is the scientific method. In actuality, all people in all disciplines are likely to use both types of reasoning, just at different times in their work. Scientists who conduct experiments are most likely going to use inductive reasoning in order to create an argument that every time they bring the described combination of chemicals to a certain temperature, the same result will occur. Such an argument is a generalization of the results of the repeated experiment. However, scientists who then take those generalized theories and show that the result would be different if the variables were slightly changed are then using deductive reasoning to move from a general theory to specific instances. And all other disciplines use both types of reasoning equally well for different purposes. What matters most to the validity of the arguments is that a person chooses the most appropriate type of reasoning for the kinds of data available and for the kind of argument or claim needed. When you study in any discipline, you will need to train your mind to think and reason in both ways and to look for the strength and soundness of the arguments presented in your studies.

You will learn more about disciplines and different strategies for learning as you read further in this book and study more in college. And as you learn more, you should start with the knowledge that thinking and learning varies from discipline to discipline, that scholars in each discipline value different types of topics, writings, and methods, and that what is a successful strategy for one discipline may need to be altered for another discipline. Knowing about disciplinary knowledge and reasoning skills before you begin is a huge foundation for learning in any field.

Cross-Check

- Prepare a foundation for your learning: Know before you go
  - What do you already know about a topic?
  - How does it relate to other topics?
  - What else do you need to learn about a topic?
- Understand genres
  - Genres are forms specific to a given field.
  - Different genres involve different information and formats to present information.
  - Common genres vary among the different disciplines.

- Practice preliminary familiarization in unfamiliar fields and genres
  - Skim through the reading for titles, headings, sub-headings, and author information.
  - For new genres, read several instances of that genre—preliminary familiarization—so that you might develop a sense of what works.
- Recognize that disciplines value different modes of thinking, topics, methods, and texts
  - A discipline, by definition, is different from a major or from a career choice.
  - Any academic discipline is a branch of instruction with a general regimen of unique reasoning, methods, topics, and texts.
  - Learn what written documents and readings are valued in a discipline by asking faculty and experts in that field what they read and write.
- Use primary research to gather previously unknown information about a topic
  - Learn disciplinary guidelines for safety, ethics, and research rigor before you start.
- Distinguish between two types of reasoning
  - Deductive reasoning means to move from generalized knowledge to specific instances.
  - Inductive reasoning means to gather repeated instances into a general knowledge or theory.

2

READING ACROSS DISCIPLINES
Reading for Learning, for Analysis, and for Argument

I f you are like most college students, you expect to do some reading while in college. You may know that you need to read in order to study for exams, to conduct research, or to stay connected with college life, like reading your emails, your school's newspaper, or reading anything else that allows you to stay up-to-date with the events on your campus.

However, you may at times find yourself unprepared for the amount of reading that is expected of you daily in your courses. Most college instructors assign 9 hours of homework, mostly in the form of reading the textbooks and other texts, for each 3-credit hour course. So, if you are enrolled in 5 courses, each worth 3 credit hours, you would have approximately 45 hours of homework/reading each week. That is the equivalent of a full-time job. You may not be prepared to spend that much time reading and want to look for ways to make the task easier and more efficient. One thing you can do to make reading an easier and faster task is to realize that it has several different purposes, and each purpose has different strategies associated with it to make your reading more efficient and effective.

When you read newspaper articles, magazine stories, novels, short stories, and poetry while waiting in a physician's office, flying in an airplane, on vacation, or simply relaxing, you are reading for entertainment. Just because this kind of reading has a main purpose of entertainment does not mean that it is wasted effort. On the contrary, any kind of reading—even entertainment reading—develops cognitive skills and language familiarity. When you read for leisure, you may skip certain parts of the text, perhaps long passages of description or a character's state of mind. Perhaps you only read the action, or plot-driven, passages. If you are an impatient reader, you may skip to the end of the book to find out how the tension of the story is resolved or who committed the crime. Whatever your style of entertainment reading, you probably find it a much faster form of reading than academic reading, in part because you have developed efficient, but often subconscious, strategies that suit your purposes for leisure reading.

READING FOR LEARNING

In contrast to reading for fun, your academic reading has a different purpose: to teach. When you engage in this style of reading, you are reading to understand the author's meaning. It can be a much slower type of reading than reading for leisure. Reading is meant to supplement your work in the classroom. Your instructor can teach you many things, but you can learn even more when you also read to learn.

Consider the advantages of reading for learning. Think of how slow life would be if all we could learn from others had to be done in a face-to-face mode, if you had to wait for wiser people to find time to impart everything you needed to know. Reading for meaning makes your learning faster and much more efficient than waiting to be told how to do everything. Do not rely on your instructors to teach you everything you need to know to pass an examination. Do not simply listen to their lectures without reading in your assigned textbook. Classroom activities and assigned readings complement and inform one another. To be a successful learner and student, listen to class lectures and read your assigned texts carefully. You can employ strategies to make your academic reading more effective and much less time consuming.

Strategies for Reading

Preparing

Before you begin to read a text, ask yourself:

- What is the topic of this text?
- What other topics are likely to be associated with this topic?
- What do I already know about this topic and what specific things do I need to learn?
- What do I know about this author?

After you've answered some preliminary questions, pick up the text, article, book, or chapter. Skim through the headings and sub-headings to find out how the text is organized. The organization of information can provide important clues, like road signs on a highway, that can make your task of traveling through the text less stressful. When you know what is ahead, you know what to look for in your text. Look for a summary or abstract at either the beginning or ending of the chapter. Read the summary first, so that you know the main points of the chapter and can recognize them later when you read the whole chapter. Grab a dictionary so that you can quickly look up unfamiliar words. After reading the summary, ask yourself if you are puzzled by any of that information. You may need to slow down when reading the text so that you can more fully understand what the author is saying. Here is an excerpted example of a student's thoughts in preparing to read "The Coming Age" by Jacques Barzun:

The Coming Age

Jacques Barzun

Herewith an undated and anonymous document from the late twentieth century. It is entitled "Let Us End with a Prologue."

The shape and coloring of the next era is beyond anyone's powers to define; if it were guessable, it would not be new. But on the character of the interval between us and the real tomorrow, speculation is possible. Within the historian lives a confederate who is an incurable pattern-maker

I wonder what this title means. Is he referring to "the future" or to someone's actual age?

I don't know anything about this author. I wonder if I should look up some information about him or her?

I notice that this essay starts and ends with these italicized comments. I wonder why? What are they supposed to mean?

and willing to risk the penalties against fortune-telling. Let the transitional state be described in the past tense, like a chronicler looking back from the year 2300.

The population was divided roughly into two groups; they did not like the word "classes." The first, less numerous, was made up of the men and women who possessed the virtually inborn ability to handle the products of techne and master the methods of physical science, especially mathematics—it was to them what Latin had been to the medieval clergy. This modern elite had the geometrical mind that singled them out for the life of research and engineering. Lord Bacon had predicted that once the ways and biases of science were enthroned, this type of mind would be found relatively common. Dials, toggles, buzzers, gauges, icons on screens, light-emitting diodes, symbols and formulas to save time and thought –these were for this group of people the source of emotional satisfaction, the means of rule over others, the substance of shoptalk, the very joy and justification of life.

Here's a word I don't recognize. I'll need a dictionary for this essay.

The mind was shaped and the fancy filled by these intricacies as had been done in an earlier era by theology, poetry, and the fine arts. The New Man saw the world as a storehouse of all items retrievable through a keyboard, and whoever added to the sum was in high repute. He, and more and more often She, might be an inventor or theorist, for the interest in hypotheses about the creation of the cosmos and the origin of life persisted, intensified, from the previous era. The sense of being close to a final formulation lasted for over 200 years.

As I skim this essay, I see many terms that the author has capitalized. I wonder why these phrases need to be capitalized. Are they important phrases? Are they proper nouns?

It is from this class—no, group—that the governors and heads of institutions were recruited. The parallel with the Middle Ages is plain—clerics in one case, cybernists in the other. The latter took pride in the fact that in ancient Greek cybernetes meant helmsman, governor. It validated their position as rulers of the masses, which by then could neither read nor count. But these less capable citizens were by no means barbarians. To be sure, schooling would have been wasted on them; that had been proved in the late twentieth century. Some now argue that the schooling was at fault, not the people; but when the teachers themselves declared children unteachable, the Deschooling Society movement rapidly converted everybody to its view. . . .

Another one of these capitalized phrases. What does this one mean?

Engaging

As you read or engage in the text, ask yourself if your predictions about the topic and the main points held true.

- Has anything changed between what you expected the text to say and what it actually is saying?

- Are there words that you do not understand and need to look up?

- What is the author's main point? What is his or her evidence for that main point?
- To what other topics does the author connect the topic?
- What is the background or context of understanding this topic?

For example, you might be familiar with the topic of earth worms in a biological sense, but if the author presents the topic within an economic context, like how earth worms save organic gardeners effort in aerating the soil and thus are worth quite a bit of money to the organic gardening industry, you might be very surprised as a reader and find yourself needing to re-read some of the claims and the context in order to understand fully the author's topic.

As you read, note, underline, and highlight important information. If you need to look up a word in the dictionary, write the definition nearby in the margin. When you find the author's main point or thesis, underline or highlight it. Mark the evidence and reasons that support the author's main point. If you are confused, write your questions in the margin. If you see places where the author is contradictory, circle those points and draw a line to connect them. Doing so will serve as a reminder later on of specific locations in the text where you need to re-read. If you find yourself surprised by a point, put an exclamation point in the margin.

Upon a first reading, you might find yourself merely understanding the content without questioning the author's points, perspective, or evidence. However, as you become a more skillful critical reader, you should engage in a dialogue with the text after you fully comprehend the piece. You might begin to question the author's evidence or the assumptions he or she makes about readers. Jot down those reactions in the margins as well.

Remember that unlike leisure reading, when reading for learning, you should actively engage in marking, questioning, and summarizing the text. You may wish to keep a notebook, note cards, or a document file in which you record your thoughts regarding the text. If you read online or on an e-reader, you might record your thoughts on a voice recorder, in a separate document file, or in a handwritten notebook. Maintaining your notes will help you both remember the material and deepen your engagement with the text as you continue to work with it. Here is an example of a student's thoughts and notes while reading the same essay, "The Coming Age," by Jacques Barzun:

The Coming Age

Jacques Barzun

Herewith an undated and anonymous document from the late twentieth century. It is entitled "Let Us End with a Prologue."

The shape and coloring of the next era is beyond anyone's powers to define; if it were guessable, it would not be new. But on the character of the interval between us and the real tomorrow, speculation is possible. Within the historian lives a confederate who is an incurable pattern-maker and willing to risk the penalties against fortune-telling. Let the transitional state be described in the past tense, like a chronicler looking back from the year 2300.

So, this essay will be a prophecy of the future, while pretending to be looking into the past. Tricky.

The population was divided roughly into two groups; they did not like the word "classes." The first, less numerous, was made up of the men and women who possessed the virtually inborn ability to handle the products of *techne* and master the methods of physical science, especially mathematics—it was to them what Latin had been to the medieval clergy.

This word means "craftsmanship" or skill. I wonder why the author uses the Latin word instead of the plain English word?

This modern elite had the geometrical mind that singled them out for the life of research and engineering. Lord Bacon had predicted that once the ways and biases of science were enthroned, this type of mind would be found relatively common. Dials, toggles, buzzers, gauges, icons on screens, light-emitting diodes, symbols and formulas to save time and thought—these were for this group of people the source of emotional satisfaction, the means of rule over others, the substance of shoptalk, the very joy and justification of life.

This whole part reminds me of Alan Turing's essay about computers and his prediction of artificial intelligence.

The mind was shaped and the fancy filled by these intricacies as had been done in an earlier era by theology, poetry, and the fine arts. The New Man saw the world as a storehouse of all items retrievable through a keyboard, and whoever added to the sum was in high repute. He, and more and more often She, might be an inventor or theorist, for the interest in hypotheses about the creation of the cosmos and the origin of life persisted, intensified, from the previous era. The sense of being close to a final formulation lasted for over 200 years.

Again, this idea about the age and power of technology seems to be reflected in Alan Turing's essay.

It is from this class—no, group—that the governors and heads of institutions were recruited. The parallel with the *Middle Ages* is plain—clerics in one case, cybernists in the other. The latter took pride in the fact that in ancient Greek cybernetes meant helmsman, governor. It validated their position as rulers of the masses, which by then could neither read nor count. But these less capable citizens were by no means barbarians. To be sure, schooling would have been wasted on them; that had been proved in the late twentieth century. Some now argue that the schooling was at fault, not the people; but when the teachers themselves declared children unteachable, the Deschooling Society movement rapidly converted everybody to its view. . . .

Here the author is pointing out that history repeats itself; the same patterns appear throughout the centuries.

Reviewing

After reading, continue using strategies to help you learn from the text: close the book and summarize in one or two sentences the main point or thesis of the text. Then ask yourself some questions applying the information to your current understanding of the topic:

- How might this information be useful to you?
- What was surprising?
- What confused you?
- What else do you need to learn about this topic?
- What did the author NOT discuss?
- Re-read your notes and comments from the margin. Can these help you remember and learn from the text?

Here is a sample of the student's comments after reading the same essay by Jacques Barzun:

Summary

In this essay, the author, Barzun, takes a fanciful look into the future, by predicting what he thinks will come of society. Even though he is an historian, he tries to predict what the future will be like, and he does this by comparing our current time with the previous historic era, the Middle Ages. His main point is that society will return to a love of the arts, like literature and photography, and that this renewed interest in the artistic human endeavor will save humanity from war, social tyranny, and worse, boredom. Barzun says that an obsession with technologies will compete with a love of the arts and creativity. He predicts that, through technological advances, society will learn to control nature, eliminate mistakes, and perfect the economic marketplace. However, Barzun says that this view of perfection will be flawed and will function much like the feudal system of the Middle Ages, in that all of society will work to enhance the economic status of the few corporate leaders. Perfection in technologies will blind us in thinking that our new world is perfect, but in reality it will be more strict and more controlled. Eventually, he argues, this society will win out over less stable nations, who will kill off each other. The world will appear boring. When it does, society will seek a renewed interest in the arts and will return to a more creative era, like the Renaissance.

Tone

Throughout this essay, Barzun strikes a frivolous, almost sarcastic tone frequently appearing to make fun of both the cybernetes and the unschooled citizens, the idea of peace, and the idea of curing illness. In the end, he even seems to make fun of those people, the lovers of literature and art, whose obsession with creativity will save society from certain boredom. Mostly, he seems to make fun of anyone who holds a single-minded obsession and demands that all of society follow that belief. He even pokes some fun at historians, and he must surely consider himself one of that group, when he states that historians are "incurable pattern-makers."

Consideration of Effectiveness

While Barzun makes some good points by comparing current and future societies with past eras, I wonder what he forgets to say. Is his view a bit narrow-minded? He seems mostly to be talking about the societies of the western hemisphere, especially those that have already thoroughly invested in technological uses. He makes very little reference to Eastern or Middle Eastern societies, except to say that some of the Eastern ideals will mingle with those of the Western societies in literature and the arts, or to say that societies not aligned with a Western alliance will eliminate each other through fighting. If we were to find a similar person from a non-Western society who wanted to give an educated hypothetical view of the future, I think this prediction would be very different from Barzun's.

Using these strategies can make time spent reading for learning more effective and efficient.

READING THE AUTHOR'S LOGIC: LOGICAL FALLACIES

As you encounter information and build on your foundational knowledge, you should also be prepared to encounter flawed knowledge or faulty reasoning. Perhaps you are already familiar with the term "logical fallacies," a flawed argument. There are over 200 recognized logical fallacies. Rather than spend time memorizing all the types just so you can avoid them, you should know that the most common logical fallacies can be grouped into four categories: evidence, relevance, language, and structure.

Evidence

Some fallacies are flawed from a lack of evidence. The argument may be true, but there is not enough evidence to declare it true at the point that the argument is made; for example, in a hasty generalization, someone might claim that because his income taxes had increased, the current governing body had increased taxes for all citizens. Such an argument might be true, if you could find the legislation to show that it had happened or if you could look at the income tax returns of all citizens. More than likely, however, one event cannot be shown to hold true for all cases. More information would be needed before you could logically make such a claim. This category may also include faulty arguments that ignore evidence to support a counter argument. When you encounter claims about knowledge, you should always ask yourself, "Is there enough evidence to make this claim? Has this event only happened once? If so, perhaps we should wait to see if the event occurs repeatedly before we make a claim about the evidence? Is there opposing evidence to this claim? Is some evidence missing?"

Relevance

Some arguments are fallacious because they lack relevance to the main idea. In these arguments, the claim usually tries to win by diverting attention to something that is not relevant to the topic. Such arguments might say that we should not vote for a political candidate because she knows several Communists. While we might not like the values of Communism, to make a logical choice for the election, we should examine a political candidate's stated values, promises, and voting record, rather than the people she knows. It is important when encountering claims or knowledge that you always ask yourself, "What is the real topic? Is this claim about the real topic? Is there any relevance between the claim and the topic? Is that relevance direct or only distantly and hazily connected? Have I learned anything of relevance and value about the real topic in this argument?" With any claim or argument made, you should be aware that many arguments try to win, not by directly explaining the topic, but by diverting your attention to other irrelevant claims.

Language

Other faulty arguments try to be persuasive by playing tricks with words; these arguments are called fallacies of language because they try to be persuasive primarily on the basis of language's complexity, misuse, or ambiguity. Often these tricks of language can be used for humor or with savvy persuasive tactics, called rhetorical strategies, to add flair and elegance to one's argument. However, language can also be used to mislead, simply on the basis of its own imprecise nature. When language is used to convey information, that is communication. When using language to convey inaccurate information or irrelevant information, that fallacy would be one of improper evidence or irrelevant information. However, when arguments use linguistic confusion like insinuations, when language is used as the primary tool of mis-arguing, that fallacy is one of language trickery. When you think about claims of knowledge, you should ask yourself, "Are the words, definitions, and meanings being used correctly? Am I being led astray or diverted from the original argument by language trickery?"

Structure

A final and perhaps most difficult category of fallacy to describe is one in which the structure of the argument is faulty in some way. All arguments, to be logical, follow certain forms; when one of the form elements is missing or misplaced, then the argument is faulty. Compare this famous argument with the argument that follows: "All men are mortal; Socrates was a man; therefore, Socrates was mortal." This argument is used as an example of proper form or structure in logic. Here is the second example: "All men are mortal; Socrates was mortal; therefore, Socrates was a man" in which elements of the original are misplaced, creating an argument that could be shown to be false, as in Socrates could have been a woman. Such mis-structured arguments are hard to detect because it takes a long-term dedication to the study of logical forms in order to be aware of all the ways in which arguments can be badly structured. Nevertheless, you can learn to recognize some faulty structural arguments by asking yourself, when you encounter knowledge claims, "Is this argument constructed in a way that makes sense? Is something wrong with this claim? Perhaps I need more time to think about and mull over this claim before I agree to it?"

READING VISUAL AIDS

Reading for learning means more than paying attention to the words. You must also be able to "read" visuals and incorporate them into your own work appropriately. Visual aids make information easier for readers to understand. Additionally, they often aid conciseness, as visual aids can provide a lot of information in a small space, information that would take too long to put into words.

There are several types of visual aids you are likely to encounter and use. Tables give precise numeric data, data that otherwise would be hard to remember or comprehend if written in prose form. Tables, like the periodic table of chemical elements, usually convey a lot of numeric information in a small amount of space. For example, an engineer might want to use a table to show that a 16-gauge nail can hold 22.568 pounds of pressure, that a 12-gauge nail can withstand 26.894 pounds of pressure, and that an 8-gauge nail can withstand 25.086 pounds of pressure. These exact numeric measurements will be extremely important to someone who is designing and constructing a building. Charts and graphs, on the other hand, are used to compare data, some of which can be numeric. Another engineer might want to use a chart, perhaps a pie chart, to show that of the total pounds of nails used in a construction project, only 30% were 16-gauge nails, while another 65% were 12-gauge nails, and only 5% were 8-gauge nails. In such a chart, the purpose is to compare that overall usefulness of the types of nails to the whole project, rather than to know specific numeric details.

You can also use a table to show multiple entries of precise data. The table below shows how teachers use certain types of computer software currently or plan to use it in the

1 Press. Sftw.		2 Word process		3 Dsktp Pub		4 hypermedia		5 Sprdsht	
now	later	now	later	now	later	now	later	now	later
1	3	5	5	2	3	1	4	2	4
2	3	2	3	2	3	3	3	2	2
4	3	4	4	3	5	3	5	4	4
4	4	4	4	2	3	4	4	2	2
2	3	4	4	2	3	1	2	1	3
3	4	4	4	3	4	3	4	4	0
1	2	4	4	3	4	1	2	1	4
4	5	5	5	4	5	4	5	0	0
1	3	4	0	1	4	1	3	0	0
2	4	4	4	2	4	2	4	2	4
2	4	5	4	1	3	1	3	1	3
3	4	4	4	1	4	2	4	2	4
4	4	5	5	4	4	4	4	4	4

future. This data could be very worthwhile to computer programmers, software designers, curriculum designers, and education scholars.

Here is an example of a chart used to show comparisons of the same data as mentioned on the previous page (see table). In it, you can clearly see how each entry stands in relation to the other entries.

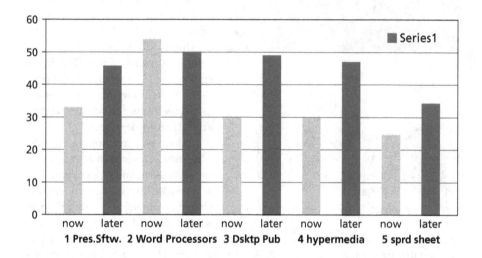

A diagram can be useful to show specific details, for example, showing the steps for changing the oil in an automobile. Photographs capture background details that a diagram cannot. Maps can be used to show geographic detail, directions, or comparison of geographic information.

Below is an example of a detailed diagram, drawn by a medical illustrator, in which you can visualize details of the human eye that may normally be inaccessible:

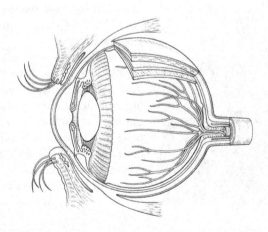

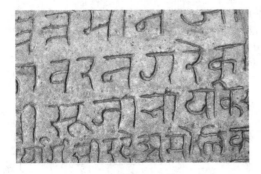

This photograph of ancient pre-Sanskrit writing found carved into stone in southern India gives detailed information to archeologists and historians studying the ancient language and Indian culture to aid in their studies.

In the map of Kentucky shown here, one can read the western counties of the state of Kentucky as they are divided into districts by the US Attorney General's Office. This information would be vitally helpful for a citizen of Kentucky wondering where to look for the nearest and most appropriate US Attorney General's Office.

Source: www.justice.gov/usao/kyw/office_overview/

Along with reading visual aids, which are designed with the purpose of conveying facts and other information in a concise and quickly understood manner, you may also be required to read other kinds of visuals, like the fine artwork of paintings, drawings, textile art, and etchings. These kinds of visuals, while still used to convey information, are likely to be mindful of aesthetic standards, often showing new artistic techniques, and often conveying emotions and concepts. When you read

these types of visuals, you should ask yourself what you can learn from this piece of art. What artistic techniques are being displayed? What is the artist's purpose? What is the artist trying to tell you? Is there a particular mood, thought, or sensation that the artist might be trying to evoke? To the left is a famous painting, "Woman with a Parasol," by Claude Monet. Monet used the technique of short, vibrant brush strokes to create a feeling of movement.

Another type of visual you are probably familiar with is the advertisement. Rather than dismissing them as unworthy of scrutiny, consider examining ads to see what you can learn about how marketers attempt to persuade the viewer. Is the product being compared to other similar products? What specific traits are compared? What traits are not mentioned? Do the sources of information, like the nutritional label or the list of ingredients, lend support to the claims made about the product? Do they give evidence to other unspoken claims about the product?

Following is an example of an advertisement that attempts to sell a variety of products designed especially for infants and toddlers. The ad is informative, stating in multiple locations that the products manufactured by Organix contain 100% organic ingredients. At the same time, it uses a less serious tone in its use of the phrase "No Junk Promise." Note the emphasis on ingredients, as shown in the images of corn and wheat at the top of the ad and the words "100% organic nutrition" in the upper right corner and again in the paragraph under the images. While the products manufactured by Organix are not directly compared to other infant foods and toddler snacks, the ad insinuates that foods and snacks not made the same way—100% organic—might not be as tasteful or as

healthy. This advertisement, like many others, emphasizes only a few traits. It focuses on a few characteristics, pure ingredients and happy consumers (children), but fails to mention several others, such as how many non-nutritive additives the foods and snacks contain, cost, and accessibility in grocery stores. Overall, the ad focuses on the benefits of its products' ingredients and relies on its organic claims, while also showing that those who purchase and consume these products are happy individuals.

Other visual aids that appear within a document, like headings, bulleted lists, and numbered lists, are also useful for quickly showing the reader the pattern of organization within a text.

READING INTERNET SITES AND DETERMINING CREDIBILITY

The Internet is a tool widely used by students and instructors alike. However, not everything worth knowing can be found on the Internet; a lot of great information can still be found in print as well.

Quality or veracity is not a requirement for most Internet sites. In fact, there are many Internet sites espousing useless or even false information. As you are reading for information on the Internet, you will need a plan for determining what information is likely to be reliable and which sites should be disregarded.

Consider the site's domain name. A *.com* site is a commercial page that may be selling information or products; originally *.com* sites were always commercial enterprises, but now many sites can be .*com* sites without being licensed businesses. Sometimes these sites, like the online *New York Times,* will be in the business of providing accurate information. In general, however, most .*com* sites are more focused on business and less concerned with providing accurate information to researchers.

An organization's web site, like that of a non-profit organization, is .*org*, and its primary purpose will be to give information about itself or about its topic. Sometimes these sites have advertisements that try to sell you a product, but the primary purpose of a .*org* site is not to increase profits, although that may be a secondary purpose. Partisan organizations such as the National Rifle Association and the Sierra Club often have .*org* addresses. While the information presented by large and well-respected organizations is likely to be accurate, it is not usually neutral. Information is usually presented in a manner consistent with an organization's aims.

An educational site, .*edu*, is hosted by an educational organization, which may or may not support all the information put forth by its members, many of whom are likely to be students. Many of these .*edu* sites are reliable sources of information, especially about the educational institution, but be aware that students, who may not be experts in any subject, can often post ideas on their .*edu* web sites.

The government also sponsors sites with the domain .*gov*; most of that information can be trusted because it is usually screened prior to publication online.

As you read through internet sites be aware that the primary purpose of the site can impact the reliability of the site's information. Look for telltale signs that will help you determine the reliability of a web site. Sites whose purpose is to publish reliable information will:

- use a reasonable, truthful tone not overwhelmed with emotional language
- usually not be swamped with sales ads
- usually keep their ads in a separate section of the screen visually set off from the information of the web site
- tell where they got their information
- provide live links to other places where you can get information
- say when they last updated their information
- provide accurate and clear information about the aims of the sponsoring company or organization
- offer readers a way to contact them

Be aware of your reading strategies when you gather information from the Internet. Most web pages hold small paragraphs of information, requiring you to scroll and click through several pages within the site to view all available information about the topic. In contrast, a textbook holds a lot of information on a single page, requiring you to switch pages much less often. Some sites use embedded links within a page, with a small listing of these links listed at the top like a table of contents. Even after you find useful information, consider reading other linked pages; you do not want to overlook important information. Reading on the Internet is a different skill than reading in a textbook or other text, even when your purpose—to learn something about a topic—is the same. In short, the Internet can be a useful tool for learning if you take the time to evaluate the quality of the information being presented.

READING FOR ANALYSIS

Analyzing how authors write as well as what they write can help you improve your own writing and learning. Examining the persuasive strategies underlying a writer's message can deepen your understanding of the writer's perspective and help you learn new strategies you can employ in your own writing. When writing in a new genre, read examples of that genre before writing. For example, if you are writing a scientific report—a genre style that may be new to you—read other reports first so you can learn what can be done within that genre. There are strategies for learning this kind of analysis, and practicing them will make such analysis become second nature to you.

Strategies for Analytic Reading

Saying versus Doing

Ask yourself two questions for each paragraph that you read: what is the author saying (reading for meaning), and what is the author doing (reading for analysis). For each paragraph, write the answers to these questions in the margin or on a separate document. For example, if you were reading the introduction to an essay about brown pelicans, you might answer these two questions like this: "Here the author is saying that brown pelicans are an endangered species, and that as a species they are very special," and "Here the author is introducing the main topic (brown pelicans) and giving the thesis statement (brown pelicans are an important species, too important to be ignored). In a following paragraph you might write these two answers: "Here the author is saying that brown pelicans have lived in the Gulf of Mexico for centuries," and "Here the author is giving some background information about the geographic range of pelicans, and the author is perhaps leading the reader to more background information, like the nesting habits of the pelicans." As you begin using this strategy, you may have to guess about what the author is doing, but with practice, you will become more confident in your responses. By answering the two questions, you learn to separate the two purposes you have for reading. More importantly, you learn to analyze the composing strategies of the author: how authors introduce topics, how they give background information, how they move from one sub-topic to another, how they cite their expert resources, etc. By learning to read or to critically analyze the writing strategies of others, you broaden your own bag of writing strategies.

An Author's Thesis

Another strategy of analytic reading is to locate the author's thesis. What is the main point, claim, or thesis of the essay? In expository writing, which is intended primarily to inform, the authors usually want to convince the readers of some point, to persuade readers that the author's opinion or discovery of facts is true. After reading an essay or text, ask yourself,

- "What is the author's purpose?"
- "What does the author want me to know?"
- "What is the author trying to persuade me to believe?"
- "What is the author's main point?"

All of these questions will help you determine that author's main point. This point is the author's thesis statement, and generally that thesis statement is a claim, an arguable point.

In other words, few authors publish works that offer no new information or opinions. If the only information presented is facts already known to be true, then there isn't much point in reading. Thus, an author's claim is often a point or position to which one could reasonably respond, "No, I disagree." Once you have determined the main point, go back to the essay and find the sentence or sentences where the author makes that claim. Where is it located in the piece? Does the author tell you the thesis statement in the opening lines? At the end of the introduction? At the conclusion of the essay? Does the author repeat the thesis during the essay, and if so, is the repetition worded exactly from the original, or does the author paraphrase the thesis statement so as not to be redundant? Is the thesis statement contained in one sentence or in two or three?

Support for the thesis   After you find the author's main point or thesis, ask yourself how the author built up to the thesis: How does the author move from introducing the topic to making an argument about the topic? Does the author give an opposing view of the topic before the thesis? After the thesis? Not at all?

What about the support the writer provides for the claim? Does the author show evidence for his claim? What kinds of reasons does he or she use to prove to you that the thesis is true? What kinds of details are used to describe the evidence: logical reasons, expertise, examples, numbers, statistics, or sensory details? What kinds of alternative perspectives, interpretations, or opinions are given? What kinds of evidence is given to support those alternative views? Asking these questions can help you analyze the author's argument and evidence for believing his or her thesis. And once you know how to recognize other authors' argument strategies, you can try some of these strategies in your own writing.

An Author's Organizational Pattern

Another analytic strategy is to examine the author's organizational pattern. Make an outline of the essay or text by noting the main point for each paragraph. Also note the thesis in that outline. Once you have these, you can review your outline for a pattern of organization. Does the author go from the least important point to the most important point? Vice versa? Does the author organize the information chronologically, perhaps telling the history of a topic? Does the author organize the information spatially, perhaps by describing the rooms of a house or the viewing of a painting? Does the author organize the essay by moving from general to specific information, for example, background or contextual knowledge to more specific information? Is the essay organized by classifying or alternatively by analyzing or examining the parts of something? Does the author define a topic and tell about its essence or nature? All of these are common patterns of organization that can often be recognized by repeatedly reading for analysis. However, some authors organize information in ways that are less common or less easily recognized. If, when you write an outline of a text, you do not recognize a pattern, do not be frustrated. Consider whether the information is presented in a way that makes sense for the topic or for a specific audience. Again, reading analytically can be a way of examining how other authors organize the information in their texts and thinking about whether those same strategies of organization might be helpful for your own writing.

Following is a sample student outline of the first eleven paragraphs of Shelby Steele's essay, "The New Sovereignty," found in Chapter 7.

Outline of Shelby Steele's "the New Sovereignty"
- a. Introduction: a story about giving a public presentation that was not well received, i.e. people were silently resistant
    - i. He challenged the notion of how diversity was pursued in this country
    - ii. He challenged the goals of the Civil Rights Movements and subsequent leaders of the 1960s that presumed collective entitlement, which was not called for in the Constitution
    - iii. He called this concept of collective entitlement the New Sovereignty, and his audience began to show some resistance to his idea
- b. He showed the evidence of this Sovereignty when he talked about all the many academic programs and departments devoted to minority entitlements, moving into a strong claim: "This push for equality among groups necessarily made for an inequality among individuals that prepared the ground for precisely the racial, gender, and ethnic divisiveness that, back in the Sixties, we all said we wanted to move beyond"
    - i. Again, he returns to the events of the public presentation, in which a woman approached afterwards to challenge his ideas
    - ii. The woman walked away after telling him that he was naïve and gave him a look that he interpreted as saying that he was "the enemy"
- c. He gives more evidence about the increase in the number of academic programs devoted to minority group entitlement
- d. He gives a brief history as background to how this concept of collective entitlement developed
- e. Given these pieces of evidence, he makes the claim that this collective entitlement misses the point of fully redressing the wrongs of minority persons—"Only inclusion answers history's exclusion"

Note to self: Steele is following a specific pattern of organization—chronological—in this Introduction to his essay. In many ways, he also uses other familiar introduction strategies: telling a story, giving some history of the topic, giving some evidence to lead up to his main point, etc.

f. He returns to the story of the challenging woman to show that she had misunderstood his point, came to see him as the enemy, because she was more interested in maintaining her territorial power.

g. He ends the Introduction by arguing that these programs devoted to collective entitlement have become sovereign, self-protective, power-hungry dictatorships. He implies that challenging the power or purpose of these fiefdoms (as he did in his presentation) was to be perceived as someone opposing the rights of fairness and justice, that to challenge the group entitlement concept is to be seen as the enemy, that these groups and the perception of the justice behind all that they stand for has blinded our nation to the real need for fairness to all people.

Finally, examine how the author concludes the piece. As a reader, were you unprepared for the ending? Or did you recognize that the conclusion was near? How did the author prepare you for finishing this piece? Did the author repeat the thesis and some of the evidence for that claim in the conclusion, reminding you of the most important piece of information you could carry with you? Did the author finish a story, metaphor, or character analysis begun much earlier in the essay so as to make the essay feel as though it had gone full-circle? Did the author imagine future possibilities in regard to the topic? Did the author summarize the main points of the essay? All of these are common strategies that authors use to wrap up their discussions, strategies that you can learn to recognize and use for your own writing.

In this excerpt from "The New Sovereignty" by Shelby Steele, a student critically analyzes Steele's essay by identifying the thesis, some writing strategies such as setting off definitions with dashes, and some of the movement of the essay's ideas.

Saying/Doing: Here, Steele is saying the facts about the quantity of minority-studies academic programs in America. Here, Steele is showing that this idea—the rise of status among collective groups—is widespread; he is giving evidence to his claim.

Saying/Doing: Here Steele is telling the story of the rise in collective entitlements ("First . . . Then . . ."). Here Steele is showing that what might have begun as a good idea (to redress grievances) became a shallow, fallacious demand for territory and autonomy. He is showing that the trend toward collective

. . . Today there are more than five hundred separate women's-studies departments or programs in American colleges and universities. There are nearly four hundred independent black-studies departments or programs, and hundreds of Hispanic, Asian, and Native American programs. . . .

I do think I know how it all came to this—how what began as an attempt to address the very real grievances of women wound up creating newly sovereign fiefdoms like this women's studies department. First there was collective entitlement to redress the grievances, which in turn implied a sovereignty for the grievance group, since sovereignty is only the formalization of collective entitlement. Then, since sovereignty requires autonomy, there had to be a demand for separate and independent stature within the university (or some other institution of society). There would have to be a separate territory with the trappings that certify sovereignty and are concrete recognition of the grievance identity—a building or suite of offices, a budget, faculty, staff, office supplies, letterhead, et cetera.

And so the justification for separate women's and ethnic-studies programs has virtually nothing to do with strictly academic matters and everything to do with the kind of group-identity politics in which the principle of collective entitlement has resulted. My feeling is that there can be no full redress of the woeful neglect of women's intellectual contributions until those contributions are entirely integrated into the very departments that neglected them in the first place. The same is true for America's minorities. Only inclusion answers history's exclusion. But now the sovereignty of grievance-group identities has confused all this. . . .

In our age of the New Sovereignty the original grievances—those having to do with fundamental questions such as basic rights—have in large measure been addressed, if not entirely redressed. But that is of little matter now. The sovereign fiefdoms are ends in themselves—providing career tracks and bases of power. This power tends to be used now mostly to defend and extend the fiefdoms, often by exaggerating and exploiting secondary, amorphous, or largely symbolic complaints. In this way, America has increasingly become an uneasy federation of newly sovereign nations. . . .

entitlement in the demand for liberty and autonomy has become the very thing that it attempted to overcome—arbitrary power over others.

Here, Steele moves from his earlier premises—that our nation has seen a rise in autonomous, collective minority groups and that such groups are like sovereign fiefdoms—to his conclusion—that such demands neglect the fundamental ideal of redressing discrimination against individuals.

One of Steele's points for this section of the essay.

Here, Steele restates this claim more concisely and more broadly construed to mean more than just women's studies programs.

Steele seems to use many phrases set off with dashes. Such phrases work to explain the concept immediately preceding the dash to help readers understand his concepts.

Another phrase set off by dashes.

Here Steele is saying that the autonomy of these academic fiefdoms has run amok, but he gives no real evidence, in this section, to this claim. How have they exaggerated and exploited complaints?

His main point? His thesis statement? If so, the preceding stuff implies a lot more about this single statement than what is stated here.

Awareness of composing strategies, like stating (and restating) a thesis, using phrases set off by dashes to give immediate definitions or explanations, showing evidence to support a point, and moving among ideas, will make your work as a reader and a writer much more effective, efficient, and perhaps even more enjoyable. Examining these strategies will help you become aware of how an author is persuading you to determine what are or are not effective strategies and how you can employ these same effective strategies in your essays.

ANALYZING ARGUMENTS

Argumentative texts deserve special consideration when reading critically because they are widely read and written in college classes. This type of text usually includes an arguable thesis and offers solid evidence and sound, valid logic for the argument. In this way, argumentation differs from an essay that attempts to persuade through personal opinion in which no solid evidence may be offered, from a narrative account in which no arguable thesis is offered, or from a definition essay in which the main point—to explain and define an issue—may not be an arguable thesis. The main purpose of an argumentation essay is to argue, often passionately and with clarity of purpose, a debatable point so as to persuade the readers to believe the point or to promote action among the readers.

Argumentation as a style of written text is also different from the kinds of arguments you might engage in with your parents, your siblings, or your friends. Such arguments are typically oral and often arise spontaneously as topics of conversation inspire you to speak up. While such oral arguments are often passionate and purposeful, for example, arguing to your parents that you should not be grounded because you missed coming home by their set curfew, rarely are they logically organized, planned thoroughly ahead of time, and/or backed by sound and valid evidence to support the argument. Rather, it is careful planning, evidence, and logic to support an arguable point that make argumentative texts compelling to academia.

Further, the specialized nature of argumentation requires its own vocabulary. While the study of these terms can be quite intense and lengthy, you should learn some of the fundamental terms as a general foundation for discussing argumentation. As you acquaint yourself with these terms, you will become more adept at identifying these elements in different texts.

- Claim, thesis, or argument: the main point of the text. For an argumentative text, it must be a point that is arguable by a reasonable person. For example, main points that are statements of fact ("it is not raining today") or statements of personal opinion ("my favorite color is purple") are not considered arguments, as most reasonable people would not attempt to argue against a statement of fact or a statement of personal opinion. In the natural science disciplines, many texts are published which are not argumentative because these texts, like field observation reports and reports of laboratory experiments, often have as their main points statements of facts. In the social sciences and humanities disciplines, arguments as thesis statements are much more common, as in the excerpt from St. Thomas Aquinas, "Summa Theologica," in which he states his positions as answers to questions regarding faith.

- Grounds, evidence, and justification: the reasons given to support the argument. If an argument is to be believed by a reasonable person, it should offer some reasons or evidence to justifiably prove the argument. After you identify an argument, you can ask, "On what grounds should I believe this argument?" What evidence does the author give to support his or her argument? For example, in the essay "Maid to Order," Barbara Ehrenreich offers the evidence of her experience as a hired maid to partly prove her argument that the trend toward outsourcing housework, once seen as the epitome of women's liberation, actually reinforces slave-like workloads, pitifully poor wages, and the reification of the lower class.

- Warrants: the underlying assumptions that connect the evidence to the argument. Some grounds given are not necessarily or directly relevant to a claim, although in the author's mind the evidence may be indirectly connected. For example, if you were to claim that housework is slave labor, you would need to give evidence to both parts of this claim—what defines slave labor and what is so bad about housework. It would not be enough to show that housework is hard or labor intensive to claim that it is slave labor, because labor-intensive work does not necessarily back up or offer a direct warrant to the claim of slave labor. When you encounter claims, evidence, or grounds, you should ask what warrants logically connect the evidence to the argument. In William Deresiewicz's "Faux Friendship," the author claims that friendship has lost its substance and has become an empty distraction. His warrant is that Facebook and other social networking sites have multiplied the number of friendships people have and created a model of friendship that discourages emotional intimacy. In this way, he has two assumptions that form the foundation of the relevant use of his evidence.

- Appeals to reason, emotion, and authorial ethics: the ways in which arguments develop their ideas through logic (reason), emotional attachments, and authorial expertise and ethics. Most argumentative essays attempt to persuade readers using three types of appeals: logic to show that the argument necessarily follows from the premises and evidence, strategies designed to strengthen our emotional attachment to the issue, and the expertise of the author's background to show that he or she is knowledgeable and trustworthy. Many essays use a combination of all three types of appeals to argue their points. In his essay "Happiness Is a Worn Gun," author Dan Baum uses all three appeals to show that many of the arguments for and against the right to carry guns are simplistic, one-sided views of what is, in fact, a very complex issue. He also shows the ways in which many people are emotionally attached, sometimes illogically so, to the image of gun freedom, when he claims, "Alas, the very word 'gunfight' is sexy." And he offers his own experiences as a gun enthusiast for more than 45 years to show that he is ethically conscious and knowledgeable about the gun issue to legitimately write a lengthy examination of the issues surrounding the right to carry guns.

- Refutation: recognizing and examining opposing viewpoints. If an author passionately argues his or her point and offers relevant evidence to support that point, many people might be persuaded to believe the argument. However, readers who were originally and staunchly opposed to the argument would not likely be persuaded. Such readers would need to see how their original beliefs were invalid in order to be persuaded to an opposing argument. When you read, you should look for the ways in which a carefully planned argumentative essay refutes opposing viewpoints, rather than relying on the single view of the argument and evidence to be persuasive. For example, in the Deresiewicz essay referred to above, a careful reader could argue against Deresiewicz's warrants that the number of friends compromises the quality of friendship and that communication on the computer is limited, which are two assumptions that Deresiewicz fails to fully examine.

Methods of Argument

Much of the terminology above is drawn from the Toulmin method of argumentation. This system, developed by philosopher Stephen Toulmin and explained in his 1958 book *The Uses of Argument*, represented a departure from traditional formal logic. Toulmin's style instead offers a practical application of logic to create an argument using several steps. In its simplest form, a Toulmin argument consists of these elements:

- Claim: a debatable point that offers a reasonable, defendable position on a topic. *Electronic books should be sold to consumers at lower prices than paper books.*

- Grounds or data: reasons and evidence offered in support of the claim. *Paper books have become more expensive to produce, while electronic books cost less per unit to produce.*

- Warrants: often unspoken, these underlying assumptions connect the data to the claim. Although warrants are often widely held values or assumptions, they may themselves need to be justified. *Lower prices are more desirable. Prices charged to consumers should be roughly analogous to the costs of producing those products; items that cost more to produce should carry a higher price tag, and items that cost less to make should have a lower price.*

- Qualifications: terms that modify the scope of the argument to make it more palatable or defendable. ***Some*** *electronic book titles should be sold to consumers at lower costs than paper books.*

- Rebuttals: counterarguments to address opposing viewpoints. *Electronic books should be priced the same as paper books because although electronic books do not require expenditures on paper or printing, they may require additional expenditures on technology.*

In addition to using a Toulmin argument to create your own argument, you can also apply that same practical logic to others' writing to analyze the soundness of their arguments.

Another commonly used form is Rogerian argument. Named for psychologist Carl Rogers, this variety of argument focuses less on winning or pushing readers to accept a claim and more on establishing common ground with readers who might not agree with you. A Rogerian argument might be appropriate when addressing an emotionally charged topic or another situation when forceful attempts to persuade might alienate readers. A Rogerian argument begins by establishing common ground between those holding opposing views and the writer. In other types of argumentation, a statement of your claim would likely follow this introduction, but in the Rogerian style you defer stating your own position until later in your piece. Instead, you proceed by characterizing the opposition's position on the issue as neutrally as possible with the intention that readers with opposing perspectives feel heard by you. Only after demonstrating your clear and neutral understanding of the reader's perspective would you then neutrally state your own position on the issue. Then, you would conclude the argument by emphasizing the benefits to the reader of adopting your position. When writing to an audience you know will be hostile to your ideas or when addressing a highly controversial or emotional issue, you might consider using a Rogerian argument, with its emphasis on understanding the readers' needs.

Argumentation in the Disciplines

Because disciplines value different kinds of information and purposes, they have developed different genres and styles of writing for their communications. As such, argumentation, as it is described above, may not always be an appropriate form of text for some disciplines, or when used, the argumentative style is adapted to the unique purposes of the discipline.

In the Humanities disciplines, argumentation is valued and used often. Disciplines such as Philosophy, Literature, Art, Foreign Languages, History, and Theatre emphasize close reading of works, such as a novel or a painting. Most scholars begin with a tentative argument, a hypothesis that they want to develop. They take notes as they scrutinize the work and categorize these notes into similar themes. These notes become the grounds for their argument. They may also examine the context and background of the text or compare related works. After thinking through their evidence, they look at their possible hypothesis and work to connect this gradually forming argument to their evidence. They may revise their initial hypothesis, developing it into a stronger argument, or they may need to overhaul it completely based on the evidence. Because these scholars' work is based on close reading and understanding of the scrutinized text, their arguments are likely to be those that emphasize unique and individual interpretation, persuading audience members that the close reading done of the text is an important, unique piece of scholarship. They usually emphasize how their argument is different than prior argumentative scholarship concerning the same text, author, artist, or historical era.

The Social Science disciplines, like Sociology, Political Science, Psychology, and Anthropology, also value argumentation, although in a different style than the argumentative essay described above. The social sciences emphasize the data gathered and evidence built, with the argument or thesis arising from the evidence. The argument is likely to propose a new understanding of the data, although the data may come from a commonly studied social situation. The argument may emphasize less the uniqueness of the view and instead try to show that the argument being made is similar to other comparable studies. Social science texts would try to show why the argument is valuable to other social science scholars. Scholars in these fields place more emphasis on the evidence and the warrants for the evidence rather than on the argument made. While the argument is important to social science scholars, they are more likely to read carefully how the data were gathered and how the evidence connects to the argument.

In the Physical and the Applied Sciences, much more emphasis is placed on evidence and the methods of gathering evidence than on the argument made. In fact, many texts in the physical science disciplines might not be considered argumentative because they primarily report facts and factual observations. However, many scientists do publish essays or other documents that are argumentative in style. They might attempt to persuade readers that new research should be funded, that previously published scientific reports that had been overlooked were in fact highly important, or that new scientific information is valuable to others or to the public. Because scientists often report factual information, their writing may not be regarded as argumentation. But even factual scientific information can be quite controversial and be presented in an argumentative style. Consider writing regarding climate change or stem cell research; arguments abound in those highly controversial topics of scientific research. In fact, the more controversial the topic or the more groundbreaking a scientist perceives his or her work to be, the more likely the document reporting that research is to have a strongly written claim and strongly written warrants given for the argument. Typically, scientific texts emphasize evidence and the gathering of evidence as the primary element of the text with the argument or thesis statement considered almost self-evident. However, as the topic becomes more controversial or significant, the argument of the document is likely to acquire more, perhaps repeated, emphasis in the text.

When you read arguments, you should identify the arguable point, the logic and other appeals used, and connect the evidence and grounds to the arguable thesis. Doing so will help you analyze the validity of the author's ideas, recognize the style of argumentation used, and develop your own ideas for writing in argumentation essays.

Cross-Check

READING FOR LEARNING

- There are three distinct purposes for reading: to be entertained, to learn, and to analyze, and each reading purpose has strategies for making that task more efficient.
- When you are reading for meaning, you can use preparatory strategies, engagement strategies, and review strategies.
  - Preparatory strategies include reviewing already known information about the topic and the author, identifying your expectations for the text, skimming through the essay's headings, having useful resources, like a dictionary, at hand, and reading the chapter summary first.
  - Engagement strategies include actively highlighting important sentences, writing definitions of difficult words in the margins, circling and drawing lines between connecting or conflicting parts of a text, and keeping notes about your reaction, response, or questions of the text.
  - Review strategies include summarizing the main information of the text, reviewing a chapter summary, and recognizing what other information you still need to get.
- In thinking about an author's meaning, be aware of logical fallacies: evidence, relevance, language, and structure.
- Be sure to read visual aids, like charts, graphs, tables, diagrams, and even headings, which can give you important information in concise form.
- Reading from the Internet in order to learn can be a useful tool, but it requires a conscious awareness of and evaluation of different sites, as well as a shift in reading strategies.

READING FOR ANALYSIS AND ARGUMENT

- Reading for analysis helps you recognize possible strategies for writing that you can use in your own writing.
  - Reading and reviewing samples of a genre can help someone who is writing for the first time in that genre.
- Ask yourself, "What is the author saying?" and "What is the author doing?"
- Recognize and identify the specific location of the author's thesis.
  - Is this a thesis statement of fact, of personal opinion, of interpretation, or of an arguable point?

- ○ Determine how that author built up to and gave credence to the thesis statement.
- ○ Determine how the author expands and explains that point.
- Create an outline of the text to better determine the organizational pattern used by the author.
- Examine the conclusion of the text so as to identify possible strategies for writing your own conclusions.
- Identify if the text is a sample of argumentation and identify the strategies used.
  - ○ A thesis statement is usually an arguable point; ask yourself what could be the opposing side to the argument of the essay.
  - ○ What is the main argument? Is it an arguable point?
  - ○ Identify the reasons and evidence given to support the author's thesis.
  - ○ Distinguish the warrants or assumptions that back up the evidence.
  - ○ Determine how the argument is justified.
  - ○ Examine the logic of the argument. Are any fallacies noted? Does the conclusion logically follow from the evidence and propositions?

3

WRITING AND RESEARCHING
Genres, Practices, and Processes

Writing encompasses more than just the act of putting words on paper. Writing combines reading and knowing, thinking and listening. It involves reflecting on previous experiences, learning and reading about new ones, thinking about what your readers want to know about you and your chosen topic, and conveying your ideas to other people.

WRITING CONVENTIONS

As you learn to write in different disciplines, you will see that writing is governed by conventions, commonly referred to as rules, guidelines, and strategies: governing principles for writing.

Rules

Rules are mandates ("Always start a sentence with a capital letter" or "A sentence should always have a subject and a verb") that should only very rarely be broken. While you may find rules fussy and time-consuming, understanding these rules actually makes writing easier. Once you have memorized the rules, they become habitual, so you can focus less on following basic rules and devote more time focusing on ideas.

Rules also make the task of reading easier for your audience. Imagine how difficult it would be to read a twenty-page chapter if the author did not use capital letters, punctuation, or paragraph breaks to signal the completion of one thought and the beginning of a new thought. Over time, readers and writers have accepted certain conventions of writing such as punctuation, indentation, and capitalization to convey meaning to readers. These conventions have become rules, and they make the tasks of reading and writing easier to understand. It is true that some writers break such rules; however, these writers usually have philosophical or political reasons for doing so, reasons that give their writing depth and richness. Such effective rule-breaking, however, is rare, and novice writers are cautioned against this practice. When you have questions, you can consult a handbook, which provides guidance on understanding and implementing the rules and conventions of writing.

Guidelines

Other conventions are less strict than rules, so they would be more appropriately called guidelines. These conventions can be adapted to suit different purposes. For example, it is a common convention that a paragraph consists of several sentences. Some instructors might even go so far as to specify an ideal paragraph length. However, paragraphs can come in many different lengths: as short as one sentence or as long as a page. For example, in Emily Bernard's essay "Teaching the N-Word," the author uses several paragraphs that are shorter than four sentences and several long paragraphs. One paragraph is only a 5-word sentence: "Tonight, David orders a cosmopolitan." Such a sentence is as terse and concise a paragraph as you might find in any essay. It carries the entire weight of the idea that David has altered his habitual dining and drinking choices and that this new choice is significant.

One essential feature of a paragraph is a topic sentence, which states the paragraph's main point. A topic sentence also connects the subject of the paragraph to the main idea of the essay and may forecast the structure of the remaining sentences of the paragraph. The remaining sentences of the paragraph expand, exemplify, explain, or substantiate the topic sentence of the paragraph. If that one sentence is enough to explain the paragraph's topic fully, then no further sentences are necessary to complete the paragraph.

Another common guideline is that a thesis statement should be the last sentence of the introduction. While this is a fine habit, it is not a strict rule. Instead, careful readers can find thesis statements in different places depending on the writing genre. In a mystery novel, the main point of identifying the criminal usually comes near the end of the book, not at the beginning. Many published essays have thesis statements placed outside the introductory paragraph, as you will learn later in this chapter ("Developing a Thesis Statement"). A thesis statement announces the author's arguable belief about the topic. For some topics and audiences, it may take several paragraphs or pages of examining the topic before the author can reasonably explain his or her main point about the topic. Other essays effectively place the thesis statement as the first sentence, a good strategy for timed essay examinations when the topic is clearly stated in the exam question.

Guidelines such as these make the job of reading easier for the audience, but these conventions are more elastic than rules, allowing you room to maneuver, adapt, and shape your writing to suit your purpose. Guidelines like paragraph length, essay length, placement of topic sentence or thesis, and sentence length make your job as a writer easier, too. Once you know the guidelines for writing in a genre, you can apply them to your own compositions in that genre. However, the flexibility of guidelines also allows you to be creative and adaptable as a writer; when you know when, why, and how to change writing guidelines, you are a more effective writer. Such understanding comes from practicing critical reading and writing skills regularly.

Strategies

Strategies are conventions that are much less strict and formulaic than rules and guidelines. Instead, strategies are based more on individual preferences and processes than on commonly agreed upon conventions. For example, many writers find it helpful to make an outline before composing, while other writers find outlines confusing and limiting. Some writers correct their mistakes in punctuation, grammar, and spelling only after they have finished several drafts, while other writers find it more effective to correct as they compose. Some writers write the body (main part) of their texts first, and then write the introduction or conclusion later, while others find it easier to draft the introduction first before writing the body and conclusion.

Strategies help writers develop their work, rather than dictate format. In other words, use strategies to brainstorm for ideas and compose; use guidelines to organize and structure what you've written; and use rules to proofread and edit your final draft. As a writer, consider reflecting on your personal writing processes: how you like to write, methods that work for you, new strategies and processes to try, strategies that work well for some situations and genres but need changing for other genres. You should also try to vary and develop your strategies so that you have several different ones to help you when writing difficulties arise.

Learning the differences among rules, guidelines, and strategies for writing happens when you read critically (How do other authors write?) and when you spend time and effort practicing your own writing. Additionally, handbooks and rhetorics (books of strategies and guidelines) can help you grow as a writer. Working with a group of other writers, classmates, and peers can also help you understand how your writing is understood (or misunderstood, as the case may be) by real readers. Above all, be aware of your writing—of how you put words together, of how you think about and prepare to write, of how your writing will be read and understood by your audience. Before you set your mind to breaking or adapting rules and conventions for your writing, learn the most common rules and guidelines and the reasons behind those parameters so you can learn when to adhere to them strictly and when to deviate from them.

WRITING AS A CYCLICAL PROCESS

In most college-level writing classes, you will learn that writing is a process. Writing is more than a single event, more than just putting words on paper. Instead, writing combines varied activities all focused on the goal of producing an effective written communication about ideas or experiences. These activities are all part of the writing process: from coming up with ideas—called invention techniques—to researching, composing, organizing, editing, and submitting (or publishing) your ideas. Rather than envisioning these ideas as sequential steps, understand them as recurring, cyclical activities. They do not necessarily follow a certain order, nor do they occur only once in any writing project. These activities may occur in any order or be repeated in any sequence for the text to be effective. Experienced writers know that research may be required at multiple points in the process of writing, as reading about one's topic at the start of the process may not be sufficient, as questions can arise at any point in the writing process. Likewise, drafting and revising are often repeated activities for experienced, effective writers. The point is this: writing is a process that involves many different activities, and you may engage in them repeatedly at different points in the process.

Planning and Invention

To be successful with any writing project, a writer needs to plan the ideas to be put into the text. For the most part, this planning—what is often called invention—occurs from learning and reading about one's topic. But planning also involves more than simply thinking and reading: it involves developing a systematic approach for completing a piece of writing. You might read and think about many different ideas but never put those ideas into words. However, when you have a purpose—when you are assigned a writing project in a class or you desire to explain ideas to effect a change in readers' behaviors or thoughts—then you should engage in planning strategies to make your writing process more effective and efficient. Planning strategies include outlining ideas, making notes about what is already known and what still needs to be learned, analyzing what the audience expects to learn from the text, and thinking about the main point—the thesis statement—of the topic.

Outlining

You may choose to plan your writing by creating an outline of your ideas. Many writers use outlines for long, complex writing projects, but may not use one with simpler, more familiar projects. To create an outline:

- Write out all the ideas that you have about a topic. Then, sift through these ideas so only the most relevant remain, while other interesting yet irrelevant ideas are put aside.
- Focus on the main idea or main argument about the topic, and list it first.
- List the other ideas in the order of how they relate to the main idea:
  - Will they work as evidence to support or prove the main idea?
  - Will they help to explain the context, background, or history of the main topic?
  - Will they help to summarize the main points?
  - Will they argue against or oppose the main idea?
- Once you determine how these ideas function in relation to the main point, arrange them in similar categories, putting all evidentiary ideas (those ideas that support or prove the main idea) together; background or contextual knowledge usually comes early in the text, and summary-like ideas help to finish the text.

Such outlines help writers stay on track and focused on their task, but they are not meant to be strict formulas from which writers can never deviate. If you find that your outline prevents you from stating pertinent points about your topic, then you need to revise your outline, not necessarily your whole project. Here is a sample outline for an essay written to defend gay marriages:

Introduction: brief story about attending a commitment ceremony (gives topic, creates interest for reader)

Thesis: Like heterosexual American citizens, homosexual people deserve the right to be legally married, in order to receive the various legal advantages of other married couples.

Point One: about advantages: receiving tax benefits

Point Two: about advantages: receiving employee/work-related benefits, like health insurance

Point Three: about advantages: legal responsibility and rights in regard to inheritance, hospital visitations, etc.

Point Four: about advantages: legal right to freedom of choice

Conclusion: The legal advantages that homosexual couples could share with their heterosexual counterparts would give them a stronger sense of security, fiscal responsibility, and freedom.

Using Heuristics

One systematic technique for determining what you already know and what you still need to learn is the use of heuristics. These are systematic sets of questions that help a writer focus on the areas of knowledge surrounding a topic. Many different types of heuristics exist, more than can be explained here, but knowing just a few of these will help you systematically think about a topic.

Particle/Wave/Field Heuristic

One common heuristic is the tagmemic, or particle/wave/field heuristic, which borrows terminology from the field of physics. Applying this heuristic asks you to consider:

- Particle: describe the topic or object as clearly and precisely as possible.
- Wave: describe how the topic has evolved over time, its past, present, and future.
- Field: describe the larger context for this topic, how it relates to other issues beyond itself, including other fields, systems it belongs to, or purposes it serves.

For example, if your topic is laboratory testing on animals, your **particle answer** might be

Animal testing covers a wide range of different types of practices, purposes, and laboratories. Some laboratories have strict policies for the humane treatment of their animals, but other laboratories subject the animals to needless pain and torture. Some laboratories use animals to test experimental medications while other laboratories use animals to test physical reactions and painful levels of cosmetics, shampoos, and other skin care products.

For your **wave answer**, you might point out that

laboratory testing on animals used to be much less regulated than it is now. Now there are standards for animal care, laboratory maintenance, and licenses and permits required by local and state legislation.

For your **field answer**, you might discuss how

animal testing is connected to veterinary care, pharmaceutical development, and movements that support the humane treatment of animals.

As you answer these questions, you may realize that you need to research the laws governing animal testing in your region; you may also want to determine the prevalence of animal laboratories in your area or in the nation. In this way, using a heuristic can help you recognize what you already know and remind you of what you still need to research.

Aristotle's Topics

Another commonly used heuristic is Aristotle's topics. Applying these categories to your subject can help you understand how much you know about your topic and what you might still want to learn or how to proceed with your research.

- Definition: describe key terms related to your topic. *"Gun control" involves the regulation by the government of the rights of individuals to own and use firearms.*

- Comparison: describe how the topic is similar to and different from other closely related subjects. *Gun control is like other regulations regarding how people operate potentially dangerous equipment, like cars. Unlike driving regulations, which are usually the purview of state and local governments, the Second Amendment guarantees citizens the right to bear arms, which is usually interpreted to mean the right to possess firearms.*

- Relationship: describe the causes and effects related to the topic. *Incidents of gun violence have urged proponents to call for stricter gun control measures; the apparent constitutionality of possessing firearms has led to gun advocates calling for decreased gun control. The effect of this polarization has been an ongoing debate in this country regarding the place of guns in our society.*

- Testimony: describe experts' opinions on the topic. *Both sides have experts willing to testify to the rightness of the respective positions.*

- Circumstance: under what conditions is the topic possible, impossible, likely, or probable. *Compromises occur regularly on both sides of the debate, but complete satisfaction and agreement on the issue is improbable (and may be impossible).*

Similarly, other disciplines have sets of questions or heuristics that are more specific to that discipline. For example, in Economics, one learns to question the cost, effectiveness, and output surrounding a topic; in the field of Sociology, one questions the function, inter-relationship, and conflict surrounding a topic; in the Humanities disciplines, it is common to consider how race, class, and gender affect the topic or the development of the topic. These are narrow perceptions of these disciplines, but if you learn that many disciplines have certain sets of questions which are pertinent to their areas of study, you will learn to recognize other heuristics as you study in those disciplines, and you will learn to use these heuristics to help you plan your writing projects in those fields. Using a systematic set of questions like the examples above to determine what you already know and what still needs to be learned will help you focus on a wide range of ideas.

Analyzing Your Audiences

Many college students enter a writing assignment thinking that the only person they need to convince is the instructor who assigned the writing task. While the instructor who will evaluate the assignment does need to be convinced, persuaded, or otherwise impressed by your writing, consider audience as a broader and more complex issue than determining what your instructor wants. Primary audiences include real people who will read your texts, like your instructor and your peers; indirect or secondary audiences are people who might, if given a chance to read your writing, be interested in your topic; and tertiary audiences are those imagined people who would never read your text but are interested in your subject. You should consider all of these groups, both real and imaginary, as members of your audience who need to be convinced of your claims. For example, if you were writing about how exercise improves health, you might consider addressing your work to the director of the Health Center on your campus to convince him or her to implement a campus plan for students and employees to increase their exercise. Your real audience would remain your instructor and classmates, but the primary audience would also include the director of the campus health center. Your secondary audience would be students and employees who would need to be convinced to increase their exercise and trained in the most appropriate ways to do so. Your secondary audience might also include the employees of the campus health center who would implement your ideas. Your tertiary audience might be people at other universities or members of society at large who would benefit from increased exercise. The first two levels of audience must be considered when writing your text, and it sometimes helps to consider a tertiary audience, too.

To analyze your audience, you need to ask yourself these questions:

- *Who are my audiences? Who is my primary audience? Secondary audience? Tertiary audience? Are these audience members real or imagined? Will they really read my text or can I imagine them reading my text?*

- *What demographic information do I know about my audience? Are they likely to be older than me? Where do they reside and is this geographic region likely to have different ideas, values, and beliefs than me? What level of education will these people have?*

- *What will my audiences likely already know about my topic? What will they not know? What kinds of ideas will they expect to learn in my text? What will I need to teach them?*

- *What beliefs or views of my topic will my audience already have? Will they be receptive, neutral, or hostile to my claim? How much will I need to refute their preconceived notions of the topic?*

- *What kinds of evidence, grounds, or appeals will most likely work with my audiences? How can I organize my ideas and evidence so as to be most persuasive to these groups of people?*

After thinking through these questions about your audiences, you can determine their needs and expectations. You will probably discover that certain information or a particular approach is essential for inclusion in your text, depending on your purpose, genre, and topic, while other information and issues of style will be less important. Thinking about your audiences and planning for their needs will help you develop the most effective document for the task.

Writing Arguments

As discussed in Chapter 2, argumentation is a valued mode of writing in many college courses, both to read and to write. You will be asked to write essays in which you will argue with evidence, grounds, warrants, and logic to persuade your audience to believe your claim. Based upon the discipline of the class and the genre of the text to be written, you will need to adapt your argumentation style to the disciplinary and genre expectations of your audience. The key element in all argumentative writing is to emphasize how your main claim is valuable and important to your audience, to explain why they should believe your claim. To do so, you will need to write powerful, arguable thesis statements, explain clearly and with detail about your evidence, show how your evidence connects to your argument, and explain what assumptions or beliefs underlie your evidence and claims.

Developing a Thesis Statement

One main invention strategy of any writing project is to develop your main point or argument, commonly called a thesis statement. To write a thesis statement, you first need to plan your ideas, although you may return to these planning activities even after you have determined your main point. You will also need to think about your audience's knowledge about a topic, their purposes for reading, what they expect to learn from reading your work, and how they expect information to be presented in your text.

A thesis statement announces the writer's belief or opinion about a topic. It is rare that an effective thesis statement will actually use the words, "I believe that . . . ." because readers understand the thesis is a statement of the author's beliefs. A thesis statement is arguable, so a reader could conceivably argue against it or oppose it. Thesis statements are not commonly known facts. While the idea that the earth revolved around the sun was controversial in Galileo's time, controversial enough to have him imprisoned, such a main point now would be uninteresting and border on the absurd. Readers already know this fact, so as a thesis statement it would be ineffective.

To determine if your thesis statement is arguable, consider what your audience already knows and what they will want to learn about your topic as they read. Also, consider what other points you will need to use in order to prove your argument to your audience. It is not enough to state simply your thesis statement, you must also marshal your evidence so as to substantiate your claim. Developing your thesis statement early in the writing process will help you determine what else you will need to learn about your topic to be persuasive to your audience.

RESEARCHING

Researching can occur at almost any stage during the writing process. If you begin knowing little about a topic, you are likely to research early in the writing project. If you are already familiar with the subject, you may research later in the project, or even after you have completed a first draft of your text. You may find that once you begin to revise that you need to find more information about your topic in order to effectively revise your discussion.

To research a topic, you should become familiar with several different methods of gathering information—from library resources to electronic resources; from expert testimony to conducting your own primary research of surveys, questionnaires, interviews, experiments, and other empirical research gathered from the field.

Types of Research

Primary research involves discovering previously unknown facts. Different disciplines have different methods of conducting primary research, which you will learn as you study in those fields. Generally, scientific disciplines engage in experimental research (like experiments conducted in laboratories) or field research (like observations of wild animal behaviors, plant growth, or geological excavations); social science disciplines use research that is more people-focused, like surveys and interviews, or observation of behaviors such as teen smoking and peer group pressure; humanities disciplines likely engage in close reading and interpreting of the literary text, art work, or musical composition, such as a study of biblical references in Shakespeare's sonnets or an account of how early childhood activities shaped the musical career of Beethoven.

Secondary research involves learning what other scholars or researchers have already discovered about a topic. Typically, these scholars are considered experts, and when you quote their research, you are using expert testimony to bolster your ideas. While you can and should find a good bit of scholarship in your textbooks, you should also become familiar with library and electronic resources to find more information. Your campus library will usually have several different resources to help you gather knowledge. These resources are listed under "Starting Your Research" below. Librarians, who are trained to find information, usually know the best places to find scholarship on your subject.

A type of research not commonly taught but frequently consulted is that of tertiary research, which is the most distanced (removed from engaging primarily and directly with one's topic) type of research. It is the gathering and categorizing of data about secondary research in a systematic way. For some professional researchers, it can be meta-analyses of huge piles of secondary research, like massive epidemiological studies of the published research about the effects of hormone replacement therapy across the nation. If you were a public health researcher interested in the effects of estrogen given to women ages 40 and older, as a primary researcher you would study these effects on a local group of female patients and you would publish these results. Secondary research would be to gather many of these published research reports about the effects of estrogen on middle-aged women. Tertiary research would gather all the primary and secondary research reports published, engage in a systemized analysis, typically some kind of statistical formula, and would show the results of this systematic analysis, with the goal of showing the overall effects of this hormone replacement treatment on a large section of the population.

Starting Your Research

Typically your class assignment or purpose in writing will determine which type of research gathering—primary, secondary, or tertiary—you will use. For most college writing assignments, you will be expected to conduct secondary research, and doing so requires some planning ahead of time. How do you go about finding these published research articles? Where should you start? Should you use one or several different search strategies? To do a good job with your research activity and to keep from feeling overwhelmed, you should become very familiar with your academic library resources—both in person and online. Typically, academic librarians are skilled researchers eager to help you find the best resources for your topic. You might begin your research process by making an appointment to meet with a librarian to talk through your research ideas.

Libraries typically offer many types of research materials to students, and librarians can help you locate these items. Some of the most commonly consulted library resources are

- Books: available in print and sometimes electronically. Many books circulate but reference titles are often restricted to library use only and cannot be checked out.

- Journals: available in print or electronically. Recent issues of journals are usually available in print as individual copies. Full volumes of journals are later bound like books. Journals, too, may be designated for library use only.

- Databases: these electronic resources might be general resources, like *Academic Search Complete*, that contain sources including magazines, journals, and newspapers on a wide array of topics, or they might focus on a specific discipline. Databases often contain some or all of the indexed sources as full-text, so you can print or email a piece directly from the database.

- Indexes: available in print or electronically. These lists or databases are usually organized by topic or discipline and provide citation information for the listed materials. Using that information, you then find the book or article in the library.

Your university's librarians may offer classes or individualized consultation sessions to assist you in learning the most commonly used resources for a particular discipline.

When it comes to finding sources, remember that libraries are organized to help patrons easily find information. Most libraries maintain an online electronic version of the now-extinct card catalog: important pieces of information about all the material—books, magazines, newspapers, journals, documents, videos, recordings, etc.—that the library owns. Catalog entries include the names of authors, editors, producers; titles of documents, books, articles, columns, movies, songs; publication dates and acquisition dates; publisher; the location of the material; and the current status (e.g. checked out or on hold). Keep in mind, however, that catalogs only list items that the library actually has in its possession. There are many other sources that you can find through your library's database system which may not be listed in its catalog. Electronic catalogs typically allow you to search by topic, name of author or editor, title, or keyword. Here is a sample of a card catalog screen in which video games is entered as a subject:

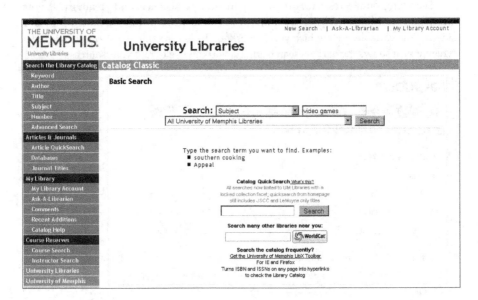

In the example above, the topic "video games" was entered as a subject, for which 22 entries were found within the university library system; the same topic was entered as a title, for which only 4 entries listed that phrase in their titles. The same topic was entered as a keyword, for which 88 entries were listed, many of which were indirectly connected to the topic of video games. If you do not find many sources on your first search, try using the different types of searches (title, subject, keyword, author, etc.) with your topic.

Academic libraries also offer online indexes and databases, like *Wilson Web Database*, *Lexis-Nexis*, and *JSTOR*, in which you can find sources that are external to the physical library. A database is an organized collection of information, typically housed electronically or digitally, and usually is a listing of publications. An index, much like a database, is an organized system to find information; indexes may or may not be electronic. Many come in printed forms, as well. Like electronic catalogs, online indexes can be searched by subject, keywords, author, title of book or journal, title of article, publication dates, etc. Many of the listed sources you can access immediately online; other sources you might have to request through the library's interlibrary loan system, a process by which your library will borrow for a limited time a copy of the specific resources you are requesting.

You can also search for brief descriptions of sources, summaries or abstracts, and by full-text availability. All of these types of information can help you find useful sources for your research project. Keep in mind that indexes will give you information only about publications that are categorized by that particular index. There may be other publications on your topic that are not listed in an index. You may need to search through several different indexes and databases to get the best overall view of the information available on your topic. Also be aware that indexes will list information for which your library may not have access, in which case you would need to request these sources through your library's interlibrary loan department.

Searching online resources requires patience, persistence, and creativity. If your searches are yielding unsatisfactory results, you can adapt your research strategies by considering the variables with which you're working. Here is a sample of an electronic index screen which shows the various search criteria you can use to find your sources:

This particular search found 16 articles in scholarly journals and, when the "scholarly journal" option was unchecked, over 190 articles, many of which were in trade magazines, like *Business Week* and *National Mortgage News*. Note also the date of publications researched was very limited: to articles only before 1999.

Narrowing Your Topic

For both print and electronic researching, start with a specific topic rather than a broad term. For example, if you wanted to research the issue of racial discrimination, you would find thousands of entries. Instead, if you narrow and focus that term, for example "racial discrimination, academic institutions, Oregon," you would find fewer hits, but those that come up would be more relevant and useful. If you find too many or too few references, you should limit your topic term (i.e. from "northwestern states" to "Oregon"), or by date, document type, or subject area so as to find more relevant references. As you read through the cited references, you may also recognize that you need to re-adapt your research terms to make them more relevant to your sources and to current knowledge about the topic. Here is a sample screen of this narrowed, specific search described in *Wilson Web Omnifile*:

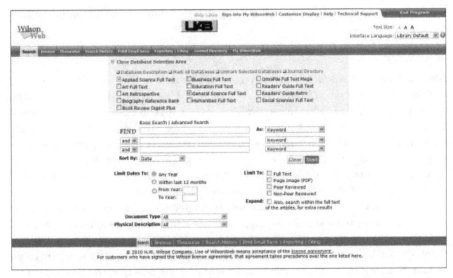

This particular search returned 2 listings, one of which was accessible as a full text. However, by changing the searched keyword terms from "academic/discrimination/Oregon" to "academic/racial/discrimination," more than 150 articles were found. Depending on your topic, your purpose in writing, and your claim, you will need to continually revise and narrow your search terms until you find the sources most suitable for your text.

Secondary research will take time. Some writers like to begin their research immediately on the Internet, going first to such sites as *Wikipedia* and other informative sites. In some instances, these may be fine places to start, but you must evaluate the veracity, validity, and quality of the information given (see Chapter 2), and expand your research beyond these preliminary sites. High quality, informational web sites, for example, almost always list references; you might use these references to learn more in-depth or valid information about your topic than what is available in *Wikipedia*. Here is a checklist of strategies for determining the worth of a source:

1. Does the source give a comprehensive view of the topic? Avoid sources that seem too short, narrowly focused, or one-sided.
2. Does the source present general, well-known information or specific information? Dig deeper than those sources that give only general information.
3. Does the source provide evidence for its claims? Is the evidence fair, logical, and truthful?
4. Does the source give credit to its sources? Avoid those sources that appear unrealistically knowledgeable and do not cite their sources.
5. Does the source seem credible and reliable? Is the author a credible expert in this field? Avoid sources whose ideas seem too far-fetched to be reasonable for your audience.
6. Do other sources support most of the information given in one source? Strive for a balance between sources that focus on well-known information and those that offer additional or fresh perspectives.
7. What is the purpose of the source? Reject those sources whose only purpose is to sell you a product or promote a political candidate.
8. Is the source chronologically pertinent to your topic? Avoid sources that are out of date.

Taking Notes

After you find several sources, read through them for information, facts, ideas, opinions, statistics, or other types of knowledge about the topic. As you read, take careful notes. Consider keeping notes either on separate pieces of paper, like note cards or document files, or directly on the printed copies of the references. Whatever your method, be aware that you may be called upon to produce these notes and you may need to prove the veracity of your research to your instructor, your audience, or your publisher. Many writers have gotten into trouble by not keeping careful notes, and have been accused of lying or plagiarizing when they could not produce notes on their research.

Many researchers and writers compose annotated bibliographies to organize their references and source materials. An annotation, in this sense, is a summary or abstract of the article, book chapter, or book. Typically such annotations begin with a bibliographic entry for the publication (author, title, date, pages) and include a paragraph or two detailing the author's thesis statement and the points used to support that thesis. Sometimes an annotation includes an evaluative comment about the worth of this article for a specific research purpose or audience. A list of annotations arranged in alphabetical order comprises an annotated bibliography, which can serve as a valuable reference when you are writing a research essay and creating a bibliography. Be careful: many sources are published with an abstract or summary already in place. While these are helpful for reading, do not rely on or copy these abstracts for your research notes. Using the same words from the abstract in your paper without citing this abstract as one of your sources is plagiarism. Instead of copying, write your own summaries or annotations, focusing on how each article relates to the points you want to make in your research project. Here is a sample annotation in which this author specified the main audience of the original article in order to evaluate its usefulness for her project:

Nelson, Erin. "What Roe v. Wade Should Have Said." *Osgoode Hall Law Journal* 44.4 (2006): 759–65. Print.

Erin Nelson asserts that there is much controversy in the Roe v. Wade decision, which granted American women a constitutional right to terminate a pregnancy. She offers three purposes for examining this decision: to provide a vehicle through which to "reexamine the premises of Roe and fundamental rights jurisprudence at the beginning of a new century"; to offer a means to experiment with the theories of constitutional interpretation supported by many of the contributors in the aftermath of Roe, and finally, to provide a forum for addressing questions about the role of the judiciary that have arisen since the Roe decision. She referenced a project that asked a number of constitutional scholars to write opinions on Roe based only on materials available when the case was being decided. This article is for students in constitutional law and anyone interested in the abortion movement.

SYNTHESIZING AND INCORPORATING BORROWED MATERIAL WITHOUT PLAGIARIZING

As you conduct secondary research, organize your gathered research into similar categories: scholars who give current information, statistical information, testimonial experiences or narrative accounts, or theoretical perceptions. It is important for the effectiveness of your writing and for the clarification of the topic for your reader that you cite your references according to similar information given, rather than according to the order in which you found them.

As you organize your information into categories, make notes about how each reference relates to another one, and then write how those two or three references connect, a strategy called **synthesizing.** This is an important step for your readers: rather than simply listing your sources, take the time to show how each connects to the others and to your ideas. Your text—your thesis statement, your evidence, your background knowledge, your conclusions—will be clear to your readers and more effective in your goal of persuading your audiences to believe you.

As you read and gather your references, think about how your ideas can build, stretch, deepen, revitalize, or oppose the ideas of those scholars who have researched your topic before you. Think about how you can use this source to help you prove your point or how you can use it to show that newer information is critical to a valid understanding of the topic. It is important in your development as a scholar and writer that you offer evidence pertinent to your subject to develop your argument. As a writer, show that you have learned from and can build on the ideas of previous scholars. Such work indicates that you are capable of learning from others and that you are giving others credit for their work. Further, citing your sources will show that you are a legitimate scholar, in that you want to acknowledge the work of other experts. Most importantly, as a student, citing all of your sources will keep you from being prosecuted for plagiarism. Taking careful notes and labeling all sources correctly will help when you write your text so that you can find the correct citation information quickly and easily.

Paraphrasing, Summarizing, and Quoting

To use the ideas of others, you can quote, paraphrase, or summarize their ideas in your writing. **Summarizing** uses your own words to shorten the ideas of the original author, rather than using his or her own words. A good summary focuses on the main point of the original piece and briefly mentions the points or evidence used to support the main idea. When summarizing, you should identify the author of the source, even if you are using your own words. There are no specific rules for the correct length of a summary; length is determined by the length of the original piece and how you are using this source. Despite its conciseness, however, a summary must accurately represent the original article. You would write a summary when the original text is long but you need to tell your readers, briefly, only the main ideas of the author. If the original text is short, you may find that a summary of that piece is too short, and a paraphrase might be more appropriate.

Paraphrasing is similar to summarizing in that you use your own words to give the ideas of the original author; you would not use the author's own words. However, paraphrases usually relate the ideas of a specific portion of a text, rather than the main point emphasized in a summary. Further, paraphrasing is not merely swapping out the author's words for synonyms of your own. To paraphrase correctly—and to avoid plagiarizing—you must change both the vocabulary and the sentence structure of the original work. Paraphrasing works well for ideas that are complex or are written at a vocabulary level that is beyond the easy comprehension of your readers. In such cases, you would use your own more easily understood words to convey the complex ideas of the original article. In a paraphrase, you still need to identify the author of the original article. When you paraphrase, you may find that your written paraphrase is longer than the original text. Thus, you would probably not use a paraphrase for a long article but for a particular section of an article; to discuss the entire article, a summary would work more effectively.

Quoting uses the author's exact words enclosed in quotation marks. Again, you must identify the author of your source. When you quote, you use however much of the original source material you determine is necessary to get the author's point across to your readers. Typically, quoting is used when you cannot find better words of your own to convey the author's ideas or when you are writing a close analysis of the original words, as in a literary analysis. Be careful to use the exact words of the author and to use them in their original context and meaning; it is unethical to use an author's words in ways that distort the original meaning. For example, a congressperson who states, "I would support an increase in the income tax, but it would be disastrous to my constituents," would be misquoted if a disreputable reporter wrote this of the congressperson's opinions: Congressperson X supports an increased income tax when he states, "I . . . support an increase in the income tax." Such a quote does use the original exact words, but removes them from their original context and meaning.

Citing sources correctly and ethically requires careful attention to detail and patience in developing and composing your text. Here is an example of some poorly cited paraphrases and quotes, followed by a well-cited quotation:

Original Source: Starr, Paul. "End of a Mandate." *The Struggle for Medical Care*. New York: Basic Books. 1982.

"From psychiatry criticism spread to medicine at large. It had long been known that medical care, especially when compared with the environment or social behavior, has relatively modest effect on mortality rates. Nonetheless, the idea that Americans were getting a diminishing return from their increasing investment in medical care hit with the force of a thunderclap in the mid-1970s. It suddenly struck intellectuals and policy makers of diverse persuasions that this was the answer to those who constantly wished to expand access to medical care. 'The marginal value of one—or one billion—dollars spent on medical care will be close to zero in improving health,' wrote the neoconservative Aaron Wildavsky in a clever essay that gave the title *Doing Better and Feeling Worse* to an influential volume on health care sponsored by the Rockefeller Foundation" (409).

Problematic Source Use

1. Medicine has come under much criticism because it has little effect on mortality rates. (Poor use of source—does not give credit to the original author, Paul Starr)

2. According to Paul Starr, medicine came under much criticism in the 1970's because it had only a modest effect on mortality rates. (Poor use of source—uses exact words without inserting quotation marks)

3. Policy makers of the 1970's had little desire to invest more money into medical access because society received very little benefit in terms of better health. (Good paraphrase, but credit needs to be given to original author, Paul Starr, whose ideas these were)

4. According to Starr, "the force of a thunderclap in the mid-1970's . . . struck intellectuals and policy makers of diverse populations." (Misquoting the original source, taking the words out of their original meaning)

5. From psychiatry criticism spread to medicine at large. It had long been known that medical care, especially when compared with the environment or social behavior, has relatively modest effect on mortality rates. Nonetheless, the idea that Americans were getting a diminishing return from their increasing investment in medical care hit with the force of a thunderclap in the mid-1970's. (Poor use of source—the exact words were used without using quotation marks or giving credit to original author)

6. According to Starr, medical care, it had long been suspected, when contrasted with living conditions or behavior, has fairly little impact on mortality rates. (Poor paraphrase—although the author is mentioned and some vocabulary is changed, the sentence structure remains essentially the same as the original)

Clear, Ethical Source Use

7. According to Starr, policy makers of the 1970s had little desire for an "increasing investment in the medical care" because they were seeing "a diminishing return" (409). (Good use of a source—uses exact words with quotation marks, fully cites the source, and is true to the original meaning)

8. Policy makers of the 1970s, according to Starr, portrayed minimal changes to mortality rates relative to medical funding as a lack of return on investment, helping them justify withholding increases in financial support for health care (409). (Good paraphrase—maintains the sense of the original but changes the sentence structure and vocabulary of the original piece)

All of these uses require that you state, either in the sentence or in parentheses at the end of the borrowed material, from whom you borrowed the material. Competent writers usually combine two or more of these techniques when they borrow someone else's ideas. For example, if you read an article whose ideas would be useful in your essay, you would not want to paraphrase the entire article, which would be too long to include in your writing project; however, if you summarized most of the article while paraphrasing some main points and quoting specific passages for which you cannot find other words, then you could effectively get most of the article's ideas into a short section of your essay while still showing you are an ethical and competent scholar who can borrow other scholars' ideas and build on them.

When you use other people's ideas and words, be sure to document these sources according to the style that your instructor or discipline has specified, usually MLA (Modern Language Association) style in the Humanities disciplines and APA (American Psychological Association) in the sciences. Both of these documentation styles are discussed in detail later in this chapter.

ORGANIZING IDEAS

When you compose your ideas, you will want to organize them to make the job of understanding your text easy for your readers. When written ideas are organized in familiar patterns, readers will be more likely to understand intuitively how points will be connected. When you organize your ideas, position them in patterns that make sense and that are widely acceptable.

Here is a list of common organizational patterns:

- General to specific: give a general idea, followed by specific examples, reasons, details, numbers, etc.
- Specific to general: give specific examples, reasons, details, numbers, etc., followed by a general idea
- Spatial: works well for describing physical and visual objects, like art work, architecture, rooms, geometry, etc.
- Chronological: works well for narrating action, a story, or explaining a process.
- Definition: define the term, tell when it happens, what it's not, where it's likely to occur, examples of, etc.
- Division: break an idea into separate parts and explicate each part
- Classification: group separate items into similar categories
- Least important to most important: leave your reader with your most important point last
- Most important to least important: if your reader has little time to read, give the most important point first, frequently used in journalism
- Comparison and contrast: AAABBB or ABABAB

Some disciplines have ready-made patterns of organization; for example, in the sciences, articles typically follow one of two patterns, either IMRAD or IRDAM. These are acronyms for the order of specified sections: introduction, methodology, results, and discussion, or less commonly, introduction, results, discussion and methods. All of these organizational strategies, whether or not specified by a discipline, are all commonly perceived patterns of information. When readers understand how ideas relate to each other through familiar patterns of organization, they are more likely to be persuaded to believe your thesis, to reach the goal of your text, than when they stumble over your ideas, wondering how each point is connected to the other ideas.

To determine the best pattern of organization, you might outline using several different patterns. You will also need to consider how your ideas relate to each other: do some oppose or contradict each other? Do some ideas extend previous ones? Are some ideas more important or more trivial than others? Determining how your main points and sub-points connect and relate to each other will help you find a suitable pattern of organizing your text.

Transitioning between Ideas

Once you have established how your ideas connect to each other, you will be able to give the reader signals—called **transitions**—about the connections between your sub-points. Transitions are words or phrases that indicate to your reader that you are moving from one idea to another connected one, typically demonstrating how these ideas are connected. Words and phrases such as *therefore, in conclusion, however, subsequently,* and *further* are used to signal a certain type of relationship between ideas as you move from one to another: addition, example, contrast, comparison, concession, result, summary, sequence, and place. Knowing how your ideas connect will help you choose which category or word to use. Transitions are usually placed at or near the beginning of sentences or paragraphs. With each transition, you will help to clarify your ideas, making them more understandable for your reader. Following is a sample paragraph that uses several transitional words and phrases (italicized):

> Before the days of extreme sports, people participated in more traditional athletic events, usually in team sports, like baseball, football, and basketball. *Of course*, the player was required to pay careful attention to the other team members if the team were to be successful. *Moreover*, while watching the other players like the quarterback, players would make their own choices of actions or plays to make. When the quarterback would give brief instructions of the next play to make, *for example*, every member of the team would make split-second decisions about which member of the opposing team to tackle, who to watch, and when to run, while following the quarterback's directions in order to make the most of the team's efforts in that play. Such coordinated activity increases a player's ability to listen and collaborate with others. *In contrast*, newer extreme sports, usually based on the individual's own decisions and actions, do not strengthen this kind of coordinated collaboration. All athletes in these extreme sports see the competition through their own goal to win. *Thus*, extreme sports cannot be considered an effective means for enhancing teamwork and collaboration.

Here are some commonly used transitional words and phrases, categorized according to their relationships with other ideas.

Addition	Also, in addition, too, moreover, and, besides, further, furthermore, equally important, next, then
Example	For example, for instance, thus, as an illustration, namely, specifically
Contrast	But, yet, however, on the other hand, nevertheless, nonetheless, conversely, in contrast, on the contrary, still, at the same time
Comparison	Similarly, likewise, in like manner, in the same way, in comparison
Concession	Of course, to be sure, certainly, naturally, granted
Result	Therefore, thus, consequently, so, accordingly, due to this, as a result
Summary	Hence, in short, in brief, in summary, in conclusion, finally, on the whole
Chronology	First, second, firstly, secondly, next, then, finally, afterwards, before, soon, later, during, meanwhile, subsequently, immediately, at length, eventually, in the future, currently
Place	In the front, in the foreground, in the back, in the background, at the side, adjacent, nearby, in the distance, here, there

Working with Visual Aids

Another strategy for making ideas clear for your reader is to use visual aids when appropriate for your topic. While some disciplines, such as philosophy, literature, and history, rarely need visual aids to make their points, you will find that these disciplines discuss subjects that are somewhat difficult to visualize, like the concepts of justice, inhumanity, the existence of God, or other abstract notions. Other disciplines, such as chemistry, economics, sociology, and medicine, use visual aids with more frequency. Tables and charts can be very helpful for giving exact numbers and data to your readers in a concise, memorable, easily located format. Graphs are used for data that is often compared to itself, either by separating the data into components or by comparing data from similar topics, like comparing gross national revenue by state or by previous years. Diagrams or pictures are useful for showing how to complete a process, like installing a new door on your house or constructing your new gas grill. Other visual aids, like photographs, can be helpful for showing the detail of a topic.

To use a visual aid, determine whether or not your information could be made clearer or more understandable to your reader. If you determine that readers could be helped with a visual aid, you then should decide, based on the data that you have gathered or the information you want to give, which visual aid is most appropriate for your information. Always use visual aids to supplement or support your prose, not to detract from or take the place of your words. A combination of text and visual aids should work together to give your ideas and information to your reader, not take the place of each other. Never rely on charts or graphs alone to give information to your reader, as some readers will skip these elements. Alternatively, do not rely on prose alone to give important information that would be best understood in table format.

Place any visual aid as close to the paragraph in which you explain that same data. Alert your reader to the visual aid with a phrase like "In the following table" or "(See Figure XX)." Certain types of software, like word processing or spreadsheet programs, may already have options for creating some kinds of visual aids, which can make your job of inserting these aids in your text much easier. Finally, if you find a visual aid on the Internet or in a source and you want to use that visual aid, you must cite that chart, table, graph, or image just like you would cite the words of a source, by giving credit to the original source.

REVISING, EDITING, AND PROOFREADING

By no means do revising and editing always come at the end of a writing project. Many writers return to previous strategies after revising and editing their project and may return to revising and editing after several rounds of planning, researching, and drafting. Do not expect that you will write the perfect text the first time that you put your ideas into prose. Instead, plan on writing and re-writing your text several times to make it as polished, effective, and persuasive as possible.

Revising means to re-think or re-see one's a topic from a different perspective. While it could mean a large-scale rethinking and rewriting of the topic, revision usually entails re-seeing smaller sections or sub-points of a subject. Perhaps you will need to add some additional research or references to one of your sub-points, or maybe you will need to re-organize your points. You may discover that using a heuristic will help you envision new ways of thinking about or writing about a topic; perhaps your text discusses the current and future existence of a topic, and by using a heuristic, you learn that discussing your subject in terms of its history would also be beneficial for your readers.

Revising can also involve reorganizing your ideas into more appropriate paragraphs or adding more explanation about a topic. One good strategy is to ask of each sentence and/or paragraph: What is this sentence (or paragraph) doing? What is it saying? As you answer these questions about your own writing, you will see places where you can move, alter, delete, or add parts of your text. In short, when you revise your writing project, think of revision in terms of re-seeing new dimensions or perspectives rather than in terms of finding new words. Revising usually happens at the level of whole paragraphs or sets of related paragraphs rather than individual sentences.

Editing involves rewriting sentences or phrases so as to clarify your meaning. It can require deleting unnecessary phrases, substituting one word for a whole phrase, making a sentence more concise, lengthening a sentence or phrase so as to add more clarity, adding transitional words or phrases, finding more appropriate words, combining sentences, and eliminating repeated ideas. Editing usually occurs at the sentence level.

Proofreading is the last step in the writing process. When you proofread, you correct mistakes in wording, punctuation, or grammatical structure. Usually this involves fixing spelling or typographical mistakes and punctuation errors, eliminating repeated words, correcting subject-verb disagreements, and other grammatical errors. Because proofreading requires slow, careful reading, many writers call on the expertise of a classmate or another reader to help them find their mistakes.

Another proofreading strategy is to read one's text backwards and aloud, which forces a reader to slow down and pay attention to each word as it is spoken. This strategy can be helpful for those writers who compose and read quickly. Even if you engage in some proofreading before re-drafting parts of or the whole essay, you should always re-proofread as the final step in your writing process.

DOCUMENTING SOURCES

In your writing, you must clarify to readers which ideas are yours and which ideas you have borrowed from other sources. To accomplish this goal of giving credit to others, you document sources both in the text of your essay, using signal phrases and parenthetical citations, and on a bibliography called either the works cited (MLA) or reference list (APA).

Occasionally, confusion arises about what ideas you are obligated to cite.

Information that does not need to be cited:

- Common knowledge: George Washington was the first president of the United States
- Well-known, easily verifiable, undisputed facts: 3.14 is pi; William Blake wrote "The Sick Rose"
- Your own ideas and perspective

Information that must be cited:

- Other people's words and ideas
- Other people's perspectives, even if they also involve well-known facts: for example, a particular interpretation of Blake's poem
- Obscure or disputed facts and information

In general, if there is a question about whether a citation is needed, go ahead and include one. While over-citing in an essay can be irksome for readers, it is not wrong to cite material that does not need to be cited. Omitting required citations, however, may lead to charges of plagiarism.

When incorporating the words and ideas of other people into your writing, as discussed earlier, you may summarize, paraphrase, or quote. Summaries, paraphrases, or quotes are also usually accompanied by signal phrases, which indicate to readers that you are using someone else's ideas, and then parenthetical citations, which give readers additional information about the source.

In MLA the parenthetical citation usually consists of the author's last name and page or paragraph number: (Foster 3). In APA the parenthetical citations for summaries and paraphrases consist of the author's last name and year of publication: (Foster, 2004). For direct quotations in APA, parenthetical citations contain the author's last name, year of publication, and the page number: (Foster, 2004, p. 3).

Signal phrases indicate to your reader that you are incorporating someone else's ideas and how those concepts relate to your own perspective. They usually consist of the author's name and a verb, which may also indicate the author's attitude toward the topic.

Some verbs you might use in a signal phrase:

- agrees
- argues
- asserts

- denies
- indicates
- implies
- notes
- says

If you mention the author's name in your signal phrase, you don't need to repeat it in the parenthetical citation: Rogers notes that . . . (22).

Quoted material must make sense in the context of your writing. You must include all the necessary information for readers, and the grammar and punctuation of direct quotations must be exactly as it appears in the quoted material. If you need to omit information from a direct quotation, use ellipsis marks to indicate material is missing.

If you need to change or add words or word parts to make a direct quotation make sense in your sentence, use square brackets to indicate what you have added or changed:

ORIGINAL: "Beginning readers can find the novel mystifying, irritating, and highly peculiar" (Foster 3).

WITH CLARIFYING INFORMATION: "Beginning readers can find [Pynchon's *The Crying of Lot 49*] mystifying, irritating, and highly peculiar" (Foster 3).

MLA Documentation

The Modern Language Association (MLA) style of documentation is widely used in modern language, humanities, and literature classes. This style emphasizes the author's name and location of cited material within the text. Like many documentation styles, MLA requires two parts to its documentation: in-text (or parenthetical) citations and a list of all the sources used in the essay, called the works cited. All the parenthetical citations in your paper must have a corresponding entry on the works cited page, where full bibliographic information for each source is given.

In-Text Citations

Parenthetical citations usually include the author's last name and page or paragraph number. Often, online material has no page or paragraph numbers, so that information is omitted from parenthetical citations if it is not provided.

Direct quotation from a book with one author, author mentioned in signal phrase:
Foster argues, "the real reason for a quest is always self-knowledge" (3).

Direct quotation from a book with one author, author not mentioned in signal phrase:
"The real reason for a quest is always self-knowledge" (Foster 3).

Paraphrase from a book with one author, author mentioned in signal phrase:
Characters rarely go on quests for their stated purpose, Foster notes, but instead use them to engage in self-discovery (3).

Book with two or three authors:
Authors' names in signal phrase:

> Levitt and Dubner call the real-estate agent "a different breed of expert than a crimi-
> nologist, but she is every bit the expert" (5).

Authors' names in parenthetical citation:

> A real-estate agent is seen by some as "a different breed of expert than a criminologist,
> but she is every bit the expert" (Levitt and Dubner 5).

In parenthetical citations for sources with four or more authors, you can list all the authors'
names, or name only the first author followed by the abbreviation *et al.*:

> (O'Brien, Dowell, Mostofsky, Denckla, and Mahone 657)
> (O'Brien et al. 657)

Articles in periodicals:
Include the page numbers from the publication:

> Garry Trudeau's comic strip "Doonesbury" has addressed numerous controversial
> domestic and international political issues during its 40-year run (Murphy 257).

Newspaper article:
Include the section letter or number with the page number:

> "This year proved that . . . Kristen Stewart does, in fact, possess more than just that
> one uninterested Bella-Swan-frozen face" (O'Connor E1).

Work with a group author:
Use the group's name as the author. In this example, there is no page or paragraph number provided, so no parenthetical citation is needed.

> According to the National Association of Anorexia Nervosa and Associated
> Disorders, treatment for anorexia can cost over $30,000 per month.

Work with no author listed:
Use in place of the author's name the full title or a shortened version of the title if it is long.

> The number of Christians practicing throughout the Holy Land appears to be
> decreasing ("Christians in the Middle East").

Play:
Cite the act, scene, and line in parentheses:

> In *Richard III* Anne asks Richard, "What black magician conjures up this fiend, / To
> stop devoted charitable deeds?" (1.2.34-35).

Poem:
Cite the line numbers, not page numbers, in parentheses. Include the word *line(s)* only in
the first parenthetical reference to indicate that you are citing line numbers.

Blake ends "The Sick Rose" on an ominous note: "And his dark secret love / Does thy life destroy" (lines 7–8).

Long quotation (block quotation):

For a quotation longer than four lines, you set it off from the rest of the text by indenting the whole selection by 1 inch (10 spaces) from the left margin. The parenthetical citation follows the end punctuation.

Foster cautions his readers to maintain flexibility regarding absolutes in literature:

> For one thing, as soon as something seems to always be true, some wise guy will come along and write something to prove that it's not. If literature seems to be too comfortably patriarchal, a novelist like the late Angela Carter or a poet like the contemporary Eavan Bolans will come along and upend things just to remind readers and writers of the falseness of our established assumptions. (6)

Works Cited Entries:

The list of works cited comes at the end of your paper on a new page.

Steps for creating the works cited list:

- After the text of your paper ends, start a new page for the works cited list.
- Double-space the list. Do not include extra spaces between entries.
- Include a header with your last name and page number in the upper right corner of the page. Continue the numbering from the previous page.
- Head the page with the words "Works Cited" centered at the top of the list.
- Alphabetize entries by the first word of each entry, usually the author's last name. If you have entries that start with a title or some other word, alphabetize by the first word, ignoring *a, an,* and *the.*
- Use a hanging indent: indent each line after the first five spaces (½ inch). Only the first line of each entry begins at the left margin.

Sample Works Cited Entries: MLA

Books

Basic information for an entry for a book or selection from a book:

- Author's name, last name first
- Title of the chapter or section, if any
- Title of the book
- Publication information: city of publication, name of publisher, year of publication
- Medium ("Print" for a source in hard copy)

Book by a single author

Foster, Thomas C. *How to Read Literature Like a Professor*. New York: Quill-HarperCollins, 2004. Print.

Two or more works by the same author

Weir, Alison. *The Lady in the Tower: The Fall of Anne Boleyn*. New York: Ballantine-Random, 2010. Print.

—. *Queen Isabella*. New York: Ballantine-Random, 2005. Print.

Multiple authors

The first author's name is listed last-name first, and subsequent authors' names are listed in regular order.

Levitt, Stephen, and Steven J. Dubner. *Freakonomics: A Rogue Economist Explores the Hidden Side of Everything*. New York: William Morrow, 2006. Print.

An entire anthology

Use the editors' rather than authors' names, followed by the abbreviation "ed."

Zemliansky, Pavel, and Wendy Bishop, ed. *Research Writing Revisited: A Sourcebook for Teachers*. Portsmouth: Boynton/Cook, 2004. Print.

Work in an anthology

List the author of the individual work as the author, and list the editor after the title of the overall work.

Emerson, Barbara W. "Coming of Age: Civil Rights and Feminism." *The Feminist Memoir Project*. Ed. Rachel Blau Duplessis and Ann Snitow. New Brunswick: Rutgers UP, 1998. 54–70. Print.

Article in reference work

"Monodrama." *Merriam-Webster's Collegiate Dictionary*. 11th ed. 2004. Print.

For a less commonly used reference work, give full citation information:

McCutcheon, Marc. "House Construction." *Descriptionary*. 2nd ed. New York: Facts on File, 2000. Print.

Book with no author listed

Start the entry with the title of the work:

Family Favorite Crossword Puzzles. Norwalk: Penny Press, 2009. Print.

Periodicals   Basic information needed for a works cited entry for a periodical:

- Author's name, last name first
- Title of the article enclosed in quotation marks
- Title of the journal or magazine in italics

- Volume and issue numbers, separated by a period, for academic journals
- Date of publication
- Page numbers. If an article runs more than one page on non-consecutive pages, include only the first page followed by a plus sign: 55+
- Medium ("Print" for a hard copy journal or magazine)

Article from an academic journal

Williams-Forson, Psyche. "Other Women Cooked for My Husband: Negotiating Gender, Food, and Identities in an African-American/Ghanaian Household." *Feminist Studies* 36.2 (2010): 435–61. Print.

Article from a journal numbered by issue

Use issue number in place of volume and issue:

Roy, Wendy. "The Word is *Colander*: Language Loss and Narrative Voice in Fictional Canadian Alzheimer's Narratives." *Journal of Canadian Literature* 203 (2009): 41–61. Print.

Article from a magazine

For a magazine published monthly, list only month and year for the date:

Murphy, Cullen. "American Comic." *Vanity Fair* Dec. 2010: 257. Print.

For weekly or biweekly magazines, use the day, month, and year for the date:

Gregory, Sean. "The Buck Stops Here." *Time* 20 Dec. 2010: 55–56. Print.

Newspaper article

O'Connor, Clint. "Honoring the Good, the Bad, and the Weird." *Cleveland Plain-Dealer* 19 Dec. 2010: E1+. Print.

Article with no author listed

"The Disposable Academic." *Economist* 18 Dec. 2008: 13. Print.

Electronic sources

- Author or editor's name
- Title of the section of the work, if any
- Title of overall work
- Name of publisher or sponsoring organization (use the abbreviation "N.p." if unavailable)
- Date of publication or last update (sometimes only a year is available; if no date is available use the abbreviation "N.d.")

- Medium (usually "Web")
- Date you accessed the material

Many online sources don't provide all these pieces of information, but include as much as you can with the aim of giving readers enough information to find the same sources.

MLA no longer calls for including URLs for sources, but if you must include one, give the information in angle brackets at the end of the entry:

<http://www.mlb.ilstu.edu/ressubj/subject/intrnt/apa.htm>

Break the URL only after a slash if the whole address won't fit on one line.

Entire website

Palya, William, ed. *Encyclopedia of Psychology*. Dept. of Psychology, Jacksonville State U, 28 Nov. 2010. Web. 18 Dec. 2010.

This source does not have an author or editor, so the entry begins with the title. Also, no date of publication or last update is given, so "N.d." is used.

Susan G. Komen for the Cure Greater Cincinnati. Susan G. Komen for the Cure. N.d. Web. 18. Dec. 2010.

Personal website

This entry does not have a sponsoring organization, so the abbreviation "N.p." is used in its place.

Buckell, Tobias. Home page. N.p. 2010. Web. 18. Dec. 2010.

Part of a website

In this entry, an organization is listed as the author.

National Association of Anorexia Nervosa and Associated Disorders. "About Eating Disorders." National Association of Anorexia Nervosa and Associated Disorders. 2010. Web. 18 Dec. 2010.

Online scholarly journal article

Carens, Timothy L. "Serpents in the Garden: English Professors in Contemporary Film and Television." *College English* 73.1 (2009): 9–27. Web. 17 Dec. 2010.

Online newspaper article

Steinberg, Jacques. "Is Going to an Elite College Worth the Cost?" *New York Times*. New York Times, 17 Dec. 2010. Web. 19 Dec. 2010.

Article from online database

Cox, Pamela L., Barry A. Friedman, and Ann-Lorraine Edwards. "*Enron: The Smartest Guys in the Room*—Using the Enron Film to Examine Student Attitudes towards Business

Ethics." *Journal of Behavioral and Applied Management* 10.2 (2009): 263–90. *Academic Search Complete.* Web. 17 Dec. 2010.

Online book or section of an online book

An online book entry includes the original publication information (city, publisher, and year) followed by the sponsoring organization, medium, and date of access.

Hawthorne, Nathaniel. "The Prison Door." *The Scarlet Letter.* N.p. Boston: Ticknor, 1850. *Bartleby.com.* Web. 17 Dec. 2010.

Blog

After the author and title of the entry (or the words "Blog entry"), include the title of the blog and the name of the sponsoring organization (or "N.p." if there is none).

Hamermesh, Daniel. "Lazy Academics." *Freakonomics Blog.* New York Times. 14 Dec. 2010. Web. 18 Dec. 2010.

Online video

Vault Video. "Interview Dos and Don'ts." *You Tube.* You Tube. 4 May 2007. Web. 17 Dec. 2010.

Other sources

Email

Stevens, Ronald. "RE: Guidelines for Editorial Work." Message to author. 4 Dec. 2010. Email.

Personal interview

Jones, Teresa. Personal interview. 2 Dec. 2010.

Advertisement

Lysol Neutra Air Fabric Mist. Advertisement. *Ladies' Home Journal* Nov. 2010: 89. Print.

Art

Hopper, Edward. *High Noon.* Oil on canvas. 1949. Dayton Art Institute, Dayton.

Film, Video, or DVD

Black Swan. Dir. Darren Aronofsky. Perf. Natalie Portman, Mila Kunis, and Vincent Cassel. Fox Searchlight, 2010. Film.

To cite a particular person's contribution to a film, cite that person first:

Portman, Natalie, perf. *Black Swan.* Dir. Darren Aronofsky. Fox Searchlight, 2010. Film.

Television show

Include the title of the episode, title of the show, relevant contributors (director, performer, writer); the network, station and city, and date of broadcast; and the medium.

"Hush." *Buffy the Vampire Slayer*. Dir. Joss Whedon. Perf. Sarah Michelle Gellar. WB. WBDT, Dayton, 14 Dec. 1999. Television.

Sethi 1

Instructor Name

Course Name

September 2, 2012

Do We Have Free Will through Nature or by God?

Religion, morality, and free will are key aspects embedded in everyday life. Have you ever wanted to do something bad? Disobeyed your parents? That is practicing your free will. Everyone is different; therefore we all have different beliefs. Whether you believe in religion, morality, or free will, or even all three, we all have different views on each of the three subjects. Some people have stronger feelings on one subject over another. Nietzsche had stronger feelings on morality, whereas Murdoch leans toward religion, but they both express feelings on free will. Whether we believe that free will is a gift from God, or a part of nature, we all have it bestowed in us at the beginning of our life.

Religion has been a part of my life for as long as I can remember. It scares me to think of a day in my life without religion. I believe strongly in my religion and am willing to share my beliefs on religion with anyone interested; I am also open-minded to ideas from other religions, whether Jewish, Mormon, Muslim, or Protestant. I do not wish to push my religion on anyone. Everyone has different beliefs, and I respect that. Ironically a virtue of my religion is not to be boastful or show off my religion; it is considered personal gain and greedy. I live to serve the Lord, not my own personal gain. Many people believe in religion; according to some estimates, as many as 80% of people worldwide believe in some kind of religion (wiki.answers.com). So if there are billions of people who believe in religion, whether or not individual people believe in some form of religion or not, most people do; it is a huge part of global culture.

Morality is very important in the life of every single person here on this earth. Without morals the world would be a dangerous and crazy place. Morals keep us from stealing, murdering, lying, and molesting. We know that certain things are wrong, or immoral; no one really knows why we know these things. Morals were given to us before we were born; God gave us these things that we all know to be true. Murdoch states that God gave us virtues and morality, whereas Nietzsche says that we learn morality through nature. God gave us morals, and he created nature. Therefore morals are everywhere in nature, and more importantly in each and every one of us. Without morals, humankind would be nothing to brag about.

Free will is a wonderful thing that is given to all of us. The most wonderful thing about a human is his freedom of choice. God gave us morals and virtues before birth, but the greatest thing he gave us is a choice of whether or not we follow those morals. According to Murdoch, the gift of free choice is given by God. Nietzsche believes that free will is a part of nature, whether it is learned through nature or just part of it. Through religion, we have been taught that God gave us free will. If God created nature and he created us, then why would free will not be a part of nature and a part of each and every one of us? Nietzsche believes that free will is part of nature; that is true, but God put it there. Whether or not you believe that free will is part of nature or given to us by God, it is everywhere. We all see free will in everything that we engage in, everyday it plays a part in our lives. No matter where we get our free will from, it is a wonderful thing that is to be treasured.

In Nietzsche's "Morality as Anti-Nature" the emphasis is that God is not real. Everyone has their own opinion, and we ought to respect that. There are points in the excerpt that do make sense, despite his denial of God and religion. Nietzsche is very straightforward in his work. It is easy to comprehend and evaluate. The third paragraph in the third section of "Morality as Anti-Nature" is very disturbing but easy to understand.

Peace of soul is something everyone who believes in religion strives for, and most people who don't believe. Nietzsche strikes down this peace of soul in the third section, "Peace of soul is merely a misunderstanding, which lacks only a more honest name" (Nietzsche 2). Nietzsche says that peace of soul can be many things, such as a sunset or signs of rain to a farmer. Nietzsche does not see that God is present in everything. Peace of soul can be found in just about anything, like Nietzsche states, but the reason for that is that God is present in everything. A non-believer would probably agree with this article, and that things are just the way they are because that is the way they are. Someone who believes in religion finds that there is an explanation for peace of soul and that explanation is God, no matter what religion he or she believes in.

According to Nietzsche, humans need enemies; self preservation depends on opposition. Whether we believe it or not, we all need enemies; human instinct is fine-tuned by enemies and challenges. Nietzsche says that the church tries to destroy enemies; he is simply misunderstanding the church. "Acting and thinking in the opposite way from that which has been the rule" (Nietzsche 1). The church gives us rules to preserve ourselves and better ourselves. The church helps us understand opposition, to better the use of it. Nietzsche says the church is taking away opposition and enemies, which will make us weak. The church helps us use the opposition to our advantage, so that we can learn from it and better serve the lord, or our religion, whatever it may be.

Murdoch's, "Morality and Religion" is in many ways opposite to Nietzsche's "Morality as Anti-Nature." In Murdoch's article, virtue is in everything, which comes from the fact that God is in everything. "An idea of virtue, which need not be formally reflective or clarified, bears some resemblance to religion, so that one might say either that it is a shadow of religion, or religion is a shadow of it" (Murdoch 2). Religious ideas are present in everything that we see and do, so maybe religion is right. Murdoch realizes that many times we are virtuous without knowing it: "A saint may perhaps be good by instinct and nature, though saintly figures are also revered as reformed sinners. Perhaps the world itself begins to seem pretentious and old-fashioned" (Murdoch 1). Murdoch agrees with Nietzsche on the fact that instinct and nature and opposition makes us good and virtuous, but Murdoch says that religion is the reason for that. God is everywhere, in nature, in opposition, in sin, and everything we do. Murdoch's article simply explains that the reason we are virtuous and good by nature is because of God. Free will is based upon faith in God.

Religion, morality, and free will are key aspects imbedded in everyday life. Nietzsche's "Morality as Anti-Nature" focuses on instinct and opposition

Sethi 5

as the reasons for morality and free will. Alternatively, Murdoch's "Morality and Religion" explains that faith is imbedded in our instinct, in nature, and in opposition, making us virtuous, giving us morals and free will. Free will is one of the most wonderful things in life. Whether we believe it comes from nature and opposition or from faith, we all know that free will is present in everything that we do; we should all be thankful for it.

Works Cited

Murdoch, Iris. "Morality and Religion." *A World of Ideas: Essential Readings for College Writers*. Ed. Lee A. Jacobus. Boston: Bedford/St. Martin's, 2010. 729–743. Print.

Nietzsche, Friedrich. "Morality as Anti-Nature." *A World of Ideas: Essential Readings for College Writers*. Ed. Lee A. Jacobus. Boston: Bedford/St. Martin's, 2010. 713–727. Print.

Okamimiyazaki. "How Many People Are Religious?" *Wiki Answers.com*. 10 Sept. 2009. Web. 18 Dec. 2010.

APA Documentation

American Psychological Association (APA) documentation style is used frequently in fields such as education, psychology, and other social sciences. APA reference list entries emphasize the currency of the sources. All sources that may be retrieved by readers must be cited on the reference list. Personal communication such as emails and personal interviews that cannot be recovered by your readers is cited only in the text, with no corresponding entry on the reference list.

Parenthetical citations usually include the author's last name and year of publication. If you directly quote from the original, also include the page number where the quoted material can be found. Often, online material has no page numbers, so that information is omitted from parenthetical citations if it is not provided.

While APA and MLA are similar, there are important differences between the bibliographic entries in the two styles. In APA:

- Authors' names are listed last name, then first and middle initials only, making all entries gender neutral.
- Dates of publication are the second element in most entries, emphasizing source currency.
- Book and article titles use sentence capitalization: *Freakonomics: A rogue economist explores the hidden side of everything.*
- Article and chapter titles are NOT enclosed in quotation marks.

In-Text Citations

Direct quotation from a single-author book, author mentioned in signal phrase

Burns argues that Rand "was also one of the first American writers to celebrate the creative possibilities of modern capitalism and to emphasize the economic value of independent thought" (2009, p. 3).

Direct quotation from a single-author book, author not mentioned in signal phrase

Ayn Rand "was also one of the first American writers to celebrate the creative possibilities of modern capitalism and to emphasize the economic value of independent thought" (Burns, 2009, p. 3).

Paraphrase, author mentioned in signal phrase

Unlike other American writers of the time, Ayn Rand assigned economic value to individuals' intellectual work (Burns, 2009).

Articles in periodicals

Include the page numbers from the publication if quoting directly:

Garry Trudeau's comic strip "Doonesbury" has addressed numerous controversial issues, "from Vietnam to Iraq, from drug use to gay marriage," during its 40-year run (Murphy, 2010, p. 257).

Newspaper article

Include the section letter or number with the page number

> "This year proved that . . . Kristen Stewart does, in fact, possess more than just that one uninterested Bella-Swan-frozen face" (O'Connor, 2010, E1).

Work with a group author

Use the group's name as the author; in this example it is mentioned in a signal phrase.

> According to the National Association of Anorexia Nervosa and Associated Disorders, treatment for anorexia can cost over $30,000 per month (2010).

Work with no author listed

Use in place of the author's name the full title or a shortened version of the title if it is long.

> The number of Christians practicing throughout the Holy Land appears to be decreasing ("Christians in the Middle East," 2010).

Long quotation (block quotation)

A quotation of forty or more words should be set off from the rest of the text by indenting it ½ inch (5 spaces) from the left margin. No quotation marks enclose the block quotation. The parenthetical citation goes at the end of the paragraph after the end punctuation.

> Burns offers this assessment of Rand's portrayal of government:
>
> > In her work, the state is always a destroyer, acting to frustrate and inhibit the natural ingenuity and drive of individuals. It is this chiaroscuro of light and dark—virtuous individuals battling a villainous state—that makes her compelling to some readers and odious to others. (2009, p. 3)

Personal communication

Personal communication such as email, personal interviews, or other communications that readers could not access independently are cited in the text only. Include the author's name, the designation *personal communication,* and the date in parentheses:

> (J. Smith, personal communication, December 2, 2010)

Unlike all other types of sources, there is no corresponding entry on the reference list.

Reference list entries

The list of references comes at the end of your paper. After your last paragraph, begin a new page for the references.

> Steps for creating the reference list:

- Double-space the list. Do not include extra spaces between entries.
- Include a header with your shortened version of the paper's title and page number in the upper right corner of the page. Continue numbering from the previous page.

- Head the page with the word "References," centered at the top of the page.
- Alphabetize entries by the first word of each entry, usually the author's last name. If you have entries that start with a title or some other word, alphabetize by the first word, ignoring *a, an,* and *the.*
- Do not include sources that readers cannot retrieve independently, such as an email sent to you. Cite such personal communication only in the text of the essay.
- Use a hanging indent: indent each line after the first five spaces (½ inch). Only the first line of each entry begins at the left margin.

Sample Reference List Entries: APA

Books

Basic information for book entries:

- Author's name, last name first. Use first and middle (if given) initials only.
- Year of publication in parentheses
- Title of the book in italics, capitalizing like a sentence
- Publication information (city and publisher)

Book with a single author

   Burns, J. (2009). *Goddess of the market: Ayn Rand and the American right.* Oxford: Oxford UP.

Two or more works by the same author

List them chronologically.

   Weir, A. (2005). *Queen Isabella.* New York: Ballantine-Random.
   Weir, A. (2010). *The lady in the tower: The fall of Anne Boleyn.* New York:
      Ballantine-Random.

If there are multiple works by the same author published the same year, list them alphabetically by title and add distinguishing letters (a, b, c, etc.) to the year.

   Harris, C. (2009a). *Dead and gone.* New York: Penguin.
   Harris, C. (2009b). *A touch of dead.* New York: Ace.

Book with two to six authors

   Levitt, S. D., & Dubner, S.J. (2006). *Freakonomics: A rogue economist explores the hidden side of everything.* New York: William Morrow, 2006. Print.

For works with more than six authors, list only the first six and then use the abbreviation *et al.*

Book with an organization or government as author

List the organization as the author. If the same organization is also the publisher, as in this example, use the word *Author* rather than repeating the organization's name.

Department of Health and Human Services. (2004). *Autism spectrum disorders: Pervasive developmental disorders*. Washington, D.C.: Author.

Book with no author listed

Begin with the title, followed by the date of publication in parentheses. Alphabetize on the reference list by the first word of the title, ignoring *a, an*, and *the*.

Family Favorites Crossword Puzzles. (2009). Norwalk, CT: Penny Press.

Periodicals

Basic format for periodicals

- Author's name, last name first. Use first and middle (if given) initials only.
- Date of publication in parentheses
- Title of the article using sentence capitalization, NOT enclosed in quotation marks
- Title of the journal in italics with important words capitalized
- Volume in italics (sometimes followed by issue number in parentheses)
- Page numbers

Article from journal

Treas, J. & Giesen, D. (2000). Sexual infidelity among married and cohabiting Americans. *Journal of Marriage and Family*, 62, 48–60.

Article from journal paginated by issue

Overall, C. (1998). Monogamy, nonmonogamy, and identity. *Hypatia* 13(4), 1–17.

Article in a magazine

For monthly magazines, include the year and month for the date. Include the volume number in italics and page numbers of the article after the title.

Murphy, C. (2010, December). American comic. *Vanity Fair, 604*, 257.

For weekly magazines, include the year, month, and day for the date.

Gregory, S. (2010, December 20). The buck stops here. *Time, 176*, 55–56.

Article with no author

The disposable academic. (2010, December 18). *Economist, 397*, 13.

Newspaper article

Unlike citations for other sources in APA, in those for newspaper articles, in reference list entries you use the designations "p." for page number and "pp." for page numbers.

For multiple-page articles, separate continuous pages with a hyphen (E1-E2) and non-consecutive page numbers with a comma, as in the following example.

> O'Connor, C. (2010, December 19). "Honoring the good, the bad, and the weird." *Cleveland Plain-Dealer*, pp. E1, E9.

Electronic sources:
Basic format for electronic sources:

- Author's or editor's name, last name first followed by first and middle initials
- Date of publication or last update
- Title of document
- Print publication information (if any)
- Title of site
- Date of access or retrieval
- Name of sponsoring organization (if any)
- URL or DOI (Digital Object Identifier)

Many online sources don't provide all these pieces of information, but include as much as you can in your reference list entries with the aim of giving readers enough information to find the same sources.

Entire website
Use the abbreviation "Ed." in parentheses to indicate that the person listed is an editor rather than author. End the entry with the retrieval information and URL.

> Palya, W. (Ed.). (2010). *Encyclopedia of psychology*. Retrieved from http://www. psychology.org

Part of website
> Jacofsky, M. D., Santos, M. T., Khemlani-Patel, S., & Neziroglu, F. (2010). The symptoms of anxiety. In *What is anxiety?* Retrieved from http://www.mentalhelp. net/poc/view_doc.php?type=doc&id=38467&cn=1

If no author or editor is listed, you can use the name of the sponsoring organization as the author.

Article from online periodical with no print version
End the entry with the retrieval information and the URL (as shown on the next page) or DOI.

Camden, S. G. (2009, January 31). Obesity: An emerging concern for patients and nurses. *Online Journal of Issues in Nursing, 14*(1). Retrieved from http://www .nursingworld.org/MainMenuCategories/ANAMarketplace/ANAPeriod icals/OJIN/TableofContents/Vol142009/No1Jan09/Obesity-An-Emerging-Concern.aspx

Article from online periodical also appearing in print

For online journal, magazine, or newspaper articles with identical print and electronic versions, you may simply add the designation [Electronic version] after the title.

Carens, T. L. (2009). Serpents in the garden: English professors in contemporary film and television [Electronic version]. *College English, 73*, 9–27.

If the online version differs from the print, give the DOI or URL (shown below)

Carens, T. L. (2009). Serpents in the garden: English professors in contemporary film and television. *College English, 73*, 9–27. Retrieved from http://www.ncte.org/ journals/ce/issues/v73-1

Article retrieved from database with no DOI

In most cases, you can simply cite the article as you would for a print source. You may include the name of the database at the end of the entry to help readers locate the document.

O'Brien, J. W., Dowell, L.R., Mostofsky, S.H., Denckla, M.B, and Mahone, M.E. (2010). Neuropsychological profile of executive function in girls with attention deficit/hyperactivity disorder. *Archives of Clinical Neuropsychology, 25*(7). 656–670. Retrieved from Academic Search Complete database.

Article retrieved from database with DOI

Cohen, E.J. (2005). "Kitchen witches: Martha Stewart: Gothic housewife." *Journal of Popular Culture 38*(4), 650–677. doi: 10.1111/j.0022-3840.2005.00134.x

Online Video

In this entry, an organization is listed as the author. Include a brief label in square brackets after the title to describe the nature of the video.

Vault Video. (2007, May 4). *Interview dos and don'ts* [Instructional video]. Retrieved from http://www.youtube.com/watch?v=S1ucmfPOBV8

If individuals are listed as writers, producers, etc., list their names as the authors, followed by their role in parentheses:

Jones, R. (Writer), & Norton, K.B. (Producer).

Film, Video, or DVD

Include the descriptive label "Motion picture" in square brackets. End the entry with the country and studio.

> Franklin, S. (Producer), & Aronofsky, D. (Director). (2010). *Black swan* [Motion picture]. United States: Fox Searchlight.

Television Show

Begin entry with the names of the writer and director. Include a descriptive label in square brackets after the episode title. Then type "In" and give producer's name, their title in parentheses, and the title of the series. End the entry with the city and network.

> Whedon, J. (Writer & Director). (1999). Hush [Television series episode]. In G. Davies & D. Fury (Producers), *Buffy the vampire slayer*. Dayton: WB.

Cross-Check

Familiarize yourself with the genres that you will be expected to use in different disciplines. Such familiarization will help you envision the kinds of texts you could write.

- Every genre has a purpose and a structure that functions for the community in which it is used.
- Writing is governed by rules, guidelines, and strategies. Most rules should not be broken, but guidelines can give an author room for creativity and adapting the text to the purpose. Recognize rules and guidelines for writing as you read, and practice different guidelines in your writing.
- Strategies for writing can vary widely, depending on the purpose and process of your text.
- Writing is a cyclical process, involving many different activities, most of which can occur and reoccur at several different stages of any writing project.
  - Planning one's writing project, through reading, researching, and thinking about the topic is an important activity for writing. Such strategies as outlining and using heuristics can be helpful tools.
  - A thesis statement should state the author's arguable belief about a topic. It is the central or main point of almost any text.
  - Take careful notes while researching a topic to show how your ideas connect to previously published ideas and to correctly cite your sources.
  - Plagiarizing is unacceptable. Your writing should show that you are a competent thinker and scholar who can learn from the ideas of previous scholars and can give those scholars credit for their original work.

- Use organizational patterns for your ideas that will be familiar to your readers. Such patterns help to make your ideas more understandable.
- Use transitional words and phrases to show your readers how your ideas connect or relate to each other.
- Visual aids should supplement, not supplant, your prose. Your words and images should work together to make your information clearer to your audience.
- Revising, editing, and proofreading are different activities, all of which can make your writing more effective and meaningful for your readers.

- Give yourself plenty of time to write and to rewrite. Each writing project deserves close attention from you, if you expect favorable reactions from your readers.

4 NATURE, GENETICS, AND THE PHILOSOPHY OF SCIENCE

In his 1959 lecture "The Two Cultures and the Scientific Revolution," scientist and novelist C. P. Snow famously lamented the fact that modern intellectual culture had largely divided itself into two distinct cultures—a scientific culture and a literary culture—and that the gap between these two cultures was not only widening, but was inhibiting intellectual progress. In one of the better known passages from that lecture, Snow pointed out that for a student of the humanities to not know the Second Law of Thermodynamics—and being indifferent in his or her ignorance—was akin to a student of the sciences having never read a play by Shakespeare and being indifferent about it.

Snow's lecture, still a matter of debate and discussion to this day, crystallized a tension that had been growing between the sciences and the humanities, both broadly conceived, since the nineteenth century—and even earlier in one guise or another—between seemingly conflicting intellectual pursuits. The word *seemingly* is used here, for it has been rigorously argued many times and in many ways during the past half-century that there is no clear distinction between these two academic cultures. Nevertheless, in the spirit of Snow's dichotomy, one might argue that the sciences focus on the *hows* of existence, whereas the humanities (literature, history, philosophy, art) focus on the *whys* of existence. The natural scientist looks at the bird and tries to understand *how* the bird flies or sings. The philosopher or artist looks at the bird and tries to understand why the flight of the bird inspires the observer and the song of the bird brings joy to the listener.

Without engaging in the history of the debate generated by Snow in 1959, one might simply note that Snow's basic point is well taken: that it is a shame that more students of the humanities aren't better versed in scientific knowledge, and that more students of the sciences are not better versed in literature, language, history, and the arts. There is little doubt that one's education is incomplete without some broad knowledge across the natural, social, and formal sciences as well as the humanities, including literature, foreign languages, philosophy, art, and history. (This belief is the philosophical basis of a liberal arts education, and is embodied in many universities today through a series of core requirements for every student that require selected classes from a number of different disciplines, not just those taken in the student's major area.)

What does it mean to have scientific knowledge? Is it enough to be able to point out that the Second Law of Thermodynamics states that over time entropy increases in systems? What, after all, does this mean? What is entropy? If one doesn't know what entropy is, can one still be considered scientifically *literate*? The implications of these questions are profound, for they suggest that there is indeed a divide in contemporary culture between those who possess a certain degree of knowledge about the physical, chemical, and biological properties of the world, and those who do not. The issue of what it means to be scientifically literate is further complicated by the fact that what we call knowledge is a relative term. In fact, to generate knowledge, one must have a way to identify knowledge once it has been generated, and one must have a theory about the proper way to generate knowledge. Much is said in high school and college classrooms about the scientific method, and this methodology has proven highly effective for generations in providing a roadmap for the scientific acquisition of new knowledge. When one uses the scientific method, one first formulates a hypothesis—a statement expressing some principle that explains a given set of data. One then tests the hypothesis through carefully controlled experiments. If the empirical data generated by the tests were predicted through logical application of the hypothesis, then the hypothesis gains a certain amount of credibility. Repeated successful tests increase the validity of the hypothesis. If, on the other hand, the test data contradicts that which the hypothesis predicted, then the hypothesis is either revised or discarded and the process begins again. A hypothesis that proves repeatedly accurate in its predictive capability becomes a theory and joins other theories that have been validated through test results as part of the mass of scientific knowledge that offers a lens through which to understand the natural world in which we operate.

If only it were that simple. The problem with the scientific method is that it still has to be framed in a theory of knowledge itself. We *know* the laws of thermodynamics because we can demonstrate them experimentally. But we also *know* we love our parents or our children, or that we are loyal to our friends. These are different kinds of knowledge emerging from different theories of knowledge. We might consider one form of knowledge more important than another, more personal, or more appropriate to different circumstances. We might even argue about which is, in fact, *knowledge*. Without such a theory of knowledge, one will not know if one has discovered anything of any value whatsoever. Moreover, even the scientific method must start with a hypothesis—where does it come from? Must it derive logically from prior theories, or can it just be something someone invents out of nothing?

THE DISCIPLINE YOU EXPERIENCE

Traditionally, the disciplines that comprise the *natural sciences* include chemistry, physics, biology, astronomy, and the earth sciences. As with so many other academic disciplines, these categories overlap and interrelate, and include dozens and dozens of sub-disciplines (such as astrophysics, geology, geochemistry, meteorology, bioinformatics, ecology, physiology, zoology, organic chemistry, inorganic chemistry, optics, fluid dynamics, and many, many others, some so specialized that they are rarely even heard of outside of the university). In general terms, the disciplines that fall under the category of the *natural* sciences are distinguished from those disciplines generally grouped under the heading *social* sciences (which would include psychology, sociology, political science, and anthropology, as well as gender and sexuality studies). They are also distinguished from what are sometimes called the *formal* sciences (such as mathematics, logic, computer science, and statistics), as well as from the *applied* sciences (such as agriculture, engineering, military science, and the health sciences). The natural sciences are those disciplines that seek to understand nature—the external world that we observe and interact with every moment of our lives—through a rigorously applied experimental methodology commonly known as the *scientific method*. The natural sciences are naturalistic insofar as they seek to explain the world through the application of reason or critical thinking to the evidence of the senses—to data that has been seen, heard, touched, tasted, or smelled (in other words, to *empirical* data). The social sciences attempt to do the same thing, but in an effort to explain *human* nature, rather than nature itself. The formal sciences are those abstract principles of reasoning that are disconnected from the empirical world—they are *a priori*, principles derived independent of empirical data—and provide a framework for describing the law-bound relationships that explain empirical phenomena. In the applied sciences, principles generated in the natural, social, and formal sciences are used to develop real-world applications and technologies that alter our interaction with the society in which we live. Everything from mousetraps to suspension bridges to vaccines to cell phones are the products of the practical application of natural, social, and formal scientific principles.

Practically speaking, there are five disciplines commonly categorized as natural sciences. Within each are numerous sub-disciplines, but the five main categories include:

- Chemistry, which is the study of the materials that comprise all of physical matter, as well as the chemical changes and reactions that matter undergoes when heated, chilled, expanded, contracted, or combined with other chemicals. Chemists examine the atomic and molecular structures of matter, and describe the molecular changes that chemicals exhibit when manipulated, whether those chemicals are organic (living things) or inorganic (non-living things) in nature.

- Physics, which studies the principles and laws that govern the behaviors and features of all of the elements that make up the universe, from the smallest fundamental particles to the largest galactic structures. Physics looks not just at matter, but at the forces that influence matter. Physicists look at the relationship between energy, space, and time, and how these things relate to the physical material of the universe. Physicists study such diverse things as quantum mechanics, general relativity, and thermodynamics.

- Biology, which is the study of life of all kinds, from microscopic unicellular creatures to the largest land mammals. Biologists study the mechanisms of life from the molecular level on up, and this includes the study of evolution, reproduction, development, and physiology, as well as genetics, zoology, anatomy, and numerous other sub-disciplines.

- Astronomy, which examines the large scale structures that make up the universe in which we live, from planets to moons to solar systems, galaxies, and beyond. Astronomers study the formation of stars and planets, examine the chemical properties of celestial objects, and theorize about the genesis of the universe itself.

- Earth Sciences, which is the umbrella term for all of those interrelated disciplines that take as their subject the physical properties of the Earth itself. This includes such disciplines as geology, meteorology, oceanography, and ecology. Those who make the Earth itself their object of study are interested in soil composition, weather patterns, the properties of minerals, the mechanics of crystal formation, and physical geography.

The natural sciences impact our lives in countless ways: they are not esoteric disciplines that few can understand and relate to. Every time one uses any piece of technology—from the most sophisticated computer to the most humble household cleaning product, one is engaging physics, biology, and chemistry. But one need not turn to the applied sciences in order to come face to face with the implications of the natural sciences for our daily lives. Indeed, contemporary debates over cloning, gene therapies, modern reproductive technologies, and cybernetics are the social and intellectual byproducts of new developments and discoveries in the natural sciences. The discipline of biology—and its related subdisciplines of cell theory, genetics, and evolutionary theory—have brought to the forefront of human culture questions regarding the practical and ethical dimensions of the physical manipulation of the human body.

REFLECTING ON THIS CHAPTER

Despite the hundreds of different avenues of research within the disciplines and subdisciplines of the natural sciences, all of them share a common goal: the generation of new, better knowledge about the physical world in which we live. As you read the selections in this chapter about the nature of scientific knowledge and the meaning of scientific literacy; the implications of new developments in genetics, cybernetics, and evolutionary theory; the role that individual human perspective plays in our scientific understanding of the world; and the responsibilities of the scientific community when it comes to shaping the opinions—religious and otherwise—of the populace, consider the following questions:

- What is the central issue or problem the author attempts to explore or solve? What claims does the author make, and does the author make a convincing argument in support of those claims?

- It is common in popular culture for those who work in the natural sciences to be seen as a select group of "rocket scientists" who deal with esoteric concepts beyond the realm of average human understanding. How do the selections in this chapter either support or challenge this stereotype?

- How do these selections compare and contrast? What central issues and themes emerge from these selections when taken as a group?

- What are the various writing strategies the authors employ? What rhetorical tools do they use to persuade us? If you found a selection convincing, what made it so?

- Do you detect any logical flaws in the arguments developed by the authors of these selections? Can you find any inconsistencies or biases? Are there any contradictions within each selection? What recommendations would you make to the author about how he or she might improve their writing?

Scientific Literacy, What It Is, Why It's Important, and Why Scientists Think We Don't Have It

Emily Martin, Bjorn Claeson, Wendy Richardson, Monica Schoch-Shana, and Karen-Sue Taussig

Emily Martin (born 1944) is currently a Professor of Anthropology at New York University where she works closely with the Institute for the History of the Production of Knowledge. She is one of the founding editors of the journal Anthropology Now, *which seeks to make the discipline of anthropology more accessible to a broad audience and show the immediacy and relevancy of anthropology in the contemporary socio-cultural environment. Martin is the author of several books, including* The Cult of the Dead in a Chinese Village *(1973),* Chinese Ritual and Politics *(1981),* The Woman in the Body *(1987), and* Flexible Bodies: Tracking Immunity in American Culture from the Days of Polio to the Age of AIDS *(1994). The following piece was co-authored by Martin and several of her graduate students when she was a professor at Johns Hopkins University. In the following excerpted essay, Martin and her students take up the notion of what it means to be scientifically literate. They question whether some members of the scientific community have a clear understanding of the cultural and environmental forces that must be taken into account when one determines the quality of one's scientific knowledge. The subject of scientific literacy has broad implications for the research and writing we do at every level, from multi-million dollar medical research laboratories to the research done every day in college classrooms across all disciplines.*

1   "Science matters" we have been told in a recent spate of publications. In *Science Matters: Achieving Scientific Literacy,* "science literacy" is defined as "the knowledge you need to understand public issues . . . to put new [scientific] advances into a context that will allow you to take part in the national debate about them" (1991 a:xii). Unproblematic as this definition might seem at first glance, the authors contend that by any measure, "Americans as a whole simply have not been exposed to science sufficiently or in a way that communicates the knowledge they need to have to cope with the life they will have to lead in the twenty-first century" (xv). This dire (and, we would like to argue, unfair) diagnosis becomes more understandable when one confronts the extremely narrow and technocratic content of the knowledge contained in *Science Matters* and most other books about science literacy. For example, in media publications spun off from *Science Matters,* readers are given a "pop quiz" that tests scientific literacy, a quiz that the great majority of Americans at all educational levels would fail (Hazen and Trefil 1991b). One question from the quiz is:

2   The blueprint for every form of life is contained in

     a. The National Institutes of Health near Washington, D.C.

     b. DNA molecules

     c. Proteins and carbohydrates

     d. Viruses

3   For Hazen and Trefil, the correct answer, measuring a person's ability to understand public issues and function responsibly as citizens, is b. But in a broader, and more socially and culturally informed, definition of science literacy, one might wish people to debate the postulated role of DNA as the blueprint for every form of life. Following the lead of Ruth Hubbard and Eliza Wald in *Exploding the Gene Myth*, for example, one might hope that people would appreciate how little about every life form is actually determined by the gene.

4   Following the lead of Bruno Latour, one might want people to understand how much the establishment of science "facts" owe[s] to the funds and credibility given particular researchers by institutions like the one mentioned in answer a, the National Institutes of Health near Washington, DC (Latour 1987).

5   Even though some publications on science literacy contain references to social and cultural issues, these issues are usually posed as afterthoughts, or at least as reflections to ponder after the real science is mastered. For example, in *Benchmarks for Science Literacy*, the summary section on "health technology" for high-school students lists six paragraphs of facts about the genetics, immunology, and epidemiology of health. Not until the seventh paragraph do we read that "biotechnology has contributed to health improvement in many ways, but its cost and application have led to a variety of controversial social and ethical issues" (American Association for the Advancement of Science 1993:207).

6   In our social anthropological research we are uncovering another picture of what science literacy might consist of by asking nonscientists, at all educational levels and from a variety of ethnic and socioeconomic settings, to tell us in their own terms what they know about health and their bodies, in particular about immunity and the immune system.

7   We introduce four stories we were told about the immune system by people in four quite different contexts.

8   Story 1. Professor Keller, a scientist and a professor of microbiology at a large northeastern university, is teaching an undergraduate class on the biology of cancer and AIDS. He seeks to alleviate his students' sense of helplessness in the face of both social expectations and health-endangering illnesses by encouraging students to look within themselves to guide their lives and to find the resources to maintain their health. The class, which he teaches every semester to about five hundred people, is known by students as "the best class on campus."

9   Professor Keller brings to the class a critical awareness of the limits of Western medical science. In particular, he stresses its lack of understanding of the powers inherent in the human body. He raises questions about the causes of cancer and other illnesses and suggests the possibility that Western medicine cannot answer these questions. He tells stories about miraculous recoveries from illnesses and invites to the class ordinary men and women who have performed feats of self-healing deemed impossible by the medical establishment, thus suggesting everything we do not know about healing. And he criticizes the medical establishment for being "completely interested in keeping all alternatives off the books."

10   The purpose of the class, then, is to teach students "other ways of thinking" about the body, self, health, illness, and death and to "empower" students by giving them a sense of their internal capacity for control over their lives, a capacity that is ignored or denied

by medical science. To this end he uses "biology as . . . a common language"; he "talks the language that [the students] are ready to hear" and "interweaves it with stuff that they are not ready to hear, but that they will accept because it is interwoven."

11   Mike took Professor Keller's class two years ago. Now, in his final year of college, he ponders the possibilities that lie ahead.

12   The class empowered Mike to "go into" and believe in himself.

13   But Mike believes Professor Keller's presentation of the immune system had little impact on him. Mike could see no connection between himself and an immune system that seemed to be existing independently inside his body.

14   The microprocesses of the immune system may be "amazing [and] overwhelming," but, to him, they are distant, and not empowering.

15   In contrast to Mike, Elizabeth came to Professor Keller's class with a conception of the world as a series of separate, but interconnected layers.

16   Her immune system may be a "separate community in there," like her other organs, but she is nevertheless able to relate to it and interact with it.

17   This sense of connection with her immune system creates the possibility for her empowerment. For Elizabeth, the immune system is more than a mechanism of use only in emergencies to "fight diseases." She interacts with it on a "day-to-day" basis. During their twenty years together, she says, she and her immune system have gotten used to each other.

18   Rather than changing her life to meet the needs of her immune system, she has been able to train it to accommodate her life. In the context of her conception of the interconnectedness of the world and her day-to-day interaction with her immune system, scientific knowledge of the immune system becomes empowering. For her, the immune system is, indeed, the "scientific version of . . . an angel or a protector."

19   Story 2. Two of our informants, George and Phillip, are a gay white male couple in their early twenties. Coming of age sexually in the first decade of the AIDS epidemic, these two men have known gay circles as places in which conversations about the immune system are commonplace. Interest in a possible lover readily becomes an interest in whether or not he has been tested for HIV and whether or not he will wear a condom. Concern over a friend or acquaintance with AIDS easily becomes worry over his falling T-cell count. While Keller's students may gain a sense of empowerment from his lectures on the immune system, Phillip and George, who have witnessed the loss of a generation of gay men to AIDS and who have heeded the safe-sex campaign among gays, speak more of vulnerability. In their descriptions of the immune system and AIDS, they draw heavily upon an idiom of boundaries. Their talk of boundaries, safety, and risk, used in depicting the body and the threat of HIV, is consonant with their descriptions of danger on a different scale, danger that threatens the neighborhood through crime.

20   Phillip laments that AIDS and a preoccupation with protecting oneself, that is, wearing a condom, is at odds with love, which is an act of letting down one's barriers.

21   The biology of sex and of HIV mandates a barrier, the condom, between two bodies, while the sociality of lovemaking mandates openness between two people.

22   His partner, George, also emphasizes that caution toward HIV entails not only vigilance against possible points of entry, but also care toward the fluid medium containing

HIV. He draws upon an example from his own life, recounting the time he threw away an exacto knife at his office after a coworker cut himself with it. He defends his act to Phillip, who thinks him somewhat paranoid, by arguing that HIV is highly contagious because of its presence in fluids and because of fluid's special quality of permeating boundaries. It is the "bodily fluids" of others, from outside, he suggests, that one must avoid getting inside oneself.

23   In thinking through issues of health and illness, Phillip and George employ notions of barriers and their permeation by bodily fluids. Talk of vulnerability shifts easily, however, from the level of the body to that of the neighborhood. Just as skin is seen to circumscribe the body, protecting a vulnerable interior from exterior threats, so are streets seen to delineate the margins of a neighborhood, marking good areas from bad. When describing their area of the central city, George and Phillip give street names to outline the "safe" portion of the neighborhood. George notes that not only have gentrification efforts on streets south and west of the lines of safety failed but also that bad areas are encroaching upon good ones.

24   Two related themes are apparent. First, boundaries mark off or contain an area of safety. In one's neighborhood, one knows what streets to avoid and at what streets bad areas appear to begin. Second, if one knowingly crosses such borders, one must assume the risk of harm. Cross the street and you may be asking for trouble.

25   The same could be said of risky sexual practices and contracting HIV.

26   Others share the concerns of Phillip and George about crime in the neighborhood. They also hold similar cognitive maps of dangerous and safe zones in the area. Residents and business owners, for instance, have organized a citizens' patrol of the neighborhood streets at night to supplement the surveillance provided by the police department. A fatal shotgun blast to the face of a young gay man who was leaving an after-hours nightclub in late spring of 1990 was the event instigating the patrols. In this murder, people saw a number of dangers that the neighborhood unfortunately hosts. Some gays and lesbians considered it another example of the increasing violence directed toward the homosexual community during a time marked by a fear of AIDS. A few considered it the plight of a neighborhood not cohesive enough to exclude such outsiders as criminals.

27   Concern over bad areas spilling into good ones and criminal elements circulating within the neighborhood prompted residents to be keenly watchful of activities in their area. Phillip and George are similarly vigilant against the threats that may lie outside their "little, cozy square." Apprehension about the breach of boundaries, however, also marks their appraisal of the threat that HIV poses to the body. Mindful of their safety on the streets and cautious about any contact with "bodily" fluids that may contain HIV, Phillip and George elaborate the social significance of boundaries.

28   Story 3. Another informant, Bill, also made references to boundaries in his discussion of the immune system, relating "borders" of the body to those of nation-states. Bill is a white man in his thirties. He lives with his wife, originally from Argentina, in a small row house. Theirs was one of the first racially integrated neighborhoods in Baltimore. The residents are both renters and owners and many live openly as gay couples.

29   Bill's fascination with questions of local autonomy and centralized power were plain when we asked what he knew about the immune system. At first he was reserved and

responded, "I don't think I think much about the immune system per se. . . . I mean the immune system is all these little white blood cells running around eating up all the bad shit in your body right? That's my understanding of the immune system technically speaking."

30   As Bill oriented his thoughts around a metaphor of organized systems of authority, however, he became excited and the immune system took on a larger significance.

31   Having compared the immune system to a social system, Bill has given it a culture that can be compared to our own. If the metaphor of the police state makes the immune system comprehensible to Bill, at the same time it also becomes a commentary on political organization. It allows him to relate different states of the body to different political systems. As he exclaimed, "I'm sure there are diseases [in which] the immune system ends up destroying the body. . . . It's more like an Argentina or a Bulgaria kind of immune system."

32   Through his use of a body-country metaphor Bill reveals his conceptions of both bodies and nations as bounded and independent.

33   As a closed system, the body must protect its boundaries. The body when sick, like a nation at war, is threatened by what Bill describes as, "a foreign organism . . . that is competing for the body's resources in some way or another."

34   By using a social metaphor to describe the body, it becomes a system with logic, an aggregate of players with motivations and intentions.

35   The words he uses to describe the world of the body also orient his understanding of social interaction and global politics. The role of the politician can move from the global politics of the cold war to the global politics described in the immune system.

36   In order to communicate his understanding of the immune system and orient his thoughts, Bill has chosen the image of the nation-state. To Bill the topic of the immune system is versatile and allows him to move the discussion from health and illness to issues of global politics and the rights of the individual. Discussion of the immune system becomes a forum to think not only about our bodies and scientific "facts," but about political structures and what positions we must take to understand the rights of others. But these are not just arbitrary subjects held together by a central metaphor, they are also interconnected queries of great relevance to Bill. By speaking about the immune system, Bill was able to convey his views on the interrelations of preventative health, national priorities, and individual rights.

37   Story 4. Unlike Bill, for whom AIDS is one of many questions about individual rights and national structures, for Mara, AIDS and the problems of immunity are of primary concern. Mara is a thirty-one-year-old white woman who works as a technical writer for an engineering firm, volunteers by writing grant applications for a local performing arts group, and lives with her husband in a quiet Baltimore neighborhood. All four of Mara's college roommates have died from AIDS. In 1989 Mara became the primary care giver for another close friend who was sick with AIDS. She was with him when he died in a hospice the day after her thirtieth birthday. He was over six feet tall and weighed seventy pounds when he died.

38   Mara's familiarity with the language of science seems to come from her experience with AIDS. She is extremely well informed about the disease, how it is transmitted, and different possibilities for treatment. She is able to clearly articulate her understanding of what she thinks happens inside the body of someone with AIDS. She told us that what she

imagines happens inside the body of someone with AIDS has "changed" with the course of the disease.

39   Mara's concern is about the effects of the disease on society. She believes that AIDS is something society may not be able to withstand. She told us that she feels "like we all have AIDS . . . whether we have the virus or not." When asked to elaborate on her suggestion that everybody has AIDS, Mara said, "I really believe that we all have AIDS. I mean, I don't believe that I carry the virus in my body, and I've proven that to myself by getting tested, but my life has been changed forever by AIDS, and I feel that by the time the crisis is over, if it's ever over, and that I'm not sure about, everyone will be touched by it, directly affected by it."

40   While Mara sees the effects of AIDS moving easily through society, she doesn't think that the virus is very contagious. She describes the disease as "just a virus."

41   Mara sees her role as an activist as "something that is every day, all day. . . . I feel like I do it every day. But you know, that's what an activist does."

42   She also sees her role on what she calls a "microlevel" and describes her boss who "told AIDS jokes and made comments" when she first started working with him and now she describes him as "real sensitized to [AIDS], and real supportive and . . . share[s] with me . . . issues of his own, having to do with a brother who died of cancer at twenty." In spite of the horror she finds in the reality of AIDS, she also expresses hope about possibilities for new kinds of collective awareness.

43   Mara discusses her experiences with death by talking about caring for her friend and being with him when he died. Significantly, although she sees the effects of AIDS as "every nightmare that . . . could happen to the human body" and as a "holocaust," she describes her friend's death as "really an amazing and positive experience."

44   For Mara, death is not only about dying. Her concept of death is imbued with a concept of transcendence and involves ideas about strength and birth.

45   Logically following from her ideas about death, Mara does not see the body as a boundary. Mara's discussion of her relationships with her friends who have died illustrates her ideas about metaphysical relationships. One of Mara's concerns is about keeping the memory of her friends alive. She feels their presence in her life and makes a point of talking about them.

46   These stories illustrate that science literacy is much more than merely knowing some basic "facts" and simple concepts (Hazen and Trefil 1991a:xix). Individuals use "facts" in very different ways and often make them work with their particular local circumstances as well as express their most overarching views of the world. Bill uses "facts" he has learned about the immune system to construct broader visions about the nature of social and political forms that relate to his political views and actions. Mara weaves "facts" she has learned about the immune system into profoundly moral and metaphysical views of the meaning of life and death. These views enable her to maintain both important relationships in her life and hope of a better society.

47   In these stories people use scientific "facts" to create knowledge about a whole range of topics. For George and Phillip, to talk about the immune system is to talk above all about boundaries. Talk of boundaries appeared in another area of our research, participant-observation in a laboratory pursuing immunological research. In this research setting, the central tenet of contemporary immunology is the ability of the immune system to distinguish self from nonself. As our examples have just shown, when nonscientists talk about

the immune system they also talk above all about boundaries. Those between the self and others—spatial, racial, gendered, class, and relational—and how these various boundaries can clash or be superimposed in complex ways. The concept of the boundary between self and nonself is a touchstone for broader social meanings. Since we find such concepts so commonly in interviews, it raises the question of whether the central role of boundaries in current research immunology is not culturally based in its inception.

48   This position is explicit in Keller's view of his course. He intends much more than "facts" to be conveyed by his scientific account of the immune system. The students respond in kind. Certainly Mike did not take away "facts" about the immune system from his biology course, but rather the idea that in life one should "go into" and believe in one's self.

49   The "facts" of science, important as they are, can never be more than tiny pieces of the maps that people devise to guide them in life. Even if we could all magically be made to "know" the answers to the science pop quiz, the process of our coming to know those "facts" would entail our embedding them in the diverse social, political, moral, and metaphysical meanings with which we construct our daily lives.

QUESTIONS ON MEANING

1. Why do you think that the authors are concerned that in the summary section of *Benchmarks for Science Literacy* the phrase "biotechnology has . . . led to a variety of controversial social and ethical issues" does not appear till the seventh paragraph?

2. What is *local knowledge* and what is its relationship to scientific literacy?

3. How do the four stories related by the authors illustrate the concept of "local knowledge"?

4. In each of the four stories, a central metaphor is developed as a useful tool for describing the human immune system and its relationship to the AIDS epidemic. What is the central metaphor proposed by each of the following:
    A. Professor Keller
    B. George and Phillip
    C. Bill
    D. Mara

5. What is the relationship, according to the authors, between knowing "facts" and scientific literacy?

6. What do the authors speculate that the scientific community might need to reconsider as it thinks about the relative scientific literacy of the populace?

QUESTIONS FOR DISCUSSION

1. The authors begin their essay by quoting a definition of science literacy developed by Hazen and Trefil in their book *Science Matters: Achieving Scientific Literacy*. What is that definition? Is it an effective definition? Would you define it differently?

2. Hazen and Trefil argue that "Americans as a whole simply have not been exposed to science sufficiently or in a way that communicates the knowledge they need to have to cope with the life they will have to lead in the twenty-first century." Do you agree with Hazen and Trefil? If so, what knowledge do Americans lack in order to succeed in the twenty-first century?

3. The authors find the claim made by Hazen and Trefil in the above question both dire and unfair. Do you agree? Based on your reading of their essay, why do you think the authors believe the characterization of Hazen and Trefil is unfair?

4. What is your view of the human immune system? Is it similar to, or different from, the view taken by the different subjects in the essay?

LOOKING AT RHETORIC

1. The authors use immunology—particularly as it relates to AIDS and HIV—as their test case. Would it have made a difference if they had selected a different subject for their test case? Does the focus on AIDS and HIV make the essay more or less interesting to you?

2. Note how knowledge—in the form of a type of literacy—is presented by the authors as, in a sense, cross-disciplinary. How do they make the case for the cross-disciplinary nature of scientific literacy? Do they build a reasonable case for the cross-disciplinary nature of scientific literacy?

3. With each of the four interview subjects (Professor Keller, George and Phillip, Bill, and Mara) the authors give us some information about who they are. Is this information important? How does this information shape the way in which we, as readers, evaluate the metaphors they use? Knowing this information, does it make you more or less inclined to value their perspectives on AIDS and HIV?

WRITING ASSIGNMENTS

1. Both the *scientific concept* and the *viewpoint of the individual* are important components of understanding scientific literary. Draft an essay in which you explain what the authors have to say about the blending of these two things in determining what scientific literary is. Do you agree with the authors? Do you believe that one or the other of these things is less important than the other? Is there a third element, perhaps, that the authors have overlooked but which should be a part of this equation?

2. Research the concept of scientific literacy. What are some different ways in which people have defined the concept? Draft an essay in which you compare and contrast three different definitions. Then, develop you own definition of scientific literacy and argue for its merits.

3. In pairs or in groups, choose another topic in the sciences and develop a few interview questions that could be used in order to gauge peoples' literacy on the topic. As a group, select four people from varying backgrounds to interview and conduct those interviews. Then, individually write an essay in which you compare the results of the case study performed by your group with the case study about immunology presented by the authors. Do your findings support the claims of the authors in their essay? Why or why not?

The Historical Structure of Scientific Discovery

Thomas Kuhn

Thomas Kuhn (1922-1996) has long been regarded as one of the premier philosophers of science of the twentieth century. His work on the development of scientific knowledge sits alongside the works of Karl R. Popper and Paul Feyerabend as among the most influential bodies of thought about the nature of scientific knowledge of the past hundred years. Kuhn received his Ph.D. in Physics in 1949 from Harvard University and quickly turned his attention away from experimental physics, focusing instead on the history and philosophy of science. His most influential—and famous—book was his first: The Structure of Scientific Revolutions *(1962). In this work, Kuhn advanced the idea that would largely define his career: the notion that scientific knowledge does not progress in strictly linear fashion to ever-increasing clarity about the nature of reality, but, instead, features moments of crisis in which newly observed phenomena cause the scientific community to have to rethink the whole set of assumptions about the structure of the natural world. These "paradigm shifts," as Kuhn called them, are the revolutionary moments in the history of science in which one world view is replaced by another. The following essay was published the same year as* The Structure of Scientific Revolutions *and sets forth in simple terms the reasoning that led Kuhn to his notion of the paradigm shift as a defining feature of the development of scientific knowledge.*

1   Many scientific discoveries, particularly the most interesting and important, are not the sort of event about which the questions "Where?" and, more particularly, "When?" can appropriately be asked. Even if all conceivable data were at hand, those questions would not regularly possess answers. That we are persistently driven to ask them nonetheless is symptomatic of a fundamental inappropriateness in our image of discovery. That inappropriateness is here my main concern, but I approach it by considering first the historical problem presented by the attempt to date and to place a major class of fundamental discoveries.

2   The troublesome class consists of those discoveries—including oxygen, the electric current, X rays, and the electron—which could not be predicted from accepted theory in advance and which therefore caught the assembled profession by surprise. That kind of discovery will shortly be my exclusive concern, but it will help first to note that there is another sort and one which presents very few of the same problems. Into this second class of discoveries fall the neutrino, radio waves, and the elements which filled empty places in the periodic table. The existence of all these objects had been predicted from theory before they were discovered, and the men who made the discoveries therefore knew from the start what to look for. That foreknowledge did not make their task less demanding or less interesting, but it did provide criteria which told them when their goal had been reached. As a result, there have been few priority debates over discoveries of this second sort, and only a paucity of data can prevent the historian from ascribing them to a particular time and place. Those facts help to isolate the difficulties we encounter as we return to the troublesome discoveries of the first class. In the cases that most concern us here, there are no benchmarks to inform either the scientist or the historian when the job of discovery has been done.

3   As an illustration of this fundamental problem and its consequences consider first the discovery of oxygen. Because it has repeatedly been studied, often with exemplary care and skill, that discovery is unlikely to offer any purely factual surprises. Therefore it is particularly well suited to clarify points of principle. At least three scientists—Carl Scheele, Joseph Priestley, and Antoine Lavoisier—have a legitimate claim to this discovery, and polemicists have occasionally entered the same claim for Pierre Bayen. Scheele's work, though it was almost certainly completed before the relevant researches of Priestley and Lavoisier, was not made public until their work was well known. Therefore it had no apparent causal role, and I shall simplify my story by omitting it. Instead, I pick up the main route to the discovery of oxygen with the work of Bayen, who, sometime before March 1774, discovered that

red precipitate of mercury (HgO) could, by heating, be made to yield a gas. That aeriform product Bayen identified as fixed air (CO_2), a substance made familiar to most pneumatic chemists by the earlier work of Joseph Black. A variety of other substances were known to yield the same gas.

4   At the beginning of August 1774, a few months after Bayen's work had appeared, Joseph Priestley, repeated the experiment, though probably independently. Priestley, however, observed that the gaseous product would support combustion and therefore changed the identification. For him the gas obtained on heating red precipitate was nitrous air (N_2O), a substance that he had himself discovered more than two years before.[1] Later in the same month Priestley made a trip to Paris and there informed Lavoisier of the new reaction. The latter repeated the experiment, both in November 1775 and in February 1774. But because he used tests somewhat more elaborate than Priestley's, Lavoisier again changed the identification. For him, as of May 1775, the gas released by red precipitate was neither fixed air nor nitrous air. Instead, it was "[atmospheric] air itself entire without alteration . . . even to the point that . . . it comes out more pure."[2] Meanwhile, however, Priestley had also been at work, and before the beginning of March 1775, he too had concluded that the gas must be "common air." Until this point all of the men who had produced a gas from red precipitate of mercury had identified it with some previously known species.

5   The remainder of this story of discovery is briefly told. During March 1775 Priestley discovered that his gas was in several respects very much "better" than common air, and he therefore reidentified the gas once more, this time calling it "dephlogisticated air," that is, atmospheric air deprived of its normal complement of phlogiston.[3] This conclusion Priestley published in the *Philosophical Transactions*, and it was apparently that publication which led Lavoisier to reexamine his own results. The reexamination began during February 1776 and within a year had led Lavoisier to the conclusion that the gas was actually a separable component of the atmospheric air which both he and Priestley had previously thought of as homogeneous. With this point reached, with the gas recognized as an irreducibly distinct species, we may conclude that the discovery of oxygen had been completed.

6   But to return to my initial question, when shall we say that oxygen was discovered and what criteria shall we use in answering that question? If discovering oxygen is simply holding an impure sample in one's hands, then the gas had been "discovered" in antiquity by the first man who ever bottled atmospheric air. Undoubtedly, for an experimental criterion, we must at least require a relatively pure sample like that obtained by Priestley in August 1774. But during 1774 Priestley was unaware that he had discovered anything except a new way to produce a relatively familiar species. Throughout that year his "discovery" is scarcely distinguishable from the one made earlier by Bayen, and neither case is quite distinct from that of the Reverend Stephen Hales, who had obtained the same gas

---

[1] J. B. Conant, *The Overthrow of the Phlogiston Theory*, pp. 34–40.

[2] Ibid., p. 23. A useful translation of the full text is available in Conant.

[3] Phlogiston: an element once (but no longer) thought to be a part of all combustible materials, which provided the mechanism for combustion and was allegedly released during combustion. Thus, "dephlogisticated air" would be air that had undergone combustion, during which process its phlogiston would have been released.

more than forty years before.[4] Apparently to discover something one must also be aware of the discovery and know as well what it is that one has discovered.

7   But, that being the case, how much must one know? Had Priestley come close enough when he identified the gas as nitrous air? If not, was either he or Lavoisier significantly closer when he changed the identification to common air? And what are we to say about Priestley's next identification, the one made in March 1775? Dephlogisticated air is still not oxygen or even, for the phlogistic chemist, a quite unexpected sort of gas. Rather it is a particularly pure atmospheric air. Presumably, then, we wait for Lavoisier's work in 1776 and 1777, work which led him not merely to isolate the gas but to see what it was. Yet even that decision can be questioned, for in 1777 and to the end of his life Lavoisier insisted that oxygen was an atomic "principle of acidity" and that oxygen gas was formed only when that "principle" united with caloric, the matter of heat. Shall we therefore say that oxygen had not yet been discovered in 1777? Some may be tempted to do so. But the principle of acidity was not banished from chemistry until after 1810 and caloric lingered on until the 1860s. Oxygen had, however, become a standard chemical substance long before either of those dates. Furthermore, what is perhaps the key point, it would probably have gained that status on the basis of Priestley's work alone without benefit of Lavoisier's still partial reinterpretation.

8   I conclude that we need a new vocabulary and new concepts for analyzing events like the discovery of oxygen. Though undoubtedly correct, the sentence "Oxygen was discovered" misleads by suggesting that discovering something is a single simple act unequivocally attributable, if only we knew enough, to an individual and an instant in time. When the discovery is unexpected, however, the latter attribution is always impossible and the former often is as well. Ignoring Scheele, we can, for example, safely say that oxygen had not been discovered before 1774; probably we would also insist that it had been discovered by 1777 or shortly thereafter. But within those limits any attempt to date the discovery or to attribute it to an individual must inevitably be arbitrary. Furthermore, it must be arbitrary just because discovering a new sort of phenomenon is necessarily a complex process which involves recognizing both *that* something is and *what* it is. Observation and conceptualization, fact and the assimilation of fact to theory, are inseparably linked in the discovery of scientific novelty. Inevitably, that process extends over time and may often involve a number of people.

9   Two last, simpler, and far briefer examples will simultaneously show how typical the case of oxygen is and also prepare the way for a somewhat more precise conclusion. On the night of 13 March 1781, the astronomer William Herschel made the following entry in his journal: "In the quartile near Zeta Tauri . . . is a curious either nebulous star or perhaps a comet."[5] That entry is generally said to record the discovery of the planet Uranus, but it cannot quite have done that. Between 1690 and Herschel's observation in 1781 the same object had been seen and recorded at least seventeen times by men who took it to be a star. Herschel differed from them only in supposing that, because in his telescope it appeared especially large, it might actually be a *comet!* Two additional observations on 17 and

---

[4] J. R. Partington, *A Short History of Chemistry*, p. 91.
[5] P. Doig, *A Concise History of Astronomy* (London: Chapman, 1950), pp. 115–116.

19 March confirmed that suspicion by showing that the object he had observed moved among the stars. As a result, astronomers throughout Europe were informed of the discovery, and the mathematicians among them began to compute the new comet's orbit. Only several months later, after all those attempts had repeatedly failed to square with observation, did the astronomer Lexell suggest that the object observed by Herschel might be a planet. And only when additional computations, using a planet's rather than a comet's orbit, proved reconcilable with observation was that suggestion generally accepted. At what point during 1781 do we want to say that the planet Uranus was discovered? And are we entirely and unequivocally clear that it was Herschel rather than Lexell who discovered it?

10   Or consider still more briefly the story of the discovery of X rays, a story which opens on the day in 1895 when the physicist Roentgen interrupted a well-precedented investigation of cathode rays because he noticed that a barium platinocyanide screen far from his shielded apparatus glowed when the discharge was in process.[6] Additional investigations—they required seven hectic weeks during which Roentgen rarely left the laboratory—indicated that the cause of the glow traveled in straight lines from the cathode ray tube, that the radiation cast shadows, that it could not be deflected by a magnet, and much else besides. Before announcing his discovery Roentgen had convinced himself that his effect was not due to cathode rays themselves but to a new form of radiation with at least some similarity to light. Once again the question suggests itself: When shall we say that X rays were actually discovered? Not, in any case, at the first instant when all that had been noted was a glowing screen. At least one other investigator had seen that glow and, to his subsequent chagrin, discovered nothing at all. Neither, it is almost as clear, can the moment of discovery be pushed back to a point during the last week of investigation. By that time Roentgen was exploring the properties of the new radiation he had *already* discovered. We may have to settle for the remark that X rays emerged in Würzburg between 8 November and 28 December 1895.

11   The characteristics shared by these examples are, I think, common to all the episodes by which unanticipated novelties become subjects for scientific attention. I therefore conclude these brief remarks by discussing three such common characteristics, one which may help to provide a framework for the further study of the extended episodes we customarily call "discoveries."

12   In the first place, notice that all three of our discoveries—oxygen, Uranus, and X rays—began with the experimental or observational isolation of an anomaly, that is, with nature's failure to conform entirely to expectation. Notice, further, that the process by which that anomaly was educed displays simultaneously the apparently incompatible characteristics of the inevitable and the accidental. In the case of X rays, the anomalous glow which provided Roentgen's first clue was clearly the result of an accidental disposition of his apparatus. But by 1895 cathode rays were a normal subject for research all over Europe; that research quite regularly juxtaposed cathode-rays tubes with sensitive screens and films; as a result, Roentgen's accident was almost certain to occur elsewhere, as in fact it had. Those remarks, however, should make Roentgen's case look very much like those of Herschel and

---

[6] L. W. Taylor, *Physics, the Pioneer Science* (Boston: Houghton Mifflin Co., 1941), p. 790.

Priestley. Herschel first observed his oversized and thus anomalous star in the course of a prolonged survey of the northern heavens. That survey was, except for the magnification provided by Herschel's instruments, precisely of the sort that had repeatedly been carried through before and that had occasionally resulted in prior observations of Uranus. And Priestley, too—when he isolated the gas that behaved almost but not quite like nitrous air and then almost but not quite like common air—was seeing something unintended and wrong in the outcome of a sort of experiment for which there was much European precedent and which had more than once before led to the production of the new gas.

13   These features suggest the existence of two normal requisites for the beginning of an episode of discovery. The first, which throughout this paper I have largely taken for granted, is the individual skill, wit, or genius to recognize that something has gone wrong in ways that may prove consequential. Not any and every scientist would have noted that no unrecorded star should be so large, that the screen ought not to have glowed, that nitrous air should not have supported life. But that requisite presupposes another which is less frequently taken for granted. Whatever the level of genius available to observe them, anomalies do not emerge from the normal course of scientific research until both instruments and concepts have developed sufficiently to make their emergence likely and to make the anomaly which results recognizable as a violation of expectation. To say that an unexpected discovery begins only when something goes wrong is to say that it begins only when scientists know well both how their instruments and how nature should behave. What distinguished Priestley, who saw an anomaly, from Hales, who did not, is largely the considerable articulation of pneumatic techniques and expectations that had come into being during the four decades which separate their two isolations of oxygen. The very number of claimants indicates that after 1770 the discovery could not have been postponed for long.

14   The role of anomaly is the first of the characteristics shared by our three examples. A second can be considered more briefly, for it has provided the main theme for the body of my text. Though awareness of anomaly marks the beginning of a discovery, it marks only the beginning. What necessarily follows, if anything at all is to be discovered, is a more or less extended period during which the individual and often many members of his group struggle to make the anomaly lawlike. Invariably that period demands additional observation or experimentation as well as repeated cogitation. While it continues, scientists repeatedly revise their expectations, usually their instrumental standards, and sometimes their most fundamental theories as well. In this sense discoveries have a proper internal history as well as prehistory and a posthistory. Furthermore, within the rather vaguely delimited interval of internal history, there is no single moment or day which the historian, however complete his data, can identify as the point at which the discovery was made. Often, when several individuals are involved, it is even impossible unequivocally to identify any one of them as the discoverer.

15   Finally, turning to the third of these selected common characteristics, note briefly what happens as the period of discovery draws to a close. A full discussion of that question would require additional evidence and a separate paper, for I have had little to say about the aftermath of discovery in the body of my text. Nevertheless, the topic must not be entirely neglected, for it is in part a corollary of what has already been said.

16   Discoveries are often described as mere additions or increments to the growing stock-pile of scientific knowledge, and that description has helped make the unit discovery seem a significant measure of progress. I suggest, however, that it is fully appropriate only to those discoveries which, like the elements that filled missing places in the periodic table, were anticipated and sought in advance and which therefore demanded no adjustment, adaptation, and assimilation from the profession. Though the sorts of discoveries we have here been examining are undoubtedly additions to scientific knowledge, they are also something more. In a sense that I can now develop only in part, they also react back upon what has previously been known, providing a new view of some previously famil-iar objects and simultaneously changing the way in which even some traditional parts of science are practiced. Those in whose area of special competence the new phenomenon falls often see both the world and their work differently as they emerge from the extended struggle with anomaly which constitutes the discovery of that phenomenon.

17   Oxygen was not the only new chemical species to be identified in the aftermath of their work. But, in the case of oxygen, the readjustments demanded by assimilation were so profound that they played an integral and essential role—though they were not by themselves the cause—in the gigantic upheaval of chemical theory and practice which has since been known as the chemical revolution. I do not suggest that every unanticipated dis-covery has consequences for science so deep and so far-reaching as those which followed the discovery of oxygen. But I do suggest that every such discovery demands, from those most concerned, the sorts of readjustment that, when they are more obvious, we equate with scientific revolution. It is, I believe, just because they demand readjustments like these that the process of discovery is necessarily and inevitably one that shows structure and that therefore extends in time.

QUESTIONS ON MEANING

1. As outlined in the first paragraph of his essay, what is the perspective on scientific discovery that Kuhn rejects?

2. Why is the attribution of discovery to a specific individual at a specific time and place often an arbitrary exercise according to Kuhn? What forces have contributed to the adoption of these seemingly arbitrary attributions of discovery according to Kuhn?

3. In a sentence, what is Kuhn's thesis?

4. Explain the key role that anomalies play in Kuhn's theory of the development of scientific knowledge.

5. What are the two normal requisites for the beginning of a period of discovery, according to Kuhn?

6. What are the three characteristics the discoveries of oxygen, Uranus, and X rays have in common?

QUESTIONS FOR DISCUSSION

1. Think about the way you have been taught about scientific discoveries in your lifetime. Did your teachers follow in the footsteps of Kuhn or in the footsteps of those Kuhn argues against?

2. How would you decide what counts as an anomaly or not? What are some of the anomalies currently posing as a challenge to modern researchers?

3. Think back over your lifetime. Has there been a "paradigm shift" during your lifetime? That is, has there been a shift in knowledge within a scientific field that has resulted in a substantial rethinking of how we think of that whole field? If not, when was the last great paradigm shift in your estimation?

LOOKING AT RHETORIC

1. All of Kuhn's examples come from the hard sciences—chemistry and physics, specifically. What does this tell you about Kuhn's attitude toward *science*? Would it weaken or strengthen his case if he pulled examples from disciplines outside the hard sciences (for example, something from the fields of psychology or sociology)? Do you believe Kuhn's thesis applies to disciplines outside of the hard sciences?

2. Take a few moments, and see if you can create an outline for Kuhn's essay. Is it easy or difficult to do so? What is it about the structure of the essay and the transitional phrases Kuhn uses that makes it easy or difficult?

WRITING ASSIGNMENTS

1. Spend some time researching the discovery of something notable in the history of science. Write an essay in which you present the history of that discovery. Did what you discover in your research confirm or challenge Kuhn's thesis about the nature of scientific discovery?

2. Recently, in the field of astronomy, Pluto—once considered the ninth planet of the solar system—was demoted, and is no longer considered a planet by many scientists. Research the history of this decision to reconsider Pluto's status in the solar system. Write an essay in which you argue for or against Pluto's status as a planet. Does changing Pluto's status constitute a paradigm shift? Why or why not?

3. In pairs or in groups, select a discipline and compose a list of what you believe the key paradigm shifts that have revolutionized the discipline over the centuries have been. Your group may have to spend some time in the library in order to do this. Then, individually, write an essay in which you summarize the history of the discipline, focusing on those moments when our understanding of the field shifted dramatically.

From *Against Method*

Paul Feyerabend

Paul Feyerabend (1924-1994) is widely regarding as one of the most influential, and controversial, of contemporary philosophers of science. Born in Austria during WWII, Feyerabend was drafted into service by the German army, and in 1945 he was shot several times. One bullet entered his spine, and Feyerabend would have to deal with the aftereffects of that wound for the rest of his life. In 1951, Feyerabend received his Ph.D. in philosophy and moved to England to study under the renowned philosopher of science, Karl Popper, whose rationalist approach to the development of scientific knowledge would later be vigorously rejected by Feyerabend. Although he lectured and taught throughout Europe and the United States, Feyerabend maintained his post as a professor of philosophy at the University of California, Berkeley, from 1958-1990. Feyerabend's first book is also his most famous: **Against Method** (1975). Feyerabend announces in his introduction to the volume that the"following essay is written in the conviction that anarchism, while perhaps not the most attractive political philosophy, is certainly excellent medicine for epistemology, and for the philosophy of science." This claim was revolutionary: logic, reason, and the so-called scientific method (considered to this day the key components of the growth and development of scientific knowledge) are not, Feyerabend argues, the methods by which scientific knowledge actually develops. Famously, Feyerabend notes that if one takes a close look at the ways in which key moments in scientific progress actually occurred, one can only conclude that when it comes to scientific discovery,"anything goes"—epistemological anarchism rules the day. In an age when even school children are introduced to the benefits of the"scientific method,"Feyerabend is against method.

1   The idea that science can, and should, be run according to fixed and universal rules, is both unrealistic and pernicious. It is *unrealistic*, for it takes too simple a view of the talents of man and of the circumstances which encourage, or cause, their development. And it is *pernicious*, for the attempt to enforce the rules is bound to increase our professional qualifications at the expense of our humanity. In addition, the idea is *detrimental to science*, for it neglects the complex physical and historical conditions which influence scientific change. It makes our science less adaptable and more dogmatic: every methodological rule is associated with cosmological assumptions, so that using the rule we take it for granted that the assumptions are correct. Naive falsificationism[1] takes it for granted that the laws of nature are manifest and not hidden beneath disturbances of considerable magnitude. Empiricism[2] takes it for granted that sense experience is a better mirror of the world than pure thought. Praise of argument takes it for granted that the artifices of Reason give better results than the unchecked play of our emotions. Such assumptions may be perfectly plausible *and even true*. Still, one should occasionally put them to a test. Putting them to a test means that we stop using the methodology associated with them, start doing science in a different way and see what happens. Case studies such as those reported in the preceding chapters show that such tests occur all the time, and that they speak *against* the universal validity of any rule. All methodologies have their limitations and the only 'rule' that survives is 'anything goes'.

2   The image of 20th-century science in the minds of scientists and laymen is determined by technological miracles such as colour television, the moon shots, the infra-red oven, as well as by a somewhat vague but still quite influential rumour, or fairy-tale, concerning the manner in which these miracles are produced.

3   According to the fairy-tale the success of science is the result of a subtle, but carefully balanced combination of inventiveness and control. Scientists have *ideas*. And they have

---

[1] Falsificationism: a "method" of producing scientific knowledge advanced by Karl Popper in his influential study *The Logic of Scientific Discovery* (1934). According to Popper, in order for a hypothesis to be considered "scientific," it must be potentially falsifiable through rational experimentation, the application of logic, and empirical observation. Statements of truth which are not subject to the test of falsifiability are not scientific statements.

[2] Empiricism: the notion that knowledge is derived through experience. Empirical information is that which comes to the individual through sensory interaction with the environment.

special *methods* for improving ideas. The theories of science have passed the test of method. They give a better account of the world than ideas which have not passed the test.

4   The fairy-tale explains why modern society treats science in a special way and why it grants it privileges not enjoyed by other institutions.

5   Ideally, the modern state is ideologically neutral. Religion, myth, prejudices *do* have an influence, but only in a roundabout way, through the medium of politically influential *parties*. Ideological principles *may* enter the governmental structure, but only via a majority vote, and after a lengthy discussion of possible consequences. In our schools the main religions are taught as *historical phenomena*. They are taught as parts of the truth only if the parents insist on a more direct mode of instruction. It is up to them to decide about the religious education of their children. The financial support of ideologies does not exceed the financial support granted to parties and to private groups. State and ideology, state and church, state and myth, are carefully separated.

6   State and science, however, work closely together. Immense sums are spent on the improvement of scientific ideas. Bastard subjects such as the philosophy of science which have not a single discovery to their credit profit from the boom of the sciences. Even human relations are dealt with in a scientific manner, as is shown by education programmes, proposals for prison reform, army training, and so on. Almost all scientific subjects are compulsory subjects in our schools. While the parents of a six-year-old child can decide to have him instructed in the rudiments of Protestantism, or in the rudiments of the Jewish faith, or to omit religious instruction altogether, they do not have a similar freedom in the case of the sciences. Physics, astronomy, history *must* be learned. They cannot be replaced by magic, astrology, or by a study of legends.

7   Nor is one content with a merely *historical* presentation of physical (astronomical, historical, etc.) facts and principles. One does not say: *some people believe* that the earth moves round the sun while others regard the earth as a hollow sphere that contains the sun, the planets, the fixed stars. One says: the earth *moves* round the sun—everything else is sheer idiocy.

8   Finally, the manner in which we accept or reject scientific ideas is radically different from democratic decision procedures. We accept scientific laws and scientific facts, we teach them in our schools, we make them the basis of important political decisions, but without ever having subjected them to a vote. *Scientists* do not subject them to a vote—or at least this is what they say—and *laymen* certainly do not subject them to a vote. Concrete proposals are occasionally discussed, and a vote is suggested. But the procedure is not extended to general theories and scientific facts. Modern society is 'Copernican'[3] not because Copernicanism has been put on a ballot, subjected to a democratic debate, and then voted in with a simple majority; it is 'Copernican' because the scientists are Copernicans and because one accepts their cosmology as uncritically as one once accepted the cosmology of bishops and cardinals.

9   Scientists do not solve problems because they possess a magic wand—methodology, or a theory of rationality*—but because they have studied a problem for a long time,

---

[3] Copernicus: a Polish astronomer who lived from 1473-1543 and whose work was instrumental in helping to shift the view of the solar system as Earth-centered to sun-centered.

because they know the situation fairly well, because they are not too dumb (though that is rather doubtful nowadays when almost anyone can become a scientist), and because the excesses of one scientific school are almost always balanced by the excesses of some other school. (Besides, scientists only rarely solve their problems, they make lots of mistakes, and many of their solutions are quite useless.) Basically there is hardly any difference between the process that leads to the announcement of a new scientific law and the process preceding passage of a new law in society: one informs either all citizens or those immediately concerned, one collects 'facts' and prejudices, one discusses the matter, and one finally votes. But while a democracy makes some effort to *explain* the process so that everyone can understand it, scientists either *conceal* it, or *bend* it, to make it fit their sectarian interests.

10   No scientist will admit that voting plays a role in his subject. Facts, logic, and methodology alone decide—this is what the fairy-tale tells us. But how do facts decide? What is their function in the advancement of knowledge? We cannot *derive* our theories from them. We cannot give a *negative* criterion by saying, for example, that good theories are theories which can be refuted, but which are not yet contradicted by any fact. A principle of falsification that removes theories because they do not fit the facts would have to remove the whole of science (or it would have to admit that large parts of science are irrefutable). The hint that a good theory *explains more* than its rivals is not very realistic either. True: new theories often predict new things—but almost always at the expense of things already known. Turning to logic we realize that even the simplest demands *are not* satisfied in scientific practice, and *could not be* satisfied, because of the complexity of the material. The ideas which scientists use to present the known and to advance into the unknown are only rarely in agreement with the strict injunctions of logic or pure mathematics and the attempt to make them conform would rob science of the elasticity without which progress cannot be achieved. We see: facts alone are not strong enough for making us accept, or reject, scientific theories, the range they leave to thought is *too wide;* logic and methodology eliminate too much, they are *too narrow.* In between these two extremes lies the ever-changing domain of human ideas and wishes. And a more detailed analysis of successful moves in the game of science ('successful' from the point of view of the scientists themselves) shows indeed that there is a wide range of freedom that *demands* a multiplicity of ideas and *permits* the application of democratic procedures (ballot-discussion-vote) but that is actually closed by power politics and propaganda. *This is where the fairy-tale of a special method assumes its decisive function.* It conceals the freedom of decision which creative scientists and the general public have even inside the most rigid and the most advanced parts of science by a recitation of 'objective' criteria and it thus protects the big-shots (Nobel Prize winners; heads of laboratories, of organizations such as the AMA, of special schools; 'educators'; etc.) from the masses (laymen; experts in non-scientific fields; experts in other fields of science): only those citizens count who were subjected to the pressures of scientific institutions (they have undergone a long process of education), who succumbed to these pressures (they have passed their examinations), and who are now firmly convinced of the truth of the fairy-tale. This is how scientists have deceived themselves and everyone else about their business, but without any real disadvantage: they have more money, more authority, more sex appeal than they

deserve, and the most stupid procedures and the most laughable results in their domain are surrounded with an aura of excellence. It is time to cut them down in size, and to give them a more modest position in society.

11   This advice, which only few of our well-conditioned contemporaries are prepared to accept, seems to clash with certain simple and widely-known facts.

12   Is it not a fact that a learned physician is better equipped to diagnose and to cure an illness than a layman or the medicine-man of a primitive society? Is it not a fact that epidemics and dangerous individual diseases have disappeared only with the beginning of modern medicine? Must we not admit that technology has made tremendous advances since the rise of modern science? And are not the moon-shots a most impressive and undeniable proof of its excellence? These are some of the questions which are thrown at the impudent wretch who dares to criticize the special position of the sciences.

13   The questions reach their polemical aim only if one assumes that the results of science *which no one will deny* have arisen without any help from non-scientific elements, and that they cannot be improved by an admixture of such elements either. 'Unscientific' procedures such as the herbal lore of witches and cunning men, the astronomy of mystics, the treatment of the ill in primitive societies are totally without merit. *Science alone* gives us a useful astronomy, an effective medicine, a trustworthy technology. One must also assume that science owes its success to the correct method and not merely to a lucky accident. It was not a fortunate cosmological guess that led to progress, but the correct *and cosmologically neutral* handling of data. These are the assumptions we must make to give the questions the polemical force they are supposed to have. Not a single one of them stands up to closer examination.

14   If we want to understand nature, if we want to master our physical surroundings, then we must use *all* ideas, *all* methods, and not just a small selection of them. The assertion, however, that there is no knowledge outside science—*extra scientiam nulla salus*—is nothing but another and most convenient fairy-tale. Primitive tribes have more detailed classifications of animals and plants than contemporary scientific zoology and botany, they know remedies whose effectiveness astounds physicians (while the pharmaceutical industry already smells here a new source of income), they have means of influencing their fellow men which science for a long time regarded as non-existent (Voodoo), they solve difficult problems in ways which are still not quite understood (building of the pyramids; Polynesian travels). There existed a highly developed and internationally known astronomy in the old Stone Age. This astronomy was factually adequate *as well as* emotionally satisfying. *It solved both physical and social problems* (one cannot say the same about modern astronomy) and it was tested in very simple and ingenious ways (stone observatories in England and in the South Pacific; astronomical schools in Polynesia—for a more detailed treatment and references concerning all these assertions cf. *my Einführung in die Naturphilosophie*). There was the domestication of animals, the invention of rotating agriculture, new types of plants were bred and kept pure by careful avoidance of cross fertilization, we have chemical inventions, we have a most amazing art that can compare with the best achievements of the present. True, there were no collective excursions to the moon, but single individuals, disregarding great dangers to their soul and their

sanity, rose from sphere to sphere to sphere until they finally faced God himself in all His splendour while others changed into animals and back into humans again (cf. Chapter 16, footnotes 20 and 21). At all times man approached his surroundings with wide open senses and a fertile intelligence, at all times he made incredible discoveries, at all times we can learn from his ideas.

15   Modern science, on the other hand, is not at all as difficult and as perfect as scientific propaganda wants us to believe. A subject such as medicine, or physics, or biology appears difficult only because it is taught badly, because the standard instructions are full of redundant material, and because they start too late in life. During the war, when the American Army needed physicians within a very short time, it was suddenly possible to reduce medical instruction to half a year (the corresponding instruction manuals have disappeared long ago, however. Science may be simplified during the war. In peacetime the prestige of science demands greater complication.) And how often does it not happen that the proud and conceited judgement of an expert is put in its proper place by a layman! Numerous inventors built 'impossible' machines. Lawyers show again and again that an expert does not know what he is talking about. Scientists, especially physicians, frequently come to different results so that it is up to the relatives of the sick person (or the inhabitants of a certain area) to decide *by vote* about the procedure to be adopted. How often is science improved, and turned into new directions by non-scientific influences! It is up to us, it is up to the citizens of a free society to either accept the chauvinism of science without contradiction or to overcome it by the counterforce of public action. Public action was used against science by the Communists in China in the fifties, and it was again used, under very different circumstances, by some opponents of evolution in California in the seventies. Let us follow their example and let us free society from the strangling hold of an ideologically petrified science just as our ancestors freed *us* from the strangling hold of the One True Religion!

16   The way towards this aim is clear. A science that insists on possessing the only correct method and the only acceptable results is ideology and must be separated from the state, and especially from the process of education. One may teach it, but only to those who have decided to make this particular superstition their own. On the other hand, a science that has dropped such totalitarian pretensions is no longer independent and self-contained, and it can be taught in many different combinations (myth and modern cosmology might be one such combination). Of course, every business has the right to demand that its practitioners be prepared in a special way, and it may even demand acceptance of a certain ideology (I for one am against the thinning out of subjects so that they become more and more similar to each other; whoever does not like present-day Catholicism should leave it and become a Protestant, or an Atheist, instead of ruining it by such inane changes as mass in the vernacular). That is true of physics, just as it is true of religion, or of prostitution. But such special ideologies, such special skills have no room in the process of *general education* that prepares a citizen for his role in society. A mature citizen is not a man who has been *instructed* in a special ideology, such as Puritanism, or critical rationalism, and who now carries this ideology with him like a mental tumour. A mature citizen is a person who has learned how to make up his mind and who has then *decided* in favour of what he thinks

suits him best. He is a person who has a certain mental toughness (he does not fall for the first ideological street singer he happens to meet) and who is therefore able *consciously to choose* the business that seems to be most attractive to him rather than being swallowed by it. To prepare himself for his choice he will study the major ideologies as *historical phenomena,* he will study science as a historical phenomenon and not as the one and only sensible way of approaching a problem. He will study it together with other fairy-tales such as the myths of 'primitive' societies so that he has the information needed for arriving at a free decision. An essential part of a general education of this kind is acquaintance with the most outstanding propagandists in all fields, so that the pupil can build up his resistance against all propaganda, including the propaganda called 'argument'. It is only *after* such a hardening procedure that he will be called upon to make up his mind on the issue rationalism-irrationalism, science-myth, science-religion, and so on. His decision in favour of science—assuming he chooses science—will then be much more 'rational' than any decision in favour of science is today. At any rate—science and the schools will be just as carefully separated as religion and the schools are separated today. Scientists will of course participate in governmental decisions, for everyone participates in such decisions. But they will not be given overriding authority. It is the *vote* of *everyone concerned* that decides fundamental issues such as the teaching methods used, or the truth of basic beliefs such as the theory of evolution, or the quantum theory, and not the authority of big-shots hiding behind a non-existing methodology. There is no need to fear that such a way of arranging society will lead to undesirable results. Science itself uses the method of ballot, discussion, vote, though without a clear grasp of its mechanism, and in a heavily biased way. But the rationality of our beliefs will certainly be considerably increased.

QUESTIONS ON MEANING

1. Why does Feyerabend believe that the idea that science should follow methods which are grounded in universal rules is *unrealistic, pernicious,* and *detrimental to science?*

2. Why does Feyerabend find falsificationism, empiricism, and rationalism limited—and limiting—as methods for generating scientific knowledge?

3. What does Feyerabend mean when he declares at the end of the first paragraph that anything goes?

4. What does Feyerabend mean by *myth,* and what is the relationship between myth and scientific knowledge?

5. According to Feyerabend, what role has the state played in the adoption of rationalist and empiricist philosophies of scientific method?

6. What, in your own words, is the fairy tale that has taken root in Western culture regarding acceptable scientific methodology?

7. According to Feyerabend, how do scientific truths become accepted by the scientific community? Does Feyerabend view this process as validating or invalidating his thesis?

8. How does the story of Copernicus illustrate Feyerabend's thesis? How about the story of the revival of traditional medicine in communist China?

QUESTIONS FOR DISCUSSION

1. Feyerabend suggests that it may be "necessary to re-examine our attitude towards myth, religion, magic, witchcraft and towards all those ideas which rationalists would like to see forever removed from the surface of the earth." Why do you think rationalists would like to see these things "removed from the surface of the earth"? Do you agree with the position of the rationalists? What is Feyerabend's opinion? Do you believe that myth or religion or witchcraft can prove useful in the generation of scientific knowledge? Why or why not?

2. Feyerabend points out that no American student can choose to study magic at school, yet all students are required to take courses in biology, physics, and chemistry. Should courses in witchcraft, magic, or other esoteric beliefs and practices be options for public school students? Conversely, should students be required to take courses in biology, chemistry, and physics?

3. Feyerabend notes that such accomplishments as the moon landing are often cited as hallmarks of scientific achievement and thus evidence of the usefulness of rationalist and empiricist scientific methodologies. What is Feyerabend's response to this argument? Do you agree with Feyerabend? Why or why not? What scientific discoveries or technological achievements would you cite as examples of the viability of the scientific method?

LOOKING AT RHETORIC

1. Both Thomas Kuhn and Paul Feyerabend are philosophers of science, and both made their mark on the intellectual world by examining how scientific knowledge develops. Compare and contrast their essays, paying particular attention to their writing styles and the ways in which they organize their thoughts. Which essay seems better organized? Which better written? Which more convincing?

2. Feyerabend frequently uses italics in his essay. What function do these italics serve? Do they contribute or detract from the essay? Do you find the italics useful or confusing as you read the essay?

3. If you were to ask your friend or roommate to read this essay by Feyerabend, do you think she or he would find it easy or difficult to read? If difficult, what features of the essay make it difficult? If you were going to rewrite this essay for a high school audience, what kinds of changes would you make?

WRITING ASSIGNMENTS

1. Research Karl R. Popper and his theory of Falsificationism. Write an essay in which you explain in what ways Feyerabend's work is a repudiation of Popper's theories. Then, develop an argument in which you demonstrate why the theories of Popper or Feyerabend are preferable to those of the other when it comes to the development of scientific knowledge.

2. Darwin's theory of natural selection revolutionized not only the biological sciences, but, indeed, challenged the way people viewed the nature of the cosmos itself, particularly in the Western world. The debates over evolutionary theory sparked by Darwin's work resonate even today, particularly in relation to conflicts over whether evolutionary theory should be presented as *fact*, or as simply one of several possible *theories* (the other major theory nowadays being some form of *creationism or intelligent design* theory). Write an essay in which you discuss the current conflicts in public education over teaching evolutionary theory. Explain in your essay how the theories of Feyerabend can provide a context within which to understand the debate.

3. In pairs or in groups, make a list of six hotly debated topics in the scientific world right now (global warming, for instance, would be one topic). As a group, discuss each topic one by one, identifying what the group believes are the major sides in the debate over each topic. Then, individually, select one of the topics and spend some time researching the current debates regarding it. After doing your research, give some consideration to whether what you have learned about the debate validates or invalidates Feyerabend's thesis about the nature of scientific methodology. Write an essay in which you examine the topic and debate what you have researched as a test case for or against Feyerabend's theories regarding the politics and methods surrounding Western science.

Interdisciplinary Connections

The Tools of Science: A World Too Small to See

M any scientific pursuits require tools. Humans are limited by biology in what can be heard with the human ear and seen with the human eye. Thus, in our ongoing effort to see further and deeper into the nature of the world around us, we have developed increasingly complex

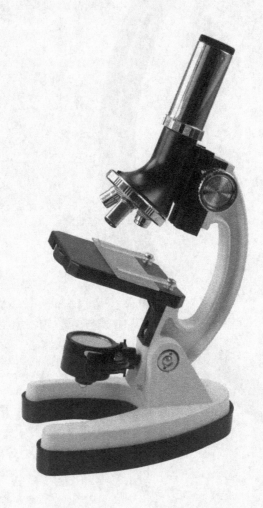

instruments that give us access to the world around us in unique ways. In terms of vision, we have tended to push in two directions: to peer outward into space in order to bring objects too far to be seen closer to us, and to peer deeper into the ever smaller objects that are the building blocks of our environment. One of the axioms of our time is that in order to see ever smaller objects, one must devise ever more complicated and large instruments. These pictures illustrate two of these devices: a simple microscope—not unlike the kind you might have used in school as you grew up—and a small section of the tremendously large, expensive, and complex Large Hadron Collider in Geneva, Switzerland, which provides access to the smallest (thus far) particles of nature. As you look at these photos, what do they suggest about the human quest for knowledge? Is the expense of building these devices worth it? What information about the nature of our environment would you like to know? Has science produced an instrument that can provide the answer you seek?

Section of the Large Hadron Collider

Unraveling the DNA Myth

By Barry Commoner

Barry Commoner (b. 1917) is a biologist at the Center for the Biology of Natural Systems at Queens College, City University of New York, where much of his work has focused on directing the Critical Genetics Projects. In his long and noted career, Commoner has written numerous books—including Science and Survival *(1966),* The Closing Circle *(1971), and* Making Peace with the Planet *(1990)—many of which focus on the relationship of humans to their environment and which call for the ethical and enlightened understanding of the integral relationship between humans and the ecological systems with which they interact. He has been a leading figure in the charge for responsible development of atomic energy, and was instrumental in bringing about the 1963 nuclear test-ban treaty. He had an unsuccessful bid for President in 1980, and has been outspokenly critical of science that does not adequately account for the complex ways in which new technologies change the environment. Without this knowledge, Commoner points out repeatedly, we run the risk of doing harm, and perhaps catastrophic damage, to ourselves and our environment. This theme appears in many of Commoner's books, and shows up in the following excerpt. The launching point of Commoner's analysis in the essay below is the work of Francis Crick, who, along with James Watson, is generally credited with discovering the double-helix structure of DNA.*

1   The wonders of genetic science are all founded on the discovery of the DNA[1] double helix—by Francis Crick and James Watson in 1953—and they proceed from the premise that this molecular structure is the exclusive agent of inheritance in all living things: in the kingdom of molecular genetics, the DNA gene[2] is absolute monarch. Known to molecular biologists as the "central dogma,"[3] the premise assumes that an organism's genome—its total complement of DNA genes—should fully account for its characteristic assemblage of inherited traits. The premise, unhappily, is false. Tested between 1990 and 2001 in one of the largest and most highly publicized scientific undertakings of our time, the Human Genome Project, the theory collapsed under the weight of fact. There are far too few human genes to account for the complexity of our inherited traits or for the vast inherited differences between plants, say, and people. By any reasonable measure, the finding (published last February) signaled the downfall of the central dogma: it also destroyed the scientific foundation of genetic engineering and the validity of the biotechnology industry's widely advertised claim that its methods of generically modifying food crops are

---

[1] Deoxyribonucleic acid: a large molecule composed of a specific sequence of four kinds of nucleotides found in the nucleus of living cells.

[2] A term applied to segments of DNA that encode specific proteins that give rise to inherited traits. Human DNA contains about 30,000 genes. The term's meaning has become increasingly uncertain.

[3] DOGMA: a theory concerning the relation among: DNA, RNA, and protein in which the nucleotide sequence of DNA exclusively governs its own replication and engenders a specific genetic unit.

"specific, precise, and predictable" and therefore safe. In short, the most dramatic achievement to date of the $3 billion Human Genome Project is the refutation of its own scientific rationale.

2   Since Crick first proposed it forty-four years ago, the central dogma has come to dominate biomedical research. Simple, elegant, and easily summarized, it seeks to reduce inheritance, a property that only living things possess, to molecular dimensions: The molecular agent of inheritance is DNA, deoxyribonucleic acid, a very long, linear molecule lightly coiled within each cell's[4] nucleus. DNA is made up of four different kinds of nucleotides,[5] strung together in each gene in a particular linear order or sequence. Segments of DNA comprise the genes that, through a series of molecular processes, give rise to each of our inherited traits.

3   Guided by Crick's theory, the Human Genome Project was intended to identify and enumerate all of the genes in the human body by working out the sequence of the three billion nucleotides in human DNA. In 1990, James Watson described the Human Genome Project as "the ultimate description of life." It will yield, he claimed, the information "that determines if you have life as a fly, a carrot, or a man." Walter Gilbert, one of the project's earliest proponents, famously observed that the 3 billion nucleotides found in human DNA would easily fit on a compact disc, in which one could point and say, "Here is a human being; it's me!" President Bill Clinton described the human genome as "the language in which God created life." How could the minute dissection of human DNA into a sequence of 3 billion nucleotides support such hyperbolic claims? Crick's crisply stated theory attempts to answer that question. It hypothesizes a clear-cut chain of molecular processes that leads from a single DNA gene to the appearance of a particular inherited trait. The explanatory power of the theory is based on an extravagant proposition: that the DNA genes have unique, absolute, and universal control over the totality of inheritance in all forms of life.

4   In order to control inheritance, Crick reasoned, genes would need to govern the synthesis of protein, since proteins form the cell's internal structures and, as enzymes, catalyze the chemical events that produce specific inherited traits. The ability of DNA to govern the synthesis of protein is facilitated by their similar structures—both are linear molecules composed of specific sequences of subunits. A particular gene is distinguished from another by the precise linear order (sequence) in which the four different nucleotides appear in its DNA. In the same way, a particular protein is distinguished from another by the specific sequence of the twenty different kinds of amino acids of which it is made. The four kinds of nucleotides can be arranged in numerous possible sequences, and the choice of any one of them in the makeup of a particular gene represents its "genetic information" in the same sense that in poker, the order of a hand of cards informs the player whether to bet high on a straight or drop out with a meaningless set of random numbers.

5   Crick's "sequence hypothesis" neatly links the gene to the protein: the sequence of the nucleotides in a gene "is a simple code for the amino acid sequence of a particular protein." This is shorthand for a series of well-documented molecular processes that transcribe

---

[4] The fundamental, irreducible unit of life.
[5] The four kinds of subunits of which nucleic acid is constructed.

the gene's DNA nucleotide sequence into a complementary sequence of ribonucleic acid (RNA)[6] nucleotides that, in turn, delivers the gene's code to the site of protein formation, where it determines the sequential order in which the different amino acids are linked to form the protein. It follows that in each living thing there should be a one-to-one correspondence between the total number of genes and the total number of proteins. The entire array of human genes—that is, the genome—must therefore represent the whole of a person's inheritance, which distinguishes a person from a fly, or Walter Gilbert from anyone else. Finally, because DNA is made of the same four nucleotides in every living thing, the genetic code is universal, which means that a gene should be capable of producing its particular protein wherever it happens to find itself, even in a different species.

6   Crick's theory includes a second doctrine, which he originally called the "central dogma" (though this term is now generally used to identify his theory as a whole). The hypothesis is typical Crick: simple, precise, and magisterial. "Once (sequential) information has passed into protein it cannot get out again." This means that genetic information originates in the DNA nucleotide sequence and terminates, unchanged, in the protein amino acid sequence. The pronouncement is crucial to the explanatory power of the theory because it endows the gene with undiluted control over the identity of the protein and the inherited trait that the protein creates. To stress the importance of this genetic taboo, Crick bet the future of the entire enterprise on it, asserting that "the discovery of just one type of present-day cell" in which genetic information passed from protein to nucleic acid or from protein to protein "would shake the whole intellectual basis of molecular biology."

7   Crick was aware of the brashness of his bet, for it was known that in living cells proteins come into promiscuous molecular contact with numerous other proteins and with molecules of DNA and RNA. His insistence that these interactions are genetically chaste was designed to protect the DNA's genetic message—the gene's nucleotide sequence—from molecular intruders that might change the sequence or add new ones as it was transferred, step by step, from gene to protein and thus destroy the theory's elegant simplicity.

8   Crick's gamble suffered a spectacular loss. In the journals *Nature* and *Science* and at joint press conferences and television appearances, the two genome research teams reported their results. The major result was "unexpected." Instead of the 100,000 or more genes predicted by the estimated number of human proteins, the gene count was only about 30,000. By this measure, people are only about as gene-rich as a mustardlike weed (which has 26,000 genes) and about twice as genetically endowed as a fruit fly or a primitive worm—hardly an adequate basis for distinguishing among "life as a fly, a carrot, or a man." In fact, an inattentive reader of genomic CDs might easily mistake Walter Gilbert for a mouse, 99 percent of whose genes have human counterparts.

9   The surprising results contradicted the scientific premise on which the genome project was undertaken and dethroned its guiding theory, the central dogma. After all, if the human gene count is too low to match the number of proteins and the numerous inherited traits that they engender, and if it cannot explain the vast inherited difference between a weed and a person, there must be much more to the "ultimate description of life" than the genes, on their own, can tell us.

---

[6] Ribonucleic acid: its various forms transmit genetic information from DNA to protein.

10   Scientists and journalists somehow failed to notice what had happened. The discovery that the human genome is not much different from the roundworm's led Dr. Eric Lander, one of the leaders of the project, to declare that humanity should learn "a lesson in humility." In the *New York Times*, Nicholas Wade merely observed that the project's surprising results will have an "impact on human pride" and that "human self-esteem may be in for further blows" from future genome analyses, which had already found that the genes of mice and men are very similar.

11   The project's scientific reports offered little to explain the shortfall in the gene count. One of the possible explanations for why the gene count is "so discordant with our predictions" was described, in full, last February in *Science* as follows: "nearly 40% of human genes are alternatively spliced." Properly understood, this modest, if esoteric, account fulfills Crick's dire prophecy: it "shakes the whole intellectual basis of molecular biology" and undermines the scientific validity of its application to genetic engineering.

12   The credibility of the Human Genome Project is not the only casualty of the scientific community's stubborn resistance to experimental results that contradict the central dogma. Nor is it the most significant casualty. The fact that one gene can give rise to multiple proteins also destroys the theoretical foundation of a multibillion-dollar industry, the genetic engineering of food crops. In genetic engineering it is assumed, without adequate experimental proof, that a bacterial gene for an insecticidal protein, for example, transferred to a corn plant, will produce precisely that protein and nothing else. Yet in that alien genetic environment, alternative splicing[7] of the bacterial gene might give rise to multiple variants of the intended protein—or even to proteins bearing little structural relationship to the original one, with unpredictable effects on ecosystems and human health.

13   The delay in dethroning the all-powerful gene led in the 1990s to a massive invasion of genetic engineering into American agriculture, though its scientific justification had already been compromised a decade or more earlier. Nevertheless, ignoring the profound fact that in nature the normal exchange of genetic material occurs exclusively within a single species, biotech-industry executives have repeatedly boasted that. In comparison, moving a gene from one species to another is not only normal but also more specific, precise, and predictable. In only the last five years such transgenic crops have taken over 68 percent of the U.S. soybean acreage, 26 percent of the corn acreage, and more than 69 percent of the cotton acreage.

14   That the industry is guided by the central dogma was made explicit by Ralph W.F. Hardy, president of the National Agricultural Biotechnology Council and formerly director of life sciences at DuPont, a major producer of genetically engineered seeds. In 1999, in Senate testimony, he succinctly described the industry's guiding theory this way: "DNA (top management molecules) directs RNA formation (middle management molecules) directs protein formation (worker molecules)." The outcome of transferring a bacterial gene into a corn plant is expected to be as predictable as the result of a corporate takeover: what the workers do will be determined precisely by what the new top management tells them

---

[7] splicing: reshuffling of the RNA transcription of a gene's nucleotide sequence that generates multiple proteins.

to do. This Reaganesque version of the central dogma is the scientific foundation upon which each year billions of transgenic plants of soybeans, corn, and cotton are grown with the expectation that the particular alien gene in each of them will be faithfully replicated in each of the billions of cell divisions that occur as each plant develops; that in each of the resultant cells the alien gene will encode only a protein with precisely the amino acid sequence that it encodes in its original organism: and that throughout this biological saga, despite the alien presence, the plant's natural complement of DNA will itself be properly replicated with no abnormal changes in composition.

15   In an ordinary unmodified plant the reliability of this natural genetic process results from the compatibility between its gene system and its equally necessary protein-mediated systems. The harmonious relation between the two systems develops during their cohabitation, in the same species, over very long evolutionary periods, in which natural selection eliminates incompatible varients. In other words, within a single species the reliability of the successful outcome of the complex molecular process that gives rise to the inheritance of particular traits is guaranteed by many thousands of years of testing in nature.

16   In a genetically engineered transgenic plant, however, the alien transplanted bacterial gene must properly interact with the plant's protein-mediated systems. Higher plants, such as corn, soybeans, and cotton, are known to possess proteins that repair DNA miscoding; proteins that alternatively splice messenger RNA and thereby produce a multiplicity of different proteins from a single gene; and proteins that chaperone the proper folding of other, nascent proteins. But the plant systems' evolutionary history is very different from the bacterial gene's. As a result, in the transgenic plant the harmonious interdependence of the alien gene and the new host's protein-mediated systems is likely to be disrupted in unspecified, imprecise, and inherently unpredictable ways. In practice, these disruptions are revealed by the numerous experimental failures that occur before a transgenic organism is actually produced and by unexpected genetic changes that occur even when the gene has been successfully transferred.

17   Most alarming is the recent evidence that in a widely grown genetically modified food crop—soybeans containing an alien gene for herbicide resistance—the transgenic host plant's genome has itself been unwittingly altered. The Monsanto Company admitted in 2000 that its soybeans contained some extra fragments of the transferred gene, but nevertheless concluded that "no new proteins were expected or observed to be produced." A year later Belgian researchers discovered that a segment of the plant's own DNA had been scrambled. The abnormal DNA was large enough to produce a new protein, a potentially harmful protein.

18   One way that such mystery DNA might arise is suggested by a recent study showing that in some plants carrying a bacterial gene, the plant's enzymes that correct DNA replication errors rearrange the alien gene's nucleotide sequence. The consequences of such changes cannot be foreseen. The likelihood in genetically engineered crops of even exceedingly rare, disruptive effects of gene transfer is greatly amplified by the billions of individual transgenic plants already being grown annually in the United States.

19   The degree to which such disruptions do occur in genetically modified crops is not known at present because the biotechnology industry is not required to provide even

the most basic information about the actual composition of the transgenic plants to the regulatory agencies. No tests, for example, are required to show that the plant actually produces a protein with the same amino acid sequence as the original bacterial protein. Yet this information is the only way to confirm that the transferred gene does in fact yield the theory-predicted product. Moreover, there are no required studies based on detailed analysis of the molecular structure and biochemical activity of the alien gene and its protein product in the transgenic commercial crop. Given that some unexpected effects may develop very slowly, crop plants should be monitored in successive generations as well. None of these essential tests are being performed, and billions of transgenic plants are now being grown with only the most rudimentary knowledge about the resulting changes in their composition. Without detailed, ongoing analyses of the transgenic crops, there is no way of knowing if hazardous consequences might arise. Given the failure of the central dogma, there is no assurance that they will not. The genetically engineered crops now being grown represent a massive uncontrolled experiment whose outcome is inherently unpredictable.

20   The results could be catastrophic.

21   Why, then, has the central dogma continued to stand? To some degree the theory has been protected from criticism by a device more common to religion than science: dissent, or merely the discovery of a discordant fact, is a punishable offense, a heresy that might easily lead to professional ostracism. Much of this bias can be attributed to institutional inertia, a failure of rigor, but there are other, more insidious, reasons why molecular geneticists might be satisfied with the status quo; the central dogma has given them such a satisfying, seductively simplistic explanation of heredity that it seemed sacrilegious to entertain doubts. The central dogma was simply too good not to be true.

22   As a result, funding for molecular genetics has rapidly increased over the last twenty years; new academic institutions, many of them "genomic" variants of more mundane professions, such as public health, have proliferated. At Harvard and other universities, the biology curriculum has become centered on the genome. But beyond the traditional scientific economy of prestige and the generous funding that follows it as night follows day, money has distorted the scientific process as a once purely academic pursuit has been commercialized to an astonishing degree by the researchers themselves. Biology has become a glittering target for venture capital; each new discovery brings new patents, new partnerships, new corporate affiliations. But as the growing opposition to transgenic crops clearly shows, there is persistent public concern not only with the safety of genetically engineered foods but also with the inherent dangers in arbitrarily overriding patterns of inheritance that are embedded in the natural world through long evolutionary experience. Too often those concerns have been derided by industry scientists as the "irrational" fears of an uneducated public. The irony, of course, is that the biotechnology industry is based on science that is forty years old and conveniently devoid of more recent results, which show that there are strong reasons to fear the potential consequences of transferring a DNA gene between species. What the public fears is not the experimental science but the fundamentally irrational decision to let it out of the laboratory into the real world before we truly understand it.

QUESTIONS ON MEANING

1. What is the central dogma of molecular biology?

2. What are Crick's two doctrines, as explained by Commoner?

3. How did the results of the Human Genome Project challenge the central dogma?

4. The experimental data discussed by Commoner stands to have a major effect on what industry? What kinds of regulations does Commoner believe are not in place to ensure that this industry is responsible in its genetic engineering efforts?

5. What alternative understanding of the importance of DNA does Commoner advocate as a counterpoint to the central dogma?

6. According to Commoner, why has the central dogma stayed immune to criticism (and revision) for so long despite the ready availability of experimental data that challenges its claims?

QUESTIONS FOR DISCUSSION

1. Before you read this article, what did you know about DNA? Did your views change as a result of reading this essay by Commoner? If so, what specifically in Commoner's work caused you to rethink your own view of the role of DNA? What might Martin and her co-authors (in their essay reprinted in this volume) say about what it would mean to be scientifically literate regarding DNA?

2. What do you believe is Commoner's primary purpose for writing this essay? Is there a central message? If so, did you find it convincing? If you did not find it convincing, why not?

3. Commoner's essay seems to have a fundamentally different purpose than the essays by Fukuyama and Sandel (both reprinted in this chapter), and yet, what viewpoints do you think they share regarding developments in biotechnology? On what points might they differ?

4. How might the theories of the development of scientific knowledge proposed by Kuhn and/ or Feyerabend provide a context in which to understand the points made by Commoner about the role of the central dogma in the biological sciences?

5. Are there any other disciplines that cling to something that might be characterized as a central dogma? Can you think of any evidence that might suggest that the dogma in question may need reevaluation? Why or why not?

LOOKING AT RHETORIC

1. Commoner clearly has some reservations about recent transformations in the field of biology. In a sentence, how would you characterize Commoner's attitude toward biology as a discipline? Go through the essay and make a list of those words, phrases, and metaphors that are evidence of Commoner's attitude.

2. Imagine that Thomas Kuhn and Paul Feyerabend were asked to respond to Commoner's essay. What do you think each of these philosophers of science would say about the issues raised by Commoner?

WRITING ASSIGNMENTS

1. Spend some time in the library researching the history of the discovery of DNA and the Human Genome Project. What more have you learned about DNA and the central dogma?

Write an essay in which you inform your audience about this history, being sure to present some of the complex opinions (both pro and con) about some of the conclusions drawn regarding the central dogma.

2. Commoner points out that one of the results of the central dogma is that it seemed to clear the path for funding for the Human Genome Project, despite the fact that experimental data existed at the time which, according to Commoner, called into question the validity of the dogma. Write an essay in which you discuss the intersection of public policy and scientific research. What guidelines, if any, should the government use when seeking to decide which scientific endeavors to fund?

3. In pairs or in groups, in light of Commoner's essay, discuss the pros and cons of increased regulation of the agricultural industry, particularly in terms of the planting of genetically engineered crops. Make two lists: one list of arguments in favor of increased regulation, one list in favor of decreased regulation. As a group, spend some time in the library gathering perspectives on the issue different from the perspective of Commoner. Discuss as a group the factors you use to determine the merits of one position over another. Then, individually write an essay in which you take a side in the debate, arguing either for or against regulation of the agricultural industry's use of genetically engineered crops.

"Why We Should Worry"

Francis Fukuyama

Francis Fukuyama (b. 1952) is a professor of International Political Economy at Johns Hopkins University, where he serves as the director of the International Development Program. He is perhaps best known for his book The End of History and the Last Man *(1992) in which Fukuyama argues that if one views the progress of history as a grand struggle between competing sociopolitical and economic ideologies, then historical progress—at least, in terms of the development of competing governmental ideologies—is nearly at an end as the basic values associated with Western democracy gradually become globalized. Fukuyama's interest in progress and development lead him to consider the ways in which new developments in the biological sciences—particularly advances in genetic engineering—may shape human social, cultural, and physical change in the coming generations. This is the subject of the book from which the following chapter is taken:* Our Posthuman Future *(2002). Published during a time when Fukuyama was a member of the President's Council on Bioethics (on which he served from 2001-2005), it asks us to consider the implications genetic engineering may have on our understanding of human nature and human rights and whether we want to pursue a course of action that would, effectively, move us, as a species, beyond* human.

> *"Take Ectogenesis. Pfitzner and Kawaguchi had got the whole technique worked out. But would the Governments look at it? No. There was something called Christianity. Women were forced to go on being viviparous."*
>
> *Aldous Huxley,* Brave New World

1   In light of the possible pathways to the future laid out in the previous chapters, we need to ask the question: Why should we worry about biotechnology? Some critics, like the activist Jeremy Rifkin and many European environmentalists, have been opposed to

innovation in biotechnology virtually across the board. Given the very real medical benefits that will result from projected advances in human biotechnology, as well as the greater productivity and reduced use of pesticides coming from agricultural biotech, such categorical opposition is very difficult to justify. Biotechnology presents us with a special moral dilemma, because any reservations we may have about progress need to be tempered with a recognition of its undisputed promise.

2   Hanging over the entire field of genetics has been the specter of eugenics—that is, the deliberate breeding of people for certain selected heritable traits. The term eugenics was coined by Charles Darwin's cousin Francis Galton. In the late nineteenth and early twentieth centuries, state-sponsored eugenics programs attracted surprisingly broad support, not just from right-wing racists and social Darwinists, but from such progressives as the Fabian socialists Beatrice and Sidney Webb and George Bernard Shaw, the communists J.B.S. Haldane and J. D. Bemal, and the feminist and birth-control proponent Margaret Sanger. The United States and other Western countries passed eugenics laws permitting the state to involuntarily sterilize people deemed "imbeciles," while encouraging people with desirable characteristics to have as many children as possible. In the words of Justice Oliver Wendell Holmes, "We want people who are healthy, good-natured, emotionally stable, sympathetic, and smart. We do not want idiots, imbeciles, paupers, and criminals."

3   The eugenics movement in the United States was effectively terminated with revelations about the Nazis' eugenics policies, which involved the extermination of entire categories of people and medical experimentation on people regarded as genetically inferior. Since then, continental Europe has been effectively inoculated against any revival of eugenics and has, in fact, become inhospitable terrain for many forms of genetic research. The reaction against eugenics has not been universal: in progressive, social democratic Scandinavia, eugenics laws remained in effect until the 1960s. Despite the fact that the Japanese conducted medical "experiments" on unwilling subjects during the Pacific War (through the activities of the infamous Unit 731), there has been a much smaller backlash against eugenics there and in most other Asian societies. China has pursued eugenics actively through its one-child population control policy and through a crude eugenics law, passed in 1995 and reminiscent of Western ones from the early twentieth century, that seeks to limit the right of low-IQ people to reproduce.

4   There were two important objections to those earlier eugenics policies that would most likely not apply to any eugenics of the future, at least in the West. The first was that eugenics programs could not achieve the ends they sought given the technology available at the time. Many of the defects and abnormalities against which the eugenicists thought they were selecting through forced sterilizations were the product of recessive genes—that is, genes that had to be inherited from both parents before they could be expressed. Many seemingly normal people would remain carriers of these genes and propagate those characteristics in the gene pool unless they could somehow be identified and sterilized as well. Many other "defects" were either not defects at all (for example, certain forms of low intelligence) or else were the result of nongenetic factors that could be remedied through better public health. For instance, certain villages in China have large populations of low-IQ children as a result not of bad heredity but of low levels of iodine in the children's diets.

5   The second major objection to historical forms of eugenics is that they were state-sponsored and coercive. The Nazis, of course, carried this to horrifying extremes by killing or experimenting on "less desirable" people. But even in the United States it was possible for a court to decide that a particular individual was an imbecile or a moron (terms that were defined, as many mental conditions tend to be, very loosely) and to order that he or she be involuntarily sterilized. Given the view at the time that a wide variety of behaviors, such as alcoholism and criminality, were heritable, this gave the state potential dominion over the reproductive choices of a large part of its population. For observers like science writer Matt Ridley, state sponsorship is the primary problem with past eugenics laws; eugenics freely pursued by individuals has no similar stigma.

6   Genetic engineering[1] puts eugenics squarely back on the table, but it is clear that any future approach to eugenics will be very different from the historical varieties, at least in the developed West. The reason is that neither of these two objections is likely to apply, leading to the possibility of a kinder, gentler eugenics that will rob the word of some of the horror traditionally associated with it.

7   The first objection, that eugenics is not technically feasible, applies only to the kinds of technologies available in the early twentieth century, like forced sterilization. Advances in genetic screening currently allow doctors to identify carriers of recessive traits before they decide to have children, and in the future might allow them to identify embryos that carry a high risk of abnormality because they have inherited two recessive genes. Information of this sort is already available, for example, to individuals from a population such as Ashkenazi Jews, who have higher than normal probabilities of carrying the recessive Tay-Sachs gene; two such carriers may decide not to marry or to have children. In the future, germ-line engineering[2] offers the possibility that such recessive genes could be eliminated from all subsequent descendants of a particular carrier. If the treatment were to become cheap and easy enough, it is possible to conceive of a particular gene being largely eliminated from entire populations.

8   The second objection to eugenics, that it was state-sponsored, is not likely to carry much weight in the future, because few modern societies are likely to want to get back into the eugenics game. Virtually all Western countries have moved sharply in the direction of stronger protection of individual rights since World War II, and the right to autonomy in reproductive decisions ranks high among those rights. The idea that states should legitimately worry about collective goods like the health of their national gene pools is no longer taken seriously but rather associated with outdated racist and elitist attitudes.

9   The kinder, gentler eugenics that is just over the horizon will then be a matter of individual choice on the part of parents, and not something that a coercive state forces on its citizens. In the words of one commentator, "The old eugenics would have required a continual selection for breeding of the fit, and a culling of the unfit. The new eugenics would permit in principle the conversion of all the unfit to the highest genetic level."

---

[1] Genetic Engineering: manipulation of the genetic code of a human, animal, or plant in order to produce some biological change.

[2] Germ-line Engineering: genetic engineering that causes changes that can be passed down to subsequent generations.

10   Parents already make these kinds of choices when they discover through amniocentesis[3] that their child has a high probability of Down's syndrome and decide to have an abortion. In the immediate future, the new eugenics is likely to lead to more abortions and discarded embryos, which is why those opposed to abortion will resist the technology strongly. But it will not involve coercion against adults or restrictions on their reproductive rights. On the contrary, their range of reproductive choices will dramatically expand, as they cease to worry about infertility, birth defects, and a host of other problems. It is, moreover, possible to anticipate a time when reproductive technology will be so safe and effective that no embryos need be discarded or harmed.

11   My own preference is to drop the use of the loaded term eugenics when referring to future genetic engineering and substitute the word *breeding*—in German, *Zuchtung*, the word originally used to translate Darwin's term *selection*. In the future, we will likely be able to breed human beings much as we breed animals, only far more scientifically and effectively, by selecting which genes we pass on to our children. *Breeding* has no necessary connotations of state sponsorship, but it is appropriately suggestive of genetic engineering's dehumanizing potential.

12   Any case to be made against human genetic engineering should therefore not get hung up on the red herring of state sponsorship or the prospect of government coercion. The old-fashioned eugenics remains a problem in authoritarian countries like China and may constitute a foreign policy problem for Western countries dealing with China. But opponents of breeding new humans will have to explain what harms will be produced by the free decisions of individual parents over the genetic makeup of their children.

13   There are basically three categories of possible objection (1) those based on religion; (2) those based on utilitarian considerations; and (3) those based on, for lack of a better term, philosophic principles. The remainder of this chapter will consider the first two categories of reservations, while Part II will deal with the philosophical issues.

RELIGIOUS CONSIDERATIONS

14   Religion provides the clearest grounds for objecting to the genetic engineering of human beings, so it is not surprising that much of the opposition to a variety of new reproductive technologies has come from people with religious convictions.

15   In a tradition shared by Jews, Christians, and Muslims, man is created in God's image. For Christians in particular, this has important implications for human dignity. There is a sharp distinction between human and nonhuman creation; only human beings have a capacity for moral choice, free will, and faith, a capacity that gave them a higher moral status than the rest of animal creation. God made a way through nature to produce these outcomes, and hence a violation of natural norms like having children through sex and the family is also a violation of God's will. While historical Christian institutions have not

---

[3] Amniocentesis: removing amniotic fluid from an amniotic sac, typically through a long needle, which allows for the examination of the cells surrounding developing tissue. Can be used to diagnose potential genetic irregularities in a developing fetus such as Tay Sachs Disease, Down syndrome, and cystic fibrosis.

always acted on this principle, Christian doctrine emphatically asserts that all human beings possess an equal dignity, regardless of their outward social status, and are therefore entitled to an equality of respect.

16   Given these premises, it's not surprising that the Catholic Church and conservative Protestant groups have taken strong stands against a whole range of biomedical technologies, including birth control, in vitro fertilization, abortion, stem cell research, cloning, and prospective forms of genetic engineering. These reproductive technologies, even if freely embraced by parents out of love for their children, are wrong from this perspective because they put human beings in the place of God in creating human life (or destroying it, in the case of abortion). They allow reproduction to take place outside the context of the natural processes of sex and the family. Genetic engineering, moreover, sees a human being not as a miraculous act of divine creation, but rather as the sum of a series of material causes that can be understood and manipulated by human beings. All of this fails to respect human dignity, and thus violates God's will.

17   Given the fact that conservative Christian groups constitute the most visible and impassioned lobby opposed to many forms of reproductive technology, it is often assumed that religion constitutes the only basis on which one can be opposed to biotechnology and that the central issue is the question of abortion. While some scientists, like Francis Collins, the distinguished molecular biologist who since 1993 has headed the Human Genome Project, are observant Christians, the majority are not, and among this latter group there is a widespread view that religious conviction is tantamount to a kind of irrational prejudice that stands in the way of scientific progress. Some think that religious belief and scientific inquiry are incompatible, while others hope that greater education and scientific literacy will eventually lead to a withering away of religiously based opposition to biomedical research.

18   These latter views are problematic for a number of reasons. In the first place, there are many grounds to be skeptical about both the practical and ethical benefits of biotechnology that have nothing to do with religion, as Part II of this book will seek to demonstrate. Religion provides only the most straightforward motive for opposing certain new technologies.

19   Second, religion often intuits moral truths that are shared by non-religious people, who fail to understand that their own secular views on ethical issues are as much a matter of faith as those of religious believers. Many hardheaded natural scientists, for example, have a rational materialist understanding of the world, and yet in their political and ethical views are firmly committed to a version of liberal equality that is not all that different from the Christian view of the universal dignity of humankind. As will be seen below, it is not clear that the equality of respect for all human beings demanded by liberal egalitarianism flows logically from a scientific understanding of the world as opposed to being an article of faith.

20   Third, the view that religion will necessarily give ground to scientific rationalism with the progress of education and modernization more generally is itself extraordinarily naive and detached from empirical reality. It was the case that many social scientists a couple of generations ago believed that modernization necessarily implied secularization. But this pattern has been followed only in Western Europe; North America and Asia have seen no inevitable decline in religiosity with higher levels of education or scientific awareness.

In some cases, belief in traditional religion has been replaced by belief in secular ideologies like "scientific" socialism that are no more rational than religion; in others, there has been a strong revival of traditional religion itself. The ability of modern societies to "free" themselves of authoritative accounts of who they are and where they are going is much more difficult than many scientists assume. Nor is it clear that these societies would necessarily be better off without such accounts. Given the fact that people with strong religious views are not likely to disappear from the political scene anytime soon in modern democracies, it behooves nonreligious people to accept the dictates of democratic pluralism and show greater tolerance for religious views.

21 On the other hand, many religious conservatives damage their own cause by allowing the abortion issue to trump all other considerations in biomedical research. Restrictions on federal funding for embryonic stem cell research were put in place by abortion opponents in Congress in 1995 to prevent harm to embryos. But embryos are routinely harmed by in vitro fertilization clinics when they are discarded, a practice that abortion opponents have been willing to let stand up to now. The National Institutes for Health had developed guidelines for conducting research in this extremely promising area without risk of raising the number of abortions performed in the United States. The guidelines mandated that embryonic stem cells should be derived not from aborted fetuses or those created specifically for research purposes, but from extra embryos produced as a by-product of in vitro fertilization, ones that would have been discarded or stored indefinitely were they not used in this fashion. President George W. Bush modified these guidelines in 2001 by limiting federal funding to only those sixty or so stem cell "lines" (that is, cells that had been isolated and that could replicate indefinitely) that had already been produced. As Charles Krauthammer has pointed out, religious conservatives have focused on the wrong issue with regard to stem cells. They should not be worried about the sources of these cells but about their ultimate destiny: "What really ought to give us pause about research that harnesses the fantastic powers of primitive cells to develop into entire organs and even organisms is what monsters we will soon be capable of creating."

22 While religion provides the most clear-cut grounds for opposing certain types of biotechnology, religious arguments will not be persuasive to many who do not accept religion's starting premises. We thus need to examine other, more secular, types of arguments.

UTILITARIAN CONCERNS

23 By *utilitarian*, I mean primarily economic considerations—that is, that future advances in biotechnology may lead to unanticipated costs or long-term negative consequences that may outweigh the presumed benefits. The "harms" inflicted by biotechnology from a religious perspective are often intangible (for example, the threat to human dignity implied by genetic manipulation). By contrast, utilitarian harms are generally more broadly recognized, having to do either with economic costs or with clearly identifiable costs to physical well-being.

24 Modern economics provides us with a straightforward framework for analyzing whether a new technology will be good or bad from a utilitarian viewpoint. We assume that all individuals in a market economy pursue their individual interests in a rational

fashion, based on sets of individual preferences that economists do not presume to judge. Individuals are free to do this as long as the pursuit of these preferences does not prevent other individuals from pursuing theirs; government exists to reconcile these individual interests through a series of evenhanded procedures embodied in law. We can further presume that parents will not seek to deliberately harm their children, but rather will try to maximize their happiness. In the words of the libertarian writer Virginia Postrel, "People want genetic technology to develop because they expect to use it for *themselves*, to help themselves and their children, to work and to keep their own humanity . . . In a dynamic, decentralized system of individual choice and responsibility, people do not have to trust any authority but their own."

25   Assuming that the use of new biotechnologies, including technologies like genetic engineering, comes about as a matter of individual choice on the part of parents rather than being coercively mandated by the state, is it possible that harms can nonetheless result for the individual or for society as a whole?

26   The most obvious class of harms are the ones quite familiar to us from the world of conventional medicine: side effects or other longterm negative consequences to the individual undergoing treatment. The reason the Food and Drug Administration and other regulatory bodies exist is to prevent these kinds of harms, through the extensive testing of drugs and medical procedures before they are released on the market.

27   There is some reason to think that future genetic therapies, and particularly those affecting the germ line, will pose regulatory challenges significantly more difficult than those that have been experienced heretofore with conventional pharmaceuticals. The reason is that once we move beyond relatively simple single-gene disorders to behavior affected by multiple genes, gene interaction becomes very complex and difficult to predict. Recall the mouse whose intelligence was genetically boosted by neurobiologist Joe Tsien but which seems also to have felt greater pain as a result. Given that many genes express themselves at different stages in life, it will take years before the full consequences of a particular genetic manipulation become clear.

28   According to economic theory, social harms can come about in the aggregate only if individual choices lead to what are termed negative externalities—that is, costs that are borne by third parties who don't take part in the transaction. For example, a company may benefit itself by dumping toxic waste in a local river but will harm other members of the community. A case like this has been made about Bt corn: it produces a toxin that kills the European corn borer, a pest, but it may also kill monarch butterflies. (This charge, it would appear, is not true.) The issue is, are there circumstances in which individual choices regarding biotechnology may entail negative externalities and thus lead to society as a whole being worse off?

29   Children who are the subjects of genetic modification, obviously without consent, are the most clear class of potentially injured third parties. Contemporary family law assumes a community of interest between parents and children and therefore gives parents considerable leeway in the raising and educating of their offspring. Libertarians argue that since the vast majority of parents would want only what is best for their children, there is a kind of implied consent on the part of the children who are the beneficiaries of greater intelligence, good looks, or other desirable genetic characteristics. It is possible, however, to think of any

number of instances in which certain reproductive choices would appear advantageous to parents but could inflict harm on their children.

QUESTIONS ON MEANING

1. What is eugenics, and how has eugenics been practiced by different societies during the past century, according to Fukuyama?
2. What are the two reasons Fukuyama believes that the objections one might have to the practice of eugenics in the past will not be equally persuasive in the future?
3. What are the religious considerations that Fukuyama outlines when considering the potential implementation of a program of genetic engineering?
4. What are the utilitarian considerations? What does Fukuyama mean by *utilitarian* considerations?
5. What is Fukuyama's conclusion regarding the necessity of preserving the human moral sense? In what ways does genetic engineering pose a threat to the moral sense? What does this have to do with human rights and with our sense of what it means to be human?

QUESTIONS FOR DISCUSSION

1. What is your opinion of eugenics? Is it acceptable or unacceptable? In what cases or under what circumstances would you find eugenics a viable option? Are there ways in which we practice eugenics already?
2. Fukuyama spends a little time talking about the role of abortion and stem cell research in terms of understanding the ethical dimensions of genetic engineering. What ethically complicated issues does Fukuyama seek to highlight through these two topics?
3. Aside from abortion and stem-cell research, are there other practices in contemporary society that are equally complicated in terms of Fukuyama's argument?
4. In terms of genetic engineering, what is the role of human free will and human choice? How does this apply to children or to the unborn? How does it apply to the relationship between a government and the people it governs? What guidelines can help us negotiate the relationship between human free will and social and ethical concerns?

LOOKING AT RHETORIC

1. What point or points is Fukuyama trying to make through the story of David Reimer? How does Reimer's story provide a context for understanding some of the ethical dimensions of genetic engineering?
2. Compare Fukuyama's essay with the selection from Sandel also reprinted in this chapter. Do they share a common viewpoint? Which makes a more convincing case? Who has the clearer thesis and the stronger arguments?

WRITING ASSIGNMENTS

1. Research the current laws and policies related to human cloning. Write an essay in which you set forth the state of current cloning policy. Then, argue for or against current policy, using as a framework some of the issues raised by Fukuyama.

2. Unless the process of biological evolution has reached its apotheosis in the production of human beings, it stands to reason that over time the human species will evolve and will eventually transform into some *post-human* species. Write an essay in which you argue either for or against the proposition that genetic engineering is merely the mechanism by which evolutionary forces are transforming the human species into a post-human species better able to negotiate social, cultural, economic, and environmental forces. Should humans fight against genetic manipulation in order to preserve their species, or should humans embrace developments in biotechnology as a means to increase evolutionary adaptation of the species?

3. In pairs or in groups, make a list of ten specific things about human beings that you believe could be improved through genetic manipulation. Then, as individuals, rank these ten potential changes according to which one would have the most radical impact on human society to the change that would have the least impact on human society. Write an essay in which you present your ranking and explain why you ranked the items in the order that you did. Then, share your essay with other members of your group.

Interdisciplinary Connections

Visions of the Posthuman

Artists have long been fascinated with the implications of genetics, evolutionary theory, and technology for the development of the human being. What will humans look like in the future? What will post humans look like? Will evolutionary development and advances in technology bring about a brighter or a darker future for the human race? Below are two artistic representations of post- or trans-human experience. What do these depictions suggest about

the merging of humans and technology? Are they peaceful or chaotic images? What might you deduce that the artist's opinion of the *posthuman* experience is? Do you find these images compelling? Do you think they represent something that might actually come to pass? What features of our current life do these images suggest will become more pronounced for future humans or *post*humans?

The Case Against Perfection

Michael J. Sandel

Michael Sandel (b. 1953) is the Anne T. and Robert M. Bass Professor of Government at Harvard University, where he teaches a very popular course entitled Justice, *which has been taken by over fourteen thousand students. Sandel is known primarily as a political philosopher, and has published several books in the field, including* Liberalism and the Limits of Justice *(1982),* Democracy's Discontent: America in Search of a Public Philosophy *(1984),* Public Philosophy: Essays on Morality in Politics *(2005), and* The Case Against Perfection: Ethics in the Age of Genetic Engineering *(2007). Like Francis Fukuyama (also included in this chapter), Sandel served on the President's Council on Bioethics from 2002-2005, and it is during that time that the following selection, "The Case Against Perfection" (2004), was published. In this essay, Sandel's interest in political philosophy intersects with his investigations into the ethical dimensions of genetic engineering.*

1   Breakthroughs in genetics present us with a promise and a predicament. The promise is that we may soon be able to treat and prevent a host of debilitating diseases. The predicament is that our newfound genetic knowledge may also enable us to manipulate our own nature—to enhance our muscles, memories, and moods; to choose the sex, height, and other genetic traits of our children; to make ourselves "better than well." When science moves faster than moral understanding, as it does today, men and women struggle to articulate their unease. In liberal societies they reach first for the language of autonomy, fairness, and individual rights. But this part of our moral vocabulary is ill equipped to address the hardest questions posed by genetic engineering.[1] The genomic revolution has induced a kind of moral vertigo.

2   Consider cloning. The birth of Dolly the cloned sheep, in 1997, brought a torrent of concern about the prospect of cloned human beings. There are good medical reasons to worry. Most scientists agree that cloning is unsafe, likely to produce offspring with serious abnormalities. (Dolly recently died a premature death.) But suppose technology improved to the point where clones were at no greater risk than naturally conceived offspring. Would human cloning still be objectionable? Should our hesitation be moral as well as medical? What, exactly, is wrong with creating a child who is a genetic twin of one parent, or of an older sibling who has tragically died—or, for that matter, of an admired scientist, sports star, or celebrity?

3   Some say cloning is wrong because it violates the right to autonomy: by choosing a child's genetic makeup in advance, parents deny the child's right to an open future. A similar objection can be raised against any form of bioengineering that allows parents to select or reject genetic characteristics. According to this argument, genetic enhancements

---

[1] Genetic Engineering: manipulation of the genetic code of a human, animal, or plant in order to produce some biological change.

for musical talent, say, or athletic prowess, would point children toward particular choices, and so designer children would never be fully free.

4   At first glance the autonomy argument seems to capture what is troubling about human cloning and other forms of genetic engineering. It is not persuasive for two reasons. First, it wrongly implies that absent a designing parent, children are free to choose their characteristics for themselves. But none of us chooses his genetic inheritance. The alternative to a cloned or genetically enhanced child is not one whose future is unbound by particular talents but one at the mercy of the genetic lottery.

5   Second, even if a concern for autonomy explains some of our worries about made-to-order children, it cannot explain our moral hesitation about people who seek genetic remedies or enhancements for themselves. Gene therapy on somatic (that is, nonreproductive) cells, such as muscle cells and brain cells, repairs or replaces defective genes. The moral quandary arises when people use such therapy not to cure a disease but to reach beyond health, to enhance their physical or cognitive capacities, to lift themselves above the norm.

6   Like cosmetic surgery, genetic enhancement employs medical means for nonmedical ends—ends unrelated to curing or preventing disease or repairing injury. But unlike cosmetic surgery, genetic enhancement is more than skin-deep. If we are ambivalent about surgery or Botox injections for sagging chins and furrowed brows, we are all the more troubled by genetic engineering for stronger bodies, sharper memories, greater intelligence, and happier moods. The question is whether we are right to be troubled, and if so, on what grounds.

MUSCLES

7   Everyone would welcome a gene therapy to alleviate muscular dystropy and to reverse the debilitating muscle loss that comes with old age. But what if the same therapy were used to improve athletic performance? Researchers have developed a synthetic gene that, when injected into the muscle cells of mice, prevents and even reverses natural muscle deterioration. The gene not only repairs wasted or injured muscles but also strengthens healthy ones. This success bodes well for human application. H. Lee Sweeney, of the University of Pennsylvania, who leads the research, hopes his discovery will cure the immobility that afflicts the elderly. But Sweeney's bulked-up mice have already attracted the attention of athletes seeking a competitive edge. Although the therapy is not yet approved for human use, the prospect of genetically enhanced weight lifters, home-run sluggers, line-backers, and sprinters is easy to imagine. The widespread use of steroids and other performance-improving drugs in professional sports suggests that many athletes will be eager to avail themselves of genetic enhancement.

8   Suppose for the sake of argument that muscle-enhancing gene therapy, unlike steroids, turned out to be safe—or at least no riskier than a rigorous weight-training regimen. Would there be a reason to ban its use in sports? These is something unsettling about the image of genetically altered athletes lifting SUVs or hitting 650-foot home runs or running a three-minute mile. But what, exactly, is troubling about it? Is it simply that we find such superhuman spectacles too bizarre to contemplate? Or does our unease point to something of ethical significance?

9   It might be argued that a genetically enhanced athlete, like a drug-enhanced athlete, would have an unfair advantage over his unenhanced competitors. But the fairness argument against enhancement has a fatal flaw: it has always been the case that some athletes are better endowed genetically than others, and yet we do not consider this to undermine the fairness of competitive sports. From the standpoint of fairness, enhanced genetic differences would be no worse than natural ones, assuming they were safe and made available to all. If genetic enhancement in sports is morally objectionable, it must be for reasons other than fairness.

MEMORY

10   Human memory is more complicated, but biotech companies, including Memory Pharmaceuticals, are in hot pursuit of memory-enhancing drugs, or "cognition enhancers," for human beings. The obvious market for such drugs consists of those who suffer from Alzheimer's and other serious memory disorders. The companies also have their sights on a bigger market: the 81 million Americans over fifty, who are beginning to encounter the memory loss that comes naturally with age. A drug that reversed age-related memory loss would be a bonanza for the pharmaceutical industry: a Viagra for the brain. Such use would straddle the line between remedy and enhancement. Unlike a treatment for Alzheimer's, it would cure no disease; but insofar as it restored capacities a person once possessed, it would have a remedial aspect. It could also have purely nonmedical uses: for example, by a lawyer cramming to memorize facts for an upcoming trial, or by a business executive eager to learn Mandarin on the eve of his departure for Shanghai.

11   Some who worry about the ethics of cognitive enhancement point to the danger of creating two classes of human beings: those with access to enhancement technologies, and those who must make do with their natural capacities. And if the enhancements could be passed down the generations, the two classes might eventually become subspecies— the enhanced and the merely natural. But worry about access ignores the moral status of enhancement itself. Is the scenario troubling because the unenhanced poor would be denied the benefits of bioengineering, or because the enhanced affluent would somehow be dehumanized? As with muscles, so with memory: the fundamental question is not how to ensure equal access to enhancement but whether we should aspire to it in the first place.

HEIGHT

12   Some parents of healthy children who are unhappy with their stature (typically boys) ask why it should make a difference whether a child is short because of a hormone deficiency or because his parents happen to be short. Whatever the cause, the consequences are the same.

13   In the face of this argument some doctors began prescribing hormone treatments for children whose short stature was unrelated to any medical problem. By 1996 such "off-label" use accounted for 40 percent of human-growth-hormone prescriptions. Although it is legal to prescribe drugs for purposes not approved by the Food and Drug Administration, pharmaceutical companies cannot promote such use. Seeking to expand its market, Eli

Lilly & Co. recently persuaded the FDA to approve its human growth hormone for healthy children whose projected adult height is in the bottom one percentile—under five feet three inches for boys and four feet eleven inches for girls. This concession raises a large question about the ethics of enhancement: If hormone treatments need not be limited to those with hormone deficiencies, why should they be available only to very short children? Why shouldn't all shorter-than-average children be able to seek treatment? And what about a child of average height who wants to be taller so that he can make the basketball team?

14   Some oppose height enhancement on the grounds that it is collectively self-defeating; as some become taller, others become shorter relative to the norm. Except in Lake Wobegon,[2] not every child can be above average. As the unenhanced began to feel shorter, they, too, might seek treatment, leading to a hormonal arms race that left everyone worse off, especially those who couldn't afford to buy their way up from shortness.

15   But the arms-race objection is not decisive on its own. Like the fairness objection to bioengineered muscles and memory, it leaves unexamined the attitudes and dispositions that prompt the drive for enhancement. If we were bothered only by the injustice of adding shortness to the problems of the poor, we could remedy that unfairness by publicly subsidizing height enhancements. As for the relative height deprivation suffered by innocent bystanders, we could compensate them by taxing those who buy their way to greater height. The real question is whether we want to live in a society where parents feel compelled to spend a fortune to make perfectly healthy kids a few inches taller.

SEX SELECTION

16   Perhaps the most inevitable nonmedical use of bioengineering is sex selection. For centuries parents have been trying to choose the sex of their children. Today biotech succeeds where folk remedies failed.

17   One technique for sex selection arose with prenatal tests using amniocentesis and ultrasound. These medical technologies were developed to detect genetic abnormalities such as spina bifida and Down syndrome. But they can also reveal the sex of the fetus—allowing for the abortion of a fetus of an undesired sex. Even among those who favor abortion rights, few advocate abortion simply because the parents do not want a girl. Nevertheless, in traditional societies with a powerful cultural preference for boys, this practice has become widespread.

18   Sex selection need not involve abortion, however. For couples undergoing *in vitro* fertilization (IVF), it is possible to choose the sex of the child before the fertilized egg is implanted in the womb. One method makes use of pre-implantation genetic diagnosis (PGD), a procedure developed to screen for genetic diseases. Several eggs are fertilized in a petri dish and grown to the eight-cell stage (about three days). At that point the embryos are tested to determine their sex. Those of the desired sex are implanted; the others are

---

[2] Lake Wobegon: a fictional town in Minnesota which is the setting for many of the tales told by Garrison Keillor in his weekly radio program, *A Prairie Home Companion*. In Lake Wobegon, all of the children are "above average."

typically discarded. Although few couples are likely to undergo the difficulty and expense of IVF simply to choose the sex of their child, embryo screening is a highly reliable means of sex selection. And as our genetic knowledge increases, it may be possible to use PGD to cull embryos carrying undesired genes, such as those associated with obesity, height, and skin color. The science-fiction movie *Gattaca* depicts a future in which parents routinely screen embryos for sex, height, immunity to disease, and even IQ. There is something troubling about the *Gattaca* scenario, but it is not easy to identify what exactly is wrong with screening embryos to choose the sex of our children.

19   One line of objection draws on arguments familiar from the abortion debate. Those who believe that an embryo is a person reject embryo screening for the same reasons they reject abortion. If an eight-cell embryo growing in a petri dish is morally equivalent to a fully developed human being, then discarding it is no better than aborting a fetus, and both practices are equivalent to infanticide. Whatever its merits, however, this "pro-life" objection is not an argument against sex selection as such.

20   The latest technology poses the question of sex selection unclouded by the matter of an embryo's moral status. The Genetics & IVF Institute, a for-profit infertility clinic in Fairfax, Virginia, now offers a sperm-sorting technique that makes it possible to choose the sex of one's child before it is conceived. X-bearing sperm, which produce girls, carry more DNA than Y-bearing sperm, which produce boys; a device called a flow cytometer can separate them. The process, called MicroSort, has a high rate of success.

21   If sex selection by sperm sorting is objectionable, it must be for reasons that go beyond the debate about the moral status of the embryo. One such reason is that sex selection is an instrument of sex discrimination—typically against girls, as illustrated by the chilling sex ratios in India and China. Some speculate that societies with substantially more men than women will be less stable, more violent, and more prone to crime or war. These are legitimate worries—but the sperm-sorting company has a clever way of addressing them. It offers Microsort only to couples who want to choose the sex of a child for purposes of "family balancing." Those with more sons than daughters may choose a girl, and vice versa. But customers may not use the technology to stock up on children of the same sex, or even to choose the sex of their firstborn child. (So far the majority of MicroSort clients have chosen girls.) Under restrictions of this kind, do any ethical issues remain that should give us pause?

22   To appreciate children as gifts is to accept them as they come, not as objects of our design or products of our will or instruments of our ambition. Parental love is not contingent on the talents and attributes a child happens to have. We choose our friends and spouses at least partly on the basis of qualities we find attractive. But we do not choose our children. Their qualities are unpredictable, and even the most conscientious parents cannot be held wholly responsible for the kind of children they have. That is why parenthood, more than other human relationships, teaches what the theologian William F. May calls an "openness to the unbidden."

23   May's resonant phrase helps us see that the deepest moral objection to enhancement lies less in the perfection it seeks than in the human disposition it expresses and promotes. The problem is not that parents usurp the autonomy of a child they design. The problem lies in the hubris of the designing parents, in their drive to master the mystery of birth.

Even if this disposition did not make parents tyrants to their children, it would disfigure the relation between parent and child, and deprive the parent of the humility and enlarged human sympathies that an openness to the unbidden can cultivate.

24   To appreciate children as gifts or blessings is not, of course, to be passive in the face of illness or disease. Medical intervention to cure or prevent illness or restore the injured to health does not desecrate nature but honors it. Healing sickness or injury does not override a child's natural capacities but permits them to flourish.

25   Nor does the sense of life as a gift mean that parents must shrink from shaping and directing the development of their child. Just as athletes and artists have an obligation to cultivate their talents, so parents have an obligation to cultivate their children, to help them discover and develop their talents and gifts. As May points out, parents give their children two kinds of love: accepting love and transforming love. Accepting love affirms the being of the child, whereas transforming love seeks the well-being of the child. Each aspect corrects the excesses of the other, he writes: "Attachment becomes too quietistic if it slackens into mere acceptance of the child as he is." Parents have a duty to promote their children's excellence.

26   The shadow of eugenics hangs over today's debates about genetic engineering and enhancement. Critics of genetic engineering argue that human cloning, enhancement, and the quest for designer children are nothing more than "privatized" or "free-market" eugenics. Defenders of enhancement reply that genetic choices freely made are not really eugenic—at least not in the pejorative sense. To remove the coercion, they argue, is to remove the very thing that makes eugenic policies repugnant.

27   Sorting out the lesson of eugenics is another way of wrestling with the ethics of enhancement. The Nazis gave eugenics a bad name. But what, precisely, was wrong with it? Was the old eugenics objectionable only insofar as it was coercive? Or is there something inherently wrong with the resolve to deliberately design our progeny's traits?

28   A number of political philosophers call for a new "liberal eugenics." They argue that a moral distinction can be drawn between the old eugenic policies and genetic enhancements that do not restrict the autonomy of the child. "While old-fashioned authoritarian eugenicists sought to produce citizens out of a single centrally designed mould," writes Nicholas Agar, "the distinguishing mark of the new liberal eugenics is state neutrality." Government may not tell parents what sort of children to design, and parents may engineer in their children only those traits that improve their capacities without biasing their choice of life plans. A recent text on genetics and justice, written by the bioethicists Allen Buchanan, Dan W. Brock, Norman Daniels, and Daniel Wikler, offers a similar view. The "bad reputation of eugenics," they write, is due to practices that "might be avoidable in a future eugenic program." The problem with the old eugenics was that its burdens fell disproportionately on the weak and the poor, who were unjustly sterilized and segregated. But provided that the benefits and burdens of genetic improvement are fairly distributed, these bioethicists argue, eugenic measures are unobjectionable and may even be morally required.

29   But removing the coercion does not vindicate eugenics. The problem with eugenics and genetic engineering is that they represent the one-sided triumph of willfulness over giftedness, of dominion over reverence, of molding over beholding. Why, we may wonder, should we worry about this triumph? Why not shake off our unease about genetic

enhancement as so much superstition? What would be lost if biotechnology dissolved our sense of giftedness?

30   From a religious standpoint the answer is clear: To believe that our talents and powers are wholly our own doing is to misunderstand our place in creation, to confuse our role with God's. Religion is not the only source of reasons to care about giftedness, however. The moral stakes can also be described in secular terms. If bioengineering made the myth of the "self-made man" come true, it would be difficult to view our talents as gifts for which we are indebted, rather than as achievements for which we are responsible. This would transform three key features of our moral landscape: humility, responsibility, and solidarity.

31   In a social world that prizes mastery and control, parenthood is a school for humility. That we care deeply about our children and yet cannot choose the kind we want teaches parents to be open to the unbidden. Such openness is a disposition worth affirming, not only within families but in the wider world as well. It invites us to abide the unexpected, to live with dissonance, to rein in the impulse to control. A *Gattaca*-like world in which parents became accustomed to specifying the sex and generic traits of their children would be a world inhospitable to the unbidden, a gated community writ large. The awareness that our talents and abilities are not wholly our own doing restrains our tendency toward hubris.

32   There is something appealing, even intoxicating, about a vision of human freedom unfettered by the given. It may even be the case that the allure of that vision played a part in summoning the genomic age into being. It is often assumed that the powers of enhancement we now possess arose as an inadvertent by-product of biomedical progress—the genetic revolution came, so to speak, to cure disease, and stayed to tempt us with the prospect of enhancing our performance, designing our children, and perfecting our nature. That may have the story backwards. It is more plausible to view genetic engineering as the ultimate expression of our resolve to see ourselves astride the world, the masters of our nature. But that promise of mastery is flawed. It threatens to banish our appreciation of life as a gift, and to leave us with nothing to affirm or behold outside our own will.

QUESTIONS ON MEANING

1. What does Sandel mean when he claims that the genomic revolution has produced a kind of moral vertigo?

2. What two reasons does Sandel give in order to demonstrate the flaws in the argument that human cloning is morally inadequate because it violates human autonomy?

3. What are the key issues raised by Sandel as he discusses using genetic engineering in order to affect muscle development, cognitive function, height, and sex selection in reproduction?

4. Is Sandel a proponent of using genetic engineering to improve the genetic outlook of unborn children? Why or why not?

5. How does the movie *Gattaca* illustrate some of the political and social implications of genetic engineering? What is Sandel's position on these sociopolitical implications? What does Sandel have to say about the role of sperm banks in modern culture?

6. What point does Sandel wish to make by introducing May's distinction between *transforming love* and *accepting love* into his essay?

7. According to Sandel, is there any form of eugenics which is acceptable?

QUESTIONS FOR DISCUSSION

1. In light of Sandel's position on genetic engineering, what are the pros and cons of pursuing research into human cloning? Are there conditions under which it would be acceptable and/ or unacceptable?

2. What is the relationship between genetic engineering and other kinds of enhancements that humans use in order to change or improve themselves? If it is legal to get a tattoo or have cosmetic surgery, should it be legal to genetically engineer oneself for superior performance either physically or mentally?

3. Sandel spends some time talking about the use of steroids to enhance physical prowess. What is Sandel's position? Do you believe steroids should be legal?

4. Does the revelation that a particular athlete has used steroids change your perception of that athlete? Would you have the same reaction if the enhancement was mental rather than physical? What if, for instance, you discovered that Einstein had used some chemical to enhance his cognitive ability: would it change how you perceive his achievements?

5. Speculate about some of the ways in which new biotechnologies might change the way in which humans both treat disease and think about abortion. Would you be in favor of using gene therapy to alter a human's genetic code in order to prevent passing an inherited abnormality to his or her children? What about abortion: would it change the way you thought about abortion if you knew someone had an abortion because tests suggested that the fetus would not have a certain color hair or a certain height? Would your reaction change if the woman had aborted because the fetus had Down Syndrome or spina bifida? What does Sandel have to say about these kinds of decisions?

LOOKING AT RHETORIC

1. Both Fukuyama, in his selection, and Sandel express some trepidation about the manner in which human culture will be altered as a result of emergent biotechnologies. On what points do they share a common outlook? On what points do they differ? Select a particular sociopolitical issue—such as abortion or cloning or stem cell research—how might both Fukuyama and Sandel respond to the issue?

2. What is the thesis of Sandel's essay? Is there a sentence in his essay which you can point to as the thesis? If not, can you state in a sentence what the implied thesis of the essay is? Take a moment to reverse-engineer the essay: can you create the outline that Sandel might have used when he wrote the essay? What does this outline tell you about what Sandel thinks is important in this essay?

WRITING ASSIGNMENTS

1. There are already numerous energy drinks and over-the-counter supplements that claim (perhaps dubiously) to enhance memory and cognitive ability. In an environment in which college entrance decisions and scholarships are so heavily reliant on grades and on standardized test scores, the notion that in the near future genetic engineering might allow for measurable increases in cognitive function is likely more a matter of when than if. Write an essay in which you discuss the social, cultural, and political ramifications of such genetic manipulation, and either support or argue against the regulation of such genetic therapies.

2. Imagine that there was a procedure developed that would allow parents to raise the IQ of their child to genius status, but the procedure was expensive so only was available to a portion of society. Should such a procedure be legal? Write an essay in which you argue for or against legalizing such a procedure.

3. Watch the movie *Gattaca*. Write an essay in which you discuss the ways in which the movie illustrates some of the key points raised by Sandel (and/or Fukuyama) in his essay. What seems to be the thesis of the movie? Does it match Sandel's thesis? Discuss both the movie and the essay as commentaries on emerging biotechnologies.

The Selfless Gene

Olivia Judson

Olivia Judson (b. 1970) is an evolutionary biologist, a journalist, a blogger for the New York Times, *and a research fellow at Imperial College in London. Her first book,* Dr. Tatiana's Sex Advice to All Creation *(2002), was a popular and humorous guide to the sexual practices of a wide variety of animal species. Judson was a student of the evolutionary biologist William Donald Hamilton at Oxford, where Judson received her doctorate. Hamilton's work had a notable influence on Judson, and she makes some of Hamilton's work the focal point of some of her speculations in the following essay, which appeared in* The Atlantic Monthly *in 2007.*

1   It's easy to see how evolution can account for the dark streaks in human nature—the violence, treachery, and cruelty. But how does it produce kindness, generosity, and heroism?

2   At 2 a.m. on February 26, 1852, the Royal Navy troopship A Birkenhead, which was carrying more than 600 people, including seven women and 13 children, struck a rock near Danger Point, two miles off the coast of South Africa. Almost immediately, the ship began to break up. Just three lifeboats could be launched. The men were ordered to stand on deck, and they did. The women and children (along with a few sailors) were put into the lifeboats and rowed away. Only then were the men told that they could try to save themselves by swimming to shore. Most drowned or were eaten by sharks.

3   The heroism of the troops, standing on deck facing almost certain death while others escaped, became the stuff of legend. But the strange thing is, such heroics are not rare: Humans often risk their lives for strangers—think of the firemen going into the World Trade Center—or for people they know but are not related to.

4   How does a propensity for self-sacrifice evolve? And what about the myriad lesser acts of daily kindness—helping a little old lady across the street, giving up a seat on the subway, returning a wallet that's been lost? Are these impulses as primal as ferocity, lust, and greed? Or are they just a thin veneer over a savage nature? Answers come from creatures as diverse as amoebas and baboons, but the story starts in the county of Kent, in southern England.

EVOLVING GENEROSITY

5   Kent has been home to two great evolutionary biologists. In the 19th century, Charles Darwin lived for many years in the village of Downe. In the 20th, William Donald

Hamilton grew up catching beetles and chasing butterflies over the rolling hills near Badgers Mount.

6   He began his career studying social behavior, and in the early '60s he published a trio of now-classic papers in which he offered the first rigorous explanation of how generosity can evolve, and under what circumstances it is likely to emerge.

7   Hamilton didn't call it generosity, though; he called it altruism. And the particular behaviors he sought to explain are acts of extreme self-sacrifice, such as when a bee dies to defend the hive, or when an animal spends its whole life helping others rear their children instead of having some of its own. To see why these behaviors appear mysterious to biologists, consider how natural selection works. In every generation, some individuals leave more descendants than others. If the reason for their greater "reproductive success" is due to the particular genes they have, then natural selection has been operating.

8   Here's an example: Suppose you're a mosquito living on the French Mediterranean coast. Tourists don't like mosquitoes, and the French authorities try to keep the tourists happy by spraying insecticide. Which means that on the coast, mosquitoes bearing a gene that confers insecticide resistance tend to leave many more descendants than those lacking it—and so today's coastal mosquitoes are far more resistant to insecticide than those that live inland.

9   Extreme altruists, by definition, leave no descendants: they're too busy helping others. So at first blush, a gene that promotes extreme altruism should quickly vanish from a population.

10   Hamilton's solution to this problem was simple and elegant. He realized that a gene promoting extreme altruism could spread if the altruist helped its close relations. The reason is that your close relations have some of the same genes as you do. In humans and other mammals, full brothers and sisters have, on average, half the same genes. First cousins have, on average, an eighth of their genes in common. Among insects such as ants and bees, where the underlying genetics work differently, full sisters (but not brothers) typically have three-quarters of their genes in common.

11   Hamilton derived a formula—now known as Hamilton's rule—for predicting whether the predisposition toward a given altruistic act is likely to evolve: $rB>C$. In plain language, this says that genes that promote the altruistic act will spread if the benefit (B) that the act bestows is high enough, and the genetic relationship (r) between the altruist and the beneficiary is close enough, to outweigh the act's cost (C) to the altruist. Cost and benefit are both measured in nature's currency: children. "Cheap" behaviors—such as when a small bird squawks from the bushes to announce it's seen a cat or a hawk—can, and do, evolve easily, even though they often benefit non-relatives. "Expensive" behaviors, such as working your whole life to rear someone else's children, evolve only in the context of close kin.

12   Since Hamilton first proposed the idea, "kin selection" has proved tremendously powerful as a way to understand cooperative and self-sacrificial behavior in a huge menagerie of animals. Look at lions. Lionesses live with their sisters, cousins, and aunts; they hunt together and help each other with child care. Bands of males, meanwhile, are typically brothers and half-brothers. Large bands are better able to keep a pride of lionesses; thus even males who never mate with a female still spread some of their genes by helping their brothers defend the pride. Or take peacocks. Males often stand in groups when they

display to females. This is because females are drawn to groups of displaying males; they ogle them, then pick the guy they like best to be their mate. Again, peacocks prefer to display with their brothers rather than with males they are not related to.

13   Kin selection operates even in mindless creatures such as amoebas. Take, for instance, the soil-dwelling amoeba Dictyostelium purpureum. When times are good, members of this species live as single cells, reproducing asexually and feasting on bacteria. But when times get tough—when there's a bacteria shortage—thousands of individuals join together into a single entity known as a slug. This glides off in search of more-suitable conditions. When it finds them, the slug transforms itself into a fruiting body that looks like a tiny mushroom; some of the amoebas become the stalk, others become spores. Those in the stalk will die; only the spores will go on to form the next amoeboid generation. Sure enough, amoebas with the same genes (in other words, clones) tend to join the same slugs: they avoid mixing with genetic strangers and sacrifice themselves only for their clones.

14   Kin selection also accounts for some of the nastier features of human behavior, such as the tendency stepparents have to favor their own children at the expense of their stepkids. But it's not enough to explain the evolution of all aspects of social behavior, in humans or in other animals.

LIVING TOGETHER

15   Animals may begin to live together for a variety of reasons—most obviously, safety in numbers. In one of his most engaging papers, Hamilton observed that a tight flock, herd, or shoal will readily appear if every animal tries to make itself safer by moving into the middle of the group—a phenomenon he termed the "selfish herd." But protection from predators isn't the only benefit of bunching together. A bird in a flock spends more time eating and less time looking about for danger than it does when on its own. Indeed, eating well is another common reason for group living. Some predatory animals—chimpanzees, spotted hyenas, and wild dogs, for example—have evolved to hunt together.

16   Many social animals thus live in huge flocks or herds, and not in family groups— or even if the nexus of social life is the family, the family group is itself part of a larger community. In species such as these, social behavior must extend beyond a simple "Be friendly and helpful to your family and hostile to everybody else" approach to the world. At the least, the evolution of social living requires limiting aggression so that neighbors can tolerate each other. And often, the evolution of larger social groupings is accompanied by an increase in the subtlety and complexity of the ways animals get along together.

17   Consider baboons. Baboons are monkeys, not apes, and are thus not nearly as closely related to us as chimpanzees are. Nonetheless, baboons have evolved complex social lives. They live in troops that can number from as few as eight to as many as 200. Females live with their sisters, mothers, aunts, and infants; males head off to find a new troop at adolescence (around age 4). Big troops typically contain several female family groups, along with some adult males. The relationships between members of a troop are varied and complex. Sometimes two or more males team up to defeat a dominant male in combat. Females often have a number of male "friends" that they associate with (friends may or may not also be sex partners). If a female is attacked or harassed, her friends will come bounding to the

rescue; they will also protect her children, play with them, groom them, carry them, and sometimes share food with them. If the mother dies, they may even look after an infant in her place.

18   Yet friendliness and the associated small acts of affection and kindness—a bout of grooming here, a shared bite to eat there—seem like evolutionary curiosities. Small gestures like these don't affect how many children you have. Or do they?

19   Among social animals, one potentially important cause of premature death is murder. Infanticide can be a problem for social mammals, from baboons and chimpanzees to lions and even squirrels. During one four-year study of Belding's ground squirrels, for example, the main cause of death for juveniles was other Belding's ground squirrels; at least 8 percent of the young were murdered before being weaned. Similarly, fighting between adults—particularly in species where animals are well armed with horns, tusks, or teeth—can be lethal, and even if it is not, it may result in severe injuries, loss of status, or eviction from the group.

20   The possibility of death by murder creates natural selection for traits that reduce this risk. For example, any animal that can appease an aggressor, or that knows when to advance and when to retreat, is more likely to leave descendants than an animal that leaps wildly into any fray. Which explains why, in many social-mammal species, you don't see many murders, though you do see males engaging in elaborate rituals to see who's bigger and stronger. Serious physical fights tend to break out only when both animals think they can win (that is, when they are about the same size).

21   Thus, among animals such as baboons, friendships mean more than a bit of mutual scratching; they play a fundamental role in an animal's ability to survive and reproduce within the group. Friendships between males can be important in overcoming a dominant male—which may in turn lead to an improvement in how attractive the animals are to females. Similarly, females that have a couple of good male friends will be more protected from bullying—and their infants less likely to be killed. Why do the males do it? Males that are friends with a particular female are more likely to become her sex partners later on, if indeed they are not already. In other words, friendship may be as primal an urge as ferocity.

BECOMING HUMAN

22   The lineage that became modern humans split off from the lineage that became chimpanzees around 6 million years ago. Eventually this new lineage produced the most socially versatile animal the planet has ever seen: us. How did we get to be this way?

23   One clue comes from chimpanzees. Chimpanzee society is the mirror image of baboon society, in that it's the females that leave home at adolescence, and the males that stay where they were born. Chimpanzee communities can also be fairly large, comprising several different sub-communities and family groups. Males prefer to associate with their brothers and half-brothers on their mother's side, but they also have friendships with unrelated males. Friends hang out together and hunt together—and gang up on other males.

24   However, unlike baboon troops, which roam around the savannah freely intermingling, chimpanzee communities are territorial. Bands of males patrol the edges of their community's territory looking for strangers—and sometimes make deep incursions into

neighboring terrain. Males on patrol move together in silence, often stopping to listen. If they run into a neighboring patrol, there may be some sort of skirmish, which may or may not be violent. But woe betide a lone animal that runs into the patrolling males. If they encounter a strange male on his own, they may well kill him. And sometimes, repeated and violent attacks by one community lead to the annihilation of another, usually smaller, one. Indeed, two of the three most-studied groups of chimpanzees have wiped out a neighboring community.

25   Chimpanzees have two important sources of premature death at the hands of other chimpanzees: They may be murdered by members of their own community, or they may be killed during encounters with organized bands of hostile neighbors.

26   Just like humans. Except that humans aren't armed with big teeth and strong limbs. Humans carry weapons, and have done so for thousands of years.

ON LOVE AND WAR

27   Darwin wondered whether lethal warring between neighboring groups might have caused humans to evolve to be more helpful and kind to each other. At first, the idea seems paradoxical. But Darwin thought this could have happened if the more cohesive, unified, caring groups had been better able to triumph over their more disunited rivals. If so, the members of those cohesive, yet warlike, groups would have left more descendants.

28   For a long time, the idea languished. Why? A couple of reasons. First, it appears to depend on "group selection." This is the idea that some groups evolve characteristics that allow them to out compete other groups, and it's long been out of favor with evolutionary biologists. In general, natural selection works much more effectively on individuals than it does on groups, unless the groups are composed of close kin. That's because group selection can be effective only when the competing groups are genetically distinct. Members of a kin group tend to be genetically similar to each other, and different from members of other kin groups. In contrast, groups composed of non-kin tend to contain considerable genetic variation, and differences between such groups are generally much smaller. Moreover, contact between the groups—individuals migrating from one to another, say—will reduce any genetic differences that have started to accumulate. So unless natural selection within the groups is different—such that what it takes to survive and reproduce in one group is different from what it takes in another—migration quickly homogenizes the genetics of the whole population.

29   A second reason Darwin's idea has been ignored is that it seems to have a distasteful corollary. The idea implies, perhaps, that some unpleasant human characteristics—such as xenophobia or even racism—evolved in tandem with generosity and kindness. Why? Because banding together to fight means that people must be able to tell the difference between friends (who belong in the group) and foes (who must be fought). In the mid-1970s, in a paper that speculated about how humans might have evolved, Hamilton suggested that xenophobia might be innate. He was pilloried.

30   But times have changed. Last year, the science journal *Nature* published a paper that tested the idea of "parochial altruism"—the notion that people might prefer to help strangers from their own ethnic group over strangers from a different group; the experiment

found that indeed they do. In addition, the idea that natural selection might work on groups—at least in particular and narrow circumstances—has become fashionable again. And so Darwin's idea about the evolution of human kindness as a result of war has been dusted off and scrutinized.

31   Sam Bowles, an economist turned evolutionary biologist who splits his time between the Santa Fe Institute, in New Mexico, and the University of Siena, in Italy, notes that during the last 90,000 years of the Pleistocene Epoch (from about 100,000 years ago until about 10,000 years ago, when agriculture emerged), the human population hardly grew. One reason for this was the extraordinary climactic volatility of the period. But another, Bowles suggests, was that our ancestors were busy killing each other in wars. Working from archaeological records and ethnographic studies, he estimates that wars between different groups could have accounted for a substantial fraction of human deaths—perhaps as much as 15 percent, on average, of those born in any given year—and as such, represented a significant source of natural selection.

32   Bowles shows that groups of supercooperative, altruistic humans could indeed have wiped out groups of less-united folk. However, his argument works only if the cooperative groups also had practices—such as monogamy and the sharing of food with other group members—that reduced the ability of their selfish members to out-reproduce their more generous members. (Monogamy helps the spread of altruism because it reduces the differences in the number of children that different people have. If, instead, one or two males monopolized all the females in the group, any genes involved in altruism would quickly disappear.) In other words, Bowles argues that a genetic predisposition for altruism would have been far more likely to evolve in groups where disparities and discord inside the group—whether over mates or food—would have been relatively low. Cultural differences between groups would then allow genetic differences to accumulate.

'THAT'S NOT THE WAY YOU DO IT'

33   If Bowles's analysis is right, it suggests that individuals who could not conform, or who were disruptive, would have weakened the whole group; any group that failed to drive out such people, or kill them, would have been more likely to be overwhelmed in battle. Conversely, people who fit in—sharing the food they found, joining in hunting, helping to defend the group, and so on—would have given their group a collective advantage, and thus themselves an individual evolutionary advantage.

34   This suggests two hypotheses. First, that one of the traits that may have evolved in humans is conformity, an ability to fit in with a group and adopt its norms and customs. Second, that enforcement of those norms and customs could have been essential for group cohesion and harmony, especially as groups got bigger (bigness is important in battles against other groups).

35   Let's start with conformity. This hasn't been studied much in other animals, but male baboons do appear to conform to the social regimens of the groups they join. For example, in one baboon troop in Kenya in the 1980s, all the aggressive males died of tuberculosis. The aggressives were the ones to snuff it because they'd eaten meat infected with bovine TB that had been thrown into a garbage dump; only the more-aggressive males ate at the

dump. After their deaths, the dynamics of the troop shifted to a more laid-back way of life. Ten years later—by which time all the original resident males had either died or moved on—the troop was still notable for its mellow attitude. The new males who'd arrived had adopted the local customs.

36   What about humans? According to Michael Tomasello—a psychologist at the Max Planck Institute, in Leipzig, Germany, who studies the behavior of human children and of chimpanzees—children as young as 3 will quickly deduce and conform to rules. If an adult demonstrates a game, and then a puppet comes in and plays it differently, the children will clamor to correct the puppet with shouts of "No, that's not the way you do it—you do it this way!" In other words, it's not just that they infer and obey rules; they try to enforce them, too.

37   Which brings me to the question of punishment.

PUNISHMENT GAMES

38   I'll be dictator. Here's how we play: An economist puts some money on the table—let's say $1,000. Since I'm dictator, I get to decide how you and I are going to split the cash; you have no say in the matter. How much do you think I'll give you?

39   Now, let's play the ultimatum game. We've still got $1,000 to play with, and I still get to make you an offer. But the game has a wrinkle: If you don't like the offer I make, you can refuse it. If you refuse it, we both get nothing. What do you think I'll do here?

40   As you've probably guessed, people tend to play the two games differently. In the dictator game, the most common offer is nothing, and the average offer is around 20 percent. In the ultimatum game, the most common offer is half the cash, while the average is around 45 percent. Offers of less than 25 percent are routinely refused—so both players go home empty-handed.

41   Economists scratch their heads at this. In the first place, they are surprised that some people are nice enough to share with someone they don't know, even in the dictator game, where there's nothing to lose by not sharing. Second, economists predict that people will accept any offer in the ultimatum game, no matter how low, because getting something is better than getting nothing. But that's not what happens. Instead, some people forgo getting anything themselves in order to punish someone who made an ungenerous offer. Money, it seems, is not the only currency people are dealing in.

42   Bring in the neuroscientists, and the other currency gets clearer. If you measure brain activity while such games are being played (and there are many variants, for the fun doesn't stop with dictators and ultimatums), you find that the reward centers of the brain—the bits that give you warm, fuzzy feelings—light up when people are cooperating. But they also light up if you punish someone who wasn't generous, or watch the punishment of someone who wasn't.

43   Whether these responses are universal isn't clear: The genetic basis is obscure, and the number of people who've had their brain activity measured is tiny. Moreover, most economic-game playing has been done with college students; the extent to which the results hold among people from different cultures and backgrounds is relatively unknown. But the results suggest an intriguing possibility: that humans have evolved both to be good at conforming to the prevailing cultural norms and to enjoy making sure that those norms

are enforced. (Perhaps this explains why schemes such as zero-tolerance policing work so well: they play into our desire to conform to the prevailing norms.)

BRINGING OUT THE BEST

44   If the evolutionary scenario I've outlined is even half right, then we should expect to find that there are genes involved in mediating friendly behavior. And there are. Consider Williams syndrome.

45   People who have Williams syndrome tend to have poor cardiovascular function and a small, pointed, "elfin" face. They are typically terrible with numbers but good with words. And they are weirdly, incautiously friendly and nice—and unafraid of strangers.

46   They are also missing a small segment of chromosome 7. Chromosomes are long strings of DNA. Most people have 46 chromosomes in 23 pairs; you get one set of 23 from your mother, and the other from your father. In Williams syndrome, one copy of chromosome 7 is normal; the other is missing a small piece. The missing piece contains about 20 genes, some of which make proteins that are important in the workings of the brain. Since one chromosome is intact, the problem isn't a complete absence of the proteins that the genes encode, but an insufficiency. Somehow, this insufficiency results in people who are too nice. What's more, they can't learn not to be nice. Which is to say, someone with Williams syndrome can learn the phrase "Don't talk to strangers" but can't translate it into action.

47   Much about Williams syndrome remains mysterious. How the missing genes normally influence behavior is unclear; moreover, the environment has a role to play, too. But despite these complexities, Williams syndrome shows that friendliness has a genetic underpinning— that it is indeed as primal as ferocity. Indirectly, it shows something else as well. Most of us are able to apply brakes to friendly behavior, picking and choosing the people we are friendly to; those with Williams syndrome aren't. They cannot modulate their behavior. This is even odder than being too friendly. And it throws into sharp relief one of the chief features of ordinary human nature: its flexibility.

48   One of the most important, and least remarked upon, consequences of social living is that individual behavior must be highly flexible and tailored to circumstance: An individual who does not know whom to be aggressive toward, or whom to help, is unlikely to survive for long within the group. This is true for baboons and chimpanzees. It is also true for us.

49   Indeed, the ability to adjust our behavior to fit a given social environment is one of our main characteristics, yet it's so instinctive we don't even notice it, let alone consider it worthy of remark. But its implications are profound—and hopeful. It suggests that we can, in principle, organize society so as to bring out the best facets of our complex, evolved natures.

QUESTIONS ON MEANING

1. Why, at first glance, does altruism seem inexplicable in light of evolutionary theories based upon Darwinian notions of natural selection? What solution to this riddle is posed by William Donald Hamilton?

2. What is Hamilton's Rule? What is kin selection?

3. What is the difference between a cheap and an expensive behavior in evolutionary terms?

4. What distinguishes group selection from individual selection? Why have most evolutionary biologists tended to focus on individual selection? What two reasons does Judson suggest kept Darwin's initial speculations about group selection out of the mainstream until recently?

5. What is parochial altruism? Why might studies of parochial altruism be controversial in contemporary society? What did the work of Sam Bowles demonstrate? How does the concept of conformity relate to this issue? What about punishment?

6. What does Williams Syndrome seem to suggest about the evolution of altruistic behavior?

QUESTIONS FOR DISCUSSION

1. Judson seems to conclude her essay by shifting slightly from evolutionary biology to social commentary. What social message does she conclude with? Do you share Judson's opinion? What do you think Judson sees in contemporary society that has caused her to end her essay in this manner?

2. Do Judson's speculations about the biological basis of altruism seem to match your experience? Does evidence of human kindness and goodness seem plausibly connected to natural selection in the terms Judson discusses them?

3. Can you think of human behaviors that do not seem to have any biological basis or any benefit in terms of the propagation of one's own genetic code? How might one account for charitable work, especially work for the benefit of strangers from different cultures than one's own?

4. Do treatments of humans as congruent with the animal kingdom seem reasonable to you, or do you believe that humans, by virtue of their *humanness*, have characteristics that create a fundamental break with the rest of the animal kingdom?

LOOKING AT RHETORIC

1. What kinds of evidence does Judson use to support her speculations? Is this evidence convincing? Why or why not?

2. What assumptions about human nature, about biology, about evolution seem to inform Judson's essay?

3. Judson cites several scientific authorities and recounts several experiments in the course of her essay. How do these passages contribute to her essay?

WRITING ASSIGNMENTS

1. Spend some time researching the differences between Darwinian evolutionary theory and Lamarckian evolutionary theory. Write an essay in which you explain the key differences between the two theories. Then discuss whether Judson's speculations—and, specifically, Hamilton's Rule—are better understood in terms of Darwinian or Lamarckian theory.

2. In her essay, Judson discusses a biological concept that has the potential power to explain specific sociological behaviors. Assuming that Judson is basically correct in her speculations about the basis of altruism in evolutionary biology, write an essay in which you set forth a prescription for organizing social systems in ways that move humanity toward increased altruism.

3. In pairs or in groups, without using outside resources develop a working definition of the term *heroism*. Once the group has developed its definition, discuss whether or not heroic behavior is explainable in terms of Hamilton's Rule or the other concepts discussed in Judson's essay. Then, individually, write an essay in which you build a case that heroism, as your group has defined it, either is or is not understandable in terms of evolutionary biology.

A New Theory of the Universe

Robert Lanza

Robert Lanza (b. 1956) is one of the single greatest authorities on stem cell research and on clon-ing working today. Lanza grew up in Massachusetts, and he first came to the attention of the scientific community when as a young adolescent he set up a lab in his basement and began altering the genes of chickens. He brought these early experiments to the attention of Harvard medical researchers, and was subsequently mentored through his teen years by such notable scientists as Jonas Salk and B. F. Skinner. Eventually, Lanza received his M.D. from the University of Pennsylvania, where he established a considerable—and award-winning—reputation as a scholar. Since 1999 Lanza has served as Chief Scientific Officer at Advanced Cell Technology where his research on stem cells—among other things—has paved the way for numerous medical advances. He is the author or coauthor of hundreds of scientific papers and some twenty books. One of his most recent books, Biocentrism: How Life and Consciousness are the Keys to Understanding the Universe *(2009), elaborates on themes introduced in the essay reprinted here. First published in the journal* The American Scholar *in 2007, the following selection posits that it is the discipline of biology, rather than chemistry or physics, which has the potential to do what scientists in these other disciplines have been attempting for decades: to provide a theory that explains the nature of reality itself. The key, Lanza explains in his essay, is human consciousness. Not without its critics, Lanza's theory, if true, would force the entire scientific community to rethink long-held assumptions about the world in which we live.*

1   The laws of physics and chemistry can explain the biology of living systems, and I can recite in detail the chemical foundations and cellular organization of animal cells: oxida-tion, biophysical metabolism, all the carbohydrates and amino acid patterns. But there was more to this luminous little bug than the sum of its biochemical functions. A full under-standing of life cannot be found by looking at cells and molecules through a microscope. We have yet to learn that physical existence cannot be divorced from the animal life and structures that coordinate sense perception and experience. Indeed, it seems likely that this creature was the center of its own sphere of reality just as I was the center of mine.

2   Although the beetle did not move, it had sensory cells that transmitted messages to the cells in its brain. Perhaps the creature was too primitive to collect data and pinpoint my location in space. Or maybe my existence in its universe was limited to the perception of some huge and hairy shadow stabilizing a flashlight in the air. I don't know. But as

I stood up and left, I am sure that I dispersed into the haze of probability surrounding the glowworm's little world.

3   Our science fails to recognize those special properties of life that make it fundamental to material reality. This view of the world—biocentrism—revolves around the way a subjective experience, which we call consciousness, relates to a physical process. It is a vast mystery and one that I have pursued my entire life. The conclusions I have drawn place biology above the other sciences in the attempt to solve one of nature's biggest puzzles, the theory of everything that other disciplines have been pursuing for the last century. Such a theory would unite all known phenomena under one umbrella, furnishing science with an all-encompassing explanation of nature or reality.

4   We need a revolution in our understanding of science and of the world. Living in an age dominated by science, we have come more and more to believe in an objective, empirical reality and in the goal of reaching a complete understanding of that reality. Part of the thrill that came with the announcement that the human genome had been mapped or with the idea that we are close to understanding the big bang rests in our desire for completeness.

5   But we're fooling ourselves.

6   Most of these comprehensive theories are no more than stories that fail to take into account one crucial factor: we are creating them. It is the biological creature that makes observations, names what it observes, and creates stories. Science has not succeeded in confronting the element of existence that is at once most familiar and most mysterious— conscious experience. As Emerson wrote in "Experience," an essay that confronted the facile positivism of his age: "We have learned that we do not see directly, but mediately, and that we have no means of correcting these colored and distorting lenses which we are or of computing the amount of their errors. Perhaps these subject-lenses have a creative power; perhaps there are no objects."

7   Biology is at first glance an unlikely source for a new theory of the universe. But at a time when biologists believe they have discovered the "universal cell" in the form of embryonic stem cells, and when cosmologists like Stephen Hawking predict that a unifying theory of the universe may be discovered in the next two decades, shouldn't biology seek to unify existing theories of the physical world and the living world? What other discipline can approach it? Biology should be the first and last study of science. It is our own nature that is unlocked by means of the humanly created natural sciences used to understand the universe. Ever since the remotest of times philosophers have acknowledged the primacy of consciousness—that all truths and principles of being must begin with the individual mind and self. Thus Descartes's adage: "Cogito, ergo sum." (I think, therefore I am.) In addition to Descartes, who brought philosophy into its modern era, there were many other philosophers who argued along these lines: Kant, Leibniz, Bishop Berkeley, Schopenhauer, and Henri Bergson, to name a few.

8   Today's preoccupation with physical theories of everything takes a wrong turn from the purpose of science—to question all things relentlessly. Modern physics has become like Swift's kingdom of Laputa,[1] flying absurdly on an island above the earth and indifferent to what is beneath. When science tries to resolve its conflicts by adding and subtracting

---

[1] Laputa: a fictional floating island that appears in the book *Gulliver's Travels* by Jonathan Swift.

dimensions to the universe like houses on a Monopoly board, we need to look at our dogmas and recognize that the cracks in the system are just the points that let the light shine more directly on the mystery of life.

9   Modern science cannot explain why the laws of physics are exactly balanced for animal life to exist. For example, if the big bang had been one-part-in-a-billion more powerful, it would have rushed out too fast for the galaxies to form and for life to begin. If the strong nuclear force were decreased by two percent, atomic nuclei wouldn't hold together. Hydrogen would be the only atom in the universe. If the gravitational force were decreased, stars (including the sun) would not ignite. These are just three of more than 200 physical parameters within the solar system and universe so exact that they cannot be random. Indeed, the lack of a scientific explanation has allowed these facts to be hijacked as a defense of intelligent design.[2]

10   Without perception, there is in effect no reality. Nothing has existence unless you, I, or some living creature perceives it, and how it is perceived further influences that reality. Even time itself is not exempted from biocentrism. Our sense of the forward motion of time is really the result of an infinite number of decisions that only *seem* to be a smooth continuous path. At each moment we are at the edge of a paradox known as The Arrow, first described 2,500 years ago by the philosopher Zeno of Elea. Starting logically with the premise that nothing can be in two places at once, he reasoned that an arrow is only in one place during any given instance of its flight. But if it is in only one place, it must be at rest. The arrow must then be at rest at every moment of its flight. Logically, motion is impossible. But is motion impossible? Or rather, is this analogy proof that the forward motion of time is not a feature of the external world but a projection of something within us? Time is not an absolute reality but an aspect of our consciousness.

11   This paradox lies at the heart of one of the great revolutions of 20th-century physics, a revolution that has yet to take hold of our understanding of the world and of the decisive role that consciousness plays in determining the nature of reality. The uncertainty principle[3] in quantum physics is more profound than its name suggests. It means that we make choices at every moment in what we can determine about the world. We cannot know with complete accuracy a quantum particle's motion and its position at the same time—we have to choose one or the other. Thus the consciousness of the observer is decisive in determining what a particle does at any given moment.

12   Einstein was frustrated by the threat of quantum uncertainty to the hypothesis he called spacetime, and *spacetime* turns out to be incompatible with the world discovered by quantum physics. When Einstein showed that there is no universal now, it followed that observers could slice up reality into past, present, and, future, in different ways, all with equal reality. But what, exactly, is being sliced up?

---

[2] Intelligent Design Theory: The theory that suggests that because the universe seems—to the human observer—to have features finely tuned for the generation and preservation of human life, and because these features seem to bear the hallmarks of purposeful design, the universe must be the product of a supremely intelligent designer, who most identify as God.

[3] Uncertainty Principle: the theory, generally credited to the work of the physicist Werner Heisenberg, that states that in quantum mechanics, there is an inherent unknowability or uncertainty built into nature, for one cannot know both the position and velocity of a particle at the same time.

13   Space and time are not stuff that can be brought back to the laboratory in a marmalade jar for analysis. In fact, space and time fall into the province of biology—of animal sense perception—not of physics. They are properties of the mind, of the language by which we human beings and animals represent things to ourselves. Physicists venture beyond the scope of their science—beyond the limits of material phenomena and law—when they try to assign physical, mathematical, or other qualities to space and time.

14   Time and space are easy to talk and think about. Find yourself short of either or both— late for work, standing in a stalled subway car packed with riders—and issues of time and space are obvious: "It's crowded and I'm uncomfortable and my boss is going to kill me for being late." But time and space as our source of comprehension and consciousness is an abstraction. Our day-to-day experiences indicate nothing of this reality to us. Rather, life has taught us that time and space are external and eternal realities. They bound all experiences and are more fundamental than life itself. They are above and beyond human experience.

15   As animals, we are organized, wired, to think this way. We use dates and places to define our experiences to ourselves and to others. History describes the past by placing people and events in time and space. Scientific theories of the big bang, geology, and evolution are steeped in the logic of time and space. They are essential to our every movement and moment. To place ourselves as the *creators* of time and space, not as the subjects of it, goes against our common sense, life experience, and education. It takes a radical shift of perspective for any of us to entertain the idea that space and time are animal-sense perceptions, because the implications are so startling.

16   Yet we all know that space and time are not things—objects that you can see, feel, taste, touch, or smell. They are intangible, like gravity. In fact they are modes of interpretation and understanding, part of the animal logic that molds sensations into multidimensional objects.

17   It's important here to address a fundamental question. We have clocks that can measure time. If we can measure time, doesn't that prove it exists? Einstein sidestepped the question by simply defining time as "what we measure with a clock." The emphasis for physicists is on the *measuring*. However, the emphasis should be on the *we*, the observers. Measuring time doesn't prove its physical existence. Clocks are rhythmic things. Humans use the rhythms of some events (like the ticking of clocks) to time other events (like the rotation of the earth). This is not *time*, but rather, a comparison of events. Specifically, over the ages, humans have observed rhythmic events in nature: the periodicities of the moon, the sun, the flooding of the Nile. We then created other rhythmic things to measure nature's rhythms: a pendulum, a mechanical spring, an electronic device. We called these manmade rhythmic devices "clocks." We use the rhythms of specific events to time other specific events. But these are just *events*, not to be confused with *time*.

18   Science has been grappling with the implications of the wave-particle duality ever since its discovery in the first half of the 20th century. But few people accept this principle at face value. At present, the implications of these experiments are conveniently ignored by limiting the notion of quantum behavior to the microscopic world. But doing this has no basis in reason, and it is being challenged in laboratories around the world. New experiments carried out with huge molecules called buckyballs show that quantum reality extends into the macroscopic world as well. Experiments make it clear that another weird quantum phenomenon known as entanglement, which is usually associated with the micro world, is also relevant on macro scales. An exciting experiment, recently proposed

(so-called scaled-up superposition), would furnish the most powerful evidence to date that the biocentric view of the world is correct at the level of living organisms.

19   As we have seen, the world appears to be designed for life not just at the microscopic scale of the atom, but at the level of the universe itself. In cosmology, scientists have discovered that the universe has a long list of traits that make it appear as if everything it contains—from atoms to stars—was tailor-made for us. Many are calling this revelation the Goldilocks principle because the cosmos is not too this or too that, but just right for life. Others are calling it the anthropic principle because the universe appears to be human centered. And still others are calling it intelligent design because they believe it's no accident that the heavens are so ideally suited for us. By any name, the discovery is causing a huge commotion within the astrophysics community and beyond.

20   At the moment, the only attempt at an explanation holds that God made the universe. But there is another explanation based on science. To understand the mystery, we need to reexamine the everyday world we live in. As unimaginable as it may seem to us, the logic of quantum physics is inescapable. Every morning we open our front door to bring in the paper or to go to work. We open the door to rain, snow, or trees swaying in the breeze. We think the world churns along whether we happen to open the door or not. Quantum mechanics tells us it doesn't.

We two human beings with nearly identical perception tools are experiencing the same harsh lighting and uncomfortable sounds.

21   You get the idea. But how can this really be? You wake up every morning and your dresser is still across the room from your comfortable spot in the bed. You put on the same pair of jeans and favorite shirt and shuffle to the kitchen in slippers to make coffee. How can anyone in his right mind possibly suggest that the great world out there is constructed in our heads?

22   What we interpret as the world is brought into existence inside our head. Sensory information does not impress upon the brain, as particles of light impress upon the film in a camera. The images you see are a construction by the brain. Everything you are experiencing right now (pretend you're back on the subway) is being actively generated in your mind—the hard plastic seats, the graffiti, the dark remnants of chewing gum stuck to the floor. All physical things—subway turnstiles, train platforms, newspaper racks, their shapes, sounds, and odors—all these sensations are experienced inside your head. Everything we observe is based on the direct interaction of energy on our senses, whether it is matter (like your shoe sticking to the floor of a subway car) or particles of light (emitted from sparks as a subway train rounds a corner). Anything that we do not observe directly, exists only as potential—or mathematically speaking—as a haze of probability.

23   The mystery is plain. Neuroscientists have developed theories that might help to explain how separate pieces of information are integrated in the brain and thus succeed in elucidating how different attributes of a single perceived object—such as the shape, color, and smell of a flower—are merged into a coherent whole. These theories reflect some of the important work that is occurring in the fields of neuroscience and psychology, but they are theories of structure and function. They tell us nothing about how the performance of these functions is accompanied by a conscious experience; and yet the difficulty in understanding consciousness lies precisely here, in this gap in our understanding of how a subjective experience emerges from a physical process. Even Steven Weinberg concedes that although consciousness may have a neural correlate, its existence does not seem to be derivable from physical laws.

24   Physicists believe that the theory of everything is hovering right around the corner, and yet consciousness is still largely a mystery, and physicists have no idea how to explain its existence from physical laws. The questions physicists long to ask about nature are bound up with the problem of consciousness. Physics can furnish no answers for them. "Let man," declared Emerson, "then learn the revelation of all nature and all thought to his heart; this, namely; that the Highest dwells with him; that the sources of nature are in his own mind."

25   Space and time, not proteins and neurons, hold the answer to the problem of consciousness. When we consider the nerve impulses entering the brain, we realize that they are not woven together automatically, any more than the information is inside a computer. Our thoughts have an order, not of themselves, but because the mind generates the spatio-temporal relationships involved in every experience. We can never have any experience that does not conform to these relationships, for they are the modes of animal logic that mold sensations into objects. It would be erroneous, therefore, to conceive of the mind as existing in space and time before this process, as existing in the circuitry of the brain before the understanding posits in it a spatio-temporal order. The situation is like playing a CD— the information leaps into three-dimensional sound, and in that way, and in that way only, does the music indeed exist.

QUESTIONS ON MEANING

1. How does the epigraph from Loren Eisely set the stage for the rest of the essay?

2. What is the thesis of Lanza's essay? What arguments does he use to back up his thesis?

3. Why have chemistry and physics failed in their attempts to completely explain the nature of the universe?

4. What is biocentrism? According to Lanza, what is the relationship between biocentrism and science's quest for a grand unified theory of nature?

5. What is the uncertainty principle, and how does it relate to human consciousness, according to Lanza? How does the uncertainty principle help us resolve or understand Zeno's paradox of the arrow? How does Lanza's theory find support in experimental data regarding quantum weirdness?

6. What view of consciousness does Lanza propose? How is this view of consciousness different from the typical view of human consciousness? How does it differ from your own view?

7. What is the anthropic principle? According to Lanza, there are two explanations for the anthropic principle: one is that God made the universe. What is the other?

QUESTIONS FOR DISCUSSION

1. Do you believe things exist outside of human perception? If all human life suddenly disappeared in the universe, would the universe still exist? Do your beliefs about the role of perception and/or consciousness differ from those of Lanza?

2. If, as Lanza suggests, space and time are only metaphors that do not necessarily correspond with reality itself, then what is reality? Does Lanza's metaphor of the record album as a depiction of time seem reasonable to you? Why or why not?

3. One criticism of Lanza's theory is that Lanza asserts the vital importance of consciousness in his biocentric theory of reality, but he never actually explains what *consciousness* is. Do you find this criticism valid? What do you believe consciousness *is*?

LOOKING AT RHETORIC

1. How do the philosophies of Kuhn and Feyerabend provide a context for understanding the significance of Lanza's theories? In particular, does Lanza's theory of biocentrism represent a paradigm shift in scientific thinking?

2. Lanza's piece draws on several different disciplines in order to advance it's thesis. As a reader, what academic disciplines are most often invoked in the essay? What disciplines feed into Lanza's arguments?

WRITING ASSIGNMENTS

1. Spend some time online and in the library learning about different attempts by scientists over the past century to develop a grand unification theory. Select three of the most prominent of these theories and write an essay in which you explain each of these three theories to your audience.

2. Lanza's theory is heavily dependent upon the concept of consciousness. Write an essay in which you define consciousness and explore the ways in which consciousness influences our perception of the world. For a research-based paper, spend some time in the library learning about the leading theories of the origin of human consciousness among the scientific world today. Compare and contrast these theories. Do these theories support or challenge Lanza's theory about the nature of reality? Is Lanza's theory dependent upon a certain definition of consciousness?

3. In pairs or in groups, create a series of questions that could be used in order to interview a chemist or a physicist about Lanza's theory of biocentrism. Then, as a group, conduct the interview with a professor of chemistry or physics at your university, making sure to take good notes at the interview. Be sure, as part of the interview, to ask the subject of the interview about his/her opinions regarding the quest for a grand unification theory and about whether he or she believes biocentrism holds promise as an explanation for the ultimate nature of reality. Then, as individuals, write an essay in which you report the results of your interview and point out where the subject of your interview agrees with and disagrees with Lanza.

My God Problem—and Theirs

Natalie Angier

Natalie Angier (b. 1958) is a Pulitzer Prize winning journalist for The New York Times, *where she has reported on developments in evolutionary biology, genetics, medicine, and other topics in the sciences. She is the author of several books, including* **Natural Obsessions** *(1988),* **The Beauty of the Beastly** *(1995),* **Woman: An Intimate Geography** *(1999), and* **The Canon: A Whirligig**

Tour of the Beautiful Basics of Science *(2007). Angier has served as an adjunct professor of science writing at New York University, and is currently serving as an A. D. White Professor-at-Large with Cornell University. Angier has won multiple awards for her science reporting, and is generally considered one of the finest journalists of science working today. The following essay was published in* The American Scholar *in 2004 as part of the journal's ongoing* The Scientific Method *department. In this essay, Angier tackles the seeming conflict between science and religion. Why is it, Angier asks, that scientists feel so strongly that the religious community accept the theory of evolution, but these same scientists don't press for a campaign against such biblical staples as the virgin birth and the resurrection of Jesus Christ? Part of the answer, suggests Angier—herself a vocal atheist—is a simple matter of economics.*

1   In the course of reporting a book on the scientific canon, and pestering hundreds of researchers at the nation's great universities about what they see as the essential vitamins and minerals of literacy in their particular disciplines, I have been hammered into a kind of twinkle-eyed cartoon coma by one recurring message. Whether they are biologists, geologists, physicists, chemists, astronomers, or engineers, virtually all my sources topped their list of what they wish people understood about science with a plug for Darwin's dandy idea.

2   Would you please tell the public, they implored, that evolution is for real? Would you please explain that the evidence for it is overwhelming, and that an appreciation of evolution serves as the bedrock of our understanding of all life on this planet?

3   In other words, the scientists wanted me to do my bit to help fix the terrible little statistic they keep hearing about, the one indicating that many more Americans believe in angels, devils, and poltergeists than in evolution. According to recent polls, about 82 percent are convinced of the reality of heaven (and 63 percent think they're headed there after death); 51 percent believe in ghosts; but only 28 percent are swayed by the theory of evolution.

4   Scientists think this is terrible, the public's bizarre underappreciation of one of science's great and unshakeable discoveries—how we and all we see came to be—and they're right.

5   Yet I can't help feeling tetchy about the limits most of them put on their complaints. You see, they want to augment this particular figure—the number of people who believe in evolution—without bothering to confront a few other salient statistics that pollsters have revealed about America's religious cosmogony. Few scientists, for example, worry about the 77 percent of Americans who insist that Jesus was born to a virgin, an act of parthenogenesis[1] that defies everything we know about mammalian genetics and reproduction. Nor do the researchers wring their hands over the 80 percent who believe in the resurrection of Jesus, the laws of thermodynamics be damned.

6   No, most scientists are not interested in taking on any of the mighty cornerstones of Christianity. They complain about irrational thinking, they despise creationist "science," they roll their eyes over America's infatuation with astrology, telekinesis, spoon bending, reincarnation, and UFOs, but toward the bulk of the magic acts that have won the imprimatur of inclusion in the Bible, they are tolerant, respectful, big of tent. Indeed, many are

---

[1]Parthenogenesis: asexual reproduction in which a female is able to fertilize an egg without interaction with a male of the species.

quick to point out that the Catholic Church has endorsed the theory of evolution, and that it sees no conflict between a belief in God and the divinity of Jesus and the notion of evolution by natural selection. If the Pope is buying, the reason for most Americans' resistance to evolution must have less to do with religion than with a lousy advertising campaign.

7   So, on the issue of mainstream monotheistic religions and the irrationality behind many of religion's core tenets, scientists often set aside their skewers, their snark, and their impatient demand for proof, and instead don the calming cardigan of a kiddie-show host on public TV. They reassure the public that religion and science are not at odds with one another, but rather that they represent separate "magisteria," in the words of the formerly alive and even more formerly scrappy Stephen Jay Gould. Nobody is going to ask people to give up their faith, their belief in an everlasting soul accompanied by an immortal memory of every soccer game their kids won, every moment they spent playing fetch with the dog. Nobody is going to mock you for your religious beliefs. Well, we might if you base your life decisions on the advice of a Ouija board; but if you want to believe that someday you'll be seated at a celestial banquet with your long-dead father to your right and Jane Austen to your left—and that she'll want to talk to you for another hundred million years or more— that's your private reliquary, and we're not here to jimmy the lock.

8   Consider the very different treatments accorded two questions presented to Cornell University's "Ask an Astronomer" Web site. To the query, "Do most astronomers believe in God, based on the available evidence?" the astronomer Dave Rothstein replies that, in his opinion, "modern science leaves plenty of room for the existence of God . . . places where people who do believe in God can fit their beliefs in the scientific framework without creating any contradictions." He cites the Big Bang as offering solace to those who want to believe in a Genesis equivalent, and the probabilistic realms of quantum mechanics as raising the possibility of "God intervening every time a measurement occurs," before concluding that, ultimately, science can never prove or disprove the existence of a god, and religious belief doesn't—and shouldn't—"have anything to do with scientific reasoning."

9   How much less velveteen is the response to the reader asking whether astronomers believe in astrology. "No, astronomers do not believe in astrology," snarls Dave Kornreich. "It is considered to be a ludicrous scam. There is no evidence that it works, and plenty of evidence to the contrary." Dr. Kornreich ends his dismissal with the assertion that in science "one does not need a reason not to believe in something." Skepticism is "the default position" and "one requires proof if one is to be convinced of something's existence."

10   In other words, for horoscope fans, the burden of proof is entirely on them, the poor gullible gits; while for the multitudes who believe that, in one way or another, a divine intelligence guides the path of every leaping lepton, there is no demand for evidence, no skepticism to surmount, no need to worry. You, the religious believer, may well find subtle support for your faith in recent discoveries—that is, if you're willing to upgrade your metaphors and definitions as the latest data demand, seek out new niches of ignorance or ambiguity to fill with the goose down of faith, and accept that, certain passages of the Old Testament notwithstanding, the world is very old, not everything in nature was made in a week, and (can you turn up the mike here, please?) Evolution Happens.

11   And if you don't find substantiation for your preferred divinity or your most cherished rendering of the afterlife somewhere in the sprawling emporium of science, that's fine, too. No need to lose faith when you were looking in the wrong place to begin with.

Science can't tell you whether God exists or where you go when you die. Science cannot definitively rule out the heaven option, with its helium balloons and Breck hair for all. Science in no way wants to be associated with terrifying thoughts, like the possibility that the pericentury of consciousness granted you by the convoluted, gelatinous, and transient organ in your skull just may be the whole story of you-dom. Science isn't arrogant. Science trades in the observable universe and testable hypotheses. Religion gets the midnight panic fêtes. But you've heard about evolution, right?

12   So why is it that most scientists avoid criticizing religion even as they decry the supernatural mind-set? For starters, some researchers are themselves traditionally devout, keeping a kosher kitchen or taking communion each Sunday. I admit I'm surprised whenever I encounter a religious scientist. How can a bench-hazed Ph.D., who might in an afternoon deftly purée a colleague's PowerPoint presentation on the nematode genome into so much fish chow, then go home, read a two-thousand-year-old chronicle, riddled with internal contradictions, of a meta-Nobel discovery like "Resurrection from the Dead," and say, gee, that sounds convincing? Doesn't the good doctorate wonder what the control group looked like?

13   Scientists, however, *are* a far less religious lot than the American population, and the higher you go on the cerebro-magisterium, the greater the proportion of atheists, agnostics, and assorted other paganites. According to a 1998 survey published in *Nature*, only 7 percent of members of the prestigious National Academy of Sciences professed a belief in a "personal God." (Interestingly, a slightly higher number, 7.9 percent, claimed to believe in "personal immortality," which may say as much about the robustness of the scientific ego as about anything else.) In other words, more than 90 percent of our elite scientists are unlikely to pray for divine favoritism no matter how badly they want to beat a competitor to publication. Yet only a flaskful of the faithless have put their nonbelief on record or publicly criticized religion, the notable and voluble exceptions being Richard Dawkins of Oxford University and Daniel Dennett of Tufts University. Nor have Dawkins and Dennett earned much good will among their colleagues for their anticlerical views; one astronomer I spoke with said of Dawkins, "He's a really fine parish preacher of the fire-and-brimstone school, isn't he?"

14   Even a recent D&D-driven campaign to spruce up the image of atheism by coopting the word "bright"—to indicate, as Dawkins put it in a newspaper piece, "a person whose world view is free of supernatural and mystical elements"—has yet to gain much candlepower. Admittedly, the new lingo has problems. To describe oneself at a cocktail party as "a bright," however saucily and sunnily the phrase is delivered, makes one sound like a member of a Rajneeshee-style[2] cult, not exactly the image a heathen wants to project.

15   But I doubt that semantics is what keeps most scientists quiet about religion. Instead, it's probably something closer to that trusty old limbic reflex called "an instinct for self-preservation." For centuries science has survived quite nicely by cultivating an image of reserve and objectivity, of being above religion, politics, business, table manners. Scientists want to be left alone to do their work, dazzle their peers, and hire grad students to wash

---

[2]Rajneeshee-style: that is, in the manner of the religious sect that formed around the Indian mystic *Osho* (also known as Bhagwan Shree Rajneesh).

the glassware. When it comes to extramural combat, scientists choose their crusades cautiously. Going after Uri Geller[3] or the Raelians[4] is risk-free entertainment, easier than making fun of the sociology department. Battling the creationist camp has been a much harder and nastier fight, but those scientists who have taken it on feel they have a direct stake in the debate and are entitled to wage it, since the creationists, and more recently the promoters of "intelligent design" theory, claim to be as scientific in their methodology as are the scientists.

16   But when a teenager named Darrell Lambert was chucked out of the Boy Scouts for being an atheist, scientists suddenly remembered all those gels they had to run and dark matter they had to chase, and they kept quiet. Lambert had explained the reason why, despite a childhood spent in Bible classes and church youth groups, he had become an atheist. He took biology in ninth grade, and rather than devoting himself to studying the bra outline of the girl sitting in front of him, he actually learned some biology. And what he learned in biology persuaded him that the Bible was full of . . . short stories. Some good, some inspiring, some even racy, but fiction nonetheless. For his incisive, reasoned, scientific look at life, and for refusing to cook the data and simply lie to the Boy Scouts about his thoughts on God—as some advised him to do—Darrell Lambert should have earned a standing ovation from the entire scientific community. Instead, he had to settle for an interview with Connie Chung, right after a report on the Gambino family.

17   Scientists have ample cause to feel they must avoid being viewed as irreligious, a prionic[5] life-form bent on destroying the most sacred heifer in America. After all, academic researchers graze on taxpayer pastures. If they pay the slightest attention to the news, they've surely noticed the escalating readiness of conservative politicians and an array of highly motivated religious organizations to interfere with the nation's scientific enterprise—altering the consumer information Web site at the National Cancer Institute to make abortion look like a cause of breast cancer, which it is not, or stuffing scientific advisory panels with anti-abortion "faith healers." Recently, an obscure little club called the Traditional Values Coalition began combing through descriptions of projects supported by the National Institutes of Health and complaining to sympathetic congressmen about those they deemed morally "rotten," most of them studies of sexual behavior and AIDS prevention. The congressmen in turn launched a series of hearings, calling in institute officials to inquire who in the Cotton-pickin' name of Mather cares about the perversions of Native American homosexuals, to which the researchers replied, um, the studies *were* approved by a panel of scientific experts, and, gee, the Native American community has been underserved and it is having a real problem with AIDS these days. Thus far, the projects have escaped being nullified, but the raw display of pious dentition must surely give fright to even the most rakishly freethinking and comfortably tenured professor. It's one thing to monkey with descriptions of Darwinism in a high school textbook . . . but

---

[3]Uri Geller: a mystic and entertainer who demonstrates his allegedly psychic abilities by using powers of telekinesis to bend spoons and perform other feats.

[4]Raelians: a religious sect that believes human life was created by extraterrestrials.

[5]Prionic: a prion is a type of infectious agent.

to threaten to take away a peer-reviewed grant! That Dan Dennett; he *is* something of a pompous leaf-blower, isn't he?

18　　Yet the result of wincing and capitulating is a fresh round of whacks. Now it's not enough for presidential aspirants to make passing reference to their "faith." Now a reporter from *Newsweek* sees it as his privilege, if not his duty, to demand of Howard Dean,[6] "Do you see Jesus Christ as the son of God and believe in him as the route to salvation and eternal life?" In my personal fairy tale, Dean, who as a doctor fits somewhere in the phylum Scientificus, might have boomed, "Well, with his views on camels and rich people, he sure wouldn't vote Republican!" or maybe, "No, but I hear he has a Mel Gibson complex." Dr. Dean might have talked about patients of his who suffered strokes and lost the very fabric of themselves, and how he has seen the centrality of the brain to the sense of being an individual. He might have expressed doubts that the self survives the brain, but, oh yes, life goes on, life is bigger, stronger, and better endowed than any Bush in a jumpsuit, and we are part of the wild, tumbling river of life, our molecules were the molecules of dinosaurs, and before that of stars, and this is not Bulfinch mythology, this is corroborated reality.

19　　Alas for my phantasm of fact, Howard Dean, M.D., had no choice but to chime, oh yes, he certainly sees Jesus as the son of God, though he at least dodged the eternal life clause with a humble mumble about his salvation not being up to him.

20　　I may be an atheist, and I may be impressed that, through the stepwise rigor of science, its Spockian[7] eyebrow of doubt always cocked, we have learned so much about the universe. Yet I recognize that, from there to here, and here to there, funny things are *everywhere*. Why is there so much dark matter and dark energy in the great Out There, and why couldn't cosmologists have given them different enough names so I could keep them straight? Why is there something rather than nothing, and why is so much of it on my desk? Not to mention the abiding mysteries of e-mail, like why I get exponentially more spam every day, nine-tenths of it invitations to enlarge an appendage I don't have.

21　　I recognize that science doesn't have all the answers and doesn't pretend to, and that's one of the things I love about it. But it has a pretty good notion of what's probable or possible, and virgin births and carpenter rebirths just aren't on the list. Is there a divine intelligence, separate from the universe but somehow in charge of the universe, either in its inception or in twiddling its parameters? No evidence. Is the universe itself God? Is the universe aware of itself? We're here. We're aware. Does that make us God? Will my daughter have to attend a Quaker Friends school now?

22　　I don't believe in life after death, but I'd like to believe in life before death. I'd like to think that one of these days we'll leave superstition and delusional thinking and Jerry Falwell[8] behind. Scientists would like that, too. But for now, they like their grants even more.

---

[6]Howard Dean: Vermont doctor and politician who ran an unsuccessful campaign for President in 2004.

[7]Spockian: that is, after the manner of the always logical Mr. Spock from the television series *Star Trek*, one of whose trademarks was a single eyebrow raised in skepticism.

[8]Jerry Falwell: American Baptist minister and well-known televangelist and political and social commentator.

QUESTIONS ON MEANING

1. What scientific concept or theory, according to Angier, are scientists most concerned that the public accept as fact?

2. According to Angier, why aren't scientists (in general) interested in tackling public beliefs regarding the resurrection of Christ and the virgin birth?

3. What seems to be Angier's opinion of scientists who also hold religious faith?

4. How did the scientific community let down Darrell Lambert, according to Angier?

5. What, in the end, would you say is Angier's thesis? What is her central message?

QUESTIONS FOR DISCUSSION

1. Why do you think scientists, as reported by Angier, are so adamant that Darwin's dandy idea be defended and explained to the general population? What is it about evolutionary theory that is unique among the field of scientific endeavor? What is at stake in the ongoing cultural debate over the acceptance of evolutionary theory as fact (rather than as theory)?

2. What do you think would be the public reaction if scientists responded publicly to religious issues the way they have responded publicy to issues such as astrology? Would it change your opinion of scientists if they treated the virgin birth and astrology equally in public discourse? Do you think they are equivalent concepts? Why or why not?

LOOKING AT RHETORIC

1. Throughout the essay, what tone does Angier take toward scientists, and what tone does she adopt when discussing religious believers? Point to moments in the essay in which those tones and/or opinions come to the forefront. Do you believe Angier's characterizations of the scientific community and of the religious community are fair and accurate? How is the tone in this piece similar to, or different from, other selections in this chapter?

2. This essay begins with a passage about scientific literacy. Does Angier's essay support or not the treatment of scientific literacy presented by Martin and her co-authors in the first selection of this chapter? Or, do the two essays make entirely different points about scientific literacy?

WRITING ASSIGNMENTS

1. Religious faith and scientific pursuit have, in the eyes of many intellectual historians, been at war for centuries. Spend some time in the library researching the history of Galileo and his relationship with the Roman Catholic Church. Then, draft an essay in which you discuss the history of Galileo's interaction with the church and discuss whether you think that the situation Angier describes regarding Darwinian evolutionary theory is similar to, or different from, Galileo's situation. What do each of these situations suggest about the relationship between science and faith?

2. Early in her essay, Angier makes a reference to Stephen Jay Gould's notion of "magisteria." Research Gould's concept and write an essay in which you define Gould's concept of the magisteria and argue either for or against Gould's concept. Point out whether Angier's essay violates Gould's principle or not. In light of Gould's magisteria, do you find Angier's essay more or less convincing? Explain why in your essay. Write a response to Angier's essay from the point of view of someone of religious faith. How would someone with a religious worldview respond to Angier's arguments?

3. Write a response to Angier's essay from the point of view of someone of religious faith. Or, alternatively, write a response to Angier's essay from the point of view of a scientist. In either version of this essay, clarify how you think someone from either point of view might respond to Angier's arguments.

4. In pairs or in groups, discuss the story of Darrell Lambert. Does the group believe that the scientific community let Lambert down? Why or why not? Then, individually, write an essay in which you argue whether the scientific community's treatment of Lambert was justified, or whether the scientific community had an ethical obligation to handle the situation differently.

Thinking Crosscurrently

As interesting as it is to speculate about the ways in which evolutionary processes and genetic engineering will reshape human biology in the future, one should not overlook the implications that genetic manipulations have on daily life. As technology catches up with the imaginations of previous generations of science fiction writers, speculative philosophers, and futurologists, new questions come to the forefront that force responsible thinkers to think of science in terms of ethics, religion, psychology, art, history, and even pop culture. Science does not happen in a vacuum: it touches all aspects of our intellectual life. As you think about the selections in this chapter, consider the following questions:

- What is the relationship between science and religion? Do these two intellectual endeavors work together in harmony or are they in a constant state of conflict? Or do they simply have nothing to do with each other? What role does science play in the various attempts to either prove or disprove the existence of God? What perspectives might Robert Orsi or Kwasi Wiredu to these questions? How about William Paley or St. Thomas Aquinas?

- How important is the field of human biology to the development of modern educational theories and practices? What perspectives might Christina Hoff Sommers or Malcolm Gladwell bring to our understanding of the relationship between biology and education?

- Certainly, the fact that humans are physical beings has not been lost on artists over the centuries, who have made human biology a consistent and provocative focus of countless paintings, sculptures, poems, and novels. Why do you think the human form has proven so compelling for so many artists? How do the short stories by Kate Chopin and James Joyce comment on the physical nature of human beings? How about the story by James Tiptree? How is the physical nature of the human body portrayed in the different paintings reprinted in the selection on "Art and Medicine"?

- What is the impact of evolutionary theory on business practice? What perspectives on the ways in which our biological natures influence the way business is conducted might Terry Burnham and Jay Phelan, Barbara Ehrenreich, or Paul Krugman have?

5 BUSINESS AND ECONOMICS

What is money? How does it work? Why do we have it? In one sense, it is simply paper. A five dollar bill is the same size as a one dollar bill. It is made of the same thing. The markings and the picture are different but they are printed with the same ink. Bills used to tell us, in print, that they were redeemable in gold. However, we are no longer on a "gold standard" (what economists call a monometallic monetary system) but a "paper standard," where the amount of money in our economy is carefully regulated by the Federal Reserve Bank, through its relationship to the banks that hold much of our wealth.

In fact, "currency," the printed bills we call money, are only a small percentage of the money supply. The largest portion of that money supply is merely a number recorded on a ledger, the checking accounts people have. Money is abstract spending power, and sometimes there is more or less of it in the economy as a whole. The more there is in relation to the amount of goods and services, the more inflation. The less there is, the greater our risk of recession and depression. Money is a human creation, a medium of exchange, a way to make it easier for us to trade. It is surely simpler for me to hand you a five dollar bill for a sack of flour than a dead chicken. You'll take the money because you can buy whatever you want with it. You may not want the chicken, and I'll have to spend a lot of time trying to find someone with flour who wants my chicken.

Money and exchange is one of the first concepts you learn in economics, but you will quickly learn others: the relationship of supply and demand, how market prices emerge in a free economy, how surpluses and shortages come about, why we have inflationary and recessionary periods. It is important stuff because it affects us daily in the most tangible ways, in our stomachs and in our minds, in the things we need and want. Most of us agree with the adage, "The best things in life are free." But practically we know that much of what we need is not without its price, and some of what we want is not either. So understanding the nature of economic behavior helps us as we adapt to our world. But economics is only one part of "business" broadly construed. There is also management theory and practice, marketing, labor relations, production management, accounting and finance, and a host of other areas. How do we interact with one another in a material world? How do we divide up the work to be done? How do we compensate it? Trade and commerce is the engine that drives the daily operation of a civilization. They may not be its soul but they are the vital organs of its body. To understand them is to understand an important aspect of our relationship to the tangible world.

THE DISCIPLINE YOU EXPERIENCE

Adam Smith, an economist who lived in the eighteenth century, is often considered to be the founder of the discipline. Economists, CEOs, finance experts, and marketing specialists refer to his ideas even today. But he didn't consider himself an economist or a businessman. He was primarily a philosopher preoccupied with human behavior. As we live and trade in the world of material things, how will we behave when we compete for resources? One of the first principles of business and economics is that resources are scarce relative to wants. Another is that individuals have different tastes and preferences. These and other "behavior postulates" form the basis for exchange in an economic system. But Adam Smith wrote before the Industrial Revolution, that transformative moment in history when the modern world came into being, when modern cities were born, when factories produced the bulk of our wealth, when machines and technology became an essential part of our daily lives. None of these events changed the essential truths Smith discovered about human economic behavior, but the picture has become much more complicated. We now have a banking and financial system that is the framework through which modern society conducts its business. There are stock markets worldwide, bond markets, equities exchanges, commodities markets, trade balances, the interaction of manufacturing, agricultural, and service economies, all functioning in the context of an increasingly integrated "world economy" that calls the assumed separation of nations into question.

We have come a long way from the flour and the chicken. We live in the world of the corporation, the stock and bond holder, the CEO, the middle manager, and the employed and unemployed worker. At the center of this we live and breathe, acting in accordance with our desires and hopes, responding to the moral and ethical problems of a complicated world. To study business and economics is to understand how the world works at a very functional level: how goods are exchanged, what money is and how it flows, how leadership is effectively conducted in a corporate context, how to sell the goods and services we have. But to really understand these things, and to live ethically in a world of scarce resources, even to maintain ourselves collectively in a civilized society, we must ponder and contemplate the human condition that drives it all: the needs, the motives, and the fundamental human nature that informs our actions as material beings in a material world.

Thus, we can see how the study of business and economics permits us to make decisions daily, both at a practical and a personal level. In universities, economics has a complicated relationship with business. As a social science, economics departments are sometimes housed within the social sciences or the humanities, but their affiliation with others aspects of business is obvious, and more often the discipline of economics has a presence in schools of business administration, which typically offer undergraduate degrees in business, specialized degrees in economics, graduate degrees in particular fields of business, and the Master of Business Administration (MBA). In contrast to disciplines in the humanities, social sciences, or physical sciences, business and economics related courses lead to "professional degrees," that is, programs that prepare the student for the workplace in a tangible way, often though not always teaching the specific skills that will be used in the world of work. There are a variety of related topics that exist in a business program, often integrating into the undergraduate and even the graduate business degree. Among them are the following:

- Economics, including the study of microeconomics (the study of "the firm," and the complex patterns relating to supply and demand) and macroeconomics (the study of the business cycle as well as the banking and finance systems).

- Management and organization theory, including the study of leadership styles and approaches as they relate to specific types of organizations.

- Marketing, involving the techniques for presenting products to the public in a competitive environment.

- Finance, which involves the study of the banking systems as well as complex financial markets such as the stock market, bond markets, commodities exchanges, and others.

- Accounting, involving the practical methods for recording funds internal and external to a company's operations, including tax preparation and presentation.

- Production and operations management, the particular skills and practices related to manufacturing, production, and inventory.

There are a number of courses in colleges and universities that explore these subjects. They include the aforementioned economics courses, as well as courses such as Money and Banking, Price Theory, Data Analysis and Decision Making, Organizational Behavior, Financial Reporting and Accounting, International Business and Law, Human Resource Management, and Business and Society, among many others. All of these subjects prepare the student of business and economics for some of the tasks they will perform when they leave school, and in the process these courses help them understand the relationship of human communities and the behaviors that motivate them, in a world of goods, services, and exchange.

REFLECTING ON THIS CHAPTER

Given the diversity of the business world and the schools that train students to work successfully within it, a number of fascinating concerns emerge in the selections in this chapter. As you read, consider these questions:

- What is the essential issue or problem the author attempts to explore or solve? What sub-discipline of business and economics are they working within?

- Given that the academic disciplines within business and economics are relatively new, what other fields of study are involved in the selection, areas such as philosophy, ethics, psychology, and biology?

- How do these various selections compare and contrast? What central themes emerge? Are there ethical and moral issues that emerge as the authors discuss the realities of the business world?

- What are the various writing strategies the authors employ? What tools do they use to persuade us? If you found a selection convincing, what made it so?

- Do you detect any flaws in the arguments? Can you find any logical fallacies? Are there any overt biases? Remember, a bias is not the same as a point of view. A strongly persuasive argument can be unbiased if it honestly presents and analyzes the available data and information.

Maid to Order

The Politics of Other Women's Work

By Barbara Ehrenreich

Barbara Ehrenreich (b. 1941) is a columnist and author of numerous books. She deals primarily with economic and social issues and identifies herself as a "social democrat," though her initial training was in the sciences. Her work engages disciplines ranging from sociology, to economics, to public policy. She graduated from Reed College in 1963 with a degree in physics, and in 1968 she earned a Ph.D. in cell biology from Rockefeller University. She became active in politics and social protest in the 1960's and 1970's and began a career in writing. Among her many books, Nickel and Dimed: On (Not) Getting By in America *(2001) was particularly popular, as she explored the problem of college educated workers experiencing economic problems and the decline of the "promise" normally associated with higher education. In 2006, she founded United Professionals, an organization dedicated to the concerns of educated workers who "find their lives disrupted by forces beyond their control." She is an honorary co-chair of the Democratic Socialists of America and serves on the editorial board of* The Nation. *The following excerpt is from an essay published in* Harper's. *It explores the personal, social, and economic implications that emerge from the use of domestic labor among the upper middle-class.*

1   In line with growing class polarization, the classic posture of submission is making a stealthy comeback. "We scrub your floors the old-fashioned way," boasts the brochure from Merry Maids, the largest of the residential-cleaning services that have sprung up in the last two decades, "on our hands and knees." This is not a posture that independent "cleaning ladies" willingly assume—preferring, like most people who clean their own homes, the sponge mop wielded from a standing position. In her comprehensive 1999 guide to home-making, *Home Comforts*, Cheryl Mendelson warns: "Never ask hired housecleaners to clean your floors on their hands and knees; the request is likely to be regarded as degrading." But in a society in which 40 percent of the wealth is owned by 1 percent of households while the bottom 20 percent reports negative assets, the degradation of others is readily purchased. Kneepads entered American political discourse as a tool of the sexually subservient, but employees of Merry Maids, The Maids International, and other corporate cleaning services spend hours every day on these kinky devices, wiping up the drippings of the affluent.

2   I spent three weeks in September 1999 as an employee of The Maids International in Portland, Maine, cleaning, along with my fellow team members, approximately sixty houses containing a total of about 250 scrubbable floors—bathrooms, kitchens, and entry-ways requiring the hands-and-knees treatment. It's a different world down there below knee

level, one that few adults voluntarily enter. Here you find elaborate dust structures held together by a scaffolding of dog hair; dried bits of pasta glued to the floor by their sauce; the congealed remains of gravies, jellies, contraceptive creams, vomit, and urine. Sometimes, too, you encounter some fragment of a human being: a child's legs, stamping by in disgust because the maids are still present when he gets home from school; more commonly, the Joan & David–clad feet and electrolyzed calves of the female homeowner. Look up and you may find this person staring at you, arms folded, in anticipation of an overlooked stain. In rare instances she may try to help in some vague, symbolic way, by moving the cockatoo's cage, for example, or apologizing for the leaves shed by a miniature indoor tree. Mostly, though, she will not see you at all and may even sit down with her mail at a table in the very room you are cleaning, where she would remain completely unaware of your existence unless you were to crawl under that table and start gnawing away at her ankles.

3   Housework, as you may recall from the feminist theories of the Sixties and Seventies, was supposed to be the great equalizer of women. Whatever else women did—jobs, school, child care—we also did housework, and if there were some women who hired others to do it for them, they seemed too privileged and rare to include in the theoretical calculus. All women were workers, and the home was their workplace—unpaid and unsupervised, to be sure, but a workplace no less than the offices and factories men repaired to every morning. If men thought of the home as a site of leisure and recreation—a "haven in a heartless world"—this was to ignore the invisible female proletariat that kept it cozy and humming. We were on the march now, or so we imagined, united against a society that devalued our labor even as it waxed mawkish over "the family" and "the home." Shoulder to shoulder and arm in arm, women were finally getting up off the floor.

4   In the most eye-catching elaboration of the home-as-workplace theme, Marxist feminists Maria Rosa Dallacosta and Selma James proposed in 1972 that the home was in fact an economically productive and significant workplace, an extension of the actual factory, since housework served to "reproduce the labor power" of others, particularly men. The male worker would hardly be in shape to punch in for his shift, after all, if some woman had not fed him, laundered his clothes, and cared for the children who were his contribution to the next generation of workers. If the home was a quasi-industrial workplace staffed by women for the ultimate benefit of the capitalists, then it followed that "wages for housework" was the obvious demand.

5   But when most American feminists, Marxist or otherwise, asked the Marxist question cui bono? they tended to come up with a far simpler answer—men. If women were the domestic proletariat, then men made up the class of domestic exploiters, free to lounge while their mates scrubbed. In consciousness-raising groups, we railed against husbands and boyfriends who refused to pick up after themselves, who were unaware of housework at all, unless of course it hadn't been done. The "dropped socks," left by a man for a woman to gather up and launder, joined lipstick and spike heels as emblems of gender oppression. And if, somewhere, a man had actually dropped a sock in the calm expectation that his wife

---

[1] Cui bono: In the Latin, "To whose benefit?" An adage used to suggest that the entity responsible for something may not be who it seems to be.

would retrieve it, it was a sock heard round the world. Wherever second-wave feminism[2]
took root, battles broke out between lovers and spouses over sticky countertops, piled-up
laundry, and whose turn it was to do the dishes.

6   The radical new idea was that housework was not only a relationship between a
woman and a dust bunny or an unmade bed; it also defined a relationship between human
beings, typically husbands and wives. This represented a marked departure from the more
conservative Betty Friedan, who, in *The Feminine Mystique,* had never thought to enter the
male sex into the equation, as either part of the housework problem or part of an even-
tual solution. She raged against a society that consigned its educated women to what she
saw as essentially janitorial chores, beneath "the abilities of a woman of average or normal
human intelligence," and, according to unidentified studies she cited, "peculiarly suited to
the capacities of feeble-minded girls." But men are virtually exempt from housework in *The
Feminine Mystique*—why drag them down too? At one point she even disparages a "Mrs.
G.," who "somehow couldn't get her housework done before her husband came home at
night and was so tired then that he had to do it." Educated women would just have to
become more efficient so that housework could no longer "expand to fill the time available."

7   Or they could hire other women to do it—an option approved by Friedan in *The
Feminine Mystique* as well as by the National Organization for Women, which she had
helped launch. At the 1973 congressional hearings on whether to extend the Fair Labor
Standards Act to household workers, NOW testified on the affirmative side, arguing that
improved wages and working conditions would attract more women to the field, and offering the seemingly self-contradictory prediction that "the demand for household help inside
the home will continue to increase as more women seek occupations outside the home."
One NOW member added, on a personal note: "Like many young women today, I am in
school in order to develop a rewarding career for myself. I also have a home to run and
can fully conceive of the need for household help as my free time at home becomes more
and more restricted. Women know [that] housework is dirty, tedious work, and they are
willing to pay to have it done. . . . " On the aspirations of the women paid to do it, assuming
that at least some of them were bright enough to entertain a few, neither Friedan nor these
members of NOW had, at the time, a word to say.

8   So the insight that distinguished the more radical, post-Friedan cohort of feminists
was that when we talk about housework, we are really talking, yet again, about power.
Housework was not degrading because it was manual labor, as Friedan thought, but because
it was embedded in degrading relationships and inevitably served to reinforce them. To
make a mess that another person will have to deal with—the dropped socks, the toothpaste
sprayed on the bathroom mirror, the dirty dishes left from a late-night snack—is to exert
domination in one of its more silent and intimate forms. One person's arrogance—or indifference, or hurry—becomes another person's occasion for toil. And when the person who is
cleaned up after is consistently male, while the person who cleans up is consistently female,
you have a formula for reproducing male domination from one generation to the next.

---

[2] second-wave feminism: Often referred to as "the Women's Liberation Movement," the period of feminist
activity that began in the 1960's and continued into the 1970's, often considered to be initiated by Betty
Friedan's *The Feminine Mystique* (1963).

9   Hence the feminist perception of housework as one more way by which men exploit women or, more neutrally stated, as "a symbolic enactment of gender relations." An early German women's liberation cartoon depicted a woman scrubbing on her hands and knees while her husband, apparently excited by this pose, approaches from behind, unzipping his fly. Hence, too, the second-wave feminists' revulsion at the hiring of maids, especially when they were women of color: At a feminist conference I attended in 1980, poet Audre Lorde chose to insult the all-too-white audience by accusing them of being present only because they had black housekeepers to look after their children at home. She had the wrong crowd; most of the assembled radical feminists would no sooner have employed a black maid than they would have attached Confederate flag stickers to the rear windows of their cars. But accusations like hers, repeated in countless conferences and meetings, reinforced our rejection of the servant option. There already were at least two able-bodied adults in the average home—a man and a woman—and the hope was that, after a few initial skirmishes, they would learn to share the housework graciously.

10   A couple of decades later, however, the average household still falls far short of that goal. True, women do less housework than they did before the feminist revolution and the rise of the two-income family: down from an average of 30 hours per week in 1965 to 17.5 hours in 1995, according to a July 1999 study by the University of Maryland. Some of that decline reflects a relaxation of standards rather than a redistribution of chores; women still do two thirds of whatever housework—including bill paying, pet care, tidying, and lawn care—gets done. The inequity is sharpest for the most despised of household chores, cleaning: in the thirty years between 1965 and 1995, men increased the time they spent scrubbing, vacuuming, and sweeping by 240 percent—all the way up to 1.7 hours per week—while women decreased their cleaning time by only 7 percent, to 6.7 hours per week. The averages conceal a variety of arrangements, of course, from minutely negotiated sharing to the most clichéd division of labor, as described by one woman to the *Washington Post*: "I take care of the inside, he takes care of the outside." But perhaps the most disturbing finding is that almost the entire increase in male participation took place between the 1970s and the mid-1980s. Fifteen years after the apparent cessation of hostilities, it is probably not too soon to announce the score: in the "chore wars" of the Seventies and Eighties, women gained a little ground, but overall, and after a few strategic concessions, men won.

11   Enter then, the cleaning lady as dea ex machina,[3] restoring tranquillity as well as order to the home. Marriage counselors recommend her as an alternative to squabbling, as do many within the cleaning industry itself. A Chicago cleaning woman quotes one of her clients as saying that if she gives up the service, "my husband and I will be divorced in six months." When the trend toward hiring out was just beginning to take off in 1988, the owner of a Merry Maids franchise in Arlington, Massachusetts, told the *Christian Science Monitor*, "I kid some women. I say, 'We even save marriages. In this new eighties period you expect more from the male partner, but very often you don't get the cooperation you would like to have. The alternative is to pay somebody to come in. . . .'" Another Merry Maids franchise owner has learned to capitalize more directly on housework-related spats;

---

[3] Dea ex machina: a variation of deus ex machina. In Latin, literally "God from the machine." The term is used by Aristotle in *Poetics* to describe the inappropriately miraculous resolution of a plot in drama. In this ironic use of the term, the god is female.

he closes between 30 and 35 percent of his sales by making follow-up calls Saturday mornings, which is "prime time for arguing over the fact that the house is a mess." The micro-defeat of feminism in the household opened a new door for women, only this time it was the servants' entrance.

12   In 1999, somewhere between 14 and 18 percent of households employed an outsider to do the cleaning, and the numbers have been rising dramatically. Mediamark Research reports a 53 percent increase, between 1995 and 1999, in the number of households using a hired cleaner or service once a month or more, and Maritz Marketing finds that 30 percent of the people who hired help in 1999 did so for the first time that year. Among my middle-class, professional women friends and acquaintances, including some who made important contributions to the early feminist analysis of housework, the employment of a maid is now nearly universal. This sudden emergence of a servant class is consistent with what some economists have called the "Brazilianization" of the American economy: We are dividing along the lines of traditional Latin American societies—into a tiny overclass and a huge underclass, with the latter available to perform intimate household services for the former. Or, to put it another way, the home, or at least the affluent home, is finally becoming what radical feminists in the Seventies only imagined it was—a true "workplace" for women and a tiny, though increasingly visible, part of the capitalist economy. And the question is: As the home becomes a workplace for someone else, is it still a place where you would want to live?

QUESTIONS ON MEANING

1. What are some of Ehrenreich's experiences when working for the Maids International? Why does she choose to take this job?
2. What position did the National Organization for Women (NOW) take during the 1973 congressional hearings on whether to extend the Fair Labor Standards Act to household workers?
3. Why did second-wave feminists have difficulties with women hiring domestic help as they entered the professional work force?
4. What does she mean when she refers to the micro defeat of feminism?
5. How has the hiring away of domestic work affected parent/child relationships?

QUESTIONS FOR DISCUSSION

1. Is the rise of the use of domestic labor among professional working women a betrayal of the feminist movement?
2. Is there anything to be gained when families, including children, share in the housework? What, if anything, is lost when they hire domestic help?
3. What social and economic losses might occur if the affluent didn't hire domestic help? How might we compensate for these losses?
4. Has the progressive movement of the 1960's and 1970's tended to privilege the interests of the upper middle class, particularly women, at the expense of economically disadvantaged groups, and if so, how?

LOOKING AT RHETORIC

1. Ehrenreich frequently quotes numerical data pointing to trends in human behavior. How effective is this rhetorical strategy in helping her make her argument?

2. Early in the article, she makes it clear that she has worked as a maid as a part of her research. How does she use this experience in her essay? How does it inform her point of view?

3. She uses only a few specific examples but instead evokes general categories such as the upper middle class and the servant class. In what way does this level of abstraction enhance or detract from her main idea?

WRITING ASSIGNMENTS

1. Research sources in economics, contemporary history, and sociology that deal with the use of manual labor by the middle class. Identify a circumstance in which you have observed this labor relationship in real life. In what way is it mutually beneficial? In what way is it unjust or exploitative?

2. Identify a situation in which you purchased the manual labor of another. This could include anything, including buying a hamburger at McDonald's. Write an essay in which you justify that purchase on ethical grounds. Who benefits and how? If you cannot justify it, write an essay arguing why.

3. In pairs or in groups, make a list of domestic chores in a typical household. Individually, write an essay in which you explore what might be gained or lost by the family collectively performing them. Remember, there are loses Ehrenreich identifies: no soccer practice, less time for piano lessons, less time for SAT prep. Make an argument for or against hiring domestic help. You may take an intermediary position, hiring for some things and not for others.

Economic Freedom and
Political Freedom

Milton Friedman

Milton Friedman (1912-2006) was the most important public voice of "monetarism," the theory that the money supply is the most important force behind economic growth. His work has implications in disciplines ranging from economics and business to public policy and history. He graduated from Rutgers University where he studied mathematics and developed an early interest in economics, partly as a result of the Great Depression. He earned his M.A. at the University of Chicago in 1933 and his Ph.D. from Columbia University in 1946. He held academic posts at the University of Wisconsin, Madison and the University of Chicago. He was initially sympathetic to John Maynard Keynes. He soon changed his position, concluding that the money supply together with the free operation of markets would consistently maximize economic potential. In time, he became the major spokesman for this position, and he consulted at the highest levels of the United States government and was a senior research fellow at the Hoover Institution. Friedman was awarded the Nobel Prize for Economic Science in 1976. Taken from Chapter One of his most famous book Capitalism and Freedom *(1962), which was partially co-authored by his wife Rose Friedman, the following excerpt explores the relationship of political and economic freedom, arguing that they are closely related and co-implicated.*

1   It is widely believed that politics and economics are separate and largely unconnected; that individual freedom is a political problem and material welfare an economic problem; and that any kind of political arrangements can be combined with any kind of economic arrangements. The chief contemporary manifestation of this idea is the advocacy of *"democratic socialism"*[1] by many who condemn out of hand the restrictions on individual freedom imposed by "totalitarian socialism" in Russia, and who are persuaded that it is possible for a country to adopt the essential features of Russian economic arrangements and yet to ensure individual freedom through political arrangements. The thesis of this chapter is that such a view is a delusion, that there is an intimate connection between economics and politics, that only certain combinations of political and economic arrangements are possible, and that in particular, a society which is socialist cannot also be democratic, in the sense of guaranteeing individual freedom.

2   Economic arrangements play a dual role in the promotion of a free society. On the one hand, freedom in economic arrangements is itself a component of freedom broadly understood, so economic freedom is an end in itself. In the second place, economic freedom is also an indispensable means toward the achievement of political freedom.

3   The first of these roles of economic freedom needs special emphasis because intellectuals in particular have a strong bias against regarding this aspect of freedom as important. They tend to express contempt for what they regard as material aspects of life, and to regard their own pursuit of allegedly higher values as on a different plane of significance and as deserving of special attention. For most citizens of the country, however, if not for the intellectual, the direct importance of economic freedom is at least comparable in significance to the indirect importance of economic freedom as a means to political freedom.

4   The citizen of Great Britain, who after World War II was not permitted to spend his vacation in the United States because of exchange control, was being deprived of an essential freedom no less than the citizen of the United States, who was denied the opportunity to spend his vacation in Russia because of his political views. The one was ostensibly an economic limitation of freedom and the other a political limitation, yet there is no essential difference between the two.

5   The citizen of the United States who is compelled by law to devote something like 10 per cent of his income to the purchase of a particular kind of retirement contract, administered by the government, is being deprived of a corresponding part of his personal freedom. How strongly this deprivation may be felt and its closeness to the deprivation of religious freedom, which all would regard as "civil" or "political" rather than "economic", were

---

[1] Democratic socialism: a form of economic and political arrangement in which democratic practices are maintained in an environment of active government participation in the economy, through regulation of markets, taxes, and the providing of social services. Common among most contemporary Western European countries.

dramatized by an episode involving a group of farmers of the Amish[2] sect. On grounds of principle, this group regarded compulsory federal old age programs[3] as an infringement of their personal individual freedom and refused to pay taxes or accept benefits. As a result, some of their livestock were sold by auction in order to satisfy claims for social security levies. True, the number of citizens who regard compulsory old age insurance as a deprivation of freedom may be few, but the believer in freedom has never counted noses.

6   A citizen of the United States who under the laws of various states is not free to follow the occupation of his own choosing unless he can get a license for it, is likewise being deprived of an essential part of his freedom. So is the man who would like to exchange some of his goods with, say, a Swiss for a watch but is prevented from doing so by a quota. So also is the Californian who was thrown into jail for selling Alka Seltzer at a price below that set by the manufacturer under so-called "fair trade" laws. So also is the farmer who cannot grow the amount of wheat he wants. And so on. Clearly, economic freedom, in and of itself, is an extremely important part of total freedom.

7   Viewed as a means to the end of political freedom, economic arrangements are important because of their effect on the concentration or dispersion of power. The kind of economic organization that provides economic freedom directly, namely, competitive capitalism, also promotes political freedom because it separates economic power from political power and in this way enables the one to offset the other.

8   Historical evidence speaks with a single voice on the relation between political freedom and a free market. I know of no example in time or place of a society that has been marked by a large measure of political freedom, and that has not also used something comparable to a free market to organize the bulk of economic activity.

9   Because we live in a largely free society, we tend to forget how limited is the span of time and the part of the globe for which there has ever been anything like political freedom: the typical state of mankind is tyranny, servitude, and misery. The nineteenth century and early twentieth century in the Western world stand out as striking exceptions to the general trend of historical development. Political freedom in this instance clearly came along with the free market and the development of capitalist institutions. So also did political freedom in the golden age of Greece and in the early days of the Roman era.

10   History suggests only that capitalism is a necessary condition for political freedom. Clearly it is not a sufficient condition. Fascist Italy and fascist Spain, Germany at various times in the last seventy years, Japan before World Wars I and II, tzarist Russia in the decades before World War I—are all societies that cannot conceivably be described as politically free. Yet, in each, private enterprise was the dominant form of economic organization. It is therefore clearly possible to have economic arrangements that are fundamentally capitalist and political arrangements that are not free.

11   Even in those societies, the citizenry had a good deal more freedom than citizens of a modern totalitarian state like Russia or Nazi Germany, in which economic totalitarianism is combined with political totalitarianism. Even in Russia under the Tzars, it was possible for some citizens, under some circumstances, to change their jobs without getting

---

[2] Amish: sect of Christianity that began in Switzerland and migrated to America in the eighteenth century. Known for plain dress, simple living, and pacifism.

[3] Federal old age programs: a reference to the Social Security and Medicare Programs.

permission from political authority because capitalism and the existence of private property provided some check to the centralized power of the state.

12   The relation between political and economic freedom is complex and by no means unilateral. In the early nineteenth century, Bentham[4] and the Philosophical Radicals were inclined to regard political freedom as a means to economic freedom. They believed that the masses were being hampered by the restrictions that were being imposed upon them, and that if political reform gave the bulk of the people the vote, they would do what was good for them, which was to vote for laissez faire. In retrospect, one cannot say that they were wrong. There was a large measure of political reform that was accompanied by economic reform in the direction of a great deal of laissez faire. An enormous increase in the well-being of the masses followed this change in economic arrangements.

13   The triumph of Benthamite liberalism in nineteenth-century England was followed by a reaction toward increasing intervention by government in economic affairs. This tendency to collectivism was greatly accelerated both in England and elsewhere, by the two World Wars. Welfare rather than freedom became the dominant note in democratic countries. Recognizing the implicit threat to individualism, the intellectual descendants of the Philosophical Radicals — Dicey, Mises, Hayek, and Simons, to mention only a few—feared that a continued movement toward centralized control of economic activity would prove *The Road to Serfdom*, as Hayek entitled his penetrating analysis of the process. Their emphasis was on economic freedom as a means toward political freedom.

14   Events since the end of World War II display still a different relation between economic and political freedom. Collectivist[5] economic planning has indeed interfered with individual freedom. At least in some countries, however, the result has not been the suppression of freedom, but the reversal of economic policy. England again provides the most striking example. The turning point was perhaps the "control of engagements" order which, despite great misgivings, the Labour party found it necessary to impose in order to carry out its economic policy. Fully enforced and carried through, the law would have involved centralized allocation of individuals to occupations. This conflicted so sharply with personal liberty that it was enforced in a negligible number of cases, and then repealed after the law had been in effect for only a short period. Its repeal ushered in a decided shift in economic policy, marked by reduced reliance on centralized "plans" and "programs," by the dismantling of many controls, and by increased emphasis on the private market. A similar shift in policy occurred in most other democratic countries.

15   The proximate explanation of these shifts in policy is the limited success of central planning or its outright failure to achieve stated objectives. However, this failure is itself to be attributed, at least in some measure, to the political implications of central planning and to an unwillingness to follow out its logic when doing so requires trampling rough-shod on treasured private rights. It may well be that the shift is only a temporary interruption in the collectivist trend of this century. Even so, it illustrates the close relation between political freedom and economic arrangements.

---

[4] Jeremy Bentham (1748-1832): English jurist, intellectual, and social theorist best known for his challenge to the idea of "natural law" and "natural rights."

[5] Collectivist: a central feature of democratic socialism, a form of social and economic behavior in which individuals work with others in the service of the collective material good. Contrasts with "individualist."

16   Historical evidence by itself can never be convincing. Perhaps it was sheer coincidence that the expansion of freedom occurred at the same time as the development of capitalist and market institutions. Why should there be a connection? What are the logical links between economic and political freedom? In discussing these questions we shall consider first the market as a direct component of freedom, and then the indirect relation between market arrangements and political freedom. A byproduct will be an outline of the ideal economic arrangements for a free society.

17   As liberals, we take freedom of the individual, or perhaps the family, as our ultimate goal in judging social arrangements. Freedom as a value in this sense has to do with the interrelations among people; it has no meaning whatsoever to a Robinson Crusoe on an isolated island (without his Man Friday). Robinson Crusoe[6] on his island is subject to "constraint," he has limited "power," and he has only a limited number of alternatives, but there is no problem of freedom in the sense that is relevant to our discussion. Similarly, in a society freedom has nothing to say about what an individual does with his freedom; it is not an all-embracing ethic. Indeed, a major aim of the liberal is to leave the ethical problem for the individual to wrestle with. The "really" important ethical problems are those that face an individual in a free society—what he should do with his freedom. There are thus two sets of values that a liberal will emphasize—the values that are relevant to relations among people, which is the context in which he assigns first priority to freedom; and the values that are relevant to the individual in the exercise of his freedom, which is the realm of individual ethics and philosophy.

18   The liberal conceives of men as imperfect beings. He regards the problem of social organization to be as much a negative problem of preventing "bad" people from doing harm as of enabling "good" people to do good; and, of course, "bad" and "good" people may be the same people, depending on who is judging them.

19   The basic problem of social organization is how to co-ordinate the economic activities of large numbers of people. Even in relatively backward societies, extensive division of labor and specialization of function is required to make effective use of available resources. In advanced societies, the scale on which coordination is needed, to take full advantage of the opportunities offered by modern science and technology, is enormously greater. Literally millions of people are involved in providing one another with their daily bread, let alone with their yearly automobiles. The challenge to the believer in liberty is to reconcile this widespread interdependence with individual freedom.

20   Fundamentally, there are only two ways of coordinating the economic activities of millions. One is central direction involving the use of coercion—the technique of the army and of the modern totalitarian state. The other is voluntary cooperation of individuals—the technique of the market place.

21   The possibility of coordination through voluntary cooperation rests on the elementary—yet frequently denied—proposition that both parties to an economic transaction benefit from it, *provided the transaction is bi-laterally voluntary and informed.*

---

[6] Robinson Crusoe: title character in a novel published by Daniel Defoe in 1719. Sometimes considered the first novel in English.

22   Exchange can therefore bring about co-ordination without coercion. A working model of a society organized through voluntary exchange is a *free private enterprise exchange economy*—what we have been calling competitive capitalism.

23   In its simplest form, such a society consists of a number of independent households—a collection of Robinson Crusoes, as it were. Each household uses the resources it controls to produce goods and services that it exchanges for goods and services produced by other households, on terms mutually acceptable to the two parties to the bargain. It is thereby enabled to satisfy its wants indirectly by producing goods and services for others, rather than directly by producing goods for its own immediate use. The incentive for adopting this indirect route is, of course, the increased product made possible by division of labor and specialization of function. Since the household always has the alternative of producing directly for itself, it need not enter into any exchange unless it benefits from it. Hence, no exchange will take place unless both parties do benefit from it. Cooperation is thereby achieved without coercion.

24   Specialization of function and division of labor would not go far if the ultimate productive unit were the household. In a modern society, we have gone much farther. We have introduced enterprises which are intermediaries between individuals in their capacities as suppliers of service and as purchasers of goods. And similarly, specialization of function and division of labor could not go very far if we had to continue to rely on the barter of product for product. In consequence, money has been introduced as a means of facilitating exchange, and of enabling the acts of purchase and of sale to be separated into two parts.

25   Despite the important role of enterprises and of money in our actual economy, and despite the numerous and complex problems they raise, the central characteristic of the market technique of achieving coordination is fully displayed in the simple exchange economy that contains neither enterprises nor money. As in that simple model, so in the complex enterprise and money-exchange economy, cooperation is strictly individual and voluntary *provided:* (a) that enterprises are private, so that the ultimate contracting parties are individuals and (b) that individuals are effectively free to enter or not to enter into any particular exchange, so that every transaction is strictly voluntary.

26   It is far easier to state these provisos in general terms than to spell them out in detail, or to specify precisely the institutional arrangements most conducive to their maintenance. Indeed, much of technical economic literature is concerned with precisely these questions. The basic requisite is the maintenance of law and order to prevent physical coercion of one individual by another and to enforce contracts voluntarily entered into, thus giving substance to "private." Aside from this, perhaps the most difficult problems arise from monopoly—which inhibits effective freedom by denying individuals alternatives to the particular exchange—and from "neighborhood effects"—effects on third parties for which it is not feasible to charge or recompense them. These problems will be discussed in more detail in the following chapter.

27   So long as effective freedom of exchange is maintained, the central feature of the market organization of economic activity is that it prevents one person from interfering with another in respect of most of his activities. The consumer is protected from coercion by the seller because of the presence of other sellers with whom he can deal. The seller is

protected from coercion by the consumer because of other consumers to whom he can sell. The employee is protected from coercion by the employer because of other employers for whom he can work, and so on. And the market does this impersonally and without centralized authority.

QUESTIONS ON MEANING

1. In what specific ways is economic freedom necessary for political freedom? In other words, why does Friedman consider democratic socialism a delusion?

2. Historically, how unique is political freedom? What is the more common condition in which people have lived?

3. What economic system coincides with the recent development of political freedom?

4. What is the basic problem of social organization confronted by modern societies?

5. In a free society built on the free market, how and why does cooperation occur without coercion?

6. In modern societies, why is money necessary as a medium of exchange?

QUESTIONS FOR DISCUSSION

1. Friedman objects to the coercive power of government in limiting political and economic freedom. How valid is this concern? Can the free market lead to other forms of coercion that limit human freedom?

2. What problems emerge when the government intervenes in the free market? How can we solve these problems?

3. In Friedman's terms, what does it mean to be a liberal? How is his usage different from our usual definition of the term? Why has our definition changed?

4. What role should the government play in relation to business and the economy?

LOOKING AT RHETORIC

1. How does Friedman use history to support his argument about the necessity of free markets? Does he think that relying on history is sufficient? Why or why not?

2. In the first paragraph, Friedman begins with a widely held belief that he then goes on to challenge. How does this challenge serve to structure his argument?

3. What other fields of academic interest inform economics? Consider Friedman's use of the past, as well as his discussion of the various forms of freedom.

WRITING ASSIGNMENTS

1. Using sources in economics, history, and political science research the various meanings of the word freedom, particularly political freedom and economic freedom. In observing the lives of yourself and others, do economic circumstances affect personal liberty? Are there ways in which the government restricts economic behavior and thus personal choices? Conversely, does government involvement in the economy in any way enhance an individual's freedom?

2. Argue for or against Friedman's claim that the single purpose of government is to act as umpire in the game of free enterprise. Are there ways we might think of government being a player in that game? If so, what are they? If not, why not?

3. In pairs or in groups, make a list of important personal freedoms, individual rights that are essential. Individually, write an essay exploring how the government's involvement in controlling business limits or enhances any one of these rights.

The End of Laissez-Faire

John Maynard Keynes

John Maynard Keynes (1883-1946) is regarded as one of the most important economists of the twentieth century. His writings address issues related to business and economics, as well as history and public policy. He took his degree in mathematics from Cambridge in 1905. After leaving the university, he worked in British Civil Service, and for many years alternated between the government and teaching. At the close of World War I, he was the Treasury Department's representative at the negotiations at Versailles but resigned his position, concluding that the treaty was excessively burdensome to the Germans. Most historians concur and argue that the economic effects of the agreement contributed to the rise of the Adolph Hitler and Nazi Party. Returning to teaching and writing in 1919, Keynes became a member of the famous Bloomsbury group of intellectuals, writers, and artists, which included Virginia Woolf, Bertrand Russell, and E. M. Forster. In the following selection, Keynes argues that government spending is an important tool in affecting employment and economic growth. Always a supporter of free markets, he nevertheless claims that state intervention is essential to the health of modern capitalism. These principles influenced contemporary economists and a number of American presidents, including Franklin Delano Roosevelt, John F. Kennedy, Lyndon B. Johnson, Bill Clinton, and Barack Obama.

1   Let us clear from the ground the metaphysical or general principles upon which, from time to time, *laissez-faire*[1] has been founded. It is *not* true that individuals possess a prescriptive "natural liberty" in their economic activities. There is *no* "compact" conferring perpetual rights on those who Have or on those who Acquire. The world is *not* so governed from above that private and social interest always coincide. It is *not* so managed here below that in practice they coincide. It is *not* a correct deduction from the Principles of Economics that enlightened self-interest always operates in the public interest. Nor is it true that self-interest generally *is* enlightened; more often individuals acting separately to promote their own ends are too ignorant or too weak to attain even these. Experience does *not* show that individuals, when they make up a social unit, are always less clear-sighted than when they act separately.

---

[1] Laissez-faire: a set of economic conditions in which individuals and markets operate freely without government regulation or intervention.

2   We cannot, therefore, settle on abstract grounds, but must handle on its merits in detail, what Burke[2] termed "one of the finest problems in legislation, namely, to determine what the State ought to take upon itself to direct by the public wisdom, and what it ought to leave, with as little interference as possible, to individual exertion." We have to discriminate between what Bentham,[3] in his forgotten but useful nomenclature, used to term *Agenda* and *Non-Agenda*, and to do this without Bentham's prior presumption that interference is at the same time, "generally needless" and "generally pernicious." Perhaps the chief task of Economists at this hour is to distinguish afresh the *Agenda* of Government from the *Non-Agenda*; and the companion task of Politics is to devise forms of Government within a Democracy which shall be capable of accomplishing the *Agenda*. I will illustrate what I have in mind by two examples.

3   (1) I believe that in many cases the ideal size for the unit of control and organization lies somewhere between the individual and the modern State. I suggest, therefore, that progress lies in the growth and the recognition of semiautonomous bodies within the State—bodies whose criterion of action within their own field is solely the public good as they understand it, and from whose deliberations motives of private advantage are excluded, though some place it may still be necessary to leave, until the ambit of men's altruism, grows wider, to the separate advantage of particular groups, classes, or faculties—bodies which in the ordinary course of affairs are mainly autonomous within their prescribed limitations, but are subject in the last resort to the sovereignty of the democracy expressed through Parliament.

4   I propose a return, it may be said, towards mediaeval conceptions of separate autonomies. But, in England at any rate, corporations are a mode of government which has never ceased to be important and is sympathetic to our institutions. It is easy to give examples, from what already exists, of separate autonomies which have attained or are approaching the mode I designate—the Universities, the Bank of England, the Port of London Authority, even perhaps the Railway Companies.

5   But more interesting than these is the trend of Joint Stock Institutions, when they have reached a certain age and size, to approximate to the status of public corporations rather than that of individualistic private enterprise. One of the most interesting and unnoticed developments of recent decades has been the tendency of big enterprise to socialize itself. A point arrives in the growth of a big institution—particularly a big railway or big public utility enterprise, but also a big bank or a big insurance company—at which the owners of the capital, i.e., the shareholders, are almost entirely dissociated from the management, with the result that the direct personal interest of the latter in the making of great profit becomes quite secondary. When this stage is reached, the general stability and reputation of the institution are more considered by the management than the maximum of profit for the shareholders. The shareholders must be satisfied by conventionally adequate dividends; but once this is secured, the direct interest of the management often consists in avoiding criticism from the public and from the customers of the concern. This is particularly the

---

[2] Edmund Burke (1729-1797): Anglo-Irish intellectual. In politics and economics, he explored the balance between state control through legislation and individual freedom.

[3] Jeremy Bentham (1748-1832): English philosopher and ethicist. He applied ethical principles to social policy, arguing that "the greatest happiness to the greatest number" should influence the development of laws.

case if their great size or semimonopolistic position renders them conspicuous in the public eye and vulnerable to public attack. The extreme instance, perhaps, of this tendency in the case of an institution, theoretically the unrestricted property of private persons, is the Bank of England. It is almost true to say that there is no class of persons in the Kingdom of whom the Governor of the Bank of England thinks less when he decides on his policy than of his shareholders. Their rights, in excess of their conventional dividend, have already sunk to the neighborhood of zero. But the same thing is partly true of many other big institutions. They are, as time goes on, socializing themselves.

6   Not that this is unmixed gain. The same causes promote conservatism and a waning of enterprise. In fact, we already have in these cases many of the faults as well as the advantages of State Socialism. Nevertheless we see here, I think, a natural line of evolution. The battle of Socialism against unlimited private profit is being won in detail hour by hour. In these particular fields—it remains acute elsewhere—this is no longer the pressing problem. There is, for instance, no so-called important political question so really unimportant, so irrelevant to the reorganization of the economic life of Great Britain, as the Nationalization of the Railways.

7   It is true that many big undertakings, particularly Public Utility enterprises and other business requiring a large fixed capital, still need to be semisocialized. But we must keep our minds flexible regarding the forms of this semisocialism. We must take full advantage of the natural tendencies of the day, and we must probably prefer semiautonomous corporations to organs of the Central Government for which Ministers of State are directly responsible.

8   I criticize doctrinaire State Socialism,[4] not because it seeks to engage men's altruistic impulses in the service of Society, or because it departs from *laissez-faire*, or because it takes away from man's natural liberty to make a million, or because it has courage for bold experiments. All these things I applaud. I criticize it because it misses the significance of what is actually happening; because it is, in fact, little better than a dusty survival of a plan to meet the problems of fifty years ago, based on a misunderstanding of what some one said a hundred years ago. Nineteenth-century State Socialism sprang from Bentham, free competition, etc., and is in some respects a clearer, in some respects a more muddled, version of just the same philosophy as underlies nineteenth-century individualism. Both equally laid all their stress on freedom, the one negatively to avoid limitations on existing freedom, the other positively to destroy natural or acquired monopolies. They are different reactions to the same intellectual atmosphere.

9   (2) I come next to a criterion of *Agenda* which is particularly relevant to what it is urgent and desirable to do in the near future. We must aim at separating those services which are *technically social* from those which are *technically individual*. The most important *Agenda* of the State relate not to those activities which private individuals are already fulfilling, but to those functions which fall outside the sphere of the individual, to those decisions which are made by *no one* if the State does not make them. The important thing for Government is not to do things which individuals are doing already, and to do them a little better or a little worse; but to do those things which at present are not done at all.

---

[4] State Socialism: A mode of economic organization in which the government is a central participant in the economy. The most extreme form of this system is Marxist communism, in which the state owns the means of production.

10   It is not within the scope of my purpose on this occasion to develop practical policies. I limit myself, therefore, to naming some instances of what I mean from among those problems about which I happen to have thought most.

11   Many of the greatest economic evils of our time are fruits of risk, uncertainty, and ignorance. It is because particular individuals, fortunate in situation or in abilities, are able to take advantage of uncertainty and ignorance, and also because for the same reason big business is often a lottery, that great inequalities of wealth come about; and these same factors are also the cause of the Unemployment of Labor, or the disappointment of reasonable business expectations, and of the impairment of efficiency and production. Yet the cure lies outside the operations of individuals; it may even be to the interest of individuals to aggravate the disease. I believe that the cure for these things is partly to be sought in the deliberate control of the currency and of credit by a central institution, and partly in the collection and dissemination on a great scale of data relating to the business situation, including the full publicity, by law if necessary, of all business facts which it is useful to know. These measures would involve Society in exercizing directive intelligence through some appropriate organ of action over many of the inner intricacies of private business, yet it would leave private initiative and enterprise unhindered. Even if these measures prove insufficient, nevertheless they will furnish us with better knowledge than we have now for taking the next step.

12   My second example relates to Savings and Investment. I believe that some coordinated act of intelligent judgment is required as to the scale on which it is desirable that the community as a whole should save, the scale on which these savings should go abroad in the form of foreign investments, and whether the present organization of the investment market distributes savings along the most nationally productive channels. I do not think that these matters should be left entirely to the chances of private judgment and private profits, as they are at present.

13   My third example concerns Population. The time has already come when each country needs a considered national policy about what size of Population, whether larger or smaller than at present or the same, is most expedient. And having settled this policy, we must take steps to carry it into operation. The time may arrive a little later when the community as a whole must pay attention to the innate quality as well as to the mere numbers of its future members.

14   These reflections have been directed towards possible improvements in the technique of modern Capitalism by the agency of collective action. There is nothing in them which is seriously incompatible with what seems to me to be the essential characteristic of Capitalism, namely the dependence upon an intense appeal to the money-making and money-loving instincts of individuals as the main motive force of the economic machine. Nor must I, so near to my end, stray towards other fields. Nevertheless, I may do well to remind you, in conclusion, that the fiercest contests and the most deeply felt divisions of opinion are likely to be waged in the coming years not round technical questions, where the arguments on either side are mainly economic, but round those which, for want of better words, may be called psychological or, perhaps, moral.

15   In Europe, or at least in some parts of Europe—but not, I think, in the United States of America—there is a latent reaction; somewhat widespread, against basing Society to the extent that we do upon fostering, encouraging, and protecting the money-motive of

individuals. A preference for arranging our affairs in such a way as to appeal to the money-motive as little as possible, rather than as much as possible, need not be entirely *a priori*,[5] but may be based on the comparison of experiences. Different persons, according to their choice of profession, find the money-motive playing a large or a small part in their daily lives, and historians can tell us about other phases of social organization in which this motive has played a much smaller part than it does now. Most religions and most philosophies deprecate, to say the least of it, a way of life mainly influenced by considerations of personal money profit. On the other hand, most men today reject ascetic notions and do not doubt the real advantages of wealth. Moreover it seems obvious to them that one cannot do without the money-motive, and that, apart from certain admitted abuses, it does its job well. In the result the average man averts his attention from the problem, and has no clear idea what he really thinks and feels about the whole confounded matter.

16   Confusion of thought and feeling leads to confusion of speech. Many people, who are really objecting to Capitalism as a way of life, argue as though they were objecting to it on the ground of its inefficiency in attaining its own objects. Contrariwise, devotees of Capitalism are often unduly conservative, and reject reforms in its technique, which might really strengthen and preserve it, for fear that they may prove to be first steps away from Capitalism itself. Nevertheless a time may be coming when we shall get clearer than at present as to when we are talking about Capitalism as an efficient or inefficient technique, and when we are talking about it as desirable or objectionable in itself. For my part, I think that Capitalism, wisely managed, can probably be made more efficient for attaining economic ends than any alternative system yet in sight, but that in itself it is in many ways extremely objectionable. Our problem is to work out a social organization which shall be as efficient as possible without offending our notions of a satisfactory way of life.

17   The next step forward must come, not from political agitation or premature experiments, but from thought. We need by an effort of the mind to elucidate our own feelings. At present our sympathy and our judgment are liable to be on different sides, which is a painful and paralysing state of mind. In the field of action reformers will not be successful until they can steadily pursue a clear and definite object with their intellects and their feelings in tune. There is no party in the world at present which appears to me to be pursuing right aims by right methods. Material Poverty provides the incentive to change precisely in situations where there is very little margin for experiments. Material Prosperity removes the incentive just when it might be safe to take a chance. Europe lacks the means, America the will, to make a move. We need a new set of convictions which spring naturally from a candid examination of our own inner feelings in relation to the outside facts.

QUESTIONS ON MEANING

1. What is Keynes's perspective on the value of enlightened self-interest? In what way does he challenge its effects?

2. What is his perspective on the social benefit of individualism versus cooperation in social and economic matters?

---

[5] *A priori*: presupposed by experience.

3. At the time Keynes wrote this selection (and arguably in contemporary times), what was the chief task of economists?

4. What does Keynes mean when he argues for the separation of those services that are *technically social* from *technically individual*?

5. In the context of modern societies, what are the values and limitations of the money-motive?

6. Why are devotees of capitalism unduly conservative in considering reform that involves an active governmental role in the economy?

QUESTIONS FOR DISCUSSION

1. Given some of the complexities of modern capitalism, what problems might we identify with *laissez-faire*, with the unregulated and completely private operation of markets? Are there any significant problems?

2. Aside from restricting innovation and the productive economic benefits of the money-motive, what are some other difficulties with doctrinaire State Socialism?

3. Like Keynes, can we acknowledge capitalism as the most effective economic system, while considering it in many ways extremely objectionable? If so, what is effective about it? What is objectionable?

4. In what way might we benefit by employing thought rather than political agitation and premature experiments as the next step in economic reform?

LOOKING AT RHETORIC

1. In the first paragraph, how does Keynes challenge the commonly held assumptions about human nature upon which traditional economics is based? In what way does this establish a foundation for his controversial claims?

2. What role do the facts of contemporary history play in assisting him in making his argument? How effectively does he make those facts apply to the future as well?

3. What other fields of academic interest inform economics? Consider his commentary on human behavior, natural rights, individual versus collective action.

WRITING ASSIGNMENTS

1. Argue for or against Keynes's claim that moderate collective action through the government strengthens the economy. Seek examples to support your points.

2. In what way are you driven by the money motive? To the extent that you are, how do you justify it ethically? What other motives influence your behavior and choices? Can you effectively balance these mixed desires?

3. In pairs or in groups, make a list of essential human rights and basic features of human nature. Then discuss whether or not anything on these lists come into conflict. Individually, write an essay that uses any one (or any combination) of these to argue for the limitation or the expansion of *laissez-faire*.

Interdisciplinary Connections

Doing Business in America

What do these two images say about what it means to work in America in the early twentieth century? What do they say about American culture? What do they suggest about the American Dream itself?

Margaret Bourke White, Bread line during the Louisville Flood, 1937

http://www.masters-of-photography.com/B/bourke-white/b-w_living_full.html

Rosie the Riveter Poster

http://www.acclaimimages.com/_gallery/_pages/0420-0611-1314-4657.html

Leadership

Warts and All

By Barbara Kellerman

Barbara Kellerman earned her B.A. from Sarah Lawrence College in 1969 and her M.A. in Russian and Eastern European Studies from Yale University in 1971. She completed her M.Phil. in 1972 and her Ph.D. in 1975, also at Yale. She was the Founding Executive Director of the Kennedy School's Center for Public Leadership at Harvard University, and she has taught at Fordham, Tufts, Fairleigh Dickinson, George Washington, and Uppsala Universities. She is a frequent television commentator, author of several articles and reviews, the author and editor of numerous books including Leadership: Multidisciplinary Perspectives *(1984),* The Political Presidency: Practice of Leadership *(1984), and* Followership: How Followers are Creating Change and Changing Leaders *(2008). Kellerman's writing addresses issues ranging from economics and business to sociology and history. The following article was originally published in* The Harvard Business Review, *and it challenges the commonly held notion that effective leadership and ethical behavior go hand in hand.*

1   "We tell ourselves stories in order to live," Joan Didion once wrote, to explain the unfounded optimism human beings display. Good stories make the world more bearable. Inevitably, therefore, we want to tell—and be told—stories that make us feel better, even if that means that we don't get as complete a picture as we need.

2   People who study leaders have fallen victim to this instinct in a big way. In the leadership literature of the past several decades, almost all successful authors have fed into their readers' (and perhaps their own) yearnings for feel-good stories. Just reflect on some of the best sellers of the last 20 to 30 years: Thomas J. Peters and Robert H. Waterman, Jr.'s *In Search of Excellence;* Warren Bennis and Burt Nanus's *Leaders: Strategies for Taking Charge;* John P. Kotter's *A force for Change: How Leadership Differs from Management;* and Jay A. Conger and Beth Benjamin's *Building Leaders.* Although a few authors have recently taken exception to the blind belief in the inherent goodness of leadership—notably Sydney Finkelstein in his book *Why Smart Executives Fail and What You Can Learn from Their Mistakes*—most of the hugely successful scholars argue, often with passion, that effective leaders are persons of merit, or at least of good intentions. It almost seems that by definition bad people cannot be good leaders.

3   If most leaders were worthy people, it would be easy to understand why we accentuate the positive. But the reality is, of course, that flawed leaders are everywhere. In corporations, overweening personal ambition and greed have driven many a CEO to run afoul of the law. In the last couple of years alone, scores of powerful and successful executives have been indicted for financial wrongdoing of various kinds. Think of Andy Fastow of Enron and Dennis Kozlowski at Tyco. Even homemaking diva Martha Stewart has joined the ranks of the indicted. As the *New York Times* wryly quipped, it now "takes a scorecard to keep up with corporate scandals in America."

4   Of course, corporations don't have a corner on the market in bad leaders. Politics is replete with the most extreme of examples. Hitler, Stalin, and Pol Pot come immediately to mind all power-mad and evil but nonetheless highly effective as leaders. These extreme cases aside, stories about the failings of more reasonable public officials litter the newspaper headlines. Consider Peter Mandelson, a member of Tony Blair's cabinet, respected both for his political skills and his understanding of public policy. In 1998, Mandelson was forced to resign from the cabinet after it was revealed that he had accepted an improper loan of £373,000 to help buy a swanky home in London's Notting Hill.

5   And, certainly, it doesn't end there. Accounts of the "wayward shepherds" in the Roman Catholic Church, as one journalist put it, continue to mount. To name just two of the highest profile examples: In 2003, a grand jury alleged that Roman Catholic authorities on Long Island, New York, had long conspired to protect 58 "rogue clergymen" from facing charges of sexual abuse. And in Boston, no fewer than 86 people filed civil lawsuits against John J. Geoghan, the convicted child molester who was later murdered in prison. Again and again, the suits alleged Cardinal Bernard F. Law, archbishop of the Boston Catholic Archdiocese for 18 years, returned Geoghan to parish work although Law had evidence that Geoghan repeatedly molested boys.

6   It is impossible to deny that bad or at least unworthy people often occupy and successfully fill top leadership positions, and it is high time leadership experts acknowledge the fact. For, contrary to the expectations of these experts, we have as much to learn from people we would regard as bad examples as we do from the far less numerous good examples we're presented with these days. Is Martha Stewart's career as a successful entrepreneur any the less instructive because she may have once sold some shares on the basis of a tip-off? Does Law's gross negligence on the issue of child abuse negate the fact that during his years in Boston he effectively managed to balance his traditional view of the church with progressive positions on discrimination and poverty? In the following pages, I shall attempt to explain how we came to accept such a skewed, moralistic understanding of leadership and in doing so I hope to put the warts—and the reality—back into the picture.

LEADERS WEREN'T ALWAYS NICE

7   Although most contemporary scholarship is focused on leaders who are blemish-free, it was not always that way. Throughout history nearly all the great political theorists have recognized the reality of bad leaders, often accentuating the need to control their malicious tendencies. Influenced by religious traditions that focus on good and evil, and often personally affected by the trauma of war and internal disorder, political thinkers in former times took rather a jaundiced view of human nature.

8   Consider Machiavelli,[1] a player in fifteenth and sixteenth-century Florentine politics and often a witness to brutal warfare. Famous for his advice to political players in his classic book *The Prince*, Machiavelli outlined opportunities associated with forceful leadership.

---

[1] Niccolo Machiavelli (1469-1527): Writer and philosopher of the Italian Renaissance and one of the founders of modern political science. His work is pragmatic and realist in nature, and it has often (somewhat inappropriately) been associated with malevolence and deceit in political dealings.

For most of us, coercive leadership almost by definition equals bad leadership. But as someone who was familiar both with the ways of the world and with the human psyche, Machiavelli argued that the only truly bad leadership is weak leadership. His philosophy was predicated on the assumption that some leaders need to use force to hold personal power and to maintain public order. Machiavelli, therefore, actually admired unscrupulous leaders who exercised power and authority with an iron fist. And in *The Prince*, he wrote with apparent calm about the occasional need judiciously to apply "cruelties": "When he seizes a state, the new ruler ought to determine all the injuries that he will need to inflict. . . . Whoever acts otherwise, either through timidity or bad advice, is always forced to have the knife ready in his hand, and he can never depend on his subjects because they, suffering fresh and continuous violence, can never feel secure with regard to him."

9   Like Machiavelli, the Founding Fathers of the United States had personal experience of bad leadership, and they thought about it a great deal. Indeed, they were some of the greatest students of leadership of all time. But their reaction to bad leadership could hardly have been further from that of the author of *The Prince*. They understood that leadership is easily corrupted and often malign, and therefore they went to extraordinary lengths to construct a constitution that makes it hard for leaders to accomplish much without the negotiated consent of their followers. Thus, in contrast to modern leadership experts who focus on how leaders can be more effective, the Founding Fathers looked for ways to rein leaders in, to ensure that leaders could act only after building a coalition of partners.

10   In *The Federalist*,[2] for example, Alexander Hamilton dedicated an entire paper to exploring the differences between the proposed presidency and the distant, detested monarchy with which his American audience had struggled. The king of Great Britain was a dreaded hereditary monarch; by contrast, the American president would be elected for only four years. The king's position was sacred and inviolable, but the president could be impeached, tried, and, under certain conditions, even removed from office. In short, the U.S. Constitution was created to preclude the possibility that bad leadership could become entrenched. The very idea of checks and balances grew out of the framers' suspicion that unless the proposed government had a balance of power, then power would almost certainly be abused.

11   We know this. How could we not, after the twentieth century, with not just Stalin, Hitler, and Pol Pot but Idi Amin, Mao Tse-tung, and Slobodan Milosevic? As the late Leo Strauss, a professor of political philosophy at the University of Chicago, bitterly put it in his classic treatise *On Tyranny*, the tyrannies of the twentieth century are so horrendous that they "surpass the boldest imagination of the most powerful thinkers of the past." Having barely escaped the Holocaust, Strauss recognized what our leadership experts seem to have forgotten: Capricious, murderous, high-handed, corrupt, and evil leaders are effective and everywhere—except in the literature of business leadership.

---

[2] *The Federalist*: In the twentieth century sometimes known as *The Federalist Papers*, a series of eighty-five articles advocating the ratification of the United States Constitution. They were published in *The Independent Journal* and *The New York Packet* in 1787 and 1788. The authors were Alexander Hamilton, James Madison, and John Jay.

WHERE THE THEORY WENT WRONG

12   To grasp how dramatically we have moved in our thinking on leadership from Machiavelli and Hamilton, it is helpful to see how the words "leader" and "leadership" in everyday language have acquired an inherently positive bias. Consider Lawrence Summers's speech when he assumed the presidency of Harvard University in 2001: "In this new century, nothing will matter more than the education of future leaders." Harvard's "Statement of Values," published in August 2002, picks up this same optimism when it says that the university "aspires . . . to prepare individuals for life, work, and leadership." In both cases, the words "leader" and "leadership" have been transformed from their Hamiltonian sense. Of course, Harvard is not alone in equating the word "leader" with outstanding human qualities. Yale president Richard Levin claims that the university's goal is to become truly global by "educating leaders." As we have already seen, most popular books on business leadership also equate the term with good leadership, and many books on political leadership follow suit.

13   The start of the transformation of leadership into something overwhelmingly positive can be traced in part to James MacGregor Burns. A biographer of Franklin Delano Roosevelt, Burns is a Pulitzer Prize–winning historian and political scientist of impeccable repute. In 1978, Burns published *Leadership*, an analysis and distillation of what he had learned about the subject in his lifelong study of politics. The book had a major impact both because of Burns's stature and because it appeared just before the teaching and study of leadership began its rapid growth. In it, Burns differentiated between "leaders," who by definition take the motives and goals of followers into account, and lesser mortals whom he labeled "power wielders." Burns's position was uncompromising: "Power wielders may treat people as things. Leaders may not." Burns's definition of leadership continues to dominate the field. For example, in the 2003 introduction to his widely read book *On Becoming a Leader*, Warren Bennis restates the position he took when the book first came out in 1989: Leaders create shared meaning, have a distinctive voice, have the capacity to adapt, and have integrity. In other words, for both Bennis and Burns—and indeed for most of their colleagues—to be a leader is, by definition, to be benevolent.

14   At about the same time as Burns's book appeared, another group of leadership theorists, led by Abraham Zaleznik, a psychoanalyst on the faculty of Harvard Business School, started to draw a distinction between "leaders" and "managers." In this construction, the leader is an inspirational and aspirational figure, while the manager handles the duller tasks of administration and maintains organizational discipline. (Zaleznik's classic HBR article, "Managers and Leaders: Are They Different?" is reprinted in this issue.) But by casting the leader in such a heroic light, these leadership theorists only strengthened the confusion between leadership and goodness.

15   Business gurus were as much responding to market forces as propounding a new doctrine. During the last 25 years, the leadership field developed primarily in response to the needs of American corporations, which by the mid-1970s were running into trouble. As Rosabeth Moss Kanter put it in her book *The Change Masters*, published in 1983, "Not long ago, American companies seemed to control the world in which they operated." Now, she said, they are in a much scarier place, in which the control of oil by OPEC,

foreign competition (then primarily from Japan), inflation, and regulation "disturb the smooth workings of corporate machines and threaten to overwhelm us." In response to this growing concern, American companies turned to business schools for concrete help in fixing what was wrong, and it is around this time that the leadership industry may be said to have begun in earnest. In 1982, funds were pledged to Harvard Business School to endow the Konosuke Matsushita Professor of Leadership, and there are now similar leadership chairs at other universities, including Columbia and the University of Michigan.

16   The fact that the contemporary leadership field is an American product—an American seed planted in American soil and harvested by American scholars, educators, and consultants—has profound implications for how we understand leaders. For one thing, current views of leaders have taken on aspects of the American national character. In particular, the positive thinking that infuses our national spirit finds its way into our leadership training. So, too, does the American dedication to self-improvement. Almost without exception, America's most popular leaders have personified this sense of possibility. Ronald Reagan captured the sentiment during one of the 1980 presidential debates. Evoking Thomas Paine and John Winthrop, he declared: "I believe . . . together we can begin the world over again. We can meet our destiny—and that destiny is to build a land here that will be, for all mankind, a shining city on a hill."[3]

WHAT WE CAN LEARN FROM BAD LEADERS

17   While the optimism of a Ronald Reagan can be highly inspirational—and even effective—as Reagan's own presidency showed, it can also lead to simplistic ideas about who leaders are and what they can do. Reagan himself provides us with many examples. Biographer Lou Cannon pointed out one: "The president was so cut off from the counsel of black Americans that he sometimes did not even realize when he was offending them."

18   People can easily accept the idea that there are lessons to be found in success stories. But it's a mistake to assume that we can learn nothing from fallen leaders. Indeed, some leaders achieve great things by capitalizing on the dark sides of their souls. Richard Nixon—relegated by many to the realm of mere "power wielder" after Watergate—was able to inaugurate diplomatic relations with China by capitalizing on his famous paranoia. No one thought that a suspicious and obsessed Nixon would be soft on Communism! Even monsters can teach us something about how to lead people. Hitler, for example, was a master of manipulating communications.

19   Likewise, many a lesson can be learned from business leaders' blunders and even from their malfeasance. Take the case of Howell Raines, the former executive editor of the *New York Times*. In the last several years, no leader has fallen further faster than

---

[3] Reagan derives the notion of a "shining city on a hill" from John Winthrop (1587/8-1649), who in his sermon "A Model of Christian Charity" (delivered on board the *Arabella* in transit to the colonies) announced the purpose of the Puritan mission in the New World. Winthrop echoes St. Augustine's (354-430) *City of God*.

Raines, who was forced to resign after only 21 months on the job. According to popular analysis, Raines had to go because reporter Jayson Blair committed multiple transgressions on Raines's watch. Raines might have survived his trial by fire if only he had not had a reputation for being high-handed and callous. No one who worked for Raines loved him; some people even considered him tyrannical.

20   But in all the postmortems about what Raines did wrong, few people have stopped to ask what he did right. We can safely assume that a man like Howell Raines did not get offered the most prestigious job in American journalism without being prodigiously gifted. The fact is that Raines was one of the great talents in the newspaper business. He had experience and expertise (he won his own Pulitzer Prize), and he had a stunning record of accomplishment. Under his leadership, the *New York Times* won an unprecedented seven Pulitzers for its coverage of the issues relating to the terrorist attacks of September 11, 2001.

21   Someday, when the story is dissected more dispassionately, I believe that we will find something to learn from Howell Raines's failure. Raines was a man of first-rate functional talent—an excellent writer, accomplished editor, a man with an unparalleled news sense and knowledge of how to cover a big story. What he failed to recognize, it seems, is that expertise is only one dimension of leadership and can even be a misleading one. Rewarding only technical merit and ambition, as Raines did, leads to a distorted kind of management and a lack of checks and balances on the team.

22   Raines, of course, isn't the only fallen leader from whom we can learn. On June 4, 2002, Manhattan District Attorney Robert Morgenthau announced the indictment of former Tyco CEO Dennis Kozlowski for allegedly evading more than $1 million in taxes on purchases of fine art. It was not that Kozlowski needed to shortchange the government; in 1999, his total pay was around $170 million. Rather, it was that after a remarkably successful run as a corporate leader, Kozlowski's impudence caught up with him.

23   Much has been made in the press of Kozlowski's lavish purchases—his $6,000 shower curtain, $17,000 traveling toilet box, $1,650 appointment book, and his $15,000 dog-shaped umbrella stand. But there was another side to the man. For in addition to throwing a multi-million-dollar birthday party for his wife on company money, Kozlowski was a very gifted CEO whom businesspeople once talked about as a second Jack Welch. Since 1992, Kozlowski oversaw an ambitious campaign in which Tyco acquired more than $50 billion in new businesses. Indeed, the habit of successfully swallowing up companies landed Kozlowski on the cover of several business magazines, one of which dubbed him "The Most Aggressive CEO."

24   As with Raines, Kozlowski's strengths and weaknesses were inextricably linked. A leader who was driven by a high-stakes mentality, Kozlowski showed almost no fear when taking enormous risks, a tactic that often paid off in his acquisition strategy. But that same mind-set led to excruciating misjudgments in his personal life, eventually ruining his career. Could Kozlowski have had the good side of leadership without the bad? Probably not, for most leaders have both. It is when they are unaware of their darker sides, and so fail to guard against them, that they fall from grace. Once again, the real problem is not so much that leaders have their dark side, rather it is that they—and everyone else—choose to pretend they don't.

25   Scholars should remind us that leadership is not a moral concept. Leaders are like the rest of us: trustworthy and deceitful, cowardly and brave, greedy and generous. To assume that all good leaders are good people is to be willfully blind to the reality of the human condition, and it severely limits our scope for becoming more effective at leadership. Worse, it may cause the leaders among us to kid themselves into thinking that, because they are leaders, they must be trustworthy, brave, and generous and that they are never deceitful, cowardly, or greedy. That way lies disaster, for as we should all have learned by now, it is only when we recognize and manage our failings that we can achieve greatness—as people and as a society. Knowing that, then we can begin to explore the more interesting questions of leadership: Why do leaders behave badly? Why do followers follow bad leaders? How can bad leadership be slowed or even stopped?

QUESTIONS ON MEANING

1. How did Machiavelli define bad leadership and how were his ideas different from the American Founding Fathers?
2. Why is the American Constitution built on the assumption that most leadership will be immoral in nature? Immoral in what way?
3. According to Abraham Zaleznik, psychoanalyst on the faculty of Harvard Business School, what is the difference between a leader and a manager?
4. How have modern notions of effective leadership taken on aspects of the American national character?
5. How does the assumption that all good leaders are moral corrupt the leaders themselves?

QUESTIONS FOR DISCUSSION

1. Beyond what not to do, what can we learn from bad leaders? What makes them bad?
2. In what way is it helpful to accept that good leaders might be bad people? Should we accept this?
3. What does Kellerman mean when she says leadership is not a moral concept?
4. Does taking an optimistic view of human nature help or hinder us in our organizational and personal lives?

LOOKING AT RHETORIC

1. Throughout the essay, the author uses examples of political leaders such as Hitler, Stalin, Mao Tse-tung, and Pol Pot, as well as business leaders such as Dennis Kozlowski. How does she employ these examples? What does she do with them?
2. Kellerman begins the article with a quotation from Joan Didion that suggests something about the "real" nature of the world. In what way does this reference form a foundation for her argument?
3. What other fields of academic interest inform her article? Consider her references to Leo Strauss and Abraham Zaleznik.

WRITING ASSIGNMENTS

1. Argue for or against Kellerman's claim that negative personal attributes often lead to effective leadership. Consider especially her reference to Richard Nixon's paranoia leading to his negotiation with China.

2. Identify a leader you have served under, such as a teacher, a coach, a supervisor at work. Consider the details of their job and the work situation. What personal qualities made them an effective or ineffective leader?

3. In pairs or in groups, make a list of qualities necessary for effective leadership. Try to avoid the pitfalls Kellerman identifies in many books on leadership by identifying both ethical and unethical characteristics. Individually, revise and trim that list. Then write an essay in which you describe a situation at work (or in any other context in which leadership is involved). Deal with how those qualities come into play in solving a problem. Explore the moral dimension of leadership.

Irrational Exuberance

Paul Krugman

Paul Krugman (b. 1953) is a well-known and highly respected contemporary economist. He earned his B. A. in Economics from Yale University in 1974 and his Ph.D. from Massachusetts Institution of Technology (MIT) in 1977. He worked briefly for the Reagan White House as a staff member for the Council for Economic Advisors, but he has spent the bulk of his career in academic posts at Yale, Berkeley, MIT, the London School of Economics, Stanford, and finally as Professor of Economics and International Affairs at Princeton. He won the Nobel Prize for Economics in 2008 for his study of international trade theory, and over the years he has developed a reputation both as a scholar and as a columnist for The New York Times, *making significant contributions to the public understanding of contemporary economic issues. He is primarily concerned with business and economics, but his writings have implications in government and public policy. The following was actually taken from two columns in* Fortune Magazine, *which were later collected in his volume* The Great Unraveling *(2003). "Irrational Exuberance" is the title of the first chapter, in which he deals with the common errors committed by investors in boom markets and explores their relationship to natural human behavior.*

1   I like the theory of efficient financial markets as much as anyone. I don't begrudge Robert Merton and Myron Scholes[1] the Nobel Prize they just received for showing how that theory can help you price complex financial instruments. But unless you spent the past five months in a Tibetan monastery, you must have noticed that markets have been behaving pretty strangely of late. As recently as June the "miracle" economies of Southeast Asia could do no wrong—investors cheerfully put billions into local stock markets. By October

---

[1] Robert Merton (b. 1944) and Myron Scholes (b. 1941): Winners of the 1997 Sveriges Riksbank Prize in Economic Sciences in Memory of Alfred Nobel.

those same investors were in full flight; after all, everyone could see how corrupt and badly managed those economies were. When the IMF[2] and the World Bank[3] held their September meeting in Hong Kong, everyone congratulated the hosts on their economic policies, which had insulated them from the turmoil to the south and maintained prosperity through the handover to China. A month later Hong Kong had not only crashed but had briefly brought Brazil and much of the rest of the world down with it.

2   What is the market up to? Well, I recently had a chance to listen to the market, or at least a fairly large part of it, when I attended a meeting of money managers. Collectively they control several hundred billion dollars, so when they talked, I listened. Mainly I wanted to know why such smart men and women—and they must be smart because if they aren't smart, why are they rich?—do such foolish things. Here's what I learned: the seven habits that help produce the anything-but-efficient markets that rule the world:

1. Think short term. A few people in that meeting tried to talk about the long term—about what kind of earnings growth U.S. corporations might be able to achieve over the next five years. This sort of thing was brushed aside as too academic. But wait: Any economist will tell you that even a short-term investor should look at the long run. This year's stock price depends on this year's earnings plus what people think the price will be next year. But next year's price will depend on next year's earnings plus what people next year expect the price to be the following year. . . . Today's price, then, should take into account earnings prospects well into the future. Try telling that to the practitioners.

2. Be greedy. Many of the people kept talking about how they expected a final "meltup" in prices before the big correction and how they planned to ride the market up for awhile longer. Well, maybe they were right, but if you really think stocks are overvalued, how confident should you be about your ability to time the inevitable plunge? Trying to get those extra few percent could be a very expensive proposition.

3. Believe in the greater fool. Several money managers argued that Asian markets have been oversold, but that one shouldn't buy in until those markets start to turn around—just as others argued that the U.S. market is overvalued, but they didn't plan to sell until the market started to weaken. The obvious question was, If it becomes clear to you that the market has turned around, won't it be clear to everyone else? Implicitly, they all seemed to believe that the strategy was safe because there is always someone else dense enough not to notice until it really is too late.

4. Run with the herd. You might have expected that a group of investors would have been interested to hear contrarian views from someone who suggested that the U.S.

---

[2] IMF: International Monetary Fund, the international organization that oversees the global financial system, particularly as it relates to exchange rates.
[3] World Bank: the international financial institution that offers loans to underdeveloped countries with the presumed goal of reducing poverty.

is on the verge of serious inflationary problems, or that Japan is poised for a rapid economic recovery, or that the *European Monetary Union*[4] is going to fail—which would have offered a nice challenge to conventional wisdom. But no: The few timid contrarians were ridiculed. The group apparently wanted conventional wisdom reinforced, not challenged.

5. Overgeneralize. I was amazed to hear the group condemn Japanese companies as uncompetitive, atrociously managed, unable to focus on the bottom line. But surely it can't be true of all Japanese companies; guys who managed to export even at 80 yen to the dollar must have at least a few tricks up their sleeves. And wasn't it only a couple of years ago that Japanese management techniques were the subject of hundreds of adulatory books and articles? They were never really that good, but surely they are better than their current reputation.

6. Be trendy. I came to the meeting expecting to hear a lot about the New Economic Paradigm, which asserts that technology and globalization mean that all the old rules have been repealed, that the inflation-free growth of the past six years will continue indefinitely, that we are at the start of a 20-year boom, etc. That doctrine is basically nonsense, of course—but anyway I quickly determined that it is, as they say in *Buffy the Vampire Slayer*, "so five minutes ago." All the rules have changed again: Now we stand on the brink of a dreadful epoch of global deflation, and despite its previous track record of engineering recoveries, there is nothing the Fed can do about it. You see, it's a new new economy.

7. Play with other people's money. If, as I said, the people at that meeting were very smart, why did they act in ways that seem so foolish? Part of the answer, I suspect, is that they are employees, not principals; they are trying to make money and careers for themselves. In that position, it is hard to take a long view: In the long run, even if you aren't dead, you probably won't be working in the same place. It is also difficult for someone managing other people's money to take an independent line. To be wrong when everyone else is wrong is not such a terrible thing: You may lose a bonus but probably not your job. On the other hand, to be wrong when everyone else is right . . . So everyone focuses on the same short-term numbers, tries to ride the trends, and buys the silly economic theory du jour.

3   Listening to all that money talking made me very nervous. After all, these people can funnel money into a country's markets, then abruptly pull that money out—and create a boombust cycle of pretty spectacular proportions. I don't think they can do it to the U.S.— in Greenspan I trust—but I am not 100% sure.

4   One thing that I am sure of is that the Asian leaders who have been fulminating against the evil machinations of speculators have it wrong. What I saw in that room was not a predatory pack of speculative wolves: It was an extremely dangerous flock of financial sheep.

---

[4] European Monetary Union: the collaboration of a number of European countries under a single currency.

THE ICE AGE COMETH

Fortune, *May 25, 1998*

5   The more I look at the amazing rise of the U.S. stock market, the more I become convinced that we are looking at a mammoth psychological problem. I don't mean mammoth as in "huge" (though maybe that too), but as in "elephant." Let me explain.

6   If you follow trends in psychology, you know that Freud is out and Darwin is in. The basic idea of "evolutionary psych"[5] is that our brains are exquisitely designed to help us cope with our environment—but unfortunately, the environment they are designed for is the one we evolved and lived in for the past two million years, not the alleged civilization we created just a couple of centuries ago. We are, all of us, hunter-gatherers lost in the big city. And therein, say the theorists, lie the roots of many of our bad habits. Our craving for sweets evolved in a world without ice cream; our interest in gossip evolved in a world without tabloids; our emotional response to music evolved in a world without Celine Dion. And we have investment instincts designed for hunting mammoths, not capital gains.

7   Imagine the situation back in what ev-psych types call the Ancestral Adaptive Environment. Suppose that two tribes—the Clan of the Cave Bear and its neighbor, the Clan of the Cave Bull—live in close proximity, but traditionally follow different hunting strategies. The Cave Bears tend to hunt rabbits—a safe strategy, since you can be pretty sure of finding a rabbit every day, but one with a limited upside, since a rabbit is only a rabbit. The Cave Bulls, on the other hand, go after mammoths—risky, since you never know when or if you'll find one, but potentially very rewarding, since mammoths are, well, mammoth.

8   Now suppose that it turns out that for the past year or two the Cave Bulls have been doing very well—making a killing practically every week. After this has gone on for a while, the natural instinct of the Cave Bears is to feel jealous, and to try to share in the good fortune by starting to act like Cave Bulls themselves. The reason this is a natural instinct, of course, is that in the ancestral environment it was entirely appropriate. The kinds of events that would produce a good run of mammoths—weather producing a good crop of grass, migration patterns bringing large numbers of beasts into the district—tended to be persistent, so it was a good idea to emulate whatever strategy had worked in the recent past.

9   But now transplant our tribes into the world of modern finance, and—at least according to finance theory—those instincts aren't appropriate at all. Efficient markets theory tells us that all the available information about a company is supposed to be already built into its current price, so that any future movement is inherently unpredictable—a random walk. In particular, the fact that people have made big capital gains in the past gives you absolutely no reason to think they will in the future. Rational investors, according to the

---

[5]"evolutionary psych": Evolutionary psychology, a research area in the discipline of psychology that explores human behavior in the context of evolutionary biology.

theory, should treat bygones as bygones: if last year your neighbor made a lot of money in stocks while you unfortunately stayed in cash, that's no reason to get into stocks now. But suppose that, for whatever reason, the market goes up month after month; your MBA-honed intellect may say, "Gosh, those P/Es[6] look pretty unreasonable," but your prehistoric programming is shrieking, "Me want mammoth meat!"—and those instincts are hard to deny.

10   And those instincts can be self-reinforcing, at least for a while. After all, whereas an increase in the number of people acting like Cave Bulls tended to mean fewer mammoths per hunter, an increase in the number of modern bulls tends to produce even bigger capital gains—as long as the run lasts. Any broker can tell you that in the last few months the market has been rising, despite mediocre earnings news, because of fresh purchases by ever more people distraught about having missed out on previous gains and desperate to get in on the action. Sooner or later the supply of such people will run out; then what?

11   O.K., O.K., I know that this isn't supposed to happen. Sophisticated investors are supposed to take the long view, and arbitrage[7] away these boom-bust cycles. And maybe, just maybe, the market is where it is because wise and far-seeing people have understood that the New Economy can produce growing profits forever, and that the rise of mutual funds has eliminated the need for old-fashioned risk premis. But my sense is that people who try to take a long view have been driven to the edge of extinction by the sheer scale of recent gains, and that the supposed explanations you now hear of why current prices make sense are rationalizations rather than serious theories.

12   The whole situation gives me the chills. It could be that I just don't get it, that I'm a Neanderthal too thick-skulled to understand the new era. But if you ask me, I'd say that there's an Ice Age just over the horizon.

QUESTIONS ON MEANING

1. What is the problem with short term thinking and excessive greed when they influence investors' behavior?
2. Why does investing other people's money lead to faulty judgment among professional investors?
3. What does Krugman mean when he says "Freud is out and Darwin is in"? How does he apply this to financial markets?
4. Why is our evolutionary psychology poorly adapted to modern financial markets?
5. Why are people who take the long view driven to extinction as investors in contemporary financial markets?

---

[6] P/E's: price-to-earnings ratio, a measure of the price paid per share of stock to the annual net income earned.
[7] Arbitrage: a financial and investment practice of taking advantage of price differentials between two different markets.

QUESTIONS FOR DISCUSSION

1. Do Krugman's seven habits of highly defective investors contribute to difficult economic circumstances for all of us? If so, how? If not, what are some other possibilities?

2. How valid is the author's use of evolutionary psychology as it relates to economic behavior? Are we hunter-gatherers ill-adapted to the modern economic world?

3. Is there anything unethical about a situation in which investors make their living playing with other people's money? If so, why? If not, why not?

4. Krugman argues that investors typically respond to a herd instinct, following boom markets when it's too late. Do you think this is true? If so, how do we guard against it?

LOOKING AT RHETORIC

1. In the first section, Krugman lists seven habits of poor investors. Does this linear pattern of organization help him clarify his ideas?

2. What role do current events play in these two columns, both of which appeared in a popular investment magazine? Are there universal economic principles that apply in all times and places which can be taken from his study of recent circumstances? If so, does he make them clear?

3. What other fields of academic interest inform his economics? Consider his references to Freud and Darwin, as well as to cave bulls and cave bears.

WRITING ASSIGNMENTS

1. Argue for or against Krugman's use of evolutionary psychology, the idea that our instinctual behaviors are poorly adapted to the modern world. Use research to support your points, and if you disagree, what other explanation for the problems he deals with can you offer?

2. You may or may not have invested money in markets, but have you ever felt yourself responding to the herding instinct? If so, why do you do this? If not, why do others? When necessary, what can you do to resist this impulse?

3. In pairs or in groups, make a list of herd behaviors, things you feel compelled to do because others do them. Individually, write an essay exploring why people tend to act this way. Then develop a strategy for responding differently when it is reasonable to do so.

Information Asymmetry

Steven D. Levitt and Stephen J. Dubner

Steven D. Levitt (b. 1967) is an American economist who has established a reputation in the field of price theory and has done significant work dealing with the economics of criminality, specifically the relationship of legalized abortion and crime. He graduated from Harvard in 1989, receiving his Ph.D. from Massachusetts Institute of Technology (MIT) in 1994.

He currently teaches at the University of Chicago as the William B. Ogden Distinguished Professor of Economics, where he is the director of The Becker Center on Price Theory. In 2003, he was the recipient of the John Bates Clark Medal, awarded by the American Economics Association to the Best U. S. Economist under the age of forty. Stephen J. Dubner (b. 1963) is an American journalist who has written for The New York Times Magazine, The New York Times, The New Yorker, Time Magazine, *and* Slate, *among others. He has written many articles on a diverse array of subjects, including economics, sports, foreign policy, and even religion, drawing the latter in part from the personal experience of his family's conversion from Roman Catholicism to Judaism. He graduated from Appalachian State University in 1984 and earned an MFA in writing from Columbia University in 1990. Levitt and Dubner co-authored the bestselling book* Freakonomics: A Rogue Economist Explores the Hidden Side of Everything *(2005), from which the following excerpt is taken. Their writing engages questions of business in the context of the social sciences. This selection considers how sellers in a free enterprise system use information to their advantage, and how the Internet is changing the buyer and seller relationship.*

1   The Internet, powerful as it is, has hardly slain the beast that is information asymmetry. Consider the so-called corporate scandals of the early 2000s. The crimes committed by Enron included hidden partnerships, disguised debt, and the manipulation of energy markets. Henry Blodget of Merrill Lynch and Jack Grubman of Salomon Smith Barney wrote glowing research reports of companies they knew to be junk. Sam Waksal dumped his ImClone stock when he got early word of a damaging report from the Food and Drug Administration; his friend Martha Stewart also dumped her shares, then lied about the reason. WorldCom[1] and Global Crossing[2] fabricated billions of dollars in revenues to pump up their stock prices. One group of mutual fund companies let preferred customers trade at preferred prices, and another group was charged with hiding management fees.

2   Though extraordinarily diverse, these crimes all have a common trait: they were sins of information. Most of them involved an expert, or a gang of experts, promoting false information or hiding true information; in each case the experts were trying to keep the information asymmetry as asymmetrical as possible.

3   The practitioners of such acts, especially in the realm of high finance, inevitably offer this defense: "Everybody else was doing it." Which may be largely true. One characteristic of information crimes is that very few of them are detected. Unlike street crimes, they do not leave behind a corpse or a broken window. Unlike a bagel criminal—that is, someone who eats one of Paul Feldman's bagels but doesn't pay—an information criminal typically doesn't have someone like Feldman tallying every nickel. For an information crime to reach the surface, something drastic must happen. When it does, the results tend to be pretty revealing. The perpetrators, after all, weren't thinking about their private actions being made public. Consider the "Enron tapes," the secretly recorded conversations of

---

[1] WorldCom: American telecommunications company that grew significantly in the 1990's but failed amidst corruption and accounting fraud, resulting in the largest chapter eleven bankruptcy in United States history.
[2] Global Crossing: Telecommunications company that provides worldwide computer networking service, known in the past for the lavish spending of its executives and their political contributions. The company was purchased by Singapore Technologies Telemedia, thus avoiding bankruptcy.

Enron employees that surfaced after the company imploded. During a phone conversation on August 5, 2000, two traders chatted about how a wildfire in Califomia would allow Enron[3] to jack up its electricity prices. "The magical word of the day," one trader said, "is 'Burn, Baby, Burn.'" A few months later, a pair of Enron traders named Kevin and Bob talked about how Califomia officials wanted to make Enron refund the profits of its price gouging.

> KEVIN: They're fucking taking all the money back from you guys? All the money you guys stole from those poor grandmas in Califomia?
> BOB: Yeah, Grandma Millie, man.
> KEVIN: Yeah, now she wants her fucking money back for all the power you jammed tight up her ass for fucking $250 a megawatt hour.

4   If you were to assume that many experts use their information to your detriment, you'd be right. Experts depend on the fact that you don't have the information they do. Or that you are so befuddled by the complexity of their operation that you wouldn't know what to do with the information if you had it. Or that you are so in awe of their expertise that you wouldn't dare challenge them. If your doctor suggests that you have angioplasty—even though some current research suggests that angioplasty often does little to prevent heart attacks—you aren't likely to think that the doctor is using his informational advantage to make a few thousand dollars for himself or his buddy. But as David Hillis, an interventional cardiologist at the University of Texas Southwestern Medical Center in Dallas, explained to the *New York Times*, a doctor may have the same economic incentives as a car salesman or a funeral director or a mutual fund manager: "If you're an invasive cardiologist and Joe Smith, the local internist, is sending you patients, and if you tell them they don't need the procedure, pretty soon Joe Smith doesn't send patients anymore."

5   Armed with information, experts can exert a gigantic, if unspoken, leverage: fear. Fear that your children will find you dead on the bathroom floor of a heart attack if you do not have angioplasty surgery. Fear that a cheap casket will expose your grandmother to a terrible underground fate. Fear that a $25,000 car will crumple like a toy in an accident, whereas a $50,000 car will wrap your loved ones in a cocoon of impregnable steel. The fear created by commercial experts may not quite rival the fear created by terrorists like the Ku Klux Klan, but the principle is the same.

6   Consider a transaction that wouldn't seem, on the surface, to create much fear: selling your house. What's so scary about that? Aside from the fact that selling a house is typically the largest financial transaction in your life, and that you probably have scant experience in real estate, and that you may have an enormous emotional attachment to your house, there are at least two pressing fears: that you will sell the house for far less than it is worth and that you will not be able to sell it at all.

---

[3] Enron: American energy company that in 2001 became embroiled in scandal when its vast financial loses were hidden by accounting fraud. It is considered a major contributor to the instability of the American economy the first decade of the twenty-first century.

7   In the first case, you fear setting the price too low; in the second, you fear setting it too high. It is the job of your real-estate agent, of course, to find the golden mean. She is the one with all the information: the inventory of similar houses, the recent sales trends, the tremors of the mortgage market, perhaps even a lead on an interested buyer. You feel fortunate to have such a knowledgeable expert as an ally in this most confounding enterprise.

8   Too bad she sees things differently. A real-estate agent may see you not so much as an ally but as a mark. Think back to the study cited at the beginning of this book, which measured the difference between the sale prices of homes that belonged to real-estate agents themselves and the houses they sold for their clients. The study found that an agent keeps her own house on the market an average ten extra days, waiting for a better offer, and sells it for over 3 percent more than your house—or $10,000 on the sale of a $300,000 house. That's $10,000 going into her pocket that does not go into yours, a nifty profit produced by the abuse of information and a keen understanding of incentives. The problem is that the agent only stands to personally gain an additional $150 by selling your house for $10,000 more, which isn't much reward for a lot of extra work. So her job is to convince you that a $300,000 offer is in fact a very good offer, even a generous one, and that only a fool would refuse it.

9   This can be tricky. The agent does not want to come right out and call you a fool. So she merely implies it—perhaps by telling you about the much bigger, nicer, newer house down the block that has sat unsold for six months. Here is the agent's main weapon: the conversion of information into fear. Consider this true story, related by John Donohue, a law professor who in 2001 was teaching at Stanford University. "I was just about to buy a house on the Stanford campus," he recalls, "and the seller's agent kept telling me what a good deal I was getting because the market was about to zoom. As soon as I signed the purchase contract, he asked me if I would need an agent to sell my previous Stanford house. I told him that I would probably try to sell without an agent, and he replied, 'John, that might work under normal conditions, but with the market tanking now, you really need the help of a broker.'"

10   Within five minutes, a zooming market had tanked. Such are the marvels that can be conjured by an agent in search of the next deal.

11   Consider now another true story of a real-estate agent's information abuse. The tale involves K., a close friend of one of this book's authors. K. wanted to buy a house that was listed at $469,000. He was prepared to offer $450,000 but he first called the seller's agent and asked her to name the lowest price that she thought the homeowner might accept. The agent promptly scolded K. "You ought to be ashamed of yourself," she said. "That is clearly a violation of real-estate ethics."

12   K. apologized. The conversation turned to other, more mundane issues. After ten minutes, as the conversation was ending, the agent told K., "Let me say one last thing. My client is willing to sell this house for a lot less than you might think."

13   Based on this conversation, K. then offered $425,000 for the house instead of the $450,000 he had planned to offer. In the end, the seller accepted $430,000. Thanks to *his own agent's* intervention, the seller lost at least $20,000. The agent, meanwhile, only lost $300—a small price to pay to ensure that she would quickly and easily lock up the sale, which netted her a commission of $6,450.

14   So a big part of a real-estate agent's job, it would seem, is to persuade the home-owner to sell for less than he would like while at the same time letting potential buyers know that a house can be bought for less than its listing price. To be sure, there are more subtle means of doing so than coming right out and telling the buyer to bid low. The study of real-estate agents cited above also includes data that reveals how agents convey information through the for-sale ads they write. A phrase like "well maintained," for instance, is as full of meaning to an agent as "Mr. Ayak" was to a Klansman; it means that a house is old but not quite falling down. A savvy buyer will know this (or find out for himself once he sees the house), but to the sixty-five-year-old retiree who is selling his house, "well maintained" might sound like a compliment, which is just what the agent intends.

15   An analysis of the language used in real-estate ads shows that certain words are pow-erfully correlated with the final sale price of a house. This doesn't necessarily mean that labeling a house "well maintained" *causes* it to sell for less than an equivalent house. It does, however, indicate that when a real-estate agent labels a house "well maintained," she may be subtly encouraging a buyer to bid low.

16   Listed below are ten terms commonly used in real-estate ads. Five of them have a strong positive correlation to the ultimate sale price, and five have a strong negative cor-relation. Guess which are which.

Ten Common Real-Estate Ad Terms

Fantastic
Granite
Spacious
State-of-the-Art
!
Corian
Charming
Maple
Great Neighborhood
Gourmet

17   A "fantastic" house is surely fantastic enough to warrant a high price, isn't it? What about a "charming" and "spacious" house in a "great neighborhood!"? No, no, no, and no. Here's the breakdown:

Five Terms Correlated to a Higher Sale Price
Granite
State-of-the-Art
Corian
Maple
Gourmet

Five Terms Correlated to a Lower Sale Price

Fantastic

Spacious

!

Charming

Great Neighborhood

18   Three of the five terms correlated with a higher sale price are physical descriptions of the house itself: granite, Corian, and maple. As information goes, such terms are specific and straightforward—and therefore pretty useful. If you like granite, you might like the house; but even if you don't, "granite" certainly doesn't connote a fixer-upper. Nor does "gourmet" or "state-of-the-art," both of which seem to tell a buyer that a house is, on some level, truly fantastic.

19   "Fantastic," meanwhile, is a dangerously ambiguous adjective, as is "charming." Both these words seem to be real-estate agent code for a house that doesn't have many specific attributes worth describing. "Spacious" homes, meanwhile, are often decrepit or impractical. "Great neighborhood" signals a buyer that, well, *this* house isn't very nice but others nearby may be. And an exclamation point in a real-estate ad is bad news for sure, a bid to paper over real shortcomings with false enthusiasm.

20   If you study the words in ads for a real-estate agent's *own* home, meanwhile, you see that she indeed emphasizes descriptive terms (especially "new," "granite," "maple," and "move-in condition") and avoids empty adjectives (including "wonderful," "immaculate," and the telltale "!"). Then she patiently waits for the best buyer to come along. She might tell this buyer about a house nearby that just sold for $25,000 *above* the asking price, or another house that is currently the subject of a bidding war. She is careful to exercise every advantage of the information asymmetry she enjoys.

21   Does this make her a bad person? That's hard to say, at least hard for *us* to say. The point here is not that real-estate agents are bad people, but that they simply *are* people—and people inevitably respond to incentives. The incentives of the real-estate business, as currently configured, plainly encourage some agents to act against the best interests of their customers.

22   But like the funeral director and the car salesman and the life insurance company, the real-estate agent has also seen her advantage eroded by the Internet. After all, anyone selling a home can now get online and gather her own information about sales trends and housing inventory and mortgage rates. The information has been set loose. And recent sales data show the results. Real-estate agents still get a higher price for their own homes than comparable homes owned by their clients, but since the proliferation of real-estate web sites, the gap between the two prices has shrunk by a third.

23   It would be naive to suppose that people abuse information only when they are acting as experts or as agents of commerce. After all, agents and experts are people too—which suggests that we are likely to abuse information in our personal lives as well, whether by withholding true information or editing the information we choose to publicize.

QUESTIONS ON MEANING

1. What is a crime of information? How has the Internet served to reduce the number of these crimes?
2. How do experts that sell products or services inspire emotions in consumers? What is the primary emotion inspired?
3. Should a seller trust a real estate agent's judgment when s/he recommends a sales price?
4. What is the main difference between general rather than concrete language in real estate advertisements? How are these types of language used differently?
5. How has the Internet affected the problem of information asymmetry?

QUESTIONS FOR DISCUSSION

1. In a free enterprise system, what moral responsibility does a seller or expert have to share information with a buyer or consumer?
2. To what extent are the buyers of goods or services responsible for their lack of knowledge? In this context, is there a difference in moral responsibility for the doctor versus the real estate agent?
3. To what extent is the Internet an effective tool in making the dissemination of information symmetrical versus asymmetrical? Is there such a thing as information overload?
4. How will the information revolution created by the Internet continue to transform free-enterprise? To what extent will these effects be positive or negative?

LOOKING AT RHETORIC

1. Levitt and Dubner use both historical and hypothetical examples, developing them in great detail. Does this help to make their argument convincing?
2. Is the detailed analysis of the language of real estate advertisements useful in clarifying how information can be manipulated to create an impression?
3. In this excerpt, which deals with business and economics, the authors generally avoid specialized language. Does this help or hinder their argument?

WRITING ASSIGNMENTS

1. Research sources in business journals or books that deal with the information age. Argue for or against Levitt and Dubner's implicit claim that information asymmetry is unfair. If you consider the situation fair, provide examples from sources to support your position. If you think it is unfair, offer a strategy for creating information symmetry based upon your research.
2. Identify a circumstance when you have made a purchase without sufficient information, when you have been the victim of information asymmetry. How could you have acquired the knowledge to permit you to make a better decision?
3. In pairs or in groups, identify a large scale purchase such as a house or a car. List the items of information you need to make an effective purchase. Individually, write an instructive essay to a buyer offering specific recommendations for how to go about making the purchase.

Laughing All the Way to the Darwinian Bank

Terry Burnham and Jay Phelan

Terry Burnham holds an MBA from Massachusetts Institute of Technology (MIT), as well as a master's degree in computer science and a bachelor's degree in biophysics from the University of Michigan. He is a professor of business at Harvard University, having received his Ph.D. in business economics from Harvard in 1997. His academic efforts have emphasized the relationship of economic behavior to evolutionary biology and genetics, having worked on Wall Street and co-founded Progenics, a biotechnology firm. Jay Phelan earned his Ph.D. in biology from Harvard in 1995 as well as masters and bachelors degrees from Yale and UCLA. He is a professor of biology at the University of California, Los Angeles (UCLA). He studies and writes in the area of evolutionary genetics and aging, is renowned as a teacher, and has been featured on the BBC and Talk of the Nation. *The following excerpt is from the co-authored bestselling book* Mean Genes (2000), *which explores human behavior from the perspective of human instinct driven by genetics and evolutionary biology, thus engaging both the disciplines of business and economics and biology. They argue that positive and negative spending behavior can be traced to our evolutionary past, and that we must trick our own instincts for our own financial good.*

1   Why do we have such a hard time saving money? Take the following quiz: First, how much money would you like to save each month? Write down your answer as a percentage of your income. Second, how much money are you saving? Look at the last few months of your actual savings behavior, not your dreams about next year after you pay off your credit card debt. Write down your actual savings as a percentage of income. Now compare the two figures. The unpleasant reality is that most of us save far less than we want to.

2   Average Americans want to save 10% of their income and claim to save about 3%. If only that were true. We set a record low in February 2000, with a 0.8% savings rate. In other words, if you took home $2,000 after taxes and you saved like an average American, you spent every cent except a measly sixteen bucks.

3   The result is that Americans have little or no cash to spare. Enticed to spend by urgings everywhere we turn—from the Internet to billboards to crafty product placements on TV and in movies—we are a nation of spenders, rushing to deposit paychecks into minuscule bank accounts to cover the checks we have written.

4   To understand our spending behavior, let's visit some of the world's most accomplished savers by taking a trip to northern Europe. There we find forests where autumn arrives much as it does throughout the temperate parts of the world. Leaves change their color, temperatures plummet, and winds pick up.

5   Look down as you walk through the forest and you'll see a feverish acknowledgment of the oncoming winter. Red squirrels shift into overdrive each September, forsaking their summer life of leisure. In the course of two months, each squirrel will hide more than three thousand acorns, pinecones, and beechnuts throughout the several acres of their home range. It's hard being a squirrel.

6   Come winter, however, diligence pays off. With little food to be found on the bare trees, some squirrels are still living large. Each day they methodically move from one storage spot to the next as they ultimately recover more than 80% of their stashed snacks, enough to keep them alive until spring.

7   Hoarding for the future isn't restricted to rodents with big cheeks. It's a common response throughout the animal kingdom when lean times are ahead. Many bird species also store food in the fall. Nutcrackers, for example, bury seeds from pine trees and, like squirrels, show remarkable memory in finding their savings.

8   If there were a Savings Hall of Fame, it would contain dozens of animal species but certainly not the average American. How can humans (at least most Americans) be so much worse at preparing for lean times than squirrels, birds, and an ark full of other dim-witted creatures?

9   As described in the fable of the grasshopper and the ant, there are two strategies for dealing with abundance. The grasshopper plays all summer long while the ant works relentlessly to store food. When winter comes, the ant survives and the grasshopper dies.

10   Similarly, squirrels that work hard to store nuts survive the winter to have babies in the spring. When those babies grow up, they have the genes of their parents, genes that tell them to start burying nuts when fall comes. Animals are accomplished savers because natural selection favors the appropriately thrifty. Shouldn't the same forces have produced frugal humans? To understand the answer, we can learn by observing the behavior of people who live as foragers, as our ancestors did until recently.

11   The !Kung San[1] live in the deserts of southern Africa. Until the 1960s they lived off this harsh land as nomads, gathering plants and hunting animals much as their ancestors had for ten thousand years or more. Because some San were still hunting and gathering into the 1960s, we have detailed records of their behavior in circumstances similar to those of our ancestors.

12   The !Kung San perpetually faced uncertain supplies of water and food. Building up reserves for the future would certainly help buffer those risks. Did the !Kung San save? Absolutely. The best opportunity for this saving came in times of windfall, usually after the killing of a large animal like a giraffe. With hundreds of pounds of edible giraffe meat, a hunter with a good savings system could live for months.

13   But !Kung San hunters had no meat lockers or freezers. Even if they preserved the extra meat, neighbors would descend and devour even the largest kill in a few days. Imagine your own "popularity" if you won the lottery, and you've got a pretty good picture of a !Kung San hunter with a dead giraffe outside his hut.

14   The !Kung San's behavior provides the clue to resolving the paradox between Americans' chronic undersaving and the strong evolutionary pressure to prepare for lean times. In a world without refrigerators or banks, preparing for hard times means eating enough food to store some fat on your body.

15   How good an evolutionary saver are you? In 1981 Bobby Sands,[2] a member of the Irish Republican Army, went on a hunger strike to protest British policy. He was not a fat man to

---

[1] !Kung San: Also known as the Nyae Nyae !Kung, a group of nomadic hunter-gatherers who reside in the Kalahari Desert in Namibia.

[2] Bobby Sands: Robert Gerard Sands (1954-1981), Irish Republican Army (IRA) volunteer who died in prison, in a hunger-strike protesting the removal by the British government of "Special Category Status" for IRA prisoners.

begin with, yet it still took him sixty-six days to starve himself to death. Many of us would survive, albeit unpleasantly, for more than two months without a single morsel of food. That's a pretty impressive savings account! Perhaps we deserve a place in that Savings Hall of Fame after all.

16   For our ancestors, however, saving through markets and money was not an option. Successful people would ram as much as possible into their own stomachs and those of their genetic relatives. They might also share with non-relatives who would repay them on their good days. In such an environment, the best way to save is, paradoxically, to consume. Rather than leave some precious energy lying around to mold or be stolen, put it in your stomach and have your body convert the food into an energy savings account.

17   When you're a mammal, food is the coin of the realm. Genetic mechanisms prod squirrels to mind their nuts and elephant seals to pad their flanks. As we struggle to save money, our mammalian heritage lurks in the background. We *know* we ought to put some money in the bank, but consuming just *feels* so good.

DON'T EAT THE NEST EGG

18   Proud as we may be of our hardy forebears and their genetic legacy, most of us would be happier if we could act less like victorious cavewomen and more like Scrooge. To prosper in the industrialized world with its refrigerators and government-insured bank accounts, we need to trick our ancient genes.

19   Because we evolved to consume everything in sight, many of the most success-ful savings techniques involve hiding money from ourselves. By making ourselves feel poor, we can induce our overconsuming instincts into living more frugally. One well-known technique is carrying less cash. By doing this we fool our genes, at least a bit, into thinking there is less surplus to be consumed.

20   As a variation on this ruse, many people find multiple bank accounts useful. One account is untouchable and can accumulate savings, while the more commonly used account, usually the checking account, gets fixed transfers each month. The savings account should be as hidden as possible. For example, it can be in another state with no associated ATM or debit card. Or at least in a bank with ATMs located only in distant locations.

21   Easy access is our enemy. Ironic as it is, the best bank for our savings may be the one that makes withdrawals as difficult as possible. We can, for example, choose an account that pays a high interest rate but has outrageous fees for every transaction.

22   People don't come into the world with instincts for appropriate financial behavior. Most of us need to learn, and this learning frequently involves some painful mistakes. We (Terry and Jay) have been there, so we know.

23   Early in his financial life, Jay discovered the joy of credit cards. Freed from the tire-some need to have actual cash for purchases, he enjoyed an extended spending spree. But he soon learned that credit-fueled feasts end with maxed-out accounts and mon-ster monthly payments that barely make dents in the balances. Each purchase felt like a one-time event—a necessity—but he quickly dug himself into a deep financial hole. (Fortunately, further digging was prevented by the financial companies canceling all of his credit lines.)

24   Jay's first solution was to switch to a card that required him to pay the entire balance each month. This led to some tough months, including last-minute scrambling to raise cash by selling CDs and books. It also brought his charging down to a manageable amount. Still, although he always scraped together just enough to stay out of debtor's prison, Jay never had a cent left over for the savings account that might someday become a down payment on the beach house he dreamed about.

25   That's when Jay's credit card company stepped in: it offered a new plan that would bill an extra amount to your credit card each month. This seems like the wrong kind of progress. How did having even more to pay help Jay save money? The trick was that the extra amount billed was invested in a mutual fund.[3] This made the monthly adventure of paying off the card even more harrowing, but it worked. He always figured out a way (and little by little it came from charging less), and by doing so he accumulated $250 every month in savings.

26   One of the most effective savings mechanisms for us is to hide money. Who are we hiding it from? From ourselves or, more precisely, from that more impulsive part of ourselves. Jay was able to begin saving only by setting up a separate account that he never saw and that was extremely difficult to access.

27   If you have a job, you are already hiding some money from yourself in the form of social security. Although it is not technically a savings plan, social security helps us save for retirement. Essentially, the more we earn, the more the government will pay us each year when we are retired. For all of its well-documented flaws, social security has worked to ease poverty among older Americans. When the program was enacted, people over 65 were the poorest segment of the American population. Now they are the richest.

28   Another proven way to save, successful precisely because it doesn't feel like saving, is to buy property. Although the average sixty-year-old American has only $8,300 in financial assets, retirees have over $35,000 in the form of home equity. Failing to keep up the mortgage payments can result in losing the property, so even terrible savers turn out to be surprisingly successful at scraping together enough to avoid default.

29   In the 1980s, Brooke Shields made a series of racy advertisements for Calvin Klein jeans. In one she says, "When I get money, I buy Calvin Klein. If I have anything left over, I pay the rent." Successful savings techniques share a bit of this seemingly warped set of priorities.

30   Effective savers can say, "When I get money, I lock some up as savings. With the money that's left over, I purchase food and shelter." People save when the money comes out of income before other needs. As long as the amount of savings is fixed and required in the form of a mortgage payment or payroll deduction, most people find a way to make ends meet. If savings are simply whatever money is left over after buying, the result is usually no savings at all.

31   Setting up mechanisms for automatic savings can be incredibly painful, but nearly everyone gets over the pain and adjusts to their new income. Mortgages and secret mutual

---

[3] Mutual fund: a form of collective investment that pools funds in stocks, bonds, and money market portfolios.

funds are just peachy for rich folks, but what about those of us who are hanging by a financial thread?

32   The trick is to pick the right time to increase the amount of hidden money. For example, when we get a raise, we can increase the contribution to our retirement account so that our take-home pay remains constant. We can whine all we want, but we know it's possible to live on the old salary because we actually did.

33   With growing government surpluses, it's also likely that we'll get a tax cut in the next few years. If so, that will be another excellent time to ratchet up the savings. Similarly, any windfalls such as tax rebates and gifts are best invested immediately.

34   The book *The Millionaire Next Door*[4] describes the behavior of average folks who became wealthy. The surprising conclusion is that most people get rich because they spend less, not because they earn more than the average. Millionaires, for instance, hold off an extra year or two before trading in their decidedly non-exotic cars and are more likely to sport a Timex on their wrist than a Rolex.

SAVING MORE

35   Why do we need so much help saving money while other behaviors come so easily? The answer is that we need little help learning behaviors that have been critical to human survival and reproduction for thousands of generations. We instinctively solve ancient problems, and it's only when our instincts fail us that we've got to buckle down and learn. For a dramatic example, consider how babies react to dangerous objects.

36   Place a loaded pistol in a playpen and the babies will play with it just like any other toy, giggle, and perhaps even place the gun in their mouth. In contrast, put a plastic snake into the playpen; the babies will cower in fear. Show a person of any age a snake—or even a picture of one—and you will elicit a dramatic response, including sweaty skin and an increased heart rate. It doesn't matter whether the person is in America, Europe, Japan, Australia, or Argentina, the response is the same. This is true even in Ireland, which has no native snakes.

37   Why do we have an instinctive fear of snakes and not of guns? In 1998, guns killed more than thirty thousand Americans; snakes killed fewer than two dozen people. In the United States, you are literally eight times as likely to be struck by lightning as killed by a snake. Nevertheless, snakes produce one of the strongest instinctual fear responses.

38   We ought to be very afraid of guns and relatively unconcerned by snakes, but we are built in just the opposite way. A bit of reflection resolves this puzzle. The genes that cause instinctual fear, like all genes, have been handed down to us from our ancestors. Snakes caused many human deaths when we lived as hunters and gatherers. In contrast, guns didn't kill a single person until very recently. Accordingly, we loathe our ancient enemy, the snake, and have no instinctual response to novel threats regardless of how deadly.

---

[4] *The Millionaire Next Door*: 1998 book by Thomas J. Stanley and William D. Danko that defines the characteristics typical of individuals who have become wealthy.

Interdisciplinary Connections

At Work in America: The Triumph and Trials of an Economic System

As you study the two images presented here, consider these questions: What does it take to make a product or to service the needs of a city? What are the obligations, the rights, and the responsibilities of workers to their employers, and of employers to their workers? What do these images suggest about the complex nature of economic enterprise?

Memphis Sanitation Workers Strike, 1968

Model T Ford Assembly Line, Highland Park Plant, 1915

QUESTIONS ON MEANING

1. To what extent does the simple observation of nature indicate that saving (hoarding for the future) is an instinctual behavior? Do modern Americans seem to follow that instinct?

2. In terms of balancing savings and consumption, why is it necessary to work against our ancestral instincts?

3. What is the most effective way to save money? In using this method, how are we tricking our primal instincts?

4. Why is it sensible to say, "I will save before I eat"?

5. What is surprising about the spending behavior of the average millionaire?

QUESTIONS FOR DISCUSSION

1. To what extent is it reasonable to trace saving and spending behavior to genetically conditioned instinct? Are there other forces involved?

2. In terms of maximizing human happiness, how much emphasis should we give to saving money?

3. To what extent is it reasonable to look to the animal world as a means of explaining human economic behavior?

4. Are there notable differences in the spending behavior of the affluent upper middle class and the less moneyed lower middle class, especially in terms of spending patterns and debt? In other words, do the affluent often follow the frugal spending patterns identified in the last paragraph?

LOOKING AT RHETORIC

1. Burnham and Phelan write in an informal, conversational tone and style. How does this contribute to the effectiveness of their argument? Does it detract from it?

2. The authors use brief paragraphs with additional line separations. Why? What are they trying to accomplish with this formal pattern?

3. The authors use examples from human anthropological history and from the natural world. Are these reasonable and logical examples to employ?

WRITING ASSIGNMENTS

1. Research sources in evolutionary biology, evolutionary psychology, economics, and sociology. Based upon what you find, argue for or against the authors' claim that our behaviors can be traced to genetically conditioned instincts observable in our ancestors. Are there social and cultural forces that operate independently of genetics? What are they?

2. When you feel the impulse to spend rather that save, why is that impulse so strong? What can you do to curb that drive? To what extent is it important to do so?

3. In pairs or in groups, make a list of unnecessary things you spend money on. Individually, trim that list to those items that apply only to you. Select an unnecessary item or activity and write an essay justifying the expenditure, making sure to take all future costs into account, that is, what you give up or incur by spending.

Why Amazon Can't Make A Kindle In the USA

Steve Denning

Steve Denning (b. 1944) is an expert in organizational leadership and management. His writings engage questions related to modern business practices, and they emphasize the necessity of rethinking the role of the manager toward more collaborative rather than authoritarian approaches. He studied law and psychology at the University of Sydney and earned a postgraduate degree in law from Oxford University. He worked for many years as a lawyer. He then worked for an extended period in prominent management positions in the World Bank, ultimately becoming an expert in the emerging field of organizational story-telling. He published five books and founded the annual Organizational Storytelling Weekend, sponsored by the Smithsonian Institution. Many of his most important ideas regarding innovative management techniques are expressed in The Leader's Guide to Radical Management: Reinventing the Workplace for the 21st Century *(2010). The following essay is from* Forbes. *It explores the effects of outsourcing manufactured products, arguing that the consequences of this tendency are misinterpreted by economists.*

> *An economist is someone who knows the price of everything and the value of nothing.*
>
> Old joke based on Oscar Wilde's quip about a cynic

1   I recently noted how conventional cost accounting inexorably focuses executives' attention on increasing short-term profits by cutting costs.

2   The same thing happens in economics. Take a recent study that set out to shed light on the role of Chinese businesses vis-à-vis American consumers. Galina Hale and Bart Hobijn, two economists from the Federal Reserve Bank of San Francisco, did a study showing that only 2.7% of U.S. consumer purchases have the "Made in China" label. Moreover, only 1.2% actually reflects the cost of the imported goods. Thus, on average, of every dollar spent on an item labeled "Made in China," 55 cents go for services produced in the United States. So the study trumpets the finding that China has only a tiny sliver of the U.S. economy.

3   So no problem, right?

4   Well, not exactly. The tiny sliver happens to be the sliver that matters. What economists miss is what is happening behind the numbers of dollars in the real economy of people.

HOW WHOLE INDUSTRIES DISAPPEAR

5   Take the story of Dell Computer [DELL] and its Taiwanese electronics manufacturer. The story is told in the brilliant book by Clayton Christensen, Jerome Grossman and Jason Hwang, *The Innovator's Prescription*:

6   ASUSTeK started out making the simple circuit boards within a Dell computer. Then ASUSTeK came to Dell with an interesting value proposition: "We've been doing a good job making these little boards. Why don't you let us make the motherboard for you? Circuit manufacturing isn't your core competence anyway and we could do it for 20% less."

7   Dell accepted the proposal because from a perspective of making money, it made sense: Dell's revenues were unaffected and its profits improved significantly. On successive occasions, ASUSTeK came back and took over the motherboard, the assembly of the computer, the management of the supply chain and the design of the computer. In each case Dell accepted the proposal because from a perspective of making money, it made sense: Dell's revenues were unaffected and its profits improved significantly. However, the next time ASUSTeK came back, it wasn't to talk to Dell. It was to talk to Best Buy and other retailers to tell them that they could offer them their own brand or any brand PC for 20% lower cost. As *The Innovator's Prescription* concludes:

8   *Bingo. One company gone, another has taken its place. There's no stupidity in the story. The managers in both companies did exactly what business school professors and the best management consultants would tell them to do—improve profitability by focus on those activities that are profitable and by getting out of activities that are less profitable.*

AMAZON COULDN'T MAKE A KINDLE HERE IF IT WANTED TO

9   Decades of outsourcing manufacturing have left U.S. industry without the means to invent the next generation of high-tech products that are key to rebuilding its economy, as noted by Gary Pisano and Willy Shih in a classic article, "Restoring American Competitiveness" (Harvard Business Review, July-August 2009).

10   The U.S. has lost or is on the verge of losing its ability to develop and manufacture a slew of high-tech products. Amazon's Kindle 2 couldn't be made in the U.S., even if Amazon wanted to:

- The flex circuit connectors are made in China because the US supplier base migrated to Asia.
- The electrophoretic display is made in Taiwan because the expertise developed from producting flat-panel LCDs migrated to Asia with semiconductor manufacturing.
- The highly polished injection-molded case is made in China because the U.S. supplier base eroded as the manufacture of toys, consumer electronics and computers migrated to China.
- The wireless card is made in South Korea because that country became a center for making mobile phone components and handsets.
- The controller board is made in China because U.S. companies long ago transferred manufacture of printed circuit boards to Asia.
- The Lithium polymer battery is made in China because battery development and manufacturing migrated to China along with the development and manufacture of consumer electronics and notebook computers.

11   An exception is Apple [AAPL], which "has been able to preserve a first-rate design capability in the States so far by remaining deeply involved in the selection of components, in industrial design, in software development, and in the articulation of the concept of its products and how they address users' needs."

A CHAIN REACTION OF DECLINE

12   Pisano and Shih continue:

> *"So the decline of manufacturing in a region sets off a chain reaction. Once manufacturing is outsourced, process-engineering expertise can't be maintained, since it depends on daily interactions with manufacturing. Without process-engineering capabilities, companies find it increasingly difficult to conduct advanced research on next-generation process technologies. Without the ability to develop such new processes, they find they can no longer develop new products. In the long term, then, an economy that lacks an infrastructure for advanced process engineering and manufacturing will lose its ability to innovate."*

13   The lithium battery for GM's [GM] Chevy Volt is being manufactured in South Korea. Making it in the U.S. wasn't feasible: rechargeable battery manufacturing left the US long ago.

14   Some efforts are being made to resurrect rechargeable battery manufacture in the U.S., such as the GE-backed [GE] A123Systems, but it's difficult to go it alone when much of the expertise is now in Asia.

15   In the same way that cost accounting and short-term corporate profits don't reflect the true health of corporations, the economists' reckoning of the impact of outsourcing production overseas misses the point. Americans are left with shipping the goods, selling the goods, marketing the goods. But the country is no longer to compete in the key task of actually making the goods.

16   Pisano and Shih have a frighteningly long list of industries that are "already lost" to the USA:

> *"Fabless chips"; compact fluorescent lighting; LCDs for monitors, TVs and handheld devices like mobile phones; electrophoretic displays; lithium ion, lithium polymer and NiMH batteries; advanced rechargeable batteries for hybrid vehicles; crystalline and polycrystalline silicon solar cells, inverters and power semiconductors for solar panels; desktop, notebook and netbook PCs; low-end servers; hard-disk drives; consumer networking gear such as routers, access points, and home set-top boxes; advanced composite used in sporting goods and other consumer gear; advanced ceramics and integrated circuit packaging.*

17   Their list of industries "at risk" is even longer and more worrisome.

WHAT'S TO BE DONE?

18   With such a complex societal problem, it's hard not to start from Albert Einstein's insight: "The significant problems that we have cannot be solved at the same level of thinking with which we created them." Many actors will have to play a role.

- Company leaders: Business leaders need to recommit themselves to continuous innovation and the values and practices that are necessary to accomplish that. i.e radical management. As Pisano and Shih write: "Whether you're the US firm IBM [IBM] with a major research laboratory in Switzerland or the Swiss company Novartis [NYSE:NVS] operating in the biotech commons in the Boston area, sacrificing such a commons for short-term cost benefits is a risky proposition."

- Accountants: Accountants need to get beyond the mental prison of cost accounting and embrace the thinking in throughput accounting that puts the emphasis on how companies can add new value, rather than just cutting costs.
- Management theorists and consultants: stop rearranging deck chairs on the Titanic of traditional management (e.g. by finding new and ingenious ways to cut costs) and start understanding and disseminating management theory that is fit for the 21st Century.
- Investors: Investors need to realize that the companies of the future are those that practice continuous innovation as Apple [AAPL], Amazon [AMZN] and Salesforce [CRM], as compared to companies practicing traditional management, such as Wal-Mart [WMT], Cisco [CSCO] OR GE [GE]. Investors need to realize that short-term financial gains are ephemeral: the companies that will generate real value are those that do what is necessary to continuously innovate.
- Government: Government has a role to play in protecting and promoting fields of expertise or what Pisano and Shih call "the industrial commons." Thus: "Government-sponsored endeavors that have made a huge difference in the past three decades include DARPA's VLSI chip development program and Strategic Computing Initiative; the DOD's and NASA's support of supercomputers and of NSFNET (an important contributor to the Internet); and the DOD's support of the Global Positioning System, to mention a handful."
- Politicians: At a time of poisonously divisive political debate, in which candidates recite anti-government mantras and call for "getting government out of the way of the private sector," it is time for serious politicians to step up and examine which parts of the private sector are fostering, and which parts are destroying, the economy of the country. They must stop embodying E. E. Cummings', definition of a politician as *"an ass upon which everyone has sat except a man."*
- Economists: Economists need to realize that merely adding up the numbers is not enough. They have to look at the meaning behind the numbers. When they trumpet their finding that "Chinese goods are only 1% of the U.S. economy," it's akin to saying "we kept the house but gave away the keys."

QUESTIONS ON MEANING

1. Given that many consumer products are made in China but much of the money spent on Chinese goods is for services provided in the United States, why does Chinese trade still present a problem for the U. S. economy?
2. Why has Apple been successful in keeping much of its design jobs in the United States?
3. What is the chain reaction of decline?
4. What are some of the industries that have already been lost by outsourcing?
5. Who are the actors that will need to help solve the problem of outsourcing and its effects on the U. S. economy?
6. How do economists need to change in terms of how they read and interpret numerical data when it comes to foreign competition with U. S. companies?

QUESTIONS FOR DISCUSSION

1. Should the increased success of foreign corporations such as China and Taiwan in the area of manufacturing be a concern for Americans?

2. Is the fact that America is moving toward a service based rather than a manufacturing based economy such a bad thing? What are the potentially positive and negative effects of outsourcing?

3. If the weakening of the manufacturing sector is a negative thing for the U. S. economy, how have labor unions helped to prevent this? How have they contributed to it?

4. Given that America tends to consume more than most of the world, particularly developing countries, do we have a moral obligation to allow for outsourcing as a means of distributing wealth to those who need it in other parts of the world?

LOOKING AT RHETORIC

1. How do you respond to Denning's conversational tone and his use of the first-person narrator? Does this enhance or detract from the credibility of his argument?

2. How effective is his use of extended quotes from other sources in terms of readability and the reliability of his argumentative claims?

3. How do you respond to use of bulleted lists? Do they help you comprehend his ideas more completely?

WRITING ASSIGNMENTS

1. Research the historical role of trade tariffs in managing foreign trade. Argue for or against the use of trade tariffs that increase the cost of foreign goods for Americans and encourage the purchase of U. S. manufactured goods.

2. Argue for or against the idea that Americans should decrease consumer spending in order to allow for the greater distribution of wealth and opportunity worldwide.

3. In pairs or in groups, make a list of some of the consumer products you commonly buy. Discuss why you buy them and how necessary you think they are to your happiness. Out of class, determine whether they are identified as a foreign product or a domestic product. Individually, select one and explore more completely how much of the production, distribution, sales, and service of that product come from American workers. Write an essay in which you argue for or against the purchase of that product.

Thinking Crosscurrently

BUSINESS AND ECONOMICS

Business and economics are a part of our daily lives. They influence many of our decisions and affect our ability to sustain ourselves and enjoy life. While certain people work in the private sector and others in the public sector, all of us do business and function as economic beings. Economics is a social science, dealing with the complex ways human beings inter-act, what they hope for, what they aspire to accomplish. Economics and business are very human, and they influence government and public policy, are informed by the physical sciences, motivate educational reform, and even find expression in art and literature. As you read the selections in this chapter, consider the following questions:

- In a capitalistic system built on free enterprise, what social responsibility does business have to serve the public good, through charity, taxes, and other philanthropic endeavors? How might John Dewey, Susan Linn, Caitlyn Flanagan, and Emily Martin answer this question? What might they have to say about the role of business in creating a free and just society?

- What are the human consequences, positive and negative, of the free enterprise system, and are there any limits that should be placed upon it? What might Herman Melville or Henry David Thoreau think about the role of business in creating and restricting human freedoms? Would Barry Commoner think differently? Why or why not?

- Who should have the greatest influence on the development of public policy in the government? Because they are experienced and successful in creating wealth, should business people and CEO's drive the development of government programs? Or should experts in social policy from the academic and non-profit sector have a greater say? Should we elect business people to public office on a regular and consistent basis? What might David Mamet or Diane Ravitch think about these questions?

- What is the ultimate purpose of wealth? How much does a thriving and wealthy economy contribute to human happiness? To a just society? Is there a balance that we might achieve between generating wealth through competition and seeking other benefits through collectivism? Can we safely assume that a vibrant wealthy society will lead to happier, more cooperative communities? They don't address the questions directly, but what might Thomas Jefferson, Abraham Lincoln, Shelby Steele, and even Oscar Wilde have to say?

6 GOVERNMENT, POLITICAL SCIENCE, AND PUBLIC POLICY

What are natural rights? How can we prove we have them? Darwin's concept of "natural selection," often expressed in the words of his contemporary, Herbert Spencer, as "survival of the fittest," implies that natural rights are questionable, that the only right we have is the right to fight, for food, for a mate, for control over territory. If we lose, we lose, and winners and losers in the natural world are as common as the air we breathe. But our own Declaration of Independence (written by Thomas Jefferson in consultation with a group of wise and savvy men of politics) states that we are endowed by our Creator with certain "inalienable rights" that include "Life, Liberty, and the pursuit of Happiness." Jefferson takes this concept from seventeenth and eighteenth-century natural rights theory, specifically from John Locke, who expressed the idea in slightly different and more practical terms: as "life, liberty, and property." Jefferson says, "We hold these truths to be self-evident." But are they?

Concepts of "natural" and "civil" rights form the basis for how we structure modern democratic societies. We cherish them. We hold them true without questioning them, because history has taught us that in their absence the world can be a brutish place. The study of government, political science, and public affairs explores and scrutinizes these ideals, examines their history, their validity, as well as when and how we can effectively put them into practice. At their inception in modern history, these concepts draw much from assuming a creator, and whether we are believers or not we usually retain the notion of human rights in some form. Why? Because these notions help us get along. In ethical terms, they seem to lead to the greatest happiness for us all. But how does the study of political institutions and ideas affect us on a daily basis, and how can our lives be enriched by exploring them?

THE DISCIPLINE YOU EXPERIENCE

When you drive a car you obey the rules, and some of them seem quite silly. Certainly there is no problem with a rolling stop in an intersection where you can see there is no oncoming traffic. But if a policeman sees you, he will probably give you a ticket. Perhaps the government will require you to appear, sacrifice a portion of the money you have earned, even listen to a lecture from a judge who at that moment has legal power over you, all because you didn't obey a law you think doesn't really need to exist. What happened to your freedom?

You sacrificed your "natural rights" for "civil rights," which are the more limited freedoms we collectively agree on when we decide to become a "society."

We have consented to form what the eighteenth-century social thinker Jean-Jacques Rousseau called, "The Social Contract." The study of government and political science might be seen as the exploration of how we continually negotiate the details and boundaries of that contract, how we define our relations to one another in societies and communities, both now and in the past. This exploration begins with basic assumptions about human nature. Our political perspectives strike deep; they emerge from our most basic beliefs. Or do they? Statistics demonstrate that by and large people in America remain in the political party they were raised in, believing what their parents or communities have taught them, perhaps without fully understanding the assumptions that ground those beliefs. Studying government and political science takes us into the depths, into places where our worldviews change. We may learn from experience and become skeptical of human nature, or we might decide that all human beings are essentially good. Often we see the complexity of the issues and move toward the moderate middle. In the end, we may conclude that "natural rights" is an unverifiable concept but accept its practical and ethical value. These fundamental assumptions inform the debates that lead to the creation and evolution of the political systems, institutions, and laws that affect us daily.

When we work with these foundational questions we begin to see how the study of public policy, government, and political science draw from the humanities, from philosophy and religion, and even from the arts. But in colleges and universities we contend with these issues usually within the context of political science departments or in undergraduate and graduate schools of Public Administration. These fields of study tend to be quite practical in nature, and as such they are concerned with how things work, what we can truly know, and how we act upon that knowledge. Questions about human nature are essential and interesting, and we must understand what those questions are. But we must also move beyond them and explore the concrete reality of the social and political world in which we live. There is a remarkable diversity of topics to examine in government and political science. Among them are the following:

- American politics, including the history of its ideologies and institutions, as well as its current structures and practices.

- International politics and international relations, including the many organizations such as the United Nations that negotiate relationships and conflicts worldwide.

- Comparative politics that looks at various political systems and problems that exist nationally and internationally.

- Public policy, which explores how policies and practices are formulated by diverse political institutions.

- Political theory, which examines the ideological foundations of institutions, as well as the relationship of the individual to the institutions they participate in.

There are a host of courses in colleges and universities that explore these subjects. Beyond introductory courses in government and political science, they include American

Government and Politics, World Politics, American Foreign Policy, International Relations, Electoral Power and Political Parties, Judicial Power and the Constitution, Civil Rights and Civil Liberties, among many others. All of these courses integrate to contribute to our understanding of the political world in which we live, the institutions we have created, and the social relationships that both insure and limit our freedoms.

Thus, the study of political science and government is diverse and complex but involves historical phenomena, realities and forces that affect us daily. Therefore, to understand them we must take the discipline on its own terms, as a "science," and more particularly a "social science," with a disciplinary parallel to sociology, psychology, and anthropology. Political scientists work to cultivate the "objectivity" of "hard sciences" such as biology, chemistry, and physics. They take something real and tangible, something they can observe that is nevertheless complex, and they try to reveal the cause and effect relationships that define how it works and how it affects us all. To do this, they follow a scientific method, what we call principles of "empiricism." There is some variation in how this method is applied but less in political science than in other academic disciplines. Often the sciences claim to be more rigorous, but what is certain is that they are more rule-driven. In science, you begin with a question and you formulate a hypothesis, which is a tentative idea that you can test. You experiment by attempting to disprove that hypothesis, and if you cannot, in time it becomes a theory. Very few experiments and scientific studies that are reported in the media result in theories. "Scientific" theories have a high degree of validity. Many things scientists hold as true remain theories in perpetuity. The theory of relativity and the theory of evolution are not theories because they may be untrue. Ask any credible scientist and he or she will tell you they are pretty much true. They are theories because we cannot yet explain everything about them. Only when that explanation is complete in all its details can we call a "theory" a "law." That is the scientific method political scientists attempt to follow. In doing so, they make extensive use of statistical data and methods, and they often measure things by numbers, "quantitatively."

REFLECTING ON THIS CHAPTER

A host of pertinent issues emerge in the selections in this chapter, concerns that affect us daily, things we talk about, debate, and ponder publicly and privately. As you read these sections, consider a set of broader questions.

- What are the central concerns of individual selections? What are the problems they identify and the solutions they offer, if any?

- What worldviews seem to implicitly inform the authors? How do they view human nature? Are we essentially good, bad, or are we a mixed bag of virtues and vices? How does each author create political principals and practices out of these assumptions?

- How do the ideas in these various selections compare and contrast? What central themes emerge? What human and social problems seem most pressing?

- Have your ideas and attitudes changed as a result of your reading? What topics and issues do you feel compelled to reconsider?

- What are the various writing strategies the authors employ? What tools do they use to persuade us? If you found a selection convincing, what made it so?

- Do you detect any flaws in any of the arguments? Can you find any logical fallacies? Are there any overt biases? Remember, a bias is not the same as a point of view. A strongly persuasive argument can be unbiased if it honestly presents and analyzes the available data and information.

Political Civility

David Mamet

David Mamet (b. 1947) is known mainly as a playwright and screenwriter, but he is also a novelist, essayist, and director. He attended Goddard College in Vermont and the Neighborhood Playhouse School of Theatre in New York. He began his career as an actor and a director but became successful as a playwright Off-Broadway. In addition to winning the Pulitzer Prize in 1984, he has received numerous citations, including the New York Drama Critics Circle Award and the Tony Award. He has also taught at Goddard College, The Yale School of Drama, and New York University. His writing lends itself naturally to political issues, and in the following piece, first published in The Village Voice, *he explores his own transition from political "liberal" to a moderate with conservative sympathies. His essay combines a biting satirical tone with a personal reflection informed both by current events and the complexities of American political history from its beginnings until today.*

1   John Maynard Keynes was twitted with changing his mind. He replied, "When the facts change, I change my opinion. What do you do, sir?"

2   My favorite example of a change of mind was Norman Mailer at *The Village Voice.*

3   Norman took on the role of drama critic, weighing in on the New York premiere of *Waiting for Godot.*

4   Twentieth century's greatest play. Without bothering to go, Mailer called it a piece of garbage.

5   When he did get around to seeing it, he realized his mistake. He was no longer a *Voice* columnist, however, so he bought a page in the paper and wrote a retraction, praising the play as the masterpiece it is.

6   Every playwright's dream.

7   I once won one of Mary Ann Madden's "Competitions" in *New York* magazine. The task was to name or create a "10" of anything, and mine was the World's Perfect Theatrical Review. It went like this: "I never understood the theater until last night. Please forgive everything I've ever written. When you read this I'll be dead." That, of course, is the only review anybody in the theater ever wants to get.

8   My prize, in a stunning example of irony, was a year's subscription to *New York*, which rag (apart from Mary Ann's "Competition") I considered an open running sore on the body of world literacy—this due to the presence in its pages of John Simon, whose stunning

amalgam of superciliousness and savagery, over the years, was appreciated by that reader-ship searching for an endorsement of proactive mediocrity.

9   But I digress.

10   I wrote a play about politics (*November*, Barrymore Theater, Broadway, some seats still available). And as part of the "writing process," as I believe it's called, I started thinking about politics. This comment is not actually as jejune[1] as it might seem. *Porgy and Bess*[2] is a buncha good songs but has nothing to do with race relations, which is the flag of convenience under which it sailed.

11   But my play, it turned out, was actually about politics, which is to say, about the polemic between persons of two opposing views. The argument in my play is between a president who is self-interested, corrupt, suborned, and realistic, and his leftish, lesbian, utopian-socialist speechwriter.

12   The play, while being a laugh a minute, is, when it's at home, a disputation between reason and faith, or perhaps between the conservative (or tragic) view and the liberal (or perfectionist) view. The conservative president in the piece holds that people are each out to make a living, and the best way for government to facilitate that is to *stay out of the way*, as the inevitable abuses and failures of this system (free-market economics) are less than those of government intervention.

13   I took the liberal view for many decades, but I believe I have changed my mind.

14   As a child of the '60s, I accepted as an article of faith that government is corrupt, that business is exploitative, and that people are generally good at heart.

15   These cherished precepts had, over the years, become ingrained as increasingly impracticable prejudices. Why do I say impracticable? Because although I still held these beliefs, I no longer applied them in my life. How do I know? My wife informed me. We were riding along and listening to NPR. I felt my facial muscles tightening, and the words beginning to form in my mind: *Shut the fuck up*. "?" she prompted. And her terse, elegant summation, as always, awakened me to a deeper truth. I had been listening to NPR and reading various organs of national opinion for years, wonder and rage contending for pride of place. Further: I found I had been—rather charmingly, I thought—referring to myself for years as "a brain-dead liberal," and to NPR as "National Palestinian Radio."

16   This is, to me, the synthesis of this worldview with which I now found myself disen-chanted: that everything is always wrong.

17   But in my life, a brief review revealed, everything was not always wrong, and neither was nor is always wrong in the community in which I live, or in my country. Further, it was not always wrong in previous communities in which I lived, and among the various and mobile classes of which I was at various times a part.

18   And, I wondered, how could I have spent decades thinking that I thought everything was always wrong *at the same time* I thought that people were basically good at heart? Which was it? I began to question what I actually thought and found that I do not think that people are basically good at heart; indeed, that view of human nature has both prompted and informed my writing for the last 40 years. I think that people, in circumstances of

---

[1] jejune: devoid of interest or significance.

[2] *Porgy and Bess*: Popular opera produced in 1935 by George Gershwin and Dubose Hayward, dealing with African American life in the 1920's.

stress, can behave like swine, and that this, indeed, is not only a fit subject, but the only subject, of drama.

19   I'd observed that lust, greed, envy, sloth, and their pals are giving the world a good run for its money, but that nonetheless, people in general seem to get from day to day; and that we in the United States get from day to day under rather wonderful and privileged circumstances—that we are not and never have been the villains that some of the world and some of our citizens make us out to be, but that we are a confection of normal (greedy, lustful, duplicitous, corrupt, inspired—in short, human) individuals living under a spectacularly effective compact called the Constitution, and lucky to get it.

20   For the Constitution, rather than suggesting that all behave in a godlike manner, recognizes that, to the contrary, people are swine and will take any opportunity to subvert any agreement in order to pursue what they consider to be their proper interests.

21   To that end, the Constitution separates the power of the state into those three branches which are for most of us (I include myself) the only thing we remember from 12 years of schooling.

22   The Constitution, written by men with some experience of actual government, assumes that the chief executive will work to be king, the Parliament will scheme to sell off the silverware, and the judiciary will consider itself Olympian and do everything it can to much improve (destroy) the work of the other two branches. So the Constitution pits them against each other, in the attempt not to achieve stasis, but rather to allow for the constant corrections necessary to prevent one branch from getting too much power for too long.

23   Rather brilliant. For, in the abstract, we may envision an Olympian perfection of perfect beings in Washington doing the business of their employers, the people, but any of us who has ever been at a zoning meeting with our property at stake is aware of the urge to cut through all the pernicious bullshit and go straight to firearms.

24   I found not only that I didn't trust the current government (that, to me, was no surprise), but that an impartial review revealed that the faults of this president—whom I, a good liberal, considered a monster—were little different from those of a president whom I revered.

25   Bush got us into Iraq, JFK into Vietnam. Bush stole the election in Florida; Kennedy stole his in Chicago. Bush outed a C.I.A. agent; Kennedy left hundreds of them to die in the surf at the Bay of Pigs.[3] Bush lied about his military service; Kennedy accepted a Pulitzer Prize for a book written by Ted Sorenson. Bush was in bed with the Saudis, Kennedy with the Mafia. Oh.

26   And I began to question my hatred for "the Corporations"—the hatred of which, I found, was but the flip side of my hunger for those goods and services they provide and without which we could not live.

27   And I began to question my distrust of the "Bad, Bad Military" of my youth, which, I saw, was then and is now made up of those men and women who actually risk their lives to protect the rest of us from a very hostile world. Is the military always right? No. Neither is government, nor are the corporations—they are just different signposts for the particular amalgamation of our country into separate working groups, if you will. Are these groups infallible, free from the possibility of mismanagement, corruption, or

---

[3] Bay of Pigs: Unsuccessful attempt in 1961 of U. S. trained Cuban exiles and U. S. government forces to invade Cuba and overthrow Fidel Castro.

crime? No, and neither are you or I. So, taking the tragic view, the question was not "Is everything perfect?" but "How could it be better, at what cost, and according to whose definition?" Put into which form, things appeared to me to be unfolding pretty well.

28   Do I speak as a member of the "privileged class"? If you will—but classes in the United States are mobile, not static, which is the Marxist view. That is: Immigrants came and continue to come here penniless and can (and do) become rich; the nerd makes a trillion dollars; the single mother, penniless and ignorant of English, sends her two sons to college (my grandmother). On the other hand, the rich and the children of the rich can go belly-up; the hegemony of the railroads is appropriated by the airlines, that of the networks by the Internet; and the individual may and probably will change status more than once within his lifetime.

29   What about the role of government? Well, in the abstract, coming from my time and background, I thought it was a rather good thing, but tallying up the ledger in those things which affect me and in those things I observe, I am hard-pressed to see an instance where the intervention of the government led to much beyond sorrow.

30   *But* if the government is not to intervene, how will we, mere human beings, work it all out?

31   I wondered and read, and it occurred to me that I knew the answer; and here it is: We just seem to. How do I know? From experience. I referred to my own—take away the director from the staged play and what do you get? Usually a diminution of strife, a shorter rehearsal period, and a better production.

32   The director, generally, does not *cause* strife, but his or her presence impels the actors to direct (and manufacture) claims designed to appeal to Authority—that is, to set aside the original goal (staging a play for the audience) and indulge in politics, the purpose of which may be to gain status and influence outside the ostensible goal of the endeavor.

33   Strand unacquainted bus travelers in the middle of the night, and what do you get? A lot of bad drama and a shake-and-bake Mayflower Compact. Each, instantly, adds what he or she can to the solution. Why? Each wants, and in fact needs, to contribute—to throw into the pot what gifts each has in order to achieve the overall goal, as well as status in the new-formed community. And so they work it out.

34   See also that most magnificent of schools, the jury system, where, again, each brings nothing into the room save his or her own prejudices, and, through the course of deliberation, comes not to a perfect solution, but a solution acceptable to the community—a solution the community can live with.

35   Prior to the midterm elections, my rabbi was taking a lot of flack. The congregation is exclusively liberal, he is a self-described independent (read "conservative"), and he was driving the flock wild. Why? Because a) he never discussed politics; and b) he taught that the quality of political discourse must be addressed first—that Jewish law teaches that it is incumbent upon each person to hear the other fellow out.

36   And so I, like many of the liberal congregation, began, teeth grinding, to attempt to do so. And in doing so, I recognized that I held those two views of America (politics, government, corporations, the military). One was of a state where everything was magically wrong and must be immediately corrected at any cost; and the other—the world in which I actually functioned day to day—was made up of people, most of whom were reasonably trying to maximize their comfort by getting along with each other (in the workplace, the marketplace, the jury room, on the freeway, even at the school-board meeting).

37   And I realized that the time had come for me to avow my participation in that America in which I chose to live, and that that country was not a schoolroom teaching values, but a marketplace.

38   "Aha," you will say, and you are right. I began reading not only the economics of Thomas Sowell (our greatest contemporary philosopher) but Milton Friedman, Paul Johnson, and Shelby Steele, and a host of conservative writers, and found that I agreed with them: a free-market understanding of the world meshes more perfectly with my experience than that idealistic vision I called liberalism.

39   *At the same time,* I was writing my play about a president, corrupt, venal, cunning, and vengeful (as I assume all of them are), and two turkeys. And I gave this fictional president a speechwriter who, in his view, is a "brain-dead liberal," much like my earlier self; and in the course of the play, they have to work it out. And they eventually do come to a human understanding of the political process. As I believe I am trying to do, and in which I believe I may be succeeding, and I will try to summarize it in the words of William Allen White.

40   White was for 40 years the editor of the *Emporia Gazette* in rural Kansas, and a prominent and powerful political commentator. He was a great friend of Theodore Roosevelt and wrote the best book I've ever read about the presidency. It's called *Masks in a Pageant,* and it profiles presidents from McKinley to Wilson, and I recommend it unreservedly.

41   White was a pretty clear-headed man, and he'd seen human nature as few can. (As Twain wrote, you want to understand men, run a country paper.) White knew that people need both to get ahead and to get along, and that they're always working at one or the other, and that government should most probably stay out of the way and let them get on with it. But, he added, there is such a thing as liberalism, and it may be reduced to these saddest of words: ". . . and yet . . ."

42   The right is mooing about faith, the left is mooing about change, and many are incensed about the fools on the other side—but, at the end of the day, they are the same folks we meet at the water cooler. Happy election season.

QUESTIONS ON MEANING

1. What major economist does Mamet begin his essay with? What brief ideas does he quote from that source?
2. What basic view of human beings do conservatives take? What basic view of human beings do liberals take?
3. What is the essential wisdom of the American Constitution? What does it recognize about human nature?
4. What was the author's attitude about the intervention of government in human affairs? How has it changed?

QUESTIONS FOR DISCUSSION

1. Is it essential that people are willing to change their minds? How do we benefit by this willingness, individually and collectively? Are there any negative consequences of cultivating this attitude?

2. Is it reasonable to assume that a group of deeply flawed human beings will work out their problems in a society with little leadership or governmental intervention? Why or why not? Consider Mamet's example of the stage production without a director or the stranded bus travelers.

3. Does a free-market understanding of the world work to help people get ahead and get along better than a society that advocates some governmental control in human affairs? Why or why not?

4. Under stress, are human beings basically swine, as Mamet contends, rife with greed, envy, and sloth? Can you think of examples?

LOOKING AT RHETORIC

1. Mamet uses the first person point of view and a conversational tone, as if he is speaking directly to an audience. In what way does this enhance his controversial argument? Does it?

2. Mamet blends personal experiences with references to the founding fathers and modern political figures. How well does he balance these various examples? Do they work well together? Why or why not?

3. How does Mamet's opening use of John Maynard Keynes and Norman Mailer help him in setting up the structure of his essay?

WRITING ASSIGNMENTS

1. Should human beings be characterized in the negative way that Mamet does, especially when they are under stress? Research your response using sources in history, psychology, and political science.

2. Argue for or against Mamet's claim that liberalism's idealistic view of human nature is inconsistent with its skepticism of the free market. Cite examples from your own experience or from history and current events.

3. In pairs or in groups, make two lists of essential human characteristics, one of virtues and another of vices. Then discuss the terms liberalism and conservatism. Individually, write an essay in which you define these terms. Then make an argument, something like Mamet's, for a liberal, conservative, or centrist position based directly on your lists of human traits.

The Declaration of Independence

In Congress, July 4, 1776

Thomas Jefferson

Thomas Jefferson (1743-1826), third president of the United States, was regarded as one of the "founding fathers." He served as the first Secretary of State, a minister to France, and as a congressman. He is also regarded as a central figure of the American Enlightenment, the period of intellectual rebirth, beginning in Europe in the seventeenth and eighteenth centuries, which fostered scientific and modern democratic ideals. The son of a prominent aristocratic family, he was educated at the College of William and Mary, graduating with highest honors in 1762. As an advocate for American independence from Great Britain, he was commissioned to serve on a committee to draft the Declaration of Independence. This brief but substantial pronouncement articulates the logic for independence upon the foundation of natural rights, which in turn have become the central precepts governing most modern democracies.

THE UNANIMOUS DECLARATION OF THE THIRTEEN UNITED STATES OF AMERICA

1   When in the Course of human events, it becomes necessary for one people to dissolve the political bands which have connected them with another, and to assume among the Powers of the earth, the separate and equal station to which the Laws of Nature and of Nature's God entitle them, a decent respect to the opinions of mankind requires that they should declare the causes which impel them to the separation.

2   We hold these truths to be self-evident, that all men are created equal, that they are endowed by their Creator with certain inalienable Rights, that among these are Life, Liberty and the pursuit of Happiness.[1] That to secure these rights, Governments are instituted among Men, deriving their just powers from the consent of the governed. That whenever any Form of Government becomes destructive of these ends, it is the Right of the People to alter or to abolish it, and to institute new Government, laying its foundation on such principles and organizing its powers in such form, as to them shall seem most likely to effect their Safety and Happiness. Prudence, indeed, will dictate that Governments long established should not be changed for light and transient causes; and accordingly all experience hath shown, that mankind are more disposed to suffer, while evils are sufferable, than to right themselves by abolishing the forms to which they are accustomed. But when a long train of abuses and usurpations, pursuing invariably the same Object evinces a design to reduce them under absolute Despotism, it is their right, it is their duty, to throw off such Government, and to provide new Guards for their future security.—Such has been the patient sufferance of these Colonies; and such is now the necessity which constrains them to alter their former Systems of Government. The history of the present King of Great Britain[2] is a history of repeated injuries and usurpations, all having in direct object the establishment of an absolute Tyranny over these States. To prove this, let Facts be submitted to a candid world.

3   He has refused his Assent to Laws, the most wholesome and necessary for the public good.

4   He has forbidden his Governors to pass Laws of immediate and pressing importance, unless suspended in their operation till his Assent should be obtained; and when so suspended, he has utterly neglected to attend to them.

---

[1] In using the phrase "Life, Liberty, and pursuit of Happiness," Jefferson modifies John Locke's wording "life, liberty, and property," which appears in his *Two Treatises on Government* (1689).

[2] King George the Third of Great Britain, who reigned from 1760 to 1801.

5   He has refused to pass other laws for the accommodation of large districts of people, unless those people would relinquish the right of Representation in the Legislature, a right inestimable to them and formidable to tyrants only.

6   He has called together legislative bodies at places unusual, uncomfortable, and distant from the depository of their Public Records, for the sole purpose of fatiguing them into compliance with his measures.

7   He has dissolved Representative Houses repeatedly, for opposing with manly firmness his invasions on the rights of the people.

8   He has refused for a long time, after such dissolutions, to cause others to be elected; whereby the Legislative Powers, incapable of Annihilation, have returned to the People at large for their exercise; the State remaining in the mean time exposed to all the dangers of invasion from without, and convulsions within.

9   He has endeavoured to prevent the population of these States; for that purpose obstructing the Laws for Naturalization of Foreigners; refusing to pass others to encourage their migration hither, and raising the conditions of new Appropriations of Lands.

10   He has obstructed the Administration of Justice, by refusing his Assent to Laws for establishing Judiciary Powers.

11   He has made Judges dependent on his Will alone, for the tenure of their offices, and the amount and payment of their salaries.

12   He has erected a multitude of New Offices, and sent hither swarms of Officers to harass our People, and eat out their substance.

13   He has kept among us, in times of peace, Standing Armies without the Consent of our legislature.

14   He has affected to render the Military independent of and superior to the Civil Power.

15   He has combined with others to subject us to a jurisdiction foreign to our constitution, and unacknowledged by our laws; giving his Assent to their acts of pretended Legislation:

16   For quartering large bodies of armed troops among us:

17   For protecting them, by a mock Trial, from Punishment for any Murders which they should commit on the Inhabitants of these States:

18   For cutting off our Trade with all parts of the world:

19   For imposing taxes on us without our Consent:

20   For depriving us in many cases, of the benefits of Trial by Jury:

21   For transporting us beyond Seas to be tried for pretended offences:

22   For abolishing the free System of English Laws in a neighbouring Province, establishing therein an Arbitrary government, and enlarging its Boundaries so as to render it at once an example and fit instrument for introducing the same absolute rule into these Colonies:

23   For taking away our Charters, abolishing our most valuable Laws, and altering fundamentally the Forms of our Governments:

24   For suspending our own Legislatures, and declaring themselves invested with Power to legislate for us in all cases whatsoever.

25   He has abdicated Government here, by declaring us out of his Protection and waging War against us.

26   He has plundered our seas, ravaged our Coasts, burnt our towns, and destroyed the lives of our people.

27   He is at this time transporting large armies of foreign mercenaries to compleat the works of death, desolation and tyranny, already begun with circumstances of Cruelty & perfidy[3] scarcely paralleled in the most barbarous ages, and totally unworthy the Head of a civilized nation.

28   He has constrained our fellow Citizens taken Captive on the high Seas to bear Arms against their Country, to become the executioners of their friends and Brethren, or to fall themselves by their Hands.

29   He has excited domestic insurrections amongst us, and has endeavoured to bring on the inhabitants of our frontiers, the merciless Indian Savages, whose known rule of warfare, is an undistinguished destruction of all ages, sexes and conditions.

30   In every stage of these Oppressions We have Petitioned for Redress in the most humble terms: Our repeated Petitions have been answered only by repeated injury. A Prince, whose character is thus marked by every act which may define a Tyrant, is unfit to be the ruler of a free People.

31   Nor have We been wanting in attention to our British brethren. We have warned them from time to time of attempts by their legislature to extend an unwarrantable jurisdiction over us. We have reminded them of the circumstances of our emigration and settlement here. We have appealed to their native justice and magnanimity, and we have conjured them by the ties of our common kindred to disavow these usurpations, which, would inevitably interrupt our connections and correspondence. They too have been deaf to the voice of justice and of consanguinity.[4] We must, therefore, acquiesce in the necessity, which denounces our Separation, and hold them, as we hold the rest of mankind, Enemies in War, in Peace Friends.

32   We, therefore, the Representatives of the United States of America, in General Congress, Assembled, appealing to the Supreme Judge of the world for the rectitude of our intentions, do, in the Name, and by Authority of the good People of these Colonies, solemnly publish and declare, That these United Colonies are, and of Right ought to be Free and Independent States, that they are Absolved from all Allegiance to the British Crown, and that all political connection between them and the State of Great Britain, is and ought to be totally dissolved; and that as Free and Independent States, they have full Power to levy War, conclude Peace, contract Alliances, establish Commerce, and to do all other Acts and Things which Independent States may of right do. And for the support of this Declaration, with a firm reliance on the Protection of Divine Providence, we mutually pledge to each other our Lives, our Fortunes and our sacred Honor.

---

[3] perfidy: an act or instance of disloyalty.
[4] consanguinity: a close connection or relation.

QUESTIONS ON MEANING

1. What truths are self-evident? What does he mean by self-evident?

2. What is the purpose of government? From where do those governments derive their authority?

3. From Jefferson's point of view, why is separation from Great Britain justifiable?

4. Why is King George the Third's Assent to Law important? What essential set of political principles would his assent serve?

5. In general terms, how does Jefferson define tyranny?

6. How does Jefferson's final reference to Divine Providence square with his assertions about natural human rights? What really are natural rights?

QUESTIONS FOR DISCUSSION

1. On what objective basis can we claim, as Jefferson does, that human beings have natural or inalienable rights?

2. Jefferson implicitly accepts the possibility of armed revolution against tyrannical government. How do we balance the rights of the individual with the stability of the state?

3. If natural or inalienable rights are conferred by a Creator, what are civil rights, and where do they come from?

LOOKING AT RHETORIC

1. In what way does the first paragraph set up the argument that follows? How does this contribute to the Declaration's effectiveness as a political document?

2. Why does Jefferson choose to modify John Locke's life, liberty, and property to Life, Liberty, and the pursuit of Happiness? In other words, in terms of its goals with its audience, in what way is this brief public document different from a more lengthy work of political philosophy?

3. What role does the list of abuses play in the Declaration as a whole? Is it effective or ineffective?

WRITING ASSIGNMENTS

1. What really are natural rights? Have you ever found yourself working under an authority that violated what you believe to be your fundamental rights? What were the circumstances? What were those rights and how were they violated? What makes them fundamental? Research sources in history and political science, particularly in the realm of natural rights theory.

2. Argue for or against the notion that human rights are inalienable or natural.

3. In pairs or in groups, make two lists. One should be a list of natural rights, those conferred by natural law, the Creator, or Providence. Make another list of civil rights, those conferred by the agreement of members of a society (the Bill of Rights and the American Constitution). To distinguish between them, consider how one person's natural rights might conflict with another person's. As an example, consider the segregationist restaurant owner's right to serve who he chooses, against the African American's right to participate fully in his society by eating in that restaurant. Individually, write an essay in which you accomplish one of two things; first, demonstrate how natural rights lead to more limited civil rights, or second, make an argument for how civil rights might emerge in a society on their own.

Civil Disobedience

Henry David Thoreau

Henry David Thoreau (1817-1862) was one of the leading figures of the American Transcendentalist movement, a highly influential and eclectic religious and social philosophy dominant in the nineteenth century. He was educated at the Concord Academy and at Harvard. After graduating from college, he returned home and began teaching, but later he dedicated himself to writing, partly under the influence of his mentor Ralph Waldo Emerson and British romantics such as Thomas Carlyle. His most famous book is Walden, or Life in the Woods, *written after he spent two years living in a cabin near Walden Pond. His other works include* A Week on the Concord and Merrimack Rivers *(1849),* Excursions *(1863), and* The Maine Woods *(1864). Partly motivated by his anger at slavery and the Mexican War, his most important social treatise is "Resistance to Civil Government" (1849), which was posthumously titled "On the Duty of Civil Disobedience." In this essay, Thoreau argues for the practice of what has come to be known as "passive resistance." In order to make governments just, citizens have the obligation to deny their support, both in terms of taxes and service. Controversial in its time, this essay became the foundation for the civil resistance movements of Mahatma Gandhi and Martin Luther King, Jr., who openly acknowledged Thoreau's influence.*

1   I heartily accept the motto—"That government is best which governs least," and I should like to see it acted up to more rapidly and systematically. Carried out, it finally amounts to this, which also I believe—"That government is best which governs not at all"; and when men are prepared for it, that will be the kind of government which they will have. Government is at best but an expedient; but most governments are usually, and all governments are sometimes, inexpedient. The objections which have been brought against a standing army, and they are many and weighty, and deserve to prevail, may also at last be brought against a standing government. The standing army is only an arm of the standing government. The government itself, which is only the mode which the people have chosen to execute their will, is equally liable to be abused and perverted before the people can act through it. Witness the present Mexican war,[1] the work of comparatively a few individuals using the standing government as their tool; for in the outset the people would not have consented to this measure.

2   This American government—what is it but a tradition, a recent one, endeavoring to transmit itself unimpaired to posterity but each instant losing some of its integrity? It has not the vitality and force of a single living man; for a single man can bend it to his will. It is a sort of wooden gun to the people themselves. But it is not the less necessary for this; for the people must have some complicated machinery or other, and hear its din, to satisfy that idea of government which they have. Governments show thus how successfully

---

[1] Mexican War: The United States annexed Texas in 1845, prompting a response from Mexico and leading to a war which lasted from 1846-1847.

men can be imposed on, even impose on themselves, for their own advantage. It is excellent, we must all allow. Yet this government never of itself furthered any enterprise but by the alacrity with which it got out of its way. *It* does not keep the country free. *It* does not settle the West.[2] *It* does not educate. The character inherent in the American people has done all that has been accomplished; and it would have done somewhat more if the government had not sometimes got in its way. For government is an expedient by which men would fain succeed in letting one another alone; and, as has been said, when it is most expedient the governed are most let alone by it. Trade and commerce, if they were not made of India-rubber, would never manage to bounce over the obstacles which legislators are continually putting in their way; and, if one were to judge these men wholly by the effects of their actions and not partly by their intentions, they would deserve to be classed and punished with those mischievous persons who put obstructions on the railroads.

3   But to speak practically and as a citizen, unlike those who call themselves no-government men, I ask for, not at once no government, but *at once* a better government. Let every man make known what kind of government would command his respect, and that will be one step toward obtaining it.

4   After all, the practical reason why, when the power is once in the hands of the people, a majority are permitted, and for a long period continue, to rule is not because they are most likely to be in the right, nor because this seems fairest to the minority but because they are physically the strongest. But a government in which the majority rule in all cases cannot be based on justice, even as far as men understand it. Can there not be a government in which majorities do not virtually decide right and wrong but conscience?—in which majorities decide only those questions to which the rule of expediency is applicable? Must the citizen ever for a moment, or in the least degree, resign his conscience to the legislator? Why has every man a conscience[3] then? I think that we should be men first and subjects afterward. It is not desirable to cultivate a respect for the law, so much as for the right. The only obligation which I have a right to assume is to do at any time what I think right. It is truly enough said that a corporation has no conscience; but a corporation of conscientious men is a corporation *with* a conscience. Law never made men a whit more just; and, by means of their respect for it, even the well-disposed are daily made the agents of injustice. A common and natural result of an undue respect for law is that you may see a file of soldiers, colonel, captain, corporal, privates, powder-monkeys,[4] and all, marching in admirable order over hill and dale to the wars, against their wills, ay, against their common sense and consciences, which

---

[2] settle the West: During Thoreau's time, migration to the western territories was increasing, partly under the influence of the concept of "Manifest Destiny," a term coined by John L. O'Sullivan (1813-1895) that suggests that it is America's divinely ordained destiny to settle the west and provide a place of growth for the emerging democratic nation.

[3] Conscience: Thoreau derives this notion in part from the German Romantic philosophy of Immanuel Kant (1724-1804), who argued that human beings possess an "innate moral sense" that precedes culture and experience.

[4] Powder-monkeys: In battle, boys who delivered gunpowder to cannons and artillery.

makes it very steep marching indeed and produces a palpitation of the heart. They have no doubt that it is a damnable business in which they are concerned; they are all peaceably inclined. Now, what are they? Men at all? or small movable forts and magazines at the service of some unscrupulous man in power? Visit the Navy-Yard, and behold a marine, such a man as an American government can make, or such as it can make a man with its black arts—a mere shadow and reminiscence of humanity, a man laid out alive and standing, and already, as one may say, buried under arms with funeral accompaniments, though it may be—

> *Not a drum was heard, not a funeral note,*
> *As his corse to the rampart we hurried;*
> *Not a soldier discharged his farewell shot*
> *O'er the grave where our hero we buried.*[5]

5   The mass of men serve the state thus, not as men mainly, but as machines, with their bodies. They are the standing army, and the militia, jailers, constables, posse comitatus?[6] &c. In most cases there is no free exercise whatever of the judgment or of the moral sense; but they put themselves on a level with wood and earth and stones; and wooden men can perhaps be manufactured that will serve the purpose as well. Such command no more respect than men of straw or a lump of dirt. They have the same sort of worth only as horses and dogs. Yet such as these even are commonly esteemed good citizens. Others—as most legislators, politicians, lawyers, ministers, and office-holders—serve the state chiefly with their heads; and, as they rarely make any moral distinctions, they are as likely to serve the Devil, without *intending* it, as God. A very few, as heroes, patriots, martyrs, reformers in the great sense, and *men*, serve the state with their consciences also and so necessarily resist it for the most part; and they are commonly treated as enemies by it. A wise man will only be useful as a man and will not submit to be "clay" and "stop a hole to keep the wind away," but leave that office to his dust at least:

> *I am too high-born to be propertied,*
> *To be a secondary at control,*
> *Or useful serving-man and instrument*
> *To any sovereign state throughout the world*[7]

6   He who gives himself entirely to his fellow-men appears to them useless and selfish; but he who gives himself partially to them is pronounced a benefactor and philanthropist.

7   How does it become a man to behave toward this American government today? I answer, that he cannot without disgrace be associated with it. I cannot for an instant recognize that political organization as *my* government which is the *slave's* government also.

8   All men recognize the right of revolution; that is, the right to refuse allegiance to, and to resist the government when its tyranny or its inefficiency are great and unendurable. But almost all say that such is not the case now. But such was the case, they think, in the Revolution of '75. If one were to tell me that this was a bad government because it taxed certain foreign

---

[5] Lines from the Irish poet Charles Wolfe's (1791-1823) poem "Burial of Sir John Moore at Corunna" (1817).

[6] posse comitatus: Essentially a private militia, a group of citizens that form a law enforcement group.

[7] The quoted lines in the text of the paragraph are from Shakespeare's *Hamlet*, Act V, Scene i, lines 236-237. The longer verse is from his *King John*, Act V, Scene ii, lines 79-82.

commodities brought to its ports, it is most probable that I should not make an ado about it, for I can do without them. All machines have their friction; and possibly this does enough good to counterbalance the evil. At any rate, it is a great evil to make a stir about it. But when the friction comes to have its machine, and oppression and robbery are organized, I say let us not have such a machine any longer. In other words, when a sixth of the population of a nation which has undertaken to be the refuge of liberty are slaves, and a whole country is unjustly overrun and conquered by a foreign army and subjected to military law, I think that it is not too soon for honest men to rebel and revolutionize. What makes this duty the more urgent is the fact that the country so overrun is not our own, but ours is the invading army.

9   Paley,[8] a common authority with many on moral questions, in his chapter on the "Duty of Submission to Civil Government," resolves all civil obligation into expediency; and he proceeds to say, "that so long as the interest of the whole society requires it, that is, so long as the established government cannot be resisted or charged without public inconveniency, it is the will of God that the established government be obeyed, and no longer. . . . This principle being admitted, the justice of every particular case of resistance is reduced to a computation of the quantity of the danger and grievance on the one side, and of the probability and expense of redressing it on the other." Of this, he says, every man shall judge for himself. But Paley appears never to have contemplated those cases to which the rule of expediency does not apply, in which a people, as well as an individual, must do justice, cost what it may. If I have unjustly wrested a plank from a drowning man, I must restore it to him though I drown myself. This, according to Paley, would be inconvenient. But he that would save his life, in such a case, shall lose it. This people must cease to hold slaves and to make war on Mexico, though it cost them their existence as a people.

10   In their practice, nations agree with Paley; but does anyone think that Massachusetts does exactly what is right at the present crisis?

A drab of state, a cloth-o'-silver slut,
To have her train borne up, and her soul trail in the dirt[9]

11   Practically speaking, the opponents to a reform in Massachusetts are not a hundred thousand politicians at the South but a hundred thousand merchants and farmers here, who are more interested in commerce and agriculture than they are in humanity, and are not prepared to do justice to the slave and to Mexico, *cost what it may*. I quarrel not with far-off foes but with those who, near at home, cooperate with, and do the bidding of, those far away, and without whom the latter would be harmless. We are accustomed to say that the mass of men are unprepared; but improvement is slow because the few are not materially wiser or better than the many. It is not so important that many should be as good as you as that there be some absolute goodness somewhere; for that will leaven the whole lump. There are thousands who are *in opinion* opposed to slavery and to the war who yet in effect do nothing to put an end to them; who, esteeming themselves children of Washington and Franklin, sit down with their hands in their pockets and say that they know not what to do, and do nothing; who even postpone the question of freedom to the question of free trade,

---

[8] William Paley (1743-1805): English theologian and natural philosopher who wrote on scientific as well as philosophical, ethical, and religious issues and their interrelationships.
[9] From Cyril (1575?-1626) *Revenger's Tragedy* (1607). "Drab" is an archaic term for prostitute.

and quietly read the prices-current along with the latest advices from Mexico after dinner and, it may be, fall asleep over them both. What is the price-current of an honest man and patriot today? They hesitate and they regret and sometimes they petition; but they do nothing in earnest and with effect. They will wait, well disposed, for others to remedy the evil, that they may no longer have it to regret. At most, they give only a cheap vote, and a feeble countenance and God-speed, to the right, as it goes by them. There are nine hundred and ninety-nine patrons of virtue to one virtuous man. But it is easier to deal with the real possessor of a thing than with the temporary guardian of it.

12   All voting is a sort of gaming, like checkers or backgammon, with a slight moral tinge to it, a playing with right and wrong, with moral questions; and betting naturally accompanies it. The character of the voters is not staked. I cast my vote, perchance, as I think right; but I am not vitally concerned that that right should prevail. I am willing to leave it to the majority. Its obligation, therefore, never exceeds that of expediency. Even voting *for the right* is *doing* nothing for it. It is only expressing to men feebly your desire that it should prevail. A wise man will not leave the right to the mercy of chance, nor wish it to prevail through the power of the majority. There is but little virtue in the action of masses of men. When the majority shall at length vote for the abolition of slavery, it will be because they are indifferent to slavery, or because there is but little slavery left to be abolished by their vote. *They* will then be the only slaves. Only *his* vote can hasten the abolition of slavery who asserts his own freedom by his vote.

13   I hear of a convention to be held at Baltimore, or elsewhere, for the selection of a candidate for the Presidency, made up chiefly of editors, and men who are politicians by profession; but I think, what is it to any independent, intelligent, and respectable man what decision they may come to? Shall we not have the advantage of his wisdom and honesty nevertheless? Can we not count upon some independent votes? Are there not many individuals in the country who do not attend conventions? But no: I find that the responsible man, so called, has immediately drifted from his position, and despairs of his country when his country has more reason to despair of him. He forthwith adopts one of the candidates thus selected as the only *available* one, thus proving that he is himself *available* for any purposes of the demagogue. His vote is of no more worth than that of any unprincipled foreigner or hireling native who may have been bought. O for a man who is a *man* and, as my neighbor says has a bone in his back which you cannot pass your hand through! Our statistics are at fault: the population has been returned too large. How many *men* are there to a square thousand miles in this country? Hardly one. Does not America offer any inducement for men to settle here? The American has dwindled into an Odd Fellow—one who may be known by the development of his organ of gregariousness and a manifest lack of intellect and cheerful self-reliance; whose first and chief concern, on coming into the world, is to see that the Almshouses are in good repair; and, before yet he has lawfully donned the virile garb, to collect a fund for the support of the widows and orphans that may be; who, in short, ventures to live only by the aid of the Mutual Insurance Company, which has promised to bury him decently.

14   It is not a man's duty, as a matter of course, to devote himself to the eradication of any, even the most enormous wrong; he may still properly have other concerns to engage him; but it is his duty, at least, to wash his hands of it and, if he gives it no thought longer, not to give it practically his support. If I devote myself to other pursuits and contemplations, I must first see, at least, that I do not pursue them sitting upon another man's shoulders. I must get off him first, that he may pursue his contemplations too. See what gross inconsistency is tolerated. I have heard some of my townsmen say, "I should like to have them order me

out to help put down an insurrection of the slaves, or to march to Mexico—see if I would go," and yet these very men have each directly by their allegiance and so indirectly, at least, by their money, furnished a substitute. The soldier is applauded who refuses to serve in an unjust war by those who do not refuse to sustain the unjust government which makes the war; is applauded by those whose own act and authority he disregards and sets at naught; as if the State were penitent to that degree that it hired one to scourge it while it sinned, but not to that degree that it left off sinning for a moment. Thus, under the name of Order and Civil Government, we are all made at last to pay homage to and support our own meanness. After the first blush of sin comes its indifference; and from immoral it becomes, as it were, *un*moral, and not quite unnecessary to that life which we have made.

QUESTIONS ON MEANING

1. What historical events in Thoreau's time motivate his desire for governmental reform?
2. Anarchy is broadly defined as a form of social organization without central control. Does Thoreau consider himself an anarchist? Why or why not?
3. What personal attribute do human beings possess that allows them to disobey laws they consider unjust without creating social chaos?
4. What ought to be the role of government as it relates to the individual?
5. What is the author's attitude toward majority rule? What are the potential problems with it?
6. How should the *individual* respond to social injustices when they see them?

QUESTIONS FOR DISCUSSION

1. In practical terms, how workable is Thoreau's method of social reform? What would be the consequences if we all followed it, individually or in groups?
2. What are some of the religious or metaphysical assumptions that inform Thoreau's method of social reform? In what way do they help make it workable? Do they?
3. To what extent can human *conscience* (as the author defines it) provide a means to support his radical individualism?

LOOKING AT RHETORIC

1. How does Thoreau's forceful tone detract or reinforce his argument?
2. In what way does his use of exemplification, particularly the references to slavery and the Mexican War, make his argument more or less effective? How does he formally link the examples to the argument?
3. This essay was delivered as a lecture as well as a written document. What advantages and disadvantages are there to oral versus written communication?

WRITING ASSIGNMENTS

1. How potentially effective is Thoreau's method of passive resistance, or active non-participation? Consider Mahatma Gandhi and Martin Luther King, Jr. Are there ways in which they refined and improved upon it?

2. Do individuals have the inherent right to disobey what they see as unjust laws? What would be the consequences of this? Is there any reasonable basis for concluding that this behavior would be justifiable in a society or a community?

3. In pairs or groups discuss Thoreau's method of passive resistance. Under what circumstances has it worked? Can it in the future? What are its limitations, if any? Individually, identify a circumstance in your own experience in which a rule was imposed unjustly. Write a specific plan for how you could have dealt with the problem, defining your method, process of implementation, and your expected results.

The Non-Violent Society

Mahatma Gandhi

Mohandas Karamchand Gandhi (1869-1948) was a principal leader in the early twentieth-century nationalist movement that led to Indian independence from British colonial rule. He is called Mahatma, an honorific title from Sanskrit meaning Great Soul. A devout Hindu, Gandhi married at the age of thirteen and in 1888 left for England to study law. While abroad, he was exposed to theosophists and vegetarians, many of them highly skeptical of modern society and its Enlightenment legacy. He returned to India after completing his education, and his work demonstrates the relationship among politics and religion and philosophy. He took a position as legal advisor to a businessman in South Africa and was exposed to the racial prejudice prevalent there. As a result, he began a resistance movement that increased his public exposure. While in Africa, he coined the term satyagraha, *which referred to the practice of non-violent resistance based on the idea that peace emerges as oppressor and oppressed come to recognize the sympathetic bond between them. The following selection applies this concept to social reform and the relationship of the individual and the government. Returning to India in 1915, he worked tirelessly to bring about independence from Great Britain, which occurred in 1947 when India was partitioned into Hindu and Muslim sections. Afterward, he campaigned for a united India. For his efforts, he was imprisoned numerous times and was ultimately assassinated by a Hindu extremist in 1948.*

1   I hold that nonviolence is not merely a personal virtue. It is also a social virtue to be cultivated like the other virtues. Surely society is largely regulated by the expression of nonviolence in its mutual dealings. What I ask for is an extension of it on a larger, national and international scale.

2   All society is held together by nonviolence, even as the earth is held in her position by gravitation. But when the law of gravitation was discovered, the discovery yielded results of which our ancestors had no knowledge. Even so, when society is deliberately constructed in accordance with the law of nonviolence, its structure will be different in material particulars from what it is today. But I cannot say in advance what the government based on nonviolence will be like.

3   What is happening today is disregard of the law of nonviolence and enthronement of violence as if it were an eternal law.

4   Society based on nonviolence can only consist of groups settled in villages in which voluntary cooperation is the condition of dignified and peaceful existence.

THE GOVERNMENT

5   The Government cannot succeed in becoming entirely nonviolent, because it represents all the people. I do not today conceive of such a golden age. But I do believe in the possibility of a predominantly nonviolent society. And I am working for it.

6   There remains the question as to whether in an ideal society, there should be any or no government. I do not think we need worry ourselves about this at the moment. If we continue to work for such a society, it will slowly come into being to an extent, such that the people can benefit by it. Euclid's line[1] is one without breadth, but no one has so far been able to draw it and never will. All the same, it is only by keeping the ideal line in mind that we have made progress in geometry. What is true here is true of every ideal.

ANARCHY

7   It must be remembered that nowhere in the world does a State without government exist.[2] If at all it could ever come into being, it would be in India; for, ours is the only country where the attempt has, at any rate, been made. We have not yet been able to show that bravery to the degree which is necessary and for the attainment of which there is only one way. Those who have faith in the latter have to demonstrate it. In order to do so, the fear of death has to be completely shed, just as we have shed the fear of prisons.

DEMOCRACY AND NONVIOLENCE

8   Science of war leads one to dictatorship pure and simple. Science of nonviolence can alone lead one to pure democracy.

9   Democracy and violence can ill go together. The States that are today nominally democratic have either to become frankly totalitarian, or if they are to become truly democratic, they must become courageously nonviolent.

10   Holding the view that, without the recognition of nonviolence on a national scale, there is no such thing as a constitutional or democratic government, I devote my energy to the propagation of nonviolence as the law of our life, individual, social, political, national and international.

11   I fancy that I have seen the light, though dimly. I write cautiously for I do not profess to know the whole of the Law. If I know the success of my experiments, I know also my failures. But the successes are enough to fill me with undying hope.

12   I have often said that if one takes care of the means, the end will take care of itself. Nonviolence is the means, the end for everyone is complete independence. There will be an international League only when all the nations, big or small, composing it are

---

[1] Euclid's line: From Euclid of Alexandria (approx. 325 B.C. to 265 B.C.), Greek mathematician influential in developing the understanding of Euclidian geometry. Euclid's line is one of his "elements," a breadthless length.

[2] Perhaps an allusion to the issues expressed in Thoreau's "Civil Disobedience."

fully independent. The nature of that independence will correspond to the extent of nonviolence assimilated by the nations concerned. One thing is certain. In a society based on nonviolence, the smallest nation will feel as tall as the tallest. The idea of superiority and inferiority will be wholly obliterated.

13   . . . The conclusion is irresistible that for one like me, wedded to nonviolence, constitutional or democratic government is a distant dream so long as nonviolence is not recognized as a living force, an inviolable creed, not a mere policy. While I prate about universal nonviolence, my experiment is confined to India. If it succeeds, the world will accept it without effort. There is however a bit of a BUT. The pause does not worry me. My faith is brightest in the midst of impenetrable darkness.

USE OF POWER

14   By its very nature, nonviolence cannot 'seize' power, nor can that be its goal. But nonviolence can do more; it can effectively control and guide power without capturing the machinery of government. That is its beauty.

15   There is an exception, of course. If the nonviolent non-cooperation of the people is so complete that the administration ceases to function or if the administration crumbles under the impact of a foreign invasion and a vacuum results, the people's representatives will then step in and fill it. Theoretically that is possible.

16   But the use of power need not necessarily be violent. A father wields power over his children; he may even punish but not by infliction violence. The most effective exercise of power is that which irks least. Power rightly exercised must sit light as a flower; no one should feel the weight of it.

17   The people accepted the authority of the Congress willingly. I was on more than one · occasion invested with the absolute power of dictatorship. But everybody knew that my power rested on their willing acceptance. They could set me aside at any time and I would have stepped aside without a murmur.

18   Prophets and supermen are born only once in an age. But if even a single individual realizes the ideal of ahimsa[3] in its fullness, he covers and redeems the whole society. Once Jesus had blazed the trail, his twelve disciples could carry on his mission without his presence.

19   It needed the perseverance and genius of so many generations of scientists to discover the laws of electricity, but today everybody, even children use electric power in their daily life. Similarly, it will not always need a perfect being to administer an ideal State once it has come into being. What is needed is a thorough social awakening to begin with. The rest will follow.

20   To take an instance nearer home, I have presented to the working class the truth that true capital is not silver or gold, but the labour of their hands and feet and their intelligence. Once labour develops that awareness, it would not need my presence to enable it to make use of the power that it will release.

---

[3] ahimsa: Sanskrit term meaning "to do no harm." Important tenet in many of the religions originating in Ancient India, including Hinduism, Buddhism, and Jainism.

QUESTIONS ON MEANING

1. What does Gandhi mean by the law of non-violence? Why does he call it a law?

2. What important principle do modern societies consistently ignore, and what do they enthrone instead?

3. If non-violence is a means of social change in a society, what is the end?

4. Gandhi claims that true capital is not silver or gold. What is true capital?

5. If violence can seize power and non-violence cannot, what can the practice of non-violence provide in the development of a stable government and society?

6. What is the most effective exercise of power? What image does Gandhi use to describe it?

QUESTIONS FOR DISCUSSION

1. Is Gandhi's principle of non-violence too idealistic? Can it ever really be elevated from a personal virtue to a realistic practice on a global level? In other words, if attacked, can a nation respond non-violently?

2. Is non-violence an essential ingredient of a democratic society? Can we conceive of a democratic society that is not assertively or courageously non-violent? To what extent can our own democratic society be characterized in these terms?

3. What value is there in considering non-violence a means rather than an end?

LOOKING AT RHETORIC

1. In the introduction, the essay establishes certain assumptions upon which the argument is based. What are they? How do they help to structure the essay as a treatise on social reform?

2. The essay is organized around an introduction and four topical sections. What purpose does the structure serve? In what way do these topics relate to one another?

3. What purpose do the short paragraphs serve? Does the brief length of the essay make it more or less effective?

WRITING ASSIGNMENTS

1. Consider any historical event you have learned about in which a nation has responded violently to an act of violence. Consider Gandhi's notion of non-violence as a social virtue. Argue for or against that response. What, if anything, is lost in responding violently?

2. Identify a circumstance when you have confronted aggression. If you have never experienced this, imagine a situation. Write a fictional narrative that describes your response in implementing Gandhi's practice. The results, positive or negative, are up to you.

3. In pairs or in groups, imagine a conflict that may lead to violence. Invent the circumstances. Referring to the Gandhi essay, list the advantages and disadvantages of a non-violent response. Individually, write an argumentative essay in which you lay out a strategy, similar or dissimilar to Gandhi's, to resolve the situation.

Interdisciplinary Connections

Governments and their Symbols

Below are two images that have come to have significant meaning, power, and value for the United States and for England: the Great Seal of the United States, and the Royal Coat of Arms of the United Kingdom. What do these images tell you about their respective countries? What do the images mean or symbolize? How can a mere image come to have power? Do you find these images to be fair or accurate representations of their respective countries? If you were

Great Seal of the United States

to design an image to be used as the Great Seal of the United States, what image would you draw? What details would be important to you and what would the elements of your image symbolize?

United Kingdom Royal Coat of Arms

Letter from a Birmingham Jail

Martin Luther King, Jr.

Martin Luther King, Jr. (1928-1968) is regarded as one of the most significant leaders in the American Civil Rights Movement. Growing up in the south and attending segregated schools, he nevertheless graduated from Morehouse College in 1948. He received a Bachelors of Divinity from Crozer Theological Seminary in 1951 and a doctorate from Boston University in 1955. After becoming the pastor of the Dexter Avenue Baptist Church in Montgomery, Alabama, King became increasingly involved in the emerging civil rights movement. He took a position on the executive committee of the National Association for the Advancement of Colored People (NAACP) and later became president of the Southern Christian Leadership Conference. King traveled the country speaking and marching for civil rights. In addition, he wrote five books and won the Nobel Peace Prize in 1964 for his many sacrifices in the pursuit of social justice. "Letter from a Birmingham Jail" was written after his arrest during the bus boycott, and became one of the most important written manifestos of civil rights. Having lived for years under the threat of violence, King was assassinated in 1968.

1   We know through painful experience that freedom is never voluntarily given by the oppressor; it must be demanded by the oppressed. Frankly, I have yet to engage in a direct-action campaign that was "well timed" in the view of those who have not suffered unduly from the disease of segregation. For years now I have heard the word "Wait!" It rings in the ear of every Negro with piercing familiarity. This "Wait" has almost always meant "Never." We must come to see, with one of our distinguished jurists, that "justice too long delayed is justice denied."[1]

2   We have waited for more than 340 years for our constitutional and God-given rights. The nations of Asia and Africa are moving with jetlike speed toward gaining political independence, but we still creep at horse-and-buggy pace toward gaining a cup of coffee at a lunch counter. Perhaps it is easy for those who have never felt the stinging darts of segregation to say, "Wait." But when you have seen vicious mobs lynch your mothers and fathers at will and drown your sisters and brothers at whim; when you have seen hate-filled policemen curse, kick, and even kill your black brothers and sisters; when you see the vast majority of your twenty million Negro brothers smothering in an airtight cage of poverty in the midst of an affluent society; when you suddenly find your tongue twisted and your speech stammering as you seek to explain to your six-year-old daughter why she can't go to the public amusement park that has just been advertised on television, and see tears welling up in her eyes when she is told that Funtown is closed to colored children, and see ominous clouds of inferiority beginning to form in her little mental sky, and see her beginning to distort her personality by developing an unconscious bitterness toward white people; when you have to concoct an answer for a five-year-old son who is asking, "Daddy, why do white people treat colored people so mean?"; when you take a cross-country drive and find it necessary to sleep night after night in the uncomfortable corners

---

[1] "justice too long delayed is justice denied": the words of Supreme Court Justice Earl Warren in 1954. It is a phrase derived from Walter Savage Landor's "Justice delayed is justice denied."

of your automobile because no motel will accept you; when you are humiliated day in and day out by nagging signs reading "white" and "colored"; when your first name becomes "nigger," your middle name becomes "boy' (however old you are) and your last name becomes "John," and your wife and mother are never given the respected title "Mrs."; when you are harried by day and haunted by night by the fact that you are a Negro, living constantly at tiptoe stance, never quite knowing what to expect next, and are plagued with inner fears and outer resentments; when you are forever fighting a degenerating sense of "nobodiness"—then you will understand why we find it difficult to wait. There comes a time when the cup of endurance runs over, and men are no longer willing to be plunged into the abyss of despair. I hope, sirs, you can understand our legitimate and unavoidable impatience.

3   You express a great deal of anxiety over our willingness to break laws. This is certainly a legitimate concern. Since we so diligently urge people to obey the Supreme Court's decision of 1954 outlawing segregation in the public schools, at first glance it may seem rather paradoxical for us consciously to break laws. One may well ask: "How can you advocate breaking some laws and obeying others?" The answer lies in the fact that there are two types of laws: just and unjust. I would be the first to advocate obeying just laws. One has not only a legal but a moral responsibility to obey just laws. Conversely, one has a moral responsibility to disobey unjust laws. I would agree with St. Augustine[2] that "an unjust law is no law at all."

4   Let us consider a more concrete example of just and unjust laws. An unjust law is a code that a numerical or power majority group compels a minority group to obey but does not make binding on itself. This is *difference* made legal. By the same token, a just law is a code that a majority compels a minority to follow and that it is willing to follow itself. This is *sameness* made legal.

5   Let me give another explanation. A law is unjust if it is inflicted on a minority that, as a result of being denied the right to vote, had no part in enacting or devising the law. Who can say that the legislature of Alabama which set up that state's segregation laws was democratically elected? Throughout Alabama all sorts of devious methods are used to prevent Negroes from becoming registered voters, and there are some counties in which, even though Negroes constitute a majority of the population, not a single Negro is registered. Can any law enacted under such circumstances be considered democratically structured?

6   Sometimes a law is just on its face and unjust in its application. For instance, I have been arrested on a charge of parading without a permit. Now, there is nothing wrong in having an ordinance which requires a permit for a parade. But such an ordinance becomes unjust when it is used to maintain segregation and to deny citizens the First Amendment privilege of peaceful assembly and protest.

7   I hope you are able to see the distinction I am trying to point out. In no sense do I advocate evading or defying the law, as would the rabid segregationist. That would lead to anarchy. One who breaks an unjust law must do so openly, lovingly, and with a willingness to accept the penalty. I submit that an individual who breaks a law that conscience tells him is unjust, and who willingly accepts the penalty of imprisonment in order to arouse the conscience of the community over its injustice, is in reality expressing the highest respect for law.

---

[2] St. Augustine (354-430): One of the most significant figures of the early Roman/Christian church, deeply influencing the development of its foundational theology.

8   Of course, there is nothing new about this kind of civil disobedience. It was evidenced subliminally in the refusal of Shadrach, Meshach, and Abednego to obey the laws of Nebuchadnezzar,[3] on the ground that a higher moral law was at stake. It was practiced superbly by the early Christians, who were willing to face hungry lions and the excruciating pain of chopping blocks rather than submit to certain unjust laws of the Roman Empire. To a degree, academic freedom is a reality today because Socrates practiced civil disobedience. In our own nation, the Boston Tea Party represented a massive act of civil disobedience.

9   We should never forget that everything Adolf Hitler did in Germany was "legal" and everything the Hungarian freedom fighters did in Hungary was "illegal." It was "illegal" to aid and comfort a Jew in Hitler's Germany. Even so, I am sure that, had I lived in Germany at the time, I would have aided and comforted my Jewish brothers. If today I lived in a Communist country where certain principles dear to the Christian faith are suppressed, I would openly advocate disobeying that country's antireligious laws.

10   Oppressed people cannot remain oppressed forever. The yearning for freedom eventually manifests itself, and that is what has happened to the American Negro. Something within has reminded him of his birthright of freedom, and something without has reminded him that it can be gained. Consciously or unconsciously, he has been caught up by the *Zeitgeist*[4] and with his black brothers of Africa and his brown and yellow brothers of Asia, South America, and the Caribbean, the United States Negro is moving with a sense of great urgency toward the promised land of racial justice. If one recognizes this vital urge that has engulfed the Negro community, one should readily understand why public demonstrations are taking place. The Negro has many pent-up resentments and latent frustrations, and he must release them. So let him march; let him make prayer pilgrimages to the city hall; let him go on freedom rides—and try to understand why he must do so. If his repressed emotions are not released in nonviolent ways, they will seek expression through violence; this is not a threat but a fact of history. So I have not said to my people, "Get rid of your discontent." Rather, I have tried to say that this normal and healthy discontent can be channeled into the creative outlet of nonviolent direct action. And now this approach is being termed extremist.

11   But though I was initially disappointed at being categorized as an extremist, as I continued to think about the matter I gradually gained a measure of satisfaction from the label. Was not Jesus an extremist for love: "Love your enemies, bless them that curse you, do good to them that hate you, and pray for them which despitefully use you, and persecute you." Was not Amos an extremist for justice: "Let justice roll down like waters and righteousness like an ever-flowing stream." Was not Paul an extremist for the Christian gospel: "I bear in my body the marks of the Lord Jesus." Was not Martin Luther an extremist: "Here I stand; I cannot do otherwise, so help me God." And John Bunyan: "I will stay in jail to the end of my days before I make a butchery of my conscience." And Abraham Lincoln: "This nation cannot survive half slave and half free." And Thomas Jefferson: "We hold these truths to be self-evident, that all men are created equal. . . ." So the question is not whether we will be extremists, but what kind of extremists we will be. Will we be extremists for hate

---

[3] Nebuchadnezzar (630-562 B. C.): Biblical King of Chaldea who attacked Jerusalem. In the Book of Daniel, he ordered three men to worship an idol, and when they refused they were cast into a furnace and rescued by God.

[4] *Zeitgeist*: German term that roughly translated means "the spirit of the times," referring to cultural, ethical, and intellectual ideals that dominate a given period.

or for love? Will we be extremists for the preservation of injustice or for the extension of justice? In that dramatic scene on Calvary's hill three men were crucified. We must never forget that all three were crucified for the same crime—the crime of extremism. Two were extremists for immorality, and thus fell below their environment. The other, Jesus Christ, was an extremist for love, truth, and goodness, and thereby rose above his environment. Perhaps the South, the nation, and the world are in dire need of creative extremists.

12   I had hoped that the white moderate would see this need. Perhaps I was too optimistic; perhaps I expected too much. I suppose I should have realized that few members of the oppressor race can understand the deep groans and passionate yearnings of the oppressed race, and still fewer have the vision to see that injustice must be rooted out by strong, persistent, and determined action. I am thankful, however, that some of our white brothers in the South have grasped the meaning of this social revolution and committed themselves to it. They are still all too few in quantity, but they are big in quality. Some—such as Ralph McGill, Lillian Smith, Harry Golden, James McBride Dabbs, Ann Braden, and Sarah Patton Boyle— have written about our struggle in eloquent and prophetic terms. Others have marched with us down nameless streets of the South. They have languished in filthy, roach-infested jails, suffering the abuse and brutality of policemen who view them as "dirty nigger-lovers." Unlike so many of their moderate brothers and sisters, they have recognized the urgency of the moment and sensed the need for powerful "action" antidotes to combat the disease of segregation.

13   Let me take note of my other major disappointment. I have been so greatly disappointed with the white church and its leadership. Of course, there are some notable exceptions. I am not unmindful of the fact that each of you has taken some significant stands on this issue. I commend you, Reverend Stallings; for your Christian stand on this past Sunday, in welcoming Negroes to your worship service on a nonsegregated basis. I commend the Catholic leaders of this state for integrating Spring Hill College several years ago.

14   But despite these notable exceptions, I must honestly reiterate that I have been disappointed with the church. I do not say this as one of those negative critics who can always find something wrong with the church. I say this as a minister of the gospel, who loves the church; who was nurtured in its bosom; who has been sustained by its spiritual blessings and who will remain true to it as long as the cord of life shall lengthen.

15   When I was suddenly catapulted into the leadership of the bus protest in Montgomery, Alabama, a few years ago, I felt we would be supported by the white church. I felt that the white ministers, priests, and rabbis of the South would be among our strongest allies. Instead, some have been outright opponents, refusing to understand the freedom movement and misrepresenting its leaders; all too many others have been more cautious than courageous and have remained silent behind the anesthetizing security of stained-glass windows.

16   In spite of my shattered dreams, I came to Birmingham with the hope that the white religious leadership of this community would see the justice of our cause and, with deep moral concern, would serve as the channel through which our just grievances could reach the power structure. I had hoped that each of you would understand. But again I have been disappointed. . . .

17   There was a time when the church was very powerful—in the time when the early Christians rejoiced at being deemed worthy to suffer for what they believed. In those days the church was not merely a thermometer that recorded the ideas and principles of popular opinion; it was a thermostat that transformed the mores of society. Whenever the early Christians entered a town, the people in power became disturbed and immediately sought

to convict the Christians for being "disturbers of the peace" and "outside agitators." But the Christians pressed on, in the conviction that they were "a colony of heaven," called to obey God rather than man. Small in number, they were big in commitment. They were too God intoxicated to be "astronomically intimidated." By their effort and example they brought an end to such ancient evils as infanticide and gladiatorial contests.

18   Things are different now. So often the contemporary church is a weak, ineffectual voice with an uncertain sound. So often it is an archdefender of the status quo. Far from being disturbed by the presence of the church, the powerful structure of the average community is consoled by the church's silent—and often even vocal—sanction of things as they are.

19   But the judgment of God is upon the church as never before. If today's church does not recapture the sacrificial spirit of the early church, it will lose its authenticity, forfeit the loyalty of millions, and be dismissed as an irrelevant social club with no meaning for the twentieth century. Every day I meet young people whose disappointment with the church has turned into outright disgust.

20   Perhaps I have once again been too optimistic. Is organized religion too inextricably bound to the status quo to save our nation and the world? Perhaps I must turn my faith to the inner spiritual church, the church within the church, as the true *ekklesia*[5] and the hope of the world. But again I am thankful to God that some noble souls from the ranks of organized religion have broken loose from the paralyzing chains of conformity and joined us as active partners in the struggle for freedom. They have left their secure congregations and walked the streets of Albany, Georgia, with us. They have gone down the highways of the South on torturous rides for freedom. Yes, they have gone to jail with us. Some have been dismissed from their churches, have lost the support of their bishops and fellow ministers. But they have acted in the faith that right defeated is stronger than evil triumphant. Their witness has been the spiritual salt that has preserved the true meaning of the gospel in these troubled times. They have carved a tunnel of hope through the dark mountain of disappointment.

21   I hope the church as a whole will meet the challenge of this decisive hour. But even if the church does not come to the aid of justice, I have no despair about the future. I have no fear about the outcome of our struggle in Birmingham, even if our motives are at present misunderstood. We will reach the goal of freedom in Birmingham and all over the nation, because the goal of America is freedom. Abused and scorned though we may be, our destiny is tied up with America's destiny. Before the pilgrims landed at Plymouth, we were here. Before the pen of Jefferson etched the majestic words of the Declaration of Independence across the pages of history, we were here. For more than two centuries our forebears labored in this country without wages; they made cotton king; they built the homes of their masters while suffering gross injustice and shameful humiliation—and yet out of a bottomless vitality they continued to thrive and develop. If the inexpressible cruelties of slavery could not stop us, the opposition we now face will surely fail. We will win our freedom because the sacred heritage of our nation and the eternal will of God are embodied in our echoing demands.

22   Before closing I feel impelled to mention one other point in your statement that has troubled me profoundly. You warmly commended the Birmingham police force for keeping "order" and "preventing violence." I doubt that you would have so warmly commended

---

[5] *ekklesia*: Greek root word for the term "ecclesiastical," meaning the "church," both as an institution and a spiritual ideal.

the police force if you had seen its dogs sinking their teeth into unarmed, nonviolent Negroes. I doubt that you would so quickly commend the policemen if you were to observe their ugly and inhumane treatment of Negroes here in the city jail; if you were to watch them push and curse old Negro women and young Negro girls; if you were to see them slap and kick old Negro men and young boys; if you were to observe them, as they did on two occasions, refuse to give us food because we wanted to sing our grace together. I cannot join you in your praise of the Birmingham police department.

23   It is true that the police have exercised a degree of discipline in handling the demonstrators. In this sense they have conducted themselves rather "nonviolently" in public. But for what purpose? To preserve the evil system of segregation. Over the past few years I have consistently preached that nonviolence demands that the means we use must be as pure as the ends we seek. I have tried to make clear that it is wrong to use immoral means to attain moral ends. But now I must affirm that it is just as wrong, or perhaps even more so, to use moral means to preserve immoral ends. Perhaps Mr. Connor and his policemen have been rather nonviolent in public, as was Chief Pritchett in Albany, Georgia, but they have used the moral means of nonviolence to maintain the immoral end of racial injustice. As T. S. Eliot[6] has said, "The last temptation is the greatest treason: To do the right deed for the wrong reason."

24   I wish you had commended the Negro sit-inners and demonstrators of Birmingham for their sublime courage, their willingness to suffer, and their amazing discipline in the midst of great provocation. One day the South will recognize its real heroes. They will be the James Merediths, with the noble sense of purpose that enables them to face jeering and hostile mobs, and with the agonizing loneliness that characterizes the life of the pioneer. They will be old, oppressed, battered Negro women, symbolized in a seventy-two-year-old woman in Montgomery, Alabama, who rose up with a sense of dignity and with her people decided not to ride segregated buses, and who responded with ungrammatical profundity to one who inquired about her weariness: "My feets is tired, but my soul is at rest." They will be the young high school and college students, the young ministers of the gospel and a host of their elders, courageously and nonviolently sitting in at lunch counters and willingly going to jail for conscience's sake. One day the South will know that when these disinherited children of God sat down at lunch counters, they were in reality standing up for what is best in the American dream and for the most sacred values in our Judaeo-Christian heritage, thereby bringing our nation back to those great wells of democracy which were dug deep by the founding fathers in their formulation of the Constitution and the Declaration of Independence.

25   Never before have I written so long a letter. I'm afraid it is much too long to take your precious time. I can assure you that it would have been much shorter if I had been writing from a comfortable desk, but what else can one do when he is alone in a narrow jail cell, other than write long letters, think long thoughts, and pray long prayers?

26   If I have said anything in this letter that overstates the truth and indicates an unreasonable impatience, I beg you to forgive me. If I have said anything that understates the truth and indicates my having a patience that allows me to settle for anything less than brotherhood, I beg God to forgive me.

---

[6] Thomas Stearns Eliot (1888-1965): Important twentieth-century American and British poet who addressed religious themes in a Christian context. King refers to lines from Eliot's play *Murder in the Cathedral*, which deals with the sacrifice of the medieval Archbishop of Canterbury, Thomas Becket, (1118-1170), who opposed King Henry II on matters related to church authority.

27   I hope this letter finds you strong in the faith. I also hope that circumstances will soon make it possible for me to meet each of you, not as an integrationist or a civil rights leader but as a fellow clergyman and a Christian brother. Let us all hope that the dark clouds of racial prejudice will soon pass away and the deep fog of misunderstanding will be lifted from our fear-drenched communities, and in some not too distant tomorrow the radiant stars of love and brotherhood will shine over our great nation with all their scintillating beauty.

Yours in the cause of Peace and Brotherhood,
MARTIN LUTHER KING, JR.

QUESTIONS ON MEANING

1. What are the four basic steps of a non-violent campaign? What is meant by the term purification?

2. What is the role that tension plays in social change? How does King use Socrates as an example?

3. How does King apply the Judeo-Christian principle of human sinfulness to segregation? What philosophers and theologians does he cite in making the connection? How does he use them?

4. How does King distinguish between just and unjust laws? How does he justify the civil disobedience of law?

5. What is King's attitude toward the black nationalism of figures such as Elijah Muhammad? Does he have any sympathy for these movements?

6. Why does King have problems with the attitudes of white moderates? Why does he eventually become satisfied in being called an extremist?

7. What is King's criticism of the church in America and organized religion in contemporary times?

QUESTIONS FOR DISCUSSION

1. In what specific ways does King apply Thoreau's principles of civil disobedience?

2. King argues against those who claim that the race problem will be solved in time by claiming that time itself is neutral. Can we hope that time will cure widespread social injustice? What problems emerge from activism?

3. King continually uses conscience as a foundation for moral law (which Thoreau does as well in Civil Disobedience). To what extent can we rely on conscience as a basis for moral action? Where does conscience come from?

4. Is the violation of law justified in the service of a presumed moral purpose? In our societies, how do we deal with the occasional difference between human laws and higher moral law?

LOOKING AT RHETORIC

1. In what tone does King address his unsympathetic readers in order to change their minds? How does that manner or tone change throughout the letter? Is it an effective rhetorical device?

2. King refers to personal conversations he had with his children about their experiences with racial prejudice. Are these anecdotes effective? Why?

3. This famous letter is known as one of the most important manifestos of the civil rights movement. What makes it a manifesto? What formal characteristics can you find that help you understand the manifesto as a written genre or form?

WRITING ASSIGNMENTS

1. Explore the relationship between King's ideas and those of Henry David Thoreau. In what way does King expand, develop, and apply the principles he learned from his nineteenth-century predecessor, Thoreau?

2. Considering the potential of social disorder as an outcome of activism, argue for or against King's claim that moderation in the face of social injustice in an evil in itself.

3. In pairs or groups, place yourself in King's time during the civil rights movement. Identify any one of the specific injustices perpetrated on African Americans that he cites (i.e. segregated buses or lunch counters, church or home bombings). Imagine you are members of an organization like the Southern Christian Leadership Conference. Come up with a specific method of response that you think might be effective. Individually, in essay form write a letter to the leadership of your activist group that sets out a plan of action.

How Serfdom Saved the Women's Movement

Caitlin Flanagan

Caitlin Flanagan (b. 1961) is a writer and social critic known for her controversial perspectives on domestic affairs and the contemporary women's movement, often dealing with the role of motherhood and the modern family. She studied at the University of Virginia, earning both her B.A. and M.A. in Art History. After college, she taught English and served as a high school counselor, subsequently becoming a staff writer for The New Yorker *and a contributing editor and book reviewer for the* The Atlantic Monthly. *She is a five-time finalist for the National Magazine Awards, and in 2006 she published* To Hell with All That, *an exploration of the lives and choices of modern women. She has courted controversy by challenging the choices made by working mothers, arguing that a more traditional approach to motherhood and domesticity has significant value for the family. In the following article, she explores the social and political effects that emerged as women returned to work in the 1970's, arguing that the primarily upper middle-class women's movement betrayed its own principles of reform, achieving success by relying on an underclass of immigrant domestic women workers, primarily disadvantaged ethnic minorities.*

1   I didn't know a single child who had a nanny when I was growing up. Nannies existed in English nursery rhymes and children's stories, in *Mary Poppins* and *Peter Pan*. The Brady Bunch, of course, had Alice, but she seemed to be part and parcel of the double family tragedy, never even alluded to, that had brought them all together. *The Courtship of Eddie's Father* had Mrs. Livingston, but again: tragedy. My father was always very proud of a scar on his right elbow, which he had received at the hands of an incompetent nurse who scalded him in the bath when he was an infant, and whom my grandfather had sent packing that very day. The scar proved to my father that his family had once been a tiny bit grand; it proved to me that he had been born a long, long time ago: a nurse? When I was growing up, in Berkeley in the 1960s, faculty wives—which is what my mother was—stayed home, kept house, and raised children. When my mother died, I gave a maudlin eulogy about all the days we spent together when I was small, shopping at Hink's department store and eating peeled apricots

and lying down for naps in the big bed under the gable window of her bedroom. I probably should have found something more estimable to say about her, but in the days after her death all I could think about was what a wonderful thing it had been to be raised at home, by a mother who loved me. But by the 1970s, of course, the idyll was coming to an end; many of the younger wives had begun to want out. I remember being sent in 1977, at age fifteen, to my very first psychotherapist, a young wife and mother with a capacious office on Bancroft Avenue. I can't remember a thing I talked about on all those darkening afternoons, but I do remember very clearly a day on which she suddenly sat up straight in her chair and began discussing, for reasons I could not fathom and in the most heated terms imaginable, not the vagaries of my sullen adolescence but, rather, marriage—specifically, her own. "I mean, who's going to do the shit work?" she asked angrily. "Who's going to make the pancakes?"

2   I stared at her uncomprehendingly. The only wife I knew intimately was my mother, who certainly had her discontents, but whom I couldn't even imagine using the term "shit work," let alone using it to characterize the making of pancakes—something she did regularly, competently, and, as far as I could tell, happily (she liked pancakes; so did the rest of us). But in 1978 shit work was becoming a real problem. Shit work, in fact, was threatening to put the brakes on the women's movement. Joan Didion's[1] unparalleled 1972 essay on the movement ("To make an omelette," the essay begins, "you need not only those broken eggs but someone 'oppressed' to break them") described the attempts women of the era made to arrive at an equitable division of household labor:

> They totted up the pans scoured, the towels picked off the bathroom floor, the loads of laundry done in a lifetime. Cooking a meal could only be "dog-work," and to claim any pleasure from it was evidence of craven acquiescence in one's own forced labor. Small children could only be odious mechanisms for the spilling and digesting of food, for robbing women of their "freedom." It was a long way from Simone de Beauvoir's grave and awesome recognition of woman's role as "the Other" to the notion that the first step in changing that role was Alix Kates Shulman's marriage contract ("wife strips beds, husband remakes them").

3   Alix Kates Shulman's[2] marriage contract, which I have read, is so perfectly a document of its time that it might stand alone, a kind of synecdoche for twenty years' worth of arguing and slamming doors and fuming over the notorious inability of husbands to fold a fitted sheet or get the children's breakfast on the table without leaving behind a scrim of crumbs and jelly on every flat surface in the room. Originally published in 1970, in a feminist magazine called *Up From Under*, the contract—like the women's-liberation movement itself—quickly moved from the radical margins of society to its very center: it was reprinted in the debut issue of *Ms.*, no surprise, but also in *Redbook* and *New York* and *Life*, in which it was part of a cover story on the subject of experimental marriages. (That a marriage in which the husband helped out with housework qualified as "experimental" tells you how much things have changed in the past three decades.) It was also taken seriously in some very high quarters, including the standard Harvard textbook on contract law, in which it was reprinted.

---

[1] Joan Didion (b. 1934): American novelist and essayist often known for exploring the degeneration of morality in a modern context.

[2] Alix Kates Shulman (b. 1932): American writer and feminist of the "second wave," which began in the 1960's.

4   The document, which I first encountered when I read the Didion essay as a girl, struck me as odd; I could see how a bride on the eve of her wedding could think ahead to the making and unmaking of beds (although it was only once I was deep into marriage that it occurred to me this task might be a chore, as opposed to yet another delightful aspect of married sexuality, which I could imagine only in the most thrilling terms), but there was other language in it that seemed born of actual and bitter experience. Shulman and her husband, for example, were going to divide "the week into hours during which the children were to address their 'personal questions' to either one parent or another." It was difficult for me to conceive of a bride's coming up with such a disillusioned view of the thing, even a bride fully alerted to the oppression of motherhood, but it turns out that Shulman was no bride when she wrote it. I have since learned that her marriage agreement—talk about a doomed cause—was of the post-nuptial variety.

5   Alix Kates Shulman's marriage—under way a full decade before she sat down at her typewriter, aglow with "feminist irony, idealism, audacity, and glee," and punched out the notorious contract—had been buffeted by many of the forces at play in American cultural life of the late sixties and early seventies, but she and her husband evinced an impressive ability to up the ante. He worked; she stayed home with the kids and wrote "subversive" essays, short stories, and position papers, all of which centered on her growing desire to come Up From Under. He retaliated by starting a new business venture in another state and taking up with a UC Berkeley student. She double-retaliated by taking a young lover of her own and publishing an essay about her husband's inability to bring her to orgasm, an essay that ended with the half jaunty, half exasperated imperative "Think clitoris!" At this point Alix and her husband were apparently seized by the one patently sensible idea of their entire marriage; they needed to get divorced.

6   Now the story begins to get complicated. In the early seventies there was no such thing as joint custody in the state of New York, and Alix realized that a divorce was not going to be much of a boon to her, since it would leave her with the kids full time, which would mean a heck of a lot of breakfasts to prepare and lunch boxes to pack—activities that would sorely cut into the time available for her to make pronouncements on behalf of the voiceless clitoris. When friends heard about her rotten marriage and asked her when she was going to divorce the bum, she would snappily reply, "Not until you're ready to help me take care of my kids." Thus the marriage agreement—which Shulman originally, and more accurately, wanted to title "A Divorce Dilemma and a Marriage Agreement"—was born, a way to husk the marriage of any pretense of emotional fulfillment and reduce it to a purely labor-sharing arrangement. (Her husband signed it, ran off with his coed, and then—proving himself to be one of the great masochists of the twentieth century—returned to Shulman for another full decade of punishment before they finally switched off the lights.)

    The marriage agreement virtually demanded to be ridiculed, and ridiculed it was: not only by Joan Didion but also by Russell Baker[3] and Norman Mailer.[4] (In his 1971 anti-feminist manifesto *The Prisoner of Sex*, Mailer considered the agreement at some length, concluding

---

[3] Russell Baker (b. 1925): Pulitzer Prize winning American writer of social satire and social commentary, as well as self-criticism.

[4] Norman Mailer (1923-2007): Pulitzer Prize winning American novelist, essayist, and playwright, often associated with the "new journalism" of the 1950's and 1960's.

that he "would not be married to such a woman." The potential of the agreement to serve as a lifetime protection policy against marriage to Norman Mailer makes me half want to hold onto my own copy, just to be on the safe side.) Certainly Shulman has earned herself a spot on almost any short list of very silly people. Yet I am reluctant to make too much sport of her document, or of the countless similar ones that it inspired. I am a wife and mother of young children in a very different time from Shulman's, a time that is in many respects more brutal and more brutalizing, a time that has been morally coarsening for many of us, a time that has made hypocrites of many contemporary feminists in ways that Shulman and her sisters in arms were not hypocrites. I have never once argued with my husband about which of us was going to change the sheets of the marriage bed, but then—to my certain knowledge—neither one of us ever has changed the sheets. Or scrubbed the bathtubs, or dusted the cobwebs off the top of the living-room bookcase, or used the special mop and the special noncorrosive cleanser on the hardwood floors. Two years ago our little boys got stomach flu, one right after the other, and there were ever so many loads of wash to do, but we did not do them. The nanny did.

14   How these workers became available to middle-class women is well known and amply reported, both in the press and in dozens of fine books, including Rhacel Salazar Parreñas's *Servants of Globalization* and Grace Chang's *Disposable Domestics*. But how so many middle-class American women went from not wanting to oppress other women to viewing that oppression as a central part of their own liberation—that is a complicated and sorry story. In it you will find the seeds of things we don't like to discuss much, including the elitism and hypocrisy of the contemporary feminist movement, the tendency of working and nonworking mothers to pit themselves against one another, and the way that adult middle-class life has become so intensely, laughably child-centered that in the past month I have chaperoned my children to eight birthday parties, yet not attended a single cocktail party (do they even exist anymore?).

15   To begin, let us turn to the best book ever written on American working mothers, a book that ought to be required reading in any women's-studies course: *The Equality Trap*, by Mary Ann Mason, who is a law and social-welfare professor at Berkeley. In it she reveals that there were in fact two distinct groups of mothers who entered the work force in the 1970s, for two distinct sets of reasons. There were middle-class women, fed up with housework and eager for the challenge, the respite, the intellectual engagement, of work. (Imagine my mother: it is 1976, and a casserole is defrosting on her kitchen counter, but she is far away from that counter; she is on a BART train, rocketing along to her new office at Equitable Life Insurance, pleased as punch.) It is these women, and now their daughters (imagine me, with an advanced degree and a book contract, sitting down at the computer, pleased as punch), who have driven a tremendous amount of the public debate and policy on the subject of working mothers.

16   But there was a second group of women, a quieter and more invisible group, who were not at all pleased as punch. Mason writes,

> *The dramatic shift from a manufacturing to a service economy, which occurred in the seventies, rendered the concept of a "family wage," earned by a relatively well-paid union member father, an anachronism. Their husbands' lower wages were driving mothers into the labor market in unprecedented numbers.*

The number of women in each group continued to grow, but as Mason chillingly and accurately notes,

> *The great majority of American women workers were . . . striving to make ends meet in women's occupations and were not entering high-paying male-dominated occupations such as law, medicine, and corporate management. But it was the relatively small class of women who were trying to push into the high-stakes male professions . . . [that] drove the feminist movement . . . [These women] were not greatly concerned with secretaries or poor single parents.*

Moreover, "Clusters of women rally around hot button issues like abortion rights, domestic violence, and gay parenting while academic women fret on queer theory, but there is no longer a compelling activist vision." And the pure, ugly truth of the thing: "Ironically, perhaps the only impact the feminist drive for equal rights in the workplace has had on this poorest, fastest growing segment of women is as a cheerleader for women's participation in the workplace, no matter how mean her job or how difficult her family burden."

17   The feminist movement, from its earliest days, has always proceeded from the assumption that all women—rich and poor—constitute a single class, and that all members of the class are, by virtue simply of being female, oppressed. In many regards this was once entirely true: all women were denied the vote; employment law discriminated against all women; and all women lacked the right to legal abortion. But this paradigm has led to a new assumption: that all working mothers—rich and poor—constitute a single class, that they are all similarly oppressed, and that they are united in a struggle against common difficulties. At its best this is vaguely well-intentioned but sloppy thinking. At its worst it is brutal and self-serving and shameful thinking.

18   The professional-class working mother—grateful inheritor of Betty Friedan's realizations about domestic imprisonment and the happiness and autonomy offered by work—is oppressed by guilt about her decision to keep working, by a society that often questions her commitment to and even her love for her children, by the labor-intensive type of parenting currently in vogue, by children's stalwart habit of falling deeply and unwaveringly in love with the person who provides their physical care, and by her uneasy knowledge that at-home mothers are giving their children much more time and personal attention than she is giving hers. She feels more than oppressed—she feels outraged! she wants something done about this!—by a corporate culture that refuses to let a working mother postpone an important meeting if it happens to coincide with the fourth-grade Spring Sing.

19   On the other hand, the nonprofessional-class working mother—unhappy inheritor of changes in the American economy that have thrust her unenthusiastically into the labor market—is oppressed by very different forces. She is oppressed by the fact that her work is oftentimes physically exhausting, ill-paid, and devoid of benefits such as health insurance and paid sick leave. She is oppressed by the fact that it is impossible to put a small child in licensed day care if you make minimum wage, and she is oppressed by the harrowing child-care options that are available on an unlicensed, inexpensive basis. She is oppressed by the fact

that she has no safety net: if she falls out of work and her child needs a visit to the doctor and antibiotics, she may not be able to afford those things and will have to treat her sick child with over-the-counter medications, which themselves are far from cheap. She is oppressed by the fact that—another feminist gain—single motherhood has been so championed in our culture, along with the sexual liberation of women and the notion that a woman doesn't really need a man. In this climate she is often left shouldering the immense burden of parenthood alone.

23   To the contemporary feminist, Zoe Baird was a victim principally of the national antagonism toward working mothers, and specifically of a problem common to all such women: there simply isn't enough affordable, high-quality child care in this country. (To the extent that the feminist thinks at all about the Peruvian couple in Baird's employ, it is usually to characterize them as subvictims of the same problem.) It is a problem, feminists argue, that the government ought to address posthaste. In a new book called *The Mommy Myth*, Susan J. Douglas and Meredith W. Michaels report that "for most mothers, work is an absolute necessity, and so, hello, Earth to Congress, some reliable form of childcare is also an absolute necessity." Because most of their readers don't have time to review everything that "those half-wits in the District" have to say on the subject of universal day care, the authors provide a fairly accurate overview of how the program has died a thousand deaths in Congress. They conclude, "A clear villain emerges—the far right wing in the United States." They're mostly right about that, and they're definitely right that millions of working-poor families are desperately in need of child care.

24   But guess what? We're told a single mother with a waitressing job is in exactly the same boat as a wealthy woman with a partnership in a major law firm and a similarly well employed husband. Joan K. Peters is the author of a highly regarded book called *When Mothers Work: Loving Our Children Without Sacrificing Our Selves*. It proceeds from an assumption dear to many women's hearts: "I argue that mothers should work outside the home," she tells us at the outset. "If they do not, they cannot preserve their identities or raise children to have both independent and family lives." (Good news for sweatshop workers and their children everywhere—Mom's identity as an underpaid seamstress is vital to healthy family functioning.) To Peters, as to so many of her philosophical sisters, all working mothers are united in a common struggle.

> *Whether they are applying for the post of attorney general like Zoe Baird, or moving from welfare to work, child care is a visible issue in their lives. As more employed women balk at trading their jobs for full-time motherhood, subsidized quality child care will become one of their primary political demands.*

No, it won't. The chances that someone like Zoe Baird—a woman who, at the time of her predicament, was working a huge number of hours at a highly remunerative job—would make use of subsidized child care are close to zilch. *Getting It Right*, by Laraine T. Zappert, is based on a "landmark study" of "more than three hundred women who have graduated from Stanford's Graduate School of Business," and who are "successfully taking up the challenge of life, family and career." The book is organized like a B[usiness]-school PowerPoint presentation, with chapters divided into heavily bullet-pointed sections such as "Experience," "Lessons Learned," and "Action Plan." The chapter on child care unequivocally advises readers to eschew day care in favor of employing nannies, because they are clearly the best option for professional women; in the first place, such employees "obviate the need for time-consuming pickups and deliveries." (Even the nomenclature suggests why a woman anxious about her choices in life wouldn't like day care: a good mother doesn't want to admit to having to make "deliveries" and "pickups" of her children, as though they were so many dirty shirts being sent to the laundry.) As one professional woman said, "Good help and lots of it is key to making the whole thing possible." Any moral equivocations about the larger ramifications of hiring a woman for such a job can be dispensed with quickly. Zappert points out, "The premiums offered to find and retain an excellent child-care provider are often more beneficent than any of the workplace perks that most professional women themselves enjoy." (Good thing Zoe's Peruvians didn't hear about those perks; they might have demanded access to an on-site gym and an annual executive physical.) True, such arrangements "can have a downside for the care provider." But there is always a silver lining where working mothers are involved: "Princeton sociologist Marta Tienda points out that 'because we rely on other women to take care of our children, two women can enter the labor force for every one that takes on a new job . . . all of [whom] are driving economic growth in a profound way.' " Granted, one of these two women has taken a job in which she may be paid under the table and denied Social Security set-asides, and is very probably (more good news for our booming, child-care-based economy) leaving her own children with yet a third woman in an arrangement in which cash changes hands and Social Security is never mentioned. But the professional-class working mother need not dwell on such unpleasantness: "Political economics aside," Zappert says, "it is clear from our survey that if you can do it, and particularly if you are working full time and/or have more than one child, having in-home child care can greatly decrease the stress of balancing work and life priorities."

25   So here we have the crux of the problem: ask an upper-middle-class woman why she is exploiting another woman for child care, and she will cry that she has to do it because there's no universal day care. But get a bunch of professional-class mothers together, and they will freely admit that day care sucks; get a nanny. This was a truth that Naomi Wolf—feminist, Yalie, Rhodes scholar, big thinker—learned the hard way after giving birth to her first child. In *Misconceptions*, Wolf reports,

> I never thought I would become one of those women who took up a fore-ordained place in a hierarchy of class and gender. Yet here we were, to my horror and complicity, shaping our new family structure along class and gender lines—daddy at work, mommy and caregiver from two different economic classes, sharing the baby work during the day.

Her dreams of parenthood, apparently formed while tripping across green New Haven quadrangles on her way to feminist-theory classes, were starkly different: "I had wanted us to be a mother and a father raising children side by side, the man moving into the world of children, the woman into the world of work, in equitable balance, maybe each working flexibly from home, the two making the same world and sharing the same experiences and values." She had wanted a revolution; what she got was a Venezuelan.

26   What few will admit—because it is painful, because it reveals the unpleasant truth that life presents a series of choices, each of which precludes a host of other attractive possibilities—is that when a mother works, something is lost. Children crave their mothers. They always have and they always will. And women fortunate enough to live in a society

where they have access to that greatest of levelers, education, will always have the burning dream of doing something more exciting and important than tidying Lego blocks and running loads of laundry. If you want to make an upper-middle-class woman squeal in indignation, tell her she can't have something. If she works she can't have as deep and connected a relationship with her child as she would if she stayed home and raised him. She can't have the glamour and respect conferred on career women if she chooses instead to spend her days at "Mommy and Me" classes. She can't have both things. I have read numerous accounts of the anguish women have felt leaving small babies with caregivers so that they could go to work, and I don't discount those stories for a moment. That the separation of a woman from her child produces agony for both is one of the most enduring and impressive features of the human experience, and it probably accounts for why we've made it as far as we have. I've read just as many accounts of the despair that descends on some women when their world is abruptly narrowed to the tedium and exhaustion of the nursery; neither do I discount these stories: I've felt that self-same despair.

27   In my case, the despair was lessened—greatly—by a nanny. Without her I could never have launched a second career as a writer. Her kindness, her patience, and her many (and oftentimes extreme) acts of generosity have shaped my family as much as any other force. But the implications of this solution to my domestic problems are grave, and ever since I read *Doméstica*, two years ago, I have been turning over in my mind the high moral cost of my decision. Even if one pays a fair wage, hires a legal resident of the United States, and pays both one's own share of the required taxes and the employee's, so as not to short her take-home pay (all of which I do), one is still part of a system that exposes women to the brutalities of illegal immigration, only to reward their suffering with the jobs that ease our already comfortable lives.

28   It's easy enough to dismiss the dilemma of the professional-class working mother as the whining of the elite. But people are entitled to their lives, and within the context of privilege there are certainly hard choices, disappointments, sorrows. Upper-middle-class working mothers may never have calm hearts regarding their choices about work and motherhood, but there are certain things they can all do. They can acknowledge that many of the gains of professional-class working women have been leveraged on the backs of poor women. They can legitimize those women's work and compensate it fairly, which means—at the very least—paying Social Security taxes on it. They can demand that feminists abandon their current fixation on "work-life balance" and on "ending the mommy wars" and instead devote themselves entirely to the real and heartrending struggle of poor women and children in this country. And they can stop using the hardships of the poor as justification for their own choices. About this much, at least, there ought to be agreement.

QUESTIONS ON MEANING

1. What motivated Alix Kates Shulman to create the marriage contract? How does that personal motivation make the contract a questionable idea?

2. In what way does Flanagan acknowledge that her current circumstances are different from those of other women in the beginning of the modern (second wave) feminist movement of the 1970's?

3. How did the civil rights movement that advanced the conditions of African American women affect the domestic arrangement of upper middle-class white women in the 1970's?

4. How did the forces of global capitalism help to save the women's movement?

5. What is the hidden reality of womens' entry into the work force in the 1970's? What were the two distinct groups of women? Who controlled the public debate over feminism in this time?

6. What is the high moral cost to middle-class mothers when they hire domestic workers for child care?

QUESTIONS FOR DISCUSSION

1. Flanagan implies that mothers provide an essential nurturing role to children that fathers or domestic workers cannot provide as effectively. Is this a supportable claim?

2. Is it reasonable to consider some version of a marriage contract, as Alix Kates Shulman originally outlined? Can this reduce some of the conflicts in modern marriages?

3. To what extent is the hiring of domestic immigrant workers a violation of the feminist ideal? What would these immigrant women do in the absence of available domestic employment?

4. In choosing to work and in employing others to perform child-rearing responsibilities, are women avoiding the tough moral choices that Flanagan claims?

LOOKING AT RHETORIC

1. Flanagan has made a reputation by courting controversy on the topical issue of women's roles in modern society. To what extent is her article confrontational in style and tone? Assuming that it is, does that rhetorical choice affect the quality of her argument? Does it enhance it or not?

2. The article makes extensive use of other writer's works, sometimes agreeing with them and sometimes challenging them. Is this an effective technique in making her point?

3. In what way does Flanagan's use of her own personal biography contribute to her essay? What would the article gain or lose without it?

WRITING ASSIGNMENTS

1. What are the tensions that frequently exist in modern marriages? In what way have you observed these tensions and difficulties, whether you are or have been married, whether you grew up with married parents, or observed marriages in other ways? To what extent are these tensions related to gender and gender roles? Research sources in sociology and marriage and family studies.

2. Argue for or against the claim that the use of domestic help (nannies and maids) is a violation of the principles of the women's movement.

3. In pairs or in groups, make a list of household duties that must be performed by a married couple with children. Discuss the list and revise it, considering conventional and more modern concepts of gender roles. Individually, in an essay, revise the list and formulate a marriage contract. Make an argument for why an arrangement of this sort would or would not be effective.

Interdisciplinary Connections

Images of Social Protest

No country on earth is free from social discord, and at times protests—some peaceful, some violent—are staged in order to demonstrate against a perceived social injustice. Below are two of the most famous images of individual social protest in the past century: the famous image of the lone man standing his ground in order to prevent the advance of a line of tanks in China's Tiananmen Square, and the well-known image of the "hippie" protester placing flowers in the

The "Tank Man" blocking tanks in Tiananmen Square in 1989

http://www.politicolnews.com/wp-content/uploads/2011/02/tiananmen-square-tank1.jpg

barrels of soldiers' guns in order to protest U.S. participation in the Vietnam War. As you study these images, ask yourself what kind of social injustice would you be willing to protest? Have you ever participated in a public protest or demonstration? Why or why not? Would you be willing to do what the two individuals depicted in these photographs did?

Photograph from 1967 showing a hippie placing a flower in a soldier's gun barrel in protest of the Vietnam War

http://media.photobucket.com/image/flower%20gun%20hippie/clhelement1/flower.jpg?o=1

The Black Sites

Jane Mayer

Jane Mayer (b. 1955) is an investigative journalist and an author of many books and essays dealing with the contemporary political scene. Graduating from Fieldston, an Ivy League College Preparatory Academy in 1973, she completed a degree at Yale University in 1977, continuing her studies at Oxford University. She has contributed articles to The Washington Post, American Prospect, The New York Review of Books, *and* The Los Angeles Times. *She has also co-authored two books,* Strange Justice: The Selling of Clarence Thomas *(1994) and* Landslide: The Unmaking of a President, 1984-1988 *(1989), which considers the difficulties of Ronald Reagan's second presidential term. She has also written* The Dark Side *(2008), exploring the legality and ethics of the C.I.A.'s interrogations techniques. She has worked as a reporter for* The New Yorker *since 1995. The following article, which appeared in* The New Yorker, *deals with similar issues as* The Dark Side, *investigating the practice, legality, and use value of "enhanced interrogation techniques," which were endorsed by the Bush Administration as a part of the War on Terror in the wake of the 9/11 attacks.*

1   In March, Mariane Pearl, the widow of the murdered *Wall Street Journal* reporter Daniel Pearl,[1] received a phone call from Alberto Gonzales,[2] the Attorney General. At the time, Gonzales's role in the controversial dismissal of eight United States Attorneys had just been exposed, and the story was becoming a scandal in Washington. Gonzales informed Pearl that the Justice Department was about to announce some good news: a terrorist in U.S. custody—Khalid Sheikh Mohammed, the Al Qaeda[3] leader who was the primary architect of the September 11th attacks—had confessed to killing her husband. (Pearl was abducted and beheaded five and a half years ago in Pakistan, by unidentified Islamic militants.) The Administration planned to release a transcript in which Mohammed boasted, "I decapitated with my blessed right hand the head of the American Jew Daniel Pearl in the city of Karachi, Pakistan. For those who would like to confirm, there are pictures of me on the Internet holding his head."

2   Pearl was taken aback. In 2003, she had received a call from Condoleezza Rice, who was then President Bush's national-security adviser, informing her of the same news. But Rice's revelation had been secret. Gonzales's announcement seemed like a publicity stunt. Pearl asked him if he had proof that Mohammed's confession was truthful; Gonzales claimed to have corroborating evidence but wouldn't share it. "It's not enough for officials to call me and say they believe it," Pearl said. "You need evidence." (Gonzales did not respond to requests for comment.)

---

[1] Daniel Pearl (1963-2002): American journalist who, while working as the South Asian Bureau Chief of *The Wall Street Journal*, was kidnapped and murdered in Karachi, Pakistan.

[2] Alberto Gonzales (b.1955): 80th Attorney General of the United States, appointed by President George W. Bush in 2005. He resigned amidst controversy (including alleged perjury) in 2007.

[3] Al Qaeda: an Islamic fundamentalist group founded between 1988 and 1990, responsible for terrorist attacks worldwide, including the September 11th attacks in the United States.

3   The circumstances surrounding the confession of Mohammed, whom law-enforcement officials refer to as K.S.M., were perplexing. He had no lawyer. After his capture in Pakistan, in March of 2003, the Central Intelligence Agency had detained him in undisclosed locations for more than two years; last fall, he was transferred to military custody in Guantánamo Bay, Cuba.[4] There were no named witnesses to his initial confession, and no solid information about what form of interrogation might have prodded him to talk, although reports had been published, in the *Times* and elsewhere, suggesting that C.I.A. officers had tortured him. At a hearing held at Guantánamo, Mohammed said that his testimony was freely given, but he also indicated that he had been abused by the C.I.A. (The Pentagon had classified as "top secret"a statement he had written detailing the alleged mistreatment.) And although Mohammed said that there were photographs confirming his guilt, U.S. authorities had found none. Instead, they had a copy of the video that had been released on the Internet, which showed the killer's arms but offered no other clues to his identity.

4   Further confusing matters, a Pakistani named Ahmed Omar Saeed Sheikh had already been convicted of the abduction and murder, in 2002. A British-educated terrorist who had a history of staging kidnappings, he had been sentenced to death in Pakistan for the crime. But the Pakistani government, not known for its leniency, had stayed his execution. Indeed, hearings on the matter had been delayed a remarkable number of times—at least thirty— possibly because of his reported ties to the Pakistani intelligence service, which may have helped free him after he was imprisoned for terrorist activities in India. Mohammed's confession would delay the execution further, since, under Pakistani law, any new evidence is grounds for appeal.

5   A surprising number of people close to the case are dubious of Mohammed's confession. A longtime friend of Pearl's, the former *Journal* reporter Asra Nomani, said, "The release of the confession came right in the midst of the U.S. Attorney scandal. There was a drumbeat for Gonzales's resignation. It seemed like a calculated strategy to change the subject. Why now? They'd had the confession for years." Mariane and Daniel Pearl were staying in Nomani's Karachi house at the time of his murder, and Nomani has followed the case meticulously; this fall, she plans to teach a course on the topic at Georgetown University. She said, "I don't think this confession resolves the case. You can't have justice from one person's confession, especially under such unusual circumstances. To me, it's not convincing." She added, "I called all the investigators. They weren't just skeptical—they didn't believe it."

6   Special Agent Randall Bennett, the head of security for the U.S. consulate in Karachi when Pearl was killed—and whose lead role investigating the murder was featured in the recent film *A Mighty Heart*—said that he has interviewed all the convicted accomplices who are now in custody in Pakistan, and that none of them named Mohammed as playing a role. "K.S.M.'s name never came up," he said. Robert Baer, a former C.I.A. officer, said, "My old colleagues say with one-hundred-percent certainty that it was not K.S.M. who killed Pearl." A government official involved in the case said, "The fear is that K.S.M. is

---

[4] Guantanamo Bay, Cuba: a bay located at the southeast end of Cuba, controlled by the United States under the 1903 Cuban-American Treaty. The United States military maintains a naval base there.

covering up for others, and that these people will be released." And Judea Pearl, Daniel's father, said, "Something is fishy. There are a lot of unanswered questions. K.S.M. can say he killed Jesus—he has nothing to lose."

7   Mariane Pearl, who is relying on the Bush administration to bring justice in her husband's case, spoke carefully about the investigation. "You need a procedure that will get the truth," she said. "An intelligence agency is not supposed to be above the law."

8   Mohammed's interrogation was part of a secret C.I.A. program, initiated after September 11th, in which terrorist suspects such as Mohammed were detained in "black sites"—secret prisons outside the United States—and subjected to unusually harsh treatment. The program was effectively suspended last fall, when President Bush announced that he was emptying the C.I.A.'s prisons and transferring the detainees to military custody in Guantánamo. This move followed a Supreme Court ruling, *Hamdan v. Rumsfeld*, which found that all detainees—including those held by the C.I.A.—had to be treated in a manner consistent with the Geneva Conventions. These treaties, adopted in 1949, bar cruel treatment, degradation, and torture. In late July, the White House issued an executive order promising that the C.I.A. would adjust its methods in order to meet the Geneva standards. At the same time, Bush's order pointedly did not disavow the use of "enhanced interrogation techniques" that would likely be found illegal if used by officials inside the United States. The executive order means that the agency can once again hold foreign terror suspects indefinitely, and without charges, in black sites, without notifying their families or local authorities, or offering access to legal counsel.

9   The C.I.A.'s director, General Michael Hayden, has said that the program, which is designed to extract intelligence from suspects quickly, is an "irreplaceable" tool for combatting terrorism. And President Bush has said that "this program has given us information that has saved innocent lives, by helping us stop new attacks." He claims that it has contributed to the disruption of at least ten serious Al Qaeda plots since September 11th, three of them inside the United States.

10   According to the Bush administration, Mohammed divulged information of tremendous value during his detention. He is said to have helped point the way to the capture of Hambali, the Indonesian terrorist responsible for the 2002 bombings of night clubs in Bali. He also provided information on an Al Qaeda leader in England. Michael Sheehan, a former counterterrorism official at the State Department, said, "K.S.M. is the poster boy for using tough but legal tactics. He's the reason these techniques exist. You can save lives with the kind of information he could give up." Yet Mohammed's confessions may also have muddled some key investigations. Perhaps under duress, he claimed involvement in thirty-one criminal plots—an improbable number, even for a high-level terrorist. Critics say that Mohammed's case illustrates the cost of the C.I.A.'s desire for swift intelligence. Colonel Dwight Sullivan, the top defense lawyer at the Pentagon's Office of Military Commissions, which is expected eventually to try Mohammed for war crimes, called his serial confessions "a textbook example of why we shouldn't allow coercive methods."

11   The Bush administration has gone to great lengths to keep secret the treatment of the hundred or so "high-value detainees" whom the C.I.A. has confined, at one point or another, since September 11th. The program has been extraordinarily "compartmentalized," in the nomenclature of the intelligence world. By design, there has been virtually

no access for outsiders to the C.I.A.'s prisoners. The utter isolation of these detainees has been described as essential to America's national security. The Justice Department argued this point explicitly last November, in the case of a Baltimore-area resident named Majid Khan, who was held for more than three years by the C.I.A. Khan, the government said, had to be prohibited from access to a lawyer specifically because he might describe the "alternative interrogation methods" that the agency had used when questioning him. These methods amounted to a state secret, the government argued, and disclosure of them could "reasonably be expected to cause extremely grave damage." (The case has not yet been decided.)

12   Given this level of secrecy, the public and all but a few members of Congress who have been sworn to silence have had to take on faith President Bush's assurances that the C.I.A's internment program has been humane and legal, and has yielded crucial intelligence. Representative Alcee Hastings, a Democratic member of the House Select Committee on Intelligence, said, "We talk to the authorities about these detainees, but, of course, they're not going to come out and tell us that they beat the living daylights out of someone." He recalled learning in 2003 that Mohammed had been captured. "It was good news," he said. "So I tried to find out: Where is this guy? And how is he being treated?" For more than three years, Hastings said, "I could never pinpoint anything." Finally, he received some classified briefings on the Mohammed interrogation. Hastings said that he "can't go into details" about what he found out, but, speaking of Mohammed's treatment, he said that even if it wasn't torture, as the Administration claims, "it ain't right, either. Something went wrong."

13   Since the drafting of the Geneva Conventions, the International Committee of the Red Cross has played a special role in safeguarding the rights of prisoners of war. For decades, governments have allowed officials from the organization to report on the treatment of detainees, to insure that standards set by international treaties are being maintained. The Red Cross, however, was unable to get access to the C.I.A.'s prisoners for five years. Finally, last year, Red Cross officials were allowed to interview fifteen detainees, after they had been transferred to Guantánamo. One of the prisoners was Khalid Sheikh Mohammed. What the Red Cross learned has been kept from the public. The committee believes that its continued access to prisoners worldwide is contingent upon confidentiality, and therefore it addresses violations privately with the authorities directly responsible for prisoner treatment and detention. For this reason, Simon Schorno, a Red Cross spokesman in Washington, said, "The I.C.R.C. does not comment on its findings publicly. Its work is confidential."

14   The public-affairs office at the C.I.A. and officials at the congressional intelligence-oversight committees would not even acknowledge the existence of the report. Among the few people who are believed to have seen it are Condoleezza Rice, now the Secretary of State; Stephen Hadley, the national-security adviser; John Bellinger III, the Secretary of State's legal adviser; Hayden; and John Rizzo, the agency's acting general counsel. Some members of the Senate and House intelligence-oversight committees are also believed to have had limited access to the report.

15   Confidentiality may be particularly stringent in this case. Congressional and other Washington sources familiar with the report said that it harshly criticized the C.I.A.'s

practices. One of the sources said that the Red Cross described the agency's detention and interrogation methods as tantamount to torture, and declared that American officials responsible for the abusive treatment could have committed serious crimes. The source said the report warned that these officials may have committed "grave breaches" of the Geneva Conventions, and may have violated the U.S. Torture Act, which Congress passed in 1994. The conclusions of the Red Cross, which is known for its credibility and caution, could have potentially devastating legal ramifications.

16   Concern about the legality of the C.I.A.'s program reached a previously unreported breaking point last week when Senator Ron Wyden, a Democrat on the intelligence committee, quietly put a "hold" on the confirmation of John Rizzo, who as acting general counsel was deeply involved in establishing the agency's interrogation and detention policies. Wyden's maneuver essentially stops the nomination from going forward. "I question if there's been adequate legal oversight," Wyden told me. He said that after studying a classified addendum to President Bush's new executive order, which specifies permissible treatment of detainees, "I am not convinced that all of these techniques are either effective or legal. I don't want to see well-intentioned C.I.A. officers breaking the law because of shaky legal guidance."

17   A former C.I.A. officer, who supports the agency's detention and interrogation policies, said he worried that, if the full story of the C.I.A. program ever surfaced, agency personnel could face criminal prosecution. Within the agency, he said, there is a "high level of anxiety about political retribution" for the interrogation program. If congressional hearings begin, he said, "several guys expect to be thrown under the bus." He noted that a number of C.I.A. officers have taken out professional liability insurance, to help with potential legal fees.

18   Paul Gimigliano, a spokesman for the C.I.A., denied any legal impropriety, stressing that "the agency's terrorist-detention program has been implemented lawfully. And torture is illegal under U.S. law. The people who have been part of this important effort are well-trained, seasoned professionals." This spring, the Associated Press published an article quoting the chairman of the House intelligence committee, Silvestre Reyes, who said that Hayden, the C.I.A. director, "vehemently denied" the Red Cross's conclusions. A U.S. official dismissed the Red Cross report as a mere compilation of allegations made by terrorists. And Robert Grenier, a former head of the C.I.A.'s Counterterrorism Center, said that "the C.I.A.'s interrogations were nothing like Abu Ghraib or Guantánamo. They were very, very regimented. Very meticulous." He said, "The program is very careful. It's completely legal."

19   Accurately or not, Bush administration officials have described the prisoner abuses at Abu Ghraib and Guantánamo as the unauthorized actions of ill-trained personnel, eleven of whom have been convicted of crimes. By contrast, the treatment of high-value detainees has been directly, and repeatedly, approved by President Bush. The program is monitored closely by C.I.A. lawyers, and supervised by the agency's director and his subordinates at the Counterterrorism Center. While Mohammed was being held by the agency, detailed dossiers on the treatment of detainees were regularly available to the former C.I.A. director George Tenet, according to informed sources inside and outside the agency. Through a spokesperson, Tenet denied making day-to-day decisions about the treatment of individual detainees. But, according to a former agency official, "Every single plan is drawn up by interrogators, and then submitted for approval to the highest possible level—meaning the director of the C.I.A. Any change in the plan—even if an extra day of a certain treatment was added—was signed off by the C.I.A. director."

20   By 2004, there were growing calls within the C.I.A. to transfer to military custody the high-value detainees who had told interrogators what they knew, and to afford them some kind of due process. But Donald Rumsfeld,[5] then the Defense Secretary, who had been heavily criticized for the abusive conditions at military prisons such as Abu Ghraib and Guantánamo, refused to take on the agency's detainees, a former top C.I.A. official said. "Rumsfeld's attitude was *You've* got a real problem." Rumsfeld, the official said, "was the third most powerful person in the U.S. government, but he only looked out for the interests of his department— not the whole Administration." (A spokesperson for Rumsfeld said that he had no comment.)

21   C.I.A. officials were stymied until the Supreme Court's Hamdan ruling which prompted the Administration to send what it said were its last high value detainees to Cúba. Robert Grenier, like many people in the C.I.A., was relieved. "There has to be some sense of due process," he said. "We can't just make people disappear." Still, he added, "The most important source of intelligence we had after 9/11 came from the interrogations of high-value detainees. And he said that Mohammed was "the most valuable of the high-value detainees, because he had operational knowledge." He went on, "I can respect people who oppose aggressive interrogations, but they should admit that their principles may be putting American lives at risk."

22   Yet Philip Zelikow, the executive director of the 9/11 Commission and later the State Department's top counselor, under Rice, is not convinced that eliciting information from detainees justifies "physical torment." After leaving the government last year, he gave a speech in Houston, in which he said, "The question would not be, Did you get information that proved useful? Instead it would be, Did you get information that could have been usefully gained only from these methods?" He concluded, "My own view is that the cool, carefully considered, methodical, prolonged, and repeated subjection of captives to physical torment, and the accompanying psychological terror, is immoral."

23   Without more transparency, the value of the C.I.A.'s interrogation and detention program is impossible to evaluate. Setting aside the moral, ethical, and legal issues, even supporters, such as John Brennan, acknowledge that much of the information that coercion produces is unreliable. As he put it, "All these methods produced useful information, but there was also a lot that was bogus." When pressed, one former top agency official estimated that "ninety percent of the information was unreliable." Cables carrying Mohammed's interrogation transcripts back to Washington reportedly were prefaced with the warning that "the detainee has been known to withhold information or deliberately mislead." Mohammed, like virtually all the top Al Qaeda prisoners held by the C.I.A., has claimed that, while under coercion, he lied to please his captors.

24   In theory, a military commission could sort out which parts of Mohammed's confession are true and which are lies, and obtain a conviction. Colonel Morris D. Davis, the chief prosecutor at the Office of Military Commissions, said that he expects to bring charges against Mohammed "in a number of months." He added, "I'd be shocked if the defense didn't try to make K.S.M.'s treatment a problem for me, but I don't think it will be insurmountable."

25   Critics of the Administration fear that the unorthodox nature of the C.I.A.'s interrogation and detention program will make it impossible to prosecute the entire top echelon of

---

[5] Donald Rumsfeld (b. 1932): thirteenth Secretary of Defense under Gerald Ford from 1975 to 1977 and twenty-first Secretary of Defense under George W. Bush from 2002 to 2006.

Al Qaeda leaders in captivity. Already, according to the *Wall Street Journal*, credible allegations of torture have caused a Marine Corps prosecutor reluctantly to decline to bring charges against Mohamedou Ould Slahi, an alleged Al Qaeda leader held in Guantánamo. Bruce Riedel, the former C.I.A. analyst, asked, "What are you going to do with K.S.M. in the long run? It's a very good question. I don't think anyone has an answer. If you took him to any real American court, I think any judge would say there is no admissible evidence. It would be thrown out."

26   The problems with Mohammed's coerced confessions are especially glaring in the Daniel Pearl case. It may be that Mohammed killed Pearl, but contradictory evidence and opinion continue to surface. Yosri Fouda, the Al Jazeera reporter who interviewed Mohammed in Karachi, said that although Mohammed handed him a package of propaganda items, including an unedited video of the Pearl murder, he never identified himself as playing a role in the killing, which occurred in the same city just two months earlier. And a federal official involved in Mohammed's case said, "He has no history of killing with his own hands, although he's proved happy to commit mass murder from afar." Al Qaeda's leadership had increasingly focused on symbolic political targets. "For him, it's not personal," the official said. "It's business."

27   Ordinarily, the U.S. legal system is known for resolving such mysteries with painstaking care. But the C.I.A.'s secret interrogation program, Senator Levin said, has undermined the public's trust in American justice, both here and abroad. "A guy as dangerous as K.S.M. is, and half the world wonders if they can believe him—is that what we want?" he asked. "Statements that can't be believed because people think they rely on torture?"

28   Asra Nomani, the Pearls' friend, said of the Mohammed confession, "I'm not interested in unfair justice, even for bad people." She went on, "Danny was such a person of conscience. I don't think he would have wanted all of this dirty business. I don't think he would have wanted someone being tortured. He would have been repulsed. This is the kind of story that Danny would have investigated. He really believed in American principles."

QUESTIONS ON MEANING

1. What did Khalid Sheikh Mohammad confess to and why was his confession questionable?

2. What specific claim did the Bush Administration make to justify enhanced interrogation techniques? What historical agreement would likely make those techniques illegal outside the United States?

3. What role has the International Committee of the Red Cross played in safeguarding the rights of prisoners of war?

4. Why is the C.I.A.'s interrogation program impossible to evaluate, in terms of the practices used and the quality of the information received?

5. Why does the use of enhanced interrogation techniques make it difficult to prosecute potential terrorists?

QUESTIONS FOR DISCUSSION

1. Assuming for the sake of argument that enhanced interrogation techniques were a violation of international law, are they still morally justifiable in a post 9/11 world?

2. To what extent can information acquired under torture be considered reliable? How can we distinguish between reliable and unreliable information?

3. If we assume, as C.I.A official Robert Grenier argues, that avoiding aggressive interrogation methods places American lives at risk, how do we reconcile their use with our democratic principles?

4. During the Civil War, Abraham Lincoln suspended Habeas Corpus, detaining people without trial in violation of the American Constitution. Under what circumstances can we justify this kind of compromise? Where do we draw the line?

LOOKING AT RHETORIC

1. Given that Mayer is a reporter, is her presentation of the interrogation issue unbiased? Does her use of facts and sources lend credibility and balance to her article?

2. The essay makes extensive use of quotations, from C.I.A. officials, politicians, and people affected by terrorism and torture. To what extent are they used in journalistic fashion, to report? To what extent are they used in a persuasive fashion, to make a claim about the practice of interrogation? Is the balance reasonable?

3. The article deals with a contemporary issue. Does Mayer present information in such a way that we learn something that transcends our own time, about human nature, politics, and social behavior?

WRITING ASSIGNMENTS

1. Are there circumstances under which we might justifiably violate our commonly held notions of human rights? Can we find examples of these reasonable violations in our lives, in contemporary events, or in history?

2. Argue for or against the claim that torture (whether committed by the C.I.A. or by any other governmental group in any time and place) leads to unreliable information. If you argue for the claim, why isn't some of the information useful and valuable? If you argue against the claim, how can you distinguish between reliable and unreliable information?

3. In pairs or in groups, imagine a situation in which you are in a position of an interrogator. You have been asked to get information from a potential terrorist, a person who may (or may not) be a criminal. Brainstorm a list of methods you might use to acquire information. Then divide that list into two, one a list of ethical practices and the other a list of ethically questionable practices. Write an essay in which you create an effective interrogation method. Use the lists in any way you think appropriate.

Thinking Crosscurrently

GOVERNMENT, POLITICAL SCIENCE, AND PUBLIC POLICY

The purpose of government and the role of public policy is perhaps the most commonly discussed topic in the news media, suggesting that we are all affected by the manner in which government is constructed, how it is evolving, and how we are expected to participate in a society in part defined by public policy. As we attempt to come to terms with the relationship of government and the individual citizen, we must consider complex questions related to human nature, physical science, education, and business and economics. As you read the selections in this chapter, consider the following questions:

- What is the ultimate purpose of government? What are the scope and limits of its responsibility? What might Milton Friedman and Barbara Kellerman say about the relationship of government to business and the qualities of an effective political leader?

- In what way does history inform our understanding of the values and features of effective government? What might Abraham Lincoln think about the relationship of the individual to the state and the nation? In what way does W.E.B. Du Bois's consideration of racial prejudice influence our sense of government's role in securing human rights and justice?

- What do we know of human nature from a scientific standpoint that might shape our notion of government and its role in our lives? What might Francis Fukuyama and Olivia Judson have to say about the role of genetics as it relates to how we function in societies and in other formal social contexts such as governments?

- In what way do our deepest religious and philosophical beliefs and conceptions shape our notions about the role of government in our collective lives? To what extent is an unambiguous separation of government from religion possible? What might William James think about the manner in which our deepest beliefs define the governments we institute? What would Kwasi Wiredu contribute to this discussion?

7 EDUCATION AND SOCIETY

C ivilizations are the byproduct of human beings joined together in common cause and enterprise. For the educators, social workers, sociologists, public health and safety officials, and civic leaders in our communities, a vibrant society is generally seen as one in which knowledge grows, justice flourishes, crime is minimized, the sick are cared for, and people—despite their differences and disagreements—can still work together for the benefit of their communities, their families, and themselves.

One of the questions that drive so many community-building efforts is the question of what our responsibilities are to ourselves, our neighbors, and our children. How shall we treat those with whom we are engaged in common enterprise? What are our obligations to our fellow humans? What, for instance, constitutes *just* punishment for a particular crime? Should citizens be allowed to carry concealed weapons? Is health care a right or a privilege? How shall we care for the sick, the elderly, the challenged, the poor? A common claim in our world is that education is the key to solving some of the more troubling features of the modern social landscape. What makes for a good education? What does it mean to be educated? What kinds of subjects should we be teaching? Is it more important to teach English or math, foreign languages or biology? And what should we do with a neighborhood school that simply isn't performing well?

These are among the toughest questions humans have to answer, not because we don't understand the terms of the debate or what is at stake, but precisely because they affect us on a daily basis, and the answers we give to these questions change lives in an immediate and profound sense. These are the questions that underlie everything from the Civil Rights Movement to *Don't Ask Don't Tell* to *No Child Left Behind* or *The Race to the Top* programs. The answers to these questions determine our voting trends, our social legislation, and our charitable organizations. They govern the curriculum of our schools, the sentencing of our criminals, and our acceptance or rejection of those who are not like us in some fashion. How we act toward our neighbor—whether our neighbor is rich, poor, black, white, gay, straight, Buddhist, Christian, male, female, well- or poorly-educated—defines who we are as individuals, and shapes the communities in which we live. Indeed, these attitudes and behaviors—these choices we make in our dealings with our neighbors on a daily basis—are the cornerstones of civilization itself.

THE DISCIPLINE YOU EXPERIENCE

Constructing a strong, smart, just civilization is counted among the fundamental desires of countless millions of people across the world, in every nation, throughout recorded human history, from Plato's recipe for a just society in *The Republic* to the charitable organizations that feed the hungry and clothe the poor in neighborhoods just like the one you live in right now. When compared with solving problems associated with poverty, crime, ignorance, and intolerance, building skyscrapers and designing better computer chips seem almost easy tasks. A building and a computer chip are defined products, with quantifiable dimensions and measurable inputs and outputs. But who can quantify what it means to be an educated human in a just society? By what standards should we treat our fellow human in need? How can we grow and nurture the children in our community into the engineers, philosophers, artists, and politicians of tomorrow? What does it mean to be an educated person, and what does it mean to be an educator? Clearly, no one discipline can provide the answer to all of these questions, and one often finds numerous departments, majors, and programs of study at modern colleges and universities dedicated to building a better society in which to live, including:

- Education, which is the formal, concentrated study of the theories and methodologies associated with teaching. Education majors study how one facilitates the growth and development of human knowledge at all levels, from preschool through college and beyond.

- Sociology, which is the study of society and social human interaction. Sociology looks at how communities define themselves in terms of class, family units, behavior, attitudes, laws, and a host of other issues and characteristics that give shape to human groupings and govern how humans react and respond to one another.

- Social work, which focuses on developing practical, real-world strategies for building just societies. If sociology is the theoretical study of the development of human communities, social workers strive to make human communities better. Social workers seek to improve human life by improving the systems that communities rely on for preserving a healthy, fully-functioning society.

- Gender studies/Women's studies, which are interdisciplinary programs at most colleges that take a close look at how gender and/or sex defines and directs human development and gives shape and significance to many facets of human interaction.

- Criminal justice, which focuses on dealing with criminal threats to a just society, including crime prevention, detention, and the rehabilitation of criminally maladjusted individuals.

REFLECTING ON THIS CHAPTER

The seemingly endless list of topics that fall under the province of departments of education, sociology, criminal justice, and social work are a clear reflection not only of the interest these topics have for each person, but also are a reflection of the complicated, ongoing processes of understanding the communities in which we live and of developing educational and social programs that will help us build a stronger, more just, more civil life for ourselves and our neighbors. The essays reprinted in this chapter cover a wide variety of topics from a series of interesting, challenging, even provocative points of view. They examine the relationships between special interests groups, the role of the disturbing and offensive language in the college classroom, the ongoing tensions around the world over civil rights issues, the complications of parenting in a consumer economy, and even the question of reasonable and responsible gun ownership in a civil society. As you read through these essays, consider the following questions:

- What is the central issue or problem the author attempts to explore or solve? What claims does the author make, and does the author make a convincing argument in support of those claims?

- As important as educators and social workers are to the building and maintaining of a just and civil community, they tend to be among the lower-paid professions in the United States. Why is this the case? What does this suggest about modern culture? About twenty-first-century civilization? Do any of the selections in this chapter provide insight into these questions?

- How do these selections compare and contrast? What central issues and themes emerge from these selections when taken as a group?

- What are the various writing strategies the authors employ? What rhetorical tools do they use to persuade us? If you found a selection convincing, what made it so?

- Do you detect any logical flaws in the arguments developed by the authors of these selections? Can you find any inconsistencies or biases? Are there any contradictions within each selection? What recommendations would you make to the author about how he or she might improve their essay?

The New Sovereignty

Shelby Steele

Shelby Steele (b. 1946) is an author, professor, and well known commentator on race relations. He holds a Ph.D. in English from the University of Utah as well as an M.A. in Sociology from Southern Illinois University. He is currently the Robert J. and Marion E. Oster Senior Fellow at the Hoover Institute, where he focuses on race relations. His commentaries often appear in publications such as The New York Times, Harper's, *and* The Wall Street Journal, *among many others. His books include* The Content of Our Character: A New Vision of Race in America *(1990),* A Dream Deferred: The Second Betrayal of Black Freedom in America *(1998),* White Guilt: How Blacks and Whites Together Destroyed the Promise of the Civil Rights Era *(2006), and* A Bound Man: Why We Are Excited About Obama and Why He Can't Win *(2007). Steele is the son of a black father and a white mother, both of whom were active during the Civil Rights Movement. As Steele notes in the following essay, these activities of his parents made a strong impression on him, one which, even if he didn't always appreciate it at the time, has retained its value for Steele throughout his life.*

1   Toward the end of a talk I gave recently at a large Midwestern university I noticed a distinct tension in the audience. All respectful audiences are quiet, but I've come to understand that when there is disagreement with what's being said at the podium the silence can become pure enough to constitute a statement. Fidgeting and whispering cease, pencils stay still in notetakers' hands—you sense the quiet filling your pauses as a sign of disquiet, even resistance. A speaker can feel ganged-up on by such a silence.

2   I had gotten myself into this spot by challenging the orthodoxy of diversity that is now so common on university campuses—not the *notion* of diversity, which I wholly subscribe to, but the rigid means by which it is pursued. I had told the students and faculty members on hand that in the late 1960s, without much public debate but with many good intentions, America had embarked upon one of the most dramatic social experiments in its history. The federal government, radically and officially, began to alter and expand the concept of entitlement in America. Rights to justice and to government benefits were henceforth to be extended not simply to individuals but to racial, ethnic, and other groups. Moreover, the essential basis of all entitlement in America—the guarantees of the Constitution—had apparently been found wanting; there was to be redress and reparation of past grievances, and the Constitution had nothing to say about that.

3   I went on to explain that Martin Luther King and the early civil rights leaders had demanded only constitutional rights; they had been found wanting, too. By the late Sixties, among a new set of black leaders, there had developed a presumption of collective entitlement (based on the redress of past grievances) that made blacks eligible for rights beyond those provided for in the Constitution, and thus beyond those afforded the nation's non-black citizens. Thanks to the civil rights movement, a young black citizen as well as a young white citizen could not be turned away from a college because of the color of his or her skin; by the early Seventies a young black citizen, poor or wealthy, now qualified for certain grants and scholarships—might even be accepted for admission—simply *because* of the color of his or her skin. I made the point that this new and rather unexamined principle of collective entitlement had led America to pursue a democracy of groups as well as of individuals—that collective entitlement enfranchised groups just as the Constitution enfranchised individuals.

4   It was when I introduced a concept I call the New Sovereignty that my audience's silence became most audible. In America today, I said, sovereignty—that is, power to act autonomously—is bestowed upon any group that is able to construct itself around a perceived grievance. With the concept of collective entitlement now accepted not only at the federal level but casually at all levels of society, any aggrieved group—and, for that matter, any assemblage of citizens that might or might not have previously been thought of as such a group—could make its case, attract attention and funding, and build a constituency that, in turn, would increase attention and funding. Soon this organized group of aggrieved citizens would achieve sovereignty, functioning within our long-sovereign nation and negotiating with that nation for a separate, exclusive set of entitlements. And here I pointed to America's university campuses, where, in the name of their grievances, blacks, women,

Hispanics, Asians, Native Americans, gays, and lesbians had hardened into sovereign constituencies that vied for the entitlements of sovereignty—separate "studies" departments for each group, "ethnic" theme dorms, preferential admissions and financial-aid policies, a proportionate number of faculty of their own group, separate student lounges and campus centers, and so on. This push for equality among groups, I said, necessarily made for an inequality among individuals that prepared the ground for precisely the racial, gender, and ethnic divisiveness that, back in the Sixties, we all said we wanted to move beyond.

5   At the reception that followed the talk I was approached by a tall, elegant woman who introduced herself as the chairperson of the women's-studies department. Anger and the will to be polite were at war in her face so that her courteous smile at times became a leer. She wanted to "inform" me that she was proud of the fact that women's studies was a separate department unto itself at her university. I asked her what could be studied in this department that could not be studied in other departments. Take the case of, say, Virginia Woolf: in what way would a female academic teaching in a women's-studies department have a different approach to Woolf's writing than a woman professor in the English department? Above her determined smile her eyes became fierce. "You must know as a black that they won't accept us"—meaning women, blacks, presumably others—"in the English department. It's an oppressive environment for women scholars. We're not taken seriously there." I asked her if that wasn't all the more reason to be there, to fight the good fight, and to work to have the contributions of women broaden the entire discipline of literary studies. She said I was naive. I said her strategy left the oppressiveness she talked about unchallenged. She said it was a waste of valuable energy to spend time fighting "old white males." I said that if women were oppressed, there was nothing to do *but* fight.

6   We each held tiny paper plates with celery sticks and little bricks of cheese, and I'm sure much body language was subdued by the tea-party postures these plates imposed on us. But her last word was not actually a word. It was a look. She parodied an epiphany of disappointment in herself, as if she'd caught herself in a bizarre foolishness. *Of course, this guy is the enemy. He is the very oppressiveness I'm talking about. How could I have missed it?* And so, suddenly comfortable in the understanding that I was hopeless, she let her smile become gracious. Grace was something she could afford now. An excuse was made, a hand extended, and then she was gone. Holding my little plate, I watched her disappear into the crowd.

7   Today there are more than five hundred separate women's-studies departments or programs in American colleges and universities. There are nearly four hundred independent black-studies departments or programs, and hundreds of Hispanic, Asian, and Native American programs. Given this degree of entrenchment, it is no wonder this woman found our little debate a waste of her time. She would have had urgent administrative tasks awaiting her attention—grant proposals to write, budget requests to work up, personnel matters to attend to. And suppose I had won the debate? Would she have rushed back to her office and begun to dismantle the women's-studies department by doling out its courses and faculty to long-standing departments like English and history? Would she have given her secretary notice and relinquished her office equipment? I don't think so.

8   I do think I know how it all came to this—how what began as an attempt to address the very real grievances of women wound up creating newly sovereign fiefdoms like this

women's-studies department. First there was collective entitlement to redress the grievances, which in turn implied a sovereignty for the grievance group, since sovereignty is
only the formalization of collective entitlement. Then, since sovereignty requires autonomy,
there had to be a demand for separate and independent stature within the university (or
some other institution of society). There would have to be a separate territory, with the
trappings that certify sovereignty and are concrete recognition of the grievance identity—a
building or suite of offices, a budget, faculty, staff, office supplies, letterhead, et cetera.

9   And so the justification for separate women's- and ethnic-studies programs has virtually nothing to do with strictly academic matters and everything to do with the kind of
group-identity politics in which the principle of collective entitlement has resulted. My
feeling is that there can be no full redress of the woeful neglect of women's intellectual
contributions until those contributions are entirely integrated into the very departments
that neglected them in the first place. The same is true for America's minorities. Only inclusion answers history's exclusion. But now the sovereignty of grievance-group identities has
confused all this.

10   It was the sovereignty issue that squelched my talk with the women's-studies chairperson. She came to see me as an enemy not because I denied that women writers had been
neglected historically; I was the enemy because my questions challenged the territorial
sovereignty of her department and of the larger grievance identity of women. It was not
a matter of fairness—of justice—but of power. She would not put it that way, of course.
For in order to rule over her sovereign fiefdom it remains important that she seem to
represent the powerless, the aggrieved. It remains important, too, that my objection to the
New Sovereignty can be interpreted by her as sexist. When I failed to concede sovereignty,
I became an enemy of women.

11   In our age of the New Sovereignty the original grievances—those having to do with
fundamental questions such as basic rights—have in large measure been addressed, if not
entirely redressed. But that is of little matter now. The sovereign fiefdoms are ends in
themselves—providing career tracks and bases of power. This power tends to be used now
mostly to defend and extend the fiefdom, often by exaggerating and exploiting secondary,
amorphous, or largely symbolic complaints. In this way, America has increasingly become
an uneasy federation of newly sovereign nations.

12   How did America evolve its now rather formalized notion that groups of its citizens
could be entitled collectively? I think it goes back to the most fundamental contradiction in
American life. From the beginning America has been a pluralistic society, and one drawn to
a radical form of democracy—emphasizing the freedom and equality of *individuals*—that
could meld such diversity into a coherent nation. In this new nation no group would lord
it over any other. But, of course, beneath this America of its ideals there was from the start
a much meaner reality, one whose very existence mocked the notion of a nation made singular by the equality of its individuals. By limiting democracy to their own kind—white,
male landowners—the Founding Fathers collectively entitled themselves and banished
all others to the edges and underside of American life. There, individual entitlement was
either curtailed or—in the case of slavery—extinguished.

13   The genius of the civil rights movement that changed the fabric of American life in
the late 1950s and early 1960s was its profound understanding that the enemy of black

Americans was not the ideal America but the unspoken principle of collective entitlement that had always put the lie to true democracy. This movement, which came to center stage from America's underside and margins, had as its single, overriding goal the eradication of white entitlement. And, correspondingly, it exhibited a belief in democratic principles at least as strong as that of the Founding Fathers, who themselves had emerged from the (less harsh) margins of English society. In this sense the civil rights movement re-enacted the American Revolution, and its paramount leader, Martin Luther King, spoke as twentieth-century America's greatest democratic voice.

14   All of this was made clear to me for the umpteenth time by my father on a very cold Saturday afternoon in 1959. There was a national campaign under way to integrate the lunch counters at Woolworth stores, and my father, who was more a persuader than an intimidator, had made it a point of honor that I join him on the picket line, civil rights being nothing less than the religion of our household. By this time, age twelve or so, I was sick of it. I'd had enough of watching my parents heading off to still another meeting or march; I'd heard too many tedious discussions on everything from the philosophy of passive resistance to the symbolism of going to jail. Added to this, my own experience of picket lines and peace marches had impressed upon me what so many people who've partaken of these activities know: that in themselves they can be crushingly boring—around and around and around holding a sign, watching one's own feet fall, feeling the minutes like hours. All that Saturday morning I hid from my father and tried to convince myself of what I longed for—that he would get so busy that if he didn't forget the march he would at least forget me.

15   He forgot nothing. I did my time on the picket line, but not without building up enough resentment to start a fight on the way home. What was so important about integration? We had never even wanted to eat at Woolworth's. I told him the truth, that he never took us to *any* restaurants anyway, claiming always that they charged too much money for bad food. But he said calmly that he was proud of me for marching and that he knew I knew food wasn't the point.

16   My father—forty years a truck driver, with the urges of an intellectual—went on to use my little rebellion as the occasion for a discourse, in this case on the concept of integration. Integration had little to do with merely rubbing shoulders with white people, eating bad food beside them. It was about the right to go absolutely anywhere white people could go being the test of freedom and equality. To be anywhere they could be and do anything they could do was the point. Like it or not, white people defined the horizon of freedom in America, and if you couldn't touch their shoulder you weren't free. For him integration was the *evidence* of freedom and equality.

17   My father was a product of America's margins, as were all the blacks in the early civil rights movement, leaders and foot soldiers alike. For them integration was a way of moving from the margins into the mainstream. Today there is considerable ambivalence about integration, but in that day it was nothing less than democracy itself. Integration is also certainly about racial harmony, but it is more fundamentally about the ultimate extension of democracy—beyond the racial entitlements that contradict it. The idea of racial integration is quite simply the most democratic principle America has evolved, since all other such principles depend on its reality and are diminished by its absence.

18   But the civil rights movement did not account for one thing: the tremendous release of black anger that would follow its victories. The 1964 Civil Rights Act and the 1965 Voting Rights Act were, on one level, admissions of guilt by American society that it had practiced white entitlement at the expense of all others. When the oppressors admit their crimes, the oppressed can give full vent to their long repressed rage because now there is a moral consensus between oppressor and oppressed that a wrong was done. This consensus gave blacks the license to release a rage that was three centuries deep, a rage that is still today everywhere visible, a rage that—in the wake of the Rodney King verdict, a verdict a vast majority of all Americans thought unfair—fueled the worst rioting in recent American history.

19   By the mid-Sixties, the democratic goal of integration was no longer enough to appease black anger. Suddenly for blacks there was a sense that far more was owed, that a huge bill was due. And for many whites there was also the feeling that some kind of repayment was truly in order. This was the moral logic that followed inevitably from the new consensus. But it led to an even simpler logic: if blacks had been oppressed collectively, that oppression would now be redressed by entitling them collectively. So here we were again, in the name of a thousand good intentions, falling away from the hard challenge of a democracy of individuals and embracing the principle of collective entitlement that had so corrupted the American ideal in the first place. Now this old sin would be applied in the name of uplift. And this made an easy sort of sense. If it was good enough for whites for three hundred years, why not let blacks have a little of it to get ahead? In the context of the Sixties—black outrage and white guilt—a principle we had just decided was evil for whites was redefined as a social good for blacks. And once the formula was in place for blacks, it could be applied to other groups with similar grievances. By the 1970s more than 60 percent of the American population—not only blacks but Hispanics, women, Asians—would come under the collective entitlement of affirmative action.

20   In the early days of the civil rights movement, the concept of solidarity was essentially a moral one. That is, all people who believed in human freedom, fairness, and equality were asked to form a solid front against white entitlement. But after the collaboration of black rage and white guilt made collective entitlement a social remedy, the nature of solidarity changed. It was no longer the rallying of diverse peoples to breach an oppressive group entitlement. It was the very opposite: a rallying of people within a grievance group to pursue their own group entitlement. As early as the mid-Sixties, whites were made unwelcome in the civil rights movement, just as, by the mid-Seventies, men were no longer welcome in the women's movement. Eventually, collective entitlement *always* requires separatism. And the irony is obvious: those who once had been the victims of separatism, who had sacrificed so dearly to overcome their being at the margins, would later create an ethos of their own separatism. After the Sixties, solidarity became essentially a separatist concept, an exclusionary principle. One no longer heard words like "integration" or "harmony"; one heard about "anger" and "power." Integration is anathema to grievance groups for precisely the same reason it was anathema to racist whites in the civil rights era: because it threatens their collective entitlement by insisting that no group be entitled over another. Power is where it's at today—power to set up the organization, attract the following, run the fiefdom.

21   But it must also be said that this could not have come to pass without the cooperation of the society at large and its institutions. Why did the government, the public and private institutions, the corporations and foundations, end up supporting principles that had the effect of turning causes into sovereign fiefdoms? I think the answer is that those in charge of America's institutions saw the institutionalization and bureaucratization of the protest movements as ultimately desirable, at least in the short term, and the funding of group entitlements as ultimately a less costly way to redress grievances. The leaders of the newly sovereign fiefdoms were backing off from earlier demands that America live up to its ideals. Gone was the moral indictment. Gone was the call for difficult, soulful transformation. The language of entitlements is essentially the old, comforting language of power politics, and in the halls of power it went down easily enough.

22   With regard to civil rights, the moral voice of Dr. King gave way to the demands and cajolings of poverty-program moguls, class-action lawyers, and community organizers. The compromise that satisfied both political parties was to shift the focus from democracy, integration, and developmental uplift to collective entitlements. This satisfied the institutions because entitlements were cheaper in every way than real change. Better to set up black-studies and women's-studies departments than to have wrenching debates within existing departments. Better to fund these new institutions clamoring for money because who knows what kind of fuss they'll make if we turn down their proposals. Better to pass laws permitting Hispanic students to get preferred treatment in college admission—it costs less than improving kindergartens in East Los Angeles.

23   And this way to uplift satisfied the grievance-group "experts" because it laid the ground for their sovereignty and permanency: You negotiated with *us*. You funded *us*. You shared power, at least a bit of it, with *us*.

24   This negotiation was carried out in a kind of quasi-secrecy. Quotas, set-asides, and other entitlements were not debated in Congress or on the campaign trail. They were implemented by executive orders and Equal Employment Opportunity Commission guidelines without much public scrutiny. Also the courts played a quiet but persistent role in supporting these orders and guidelines and in further spelling out their application. Universities, corporations, and foundations implemented their own grievance entitlements, the workings of which are often kept from the public.

25   Now, it should surprise no one that all this entitlement has most helped those who least need it—white middle-class women and the black middle class. Poor blacks do not guide the black grievance groups. Working-class women do not set NOW's agenda. Poor Hispanics do not clamor for bilingualism. Perhaps there is nothing wrong with middle-class people being helped, but their demands for entitlements are most often in the name of those less well off than themselves. The negotiations that settled on entitlements as the primary form of redress after the Sixties have generated a legalistic grievance industry that argues the interstices of entitlements and does very little to help those truly in need.

26   In a liberal democracy, collective entitlements based upon race, gender, ethnicity, or some other group grievance are always undemocratic expedients. Integration, on the other hand, is the most difficult and inexpedient expansion of the democratic ideal: for in opting for integration, a citizen denies his or her impulse to use our most arbitrary characteristics—race, ethnicity, gender, sexual preference—as the basis for identity, as a key

to status, or for claims to entitlement. Integration is twentieth-century America's elaboration of democracy. It eliminates such things as race and gender as oppressive barriers to freedom, as democrats of an earlier epoch eliminated religion and property. Our mistake has been to think of integration only as a utopian vision of perfect racial harmony. I think it is better to see integration as the inclusion of all citizens into the same sphere of rights, the same range of opportunities and possibilities that our Founding Fathers themselves enjoyed. Integration is not social engineering or group entitlements; it is a fundamental *absence* of arbitrary barriers to freedom.

27   If we can understand integration as an absence of barriers that has the effect of integrating all citizens into the same sphere of rights, then it can serve as a principle of democratic conduct. Anything that pushes anybody out of this sphere is undemocratic and must be checked, no matter the good intentions that seem to justify it. Understood in this light, collective entitlements are as undemocratic as racial and gender discrimination, and a group grievance is no more a justification for entitlement than the notion of white supremacy was at an earlier time. We are wrong to think of democracy as a gift of freedom; it is really a kind of discipline that avails freedom. Sometimes its enemy is racism and sexism; other times the enemy is our expedient attempts to correct these ills.

28   I think it is time for those who seek identity and power through grievance groups to fashion identities apart from grievance, to grant themselves the widest range of freedom, and to assume responsibility for that freedom. Victimhood lasts only as long as it is accepted, and to exploit it for an empty sovereignty is to accept it. The New Sovereignty is ultimately about vanity. It is the narcissism of victims, and it brings only a negligible power at the exorbitant price of continued victimhood. And all the while integration remains the real work.

QUESTIONS ON MEANING

1. What does Steele mean when he writes that he wishes to challenge the orthodoxy of diversity, but not the notion of diversity?

2. What does Steele mean by the phrase *the New Sovereignty*?

3. Why was the audience so quiet when Steele gave his lecture?

4. What fundamental change took place as the Civil Rights Movement under the leadership of Martin Luther King, Jr., in the 1960s moved into the 1970s?

5. What important lesson does Steele learn from his father when he is forced to march in a picket line? How does that lesson relate to the essay?

6. What does Steele mean when he writes that the "New Sovereignty is ultimately about vanity . . . and it brings only a negligible power at the exorbitant price of continued victimhood"?

QUESTIONS FOR DISCUSSION

1. Does your university or college have a Women's Studies Program? A Black Studies Program? A Gay and Lesbian Studies Program? Or some other program built around principles discussed in Steele's essay? If not, would you support the creation of such a program on your campus? If so, do you support them, or would you prefer to see these kinds of programs dismantled? Why or why not?

2. Steele writes that "America has increasingly become an uneasy federation of newly sovereign nations." What does Steele mean by this? Do you agree with Steele?

3. What is the relationship between democracy, as a political theory, and the New Sovereignty? Does Steele find them compatible? Do you?

4. Does America, as a socio-political institution, owe certain groups of its citizens for past grievances? Should current citizens be held to account for the policies of the past? Why or why not? Are programs like Affirmative Action a reasonable way to redress these prior grievances? Does Affirmative Action go far enough? Does it go too far? In other words, does American have an *ethical or moral responsibility* to treat certain groups differently than the rest?

LOOKING AT RHETORIC

1. What is the thesis of Steele's essay? Where does it become apparent that this is his thesis? Do you think that Steele's placement of his thesis (whether direct or implied) makes for a stronger or weaker essay? Why might Steele have chosen to introduce his thesis where he did?

2. Steele tells two key anecdotes during the course of this essay. Identify them. How do each of these anecdotes contribute to his essay? What points do they help Steele make? Are they effective?

WRITING ASSIGNMENTS

1. Spend some time researching the history of one of the following groups: the NAACP, NOW, or Act Up. Write an essay in which you give a history of the organization from its inception to its current activities.

2. Imagine that your college or university does not have a Women's Studies Program, but that a group of faculty and students on campus are calling for its creation and funding. Write an essay addressed to the administration of your school either supporting or challenging the creation of such a program on campus. As a variation on this assignment, imagine that instead of a Women's Studies Program the proposal is for a Black Studies Program? A Gay and Lesbian Studies Program? An Asian Studies Program?

3. In pairs or in groups, discuss whether you believe that there is such a thing as The New Sovereignty. As a group, debate whether Steele's portrait of The New Sovereignty accurately reflects the current socio-political situation in the United States. Then, as an individual, write an essay in which you either support or challenge Steele's position.

My Pedagogic Creed

John Dewey

John Dewey (1859–1952) was an American educational theorist, philosopher, and psychologist who exerted a tremendous influence on the many educational reforms that took place during and after his lifetime. Having graduated from the University of Vermont in 1879, he spent a short period of time as a public school teacher. He earned his Ph.D. from Johns Hopkins University, and taught at the University of Michigan and later at the University of Chicago. He began applying his

understanding of philosophy and psychology to education, writing many books, among them The
School and Social Progress *(1899),* Democracy and Education *(1916), and* Experience and
Education *(1938). He was president of the American Psychological Association and the American
Philosophical Association, as well as a long time member of the American Federation of Teachers.
In the following essay, Dewey argues that education should involve subject matter content, but only
insofar as it enhances the development of the social being, one who is prepared to act in the service
of the community and society as a whole.*

ARTICLE ONE: WHAT EDUCATION IS

1   I believe that all education proceeds by the participation of the individual in the social
consciousness of the race.[1] This process begins unconsciously almost at birth, and is continually shaping the individual's powers, saturating his consciousness, forming his habits, training his ideas, and arousing his feelings and emotions. Through this unconscious
education the individual gradually comes to share in the intellectual and moral resources
which humanity has succeeded in getting together. He becomes an inheritor of the funded
capital of civilization. The most formal and technical education in the world cannot safely
depart from this general process. It can only organize it; or differentiate it in some particular direction.

2   I believe that the only true education comes through the stimulation of the child's
powers by the demands of the social situations in which he finds himself. Through these
demands he is stimulated to act as a member of a unity, to emerge from his original nar-
rowness of action and feeling and to conceive of himself from the standpoint of the welfare of the group to which he belongs. Through the responses which others make to his
own activities he comes to know what these mean in social terms. The value which they
have is reflected back into them. For instance, through the response which is made to the
child's instinctive babblings the child comes to know what those babblings mean; they are
transformed into articulate language and thus the child is introduced into the consolidated
wealth of ideas and emotions which are now summed up in language.

3   I believe that this educational process has two sides—one psychological and one sociological; and that neither can be subordinated to the other or neglected without evil results
following. Of these two sides, the psychological is the basis. The child's own instincts and
powers furnish the material and give the starting point for all education. Same as the efforts
of the educator connect with some activity which the child is carrying on of his own initiative independent of the educator, education becomes reduced to a pressure from without.
It may, indeed, give certain external results but cannot truly be called educative. Without
insight into the psychological structure and activities of the individual, the educative process will, therefore, be haphazard and arbitrary. If it chances to coincide with the child's
activity it will get a leverage; if it does not, it will result in friction, or disintegration, or
arrest of the child nature.

4   I believe that the psychological and social sides are organically related and that education cannot be regarded as a compromise between the two, or a superimposition of one
upon the other. We are told that the psychological definition of education is barren and

---

[1]In this usage, "race" does not refer to ethnicity or race as used now but is meant to denote the human race.
A common usage in this time.

formal—that it gives us only the idea of a development of all the mental powers without giving us any idea of the use to which these powers are put. On the other hand, it is urged that the social definition of education, as getting adjusted to civilization, makes of it a forced and external process, and results in subordinating the freedom of the individual to a preconceived social and political status.

5   With the advent of democracy and modern industrial conditions,[2] it is impossible to foretell definitely just what civilization will be twenty years from now. Hence it is impossible to prepare the child for any precise set of conditions. To prepare him for the future life means to give him command of himself; it means so to train him that he will have the full and ready use of all his capacities; that his eye and ear and hand may be tools ready to command, that his judgment may be capable of grasping the conditions under which it has to work, and the executive forces be trained to act economically and efficiently. It is impossible to reach this sort of adjustment save as constant regard is had to the individual's own powers, tastes, and interests—say, that is, as education is continually converted into psychological terms. In sum, I believe that the individual who is to be educated is a social individual and that society is an organic union of individuals. If we eliminate the social factor from the child we are left only with an abstraction; if we eliminate the individual factor from society, we are left only with an inert and lifeless mass. Education, therefore, must begin with a psychological insight into the child's capacities, interests, and habits. It must be controlled at every point by reference to these same considerations. These powers, interests, and habits must be continually interpreted—we must know what they mean. They must be translated into terms of their social equivalents—into terms of what they are capable of in the way of social service.

ARTICLE TWO: WHAT THE SCHOOL IS

6   I believe that the school is primarily a social institution. Education being a social process, the school is simply that form of community life in which all those agencies are concentrated that will be most effective in bringing the child to share in the inherited resources of the race, and to use his own powers for social ends.

7   I believe that education, therefore, is a process of living and not a preparation for future living.

8   I believe that the school must represent present life—life as real and vital to the child as that which he carries on in the home, in the neighborhood, or on the play-ground.

9   I believe that education which does not occur through forms of life, forms that are worth living for their own sake, is always a poor substitute for the genuine reality and tends to cramp and to deaden.

10   I believe that the school, as an institution, should simplify existing social life; should reduce it, as it were, to an embryonic form. Existing life is so complex that the child cannot be brought into contact with it without either confusion or distraction; he is either overwhelmed by multiplicity of activities which are going on, so that he loses his own power of orderly reaction, or he is so stimulated by these various activities that his powers are prematurely called into play and he becomes either unduly specialized or else disintegrated.

---

[2]Dewey writes in a period of rapid industrialization, in which modern factories and cities are emerging, leading ultimately to contemporary technological society.

11   I believe that, as such simplified social life, the school life should grow gradually out of the home life; that it should take up and continue the activities with which the child is already familiar in the home.

12   I believe that it should exhibit these activities to the child, and reproduce them in such ways that the child will gradually learn the meaning of them, and be capable of playing his own part in relation to them.

13   I believe that this is a psychological necessity, because it is the only way of securing continuity in the child's growth, the only way of giving a background of past experience to the new ideas given in school.

14   I believe it is also a social necessity because the home is the form of social life in which the child has been nurtured and in connection with which he has had his moral training. It is the business of the school to deepen and extend his sense of the values bound up in his home life.

15   I believe that much of present education fails because it neglects this fundamental principle of the school as a form of community life. It conceives the school as a place where certain information is to be given, where certain lessons are to be learned, or where certain habits are to be formed. The value of these is conceived as lying largely in the remote future; the child must do these things for the sake of something else he is to do; they are mere preparation. As a result they do not become a part of the life experience of the child and so are not truly educative.

16   I believe that moral education centres about this conception of the school as a mode of social life, that the best and deepest moral training is precisely that which one gets through having to enter into proper relations with others in a unity of work and thought. The present educational systems, so far as they destroy or neglect this unity, render it difficult or impossible to get any genuine, regular moral training.

17   I believe that the child should be stimulated and controlled in his work through the life of the community.

18   I believe that under existing conditions far too much of the stimulus and control proceeds from the teacher, because of neglect of the idea of the school as a form of social life.

19   I believe that the teacher's place and work in the school is to be interpreted from this same basis. The teacher is not in the school to impose certain ideas or to form certain habits in the child, but is there as a member of the community to select the influences which shall affect the child and to assist him in properly responding to these influences.

20   I believe that the discipline of the school should proceed from the life of the school as a whole and not directly from the teacher.

21   I believe that the teacher's business is simply to determine on the basis of larger experience and riper wisdom, how the discipline of life shall come to the child.

22   I believe that all questions of the grading of the child and his promotion should be determined by reference to the same standard. Examinations are of use only so far as they test the child's fitness for social life and reveal the place in which he can be of most service and where he can receive the most help.

ARTICLE THREE: THE SUBJECT-MATTER OF EDUCATION

23   I believe that the social life of the child is the basis of concentration, or correlation, in all his training or growth. The social life gives the unconscious unity and the background of all his efforts and of all his attainments.

24   I believe that the subject-matter of the school curriculum should mark a gradual differentiation out of the primitive unconscious unity of social life.

25   I believe that we violate the child's nature and render difficult the best ethical results, by introducing the child too abruptly to a number of special studies, of reading, writing, geography, etc., out of relation to this social life.

26   I believe, therefore, that the true centre of correlation of the school subjects is not science, nor literature, nor history, nor geography, but the child's own social activities.

27   I believe once more that history is of educative value in so far as it presents phases of social life and growth. It must be controlled by reference to social life. When taken simply as history it is thrown into the distant past and becomes dead and inert. Taken as the record of man's social life and progress it becomes full of meaning. I believe, however, that it cannot be so taken excepting as the child is also introduced directly into social life.

28   I believe accordingly that the primary basis of education is in the child's powers at work along the same general constructive lines as those which have brought civilization into being.

29   I believe that the only way to make the child conscious of his social heritage is to enable him to perform those fundamental types of activity which makes civilization what it is.

30   I believe, therefore, in the so-called expressive or constructive activities as the centre of correlation.

31   I believe that this gives the standard for the place of cooking, sewing, manual training, etc., in the school.

32   I believe that they are not special studies which are to be introduced over and above a lot of others in the way of relaxation or relief, or as additional accomplishments. I believe rather that they represent, as types, fundamental forms of social activity; and that it is possible and desirable that the child's introduction into the more formal subjects of the curriculum be through the medium of these activities.

33   I believe that the study of science is educational in so far as it brings out the materials and processes which make social life what it is.

34   I believe that one of the greatest difficulties in the present teaching of science is that the material is presented in purely objective form, or is treated as a new peculiar kind of experience which the child can add to that which he has already had. In reality, science is of value because it gives the ability to interpret and control the experience already had. It should be introduced, not as so much new subject-matter, but as showing the factors already involved in previous experience and as furnishing tools by which that experience can be more easily and effectively regulated.

35   I believe that at present we lose much of the value of literature and language studies because of our elimination of the social element. Language is almost always treated in the books of pedagogy simply as the expression of thought. It is true that language is a logical instrument, but it is fundamentally and primarily a social instrument. Language is the device for communication; it is the tool through which one individual comes to share the ideas and feelings of others. When treated simply as a way of getting individual information, or as a means of showing off what one has learned, it loses its social motive and end.

36   I believe that there is, therefore, no succession of studies in the ideal school curriculum. If education is life, all life has, from the outset, a scientific aspect; an aspect of art and culture and an aspect of communication. It cannot, therefore, be true that the proper studies

for one grade are mere reading and writing, and that at a later grade, reading, or literature, or science, may be introduced. The progress is not in the succession of studies but in the development of new attitudes towards, and new interests in, experience.

37   I believe finally, that education must be conceived as a continuing reconstruction of experience; that the process and the goal of education are one and the same thing.

38   I believe that to set up any end outside of education, as furnishing its goal and standard, is to deprive the educational process of much of its meaning and tends to make us rely upon false and external stimuli in dealing with the child.

ARTICLE FOUR: THE NATURE OF METHOD

39   I believe that the question of method is ultimately reducible to the question of the order of development of the child's powers and interests. The law for presenting and treating material is the law implicit within the child's own nature. Because this is so I believe the following statements are of supreme importance as determining the spirit in which education is carried on:

1. I believe that the active side precedes the passive in the development of the child nature; that expression comes before conscious impression; that the muscular development precedes the sensory; that movements come before conscious sensations; I believe that consciousness is essentially motor or impulsive; that conscious states tend to project themselves in action.

    I believe that the neglect of this principle is the cause of a large part of the waste of time and strength in school work. The child is thrown into a passive, receptive or absorbing attitude. The conditions are such that he is not permitted to follow the law of his nature; the result is friction and waste.

    I believe that ideas (intellectual and rational processes) also result from action and devolve for the sake of the better control of action. What we term reason is primarily the law of orderly or effective action. To attempt to develop the reasoning powers, the powers of judgment, without reference to the selection and arrangement of means in action, is the fundamental fallacy in our present methods of dealing with this matter. As a result we present the child with arbitrary symbols. Symbols are a necessity in mental development, but they have their place as tools for economizing effort; presented by themselves they are a mass of meaningless and arbitrary ideas imposed from without.

2. I believe that the image is the great instrument of instruction. What a child gets out of any subject presented to him is simply the images which he himself forms with regard to it.

    I believe that if nine-tenths of the energy at present directed towards making the child learn certain things, were spent in seeing to it that the child was forming proper images, the work of instruction would be indefinitely facilitated.

    I believe that much of the time and attention now given to the preparation and presentation of lessons might be more wisely and profitably expended in training the child's power of imagery and in seeing to it that he was continually forming definite, vivid, and growing images of the various subjects with which he comes in contact in his experience.

3. I believe that interests are the signs and symptoms of growing power. I believe that they represent dawning capacities. Accordingly the constant and careful observation of interests is of the utmost importance for the educator.

I believe that these interests are to be observed as showing the state of development which the child has reached.

I believe that they prophesy the stage upon which he is about to enter.

I believe that only through the continual and sympathetic observation of childhood's interests can the adult enter into the child's life and see what it is ready for, and upon what material it could work most readily and fruitfully.

I believe that these interests are neither to be humored nor repressed. To repress interest is to substitute the adult for the child, and so to weaken intellectual curiosity and alertness, to suppress initiative, and to deaden interest. To humor the interests is to substitute the transient for the permanent. The interest is always the sign of some power below; the important thing is to discover this power. To humor the interest is to fail to penetrate below the surface and its sure result is to substitute caprice and whim for genuine interest.

ARTICLE FIVE: THE SCHOOL AND SOCIAL PROGRESS

40   I believe that education is the fundamental method of social progress and reform.

41   I believe that all reforms which rest simply upon the enactment of law, or the threatening of certain penalties, or upon changes in mechanical or outward arrangements, are transitory and futile.

42   I believe that education is a regulation of the process of coming to share in the social consciousness; and that the adjustment of individual activity on the basis of this social consciousness is the only sure method of social reconstruction.

43   I believe that this conception has due regard for both the individualistic and socialistic ideals.[3] It is duly individual because it recognizes the formation of a certain character as the only genuine basis of right living. It is socialistic because it recognizes that this right character is not to be formed by merely individual precept, example, or exhortation, but rather by the influence of a certain form of institutional or community life upon the individual, and that the social organism through the school, as its organ, may determine ethical results.

44   I believe that in the ideal school we have the reconciliation of the individualistic and the institutional ideals.

45   I believe that the community's duty to education is, therefore, its paramount moral duty. By law and punishment, by social agitation and discussion, society can regulate and

---

[3]"socialistic ideals" is not a reference to the economic and political ideals often referred to as Socialism or its more radical form, Marxist Communism. In this context, the term refers to a general devotion to the improvement of society.

form itself in a more or less haphazard and chance way. But through education society can formulate its own purposes, can organize its own means and resources, and thus shape itself with definiteness and economy in the direction in which it wishes to move.

QUESTIONS ON MEANING

1. What does Dewey mean when he writes that all education "proceeds by the participation of the individual in the social consciousness of the race"?

2. What are the two sides of education? What kind of relationship do they have to one another?

3. What does he mean when he says that school is primarily a social institution?

4. What role does "subject matter" play in his concept of education? How is it different than more conventional ideas about teaching disciplinary content?

5. What does he mean when he writes, "What we term reason is primarily the law of orderly and effective action"?

6. What is the primary purpose of education?

QUESTIONS FOR DISCUSSION

1. Is it reasonable to subordinate the teaching of academic subjects to activating the student's mind as a social being? Are the two approaches reconcilable?

2. What might a modern class session in English, mathematics, or social studies look like using this method?

3. Do you think that education is the community's "paramount moral duty"?

LOOKING AT RHETORIC

1. How does the structure of the creed (with the continual use of "I believe") affect the presentation of concepts? Does it serve the author's purpose?

2. Consider the use of abstract concepts such as social consciousness and the law of orderly and effective action. How do they affect the reading experience?

3. Consider the sense of moral urgency in the creed's tone. How does it affect the argument?

WRITING ASSIGNMENTS

1. In this essay, Dewey presents his readers with a creed—a statement of belief—regarding the utility and significance of the modern educational system. Using library and/or Internet resources, track down another work that presents an educational creed. Draft an essay in which you compare and contrast the creeds presented in these two essays—the one by Dewey and the one that you located through your research.

2. Argue for or against the idea that education's main purpose is to create well-adapted social beings.

3. In pairs or in groups, discuss specific class sessions you have experienced in various subjects. To what extent were they exclusively content driven and to what extent were they oriented toward developing you as a social being? Individually, write an essay in which you devise a plan for a class session that integrates subject matter with the desire to link the learner to a group or community.

The American Scholar

Ralph Waldo Emerson

*Ralph Waldo Emerson (1803-1882) was one of the most influential American thinkers of the nine-
teenth century. Often associated with the Transcendentalist and Romantic movements, Emerson
wrote essays, speeches, and treatises on various related subjects, including education, religion,
poetry, politics, and social philosophy. He attended Harvard College and taught in Boston-area
schools before becoming an ordained pastor of Boston's Second Church. Emerson eventually left his
position to pursue a career as a philosopher and a poet. In 1836, he published the small pamphlet*
Nature, *which became a founding document of the American Transcendentalist movement. In a
series of essays that followed, Emerson continued to develop these concepts. The following essay,
which was first published as a pamphlet in 1837 (and then republished in* **Nature, Addresses,
and Lectures** *(1849), states that individuals should not simply receive the knowledge of others,
but should absorb and recreate that understanding. Learning is an organic process by which human beings become whole, complete, and spiritually realized, not "divided" by pre-set curricula
designed to serve the economic interests of the Industrial Revolution.*

1   Mr. President, and Gentlemen,

2   I greet you on the re-commencement of our literary year. Our anniversary is one of
hope, and, perhaps, not enough of labor. We do not meet for games of strength or skill,
for the recitation of histories, tragedies and odes, like the ancient Greeks; for parliaments
of love and poesy, like the Troubadours;[1] nor for the advancement of science, like our
cotemporaries in the British and European capitals. Thus far, our holiday has been simply
a friendly sign of the survival of the love of letters amongst a people too busy to give to
letters any more. As such, it is precious as the sign of an indestructible instinct. Perhaps the
time is already come, when it ought to be, and will be something else when the sluggard
intellect of this continent will look from under its iron lid and fill the postponed expectation of the world with something better than the exertions of mechanical skill. Our day of
dependence, our long apprenticeship to the learning of other lands, draws to a close. The
millions, that around us are rushing into life, cannot always be fed on the sere remains of
foreign harvests. Events, actions arise, that must be sung, that will sing themselves. Who
can doubt that poetry will revive and lead in a new age, as the star in the constellation Harp
which now flames in our zenith, astronomers announce, shall one day be the pole-star[2] for
a thousand years.

3   In the light of this hope, I accept the topic which not only usage, but the nature of our
association, seem to prescribe to this day,—the AMERICAN SCHOLAR. Year by year, we come

---

[1]Troubadours: Courtly poets in the middle ages, especially in Provence, France, in the twelfth and thirteenth
centuries.
[2]Pole-star: the North Star. "Harp" referring to Lyra, a northern constellation which includes Vega, a bright star.

up hither to read one more chapter of his biography. Let us inquire what new lights, new events and more days have thrown on his character, his duties and his hopes.

4   It is one of those fables, which out of an unknown antiquity, convey an unlooked for wisdom, that the gods, in the beginning, divided Man into men that he might be more helpful to himself; just as the hand was divided in to fingers, the better to answer its end.

5   The old fable covers a doctrine ever new and sublime; that there is One Man—present to all particular men only partially; or through one faculty and that you must take the whole society to find the whole man. Man is not a farmer, or a professor, or an engineer, but he is all. Man is priest, and scholar, and statesman, and producer, and soldier. In the *divided* or social state, these functions are parcelled out to individuals, each of whom aims to stint of the joint work, whilst each other performs his. The fable implies that the individual to possess himself, must sometimes return from his own labor to embrace all the other laborers. But unfortunately, this original unit, this fountain of power, has been so distributed to multitudes, has been so minutely subdivided and peddled out, that it is spilled into drops, and cannot be gathered. The state of society is one in which the members have suffered amputation from the trunk, and strut about so many walking monsters—a good finger, a neck, a stomach, an elbow, but never a man.

6   Man is thus metamorphosed into a thing, into many things. The planter, who is Man sent out into the field to gather food, is seldom cheered by any idea of the true dignity of his ministry. He sees his bushel and his cart, and nothing beyond, and sinks into the farmer, instead of Man on the farm. The tradesman scarcely ever gives an ideal worth to his work, but is ridden by the routine of his craft, and the soul is subject to dollars. The priest becomes a form; the attorney, a statute-book; the mechanic, a machine; the sailor, a rope of a ship.

7   In this distribution of functions, the scholar is the delegated intellect. In the right state, he is, *Man Thinking*. In the degenerate state, when the victim of society, he tends to become a mere thinker, or, still worse, the parrot of other men's thinking.

8   In this view of him, as Man Thinking, the whole theory of his office is contained. Him nature solicits, with all her placid, all her monitory pictures. Him the past instructs. Him the future invites. Is not, indeed, every man a student, and do not all things exist for the student's behoof? And, finally, is not the true scholar the only true master? But, as the old oracle said, "All things have two handles. Beware of the wrong one." In life, too often, the scholar errs with mankind and forfeits his privilege. Let us see him in his school, and consider him in reference to the main influences he receives.

9   I. The first in time and the first in importance of the influences upon the mind is that of nature. Every day, the sun; and, after sunset, night and her stars. Ever the winds blow; ever the grass grows. Every day, men and women, conversing, beholding and beholden. The scholar must needs stand wistful and admiring before this great spectacle. He must settle its value in his mind. What is nature to him? There is never a beginning, there is never an end to the inexplicable continuity of this web of God, but always circular power returning into itself. Therein it resembles his own spirit, whose beginning, whose ending he never can find—so entire, so boundless. Far, too, as her splendors shine, system on system shooting like rays, upward, downward, without centre, without circumference—in the mass and in the particle nature hastens to render account of herself to the mind. Classification begins. To the young mind, every thing is individual, stands by itself. By and by, it finds how to join two things, and see in them one nature; then three, then three thousand; and so, tyrannized

over by its own unifying instinct, it goes on tying things together, diminishing anomalies, discovering roots running under ground, whereby contrary and remote things cohere, and flower out from one stem. It presently learns, that, since the dawn of history, there has been a constant accumulation and classifying of facts. But what is classification but the perceiving that these objects are not chaotic, and are not foreign, but have a law which is also a law of the human mind? The astronomer discovers that geometry, a pure abstraction of the human mind, is the measure of planetary motion. The chemist finds proportions and intelligible method throughout matter: and science is nothing but the finding of analogy, identity in the most remote parts. The ambitious soul sits down before each refractory fact; one after another, reduces all strange constitutions, all new powers, to their class and their law, and goes on forever to animate the last fibre of organization, the outskirts of nature, by insight.

10   Thus to him, to this school-boy under the bending dome of day, is suggested, that he and it proceed from one root; one is leaf and one is flower; relation, sympathy, stirring in every vein. And what is that Root? Is not that the soul of his soul?—A thought too bold—a dream too wild. Yet when this spiritual light shall have revealed the law of more earthly natures—when he has learned to worship the soul, and to see that the natural philosophy that now is, is only the first gropings of its gigantic hand, he shall look forward to an ever expanding knowledge as to a becoming creator. He shall see that nature is the opposite of the soul, answering to it part for part. One is seal, and one is print. Its beauty is the beauty of his own mind. Its laws are the laws of his own mind. Nature then becomes to him the measure of his attainments. So much of nature as he is ignorant of, so much of his own mind does he not yet possess. And, in fine, the ancient precept, "Know thyself," and the modern precept, "Study nature," become at last one maxim.

11   II. The next great influence into the spirit of the scholar, is, the mind of the Past—in whatever form, whether of literature, of art, of institutions, that mind is inscribed. Books are the best type of the influence of the past, and perhaps we shall get at the truth—learn the amount of this influence more conveniently—by considering their value alone.

12   The theory of books is noble. The scholar of the first age received into him the world around; brooded thereon; gave it the new arrangement of his own mind, and uttered it again. It came into him—life; it went out from him—truth. It came to him—short-lived actions; it went out from him—immortal thoughts. It came to him—business; it went from him—poetry. It was—dead fact; now, it is quick thought. It can stand, and it can go. It now endures, it now flies, it now inspires. Precisely in proportion to the depth of mind from which it issued, so high does it soar, so long does it sing.

13   Or, I might say, it depends on how far the process had gone, of transmuting life into truth. In proportion to the completeness of the distillation, so will the purity and imperishableness of the product be. But none is quite perfect. As no air-pump can by any means make a perfect vacuum, so neither can any artist entirely exclude the conventional, the local, the perishable from his book, or write a book of pure thought that shall be as efficient, in all respects to a remote posterity, as to cotemporaries, or rather to the second age. Each age, it is found, must write its own books; or rather, each generation for the next succeeding. The books of an older period will not fit this.

14   Yet hence arises a grave mischief. The sacredness which attaches to the act of creation— the act of thought—is instantly transferred to the record. The poet chanting, was felt to be a divine man. Henceforth the chant is divine also. The writer was a just and wise spirit.

Henceforward it is settled, the book is perfect; as love of the hero corrupts into worship of his statue. Instantly, the book becomes noxious. The guide is a tyrant. We sought a brother, and lo, a governor. The sluggish and perverted mind of the multitude, always slow to open to the incursions of Reason, having once so opened, having once received this book, stands upon it, and makes an outcry, if it is disparaged. Colleges are built on it. Books are written on it by thinkers, not by Man Thinking; by men of talent, that is, who start wrong, who set out from accepted dogmas, not from their own sight of principles. Meek young men grow up in libraries, believing it their duty to accept the views which Cicero, which Locke, which Bacon have given, forgetful that Cicero,[3] Locke[4] and Bacon[5] were only young men in libraries when they wrote these books.

15   Hence, instead of Man Thinking, we have the bookworm. Hence, the book-learned class, who value books, as such; not as related to nature and the human constitution, but as making a sort of Third Estate[6] with the world and the soul. Hence, the restorers of readings, the emendators, the bibliomaniacs of all degrees.

16   This is bad; this is worse than it seems. Books are the best of things, well used; abused, among the worst. What is the right use? What is the one end which all means go to effect? They are for nothing but to inspire. I had better never see a book than to be warped by its attraction clean out of my own orbit, and made a satellite instead of a system. The one thing in the world of value, is, the active soul—the soul, free, sovereign, active. This every man is entitled to; this every man contains within him, although in almost all men, obstructed, and as yet unborn. The soul active sees absolute truth; and utters truth, or creates. In this action, it is genius; not the privilege of here and there a favorite, but the sound estate of every man. In its essence, it is progressive. The book, the college, the school of art, the institution of any kind, stop with some past utterance of genius. This is good, say they—let us hold by this. They pin me down. They look backward and not forward. But genius always looks forward. The eyes of man are set in his forehead, not in his hindhead. Man hopes. Genius creates. To create—to create—is the proof of a divine presence. Whatever talents may be, if the man create not, the pure efflux of the Deity is not his:—cinders and smoke, there may be, but not yet flame. There are creative manners, there are creative actions, and creative words; manners, actions, words, that is, indicative of no custom or authority, but springing spontaneous from the mind's own sense of good and fair.

17   On the other part, instead of being its own seer, let it receive always from another mind its truth, though it were in torrents of light, without periods of solitude, inquest and self-recovery, and a fatal disservice is done. Genius is always sufficiently the enemy of genius by over-influence. The literature of every nation bear me witness. The English dramatic poets have Shakspearized now for two hundred years.

18   Undoubtedly, there is a right way of reading—so it be sternly subordinated. Man Thinking must not be subdued by his instruments. Books are for the scholar's idle times. When he can read God directly, the hour is too precious to be wasted in other men's

---

[3]Cicero (106–143 B. C. E.): Roman statesman and writer, often known for his oratory.
[4]John Locke (1632–1704): English philosopher and political thinker who was a founding figure in scientific empiricism as well as modern democratic social philosophy.
[5]Sir Francis Bacon (1561–1626): English statesman, philosopher, and Renaissance figure, known especially for his essays.
[6]Third Estate: The third level in a medieval social arrangement involving three social divisions in descending order of privilege: the clergy, the nobility, and the common people.

transcripts of their readings. But when the intervals of darkness come, as come they must—when the soul seeth not, when the sun is hid, and the stars withdraw their shining—we repair to the lamps which were kindled by their ray to guide our steps to the East again, where the dawn is. We hear that we may speak. The Arabian proverb says, "A fig tree looking on a fig tree, becometh fruitful."

19   It is remarkable, the character of the pleasure we derive from the best books. They impress us ever with the conviction that one nature wrote and the same reads. We read the verses of one of the great English poets, of Chaucer,[7] of Marvell,[8] of Dryden,[9] with the most modern joy—with a pleasure, I mean, which is in great part caused by the abstraction of all *time* from their verses. There is some awe mixed with the joy of our surprise, when this poet, who lived in some past world, two or three hundred years ago, says that which lies close to my own soul, that which I also had well nigh thought and said. But for the evidence thence afforded to the philosophical doctrine of the identity of all minds, we should suppose some pre-established harmony, some foresight of souls that were to be, and some preparation of stores for their future wants, like the fact observed in insects, who lay up food before death for the young grub they shall never see.

20   I would not be hurried by any love of system, by any exaggeration of instincts, to underrate the Book. We all know, that as the human body can be nourished on any food, though it were boiled grass and the broth of shoes, so the human mind can be fed by any knowledge. And great and heroic men have existed, who had almost no other information than by the printed page. I only would say, that it needs a strong head to bear that diet. One must be an inventor to read well. As the proverb says, "He that would bring home the wealth of the Indies, must carry out the wealth of the Indies." There is then creative reading, as well as creative writing. When the mind is braced by labor and invention, the page of whatever book we read becomes luminous with manifold allusion. Every sentence is doubly significant, and the sense of our author is as broad as the world. We then see, what is always true, that as the seer's hour of vision is short and rare among heavy days and months, so is its record, perchance, the least part of his volume. The discerning will read in his Plato or Shakspeare, only that least part—only the authentic utterances of the oracle—and all the rest he rejects, were it never so many times Plato's and Shakspeare's.

21   Of course, there is a portion of reading quite indispensable to a wise man. History and exact science he must learn by laborious reading. Colleges, in like manner, have their indispensable office—to teach elements. But they can only highly serve us, when they aim not to drill, but to create; when they gather from far every ray of various genius to their hospitable halls, and, by the concentrated fires, set the hearts of their youth on flame. Thought and knowledge are natures in which apparatus and pretension avail nothing. Gowns, and pecuniary foundations, though of towns of gold, can never countervail the least sentence or syllable of wit. Forget this, and our American colleges will recede in their public importance whilst they grow richer every year.

---

[7]Geoffrey Chaucer (1340–1400): One of the most important medieval English poets and author of *The Canterbury Tales*.

[8]Andrew Marvell (1621–1678): English poet.

[9]John Dryden (1631–1700): English poet and literary critic.

Interdisciplinary Connections

The Classroom: Then and Now

Here we find two depictions of college learning. The first is a painting by Raphael called "The School of Athens." The second is a photograph taken in a contemporary classroom. What do each of these images suggest about the values we attach to the college classroom experience?

Raphael, The School of Athens

http://3.bp.blogspot.com/_vEOtjqydo88/SwjL45edmfI/AAAAAAAAACQ/PGTiUxreNLo/s1600/School+of+Athens2.jpg

Which classroom looks more inviting to you? Does one image inspire you to learn more than the other? Why or why not? What details in these images give us clues to the way in which learning and the college experience has changed over time?

Classroom at the University of Toronto

QUESTIONS ON MEANING

1. According to Emerson, what has modern society done that divides human beings from their true selves?

2. What does he mean when he says that in his right state, the scholar is *Man Thinking*?

3. What role do previously written works play in developing the scholar or student? In what spirit should they read these past works?

4. What does Emerson mean when he says that books are read by thinkers, not by *Man Thinking*? What is the difference between *Man Thinking* and a bookworm?

5. In terms of reading and thinking, how does Emerson define *genius*?

QUESTIONS FOR DISCUSSION

1. What role should reading (or the education we receive through reading) play in our lives? How should it change us?

2. How should Emerson's notion of Man Thinking affect the way subjects are taught in school? How might an individual class session look different if the teacher were trying to create Man Thinking?

3. Do you think the specialized roles we are required to play in our lives confine us intellectually and spiritually, as Emerson suggests?

LOOKING FOR RHETORIC

1. Emerson's essay began as a speech. How does the personal address to the reader make the argument more or less effective?

2. The essay involves an epigrammatic style, a frequent use of short emphatic statements. How does this affect the reading experience?

3. Does the use of examples, analogies, and details enhance or detract from the essay's effectiveness?

WRITING ASSIGNMENTS

1. Emerson was one of the leading Transcendentalist philosophers in the nineteenth century. Using library and/or Internet resources, find out who the New England Transcendentalists were and what they believed. Then, try to find some information about the relationship between New England Transcendentalism and educational reform efforts in the nineteenth century. Write an essay in which you summarize your findings and talk about how some of the ideas in "The American Scholar" relate to your findings.

2. Define what Emerson means by Man Thinking. Then argue for or against this fairly modern notion of the scholar or student.

3. In pairs or in groups, discuss the way in which your experiences in school have encouraged you to be a divided being or Man Thinking. Individually, write an essay in which you design a class session, in any subject, which will encourage you to be a man, or woman, thinking.

The Myth of Helplessness

Jay P. Greene

Jay P. Greene is currently the head of the Department of Education Reform at the University of Arkansas. He received his Ph.D. in political science in 1995 and taught at the University of Houston and the University of Texas at Austin before taking a post as a Senior Fellow at the Manhattan Institute for Policy Research, where he worked from 2000-2005, before moving on to the University of Arkansas. In his 2005 book Education Myths, *from which the following selection is taken, Greene examines eighteen different beliefs about why the school system in the United States is faltering. In debunking these various myths, Greene attempts to chart a course for school improvement and student achievement.*

1   Everyone is familiar with the process by which obstacles and difficulties lying in the path to a certain goal are inevitably transformed into excuses for giving up on that goal entirely. A politician on the campaign trail will solemnly promise to adhere to a particular policy, but will later cite some new or complicating factor as an excuse to disregard this promise if doing so is politically expedient. A child will eagerly take up the study of a musical instrument—usually one that costs his parents a lot of money—only to declare it uninteresting and drop it the instant he discovers that practicing is tedious and slow to yield results. And every workplace has at least one employee who keeps finding excuses not to do difficult tasks.

2   Unfortunately, education is not exempt from what we might call the "law of convenient helplessness," the iron law of human behavior by which any difficulty becomes an excuse for inaction. Schools frequently cite a variety of social problems like poverty, broken homes, and bad parenting as excuses for their own poor performance. There is no doubt that many of our schools face big challenges caused by these problems. Even though material poverty has lessened—poor people today have higher incomes and a better standard of living than poor people a generation ago—other social problems that create obstacles to student learning have proven to be more persistent. For some, the existence of these challenges means that any effort to improve education is doomed to failure. A surprising number of commentators believe in the Myth of Helplessness—that failing schools cannot be improved so long as social problems persist. Some of them seem to think that the very idea of a "failing school" is misleading, since it is really society that has failed. But the evidence clearly establishes that schools can make a difference in students' level of educational achievement in spite of social problems.

SOCIAL PROBLEMS AS AN EXCUSE FOR INACTION

3   Richard Rothstein, former education columnist for the *New York Times*, is one of the foremost champions of the Myth of Helplessness. In one column, he laments that "parents today, by a ratio of three to one, tell pollsters that all children should be held to identical

standards." It is unreasonable, he writes, to expect poor and minority students to read and do math up to a defined minimum standard when they have not benefited from the superior parenting skills and resources of middle-class families.

4   Rothstein's successor as *New York Times* education columnist, Michael Winerip, has followed his lead in promoting the Myth of Helplessness. Commenting on the federal No Child Left Behind Act, he argues that whether schools meet federal standards will be determined by the condition of their local neighborhoods.

5   Rothstein and Winerip are the most prominent advocates of the Myth of Helplessness, but unfortunately, that myth goes far beyond their columns. Indeed, in some ways Rothstein and Winerip are voices of moderation compared to many other mainstream education commentators. They sometimes concede that schools are not totally helpless in the face of difficult social problems; others are not so conciliatory.

6   No one would deny that learning is more difficult for some students than it is for others because of factors that are beyond schools' control. Poverty, broken homes, lack of English proficiency, poor parenting, and any number of other factors pose serious educational challenges for some students. If the advocates of the Myth of Helplessness were merely cautioning us to be mindful of these difficulties, or exhorting us that while we seek to improve schools we must also try to alleviate other social problems, no one could disagree with them.

7   But they go far beyond just reminding us of the challenges resulting from social problems; they use these problems as an excuse to oppose school reforms. Rothstein's position is that no school reform can ever be effective as long as social problems persist.

8   For those who embrace this myth, the difficulties caused by social problems have become an excuse for inaction. Even Rothstein and Winerip, who do occasionally say that there is room for improvement in schools even if social problems are not alleviated, never allow these admissions to translate into concrete support for any proposal that would change the educational status quo. The Myth of Helplessness predominates—social problems are always seen as more powerful than anything schools might do to overcome them.

EVIDENCE OF PROMISING REFORMS

9   For the evidence to support the Myth of Helplessness and its attendant across-the-board opposition to changes in the educational status quo, it would have to show that no change in the status quo is effective at raising student performance in spite of the challenges posed by social problems. This is not the case. In fact, some school systems do a strikingly better job than others at overcoming the challenges posed by student disadvantages, and there are a variety of educational strategies and reforms that have been shown to work better than the status quo, even for the most disadvantaged students. Poverty, broken homes, and other social problems no doubt pose significant challenges, but the evidence simply doesn't leave room for the conclusion that these challenges are insurmountable.

SOME SCHOOL SYSTEMS DO BETTER THAN OTHERS

10   If the influence of disadvantages on student achievement were as overwhelming as the Myth of Helplessness implies, we would expect to see little variation in levels of achievement at schools serving similar student populations. That is, if two populations

of students are similar with regard to their disadvantages, we would expect them to have similar educational outcomes—highly advantaged students would have consistently high achievement, while highly disadvantaged students would have consistently low achievement. On the other hand, if schools can make a sizeable difference in students' academic outcomes in spite of their disadvantages, we might see substantial variation among the achievement of similarly disadvantages student populations.

11   Jay Greene and Greg Forster of the Manhattan Institute performed simple analysis to test the evidence on this question. First, they developed a systematic method for measuring levels of advantages and disadvantages in the student population. They combined measurements of sixteen social factors that researchers agree affect student outcomes, such as poverty, family structure, health, and students who don't speak English well. They call the combined measurement the Teachability Index, since it measures the over all "teachability" of the student population. Then they tested its validity be examining its statistical relationship with student outcomes; they found that the Teachability Index is a reliable predictor of student outcomes, indicating that it does in fact measure students' teachability.

12   Armed with this tool, they compared each state's student characteristic to its level of academic achievement. Specifically, they used each state Teachability Index score to predict the level of achievement its students would be expected to reach given their level of disadvantages, and then compared each state's actual achievement to its predicted achievement. They found a large degree of variation in how well the school systems in the various states overcome student disadvantages.

13   Greene and Forster's findings suggest that student achievement depends on more than just the levels of advantages and disadvantages that students face. This would naturally prompt us to ask what factors other than student advantages might produce higher educational outcomes. If we examine the evidence, we find that a number of school strategies have been shown to raise student achievement, even among particularly disadvantaged student populations.

ACCOUNTABILITY PROGRAMS

14   One type of reform that has been shown to work is school accountability, also known as "high-stakes testing." This type of program measures each school's performance through standardized testing and then provides rewards for schools that perform well and sanctions for schools that perform poorly. The goal is to give schools an incentive to educate all students well. Accountability has become something of a lightening rod for sharp criticism, especially from proponents of the Myth of Helplessness; Winerip in particular has been unrelenting in his attacks on high-stakes tests.

15   But the evidence shows that accountability works. Margaret Raymond and Eric Hanushek of Stanford University have demonstrated that states with high-stakes tests made significantly better test score improvements on the National Assessment of Educational Progress (NAEP), a highly reliable basic-skills test administered nationally by the U.S. Department of Education. Examining math scores, they found that high-stakes tests made a statistically significant difference in boosting both fourth-grade and eighth-grade scores over time. They also tracked a cohort of students from fourth grade in 1996 to eighth grade

in 2000 and found that this cohort had made significantly better improvements in states with high-stakes testing.

16   Another study, by Martin Carnoy and Susanna Loeb of Stanford University, came to similar conclusions. Carnoy and Loeb rated the strength of each state's accountability system according to the seriousness of its sanctions for failing schools, counting states with no sanctions as having the weakest accountability. They found that stronger accountability systems were associated with higher NAEP scores in both fourth and eighth grades, and that the improvements were even greater for black and Hispanic students than for white students.

17   The evidence also shows that high-stakes testing works not only in comfortable suburban schools, but also in failing schools with large numbers of poor and minority students. A study of high-stakes testing in Florida by Greene and Marcus Winters of the Manhattan Institute found that when chronically failing schools were threatened with sanctions if their test scores didn't improve, they made very impressive gains compared to the performance of all other schools, while similar low-performing schools not threatened with the same sanctions did not make similar gains. This is a point of particular importance, since one of the most frequent criticisms of high-stakes testing—especially from Rothstein and Winerip—is that poor students can't pass the same high-stakes tests that middle-class students can. But the opposite is actually occurring: accountability systems force school systems to focus their efforts on the failing schools and poor minority students who need help most.

SCHOOL CHOICE

18   Another kind of school reform that can help overcome the educational challenges caused by social problems is school choice. Five school voucher programs, all of them restricted to low-income students, have been studied by what is called the "random assignment" method. Random assignment is the gold standard for social science research; it provides highly reliable results because it compares groups of students that are virtually identical in every respect except whether or not they received a treatment, in this case whether or not they used a voucher. All five programs were found to have a statistically significant beneficial effect on the test scores of participating students.

19   School choice is a particularly important reform for the low-income and minority students who are facing larger challenges because of social problems. Comfortable middle-class families already exercise school choice when they choose where to live; they have the financial means to decide what neighborhood to live in based partly on the quality of the local schools. This gives neighborhoods an incentive to provide good schools, because if they don't then families will move away and property values will go down. But low-income families cannot exercise this form of school choice, so their schools can simply take them for granted. Offering school vouchers to these families gives urban schools in poor neighborhoods the same positive competitive incentives that suburban schools already face.

OTHER PROMISING REFORMS

20   High-quality early instruction is yet another education policy shown to produce positive results in spite of social problems. Research particularly supports early
intervention for young children who have difficulty learning to read. A consensus
has emerged among researchers that giving extra help to students who are behind in
reading in first and second grades significantly reduces the number of those students
who are later diagnosed as learning disabled. This is particularly relevant for the poor
minority students who are the most likely to have trouble learning to read. A group of
eight specialists led by G. Reid Lyon of the National Institutes of Health has called for
dramatic reforms in the special education system given the large body of evidence that
early reading intervention prevents the onset of educational dysfunctions that are often
attributed to learning disabilities.

21   Research has also shown that another form of early intervention, high-quality
preschool programs, can produce significantly better outcomes for poor minority
students facing social problems. A longitudinal study of the Perry Preschool Project
tracked a set of poor black preschoolers who were randomly assigned to two groups:
one that attended preschools using the "active learning" program of the High/Scope
Educational Research Foundation and another that attended no preschool. Students
who received the preschool program performed better in school, were more likely to
graduate from high school (65 percent of participants graduated, versus 45 percent in
the control group), were more likely to be employed at age forty (76 percent versus 62
percent), had higher incomes, were more likely to own homes and cars, were less likely
to go to jail or deal drugs, had longer-lasting marriages, and were less likely to bear
children out of wedlock.

22   The educational method known as "direct instruction" has also been shown to
improve student performance. Direct instruction seeks to convey a highly specific set of
knowledge and skills to students through carefully planned lessons. There is empirical
evidence that direct instruction improves test scores, raises academic achievement, and
results in better student attitudes and behavior.

23   All of these strategies have been shown to effectively improve student performance. What's more, they have all been shown to work even for the poor minority
students who face the largest educational challenges. In some cases, these strategies
have been shown to work especially well for these disadvantaged students. And these
strategies—accountability, choice, early intervention, and direct instruction—are only
four examples of effective school reforms. Other strategies could also be effective in
improving student outcomes.

24   This evidence stands in marked contrast to the Myth of Helplessness. To believe
that school reform can't succeed because of the challenges posed by social problems,
we would have to believe that no strategy—not these examples and not any other kind
of reform—will work. The evidence shows otherwise, and in light of this, we can see
the serious consequences of the Myth of Helplessness. It uses the educational disadvantages faced by many students to justify blocking reforms that have been shown to
alleviate those very disadvantages.

25   Social problems present our schools with serious challenges. Nonetheless, schools are not helpless. The evidence shows that there are many effective strategies for improving student performance, even—and sometimes especially—for the poor minority students who bear the brunt of these challenges. The Myth of Helplessness should not be allowed to stand in the way of reforms that promise to help those students who need it most.

QUESTIONS ON MEANING

1. In a sentence, how would you define the Myth of Helplessness? What is Greene's claim regarding it?

2. Greene acknowledges that poverty and other social factors play a role in student and school success. What is the difference between Greene's position and the positions of Rothstein, Winerip, Rips, and Cohen?

3. What does Greene and Forster's Teachability Index measure? What does the correlation of the Teachability Index to actual student achievement suggest to Greene?

4. What is the correlation between accountability programs and overall student achievement, according to Greene?

5. What are some of the different reforms that Greene suggests may help improve student achievement?

QUESTIONS FOR DISCUSSION

1. What role do poverty and broken homes play in a student's pursuit of an education? Are schools rendered impotent in terms of teaching some students because of these social problems?

2. What ethical responsibilities do schools have toward the students they serve?

3. Who, ultimately, is responsible for a student's educational success: schools, families, or the student?

4. Should parents be given a choice about which public school to send their children to? What happens if too many parents want to send their kids to the same school? How will the local school system or government decide which students get to attend and which will be turned away?

LOOKING AT RHETORIC

1. Examine the structure of the chapter by Greene. How is it organized? Is the organization effective? Note that the chapter essentially has three main parts. What are those parts? What does Greene try to accomplish in each part?

2. Greene's chapter takes the shape of what is often referred to as a problem/solution essay. What is the problem Greene identifies, and what is Greene's solution?

WRITING ASSIGNMENTS

1. Two recent educational initiatives established by the federal government are the *No Child Left Behind* program and the *Race to the Top* program. Spend some time in the library and online researching these programs. Draft an essay in which you compare and contrast these two programs. Argue for the effectiveness of one program over the other.

2. Write your own problem/solution essay in which you identify a key problem that you see schools struggling with and propose a solution.

3. In pairs or in groups, list five factors that improve a student's learning experience and five factors that inhibit a student's learning experience. Then, as an individual, draft an essay in the form of a prospectus for the development of an experimental school in which students, in your opinion, will have the best chance for achieving academic success. In the course of your essay, explain how your school is both similar to and different from the public schools in your town or city.

The War Against Boys

Christina Hoff Sommers

Christina Sommers (b. 1950) is a philosopher, ethicist, and cultural critic who is best known for her critique of modern feminism. She is the author of a popular ethics textbook, Vice and Virtue in Everyday Life, *as well as* Who Stole Feminism?: How Women Have Betrayed Women *(1995) and* The War Against Boys: How Misguided Feminism is Harming our Young Men *(2001). She is also the coauthor of* One Nation Under Therapy: How the Helping Culture is Eroding Self-Reliance *(2006). In the following essay, Sommers engages in a kind of academic myth-busting: she challenges claims about how schools are biased against girls. The implications of Sommers' assertions for the modern educational system are significant, and they directly challenge some long-standing beliefs about both education and society.*

1   It's a bad time to be a boy in America. The triumphant victory of the U.S. women's soccer team at the World Cup last summer has come to symbolize the spirit of American girls. The shooting at Columbine High last spring might be said to symbolize the spirit of American boys.

2   That boys are in disrepute is not accidental. For many years women's groups have complained that boys benefit from a school system that favors them and is biased against girls. "Schools shortchange girls," declares the American Association of University Women. Girls are "undergoing a kind of psychological foot-binding," two prominent educational psychologists say. A stream of books and pamphlets cite research showing not only that boys are classroom favorites but also that they are given to schoolyard violence and sexual harassment.

3   In the view that has prevailed in American education over the past decade, boys are resented, both as the unfairly privileged sex and as obstacles on the path to gender justice for girls. This perspective is promoted in schools of education, and many a teacher now feels that girls need and deserve special indemnifying consideration. "It is really clear that boys are Number One in this society and in most of the world," says Patricia O'Reilly, a professor of education and the director of the Gender Equity Center, at the University of Cincinnati.

4   The idea that schools and society grind girls down has given rise to an array of laws and policies intended to curtail the advantage boys have and to redress the harm done to girls. That girls are treated as the second sex in school and consequently suffer, that boys are accorded privileges and consequently benefit—these are things everyone is presumed to know. But they are not true.

5   The research commonly cited to support claims of male privilege and male sinfulness is riddled with errors. Almost none of it has been published in peer-reviewed professional journals. Some of the data turn out to be mysteriously missing. A review of the facts shows boys, not girls, on the weak side of an education gender gap. The typical boy is a year and a half behind the typical girl in reading and writing; he is less committed to school and less likely to go to college. In 1997 college full-time enrollments were 45 percent male and 55 percent female. The Department of Education predicts that the proportion of boys in college classes will continue to shrink.

6   Data from the U.S. Department of Education and from several recent university studies show that far from being shy and demoralized, today's girls outshine boys. They get better grades. They have higher educational aspirations. They follow more-rigorous academic programs and participate in advanced-placement classes at higher rates. According to the National Center for Education Statistics, slightly more girls than boys enroll in high-level math and science courses. Girls, allegedly timorous and lacking in confidence, now outnumber boys in student government, in honor societies, on school newspapers, and in debating clubs. Only in sports are boys ahead, and women's groups are targeting the sports gap with a vengeance. Girls read more books. They outperform boys on tests for artistic and musical ability. More girls than boys study abroad. More join the Peace Corps. At the same time more boys than girls are suspended from school. More are held back and more drop out. Boys are three times as likely to receive a diagnosis of attention-deficit hyperactivity disorder. More boys than girls are involved in crime, alcohol, and drugs. Girls attempt suicide more often than boys, but it is boys who more often succeed. In 1997, a typical year, 4,483 young people aged five to twenty-four committed suicide: 701 females and 3,782 males.

7   In the technical language of education experts, girls are academically more "engaged." Last year an article in *The CQ Researcher* about male and female academic achievement described a common parental observation: "Daughters want to please their teachers by spending extra time on projects, doing extra credit, making homework as neat as possible. Sons rush through homework assignments and run outside to play, unconcerned about how the teacher will regard the sloppy work."

8   School engagement is a critical measure of student success. The U.S. Department of Education gauges student commitment by the following criteria: "How much time do students devote to homework each night?" and "Do students come to class prepared and ready to learn? (Do they bring books and pencils? Have they completed their homework?)" According to surveys of fourth, eighth, and twelfth graders, girls consistently do more homework than boys. By the twelfth grade boys are four times as likely as girls not to do homework. Similarly, more boys than girls report that they "usually" or "often" come to school without supplies or without having done their homework.

9   The performance gap between boys and girls in high school leads directly to the growing gap between male and female admissions to college.

DECONSTRUCTING THE TEST-SCORE GAP

10   Feminists cannot deny that girls get better grades, are more engaged academically, and are now the majority sex in higher education. They argue, however, that these advantages are hardly decisive. Boys, they point out, get higher scores than girls on almost every significant standardized test—especially the Scholastic Assessment Test and law school, medical school, and graduate school admissions tests.

11   In 1996 I wrote an article for *Education Week* about the many ways in which girl students were moving ahead of boys. Seizing on the test-score data that suggest boys are doing better than girls, David Sadker, a professor of education at American University and a co-author with his wife, Myra, of *Failing at Fairness: How America's Schools Cheat Girls* (1994), wrote, "If females are soaring in school, as Christina Hoff Sommers writes, then these tests are blind to their flight." On the 1998 SAT boys were thirty-five points (out of 800) ahead of girls in math and seven points ahead in English. These results seem to run counter to all other measurements of achievement in school. In almost all other areas boys lag behind girls. Why do they test better? Is Sadker right in suggesting that this is a manifestation of boys' privileged status?

12   The answer is no. A careful look at the pool of students who take the SAT and similar tests shows that the girls' lower scores have little or nothing to do with bias or unfairness. Indeed, the scores do not even signify lower achievement by girls. First of all, according to *College Bound Seniors*, an annual report on standardized-test takers published by the College Board, many more "at risk" girls than "at risk" boys take the SAT—girls from lower-income homes or with parents who never graduated from high school or never attended college. "These characteristics," the report says, "are associated with lower than average SAT scores." Instead of wrongly using SAT scores as evidence of bias against girls, scholars should be concerned about the boys who never show up for the tests they need if they are to move on to higher education.

13   Another factor skews test results so that they appear to favor boys.

14   Nancy Cole, the president of the Educational Testing Service, calls it the "spread" phenomenon. Scores on almost any intelligence or achievement test are more spread out for boys than for girls—boys include more prodigies and more students of marginal ability. Or, as the political scientist James Q. Wilson once put it, "There are more male geniuses and more male idiots."

15   Boys also dominate dropout lists, failure lists, and learning-disability lists. Students in these groups rarely take college-admissions tests. On the other hand, the exceptional boys who take school seriously show up in disproportionately high numbers for standardized tests. Gender-equity activists like Sadker ought to apply their logic consistently: if the shortage of girls at the high end of the ability distribution is evidence of unfairness to girls, then the excess of boys at the low end should be deemed evidence of unfairness to boys.

16   Suppose we were to turn our attention away from the highly motivated, self-selected two fifths of high school students who take the SAT and consider instead a truly representative sample of American schoolchildren. How would girls and boys then compare? Well, we have the answer. The National Assessment of Educational Progress, started in 1969 and mandated by Congress, offers the best and most comprehensive measure of achievement among students at all levels of ability. Under the NAEP program 70,000 to 100,000 students,

drawn from forty-four states, are tested in reading, writing, math, and science at ages nine, thirteen, and seventeen. In 1996, seventeen-year-old boys outperformed seventeen-year-old girls by five points in math and eight points in science, whereas the girls outperformed the boys by fourteen points in reading and seventeen points in writing. In the past few years girls have been catching up in math and science while boys have continued to lag far behind in reading and writing.

17   In the July, 1995, issue of *Science*, Larry V. Hedges and Amy Nowell, researchers at the University of Chicago, observed that girls' deficits in math were small but not insignificant. These deficits, they noted, could adversely affect the number of women who "excel in scientific and technical occupations."

18   Of the deficits in boys' writing skills they wrote, "The large sex differences in writing . . . are alarming. . . . The data imply that males are, on average, at a rather profound disadvantage in the performance of this basic skill." They went on to warn,

> *The generally larger numbers of males who perform near the bottom of the distribution in reading comprehension and writing also have policy implications. It seems likely that individuals with such poor literacy skills will have difficulty finding employment in an increasingly information-driven economy. Thus, some intervention may be required to enable them to participate constructively.*

19   Hedges and Nowell were describing a serious problem of national scope, but because the focus elsewhere has been on girls' deficits, few Americans know much about the problem or even suspect that it exists.

THE INCREDIBLE SHRINKING GIRL

20   How did we get to this odd place? How did we come to believe in a picture of American boys and girls that is the opposite of the truth? And why has that belief persisted, enshrined in law, encoded in governmental and school policies, despite overwhelming evidence against it? The answer has much to do with one of the American academy's most celebrated women—Carol Gilligan, Harvard University's first professor of gender studies.

21   Gilligan first came to widespread attention in 1982, with the publication of *In a Different Voice*, which this article will discuss shortly. In 1990 Gilligan announced that America's adolescent girls were in crisis. In her words, "As the river of a girl's life flows into the sea of Western culture, she is in danger of drowning or disappearing." Gilligan offered little in the way of conventional evidence to support this alarming finding. Indeed, it is hard to imagine what sort of empirical research could establish such a large claim. But she quickly attracted powerful allies. Within a very short time the allegedly vulnerable and demoralized state of adolescent girls achieved the status of a national emergency.

22   A number of popular books soon materialized, including Myra and David Sadker's *Failing at Fairness* and Peggy Orenstein's *Schoolgirls: Young Women, Self-Esteem, and the Confidence Gap* (1994). Elizabeth Gleick wrote in *Time* in 1996 on a new trend in literary victimology: "Dozens of troubled teenage girls troop across [the] pages: composite sketches of Charlottes, Whitneys and Danielles who were raped, who have bulimia, who have pierced bodies or shaved heads, who are coping with strict religious families or are felled by their parents' bitter divorce."

23   The country's adolescent girls were both pitied and exalted. The novelist Carolyn See wrote in *The Washington Post* in 1994, "The most heroic, fearless, graceful, tortured human beings in this land must be girls from the ages of 12 to 15." In the same vein, the Sadkers, in *Failing at Fairness*, predicted the fate of a lively six-year-old on top of a playground slide: "There she stood on her sturdy legs, with her head thrown back and her arms flung wide. As ruler of the playground, she was at the very zenith of her world." But all would soon change: "If the camera had photographed the girl . . . at twelve instead of six . . . she would have been looking at the ground instead of the sky; her sense of self-worth would have been an accelerating downward spiral."

24   The description of America's teenage girls as silenced, tortured, and otherwise personally diminished was (and is) indeed dismaying. But no real evidence has ever been offered to support it. Certainly neither Gilligan nor the popular writers who followed her lead produced anything like solid empirical evidence, gathered according to the conventional protocols of social-science research.

25   Scholars who do abide by those protocols describe adolescent girls in far more optimistic terms. Anne Petersen, a former professor of adolescent development and pediatrics at the University of Minnesota and now a senior vice-president of the W. K. Kellogg Foundation, reports the consensus of researchers working in adolescent psychology: "It is now known that the majority of adolescents of both genders successfully negotiate this developmental period without any major psychological or emotional disorder, develop a positive sense of personal identity, and manage to forge adaptive peer relationships with their families." Daniel Offer, a professor of psychiatry at Northwestern, concurs. He refers to a "new generation of studies" that find 80 percent of adolescents to be normal and well adjusted.

26   At the time that Gilligan was declaring her crisis, a study conducted by the University of Michigan asked a scientifically selected sample of 3,000 high school seniors, "Taking all things together, how would you say things are these days—would you say you're very happy, pretty happy, or not too happy these days?" Nearly 86 percent of the girls and 88 percent of the boys responded that they were "pretty happy" or "very happy." If the girls polled were caught in "an accelerating downward spiral," they were unaware of it.

27   Contrary to the story told by Gilligan and her followers, American girls were flourishing in unprecedented ways by the early 1990s. To be sure, some—including many who found themselves in the offices of clinical psychologists—felt they were crashing and drowning in the sea of Western culture. But the vast majority were occupied in more-constructive ways.

"POLITICS DRESSED UP AS SCIENCE"

28   Gilligan's ideas about demoralized teenage girls had a special resonance with women's groups that were already committed to the proposition that our society is unsympathetic to women. The interest of the venerable and politically influential American Association of University Women, in particular, was piqued. Its officers were reported to be "intrigued and alarmed" by Gilligan's research. They wanted to know more.

29   In 1990 *The New York Times Sunday Magazine* published an admiring profile of Gilligan that heralded the discovery of a hidden crisis among the nation's girls. Soon

after, the AAUW commissioned a study from the polling firm Greenberg-Lake. The pollsters asked 3,000 children (2,400 girls and 600 boys in grades four through ten) about their self-perceptions. In 1991 the association announced the disturbing results, in a report titled *Shortchanging Girls, Shortchanging America*: "Girls aged eight and nine are confident, assertive, and feel authoritative about themselves. Yet most emerge from adolescence with a poor self-image, constrained views of their future and their place in society, and much less confidence about themselves and their abilities." Anne Bryant, the executive director of the AAUW and an expert in public relations, organized a media campaign to spread the word that "an unacknowledged American tragedy" had been uncovered. Newspapers and magazines around the country carried reports that girls were being adversely affected by gender bias that eroded their self-esteem. Sharon Schuster, at the time the president of the AAUW, candidly explained to *The New York Times* why the association had undertaken the research in the first place: "We wanted to put some factual data behind our belief that girls are getting shortchanged in the classroom."

30   As the AAUW's self-esteem study was making headlines, a little-known magazine called *Science News*, which has been supplying information on scientific and technical developments to interested newspapers since 1922, reported the skeptical reaction of leading specialists on adolescent development. The late Roberta Simmons, a professor of sociology at the University of Pittsburgh (described by *Science News* as "director of the most ambitious longitudinal study of adolescent self-esteem to date"), said that her research showed nothing like the substantial gender gap described by the AAUW. According to Simmons, "Most kids come through the years from 10 to 20 without major problems and with an increasing sense of self-esteem." But the doubts of Simmons and several other prominent experts were not reported in the hundreds of news stories that the Greenberg-Lake study generated.

31   The AAUW quickly commissioned a second study, *How Schools Shortchange Girls*. This one, conducted by the Wellesley College Center for Research on Women and released in 1992, focused on the alleged effects of sexism on girls' school performance. It asserted that schools deflate girls' self-esteem by "systematically cheating girls of classroom attention." Such bias leads to lower aspirations and impaired academic achievement. Carol Gilligan's crisis was being transformed into a civil-rights issue: girls were the victims of widespread sex discrimination. "The implications are clear," the AAUW said. "The system must change."

32   With great fanfare *How Schools Shortchange Girls* was released to the remarkably uncritical media. A 1992 article for *The New York Times* by Susan Chira was typical of coverage throughout the country. The headline read "BIAS AGAINST GIRLS IS FOUND RIFE IN SCHOOLS, WITH LASTING DAMAGE." The piece was later reproduced by the AAUW and sent out as part of a fundraising package. Chira had not interviewed a single critic of the study.

33   In March of last year I called Chira and asked about the way she had handled the AAUW study. I asked if she would write her article the same way today. No, she said, pointing out that we have since learned much more about boys' problems in school. Why had she not canvassed dissenting opinions? She explained that she had been traveling when the AAUW study came out, and was on a short deadline. Yes, perhaps she had relied

too much on the AAUW's report. She had tried to reach Diane Ravitch, who had then been the former U.S. Assistant Secretary of Education and was a known critic of women's-advocacy findings, but without success.

34   Six years after the release of *How Schools Shortchange Girls, The New York Times* ran a story that raised questions about its validity. This time the reporter, Tamar Lewin, did reach Diane Ravitch, who told her, "That [1992] AAUW report was just completely wrong. What was so bizarre is that it came out right at the time that girls had just overtaken boys in almost every area. It might have been the right story twenty years earlier, but coming out when it did, it was like calling a wedding a funeral. . . . There were all these special programs put in place for girls, and no one paid any attention to boys."

35   One of the many things about which the report was wrong was the famous "call-out" gap. According to the AAUW, "In a study conducted by the Sadkers, boys in elementary and middle school called out answers eight times more often than girls. When boys called out, teachers listened. But when girls called out, they were told 'raise your hand if you want to speak.'"

36   But the Sadker study turns out to be missing—and meaningless, to boot. In 1994 Amy Saltzman, of *U.S. News & World Report*, asked David Sadker for a copy of the research backing up the eight-to-one call-out claim. Sadker said that he had presented the findings in an unpublished paper at a symposium sponsored by the American Educational Research Association; neither he nor the AERA had a copy. Sadker conceded to Saltzman that the ratio may have been inaccurate. Indeed, Saltzman cited an independent study by Gail Jones, an associate professor of education at the University of North Carolina at Chapel Hill, which found that boys called out only twice as often as girls. Whatever the accurate number is, no one has shown that permitting a student to call out answers in the classroom confers any kind of academic advantage. What does confer advantage is a student's attentiveness. Boys are less attentive—which could explain why some teachers might call on them more or be more tolerant of call-outs.

37   Despite the errors, the campaign to persuade the public that girls were being diminished personally and academically was a spectacular success. The Sadkers described an exultant Anne Bryant, of the AAUW, telling her friends, "I remember going to bed the night our report was issued, totally exhilarated. When I woke up the next morning, the first thought in my mind was, 'Oh, my God, what do we do next?'" Political action came next, and here, too, girls' advocates were successful.

38   Categorizing girls as an "under-served population" on a par with other discriminated-against minorities, Congress passed the Gender Equity in Education Act in 1994. Millions of dollars in grants were awarded to study the plight of girls and to learn how to counter bias against them. At the United Nations Fourth World Conference on Women, in Beijing in 1995, U.S. delegates presented the educational and psychological deficits of American girls as a human-rights issue.

THE MYTH UNRAVELING

39   By the late 1990s the myth of the downtrodden girl was showing some signs of unraveling, and concern over boys was growing. In 1997 the Public Education Network (PEN) announced at its annual conference the results of a new teacher-student survey titled *The*

American Teacher 1997: Examining Gender Issues in Public Schools. The survey was funded by the Metropolitan Life Insurance Company and conducted by Louis Harris and Associates.

40 During a three-month period in 1997 various questions about gender equity were asked of 1,306 students and 1,035 teachers in grades seven through twelve. The MetLife study had no doctrinal ax to grind. What it found contradicted most of the findings of the AAUW, the Sadkers, and the Wellesley College Center for Research on Women: "Contrary to the commonly held view that boys are at an advantage over girls in school, girls appear to have an advantage over boys in terms of their future plans, teachers' expectations, everyday experiences at school and interactions in the classroom."

41 Some other conclusions from the MetLife study: Girls are more likely than boys to see themselves as college-bound and more likely to want a good education. Furthermore, more boys (31 percent) than girls (19 percent) feel that teachers do not listen to what they have to say.

42 At the PEN conference, Nancy Leffert, a child psychologist then at the Search Institute, in Minneapolis, reported the results of a survey that she and colleagues had recently completed of more than 99,000 children in grades six through twelve. The children were asked about what the researchers call "developmental assets." The Search Institute has identified forty critical assets—"building blocks for healthy development." Half of these are external, such as a supportive family and adult role models, and half are internal, such as motivation to achieve, a sense of purpose in life, and interpersonal confidence. Leffert explained, somewhat apologetically, that girls were ahead of boys with respect to thirty-seven out of forty assets. By almost every significant measure of well-being girls had the better of boys: they felt closer to their families: they had higher aspirations, stronger connections to school, and even superior assertiveness skills. Leffert concluded her talk by saying that in the past she had referred to girls as fragile or vulnerable, but that the survey "tells me that girls have very powerful assets."

43 The Horatio Alger Association, a fifty-year-old organization devoted to promoting and affirming individual initiative and "the American dream," releases annual back-to-school surveys. Its survey for 1998 contrasted two groups of students: the "highly successful" (approximately 18 percent of American students) and the "disillusioned" (approximately 15 percent). The successful students work hard, choose challenging classes, make schoolwork a top priority, get good grades, participate in extracurricular activities, and feel that teachers and administrators care about them and listen to them. According to the association, the successful group in the 1998 survey is 63 percent female and 37 percent male. The disillusioned students are pessimistic about their future, get low grades, and have little contact with teachers. The disillusioned group could accurately be characterized as demoralized. According to the Alger Association, "Nearly seven out of ten are male."

44 Did anything of value come out of the manufactured crisis of diminished girls? Yes, a bit. Parents, teachers, and administrators now pay more attention to girls' deficits in math and science, and they offer more support for girls' participation in sports. But do these benefits outweigh the disservice done by promulgating the myth of the victimized girl or by presenting boys as the unfairly favored sex?

45 A boy today, through no fault of his own, finds himself implicated in the social crime of shortchanging girls. Yet the allegedly silenced and neglected girl sitting next to him is likely to be the superior student. She is probably more articulate, more mature, more

engaged, and more well-balanced. The boy may be aware that she is more likely to go on to college. He may believe that teachers prefer to be around girls and pay more attention to them. At the same time, he is uncomfortably aware that he is considered to be a member of the favored and dominant gender.

46   The widening gender gap in academic achievement is real. It threatens the future of millions of American boys. Boys are not getting the help they need. In the climate of disapproval in which boys now exist, programs designed to aid them have a very low priority. This must change. We should repudiate the partisanship that currently clouds the issues surrounding sex differences in the schools. We should call for balance, objective information, fair treatment, and a concerted national effort to get boys back on track. That means we can no longer allow the partisans of girls to shape the discussion and to write the rules.

QUESTIONS ON MEANING

1. What is Sommers' thesis in this essay? What evidence and arguments does she use to prove her thesis?
2. What is the spread phenomenon? How does it relate to Sommers' argument?
3. Does SAT achievement indicate male privilege? Compare and contrast the views of Sommers and Sadker on this question.
4. What did the research of Hedges and Nowell reveal?
5. What is the call-out gap? In your experience in high school, did you notice a call-out gap?
6. How does Sommers respond to each of the three claims presented by Gilligan in her study of the development of boys?
7. What did the MetLife study conclude?

QUESTIONS FOR DISCUSSION

1. Sommers begins her essay with a catalog of statistics and trends related to the academic performance of boys compared with girls. Which did you find most surprising? Why?
2. What does some of the research presented in this essay suggest (directly or indirectly) about the role of parenting in shaping student achievement in school? What about in shaping gender roles in society? Do you think that boys are more in need of their mothers or their fathers in terms of improving their success in school and in society?
3. What could communities do to improve the chances for academic and social success for all children, both boys and girls?
4. Sommers argues at one point in her essay that bad research is being used in the interest of advancing a political agenda. What is that political agenda? Do you agree? Setting aside the cultural treatment of girls and boys, are there other aspects of contemporary life in which you believe unconvincing scientific evidence (or none at all) is being used to support a political agenda?

LOOKING AT RHETORIC

1. It is important for essay writers to engage their audience quickly—to get their attention—so as to compel their readers to continue reading the rest of the essay. How does Sommers do this? What makes the opening sentence of her essay particularly effective?

2. As one might easily imagine, Sommers' views in this essay have proven controversial and her claims have been criticized and challenged by others. Rhetorically, what are some strategies an author can use to present controversial material to an audience? Does Sommers use these strategies?

WRITING ASSIGNMENTS

1. Track down either the Sadker's *Failing at Fairness* or Gilligan's *In a Different Voice* and read it. Then, re-read Sommers' essay. Draft an essay in which you explain to your audience either Sadker's or Gilligan's thesis as well as Sommers' critique of it. Then, build an argument in which you argue for one position or the other.

2. Write a thesis-driven essay in which you either support or challenge the following proposition: the public school system is currently better suited for the academic success of girls than boys.

3. In pairs or in groups, discuss the relative validity of Carolyn See's claim that the "most heroic, fearless, graceful, tortured human beings in this land must be girls from the ages of 12 to 15." Do you agree or disagree with this claim? Why? Then, as individuals, draft an essay in which you argue either for or against See's claim.

What I Learned About School Reform

Diane Ravitch

Diane Ravitch (b. 1938) is former United States Assistant Secretary of Education and is an historian and critic of the American educational system. She graduated from Wellesley College and earned a Ph.D. from Columbia University. She began her career as an editorial assistant for the New Leader *and in 1975 began writing on the history of education. She served under Presidents George H. W. Bush and Bill Clinton. In 2005, she received the John Dewey Award from the American Federation of Teachers, the Gaudium Award from the Breukelein Institute of Brooklyn, and the Uncommon Book Award from the Hoover Institution. She is currently research professor at New York University's Steinhardt School of Culture, Education, and Human Development and is the author of numerous books, including* Left Back: A Century of Battles Over School Reform *(2000) and* The Language Police: How Pressure Groups Restrict What Students Learn *(2003). In the following chapter from* The Death and the Life of the American School *(2010), she recounts how her ideas of school reform evolved over time.*

1   In the fall of 2007, I reluctantly decided to have my office repainted. It was inconvenient. I work at home, on the top floor of a nineteenth-century brownstone in Brooklyn. Not only did I have to stop working for three weeks, but I had the additional burden of packing up and removing everything in my office. I had to relocate fifty boxes of books and files to other rooms in the house until the painting job was complete.

2   At the very time that I was packing up my books and belongings, I was going through an intellectual crisis. I was aware that I had undergone a wrenching transformation in my perspective on school reform. Where once I had been hopeful, even enthusiastic, about the

potential benefits of testing, accountability, choice, and markets, I now found myself experiencing profound doubts about these same ideas. I was trying to sort through the evidence about what was working and what was not. I was trying to understand why I was increasingly skeptical about these reforms, reforms that I had supported enthusiastically. I was trying to see my way through the blinding assumptions of ideology and politics, including my own.

3   I kept asking myself why I was losing confidence in these reforms. My answer: I have a right to change my mind. Fair enough. But why, I kept wondering, why had I changed my mind? What was the compelling evidence that prompted me to reevaluate the policies I had endorsed many times over the previous decade? Why did I now doubt ideas I once had advocated?

4   The short answer is that my views changed as I saw how these ideas were working out in reality.

5   The task of sorting my articles gave me the opportunity to review what I had written at different times, beginning in the mid-1960s. I began to see two themes at the center of what I have been writing for more than four decades. One constant has been my skepticism about pedagogical fads, enthusiasms, and movements. The other has been a deep belief in the value of a rich, coherent school curriculum, especially in history and literature, both of which are so frequently ignored, trivialized, or politicized.

6   As I flipped through the yellowing pages in my scrapbooks, I started to understand the recent redirection of my thinking, my growing doubt regarding popular proposals for choice and accountability. Once again, I realized, I was turning skeptical in response to panaceas and miracle cures. The only difference was that in this case, I too had fallen for the latest panaceas and miracle cures; I too had drunk deeply of the elixir that promised a quick fix to intractable problems. I too had jumped aboard a bandwagon, one festooned with banners celebrating the power of accountability, incentives, and markets. I too was captivated by these ideas. They promised to end bureaucracy, to ensure that poor children were not neglected, to empower poor parents, to enable poor children to escape failing schools, and to close the achievement gap between rich and poor, black and white. Testing would shine a spotlight on low-performing schools, and choice would create opportunities for poor kids to leave for better schools. All of this seemed to make sense, but there was little empirical evidence, just promise and hope. I wanted to share the promise and the hope. I wanted to believe that choice and accountability would produce great results. But over time, I was persuaded by accumulating evidence that the latest reforms were not likely to live up to their promise. The more I saw, the more I lost the faith.

7   I had not, in the first two decades of my career in education, given much thought to issues of choice, markets, or accountability.

8   Then something unexpected happened: I received a telephone call in the spring of 1991 from President George H. W. Bush's newly appointed education secretary, Lamar Alexander. Alexander, a moderate Republican, had been governor of Tennessee. The secretary invited me to come to Washington to chat with him and his deputy David Kearns, who had recently been the chief executive officer of Xerox. We met for lunch at the elegant Hay-Adams Hotel, near the White House. We talked about curriculum and standards (Secretary Alexander later joked that I talked and he listened), and at the end

of lunch he asked me to join the department as assistant secretary in charge of the Office of Educational Research and Improvement and as his counselor.

9   I went home to Brooklyn to think about it. I was a registered Democrat, always had been, and had never dreamed of working in a government job, let alone a Republican administration. I had no desire to leave Brooklyn or to abandon my life as a scholar. And yet I was intrigued by the thought of working in the federal government. Surely education was a nonpartisan issue, or so I then imagined. I decided that this would be a wonderful opportunity to perform public service, learn about federal politics, and do something totally different. I said yes, was confirmed by the Senate, moved to Washington, and spent the next eighteen months as assistant secretary and counselor to the secretary in the U.S. Department of Education.

10   During my time at the department, I took the lead on issues having to do with curriculum and standards. The federal government is prohibited by law from imposing any curriculum on states or school districts. Nonetheless, my agency used its very small allotment of discretionary funds (about $10 million) to make grants to consortia of educators to develop "voluntary national standards" in every academic subject. Our assumption was that so long as the standards were developed by independent professional groups and were voluntary, we were not violating the legal prohibition against imposing curriculum on states and school districts. And so we funded the development of voluntary national standards in history, the arts, geography, civics, science, economics, foreign languages, and English. We did this energetically but without specific congressional authorization; the absence of authorization unfortunately lessened the projects' credibility and longevity.

11   The Department of Education was committed to both standards and choice (choice was even higher on the agenda of Republicans than standards, because Republicans generally opposed national standards, which suggested federal meddling). At meetings of top staff in the department, I sat in on many discussions of school choice in which the question was not whether to support choice, but how to do so. The issue of choice had never been important to me, but I found myself trying to incorporate the arguments for choice into my own worldview. I reasoned that standards would be even more necessary in a society that used public dollars to promote school choice. The more varied the schools, the more important it would be to have common standards to judge whether students were learning. I began to sympathize with the argument for letting federal dollars follow poor students to the school of their choice. If kids were not succeeding in their regular public school, why not let them take their federal funds to another public school or to a private—even religious—school? Since affluent families could choose their schools by moving to a better neighborhood or enrolling their children in private schools, why shouldn't poor families have similar choices?

12   In the decade following my stint in the federal government, I argued that certain managerial and structural changes—that is, choice, charters, merit pay, and accountability—would help to reform our schools. With such changes, teachers and schools would be judged by their performance; this was a basic principle in the business world. Schools that failed to perform would be closed, just as a corporation would close a branch office that continually produced poor returns. Having been immersed in a world of true believers,

I was influenced by their ideas. I became persuaded that the business-minded thinkers were onto something important. Their proposed reforms were meant to align public education with the practices of modern, flexible, high-performance organizations and to enable American education to make the transition from the industrial age to the postindustrial age. In the 1990s, I found myself in step with people who quoted Peter Drucker[1] and other management gurus. I dropped casual references to "total quality management" and the Baldridge Award, both of which I learned about by listening to David Kearns[2] during my stint in the Department of Education.

13   During this time, I wrote many articles advocating structural innovations. In the past, I would have cast a cold eye on efforts to "reinvent the schools" or to "break the mold," but now I supported bold attempts to remake the schools, such as charter schools, privatization, and specialized schools of all kinds. I maintained that we should celebrate the creation of good schools, no matter what form they took or who developed them.

14   Both the Bush administration and the Clinton administration advocated market reforms for the public sector, including deregulation and privatization. Bill Clinton and the New Democrats championed a "third way" between the orthodox policies of the left and the right. People in both parties quoted *Reinventing Government* by David Osborne and Ted Gaebler as a guide to cutting down bureaucracy and injecting entrepreneurship into government. Months after his inauguration, President Clinton tasked Vice President Al Gore to devise ways to "reinvent" the federal bureaucracy, and he did. With the help of David Osborne, Gore created the National Partnership for Reinventing Government, whose purpose was to adapt private sector management techniques to the public sector. Many of its recommendations involved privatizing, cutting jobs, and implementing performance agreements in which agencies would receive autonomy from regulations in exchange for meeting targets.

15   Similar ideas began to percolate in the world of public education. The new thinking—now ensconced in both parties—saw the public school system as obsolete, because it is controlled by the government and burdened by bureaucracy. Government-run schools, said a new generation of reformers, are ineffective because they are a monopoly; as such, they have no incentive to do better, and they serve the interests of adults who work in the system, not children. Democrats saw an opportunity to reinvent government; Republicans, a chance to diminish the power of the teachers' unions, which, in their view, protect jobs and pensions while blocking effective management and innovation.

16   This convergence explained the bipartisan appeal of charter schools. Why shouldn't schools be managed by anyone who could supply good schools, using government funds? Free of direct government control, the schools would be innovative, hire only the best teachers, get rid of incompetent teachers, set their own pay scales, compete for students (customers), and be judged solely by their results (test scores and graduation rates). Good

---

[1]Peter Drucker (1909-2005): Writer and management consultant known for his ideas on management theory and practice.
[2]David Kearns (1930-2011): American businessman who was the CEO of Xerox Corporation and Deputy Secretary of the United States Department of Education.

schools under private management would proliferate, while bad schools would be closed down by market forces (the exit of disgruntled parents) or by a watchful government. Some of the new generation of reformers—mainly Republicans, but not only Republicans—imagined that the schools of the future would function without unions, allowing management to hire and fire personnel at will. With the collapse of Communism and the triumph of market reforms in most parts of the world, it did not seem to be much of a stretch to envision the application of the market model to schooling.

17   Like many others in that era, I was attracted to the idea that the market would unleash innovation and bring greater efficiencies to education. I was certainly influenced by the conservative ideology of other top-level officials in the first Bush administration, who were strong supporters of school choice and competition. But of equal importance, I believe, I began to think like a policymaker, especially a federal policymaker. That meant, in the words of a book by James C. Scott that I later read and admired, I began "seeing like a state," looking at schools and teachers and students from an altitude of 20,000 feet and seeing them as objects to be moved around by big ideas and great plans.

18   There is something comforting about the belief that the invisible hand of the market, as Adam Smith[3] called it, will bring improvements through some unknown force. In education, this belief in market forces lets us ordinary mortals off the hook, especially those who have not figured out how to improve low-performing schools or to break through the lassitude of unmotivated teens. Instead of dealing with rancorous problems like how to teach reading or how to improve testing, one can redesign the management and structure of the school system and concentrate on incentives and sanctions. One need not know anything about children or education. The lure of the market is the idea that freedom from government regulation is a solution all by itself. This is very appealing, especially when so many seemingly well-planned school reforms have failed to deliver on their promise.

19   The new corporate reformers betray their weak comprehension of education by drawing false analogies between education and business. They think they can fix education by applying the principles of business, organization, management, law, and marketing and by developing a good data-collection system that provides the information necessary to incentivize the workforce—principals, teachers, and students—with appropriate rewards and sanctions. Like these reformers, I wrote and spoke with conviction in the 1990s and early 2000s about what was needed to reform public education, and many of my ideas coincided with theirs.

20   I have long been allied with conservative scholars and organizations. My scholarly work at Teachers College and later at New York University was supported by conservative foundations, principally the John M. Olin Foundation, which never sought to influence anything I wrote.

21   In 1999, I became a founding member of the Koret Task Force at the Hoover Institution at Stanford University; the task force supports education reforms based on the principles

---

[3]Adam Smith (1723–1790): Scottish philosopher and economist known for his foundational explanation of free-market economics.

of standards, accountability, and choice. Most of the members of the task force are forceful advocates of school choice and accountability. I enjoyed the camaraderie of the group, and I loved the intellectual stimulation I encountered at the Hoover Institution. But over time I realized that I was no longer fully supportive of the task force's aims. When I told my colleagues that I felt I had to leave, they urged me to stay and debate with them. I did for a time, but in April 2009 I resigned.

22   I grew increasingly disaffected from both the choice movement and the accountability movement. I was beginning to see the downside of both and to understand that they were not solutions to our educational dilemmas. As I watched both movements gain momentum across the nation, I concluded that curriculum and instruction were far more important than choice and accountability. I feared that choice would let thousands of flowers bloom but would not strengthen American education. It might even harm the public schools by removing the best students from schools in the poorest neighborhoods. I was also concerned that accountability, now a shibboleth that everyone applauds, had become mechanistic and even antithetical to good education. Testing, I realized with dismay, had become a central preoccupation in the schools and was not just a measure but an end in itself. I came to believe that accountability, as written into federal law, was not raising standards but dumbing down the schools as states and districts strived to meet unrealistic targets.

23   The more uneasy I grew with the agenda of choice and accountability, the more I realized that I am too "conservative" to embrace an agenda whose end result is entirely speculative and uncertain. The effort to upend American public education and replace it with something market-based began to feel too radical for me. I concluded that I could not countenance any reforms that might have the effect—intended or unintended—of undermining public education. Paradoxically, it was my basic conservatism about values, traditions, communities, and institutions that made me back away from what once was considered the conservative agenda but has now become the bipartisan agenda in education.

24   Before long, I found that I was reverting to my once familiar pattern as a friend and supporter of public education. Over time, my doubts about accountability and choice deepened as I saw the negative consequences of their implementation.

25   As I went back to work in my freshly painted office and reviewed the historical record of my intellectual wanderings, deviations, and transgressions, I decided to write about what I had learned. I needed to explain why I had returned to my roots as a partisan of American public education. I wanted to describe where we have gone astray in our pursuit of worthy goals. We as a society cannot extricate ourselves from fads and nostrums unless we carefully look at how we got entangled in them. We will continue to chase rainbows unless we recognize that they are rainbows and there is no pot of gold at the end of them. We certainly cannot address our problems unless we are willing to examine the evidence about proposed solutions, without fear, favor, or preconceptions.

26   It is time, I think, for those who want to improve our schools to focus on the essentials of education. We must make sure that our schools have a strong, coherent, explicit curriculum that is grounded in the liberal arts and sciences, with plenty of opportunity for children to engage in activities and projects that make learning lively. We must ensure that students gain the knowledge they need to understand political debates, scientific phenomena, and the world they live in. We must be sure they are prepared for the responsibilities

of democratic citizenship in a complex society. We must take care that our teachers are well educated, not just well trained. We must be sure that schools have the authority to maintain both standards of learning and standards of behavior.

QUESTIONS ON MEANING

1. Why did Ravitch change her mind about the standards and accountability movement in education?
2. Why is she concerned about decentralization and corporatization in education? What are their effects?
3. What motivated her to accept the position as Assistant Secretary of Education in 1991? What did she want to accomplish?
4. What does it mean to "see like the state"? What are the effects of this vision on policy making and/or decision making in education?
5. Why did she find the idea of an educational system modeled on free market ideals so alluring? What problems does it allow the reformer to avoid?
6. What are the "essentials of education"? What should schools focus on?

QUESTIONS FOR DISCUSSION

1. Should our educational system emphasize accountability through standardized tests? What are the positives and negatives of this approach?
2. Should the business community play a significant role in defining the curriculum and goals of our educational system? What are the positive and negative effects of this approach?
3. Should the educational system allow for choice in schools and curriculum? What kinds of choice should be offered?

LOOKING AT RHETORIC

1. To what extent does Ravitch's autobiographical approach enhance her argument?
2. She writes that she has changed her mind over time, and she tells us why. How does this affect her credibility as she makes her argument?
3. What is the effect of her use of narrative or story form?

WRITING ASSIGNMENTS

1. Using Internet and library resources—or through visiting and interviewing a school administrator—find out what policies regarding national standards and accountability the middle or high school you attended follows. Write an essay in which you compare your findings with the positions taken by Ravitch in her essay.
2. Write an essay arguing for or against a set of centralized national standards for education at the primary and secondary level.
3. In pairs or in groups, discuss your experiences with tests and accountability in school. Individually, write an essay in which you use your own experience to argue for or against national standards and accountability in education.

The Baby Genius Edutainment Complex: The New Smart Baby Products

Alissa Quart

Alissa Quart is a journalist and author whose work has tended to focus on childhood development, particularly in the context of marketing and education. She is a graduate of Brown University and the Columbia School of Journalism, where she remains an adjunct professor of journalism. She is the author of Branded: The Buying and Selling of Teenagers (2003) *and* Hothouse Kids: How the Pressure to Succeed Threatens Childhood (2006). *In addition, she is a frequent contributor to* The Atlantic Monthly, The New York Times Magazine, *and the* Columbia Journalism Review. *In the following essay, taken from* Hothouse Kids, *Quart looks at the growing industry of creating educational videos and toys that are marketed to parents as products that will increase a child's intelligence, and she asks whether these products actually do the things they claim.*

> *"She's ten months old, for God's sake," I said. "I know," Seymour said.*
> *"They have ears. They can hear." The story Seymour read to Franny that*
> *night, by flashlight, was a favorite of his, a Taoist tale. To this day,*
> *Franny swears that she remembers Seymour reading it to her.*

> J. D. SALINGER, *"Raise High the Roof Beam, Carpenters"*

1   One DVD is full of images of children big and small, all holding violins, recorders, guitars, and cellos—while a song in the background insists that when playing music, children should "Do your best! And never less!" Another contains images of toddlers on a putting green or wandering around a basketball court and a baby with a golf ball, all set to bouncy music with words like *teamwork* flashing on the screen, in the hopes of inspiring a generation of toddler athletes. Another features a puppet called Vincent van Goat that introduces an infant to six primary colors and then to the colors as they appear in van Gogh's paintings *The Starry Night* and *Wheat Fields with Reaper at Sunrise*. Yet another DVD contains colorful, high-contrast imagery of babies playing with blocks and balloons, counting tomatoes, and sibilating words in English, French, and Spanish.

2   These infant and toddler DVDs may be cute or even visually striking, but their selling point is that they offer the youngest viewer—intended age sometimes as young as newborn and up—a great deal more. The *Brainy Baby Left and Right Brain* DVD set, from a company whose motto heralds "a little genius in the making," claims to "engage your child's whole brain (logic and creative) to help boost your baby's intellect." The *Right Brain* disc features classical music and focuses on "cognitive skills," among them "Rhymes, Spatial Reasoning, and Imagination, Intuition, and more!" The *Left Brain* disc has bright visuals, patterns, and shapes in red, black, and white, with letters of the alphabet, and voiceovers offering words in Spanish and French. The *Baby Prodigy* DVD claims to do nothing short of giving a child "A Head Start in Life!" The disc's back copy reads, "Did you know that you can actually

help to enhance the development of your baby's brain? The first 30 months of life is the period where a child's brain undergoes its most critical stages of evolution . . . together we can help to make your child the next Baby Prodigy!" The *So Smart!* two-disc set, suggested for infants of nine months and up, features Mozart and Vivaldi and interactive alphabet games the infant can play on the television using the remote control, while the *V. Smile* video game system promotes itself with the catchphrase "Turn Game Time into Brain Time."

3   Perhaps the best known of these products is the Baby Einstein series, which offers promotional materials swaddled in the rhetoric of stimulation: the word *multi-sensory* appears frequently. These DVDs tend to feature the alphabet or musical scales or colors, demonstrated through toys and lights and, of course, classical music. In fact, almost all of the company's DVDs are named after a crew of infantilized dead white male geniuses: *Baby Galileo, Baby Shakespeare, Baby Wordsworth,* and *Baby Van Gogh.* The Baby Einstein PR rep explains the product name by saying, "Albert Einstein exemplifies someone who was truly curious about the world around him." Her remark unwittingly undercuts the very premise of the series, suggesting not that babies can be made into Einsteins but that Einstein remained, in some sense, a baby. Additionally, I couldn't help but recall that Albert Einstein was not an early bloomer.

4   These videos are part of a DVD and toy fad that I call the Baby Genius Edutainment Complex. What I mean by the word *complex* here is two things. The first is as in "military-industrial complex": as Webster's has it, "a whole made up of complicated or interrelated parts," and "a group of obviously related units of which the degree and nature of the relationship is imperfectly known." The second is the psychological sense of the word: an exaggerated reaction to a situation. The complex is the first stage of the American passion for raising gifted children, reflecting the faith that, exposed to enough media, typically in tandem with equally stirring classes, bright children can be invented, and that precocity is the best insurance policy for one's children. The complex is also composed of products and companies now promising to urge on children's precocity.

5   This complex is relatively new. Until 1997, there were no Baby Einstein videos. By 2003, 32 percent of our nation's infants owned at least one Baby Einstein video. Ten percent of kids aged six months to two years have a television remote designed for children, according to a 2003 report by the Henry J. Kaiser Family Foundation, *Zero to Six: Electronic Media in the Lives of Infants, Toddlers and Preschoolers.* Forty-two percent of children in this age group watch a videotape or a DVD each day. According to the 2005 Kaiser report *A Teacher in the Living Room? Educational Media for Babies, Toddlers and Preschoolers,* on the average babies six months to three years spend an hour watching TV and forty-seven minutes a day on videos or computers, all despite the American Academy of Pediatrics' 1999 recommendation of no screen time at all for babies under two and no more than an hour or two of highly educational screen media for children ages two and older. No wonder, then, that developmental videos and DVDs in 2004 brought in profits of $100 million. That same year, videos and DVDs for preschool-age children earned $500 million. (From 2003 to 2004, overall sales of educational toys increased by 19 percent.)

6   One boon to the producers of children's DVDs is that the parent consumer appears more willing to buy rather than rent them because of their "repeatability"—that is, infants

and young children, unlike adults, enjoy watching the same DVD over and over again. (The irony here is that babies and toddlers like doing a lot of different kinds of things over and over again, in a level of repetition that adults might find intolerable, especially repeated actions with objects that are bright and shiny.) Chasing this opportunity, studios such as Warner Brothers have spent the last decade adding children's programming with an educational component into the mix. Baby Einstein is owned by Disney. The toy companies have also gotten into the act: Fisher-Price, a major DVD producer, is a subsidiary of Mattel. For the nation's biggest companies, the incentive to get into the edutainment DVD market is as clear as phonics. It's clear for smaller companies as well: as Dennis Fedoruk, president of Brainy Baby, says, "There's a bumper crop of new kids each month, after all."

7   But the impetus behind the Baby Genius Edutainment Complex's acceleration has not been just savvy marketing. The popularity of DVDs with classical music, pinwheels, and colorful imagery coincided with—and was also incited by—theories of infant and childhood learning that became fashionable in the early 1990s. As Liz Iftikhar, founder and president of Baby BumbleBee, puts it, the kid vid biz emerged on the back of the Mozart effect.

8   The phenomenon called the Mozart effect made its first appearance in a study done by Gordon Shaw and Frances Rauscher in 1993. One group of college students listened to ten minutes of a Mozart sonata, while another group didn't. Then both groups took a paper-folding-and-cutting test. Those who had listened to the music reportedly performed better than those who had not. Shaw and Rauscher concluded that listening to Mozart improved the students' very short-term spatial thinking. A second study in 1995 yielded similar findings.

9   The benefits of listening to Mozart soon became folk wisdom, and Mozart became even more synonymous with early learning and precocity. From the start of the renown of the Mozart effect and the tendency to refer to children with gifts as "little Mozarts," I recall being somewhat disturbed by any ambition to be Mozartian. While we can all imagine little Mozart playing blindfolded before Emperor Joseph, it is quite clear that the infant prodigy was raised by his father to be a high-rent stage show, "scattering his notes," as the music historian Paul Metzner puts it, all around Europe, and that he grew up to be a wildly creative yet also unstable young man whose incandescent exertions ultimately brought him physical deterioration and an early death. Nevertheless, the two Mozarts coexist, the parental fantasy and the Enlightenment wreck.

10   Soon the Mozart effect study's college students morphed into infants in the imaginations of kid marketers, parents, and Zell Miller, then governor of Georgia, who pushed his state to send a Mozart CD to every newborn. The idea that classical music played to infants, or even fetuses, would improve their ability to reason fed into the pitches of edutainment video companies, which in 1995 started to make ostensibly stimulating videos for babies, usually with a classical music component. One businessman, Don Campbell, even trademarked the term *Mozart Effect* in order to better sell "educational" CDs and books for infants. And the pitch has broadened beyond the music of the prodigious Wolfgang Amadeus–some of the newer videos are accompanied by the sonorous strains of Beethoven, and some offer random noise.

11   The catch to all these CDs and baby edutainment videos is that no psychologists, musicians, or musicologists have been able to duplicate the Mozart effect that Shaw

and Rauscher described. Kenneth Steele, professor of psychology at Appalachian State University, was one of the scholars who tried. In 1997, a few of his graduate students conducted similar experiments and failed to reproduce the results. Steele presumed at first that the Mozart effect was the result of individuals' arousal after listening to music. But he did not discover this to be the case. Then Steele himself tried, and he wasn't able to replicate the results, either. He eventually became the effect's greatest critic, publishing half a dozen papers decrying it, chief among them "Prelude or Requiem for the 'Mozart Effect'?" published with coauthors in *Nature* magazine in 1999. To date, the Mozart effect has failed to replicate in scientific settings at least three dozen times. Many additional scholars have noted that if any such effect does exist, it could well be due to the increased arousal that music can cause, or to the testing conditions.

12   None of this scholarly debunking has stymied the spread of the Baby Genius Complex. In fact, the complex has only expanded since the middle 1990s. Now it includes mind-enhancing baby formulas: giftedness has become digestible. In 2003 a fatty acid, DHA, suddenly made news as a wonder ingredient in baby formulas. DHA-ARA oils (docosahexaenoic acid and arachidonic acid), extracted from microbial sources such as algae and fungus, are supposed to help formulas replicate breast milk more closely than non-DHA formulas, thus increasing infant intelligence. Now a host of formulas offer DHA-ARA: Similac Advance, Nestle Good Start, Supreme with DHA and ARA, and Bright Beginnings. The Bright Beginnings pitch tells parents that the lipids added "are associated with mental and visual development." Enfamil A+ claims to be "the only formula clinically proven to result in higher early mental development scores."

13   Apparently, the creation of baby geniuses begins not at birth, but in the womb. Expecta Lipil, a pill for pregnant women, offers DHA in a prenatal form. There are also auditory prenatal enrichment products. Brent Logan, inventor of BabyPlus and author of *Learning before Birth: Every Child Deserves Giftedness*, hawks the prenatal BabyPlus system, a speaker unit that pregnant women are supposed to place in a fabric pouch that is then strapped to their abdomens: the unit gives off sixteen "scientifically designed rhythmic sounds that resemble a mother's heartbeat," according to the BabyPlus company. "The rhythm of the sounds increases incrementally and sequentially as the pregnancy progresses. The BabyPlus sound pattern introduces your child to a sequential learning process, built upon the natural rhythms of their own environment."

14   In describing his product to me, Logan promises that BabyPlus's "auditory exercises" will produce a higher-than-average IQ. The key to his pitch is the logical technique of inversion: he mentions in an interview that infants in Romania and Russia who are deprived suffer as adults, and thus infants in America who are enriched by a product like his will blossom. BabyPlus's ad copy claims that "babies and children enriched with BabyPlus are more relaxed at birth, with eyes and hands open, crying little," that they "reach their milestones earlier" and "have longer attention spans."

15   BabyPlus may be a far-out product, but like so many others, it uses parents' fears that their child might not hit milestones early or at the "normal time." Like the edutainment DVDs, it is first in a series of products claiming to promote child development and a timely march of the infant toward multilingualism and early spatial acumen. For instance, just to make sure progress is indeed timely, there is the Time Tracker, a lighted test-timer

for children aged four and up. Once you could get by with an egg timer or a stopwatch. But in the age of edutainment mass culture, that's not good enough. The Time Tracker is a plastic object shaped like a large cucumber standing on its end. It has red, yellow, and green stripes that can be programmed to light up after a certain amount of time has passed, accompanied by six sound effects. I bought it and programmed it. I was struck by a number of things regarding Time Tracker. For starters, there was the product's relative popularity—on Amazon.com it was in the top 2,000 the last time I checked. Second, I found the extension of time management—now such a concern among adults, as documented by a number of sociologists who study time use, and parents—to the toys of the youngest children meaningful. I was also struck by its similarity to a number of other objects: a lighted joystick, a miniature of the spaceship in *Close Encounters of the Third Kind*, and finally and somewhat disturbingly, although also somewhat amusingly, a sex toy.

16   The claims made by the producers of Baby Genius Edutainment DVDs and brain-feeding formulas may at times seem absurd. But the impulses that usher parents into the complex and drive them to purchase these products are utterly sincere, and the wish to raise flourishing children is so old it is practically biblical.

17   As Peggy Madsen, a parent of two in Colorado, put it to me, "Giftedness is a gift you can give." Madsen has always been terrifically determined that her children be the very smartest, and she continues to champion the use of flash cards to inspire early reading. She has written about wandering around the house, naming objects, when her children were still newborns, watching their eyes intently to make sure they understood. She believes it is thanks to her efforts that her children began attending college when they were thirteen.

18   The ambition to give "giftedness" may have quite a history, but other aspects of the complex are new. Today's complex yokes together two concepts of infant betterment—that those skills and aptitudes not provided through genetics can be worked at and developed, and that one must do so by a certain age, or the jig is up. Only in the last ten years have parents been inundated with flash cards, DVDs, toys, and games that promise to provide "just the right level" of stimulation. Parents are much more receptive to these ideas and pitches today because they are more anxious about their children's futures, which precocious achievement may assure.

19   One need only look at the history of toys to learn that educational stimulation has not always been the primary aim of children's and infants' playthings. Through the nineteenth century, children tended not to play with manufactured things. Toys were handcrafted and usually homemade, and most children had few or even no toys in the cupboard. Only the wealthy had a number of toys, and these were quite different from contemporary playthings. Diminutive replicas of women, babies, and furniture enabled children to engage the larger world at their own level, that of small bit players. Many children's toys were indistinguishable from the miniatures included in the reliquaries of the adult dead. Such toys were meant to help pass the time, not to create genius.

20   Early manufactured toys and games were a good index for how Americans conceived of childhood, and also of parents' more general wishes and impulses. The game Monopoly, for example, first produced in 1883, was an Industrial Revolution training ground whose promotional material described it as the site of "the struggle between Capital and Labor." In fact, "One of the most important changes in the play of children from large group ring

games to small group board games represented the embourgeoisement of our society," writes Stephen Kline, a professor of media studies at Simon Fraser University, in his book *Out of the Garden*. For instance, the beginning of the twentieth century saw a rise of mass-produced toys dedicated to solitary play. Lincoln Logs (invented by John Lloyd Wright, son of architect Frank), boxes of crayons (first produced by Crayola in 1903), and Erector sets (introduced in 1913) all signaled an increase in time spent indoors for children in newly prosperous families.

21   Some of these toys for solitary play were the earliest precursors of the DVDs and similar products sold by today's edutainment complex. Initially, Parker Bros., Playskool, and Milton Bradley were three toy companies specializing in "education games." A notion of playthings as maturational devices for children was on the rise, but it remained very different from the ideas behind today's ostensibly intelligence-enhancing toys. These maturational playthings did not claim to promote a child's achievement or mental gain: they could simply be dolls that taught mothering, for example. (In an article in a toy trade magazine in 1927, dolls were termed an "Antidote to Race Suicide" in that they would encourage white girls to reproduce. The teddy bear emerged in Brooklyn, New York, in 1902 and soon became faddish. It, too, was thought to have maturational benefits, but not in the sense of making children or toddlers faster learners. Rather, teddy bears were thought to be objects that spurred children's emotional growth. Teddy bears also have the benefit of being tactile, tangible, and manipulatable in a way that today's Baby Genius Edutainment Complex's DVDs and videos are not. DVDs, when playing on a screen, are by definition untouchable and mechanical. They encourage infants and toddlers to think while watching images on a box, rather than to invent and imagine a story around an object like a toy bear.

22   One of the aspects of the Baby Genius Edutainment Complex, the study of play and playthings' relationship to the development of children, also began in the late nineteenth century. Anthropologists started studying children's games as a sort of living folklore. One study of 15,000 kids in Cleveland in 1913 discovered that of a number of possible activities, "3171 were just fooling" while "531 were playing with kites," a bit of historical data that strikes me as particularly interesting in light of our contemporary attitudes toward children's mental development, where the "just fooling" time, seen as wasteful, has shrunk. At the turn of the century, toys were being used in kindergartens. The educator Maria Montessori used toys to teach math concepts, and promoted the enlightened notion that child pupils would be less obdurate about learning if work was more playlike, because when they were playing they were actively engaged. Montessori's ideas soon caught on among some educators. But the nature of toys was also debated, with academics championing free play and high-quality materials. In 1920, a professor at Columbia University's Teachers College informed a group of businessmen in the toy industry that they should make toys of better quality that appealed to the imagination—a plea not always heeded by manufacturers.

23   Complaints about toys stifling imagination rather than charging it have become ever more urgent with regard to the toys and DVDs of today. In an insolent, sparkling essay on the subject first collected in 1957 in the book *Mythologies*, the cultural critic Roland Barthes decried his era's playthings as products of "chemistry not nature." He was horrified that there were "dolls which urinate" and other toys "meant to prepare the little girl

for the causality of housekeeping, to 'condition' her to her future role as mother." These toys, Barthes wrote, "are meant to produce children who are users, not creators." He was paraphrasing what was to become a central tenet of scholars of play: self-directed play is seen as superior play, and toys where children can improvise and imagine are privileged over those that are passive and preprogrammed. Prefabricated toys of this kind condemned the child to feel, Barthes wrote, that "he does not invent the world, he uses it: there are, prepared for him, actions without adventure, without wonder, without joy. He is turned into a little stay-at-home householder who does not even have to invent the mainsprings of adult causality; they are supplied to him ready-made: he has only to help himself, he is never allowed to discover anything from start to finish."

24   After Barthes, the psychologist Erik Erikson's insights into toys and development complicated the study of playthings. Erikson wrote of the earliest and most primitive play in a child's life, "autocosmic play," where infants play with their own bodies, and going on to a toy "microsphere" or "the small world of manageable toys," which is "a harbor" for the child's ego. Ultimately, according to Erikson, the toy "thing-world" expands into the "macrosphere" of group play, or play with other children. Erikson kept underlining the point that play and play with toys is a part of identity, and the children's world of manageable toys should be shaped or intervened with as little as possible to avoid any disruption in their social learning.

25   At least in Barthes's era, children's playthings were still primarily tactile in character. Today's DVDs tend to be images of toys emanating from a television screen in programs with goofy pedantry. Still, Barthes's notion of toys as totems of a prescribed and manufactured adult world held some truth, and would only become more true with time. Already by the middle of the last century, toys had become less arcadian. They were creations devoted to novelty and expendability—in other words, trendy and makeshift: yo-yos and Davy Crockett hats and the like. In fact, today's nostalgia for a simpler time, for a time when childhood meant frolicking in more innocent pastoral climes—romping through the yard rather than through parents' DVD collections—may be an attractive construction, but it is also almost always misleading, a sort of sentimentality for an idyllic childhood that may have existed a century ago rather than one or two generations past. Beginning as early as the 1950s, toys suddenly became spin-off gear from television shows or children's films: when a child wasn't watching television, she might well be playing with action figures or other toys based on television programs, products that would allow her to re-create, in her own home, scenes from her favorite series. Along with the ever more calculated nature of children's toys, there was inevitably an increase of market-driven toy testing and research conducted by toy manufacturers.

26   This isn't to say that the "maturational" ambitions of toys vanished. For instance, the construction toy Lego advertised itself as an "instructive game." And in 1969, the ultimate maturational television program, *Sesame Street* debuted, with a line of educational toys following in its wake. The lessons of *Sesame Street*, were strongly influenced by the educational philosophy of Maria Montessori, and from the beginning *Sesame Street*'s producers, the Children's Television Workshop, made a huge effort at outreach to young children and their families in low-income areas. The show was, in fact, considered to be an extension of the 1960s "War on Poverty," funded in part by the Department of Health, Education and Welfare, as if it were a social program.

27   But in a certain sense, the early debates that swirled around *Sesame Street* are echoed today in the debates over the Baby Edutainment Complex. *Sesame Street*'s critics argued that young children benefit from imaginary play rather than watching television. Similarly, the edutainment DVDs for infants regularly run afoul of the American Academy of Pediatrics, which suggests that there should be no television watching at all for children under two. But there is a crucial difference between edutainment DVDs and *Sesame Street*. *Sesame Street* was not intended for babies (until now, that is, as a *Sesame Street* infant DVD line is readied for release), while today's DVDs are made explicitly for children two and under.

28   Companies are making these products because parents want them. Parents want them because they are concerned about their children's mental lives, thanks to the hard-sell marketing. There are deeper reasons, too, for parents' greater receptivity to such products and toys. One is a contemporary mania for infant betterment and precocity. Another is an increasing fashion for gizmos and technological improving devices for people of all ages, starting in infancy. A third reason is harder to prove but seems to me to be widespread: adults' tendency to project themselves into infant and toddler experience, as an antidote to their inability to remember that time, and perhaps to remember much of childhood at all, given the pressure to live in the future rather than the past. The gap between adults' projections onto infants' viewing experience and the true nature of that experience is large—is the baby learning or just taking in a set of bright two-dimensional images that makes little sense? And if the infant is learning from the edutainment DVD, wouldn't she learn from any repetitive experience, since infants learn through repetition? DVDs are just easier to repeat than other experiences.

29   This is part of how the Baby Edutainment Complex is the beginning of the movement to invent gifted children: it starts with parental wishes and hopes, one of which is that the infant is getting as much out of a DVD as his parents. It's also part of another aspect of childhood that will be covered in more depth elsewhere in this book—directed play has trumped free play. This is one unspoken reason why babies are now the audience for educational products. According to Brainy Baby president Dennis Fedoruk, parents are concerned about their infants' mental lives. "Parents know about that preschool window of opportunity–it's very narrow," he says. "Parents want to maximize results in their children without causing their children trouble. Listen, you can't turn back the hands of time. Once they enter kindergarten they can't have the window of opportunity any longer. It's too late."

30   Similarly, CEO and founder of the Athletic Baby Company Karen Foster tells me that her *Athletic Baby Golf* and *Athletic Baby All-Star* DVDs help parents give a head start to their kids, so that when they are actually old enough to play a sport or even to walk, "they will succeed at it." She likens her DVDs' potential effect to the effect of his father on Tiger Woods: "Everyone has heard about Tiger's imprinting from an early age by his father. . . . The earlier the age, the more successful they will be." Foster gives the standard edutainment-complex line: if infant deprivation creates negative effects, inversely, "enriching" products must automatically produce a positive effect. She mentions the child obesity epidemic frequently, as if her *Athletic Baby* DVDs are a sure cure. Even as many researchers tie obesity to sedentary habits, Foster wants parents to sit their babies down in front of a DVD to prevent—well, to prevent them from sitting around. By this logic, adults would be encouraged to keep in shape by watching the NFL on TV each Sunday afternoon.

31   The makers of the smart-baby formulas also sell their products by promising bright children. "The difference between the children who received formulas containing this ingredient and other children can be observed from each group's reading of one line on the eye chart," claimed Angela Tsetsis, director of marketing for Martek, the company that produces the "smart" fatty acid and sells it to the companies that use it in their baby formulas. "At eighteen months, we looked at the mental acuity of babies who have received the nutrient, and those babies scored higher."

32   "BabyPlus helps with imprinting," Brent Logan, the inventor, claims. "And soon, the imprinting window shuts off for the fetus and it is too late. When they are prenates, they are in an unusual different time and they are learning in a different mode." Logan and BabyPlus are extremes in the edutainment market—Logan does an unironic star turn in a British television documentary program entitled *Brave New Babies*, which he proudly sends me. But his prenatal interventionist ideology is not a fringe belief. Real mothers are buying his product. Rather than a radical maneuver, Logan's move into prenatal marketing seems like the next logical step.

33   All of these are pitches that could make a parent nervous enough to run out and buy the product. But are any of them accurate? To better understand the answer to this question, one needs to first cleave the popular ideas of infant "crucial stages," "brain cell death," "windows of time," and "brain plasticity" (today's scientized buzzword for "ability to learn") from the science and cultural history underlying them.

34   The notion that the first three years are key ones for emotional and intellectual development isn't new. Americans have long sought to command and control natural processes so as to accelerate them. This is part of our faith in man's ability to harness nature and to use time shrewdly. As Benjamin Franklin said, time is money, and the stuff life is made of. Child development pioneer Jean Piaget was famously disturbed by Americans' fixation on their children's educational velocity. A story was told to me anecdotally by Charles Nelson, a professor of pediatrics at Harvard Medical School, of Piaget's tour of American universities in the middle of the last century. When the Swiss psychologist described the cognitive stages children pass through as they mature, his American listeners asked him how they could make their children go through those stages faster. (Piaget was displeased.) In 1964, those who founded Head Start, a federally funded program for disadvantaged preschool children, emphasized the urgent nature of education in the earliest years, an undertaking that was seen as determining these children's entire futures.

35   In the last decade or so, a focus on early development and the necessity of intervention for disadvantaged children, once a social welfare plank, fueled a popular awareness (and sometimes misunderstanding) of the crucial period from zero to three. Vociferous celebrity advocates for infants, a White House conference on the subject, and the Mozart effect theory ultimately gave rise to a rash of baby products promising infant precocity.

36   As John Bruer recounts in his clear-headed derogation of the early enrichment movement, *The Myth of the First Three Years*, texts from the 1990s like *Rethinking the Brain* tended to suggest that critical periods pervade all areas of learning. In the mid-1990s, the actor Rob Reiner's national "I Am Your Child" campaign, with its slogan "The first years last forever," disseminated the zero-to-three worldview. Reiner claimed at the time that parents who don't read to their children in those first three years were diminishing the growth potential of their

brains, and that by the age of ten "your brain is cooked and there's nothing much you can do." While Reiner and his campaign claimed to address an infant's intellectual development, Bruer notes correctly that it was theories of emotional attachment as outlined by child psychologists in the late 1950s, '60s, and '70s—most famous among them the legendary British child psychologist John Bowlby—that gave Reiner's campaign its true ballast. A second event that egged the craze onward was the 1997 White House Conference on Child Development, which emphasized the effect of early childhood events on the development of a child's intelligence. A third element was a series of studies on rats and enrichment conducted by Mark Rosenzweig at the University of California, Berkeley, and William Greenough at the University of Illinois in the 1970s and '80s. Both researchers looked at how rats' brains benefit from experience. They conducted studies on the brains of rats raised in enriched environments with toys and with other rats—cages akin to the rats' natural habitat—versus the brains of rats in bare cages more akin to prison cells. The rats in the enriched cages were found to have more dendritic area in certain regions of the brain: basically, these rats were more mentally enhanced than their deprived colleagues. This research was ultimately absorbed by the popular press and applied to infants and children.

37   And then there was the Mozart effect.

38   But in the years since the middle 1990s, scholars have cast aspersions on the credence of zero-to-three as an absolute time frame. William Greenough of rat-enrichment fame was a vehement critic of the new overemphasis on early learning: he argued that his research supported the idea that the brain continues to be plastic after infancy, rather than the opposite conclusion that the time for development is limited. Indeed, many in the neuroscientific community now dismiss the idea that adult brains lose plasticity, viewing the brain as an entity that continually remodels itself. The trend in current research is to study in earnest how individuals execute cognitive tasks from ages six to ninety, and observe mental dynamics across the life span.

39   "It's important to point out that windows of development do not slam shut, as the earliest versions of 'Parents' Action for Children' and the 'Birth to Three' movement suggested," says Bradley Schlaggar, a pediatric neurologist at Washington University. "When the development windows are thought to slam shut, a parent may feel that he or she must try again with the next child. While the motivation was very justifiable—a desire to make sure every child had access to good nutrition—the message was so harsh."

40   Schlaggar and other neurologists, cognitive scientists, psychologists, and child development specialists I spoke with questioned the idea that educational toys or DVDs accomplish what their makers claim. As Professor Charles Nelson, a professor at Harvard Medical School and a preeminent scholar of the infant brain, puts it, "There is no proof of the value of the early enrichment toys and videos in terms of brain science." Nelson also consulted for Mead Johnson for a year regarding "smart" food additives and says that while DHA and ARA have been shown to improve babies' auditory and retina responses, they have not been shown to improve reading skills.

41   Scholars have also argued that the idea of hard and fast "critical periods" is overplayed. For one thing, there is a difference between brain functions that are "experience-expectant" and bound by critical periods, and those that are "experience-dependent" and not so bound. Experience-expectant means, for example, that the brain requires exposure

to light so that vision can develop properly. This experience does, in fact, need to take place at a particular point in the development of all infants. Experience-dependent learning, by contrast, is how an infant or child learns things individual to her environment—reading or weaving or dumpling-making. This sort of learning is less time-governed. As John Bruer puts it, "critical periods are less likely to exist for traits and behaviors that are unique to the experiences of individuals, social groups, or cultures."

42   According to Fred Dick, a developmental cognitive neuroscientist and a lecturer in psychology at the University of London, starting to learn second or even third languages early can be a good thing. But early doesn't mean infancy. Furthermore, teaching a child language with another child may be preferable to using videos, because a normal environment with another child "holds more information than any multimedia film." Experts tell me that today's edutainment DVDs or language-blurting toys are generally untested in how effective they are in teaching children a second language. The DVDs tend to offer only disconnected French or Spanish words; additionally, a child must be exposed to a language continuously to acquire it. Studies have shown that the ability to learn the grammar of a second language begins to decline in puberty—quite a while after the age of three. And ultimately, says Dick, one can be a successful language learner well into adulthood. "It's not as easy, but I can take up a new language when I am twenty," says Michael Merzenich, a neuroscientist at the University of California and a preeminent expert on brain plasticity. "It's not as easy *not* because I am less plastic, but because I became so damn proficient at my native language."

43   Many infant DVDs are hawked with questionable promises about time-limited opportunities for learning. Some head straight for the parental panic button, selling themselves by gesturing at the specter of "infant brain cell death." Charles Zorn, a neuropsychological education specialist, told me that he often has to reassure parents that numbers of brain cells are not a measure of a child's intelligence, knowledge, or ability to learn. The brain deliberately makes too many, then lets a bunch wither; the specific ones that wither depend on the environment the newborn encounters. In fact, cell death is actually a part of the learning process. "When you learn to read, you are killing cells to create a pathway," he says.

44   Indeed, reducing infant brain cell death is counterproductive; cell death is the main way the nervous system refines its circuits. One scholar used the example of a toddler flying an airplane and asked rhetorically, Wouldn't you rather a trained adult pilot it, even if the toddler may have more exuberant brain cells?

45   Academics who study cognition also question the value of prenatal enrichment products. Gary Marcus, a professor of psychology at New York University and author of *The Birth of the Mind*, says that while it is possible to learn something in the womb, it also isn't good to give a fetus too much stimulation. And given the paucity of long-term research on the subject, it's hard to gauge what would be overstimulating, says Marcus: "We don't know enough about early brain development to say."

46   In truth, scant neurobiology is dedicated to gifted children, and there are also few studies on the value of edutainment videos. The 2005 Kaiser Family Foundation report *A Teacher in the Living Room,* underlines the point I have heard time and again from researchers of infant brain development and education on the effect of the bright baby videos: there is little adequate scholarship on these products' value over time.

47   What researchers *can* comfortably assert is that a false set of assumptions is at work. According to the blurry logic I described earlier, the total neglect of orphans is shown to be bad, and therefore superstimulation must be good. This is a false conflation, says Nelson; deprived infants who benefit from a move to an ordinary environment are being used to indicate the benefits of enrichment to children who grow up in ordinary or even "super" environments. "For many infants, there's an a priori enrichment in their daily lives," says Nelson. "What they see in *Baby Einstein*, and all of the edutainment DVDs, exists in the baby's ordinary environment." As long as you don't put a child in a closet, nutritionally deprive him, or cause trauma to his developing brain, he will naturally learn.

48   The proposition is that, say, if disadvantaged children are helped by exposure to age-appropriate enrichment, then advantaged children will be even more enriched by exposure to supersonic educational stimuli. Data on the value of early learning intervention for disadvantaged kids is also mapped onto the value of pumped-up learning for advantaged children, including a study in which three-year-olds in Early Head Start programs performed significantly better cognitively, linguistically, and emotionally than a similarly disadvantaged control group not enrolled in Early Head Start. But just because a child who lacks the ordinary stimulation of an everyday childhood and gets a great deal of negative stimulation may experience permanent damage, that does not mean that more stimulation is better for all kids. To put it in hothouse terms, a lack of water will kill an orchid—but so will a flood. Nevertheless, the makers of baby edutainment use a blurry syllogism in their efforts to beguile parents: Deprivation is bad; therefore, the opposite of deprivation is good.

49   The final criticism that researchers have made of the Baby Genius Edutainment Complex goes beyond the fact that the DVDs are not as educational as they claim: their widening use may actually prevent more effective learning from taking place. A University of Massachusetts researcher had one sample group of infants learn to use a puppet from a live person, while the other learned by watching a DVD. The tots who received live instruction learned to use the puppet immediately, but the infant video-watchers had to repeat their viewing six times before they learned the same skill. A number of scholars have also started to investigate whether the millions of infants and children who have grown up watching educational videos have actually been damaged by their new orientation to the television. One such scholar, Rhonda Clements, a professor of education at Manhattanville College and the former president of the American Association for the Child's Right to Play, recently conducted a study that found that 70 percent of the sample's mothers said that they themselves played every day outdoors when they were children, typically tag, hopscotch, and jumping rope, as compared with 31 percent of their children. And of the mothers who said their children played outdoors, only 22 percent played for three hours at a time or longer. The study concluded that today's level of indoor activity and play, even if it involves "learning," is deleterious to the children's young bodies and minds. (The study was financed by the detergent maker Wisk—perhaps in an effort to promote an increase in dirt and grass stains.)

50   But despite negative findings about time spent watching DVDs indoors, and the fuzziness of the edutainment product makers' claims, even the most sophisticated parents can be drawn to the Baby Edutainment Complex.

51   "There are some guarantees with these products," says Lynne Varner, a forty-two-year-old newspaper writer and mom who resides in Seattle. "There aren't guarantees in

the world. My son may not see all the colors in the prism every day. He may go outside and see a green tree one day and a roaring bus the next day, but I have to hope that nature and life offer everything to him. I want our child to always be doing something that stimulates him. And so does everyone I know."

52   Varner's accumulation of educational toys started with Baby Einstein and grew from there to Baby BumbleBee toys purchased at the Imaginarium and the now-defunct Zany Brainy. The stores and products made reassuring guarantees that her kid was going to be smart, she says: Baby Einstein markets itself this way to the "überparents" she knows in Seattle and Palo Alto.

53   "I do believe that the brain has a certain clump of neurons firing, and that by the time he is five it will be too late," one women, an educated professional who is an avid consumer of these products, told me. "It sounds panicky, I know, but if those neurons are dying off . . . you have to get in there during the first three years. If my baby doesn't use it with a stimulating game or class, he is going to lose it." But her baby's neurons are going to die no matter what she does. They're supposed to die.

54   On Amazon.com, reviewers likewise emphasize that the videos are part of their responsibility to adequately enhance and stimulate their children. One writes about *Brainy Baby Left Brain*, "I come from a Montessori background and have very high standards regarding my child's education. I am discriminating about what I expose her to. The formative years are a crucial time in every child's development. . . . Now that she is three years old, she enjoys the more cognitive lessons in the video (even though it is all review for her!). . . . No longer do parents have to tolerate the use of mindless videos to 'occupy' their young ones. We now have the opportunity to actually EDUCATE our babies with a video. The child will LEARN something while watching this."

55   Another reviwer writes, "My 1-year-old is growing into a Brainy Baby, herself! How many 18-month-olds can tell you what an orangutan is, or the difference between a circle and an oval, or that the color of our van is 'silver'? My son could—from watching these videos!"

56   Of course, parents don't entirely trust the pitches from the companies. The Seattle mom recognizes that many of the pitches she receives for toys play upon her worst fears–that her children's brains will stop growing, that her children will become adults who fall through the cracks. "Unless something cataclysmic happens, our children won't be prisoners, or even drug addicts," says the mom. But she still buys *Baby Einstein*, Leapster, and the rest.

57   Many parents buy these products even as they remain skeptical about their claims. In 2004, I attended an educational-toy party in New York. The party's emcee, the self-proclaimed "Discovery Toy Lady," was named Simone Weissman. Weissman is an enthusiastic woman with curly hair, a loud girlish voice, and a more-than-passing resemblance to Bette Midler. She sold her products Tupperware-style: plastic toys, plush toys, and flash cards in a sea of primary colors, laid out before her on a table in a sunset-suffused thirtieth-floor apartment. The partygoers, women of thirty or fortyish, wore stretchy comfort clothes—not a plunging shirtdress in sight. As they drank wine, a wailing baby provided the party's sound track from behind a set of screens. While the baby cried, Discovery Toy Lady Weissman pointed out the products that provoke "fine and gross mental skills." She

moved on to a toy that used to be merely sentimental: a stuffed bear. But this teddy was named Classical Casey, and played famous melodies from six classical composers. He wasn't sold as being all about love: he also strengthened an infant's "sensory capacities," Weissman said. The mothers looked on, seemingly unimpressed by Classical Casey. No one reached for their purses, even when she showed the group flash cards called Think It Through Tiles. The cards, Weissman said, were good for studying for the ERBs–the Educational Records Bureau test for private preschool admission, tests that are given to children as young as three. The mothers at this particular party weren't planning on sending their children to private schools, but upon hearing that other mothers were using these flash cards and had seen great improvement in their children's scores, they perked up. They didn't want to fail to do due diligence for their kids. Weissman said that the cards' buyers wanted their children to have an edge. "These moms worry that their children aren't doing the right things, you know?" she said.

58   But doing things "right" isn't the whole story. It seems to me that the Baby Genius Edutainment Complex exists, in part, out of a deeper fear than that of infants losing their learning opportunities. It responds to adults' fear of children's boredom. The edutainment products are, at bottom, meant to reduce unproductive boredom.

59   But what exactly is boredom, especially in infancy and childhood? The psychotherapist and writer Adam Phillips writes in *On Kissing, Tickling, and Being Bored* that the bored child is waiting "for an experience of anticipation" and that being bored, rather than an inadequacy, is an opportunity and perhaps even a capacity: boredom is "a developmental achievement for the child."

60   "It is one of the most oppressive demands of adults that the child should be interested," writes Phillips, "rather than take time to find what interests him. Boredom is integral to the process of taking one's time." But taking one's time and waiting for desire or interest to return goes against the grain of the new improved infancy, and the regimen of infant stimulation.

61   Talking about childhood boredom is not boring—I find this out discoursing on dullness in the sun-filled office of Dona Matthews, coauthor of *Being Smart about Gifted Children: A Guidebook for Parents and Educators* and the director of Hunter College's Center for Gifted Studies and Education. Matthews is fifty-something, clad in a stripy sweater. Her office has the upbeat atmosphere common to those who work with children: a blue plate full of bright orange nectarines, an orchid, a colorful poster, and Matthews herself, with a bright smile and winningly tousled hair. "Parents are always saying, 'My kids are bored or understimulated,'" she says. "Sometimes it is a parent-induced boredom, where the parents are centered on entertaining the child." Like many in the gifted business, Matthews has the air of a Boomer Vivant. "Boredom is essential. It's important to encourage children to find things to do, and a commonality with others. We call it do-nothing time. It is necessary to be bored to find out what you really want to do." Buddhists call it non-doing.

62   There are even experts who argue that a certain amount of boredom is important for kids' development. Fred Dick, the developmental cognitive neuroscientist, notes that babies' emotional states tend to change, and thus an infant's caregivers should attend to a child but should not feel obliged to provide *constant* stimulation to their children.

63   One specialist in gifted education suggests that an adult finger can be just as stimulating for an infant as the whirling dervish of rainbows on a *Baby Einstein* DVD. Charles Zorn, the neuropsychological educational consultant, suggests that parents who aren't sold on the need for stimulating DVDs can see that the perfect educational baby toys are everywhere: keys on a chain. They jingle. Babies get excited, are aurally and visually stimulated, and learn to identify a shape that will have lifelong application. Others suggest playing with a broom and dustpan.

64   Such simple pleasures, which adults find boring—and this is part of it: our inability, as adults, to remember how easily we were entertained during our own infancies—are often just what infants need. Their systems are ready for simplicity, not for a deluge of diffuse stimuli.

65   Why the aversion to boredom? It belongs to a larger fear of emptiness, a fascination with whirring cities, technologies, a distrust of the "dull" repetitions of experience. As Patricia Meyer Spacks writes in her book of literary criticism, *Boredom*, "The diagnoses (self-diagnoses and evaluations by others) of middle class adolescents and housewives as sufferers from boredom exemplify the imaginative functions boredom serves in our culture. . . . The claim of boredom now locates the causes of conduct firmly outside the self."

66   "If sleep is the apogee of physical relaxation," writes philosopher and cultural critic Walter Benjamin, "boredom is the apogee of mental relaxation. Boredom is the dream bird that hatches the egg of experience. A rustling in the leaves drives him away. His nesting places—the activities that are intimately associated with boredom—are already extinct in the cities and are declining in the country as well."

67   Indeed, a number of childhood edutainment products are equivalent to a mechanical rustling in the leaves, a buzzing, bleeping thing called computerized enrichment that drives away the dream bird that could otherwise have hatched the egg of true human experience. What is that experience for infants? Perhaps it's keys on a chain. Perhaps it's what they see between the rails of their cribs. But it is also letting the infant alone with her thoughts, her own developing self, rather than providing external stimulus.

68   The fight against boredom, the insistence on external stimulation whenever possible, is clearly tied to a concern about time. This concern—or, perhaps, fear—drives the Baby Genius Edutainment Complex: the fear that time is being wasted, that windows of development are slamming shut, that time for learning is running out.

QUESTIONS ON MEANING

1. What is, as labeled by Quart, the Baby Genius Edutainment Complex?

2. What is the Mozart Effect? Does experimental data confirm the effect?

3. What is the role of boredom in a toddler's life? Is it something to fight against, or to allow?

4. According to some of the researches cited in this essay, are brain-cell deaths an indicator of diminishing intelligence?

5. Based on your reading of this essay, how would you define the following concepts: (1) imprinting, (2) brain plasticity, (3) crucial development states?

QUESTIONS FOR DISCUSSION

1. Quart quotes the cultural critic Roland Barthes who, when commenting on the toy trends in the 1950s said of these products that they are "meant to produce children who are users, not creators." What kids of toys is Barthes thinking of here? Did you own some of these kinds of toys as a child? What do you think Barthes means in this quote? Do you agree or disagree with Barthes? Are "edutainment" toys better or worse than the toys Barthes had in mind?

2. After reading this essay, are you more or less likely to purchase the kinds of "edutainment" products Quart discusses in this essay? Why?

3. What does the rise and growth of the edutainment industry suggest about American culture? Is Quart critical of American culture in this essay? Does your experience confirm or challenge the portrait of one piece of American culture presented in Quart's essay?

4. If you were told by an authority you trusted that using a certain product would increase the chance that your child would be smarter, would you use it? What if you were told that use of the product had a 50% chance of boosting your child's intelligence, and a 50% chance of diminishing your child's intelligence?

5. Moving beyond the pre-school years, what does Quart's essay suggest about a child's formal education? If you were a teacher, what kinds of activities would you be most likely to use in a classroom, and which least? Why?

LOOKING AT RHETORIC

1. Who is Quart's audience in this essay? Is it possible to identify her primary audience based on the way in which the essay is written? Are they audiences that would be more or less interested in Quart's essay? What is your level of interest in this essay? Do you think you'd be more or less interested in this essay five years ago? What about five years from now?

2. It is clear from Quart's essay that researchers and companies do not entirely agree over whether or not edutainment has any clear benefit for growing infants and toddlers. Which side of the question does Quart side with? Is it possible to tell? Does Quart have a clear thesis related to this question or is this an informative essay that raised a question and sets forth the opposing views without advocating for one over the other?

WRITING ASSIGNMENTS

1. Spend some time in the library and/or online researching the Montessori theory of and approach to childhood education. Write a paper in which you compare and contrast the beliefs, goals, and practice of a Montessori classroom with a traditional public school classroom. As an alternative, write the same paper, but instead of Montessori use the Reggio Emilia theory and methodology.

2. Track down examples of at least three different edutainment products mentioned in Quart's essay and analyze them. Write an essay in which you describe each of the three products and compare and contrast them. Then, argue which one of the products seems most, and which least, likely to actually keep the promises alleged in the products packaging.

3. In pairs or in groups, imagine you are a team of toy developers for a major toy manufacturer, and you have been charged with designing a toy that would not only sell well, but which would do the best possible job stimulating intellectual growth in pre-school children. Share the results of your group's work with other groups in the classroom. Then, as an individual, write an essay in which you propose to the management of the company that they develop the toy your group has developed as opposed to toys developed by other groups in class. Convince your audience (company management) that your toy has the best potential not only to sell, but to promote intellectual development in children.

Teaching the N-Word

Emily Bernard

Emily Bernard is an Associate Professor of English and Ethnic Studies at the University of Vermont. She is the editor of Remember Me to Harlem: The Letters of Langston Hughes and Carl Van Vechten *(2001) and* Some of My Best Friends: Writers on Interracial Friendship *(2004), a collection of essays about relationships between people from different racial backgrounds. She has also co-authored* Michelle Obama: The First Lady in Photographs *(2009). As the following essay demonstrates, there is a close connection between race, racism, and the language that we use. By focusing on the complex emotional responses both blacks and whites have to the "N word" in contemporary society, Bernard is able to illustrate at least one aspect of the ongoing struggle in the United States—and beyond—to understand the significance and meaning of race in this country.*

OCTOBER 2004

1   Eric is crazy about queer theory. I think it is safe to say that Eve Sedgwick, Judith Butler, and Lee Edelman[1] have changed his life. Every week, he comes to my office to report on the connections he is making between the works of these writers and the books he is reading for the class he is taking with me, African-American autobiography.

2   I like Eric. So tonight, even though it is well after six and I am eager to go home, I keep our conversation going. I ask him what he thinks about the word "queer," whether or not he believes, independent of the theorists he admires, that epithets can ever really be reclaimed and reinvented.

3   "'Queer' has important connotations for me," he says. "It's daring, political. I embrace it." He folds his arms across his chest, and then unfolds them.

4   I am suspicious.

5   "What about 'nigger'?" I ask. "If we're talking about the importance of transforming hateful language, what about that word?" From my bookshelf I pull down Randall Kennedy's book *Nigger: The Strange Career of a Troublesome Word*, and turn it so its cover faces Eric. "Nigger," in stark white type against a black background, is staring at him, staring at anyone who happens to be walking past the open door behind him.

6   Over the next 30 minutes or so, Eric and I talk about "nigger." He is uncomfortable; every time he says "nigger," he drops his voice and does not meet my eyes. I know that he does not want to say the word; he is following my lead. He does not want to say it because he is white; he does not want to say it because I am black. I feel my power as his professor,

---

[1]Eve Sedgwich, Judith Butler, and Lee Edelman: all well-known scholars working in the field of queer theory (or queer studies), which examines literature and culture in terms of their relationship to queer or non-normative sexualities and gender identifications.

the mentor he has so ardently adopted. I feel the power of Randall Kennedy's book in my hands, its title crude and unambiguous. *Say it*, we both instruct this white student. And he does.

7   It is late. No one moves through the hallway. I think about my colleagues, some of whom still sit at their own desks. At any minute, they might pass my office on their way out of the building. What would they make of this scene? Most of my colleagues are white. What would I think if I walked by an office and saw one of them holding up *Nigger* to a white student's face? A black student's face?

8   "I think I am going to add 'Who Can Say Nigger?' to our reading for next week," I say to Eric. "It's an article by Kennedy that covers some of the ideas in this book." I tap *Nigger* with my finger, and then put it down on my desk.

8   "I really wish there was a black student in our class," Eric says as he gathers his books to leave.

10   As usual I have assigned way too much reading. Even though we begin class discussion with references to three essays required for today, our conversation drifts quickly to "Who Can Say Nigger?" and plants itself there. We talk about the word, who can say it, who won't say it, who wants to say it, and why. There are 11 students in the class. All of them are white.

11   Our discussion is lively and intense; everyone seems impatient to speak. We talk about language, history, and identity. Most students say "the n-word" instead of "nigger." Only one or two students actually use the word in their comments. When they do, they use the phrase "the word 'nigger,'" as if to cushion it. Sometimes they make quotations marks with their fingers. I notice Lauren looking around. Finally, she raises her hand.

12   "I have a question; it's somewhat personal. I don't want to put you on the spot."

13   "Go ahead, Lauren." I say with relief.

14   "Okay, so how does it feel for you to hear us say that word?"

15   I have an answer ready.

16   "I don't enjoy hearing it. But I don't think that I feel more offended by it than you do. What I mean is, I don't think I have a special place of pain inside of me that the word touches because I am black." *We are both human beings*, I am trying to say. She nods her head, seemingly satisfied. Even inspired. I hope.

17   I am lying, of course.

18   I am grateful to Lauren for acknowledging my humanity in our discussion. But I do not want me—my feelings, my experiences, my humanity—to become the center of classroom discussion. Here at the University of Vermont, I routinely teach classrooms full of white students. I want to educate them, transform them. I want to teach them things about race they will never forget. To achieve this, I believe I must give of myself. I want to give to them—but I want to keep much of myself to myself. How much? I have a new answer to this question every week.

19   I always give my students a lecture at the beginning of every African-American studies course I teach. I tell them, in essence, not to confuse my body with the body of the text. I tell them that while it would be disingenuous for me to suggest that my own racial identity has nothing to do with my love for African-American literature, my race is only one of the

many reasons why I stand before them. "I stand here," I say, "because I have a Ph.D., just like all your other professors." I make sure always to tell them that my Ph.D., like my B.A., comes from Yale.

20   "In order to get this Ph.D.," I continue, "I studied with some of this country's foremost authorities on African-American literature, and a significant number of these people are white.

21   "I say this to suggest that if you fail to fully appreciate this material, it is a matter of your intellectual laziness, not your race. If you cannot grasp the significance of Frederick Douglass's[2] plight, for instance, you are not trying hard enough, and I will not accept that."

22   I have another part of this lecture. It goes: "Conversely, this material is not the exclusive property of students of color. This is literature. While these books will speak to us emotionally according to our different experiences, none of us is especially equipped to appreciate the intellectual and aesthetic complexities that characterize African-American literature. This is American literature. American experience, after all."

23   Sometimes I give this part of my lecture, but not always. Sometimes I give it and then regret it later.

SEPTEMBER 2004

24   On the first day of class, Nate asks me what I want to be called.

25   "Oh, I don't know," I say, fussing with equipment in the room. I know. But I feel embarrassed, as if I have been found out. "What do you think?" I ask them.

26   They shuffle around, equally embarrassed. We all know that I have to decide, and that whatever I decide will shape our classroom dynamic in very important ways.

27   "What does Gennari ask you to call him?" I have inherited several of these students from my husband, John Gennari, another professor of African-American studies. He is white.

28   "Oh, we call him John," Nate says with confidence. I am immediately envious of the easy warmth he seems to feel for John. I suspect it has to do with the name thing.

29   "Well, just call me Emily, then. This is an honors class, after all. And I do know several of you already. And then wouldn't it be strange to call the husband John and the wife Professor?" Okay, I have convinced myself.

30   Nate says, "Well, John and I play basketball in a pickup game on Wednesdays. So, you know, it would be weird for me to be checking him and calling him 'Professor Gennari.' "

31   We all laugh, and move on to other topics. But my mind locks onto an image of my husband and Nate on the basketball court, two white men, covered in sweat, body to body, heads down, focused on the ball.

---

[2]Frederick Douglass: African-American author who escaped from slavery, wrote one of the most famous slave narratives—*The Narrative of the Life of Frederick Douglass*—in 1845, and was active in the anti-slavery lecture circuit in the years leading up to the Civil War.

OCTOBER 2004

32   "It's not that I can't say it, it's that I don't want to. I will not say it," Sarah says. She wears her copper red hair in a short, smart style that makes her look older than her years. When she smiles I remember how young she is. She is not smiling now. She looks indignant. She is indignant because I am insinuating that there is a problem with the fact that no one in the class will say "nigger." Her indignation pleases me.

33   Good.

34   "I'd just like to remind you all that just because a person refuses to say 'nigger' that doesn't mean that person is not a racist," I say. They seem to consider this.

35   I hold up *Nigger* and show its cover to the class. I hand it to the person on my left, gesture for him to pass the book around the room.

36   "Isn't it strange that when we refer to this book, we keep calling it 'the n-word?'"

37   Lauren comments on the affect of one student who actually said it. "Colin looked like he was being strangled." Of the effect on the other students, she says. "I saw us all collectively cringing."

38   "Would you be able to say it if I weren't here?" I blurt.

39   A few students shake their heads. Tyler's hand shoots up. He always sits directly to my right.

40   "That's just bullshit," he says to the class, and I force myself not to raise an eyebrow at *bullshit*. "If Emily weren't here, you all would be able to say that word."

41   I note that he, himself, has not said it, but do not make this observation out loud.

42   "No," Sarah is firm. "I just don't want to be the kind of person who says that word, period."

43   "Even in this context?" I ask.

44   "Regardless of context." Sarah says.

45   "Even when it's the title of a book?"

46   I tell the students that I often work with a book called *Nigger Heaven*, written in 1926 by a white man, Carl Van Vechten.

47   "Look, I don't want to give you the impression that I am somehow longing for you guys to say 'nigger,'" I tell them, "but I do think that something is lost when you don't articulate it especially if the context almost demands its articulation."

48   "What do you mean? What exactly is lost?" Sarah insists.

49   "I don't know," I say. I do know. But right here, in this moment, the last thing I want is to win an argument that winds up with Sarah saying "nigger" out loud.

SEPTEMBER 2004

50   On the way to school in the morning, I park my car in the Allen House lot.

51   It is true that the library lot is nearly always full in the morning. It's also true that the Allen House lot is relatively empty, and much closer to my office. But if it were even just slightly possible for me to find a space in the library lot, I would probably try to park there, for one reason. To get to my office from Allen House, I have to cross a busy street. To get to my office from the library, I do not.

52   Several months ago, I was crossing the same busy street to get to my office after a class. It was late April, near the end of the semester, and it seemed as if everyone was outside. Parents were visiting, and students were yelling to each other, introducing family members from across the street. People smiled at me—wide, grinning smiles. I smiled back. We were all giddy with the promise of spring, which always comes so late in Vermont, if it comes at all.

53   Traffic was heavy, I noticed as I walked along the sidewalk, calculating the moment when I would attempt to cross. A car was stopped near me; I heard rough voices. Out of the corner of my eye, I looked into the car: all white. I looked away, but I could feel them surveying the small crowd that was carrying me along. As traffic picked up again, one of the male voices yelled out, "Queers! Fags!" There was laughter. Then the car roared off.

54   I was stunned. I stopped walking and let the words wash over me. *Queer. Fag.* Annihilating, surely. I remembered my role as a teacher, a mentor, in loco parentis, even though there were real parents everywhere. I looked around to check for the wounds caused by those hateful words. I peered down the street: too late for a license plate. All around me, students and parents marched to their destinations, as if they hadn't heard. *Didn't you hear that?* I wanted to shout.

55   All the while I was thinking. *Not nigger. Not yet.*

OCTOBER 2004

56   Nate jumps in.

57   "Don't you grant a word power by not saying it? Aren't we, in some way, amplifying its ugliness by avoiding it?" He asks.

58   "I am afraid of how I will be affected by saying it," Lauren says. "I just don't want that word in my mouth."

59   Tyler remembers a phrase attributed to Farai Chideya in Randall Kennedy's essay. He finds it and reads it to us. "She says that the n-word is the 'trump card, the nuclear bomb of racial epithets.' "

60   "Do you agree with that?" I ask.

61   Eleven heads nod vigorously.

62   "Nuclear bombs annihilate. What do you imagine will be destroyed if you guys use the word in here?"

63   Shyly, they look at me, all of them, and I understand. Me. It is my annihilation they imagine.

NOVEMBER 2004

64   *Some of My Best Friends*, my anthology of essays about interracial friendship, came out in August, and the publicity department has arranged for various interviews and other promotional events. When I did an on-air interview with a New York radio show, one of the hosts, Janice, a black woman, told me that the reason she could not marry a white man was because she believed if things ever got heated between them, the white man would call her a nigger.

65   I nodded my head. I had heard this argument before. But strangely I had all but forgotten it. The fact that I had forgotten to fear "nigger" coming from the mouth of my white
husband was more interesting to me than her fear, alive and ever-present.

66   "Are you bi-racial?"

67   "No."

68   "Are you married to a white man?"

69   "Yes."

70   These were among the first words exchanged between Janice, the radio host, and me.
I could tell—by the way she looked at me, and didn't look at me; by the way she kept her
body turned away from me; by her tone—that she had made up her mind about me before
I entered the room. I could tell that she didn't like what she had decided about me, and
that she had decided I was the wrong kind of black person. Maybe it was what I had written in *Some of My Best Friends*. Maybe it was the fact that I had decided to edit a collection
about interracial friendships at all. When we met, she said, "I don't trust white people," as
decisively and exactly as if she were handing me her business card. I knew she was telling
me that I was foolish to trust them, to marry one. I was relieved to look inside myself and
see that I was okay, I was still standing. A few years ago, her silent judgment—this silent
judgment from any black person—would have crushed me.

71   When she said she could "tell" I was married to a white man, I asked her how.
She said, "Because you are so friendly," and did a little dance with her shoulders.
I laughed.

72   But Janice couldn't help it: she liked me in spite of herself. As the interview progressed, she let the corners of her mouth turn up in a smile. She admitted that she had
a few white friends, even if they sometimes drove her crazy. At a commercial break, she
said, "Maybe I ought to try a white man." She was teasing me, of course. She hadn't
changed her mind about white people, or dating a white man, but she had changed her
mind about me. It mattered to me. I took what she was offering. But when the interview
was over, I left it behind.

73   My husband thought my story about the interview was hilarious. When I got home,
he listened to the tape they gave me at the station. He said he wanted to use the interview
in one of his classes.

74   A few days later, I told him what Janice said about dating a white man, that she won't
because she is afraid he will call her a nigger. As I told him, I felt an unfamiliar shyness
creep up on me.

75   "That's just so far out of . . . it's not in my head at all." He was having difficulty coming up with the words he wanted, I could tell. But that was okay. I knew what he meant.
I looked at him sitting in his chair, the chair his mother gave us. I can usually find him in
that chair when I come home. He is John, I told myself. And he is white. No more or less
John and no more or less white than he was before the interview, and Janice's reminder of
the fear that I had forgotten to feel.

76   I tell my students in the African-American autobiography class about Janice. I say,
"You would not believe the indignities I have suffered in my humble attempts to 'move
this product,' as they say in publishing." I say, "I have been surrounded by morons, and
now I gratefully return to the land of the intellectually agile." They laugh.

77   I flatter them, in part because I feel guilty that I have missed so many classes in order to do publicity for my book. But I cringe, thinking of how I have called Janice, another black woman, a "moron" in front of these white students. I do not tell my students she is black.

78   "Here is a story for your students," John tells me. We are in the car, on our way to Cambridge for the weekend. "The only time I ever heard 'nigger' in my home growing up was when my father's cousin was over for a visit. It was 1988, I remember. Jesse Jackson was running for president. My father's cousin was sitting in the kitchen, talking to my parents about the election. 'I'm going to vote for the nigger,' my father's cousin said. 'He's the only one who cares about the workingman.'"

79   John laughs. He often laughs when he hears something extraordinary, whether it's good or bad.

80   "That's fascinating," I say.

81   The next time class meets, I tell my students this story.

82   "So what do we care about in this sentence?" I say. "The fact that John's father's cousin used a racial epithet, or the fact that his voting for Jackson conveys a kind of ultimate respect for him? Isn't his voting for Jackson more important for black progress than how his father's cousin *feels?*"

83   I don't remember what the students said. What I remember is that I tried to project for them a sense that I was untroubled by saying "nigger," by my husband's saying "nigger," by his father's cousin's having said "nigger," by his parents'—my in-laws—tolerance of "nigger" in their home, years ago, long before I came along. What I remember is that I leaned on the word "feels" with a near-sneer in my voice. *It's an intellectual issue.* I beamed at them, and then I directed it back at myself. *It has nothing to do with how it makes me feel.*

84   After my interview with Janice, I look at the white people around me differently, as if from a distance. I do this, from time to time, almost as an exercise. I even do it to my friends, particularly my friends. Which of them has "nigger" in the back of her throat?

85   I go out for drinks with David, my senior colleague. It is a ritual. We go on Thursdays after class, always to the same place.

86   We never say it, but I suspect we both like the waitresses who appreciate the odd figure we cut. He is white, 60-something, male. I am black, 30-something, female. Not such an odd pairing elsewhere, perhaps, but uncommon in Burlington, insofar as black people are uncommon in Burlington.

87   Something you can't see is that we are both from the South. Different Souths, perhaps, 30 years apart, black and white. I am often surprised by how much I like his company. *All the way up here,* I sometimes think when I am with him, *and I am sitting with the South, the white South that, all of my childhood, I longed to escape.* I once had a white boyfriend from New Orleans. "A white Southerner, Emily?" My mother asked, and sighed with worry. I understood. We broke up.

88   David and I catch up. We talk about the writing we have been doing. We talk each other out of bad feelings we are harboring against this and that person. (Like most Southerners, like the South in general, David and I have long memories.) We talk about classes. I describe to him the conversation I have been having with my students about "nigger." He laughs at my anecdotes.

89   Later that evening, I am alone. I remember that David recently gave me a poem of his to read, a poem about his racist grandmother, now dead, whom he remembers using the word "nigger" often and with relish. I lie in bed and reconstruct the scene of David and me in the restaurant, our conversation about "nigger." Was his grandmother at the table with us all along?

90   I tell Hillary, another of my close friends in the department, about the fear I have every day in Burlington, crossing that street to get back and forth from my office, what I do to guard myself against the fear.

91   "Did you grow up hearing that?" she asks. Even though we are close, and alone, she does not say the word.

92   I start to tell her a story I have never told anyone. It is a story about the only time I remember being called a nigger to my face.

93   "I was a teenager, maybe 16. I was standing on a sidewalk, trying to cross a busy street after school, to get to the mall and meet my friends. I happened to make eye contact with a white man in a car that was sort of stopped—traffic was heavy. Anyway, he just said it, kind of spit it up at me."

94   "*Oh, that's why,*" I say, stunned, remembering the daily ritual I have just confessed to her. She looks at me, just as surprised.

DECEMBER 2004

95   In lieu of a final class, my students come over for dinner. One by one, they file in, John takes coats while I pretend to look for things in the refrigerator. I can't stop smiling.

96   "The books of your life" is the topic for tonight. I have asked them to bring a book, a poem, a passage, some art that has affected them. Hazel has brought a children's book. Tyler talks about *Saved by the Bell*. Nate talks about Freud. Dave has a photograph. Eric reads "The Seacoast of Despair" from *Slouching Towards Bethlehem*.

97   I read from *Annie John* by Jamaica Kincaid. Later I will wonder why I did not read "Incident" by Countee Cullen, the poem that has been circulating in my head ever since we began our discussion about "nigger." *What held me back from bringing "Incident" to class?* The question will stay with me for months.

98   The night of our dinner is an emotional one. I tell my students that they are the kind of class a professor dreams about. They give me a gift certificate to the restaurant that David and I frequent. I give them copies of *Some of My Best Friends* and inscribe each one. Eric demands a hug, and then they all do; I happily comply. We talk about meeting again as a class, maybe once or twice in the spring. The two students who will be abroad promise to keep in touch through our Listserv, which we all agree to keep going until the end of the school year, at least. After they leave, the house is quiet and empty.

99   Weeks later, I post "Incident" on our Listserv and ask them to respond with their reactions. Days go by, then weeks. Silence. After more prodding, finally Lauren posts an analysis of the poem, and then her personal reactions to it. I thank her online, and ask for more responses. Silence.

100   I get emails and visits from these students about other matters, some of them race-related. Eric still comes by my office regularly. Once he brings his mother to meet me, a

kind and engaging woman who gives me a redolent candle she purchased in France, and tells me her son enjoyed "African-American Autobiography." Eric and I smile at each other.

101   A few days later, I see Eric outside the campus bookstore.

102   "What did you think about 'Incident?"

103   "I've been meaning to write you about it. I promise I will."

104   In the meantime. *Nigger* is back in its special place on my bookshelf. It is tucked away so that only I can see the title on its spine, and then only with some effort.

QUESTIONS ON MEANING

1. Why does Bernard lie to her students about not being any more offended by the word *nigger* than they are?

2. Why do you think Bernard makes it a point to tell her students her Ph.D. is from Yale? Why is this important to her? What is she attempting to communicate to her students by revealing this information?

3. Why doesn't Bernard reveal to her students that Janice—who she had just indirectly referred to as a moron—is black?

4. Why do you think Bernard enjoys the ritual of her Thursday drinks with David, the 60-something white southerner? What happens that slightly alters their relationship? Who was more responsible for that change, Bernard or David? Why?

5. What is Bernard's primary purpose with this essay? Can you identify her purpose? Does the essay have a thesis? If so, what is it? If not, then what kind of essay is it? Do you think Bernard accomplished her purpose in this essay?

QUESTIONS FOR DISCUSSION

1. This essay deals with certain types of language use, specifically the use of a word that has such charged emotional and political meaning in the United States. Should use of this word be banned? Who should be allowed to use this word? Is it acceptable for some to use this word and not others? Why?

2. What is the relationship between the concerns of this essay and issues of freedom of speech? What about other forms of hate speech? What ethical responsibilities do we have toward our fellow citizens when it comes to using potentially offensive or hurtful language?

3. In what ways can an analysis of the history and use of the word *nigger* tell us about race relations in the United States? What can it tell us about our own feelings toward race?

4. Bernard tells the story of the time her husband heard the word *nigger* used in his home by his father's cousin. Imagine you were in that home at the time. What would you say to John's father's cousin? How would you respond?

LOOKING AT RHETORIC

1. Bernard uses a considerable amount of dialogue in this essay. How does this dialogue contribute to her objectives as a writer? Is the essay more or less interesting because of the dialogue? Is it more or less effective in communicating its message because of the dialogue?

2. Note that the essay is organized by time, and that the times are not in chronological order. Why do you think Bernard broke up the story in this way? Is it effective? How might her essay be related to the movie *Pulp Fiction*? What does she have to say about that movie in the essay itself?

WRITING ASSIGNMENTS

1. Using library and/or Internet resources, spend some time researching the history of another word that is deemed controversial in the English language (do not use the word *nigger* or one of the traditional swear words, however). Write an essay in which you talk about the history of that word and discuss the cultural implications for its use today.

2. Modeling your own writing after that of Bernard, draft an essay in which you analyze a particularly difficult social issue—related to race, religion, politics, sexuality, or some other issue of contemporary interest—by relating a story from your own life, or the life of someone close to you. Use dialogue and description when you are able. We recommend, of course, that you choose a story and an issue that you don't mind sharing with an audience. Avoid focusing on some issue of such personal gravity that you might regret revealing it to an audience. By telling your story, try to get your audience to see a particularly difficult issue in a new way.

3. In pairs or in groups, imagine you are a research group charged with coming up with a simple public policy that will govern public use of the word *nigger*. Come up with a proposed set of laws or guidelines for use of the word. Can anyone say it? If so, who? Under what circumstances? Share your set of policy statements with the other groups in class. Then, as an individual, draft an essay in which you present your guidelines and defend them. For the purposes of this exercise, imagine that you are drafting your essay in the form of a public policy press release being given by a state or federal official.

Straight Man's Burden

Jeff Sharlet

Jeff Sharlet (b. 1972) is a journalist, author, and editor whose work has tended to focus on the often uneasy marriage of religion, society, and politics. He is the author of C Street: The Fundamentalist Threat to American Democracy *(2010),* The Family: The Secret Fundamentalism at the Heart of American Power *(2008) and is the co-author of* Killing the Buddha: A Heretic's Bible *(2004). Sharlet is a frequent contributor to* Rolling Stone, Harper's, The Chronicle of Higher Education, *and numerous other magazines and journals. He has also made numerous guest appearances on a variety of television programs, including* The Daily Show, Hardball, *the* Rachel Maddow Show, *and on news segments on CNN, NPR, and the BBC. As will be evident in the following selection, Sharlet is known both for his engaging, lively style and for his willingness to dig into controversial topics on the fringe of religious culture.*

1   A young man who called himself Blessed had agreed to meet me in front of the Speke Hotel, the oldest in Kampala, Uganda's capital, but he was late, very late, and I had no way to contact him. Emailing me from a café, he'd said he didn't have a phone; calling from a pay phone, he'd said he didn't have a watch. The friends who'd put me in touch with him said he didn't have an address. I'd seen a picture of him: he had a long neck, a narrow face, and a broad smile that made him look both kind and a little sly. I wanted to talk

to him precisely because he was hard to find, because he was gay, and because he was on the run.

2   On October 14, 2009, a Ugandan member of parliament named David Bahati introduced legislation called the Anti-Homosexuality Bill. Among its provisions: up to three years in prison for failure to report a homosexual; seven years for "promotion;" life imprisonment for a single homosexual act; and, for "aggravated homosexuality" (which includes gay sex while HIV-positive, gay sex with a disabled person, or, if you're a recidivist, gay sex with anyone—marking the criminal as a "serial offender"), death. As of this writing, the bill has yet to pass, despite near-unanimous support in Parliament. But the violence has been building, a crackling fury not yet quite a fire: beatings, disappearances, "corrective" rapes of lesbians, blacklists in a national tabloid, vigilante squads and church crusades, preachers calling out "homos" in their own pews.

3   It was Blessed's pastor, a celebrity with an American following, who had outed him. "Am being hunted by my family at the moment," he'd written in an email apologizing for his inability to commit to dinner plans. "Am moving place to place now." Then, in case I didn't understand: "They want to kill me."

4   The Speke is nothing grand, just a succession of stucco arches, but smartly located midway between the business district and the president's office, just down the hill from the gated gardens of the luxury Sheraton. At night, *mzungus* (white men—aid workers, oilmen, missionaries) come to shop for twenty-dollar prostitutes at the outdoor bar. By day, the Ugandan elite meet at the sidewalk tables. They ignore the whores, regal women who sip colas while they wait for evening, and likely have no idea that the hotel also serves as one of the city's few havens for gays and lesbians.

5   Certainly Miria Matembe didn't know. I'd been looking for her too. Then one night, there she was, pointed out to me by my friend Robert, a Ugandan journalist I'd hired to show me around. "That is Honorable right there," he said. Uganda's first minister of ethics and integrity, the Honorable Matembe, now out of government, was working as a private lawyer. A small woman in a brown power suit, with short hair styled upward, she charged through the café tables with two cell phones simultaneously in action.

6   "Honorable!" I called, and ran after her. She trapped one phone between her shoulder and her ear, stared at me, and held up a finger: Stop. She crooked it: Follow. She pointed: Speak. I whispered beneath her two conversations, telling her that I'd heard she'd been at a planning meeting for the Anti-Homosexuality Bill, that I was writing about the Fellowship, and that I wanted to understand the connection.

7   "Wait!" Matembe said into her phones. Then, to me: "You are funny!" She chortled, held up five fingers, and walked away.

8   The Fellowship is the Ugandan Parliament's branch of an American evangelical movement of the same name, also called the Family. The Family differs from most fundamentalist groups in its preference for those whom it calls "key men," political and business elites, over the multitude. The bill's author, MP Bahati, the de facto leader of the Ugandan branch, has become a national star for his crusade against gays. Winston Churchill called Uganda "the pearl of Africa;" the Family agrees. In the past ten years, it has poured millions into "leadership development" there, more than it has invested in any other foreign country, and billions in U.S. foreign aid have flowed into Ugandan coffers since a Family leader

turned on the tap twenty-four years ago for President Yoweri Museveni, a dictator hailed by the West for his democratic rhetoric and by Christian conservatives for the evangelical zeal of his regime.

9   Every year, right before Uganda's Independence Day, the government holds a National Prayer Breakfast modeled on the Family's event in Washington. Americans, among them Republican Senator Jim Inhofe of Oklahoma, former attorney general John Ashcroft—both longtime Family men and outspoken antigay activists—and Pastor Rick Warren, are a frequent attraction at the Ugandan Fellowship's weekly meetings. "He said homosexuality is a sin and that we should fight it," Bahati recalled of Warren's visits.

10   Inhofe and Warren, like most American fundamentalists, came out in muted opposition to Uganda's gay death penalty, but they didn't dispute the motive behind it: the eradication of homosexuality. They may disagree on the means, favoring a "cure" rather than killing, but not the ends. For years, American fundamentalists have looked on Uganda as a laboratory for theocracy, though most prefer such terms as "government led by God." They sent not just money and missionaries but ideas, and if the money disappeared and the missionaries came and went, the ideas took hold. Ugandan evangelicals sing American songs and listen to sermons about American problems, often from American preachers. Ugandan politicians attend prayer breakfasts in America and cut deals with evangelical American businessmen. American evangelicals, in turn, hold up Ugandan congregations as role models for their own, and point to Ugandan AIDS policy—from which American evangelicals nearly stripped condom distribution altogether—as proof that public-health problems can be solved by moral remedies. It is a classic fundamentalist maneuver: move a fight you can't win in the center to the margins, then broadcast the results back home.

11   Half an hour after our first encounter, Honorable Matembe and two friends plopped down at my table. Night had come, the air was cooling, the prostitutes were rustling, and the guards—skinny men with wide-mouthed shotguns—were guiding the white SUVs of Uganda's elite in and out of the drop-off zone a few feet from our table. "You wanna talk about homos?" Matembe asked. She drew the word out for comic effect. Honorable—in Uganda even former politicians go by their honorifics—had a booming voice that rose above the *boda-boda* bikes, the careering motorcycle taxis that rule Kampala's cratered streets, but she stage-whispered a list of practices she knew to be common to homos: boy-rape, blasphemy, "golden showers." Then she threw back her head and cackled.

12   "I was the first person to fight homosexuality!" she shouted. During the late 1990s, American missionaries were rushing in, a revival sweeping the land. Ugandan Catholics and Anglicans made evangelical causes and evangelical pariahs—including homosexuality—their own. Matembe, who said she was one of the original members of Uganda's parliamentary Fellowship group, was in the vanguard.

13   "I used to come here and catch them!" She mimed sneaking up and pouncing. "People used to tell me where they were hiding." For a brief period, gay life had almost flourished in Kampala. Gay men cruised the streets, and parties at the Speke Hotel began to take on the political cast of an identity in formation. Matembe put a stop to that. "You see Matembe walk into a place," said Matembe, "and you disappear!" She sipped her beer and ate some nuts. "Eventually, of course, people went underground."

14   That was all right with her. The closet, she believed, was a fine African tradition. That made her a liberal; she didn't want to kill gays. "First of all, I am a human-rights activist," she said. "My activism is guided by godly principles. Therefore, I don't support homosexuality as a human right. Why? Because my beautiful—my godly conviction is that homosexuality is not a sin but a curse! Looking at homosexuality as a curse by God, I do not prescribe the death sentence for such people."

15   Her real problem with the bill, she said, "is it makes us all potential criminals." She was referring to a provision designed to enlist every Ugandan in the war against the gays. "Like, if I am speaking with you, and if I find you are a homosexual . . . " She'd have twenty-four hours to report me or face a prison sentence of up to three years. This, she thought, was unfair. To her.

16   She wanted to make it clear that she bore no responsibility for David Bahati's bill. Who did? American politicians and pastors, Matembe believed, their disavowals notwithstanding. "The Prayer Breakfast continues, but I no longer go to it. They were corrupted. It is the Americans! Confused as usual, exploiting." She sighed, depleted. Then she rallied, remembering the good old days. "But I was the first! I fought the homos!"

17   The owner of the hotel swooped down on the table, cutting her off. "Honorable Matembe!" he cried. He took her gently by her arm and lifted her from us, petting her and flattering her, quieting her. She was scaring away the trade.

18   The lobby was empty when Blessed arrived, an hour late. He wore crisp black slacks and a lime-green long-sleeved shirt underneath a black sweater vest, too warm for the weather. Only twenty, he tried to carry himself like an older, courtlier man. He apologized for his impeccable appearance with what he hoped sounded like a joke. "I am a bit homeless at the moment," he said, and then chuckled, as if this were merely an inconvenience. Walking up the hill to the Sheraton for dinner, he began to tell me his story.

19   He was the only son of educated parents, his father a lawyer and his mother a bureaucrat. He had a happy childhood, "normal" in every way. His parents loved him, and he loved them. They sent him to an elite boys' school in his father's hometown, and Blessed loved that too. An affectionate child, he liked to touch people, to hug, to kiss. By the age of twelve, he knew that his hugs and his kisses with other boys—not unusual in Uganda, where straight men sometimes hold hands—felt different from those with girls. And this didn't bother him. He was a good student, but his teachers told him his head was in the clouds. That sounded nice: up there, he didn't see conflict; he saw love. By the time he was fourteen he'd found six other boys in the school who felt as he did, and he loved them.

20   All of them? "Of course I loved them. Because God loves me."

21   His family was Catholic but not very religious. Neither was Blessed; he said he felt spiritual. Not in the vaguely agnostic American sense. He was like a holy fool, a boy for whom everything was sacred: church, his friendships, the rainbows over Lake Victoria, the white egrets in the trees, his books, the touches, the caresses.

22   The orgasms? Of course. Everything sweet, he believed, was holy. He began calling himself "Blessed" not long after he and his friends were turned in to their headmaster, who beat them, expelled them, and then sent them to the police. They spent forty-eight hours in jail. "It was so much fun!" Just imagine, he said—holding my eyes, his voice low— "Remember when you were sixteen?" Sixteen, forty-eight hours, the six sexiest people in the

world, as far as you were concerned, all in one cell. "I call myself 'Blessed,'" he explained, "because that's what I am, so fortunate to be born like this." Like this: gay, and so in love with the world that even in jail he forgot about the bars.

23   We'd taken an outdoor table, as far as possible from other people. Dinner was a buffet, and Blessed had heaped his plate high. He was built like a sapling, but the hillock of food disappeared and he went back for seconds. "I think you need to eat more too," he told me, though I'm more baobab than sapling. "I like white men," he added quickly, in case he'd insulted me. "Are you gay?" he asked.

24   "Well, no," I said, embarrassed, a straight man in a country ruled by would-be gay killers.

25   Blessed didn't see it like that. "Oh!" he said, "Then you have children? Let me see!" He spent ten minutes cooing over pictures of my daughter.

26   After his expulsion, he moved back to Kampala and began attending a new school. His parents wouldn't pay; Blessed washed cars. His love took on a more political form: he began organizing youth clubs to talk about sex. Not just gay sex but straight sex too, and all the shades in between. He'd never experienced sex as anything but a gift, yet he understood that most teenagers are as terrified of sex as they are drawn to it. He wanted them to know about condoms, HIV, and abortion, but he also wanted them to believe that the good parts were "good news," just like their pastors said of Christ. "I don't think Jesus is against us," he said, waving away the absurd thought with a gesture so fey I looked over my shoulder to make sure the waiter hadn't seen.

27   Around the time Blessed became Blessed, he began attending Pentecostal churches, "spirit-filled" places where you sang and danced and maybe experienced the gift of tongues, babbling in languages granted you by God. The songs were American as often as African, the churches were sprinkled with handsome *mzungus*, and there was a lot of laying on of hands. It felt cosmopolitan, modern. Blessed's favorite pastor was Martin Ssempa, who appeared in music videos in Uganda and in pulpits in the United States. Every Saturday night Ssempa led a service—a party, really—called Primetime, held at Makerere University's outdoor pool. It was fun, even though, technically, it was antifun: an abstinence rally. But Blessed, and plenty of straight kids, were there to cruise. It was hard not to—girls in their Saturday best, hot pink dresses tight around the hips and cling-ing baby T's, boys in American hip-hop style, pants low, shirts giant, young faces lean.

28   Ssempa was beautiful too, golden-skinned, the handsomest bald man you ever saw, beckoning from the stage across the pool, which glowed in the night. The band thumped and Ssempa called, as if the kids might actually walk on the water. The story he told was almost always the same: sex (it's going to be awesome!), sex (it'll be wonderful *someday*), sex (wait just a little bit longer now). And then everybody would jump. A thousand, some-times two thousand young Ugandans hopping in time as high as they could, holding on to one another lest they fall in the pool, giggling. "Holy laughter," some called it. It was a gift they believed came from the Holy Ghost, just like tongues; and some had heard about "holy kissing," another gift—not carnal!—the Spirit in the flesh. There were gay boys, and drag kings, and straight kids who might peer around the bend, all waiting, not having sex together, except when they were. "It was so hot!" said Blessed.

29   Then came the day Blessed had to choose a side. It was 2007, and he was in court, as spectator and supporter. The case being heard was called *Yvonne Oyoo and Juliet Mukasa v.*

Attorney General. Victor Juliet Mukasa, a transman—born female, living male, interested in girls—taught Blessed—the sweet, femme boy—to be a man, a gay man, without ever meeting him.

30   Like Blessed, Juliet Mukasa knew as a child that she was attracted to children of the same sex. And like Blessed she'd been raised Catholic but had joined an American-style Pentecostal church, hoping that in the music and the dancing and the Holy Ghost—the ecstasy—she would find the resolution of her desires. But Juliet Mukasa was not as skilled as Blessed at leading two lives. Dressed like a girl, she couldn't think. A pastor determined that she was possessed by a "male spirit" and asked his flock to help him heal her. As women in the pews swayed and sang for Mukasa's liberation, the exorcism took place at the altar, boys and men from the church laying on hands and speaking in tongues. They took her arms, gently then firmly, and stripped her. Slowly, garment by garment, praying over each piece of demonically polluted cloth. She'd bound her breasts. They bared them. "I cried, and every time I cried they would call it 'liberation.'" They slapped her, but it was holy slapping, and when she stood before them naked, the men's hands roaming over her and then inside, they said that was holy too.

31   Then they locked her in a room and raped her. For a week. This is considered a corrective; a medical procedure, really; a cure. When it was all over, the pastor declared that the church had freed Mukasa. Maybe, in a sense, it had. Victor Mukasa no longer believed there was a demon inside him. The demons were in the church.

32   Mukasa became a man and an activist, determined to prevent what had happened to him from happening again. In 2003, he cofounded Freedom and Roam Uganda, an organization for lesbian, bisexual, transgender, and intersex human rights. In 2005, Ugandan police, led by government officials, raided his house. They didn't find him. But a friend, Yvonne Oyoo, was there. They took her to the station. You look like a man, they said. We're going to prove you're a woman. They stripped her, fondled her breasts.

33   Mukasa fled. But in hiding and then in exile, he planned. The plan wasn't lesbian, it wasn't gay, it was . . . human, Blessed would say. It was a citizen's plan: Mukasa sued, and never was a lawsuit more like a gift of the spirit, the romance of the rule of law.

34   Blessed, of course, was a romantic boy. He thought the trial was exciting! He wanted to be there, and so did his friends. They would swish for dignity, drag for democracy, be themselves for God and Victor Mukasa. Blessed could hardly wait. What he didn't know was that his beautiful pastor, Martin Ssempa, was gathering an opposing force. Blessed, with his head in the clouds! He hadn't paid attention. When he walked into the courtroom—late, as always—he could not have faced a starker choice. "Blessed!" called his church friends. Ssempa saw him and smiled. Blessed looked down at the T-shirt he'd chosen for the occasion: a rainbow. He looked to the other side of the room. His gay friends looked back. Some of them sighed. They knew how it was. If, with his sly, earnest smile, he chose Ssempa today, they would forgive him tomorrow. If he didn't—the truth was, he didn't know. All that would follow, all that he would lose, was beyond his imagination.

35   "I don't know if I have a very strong heart," he told me. "I do not know if I am a tough man."

36   How did you make your choice, Blessed?

37   He gave me the smile, a mask for all he had lost. "I had a breakthrough." "Breakthrough," for Ugandan Christians, is a spiritual term. A gift from the Holy Ghost. Grace, in whatever shape it's needed. "I got courage."

38   Blessed sat down with the homos.

39   And then something like a miracle occurred: Victor Mukasa and Yvonne Oyoo won. The court ruled that the state had transgressed. Yes, homosexuality was illegal in Uganda, but there was still due process, even for homos, and the police had violated it. Without warrants, you cannot kick in doors, take prisoners, strip them, do what had been done to Victor Mukasa and Yvonne Oyoo.

40   Unless, that is, you change the law. Which is what a small coalition of Ugandans, inspired by American fundamentalism, set out to do. In the beginning they weren't shy about their American influences. They invited American antigay activists, most notably Scott Lively—coauthor, with Kevin Abrams, of a book called *The Pink Swastika*, which blames the rise of Nazism on homosexuals—to address Parliament, and even drafted the bill with what appeared to be the concerns of their American friends in mind. Indeed, the bill followed, with remarkable precision, the talking points not of Lively, a fringe character, but of mainstream evangelicals and conservative politicians. It singled out same-sex marriage as a threat to Ugandan heterosexuality and in an opening clause declared the bill a model for other nations—such as those where same-sex marriage was a legal possibility.

41   One camp within the antigay movement, led by Pastor Michael Kyazze, argues that Ugandans must admit that homosexuality is an internal Ugandan problem. Martin Ssempa, Kyazze's friend, had a different perspective, Kyazze told me, when I went to see him at his church. "Now, Martin, he believes it is *you*."

42   "Me?" I had worn a suit and tie, a terrible choice on a blazing day. I began to sweat.

43   Kyazze, a tall, broad man with a slight stoop and a gentle rasp, laughed and patted my hand. "No, not you, Jeff. You Americans." Kyazze, Pastor Moses Solomon Male, and I were sitting around a table in Kyazze's office. The Omega Healing Center, Kyazze's church, was small by Ugandan standards, just 2,500 regulars and a full-time school for 400 students, a spread of one-story classrooms arrayed around a garden spiked with signs reminding students of the righteous path: SAY NO TO HOMOSEXUALITY. AVOID SEX BEFORE MARRIAGE. A young teacher took my photograph beside the most ambitious proverb of all: ALWAYS SAY NO TO SEX.

44   "What Martin means," Kyazze continued, "is that the Americans, the Europeans, the Dutch, are under the control of the homo." That was a curious statement for Ssempa, since he'd received significant support from the United States, most notably at least $90,000 for his church through the federal anti-AIDS program. In 2005 and 2006 he appeared at Rick Warren's Orange County megachurch. "You are my brother, Martin, and I love you," Warren's wife declared from the stage, eyes watering.

45   Kyazze, with a more modest network of American supporters, worried that Ssempa was too close to the West. "The homosexuals can use your organizations to spread their ways," Kyazze explained. "To recruit, you see. There are many methods, you know."

46   I did; David Bahati had listed several by phone before I came to Uganda. Among the most insidious: iPods. Also, laptops and cell phones. Gay recruiters are said to offer them

the way pedophiles entice with lollipops. "But it is technology. So much more seductive," Bahati had explained. "Always the new thing."

47   "The iPad?" I'd asked.

48   "Yes, this could happen."

49   "To me?" One could dream.

50   Kyazze had bigger trouble in mind. "The homos use UNICEF—this is true!—to attempt to colonize Uganda." He meant a 2002 pamphlet, "the Teenagers Toolkit," that had referred to homosexuality as natural. He clapped his hands together. "This is absolutely correct, what I am informing you. But. It is only one half of the story!"

51   "Yes," murmured Pastor Male, Kyazze's sidekick. He was a graying, fine-boned man, given to stroking a stiff, blue-striped tie. "Is it possible that one nationality would have homosexuality and another would not? No. You see, this is an area where we disagree with Pastor Ssempa. We have democracy, and we have science. We have these two powerful weapons and—with God!—we can fight homosexuality. And we know it is here. It is in *us*."

52   Kyazze and Male are nothing if not ambitious. Their main complaint with the Anti-Homosexuality Bill is that it is actually too lenient. They see a clause forbidding the media from exposing victims of same-sex rape as evidence of a gay infiltrator within their ranks. Even James Buturo, Honorable Matembe's successor as Uganda's minister of ethics and integrity, and the current chair of the weekly Family meeting in Parliament, is suspect in their eyes. (They don't think he's gay, but they wonder whether he's protecting someone.) Like many Ugandans, both pastors believe the bill's timing has more to do with a massive corruption investigation.

53   "First," said Male, "Buturo does nothing. Then, all of a sudden, 'We must act right away!' We said, 'Please, Honorable, let us be scientific about this. The government must provide funds for a proper study. We must know how many homosexuals there are, where they are. We must be modern in our approach.' But Buturo said to us, 'We're going to kill them, so we don't have to have this inquiry.' He knows that if we study it, we will find it in the government!"

54   What about Bahati? I asked. Both men sighed.

55   "Honorable is a good boy," said Kyazze, who, at forty-nine, is thirteen years Bahati's senior. "But he is too eager. He says, 'Forget about the inquiry! We must stop them right now.' He sees the danger. He feels the evil wind of the homosexual. But the eye of the storm and the whirlwind are two different things. What we are dealing with is a moral problem." The solution required a force greater than law: Christ, transcendent, purifier of nations.

56   There was a hint of sectarian rivalry in their critique. Bahati, like Buturo, is an Anglican. Kyazze and Male are Pentecostals; when Kyazze goes to America, it's to preach in working-class mega-churches. Bahati prays quietly, eyes closed and hands folded. Male in prayer looks like the bride of Frankenstein, head tipped back, hands rigid, eyes jolted wide by the Spirit. Ethnic differences matter as well. Uganda's tribes are held together so delicately that last year the government took four radio stations off the air for allegedly inciting genocide. What they'd done, in fact, was simply to report on ethnic rioting, but in Uganda, genocide is not an abstraction. It is a living memory. In the 1970s, Idi Amin murdered hundreds of thousands of his countrymen. In the 1980s, a war between dictator Milton Obote and Museveni's bush army killed hundreds of thousands more. Museveni,

once in power, was different. He disposed of his enemies through "accidents" and frame-ups, not massacres. He wasn't a kleptocrat, but he surrounded himself with thieves—on the theory, apparently, that rich men are peaceful men. Still, he is a dictator, and dictators need enemies. For years, the enemy was a vicious rebel group called the Lord's Resistance Army, but the LRA has been reduced to a few hundred child fighters. Enter the homosexual: singular, an archetype—a bogeyman.

57   "Is the death penalty a good idea?" I'd asked a pretty girl named Sharon at Martin Ssempa's weekly abstinence rally on the campus of Makerere University.

58   "It's good because the Bible condemns it." She smiled, a flash of neat little teeth, and leaned in close to be heard over the thumping hip-hop.

59   "Have you ever met a homosexual?"

"I have never!"

60   "If you met one, would you kill him?"

61   "It's hard for me to kill." That smile. Those teeth. "It is hard for me to do it alone."

62   "But together?" She giggled and nodded.

63   David Bahati is a dapper man, not a dandy but stylish. On the afternoon of our first meeting, lunch at the Serena Hotel, he was wearing a dove-gray suit, a tie of chocolate brown stripes, and an ivory shirt. He'd chosen our table carefully; it was on an elevated platform, in the middle of the room but with a high wall behind him. He could take the corner but still be the center of attention. The maître d' knew him; the other politicians—identifiable because they were in the restaurant, one of the most expensive in Kampala—wanted to talk to him. He offered them little flutters of his fingers. But for the waitstaff, or an occasional businessman, he'd rise up out of his seat and twist around over the wall behind him, clasping hands with controlled explosions of giggles followed by terse exchanges. People liked him. They were afraid of him. He wasn't what I'd imagined (a bumpkin, a Tom Coburn, a country mouse come to the city and crying "gay!" at everything that offended him). He was something more compact, tougher: a cannier George Wallace for Uganda.

64   "David," I said, "you're a player."

65   He smiled, half-shy, half-pleased, and summoned a waiter with the same flutter he used on his colleagues, ordering for both of us in Lugandan, one of his three languages along with English and his native Rukiga, the language of Uganda's Bakiga minority.

66   The restaurant's interior was white. Windows halfway round. Outside, sculpted greenery, lily pads, spiky trees, tall grasses, like Africa on TV.

67   "You know, Bob was here," said Bahati. He gestured to a table behind us. "Bob" was Bob Hunter, the Family's spokesman on the Anti-Homosexuality Bill, a former official with the Ford and Carter administrations who, working with American politicians, had first established the organization's relationship with the Museveni regime when it came to power in 1986. Back then part of the goal he'd outlined in two lengthy memos had been to make sure that "the most Christian country in Africa not take the wrong ideological direction," but he considers himself a liberal and thought that the bill was the wrong way to address homosexuality. He also thought it was a PR problem for the Family.

68   "We sat right at that table," said Bahati. The purpose of his meeting with Hunter had been "to mend fences," Bahati said. In the weeks leading up to the 2010 National

Prayer Breakfast in February, gay-rights groups, protesting the Family's links to the Anti-Homosexuality Bill, had asked Obama not to attend. Hunter first told the press that Bahati hadn't been invited, then that he had but declined. Bahati said neither statement was true. "When Bob talked to me he was talking about the pressure the gay community is exerting on the Fellowship," Bahati had told me by phone in February. "He communicated his fear that this might cause the destruction of the National Prayer Breakfast. He was trying to control the damage. He has never said, 'David, what you are doing is a problem.' What he has said is to discuss the pressure from the gays."

69   And now?

70   "We talked about you!" He said Hunter had told him I was not to be trusted, that I was interested in the story just for money. (Hunter denies that this part of the conversation took place.) Bahati giggled, displaying a spray of teeth. A scar down the middle of his forehead gives him the appearance of having a permanently furrowed brow, but when he laughed he sounded like a boy. It was the most reassuring thing about him. Then he clamped his mouth shut, the right side of his jaw pulsing.

71   Bahati is a man of many influences. He was educated in Uganda, at Cardiff University in Wales, and at the Wharton School at the University of Pennsylvania, with financial support from a foundation in Norway. His mother died in childbirth. His father, he says, was poisoned by a business associate three years later. He lived in Kabale, a market town of forty thousand in southwestern Uganda. "I sold things you cannot understand," he told me. (That sounded dramatic, but what he meant was bananas and cigarettes.)

72   He won one scholarship after another, and he became an accountant. But he felt God wanted more from him. In 2004, on the advice of two friends who'd studied in the United States at the fundamentalist Family Research Council, he went to America to learn the art of political campaigning at the Leadership Institute, a well-funded school of "political technology" for conservative activists. *Young man*, a politician he met there—he won't say who—told him, *you need to visit the Cedars*, the Family's headquarters, a white-pillared Georgian mansion in Arlington, Virginia. When he returned home in 2006 and won his parliamentary seat, the first thing he did was look for the Ugandan Fellowship he'd learned about in America.

73   "God uses instruments to make his purpose be fulfilled," Bahati said, after we'd filled our plates. "He uses voters to lift somebody up to bring them to where you are. Eh?" *Eh*—that was his all-purpose word, good for acknowledgment, dismissal, or coercion. I nodded despite myself, confirming his self-anointing. "God puts people in a place. The Bible says in Romans 13 that all authority comes from God." He pointed his fork at me. "All authority comes from God. Eh?" Nod. "Yes," he said, smiling, as though I were an apt pupil. "For example, I didn't champion this issue, homosexuality, for the whole world. I did it for Uganda. That was me. But God!" Bahati pointed up. "God made it bigger. We are going to get the bill through, now or later. And when we do, we will *close* the door to homosexuality, and *open* society to something larger."

74   That was the crux of the matter for Bahati. To him, homosexuality is only a symptom of what he learned from the Family to be a greater plague: government by people, not by God. *The burden is on you, David*, his American friends told him. Inhofe's staff had sent word, he said, and there were others—about half a dozen American leaders who supported

his cause. He couldn't name them, though, because the gays would destroy them. (That's what they'd told Bahati.) *You must fight the battle*. "We have talked to a number of conservatives in America who believe that what we are doing is right, and that if we do not close the door to homosexuality at this time, it would be too late for us to breathe," he told me. "They wish that homosexuality was confronted and fought severely in America."

75   There was still hope for Africa. God would use the weak to teach the strong, a Bahati to send a message to America. God had given him a Word, divine insight, five years earlier, on the eve of his first journey to America. Five words, actually, Isaiah 6:8, illuminated for Bahati by Jesus: "Here am I; send me." The words of the prophet Isaiah to the Lord, the words of the Lord for Bahati; his "prayer team" had used the verse as a campaign slogan. Smartly divorced, that is, from what follows, just two verses later: *Then said I, Lord, how long? And he answered, / Until the cities be wasted without inhabitant, / And the houses without man, / And the land be utterly desolate, / And the* LORD *have removed men far away, / And there be a great forsaking in the midst of the land.*

76   Prophecy isn't kind, but Bahati was brave. He knew his bill, if passed—and in Uganda, voters wanted it passed—would lead to a great forsaking, indeed: of foreign aid, the lifeblood of what passes for an economy in a country where job seekers outnumber jobs fifty to one. People would starve. There would be no medicine for AIDS. And it might be worse than that. The dictator was old, his grip was weakening, and war might be coming. It was hard to conceive, after at least 300,000 dead under Amin and as many as half a million lost in the fight that brought Museveni to power, that Uganda would ever return to the slaughter. But they would do what God asked of them, Bahati believed. They would be a God-led nation, a light unto the world. Bahati and a pastor ally whom he'd put on the government payroll said Fellowship groups in the governments of countries across the continent—Rwanda, Burundi, Tanzania, Zambia, Congo—had requested copies of his bill, or better yet, a personal appearance. The message was spreading, with Bahati as its apostle, suddenly the most famous Ugandan since Idi Amin.

77   He wanted to bring the message back to the source. "If I came to America, what do you think would happen?"

78   "I think there would be protests," I said. In 2010 there'd been protests at the Prayer Breakfast for the first time in five decades just on the possibility that Bahati *might* show.

79   "I want to come one of these days and see. What do you think is the best way to come in? Eh?"

80   "I wouldn't make it public."

81   "Ah! So the best way would be to sneak in?"

82   "Just go as a regular traveler."

83   "But they wouldn't hurt me?" He claimed to have survived several gay poisoning attempts already. The Family, he'd been told, was also under gay attack. In Uganda the gays used poison; in America, "blackmail."

84   How did that work?

85   He couldn't explain. The gays, he said, have secret ways.

86   "Spiritual warfare?" I asked.

87   "Mm-mmm." Bahati smiled, pleased that I had invoked the dark side of his faith, the invisible work of the spirit that selects between men of God and those outside His circle. Spiritual warfare is a concept as old as the New Testament, but, through the literalist

filter of twentieth-century American fundamentalism, it has taken on magical meaning, imbuing the actions of its believers with supernatural significance. He gestured toward me, my presence in Uganda, and the dining room of the Serena, Kampala's international stage.

88   I saw where he was going. "That must mean something's going on here."

89   "Yes. Something . . . " He paused. "Invisible." Spiritual warfare, that is, the amplification of angels and their worldly counterparts, American allies. With that power came enemies.

90   "You believe in the reality of demons?" I asked.

91   "Demons, yes."

92   "Do you think homosexuality is a form of demonic possession?"

93   He giggled. "It is *modern* witchcraft," Bahati clarified. Modern witchcraft isn't a matter of chicken heads or curses, he explained; it's about information, the suppression or selective release of truths. "It is manipulation for control and dominance."

94   And what about the lies he claimed his American friends had told about his invitation to the Prayer Breakfast, his role in the organization, his visits to Washington? Were those "modern witchcraft"? No. What was the distinction? Perspective, thought Bahati. Take a lie and turn it upside down. What do you see?

95   The truth?

96   Bahati giggled again. No. "*Unnecessary* truth." Truths, that is, that are too subtle for the public to understand.

QUESTIONS ON MEANING

1. According to Sharlet's article, what is the relationship between the anti-gay movement in Uganda and American religious subculture?

2. Compare and contrast the attitude of Matembe and Bahati. Whose attitude strikes you as more just? More humane? More correct?

3. Why do Kyazze and Male believe the anti-homosexual bill is too lenient?

4. What is Sharlet's feeling toward Bahati? What words or phrases in the essay reveal Sharlet's attitude?

5. What do we learn about Bahati from the discussion he has with Robert and Chalet over a bill that would require the Ugandan media to pass a values test?

6. Compare Blessed with Bahati. What political and social values do each of these characters represent?

QUESTIONS FOR DISCUSSION

1. Does reading this essay on the treatment of gays in Uganda provide insight into the ways gays are treated in America? Why or why not? In what ways are the controversies discussed in the essay specifically Ugandan controversies? In what ways are they American controversies?

2. What is Sharlet's attitude toward The Family (aka The Fellowship)? What is his attitude toward fundamentalism? What phrases or passages in the essay reveal these attitudes? Had

Interdisciplinary Connections

Guns in America: Two Views

The second amendment to the U.S. constitution reads "well regulated Militia, being necessary to the security of a free State, the right of the people to keep and bear Arms, shall not be infringed." This statement has been a focal point for major controversy throughout the country from the time of its adoption as an amendment to the present day. To be sure, American culture has been influenced greatly by gun use and gun ownership. Below are two images related to gun culture in America. The first is an advertisement for a revolver from a century ago. The second is a recent image from an ad campaign in Chicago aimed at stopping gun violence in the city. Are these ads effective? What details about each ad contributes to its message or its effectiveness? Do you find one more provocative or convincing than the other? If you were designing an advertisement for a gun, how would you design it? On the other hand, how would you design an anti-gun ad?

Revolver Advertisement from 1904

http://www.theblogofrecord.com/wp-content/uploads/2009/08/safe-revolver-advertisement-19042.jpg

Live Boy Walking

http://www.examiner.com/pr-and-advertising-in-chicago-s-young-rubicam-targets-city-s-violence

you heard of The Family prior to reading Sharlet's essay? What, after reading the essay, is your attitude toward The Family?

3. Can public health problems like AIDS be solved by moral remedies? Why or why not? Does this story of Uganda's treatment of gays provide an answer to this question?

4. Who is the most sympathetic character in Sharlet's essay? Who is the least sympathetic? What makes them so? Were this essay written from Bahati's or Matembe's or Blessed's or Kyazze's point of view, how might it be different? What if you were asked to write this essay—how might it be different then?

LOOKING AT RHETORIC

1. This is a serious essay with a serious topic. Yet, Sharlet's tone is often light, even comical on occasion. Identify three places in the essay where Sharlet uses humor to make a serious point.

2. Sharlet introduces us to numerous characters in his essay. What rhetorical techniques does he use in order to quickly paint a picture of each person?

WRITING ASSIGNMENTS

1. Spend some time researching the controversy regarding anti-gay legislation in Uganda. Write an essay in which you update your audience on the current state of affairs, giving particular detail about what has transpired since Sharlet published his essay in September 2010.

2. Imagine that you are asked to serve as a special advisor to the President on social policy, and that you have been asked to draft a report to the President in which you advise the President about whether he or she should attend the next meeting of the annual National Prayer Breakfast. On the basis of your reading of Sharlet's essay, what is your advice to the President?

3. In pairs or in groups, discuss the extent to which the United States government attempts to legislate morality in this country. Discuss as a group whether you believe creating a Secretary of Ethics and Integrity to serve on the President's Cabinet would be a worthwhile endeavor or not. Create two lists: one of arguments for the creation of such a position; one of arguments against creating such a position. Share these arguments with the rest of the class. Then, as an individual, draft a thesis-driven essay in which you argue for or against the following claim: in the United States, the doctrine of the separation of church and state has resulted in a socio-political culture in America in which morality is left up to the individual, not the state.

Happiness is a Worn Gun

Dan Baum

Dan Baum is a freelance writer for such magazines as The New Yorker, Rolling Stone, Harper's, *and* Wired. *He is the author of several books, including* Smoke and Mirrors: The War on Drugs and Politics of Failure *(1996) and, most recently,* Nine Lives: Death and Life in New Orleans *(2009), which grew out of Baum's experiences writing essays for* The New Yorker *about post Hurricane Katrina New Orleans. In the following essay, Baum takes up the much-discussed and debated issue of gun control, giving readers a new perspective on some of the core issues involved in the gun control debate by discussing his own experience carrying a concealed firearm.*

1   Nowadays, most states let just about anybody who wants a concealed-handgun permit have one; in seventeen states, you don't even have to be a resident. Nobody knows exactly how many Americans carry guns, because not all states release their numbers, and even if they did, not all permit holders carry all the time. But it's safe to assume that as many as 6 million Americans are walking around with firearms under their clothes.

2   Good thing or bad? Most people can answer that question instinctively, depending on how they think about a whole matrix of bigger questions, from the role of government to the moral obligations we have to one another. Politically, the issue breaks along the expected lines, with the NPR end of the dial going one way and the talk-radio end the other.

3   The gun-carrying revolution started in Florida, which in 1987 had a murder rate 40 percent higher than the national average. Another state might have reacted to such carnage by restricting access to guns, but Florida's legislature went the other way. Believing that law-abiding citizens should have the means to defend themselves, it ordered police chiefs to issue any adult a carry permit unless there was good reason to deny it. In the history of gun politics, this was a big moment. The gun-rights movement had won just about every battle it had fought since coalescing in the late 1960s, but these had been defensive battles against new gun-control laws. Reversing the burden of proof on carry permits expanded gun rights. For the first time, the movement was on offense, and the public loved it. The change in Florida's law was called "shall-issue"— as in, the police shall issue the permit and not apply their own discretion. Six states already had such laws, but Florida's became the model for the twenty-nine others that followed. Most of these states recognize the permits of other shall-issue states. Nine remain "may issue" states, leaving the decision up to local law enforcement. Alaska and Arizona have laws allowing any resident who can legally own a gun to carry it concealed with no special permit. And one—can you guess which?—is silent on the whole issue, meaning anybody over sixteen from any state can walk around secretly armed inside its borders. (Most people guess Texes, but it's Vermont.) Only two states, Wisconsin and Illinois flatly forbid civilians to carry concealed guns.

4   I got hooked on guns forty-nine years ago as a fat kid at summer camp—the one thing I could do was lie on my belly and shoot a .22 rifle—and I've collected, shot, and hunted with guns my entire adult life. But I also grew up into a fairly typical liberal Democrat, with a circle of friends politely appalled at my fixation on firearms. For as long as I've been voting, I've reflexively supported waiting periods, background checks, the assault-rifle ban, and other gun-control measures. None interfered with my enjoyment of firearms, and none seemed to me the first step toward tyranny. As the concealed-carry laws changed across the land, I naturally sided with those who argued that arming the populace would turn fender benders into gunfights. The prospect of millions more gun-carrying Americans left me reliably horrified.

5   At the same time, though, I was a little jealous of those getting permits. Taking my guns from the safe was a rare treat; the sensual pleasure of handling guns is a big part of the habit. Elegantly designed and exquisitely manufactured, they are deeply satisfying to manipulate, even without shooting. I normally got to play with mine only a few times a year, during hunting season and on one or two trips to the range. The people with carry permits, though, were handling their guns all the time. They were developing an enviable competence and familiarity with them. They were *living the gun life*. Finally, last year, under the guise of "wanting to learn what this is all about," but really wanting to live the gun life myself, I began the process of getting a carry permit. All that was required was a background check, fingerprints, and certification that I'd passed an approved handgun class.

6   Both classes were less about self-defense than about recruiting us into a culture animated by fear of violent crime. We watched lurid films of men in ski masks breaking into homes occupied by terrified women. We studied color police photos of a man slashed open with a knife. Teachers in both classes directed us to websites dedicated to concealed carry, among them usacarry.org, an online gathering place where the gun-carrying community warns, over and over, that crime is "out of control."

7   In fact, violent crime has fallen by a third since 1989—one piece of unambiguous good news out of the past two decades. Murder, rape, robbery, assault: all of them are much less common now than they were then. At class, it was hard to discern the line between preparing for something awful to happen and praying for something awful to happen. A desire to carry a gun seemed to precede the fear of crime, the fear serving to justify the carrying. I asked one of the instructors whether carrying a gun didn't bespeak a needlessly dark view of mankind. "I'm an optimist," he said, "but we live in a world of assholes."

8   At the conclusion of both classes, we students were welcomed into the gun-carrying fraternity as though dripping from the baptismal font. "Thank you for being a part of this, man. You're doing the right thing," one of the teachers said, taking my hand in both of his and looking into my eyes. "You should all be proud of yourselves just for being here," said the police officer who helped with the class. "All of us thank you." As we stood shaking hands, with our guns in our gym bags and holding our certificates, we felt proud, included, even loved. We had been admitted to a league of especially useful gentlemen and ladies.

9   Partly, gun carriers are looking for political safety in numbers. Alongside a belief in rising crime lies a certainty that gun confiscation is nigh. I had a hard time finding

cartridges for my hunting rifle the past two seasons because shooters began hoarding when Barack Obama was elected president. Since then, the gun industry has had its best sales on record.

10   Shooters see their guns as emblems of a whole spectrum of virtuous lifestyle choices—rural over urban, self-reliance over dependence on the collective, vigorous out-doorsiness over pallid intellectualism, patriotism over internationalism, action over inac-tion—and they hear attacks on guns as attacks on them, personally. The Coalition to Stop Gun Violence and the Brady Campaign to Prevent Gun Violence sound like groups even the NRA could support: who wouldn't want to prevent violence? But the former was called, until 1989, the National Coalition to Ban Handguns, and the latter wants to prohibit the "military-style semi-automatic assault weapons" popular among shooters. From the point of view of gun enthusiasts, it's not gun violence these groups want to end, but gun ownership.

11   Beyond mere politics, gun carriers are evangelizing a social philosophy. Belief in rising crime, when statistics show the opposite, amounts to faith in a natural order of predators and prey. The turtle doesn't apologize for his shell nor the tiger for his claws; humans shouldn't be bashful about equipping to defend themselves. Men and women who carry guns fill a noble niche between sheep and wolf. "Sheepdogs" is the way they often describe themselves—alert, vigilant, not aggressive but prepared to do battle.

12   In both classes, and in every book about concealed carry that I read, much was made of "conditions of readiness," which are color-coded from white to red. Condition White is total oblivion to one's surroundings—sleeping, being drunk or stoned, losing oneself in conversation while walking on city streets, texting while listening to an iPod. Condition Yellow is being aware of, and taking an interest in, one's surroundings—essentially, the mental state we are encouraged to achieve when we are driving: keeping our eyes mov-ing, checking the mirrors, being careful not to let the radio drown out the sounds around us. Condition Orange is being aware of a possible threat. Condition Red is responding to danger.

13   Contempt for Condition White unifies the gun-carrying community almost as much as does fealty to the Second Amendment. "When you're in Condition White you're a sheep," one of my instructors told us. "You're a victim."

14   Having carried a gun full-time for several months now, I can attest that there's no way to lapse into Condition White when armed. Moving through a cocktail party with a gun holstered snug against my ribs makes me feel like James Bond—*I know something you don't know!*—but it's socially and physically unpleasant. I have to remember to keep adjusting the drape of my jacket so as not to expose myself, and make sure to get the arms-inside position when hugging a friend so that the hard lump on my hip or under my arm doesn't give itself away. In some settings my gun feels as big as a toaster oven, and I find myself tense with the expectation of being discovered.

15   Living in Condition Yellow can have beneficial side effects. A woman I met in Phoenix told me carrying a gun had made her more organized. "I used to lose my stuff all the time," she said. "I was always leaving my purse in restaurants, my wallet in the car, my sunglasses at friends' houses. Once I started carrying a gun—accepted that grave responsibility—that all stopped. I'm *on it* now."

16   Like her, I'm more alert and acute when I'm wearing my gun. If I'm in a restaurant or store, I find myself in my own little movie, glancing at the door when a person walks in and, in a microsecond, evaluating whether a threat has appeared and what my options for response would be—roll left and take cover behind that pillar? On the street, I look people over: Where are his hands? What does his face tell me? I run sequences in my head. If a guy jumps me with a knife, should I throw money to the ground and run? Take two steps back and draw? How about if he has a gun? How will I distract him so I can get the drop? It can be fun. But it can also be exhausting. Some nights I dream gunfight scenarios over and over and wake up bushed. In Flagstaff I was planning to meet a friend for a beer, and although carrying in a bar is legal in Arizona, drinking in a bar while armed is not. I locked my gun in the car. Walking the few blocks to the bar, I realized how different I felt: lighter, dreamier, conscious of how the afternoon light slanted against Flagstaff's old buildings. I found myself, as I walked, composing lines of prose. I was lapsing into Condition White, and loving it.

17   Condition White may make us sheep, but it's also where art happens. It's where we daydream, reminisce, and hear music in our heads. Hardcore gun carriers want no part of that, and the zeal for getting everybody to carry a gun may be as much an anti–Condition White movement as anything else—resentment toward the airy-fairy elites who can enjoy the luxury of musing, sipping tea, and nibbling biscuits while the good people of the world have to work for a living and keep their guard up.

18   I was crossing the corner of Dauphine and Kerlerec Streets in New Orleans late one evening with my gun under my jacket. (Louisiana is one of the states that recognizes a Colorado permit.) I wasn't smelling the sweet olive, replaying in my head the clackety music of Washboard Chaz, or savoring the residuum of dinnertime's oysters Pernod. I was in Condition Yellow and fully aware of two scruffy guys lounging in a doorway up ahead. "Can you help us out?" one asked. I made my usual demurral and walked on. When I got about fifteen feet away, one of them yelled, "Faggot!"

19   I've never been one to throw down because someone called me a name. But it's possible that in the old days I'd have yelled something back. At the very least, I'd have felt my blood pressure spike.

20   This time, I didn't become angry or even annoyed. A Zen-like calm overtook me. I felt no need to restrain myself; my body didn't even gesture in the direction of anger. *Pace* Claudio, my hand meant nothing to my sword. Rage wasn't an option, because I had no way of knowing where it would end, and somehow my brain and body sensed that. I began to understand why we don't hear a lot of stories about legal gun carriers killing one another in road-rage incidents. Carrying a gun gives you a sense of guardianship, even a kind of moral superiority.

21   Shall-issue may or may not have contributed to the stunning drop in violent crime since the early Nineties. The problem with the catchy *More Guns, Less Crime* construction, though, is that many other things may have helped: changing demographics, smarter policing, the burnout of the crack-cocaine wave, three-strikes laws, even—as suggested by *Freakonomics* authors Steven Levitt and Stephen Dubner—legalized abortion. And crime dropped more in some states that didn't adopt shall-issue laws than in some that did.

22   But shall-issue didn't lead to *more* crime, as predicted by its critics. The portion of all killing done with a handgun—the weapon people carry concealed—hasn't changed in decades; it's still about half. Whereas the Violence Policy Center in Washington, D.C., can produce a list of 175 killings committed by carry-permit holders since 2007, the NRA can brandish a longer list of crimes prevented by armed citizens. I prefer to rely on the FBI's data, which show that not only are bad-guy murders—those committed in the course of rape, robbery, and other felonies—way down but so are spur-of-the-moment murders involving alcohol, drugs, romantic entanglements, money disputes, and other arguments: the very types of murders that critics worried widespread concealed-carry would increase.

23   Law enforcement tends to oppose shall-issue laws, at least institutionally. A group of Iowa sheriffs agitated against a shall-issue law their governor signed in April, and Ohio's Fraternal Order of Police is objecting to a bill designed to open bars, stadiums, and other venues to concealed guns. Every street cop I've met lately, though, sees it the other way. "Absolutely I want more people armed," one told me in Las Vegas. "If I'm shooting it out with a bad guy, and an armed citizen can step in and throw fire downrange, I'm all for it." At traffic stops, a person's concealed-carry permit pops up on the computer. "That tells me they've been checked out," he said, "that they're probably someone I don't have to worry about."

24   The inclination nationwide is still to make concealed-carry permits easier, not harder, to get, and the recession may be helping the cause. In Ohio, a judge recently suggested that, in the face of law-enforcement budget cuts, people should "arm themselves." An Ohio concealed-carry activist told the *Toledo Blade* that he thinks hard economic times are "causing all these law-enforcement officers, whether they're police officers or sheriff's deputies, to get laid off, and people realize they're in a situation where they may have to be responsible for their own safety."

25   Whatever the reason, the handgun industry is pleased with the legal drift, given that the Obama-panic bubble is fading and the longterm industry trend is bleak. Young adults buy markedly fewer guns than older people. They want to be urban and digital, and guns are the opposite of that. A big push by the industry to feminize the shooting sports has fallen flat; only in hunting has women's participation increased, and even there just by a little. The bright spot in the industry remains small handguns and all of their accoutrements—holsters, belts, purses, and an entire line of clothing, 5.11 Tactical, designed to conceal weapons. Back in the mid-Nineties, when handgun sales were falling fast, *Shooting Industry* magazine wrote, "Two bright rays of sunshine gleam through the dark clouds of the slump in the firearms market. One is the landslide of 'shall-issue' concealed-carry reform legislation around the country. The other is the emergence of a new generation of compact handguns." Shall-issue saved the handgun business; sales were half again higher in 2007 than in 2000, and much of that growth was in concealable weapons.

26   Now that they've largely won the concealed-carry fight, gun-rights activists have begun a new offensive: "open-carry." Advocates for wearing guns in plain view hold armed picnics and urge people to wear their guns visibly wherever it's legal. Forty-three states let citizens carry openly, including some that remain reticent on concealed-carry and

one—Wisconsin—that doesn't allow concealed-carry at all. Open-carry became a national issue last year, when people displaying guns showed up at New Hampshire and Arizona rallies attended by President Obama. Reporters seemed surprised that police made no arrests, but open-carry is legal in both states and none of the gun carriers made threats. The open carriers are pushing it; in at least six states, citizens have sued police after being stopped for wearing a gun. In January, a group of California activists began wearing unloaded guns openly to Starbucks, but if they were expecting to get arrested or thrown out they were disappointed. They drank their lattés and left. Starbucks, a company official told reporters over and over, respects California state law, which as of this writing allows open carry as long as the guns are unloaded.

27   I've tried carrying openly a few times, wearing a loaded, long-barreled .45-caliber revolver in a hip holster to Safeway, Home Depot, Target, Whole Foods, and my local Apple Store. The only person who objected was my wife ("For Christ's sake!"). Nobody else said a word. The kids at the Apple Store, in their rectangular-framed glasses and blue T-shirts, stood right beside me as I played with an iPad for half an hour. It isn't possible that they didn't see the big handgun. More likely, it didn't interest them: a World War I revolver is pretty dull competition for a touch-screen device running a 1 GHz A4 chip and 802.11a/b/g/n Wi-Fi. At Target, I made a point of standing for a long time directly in front of a security guard. Nothing. What he saw was a balding, middle-aged man in pleated pants and glasses with a tired old gun on his hip—not a particularly threatening sight. He may have figured I was a useless cop or a ranger from the city's vast parks system. Either that, or the sight was so incongruous that he and everybody else in Target failed to register it. Then I stopped at a gritty little Mexican grocery I like, for some tortillas and *crema*, and everybody noticed, their eyes flicking over my belt and going wide. "*Señor*, is it real?" a chubby little boy asked as I locked up my bicycle. In Mexico, almost nobody gets a license to own a handgun, let alone wear one. "*¿Por qué la pistola?*" a man at the meat counter asked. "*¿Por qué no?*" I answered. He shrugged and walked away, shaking his head—not like I was dangerous, more like I was simply a *gabacho* fool. Overall, I felt less safe with the gun openly displayed than with it concealed. I worried that someone would knock me on the back of the head and steal it, or that some genuinely aggressive nutcase would challenge me to draw. Mostly, though, I felt obnoxious. In all likelihood, I was making somebody silently anxious.

28   Even in shall-issue states, guns—whether visible or concealed—are often barred from places where they seem especially inappropriate: college campuses, schools, bars, parks, churches. The list can vary from town to town. When I take a long road trip, I keep a sheaf of gun-law printouts on the front seat so I don't inadvertently walk into the wrong place with my concealed revolver. In Boulder, it's a nuisance to keep taking my gun off and finding a place to stow it when I'm going to visit the university library, toss a Frisbee in a school-yard, or see a movie on campus. I've been checked out, fingerprinted, and trusted by the state with a carry permit; having to ditch my gun feels vaguely demeaning. To those already feeling slighted, gun-free zones are a continual insult.

29   Someone bent on killing people isn't going to be dissuaded by a NO FIREARMS sign on the door. Gun carriers tend to think that such rules serve only to alert the malevolent to good places for mass shootings. And they're right that no matter how stringent our

background checks, we'll never do a perfect job of keeping guns out of the wrong hands. Guns are well-made things; the rifle I hunt with was made in 1900, the revolver I carry was made in 1956, and both are as lethal today as the day they were built. So even if the United States were to ban the import, manufacture, and sale of new ones—unlikely—there would still be some 250 million privately owned guns in the United States. Unless we're willing to send the police door-to-door to round them all up, the country is going to be awash in firearms for years to come. Thugs will push guns into the faces of convenience-store clerks, lunatics will shoot up restaurants, aggrieved workers will spray their offices with bullets, and alienated students will open fire at school. The question that interests gun activists is how we're prepared to respond. A Republican legislator in Wisconsin wanted to arm teachers so they could cut down Columbine copycats, and college students in Alaska, Colorado, Connecticut, Michigan, Texas, and Virginia are agitating for the right to carry concealed weapons on campus so they can defend themselves against the next Virginia Tech-style shooter. An armed civilian might be even more useful during a massacre than a police officer; cops hit the people they're aiming at less than half the time—in some departments much less. That might be because criminals identify police by their uniforms and so get the first shot off. A civilian might have the element of surprise.

30   My friends who are appalled at the thought of widespread concealed weapons aren't impressed by this argument, or by the research demonstrating no ill effects of the shall-issue revolution. "I don't care," said one. "I don't feel safe knowing people are walking around with guns. What about my right to feel safe? Doesn't that count for anything?"

31   To the unfamiliar, guns are noisy and intimidating. They represent the supremacy of force over reason, of ferocity over refinement, and probably a whole set of principles that rub some people the wrong way. But a free society doesn't make people give a reason for doing the things they want to do; the burden of proof falls on those who would forbid. I started out thinking widespread concealed-carry was a bad idea. But in the absence of evidence that allowing law-abiding citizens to carry guns is harmful, I come down on the side of letting people do what they want.

32   Why shouldn't being prepared to defend oneself be on the list of skills we expect of modern citizens? I've encountered five reasons not to wear a gun: you think it so unlikely you'll be attacked it's not worth the trouble or the sacrifice of Condition White; you expect the police to come to your aid in the event of trouble; wearing a gun makes you feel less safe instead of more; you've decided you couldn't take a life under any circumstance; or you don't want to contribute to a coarsening of society by preparing to kill at a moment's notice.

33   It's true that crime is down, but it's certainly not nonexistent; hideous things happen to good people every day. We carry fire insurance even though fire is uncommon; carrying a gun may be no more paranoid. Expecting police protection is delusional; they'll usually do no more than show up later to investigate. Carrying a gun is unsafe for those who haven't been properly trained, but a good class and regular practice can fix that. Only the last two reasons strike me as logically complete arguments not to go armed. Being willing to die rather than kill is an admirable and time-honored philosophical position. I'm not certain, though, how many of us would hold to it when the fatal moment was upon us. I, for one, count myself out. I'm *willing*.

34   That said, I will probably stop carrying my gun. It's uncomfortable, distracting, and freaks out my friends; it's not worth it. I miss Condition White. If I lived in a dangerous place, I might feel different, and I may continue wearing a gun when I travel to such places (at least to the ones that allow it). That some people think going unarmed makes me a traitor to the Second Amendment doesn't bother me at all. And if I'm a burden to society because I cannot jump in and stop a crime, well, I'm not qualified in CPR, advanced first aid, maritime lifesaving, or firefighting either. Social parasite that I am, I'm content to leave emergency response to the pros.

35   We may all benefit from having a lot of licensed people carrying guns, if only because of the heightened state of awareness in which they live. It's a scandal, though, that people can get a license to carry on the basis of a three-hour "course" given at a gun show. State requirements vary, but some don't even ask students to fire a weapon before getting a carry permit. We should enforce high standards for instruction, including extensive live firing, role playing, and serious examination of the legal issues. Since people can carry guns state to state, standards should be uniform. States should require a refresher course, the way Texas does, before renewing a carry permit. To their credit, most gun carriers I've talked to agree that training should improve, even if some of them get twitchy at the idea of mandates. The Second Amendment confers a right to keep and bear arms. It does not confer a right to instant gratification.

36   Going armed has connected me with an entire range of values I didn't use to think much about—self-reliance, vigilance, muscular citizenship—and some impulses I'd rather avoid, like social pessimism and irrational fear. It has militarized my life; all that locking and loading and watching over my shoulder makes me feel like a bit player in the perpetual global war in which we find ourselves. There's no denying that carrying a gun has made my days a lot more dramatic. Suddenly, I'm dangerous. I'm an action figure. I bear a lethal secret into every social encounter. I have to remind myself occasionally that my gun is not a prop, a political statement, or a rhetorical device, but an instrument designed to blow a ragged channel through a human being. From a public-safety standpoint it may matter little that lots of people are carrying guns now, but if accessorizing with firearms becomes truly *au courant*,[1] the United States will feel like a different place. We'll be less dreamy and more secretive. We'll spend more energy watching one another and less on self-obsession. We'll be a little more on-task, more cognizant of violence and prepared to participate therein. We'll also be, in our own minds, a little sexier as we make ourselves more dangerous. We'll be carrying guns for exactly the reason John Garfield did: to shoot people with, sweetheart.

QUESTIONS ON MEANING

1. What do you think Baum means by the phrase "living the gun life"?

2. What conclusions does Baum draw about carry culture from his experience in the two gun-carry courses?

3. What are the differences between conditions white, yellow, orange, and red?

---

[1]*Au courant*: literally *in the current*, meaning a trend in the present moment.

4. Statistically, according to Baum, what has been the impact of the proliferation of shall-issue states?

5. What does Baum learn from his open-carry experiments?

6. What are the five reasons Baum has encountered for *not* carrying a gun?

QUESTIONS FOR DISCUSSION

1. In your experience, is there a class-based distinction between those in and out of gun culture? What stereotypes are commonly attached to those who live the gun life? What stereotypes are typically associated with those who oppose gun culture? In what group would you place Baum? Does he fit either stereotype? Why or why not?

2. Do you live your life in Condition Yellow? Should you? Would the United States be a better place if everyone did?

3. Baum presents five reasons why people argue against carrying. Can you think of more?

4. Read over Baum's last paragraph again. Is this a reasonable set of expectations about the future? Is Baum's vision a positive or negative vision?

5. The United States has a reputation for being a violent nation. Does this bother you? If it does, what would have to change in the United States, in your opinion, to begin to shed this reputation?

LOOKING AT RHETORIC

1. In recent years it has become almost a cliché to speak of the ubiquitous gun control essay in a composition class, as if the topic has been so overdone as to warrant parody or even disdain. It has become a topic generally avoided by composition teachers. What makes this gun control essay different? Anything? What new perspectives does Dan Baum bring to the issue? In terms of the rhetoric of the piece—the way the essay is written and structured—how does Baum make the shop-worn topic of gun control new, fresh, and interesting?

2. Note how Baum frames his essay with references to John Garfield in the movie *The Fallen Sparrow*. Framing essays in this manner can prove an effective strategy, as it does in this case. How do the references to the Garfield movie quote frame the rest of the essay? What other equally effective strategies might Baum have used to introduce and conclude his essay?

WRITING ASSIGNMENTS

1. Spend some time in the library and on the Internet researching federal and state gun control laws (in at least a handful of states). Then, having given careful consideration to Baum's perspectives on the concealed carry issue, draft an essay in which you either support or challenge the notion that all states should pass shall-issue laws making it easier for ordinary citizens to get permits to carry concealed firearms. Be sure to note how different states currently handle the issues involved.

2. Find someone who owns a firearm and interview them about their attitudes regarding shall-issue and related gun control issues. Write a profile essay in which you introduce your readers to this person and share with the audience this person's views on the kinds of gun control issues raised in the essay by Baum. Following Baum's lead, contextualize your profile essay with data regarding local gun control laws and gun-related crime statistics.

3. In pairs or in groups, put together a series of guidelines that would govern the regulation concealed-carry permit distribution and practice in your state. What steps would a person have to take in order to get the permit? What laws would that person have to follow when carrying? Where would it be legal to carry? Where illegal? Then, as individuals, research the actual laws of your state regarding concealed-carry. Draft an essay as if you were proposing new legislation in your state legislature seeking to put in place the set of laws and guidelines your group developed.

The 10,000-Hour Rule

Malcolm Gladwell

Malcolm Gladwell (b. 1963) earned a bachelor's degree in history from the University of Toronto's Trinity College in 1984. He began his career with The American Spectator *and later become a reporter with* The Washington Post *before joining* The New Yorker. *Gladwell is known for many bestselling nonfiction books dealing with education and society, including* The Tipping Point *(2000),* Blink *(2005),* Outliers *(2008), and* What the Dog Saw: And Other Adventures *(2009). Gladwell's books are based in research in the social sciences, particularly social psychology, and they often present surprising conclusions that challenge common assumptions about human behavior and success. The following explores the role practice plays in the development of expertise, calling into question our frequent assumption that innate talent is the primary factor in success. Achievement seems to be the result of a combination of external influences rather than individual or in-born ability.*

1   For almost a generation, psychologists around the world have been engaged in a spirited debate over a question that most of us would consider to have been settled years ago. The question is this: is there such a thing as innate talent? The obvious answer is yes. Not every hockey player born in January ends up playing at the professional level. Only some do—the innately talented ones. Achievement is talent plus preparation. The problem with this view is that the closer psychologists look at the careers of the gifted, the smaller the role innate talent seems to play and the bigger the role preparation seems to play.

2   Exhibit A in the talent argument is a study done in the early 1990s by the psychologist K. Anders Ericsson and two colleagues at Berlin's elite Academy of Music. With the help of the Academy's professors, they divided the school's violinists into three groups. In the first group were the stars, the students with the potential to become world-class soloists. In the second were those judged to be merely "good." In the third were students who were unlikely to ever play professionally and who intended to be music teachers in the public school system. All of the violinists were then asked the same question: over the course of your entire career, ever since you first picked up the violin, how many hours have you practiced?

3   Everyone from all three groups started playing at roughly the same age, around five years old. In those first few years, everyone practiced roughly the same amount, about two or three hours a week. But when the students were around the age of eight, real differences started to emerge. The students who would end up the best in their class began to practice more than everyone else: six hours a week by age nine, eight hours a week by age twelve, sixteen hours a week by age fourteen, and up and up, until by the age of twenty they were practicing—that is, purposefully and single-mindedly playing their instruments with the intent to get better—well over thirty hours a week. In fact, by the age of twenty, the elite performers had each totaled ten thousand hours of practice. By contrast, the merely good students had totaled eight thousand hours, and the future music teachers had totaled just over four thousand hours.

4   Ericsson and his colleagues then compared amateur pianists with professional pianists. The same pattern emerged. The amateurs never practiced more than about three hours a week over the course of their childhood, and by the age of twenty they had totaled two thousand hours of practice. The professionals, on the other hand, steadily increased their practice time every year, until by the age of twenty they, like the violinists, had reached ten thousand hours.

5   The striking thing about Ericsson's study is that he and his colleagues couldn't find any "naturals," musicians who floated effortlessly to the top while practicing a fraction of the time their peers did. Nor could they find any "grinds," people who worked harder than everyone else, yet just didn't have what it takes to break the top ranks. Their research suggests that once a musician has enough ability to get into a top music school, the thing that distinguishes one performer from another is how hard he or she works. That's it. And what's more, the people at the very top don't work just harder or even much harder than everyone else. They work much, *much* harder.

6   The idea that excellence at performing a complex task requires a critical minimum level of practice surfaces again and again in studies of expertise. In fact, researchers have settled on what they believe is the magic number for true expertise: ten thousand hours.

7   "The emerging picture from such studies is that ten thousand hours of practice is required to achieve the level of mastery associated with being a world-class expert—in anything," writes the neurologist Daniel Levitin. "In study after study, of composers, basketball players, fiction writers, ice skaters, concert pianists, chess players, master criminals, and what have you, this number comes up again and again. Of course, this doesn't address why some people get more out of their practice sessions than others do. But no one has yet found a case in which true world-class expertise was accomplished in less time. It seems that it takes the brain this long to assimilate all that it needs to know to achieve true mastery."

8   This is true even of people we think of as prodigies. Mozart,[1] for example, famously started writing music at six. But, writes the psychologist Michael Howe in his book *Genius Explained*,

---

[1]Wolfgang Amadeus Mozart (1756-1791): Austrian composer and musician of the Classical Period, often considered the most gifted composer of all time.

by the standards of mature composers, Mozart's early works are not outstanding. The earliest pieces were all probably written down by his father, and perhaps improved in the process. Many of Wolfgang's childhood compositions, such as the first seven of his concertos for piano and orchestra, are largely arrangements of works by other composers. Of those concertos that only contain music original to Mozart, the earliest that is now regarded as a masterwork (No. 9, K. 271) was not composed until he was twenty-one: by that time Mozart had already been composing concertos for ten years.

9   Even Mozart—the greatest musical prodigy of all time—couldn't hit his stride until he had his ten thousand hours in. Practice isn't the thing you do once you're good. It's the thing you do that makes you good.

10   The other interesting thing about that ten thousand hours, of course, is that ten thousand hours is an *enormous* amount of time. It's all but impossible to reach that number all by yourself by the time you're a young adult. You have to have parents who encourage and support you. You can't be poor, because if you have to hold down a part-time job on the side to help make ends meet, there won't be time left in the day to practice enough. In fact, most people can reach that number only if they get into some kind of special program—like a hockey all-star squad—or if they get some kind of extraordinary opportunity that gives them a chance to put in those hours.

11   Is the ten-thousand-hour rule a general rule of success? If we scratch below the surface of every great achiever, do we always find the equivalent of the Michigan Computer Center or the hockey all-star team—some sort of special opportunity for practice?

12   Let's test the idea with two examples, and for the sake of simplicity, let's make them as familiar as possible: the Beatles, one of the most famous rock bands ever; and Bill Gates, one of the world's richest men.

13   The Beatles—John Lennon, Paul McCartney, George Harrison, and Ringo Starr—came to the United States in February of 1964, starting the so-called British Invasion of the American music scene and putting out a string of hit records that transformed the face of popular music.

14   The first interesting thing about the Beatles for our purposes is how long they had already been together by the time they reached the United States. Lennon and McCartney first started playing together in 1957, seven years prior to landing in America. (Incidentally, the time that elapsed between their founding and their arguably greatest artistic achievements—*Sgt. Pepper's Lonely Hearts Club Band* and *The Beatles* [White Album]—is ten years.) And if you look even more closely at those long years of preparation, you'll find an experience that, in the context of world-class violinists, sounds awfully familiar. In 1960, while they were still just a struggling high school rock band, they were invited to play in Hamburg, Germany.

15   And what was so special about Hamburg? It wasn't that it paid well. It didn't. Or that the acoustics were fantastic. They weren't. Or that the audiences were savvy and appreciative. They were anything but. It was the sheer amount of time the band was forced to play.

16   Here is John Lennon, in an interview after the Beatles disbanded:

We got better and got more confidence. We couldn't help it with all the experience play-
ing all night long. It was handy them being foreign. We had to try even harder, put our
heart and soul into it, to get ourselves over.

In Liverpool, we'd only ever done one-hour sessions, and we just used to do our best
numbers, the same ones, at every one. In Hamburg, we had to play for eight hours, so
we really had to find a new way of playing.

17   *Eight hours?*

18   Here is Pete Best, the Beatles' drummer at the time: "Once the news got out about that
we were making a show, the club started packing them in. We played seven nights a week.
At first we played almost nonstop till twelve-thirty, when it closed, but as we got better the
crowds stayed till two most mornings."

19   *Seven days a week?*

20   The Beatles ended up traveling to Hamburg five times between 1960 and the end of 1962.

21   "They were no good onstage when they went there and they were very good when
they came back," Norman went on. "They learned not only stamina. They had to learn an
enormous amount of numbers—cover versions of everything you can think of, not just rock
and roll a bit of jazz too. They weren't disciplined onstage at all before that. But when they
came back, they sounded like no one else. It was the making of them."

22   Let's now turn to the history of Bill Gates. His story is almost as well known as the
Beatles.' Brilliant, young math whiz discovers computer programming. Drops out of
Harvard. Starts a little computer company called Microsoft with his friends. Through sheer
brilliance and ambition and guts builds it into the giant of the software world. That's the
broad outline. Let's dig a little bit deeper.

23   Gates's father was a wealthy lawyer in Seattle, and his mother was the daughter of
a well-to-do banker. As a child Bill was precocious and easily bored by his studies. So his
parents took him out of public school and, at the beginning of seventh grade, sent him to
Lakeside, a private school that catered to Seattle's elite families. Midway through Gates's
second year at Lakeside, the school started a computer club.

24   It was an "amazing thing," of course, because this was 1968. Most *colleges* didn't have
computer clubs in the 1960s. Even more remarkable was the kind of computer Lakeside
bought. The school didn't have its students learn programming by the laborious computer-
card system, like virtually everyone else was doing in the 1960s. Instead, Lakeside installed
what was called an ASR-33 Teletype, which was a time-sharing terminal with a direct link
to a mainframe computer in downtown Seattle. Bill Gates got to do real-time programming
as an eighth grader in 1968.

25   From that moment forward, Gates lived in the computer room. He and a number of
others began to teach themselves how to use this strange new device. Buying time on the
mainframe computer the ASR was hooked was, of course, expensive—even for a wealthy
institution like Lakeside—and it wasn't long before the $3,000 taken up by the Mothers'
Club ran out. The parents raised more money. The students spent it. Then a group of
programmers at the University of Washington formed an outfit called Computer Center
Corporation (or C-Cubed), which leased computer time to local companies. As luck would
have it, one of the founders of the firm—Monique Rona—had a son at Lakeside, a year

ahead of Gates. Would the Lakeside computer club, Rona wondered, like to test out the company's software programs on the weekends in exchange for free programming time? Absolutely! After school, Gates took the bus to the C-Cubed office and programmed long into the evening.

26   C-Cubed eventually went bankrupt, so Gates and his friends began hanging around the computer center at the University of Washington. Before long, they latched onto an outfit called ISI (Information Sciences Inc.), which agreed to let them have free computer time in exchange for working on a piece of software that could be used to automate company payrolls. In one seven-month period in 1971, Gates and his cohorts ran up 1,575 hours of computer time on the ISI mainframe, which averaged out to eight hours a day, seven days a week.

27   "It was my obsession," Gates says of his early high school years. "I skipped athletics. I went up there at night. We were programming on weekends. It would be a rare week that we wouldn't get twenty or thirty hours in a period where Paul Allen and I got in trouble for stealing a bunch of passwords and crashing the system. We got kicked out. I didn't get to use the computer the whole summer. This is when I was fifteen and sixteen. Then I found out Paul had found a computer that was free at the University of Washington. They had these machines in the medical center and the physics department. They were on a twenty-four-hour schedule, but with this big slack period, so that between three and six in the morning they never scheduled anything." Gates laughed. "I'd leave at night, after my bedtime. I could walk up to the University of Washington from my house. Or I'd take the bus. That's why I'm always so generous to the University of Washington, because they let me steal so much computer time." (Years later, Gates's mother said, "We always wondered why it was so hard for him to get up in the morning.")

28   One of the founders of ISI, Bud Pembroke, then got a call from the technology company TRW, which had just signed a contract to set up a computer system at the huge Bonneville Power station in southern Washington State. TRW desperately needed programmers familiar with the particular software the power station used. In these early days of the computer revolution, programmers with that kind of specialized experience were hard to find. But Pembroke knew exactly whom to call: those high school kids from Lakeside who had been running up thousands of hours of computer time on the ISI mainframe. Gates was now in his senior year, and somehow he managed to convince his teachers to let him decamp for Bonneville under the guise of an independent study project. There he spent the spring writing code, supervised by a man named John Norton, who Gates says taught him as much about programming as almost anyone he'd ever met.

29   Those five years, from eighth grade through the end of high school, were Bill Gates's Hamburg. By the time Gates dropped out of Harvard after his sophomore year to try his hand at his own software company, he'd been programming practically nonstop for seven consecutive years. He was *way* past ten thousand hours. How many teenagers in the world had the kind of experience Gates had? "If there were fifty in the world, I'd be stunned," he says. "There was C-Cubed and the payroll stuff we did, then TRW—all those things came together. I had a better exposure to software development at a young age than I think anyone did in that period of time, and all because of an incredibly lucky series of events."

QUESTIONS ON MEANING

1. What is the main debate that psychologists have engaged in regarding skill and talent?

2. What kinds of situations and skills did psychologists explore when they developed the 10,000 hour rule?

3. What did the psychologist Michael Howe discover about Mozart that challenged the conventional wisdom about Mozart's talent?

4. What circumstances led the Beatles to accumulate 10,000 hours of practice?

5. What circumstances led Bill Gates to accumulate 10,000 hours of practice?

6. What role did the University of Washington play in Bill Gates's success?

QUESTIONS FOR DISCUSSION

1. When we discuss ability, what do we commonly assume about the importance of innate talent? How important is it compared to practice?

2. When we discuss ability, what do we commonly assume about the importance of practice? How important is it compared to innate talent?

3. Is it reasonable to compare Mozart and the Beatles? Why or why not?

4. To what extent do social class, environment, and parenting contribute to the development of expertise?

LOOKING AT RHETORIC

1. Gladwell's style might be characterized as simple and direct, yet he deals with the complex issue of human expertise and its development. Does this style enhance the effectiveness of his argument?

2. Some scientists challenge Gladwell's use of anecdotes and examples, suggesting that their validity is questionable. Does his manner of presenting evidence seem credible? In what way can it be challenged?

3. Though he uses a simple style and recognizable examples, he also chooses to quote psychological studies. Does this combination of the academic and the popular work to strengthen his argument?

WRITING ASSIGNMENTS

1. Using library and/or Internet resources, identify and research another example of a person or group that may have done something for 10,000 hours. In an essay, tell their story, either proving or contradicting Gladwell's claim about the importance of practice.

2. Argue for or against the notion that skill emerges from innate talent.

3. In pairs or in groups, make a list of activities that might require the 10,000 hour rule. Individually, write an essay in which you analyze the activity in detail. Identify the particular skills involved in the activity you choose. Write a narrative that demonstrates how a person might move from beginner to expert. Or demonstrate how expertise might be achieved without conforming to the 10,000 hour rule.

Thinking Crosscurrently

TEACHING

Educating a nation's children is a far more complicated matter than simply putting good teachers in front of eager students and letting magic happen. Yes, quality education begins in the classroom, and requires well-trained teachers and students willing to learn, but to provide a quality education on a consistent basis across the nation requires answering complex questions about civil rights and obligations, about the philosophy of education, about funding models and tax codes, and even about the biology of the human brain itself. As you read the selections in this chapter, consider the following questions:

- Is society obligated to provide a quality education to its citizens? How might Henry David Thoreau, Martin Luther King, Jr., or Caitlin Flanagan answer this question? What might they say about the relationship between education and a free and just society?

- What are the costs of providing a quality education to a nation's citizens? How might Milton Friedman or John Maynard Keynes think about the economic value of a public educational system? Would Burnham and Phelan have a different opinion? Why or why not?

- Who has the right to freely access a public education system? Should you have to be a citizen? What about illegal immigrants? What might Judith Ortiz Cofer or Belle Yang say? Should the United States educational system accommodate the needs of non-native English speakers? In what ways? To what extent? If your tax dollars supported public schools in which the language used was Spanish instead of English, would that bother you? Why or why not? What might Terry Eagleton say about this issue?

- What should be the goals of a quality educational system? When is a child considered *educated*? Are there different standards for different people? If you were a parent of a child in school and the teacher was using comic books and television and video games in the classroom, would that bother you? What might Scott McLeod or Douglas Wolk say about this? What about Noel Murray and Scott Tobias? Can two people be equally well educated and yet know very different things? How might Emily Martin answer that question?

8 COMMUNICATION AND POP CULTURE

Our world is so saturated with media and with the byproducts of popular culture that it is often difficult to distinguish ourselves from the media we engage with and the popular culture that envelopes us. They so infuse every aspect of our lives that we almost forget they are there. They are as much a part of our lives as the air we breathe, and just as invisible to us as a result. In fact, it is the efforts of researchers to make visible these invisible currents that surround us and fill our everyday lives that have given rise to the disciplines that are represented by the readings in this chapter.

Consider the average day of a college student. The morning begins as a radio alarm clock—set for 7:00 a.m.—goes off. The alarm is set to a local top forty radio station, and the song that wakes you from slumber is a danceable track from the latest album by some *American Idol* winner. You allow the radio to keep playing as you get ready in the morning, stopping once or twice to check your email to see if by some lucky chance your eight o'clock class has been cancelled that day. It hasn't. You give some careful thought to your outfit that day, choosing a particular shirt that happens to be in style and you think suits your mood that day. It's a jeans and concert tee-shirt day. You pick out your favorite tee-shirt, the one you bought at that concert a few months ago where your ears rang for three days afterwards. On your way out the door, you turn off the clock radio, but grab your iPhone and iPod. As you walk across campus to class, you pop in the ear buds and listen to a few upbeat songs by your favorite band. As you walk, you watch a YouTube video that a friend of yours had posted to your Facebook wall while you slept last night. Everywhere you look—on signs posted around campus, on the Web pages you scroll through, in the magazine you have stuffed into your backpack, on the radio between songs as you brushed your teeth, are advertisements of all kinds, kindly requesting you to purchase toothpaste, a new car, and an endless parade of other commodities. You finally arrive at your classroom. You set the iPhone on silent and turn off the iPod, but because you are early to class, you pull the magazine out of your backpack and flip through it as you wait for the professor to arrive. It's a celebrity gossip-themed magazine, and you skip to the back to read the reviews of the movies coming out that weekend. It's now 8:00 a.m. The professor strolls in, sets up a PowerPoint presentation—shining through an overhead projector mounted on the ceiling of the classroom—and class begins.

From the first moment you woke to the start of class, you have been inundated with media and have interacted in meaningful ways with popular culture. You have used a clock radio, a computer, an iPhone, an iPod, a magazine, and as class begins you are staring at a static image on a PowerPoint slide projected on a screen at the front of the classroom. You have listened to music, watched a viral video, surfed the Web, checked your email, coordinated the rhythms of your morning ritual to a variety of songs, remembered a concert you went to, picked out clothes in a deliberate fashion, read articles in a celebrity magazine, thought about what movie you'd like to see this weekend, and been subjected to dozens of advertisements seeking to convince you that one item or another would be worth your hard earned money. And your day is just getting started. By the time you will go to sleep at the end of the day you will have read a chapter of a spy novel, watched several television programs, listened to more music, played a video game, flipped through a newspaper, texted several friends, talked on the phone, sent and received numerous emails, updated your status on Facebook and uploaded a new image to use for your profile, and you've been kind enough to narrate your progress through the day with a series of tweets.

This is a typical day for you; for just about everyone, in one way or another. This is interesting simply as a statement of observation. But things get far more interesting when one starts to ask certain questions about these activities. What message were you trying to send to your classmates by wearing a concert tee-shirt to class? Did it matter who the band was you were advertising? Does it mean anything to you that you were, in fact, acting as an unpaid billboard for the band by wearing that shirt? Why do you listen to the particular music you listen to? Why an iPod instead of some other device? If someone asked you to trade in your iPhone for a Blackberry, would you? Why does it matter to you? What news sources do you take most seriously and which less seriously, and why: the evening news on television, the local newspaper, a blog, a Web site, a tweet? If you wish to read a book, does it matter to you if you actually have the book in your hands, or are you just as happy (or more happy?) reading it on a Kindle or an iPad or some other electronic device? Does the medium through which you receive the book (print or electronic) affect the way you think about what you are reading? Does it affect the way you read? Are you more or less inclined to read a print text as opposed to an electronic text?

We send and receive messages every moment of our lives. We both consume and participate in the creation of popular culture on a regular basis. Sometimes we choose to wear one brand of jeans over another not because they are more comfortable or fit better, but because they send a message to our peers about who we are. The same might be said for the music we listen to and the television shows we watch. Indeed, what one notices is that there is a direct correlation between the media we engage, the elements of popular culture we adopt as our own, and our own sense of identity. We are what we wear, who we listen to, and what we watch. There are whole sub-cultures built around who uses a particular brand of computer, or communicates through tweets, or uses Facebook, or reads a certain genre of fiction, or drives a certain kind of car.

The ubiquitous nature of pop culture has led some scholars to speculate about the significance of pop culture not just for the individual, but for whole societies as well. Pop culture and the media (television, radio, the Web, newspapers, blogs, mp3 players, cell phones, and the list goes on) through which people receive their news, music, sports, entertainment, are important tools. They are the veins through which the life blood of human society flows: information. The sending and receiving of messages—of information—is as fundamental to who we are as the biological processes that keep us alive. In fact, the claim has even been made that to be alive is defined by our ability to retain information, and we are only truly dead when our ability to act as warehouses for information ends. Information is power, it is a tool for manipulation, it is the raw essence of what we call knowledge, it is a mirror in which is reflected ourselves, our society, our culture. To study the sending and receiving of information—through the various media and means of communication available to us, and reflected in the pop culture in which we are enveloped—is to study the very things that make us human and give shape and meaning to our lives, for good or bad.

THE DISCIPLINE YOU EXPERIENCE

The academic disciplines brought together in this chapter represent several of the newest avenues of serious study to be found in the modern university—many of them are no more than fifty years old at best, and a few are far younger than that. When compared with disciplines such as chemistry and mathematics, which can trace their genesis back hundreds, even thousands, of years, a discipline such as Communication Theory, which traces its long roots all the way back to the mid-twentieth century, is one of the new kids on the academic block.

The relative youth of these areas of serious academic investigation means that these programs tend to be called many different things from one university to another, and there is no consistency in where universities place these programs. Sometimes they are housed in their own departments, but, just as commonly they are programs housed within larger academic departments, or they are developed as cross-disciplinary teaching and research centers within larger colleges. It is not unusual to find journalism and popular culture programs housed in English departments, for instance, or to find a Communication Theory program attached to a philosophy department. Often Communication or Media Studies programs will be in their own departments, but they frequently will have cross-disciplinary ties to literature, history, rhetoric, and related departments and programs. Indeed, these disciplines, by their very nature, promote cross-disciplinary investigation. To study popular culture one must also dip into media theory, film, music, sociology, psychology, marketing, economics, constitutional law, literature, art, graphic design, language, rhetoric, fashion, theater, publishing, and broadcasting in all its forms, including internet-enabled communication and all manner of communication technology.

Because the disciplines that deal with communication, media, and popular culture are all relatively new, they go by a variety of names at different colleges and universities. At your university, they may be called something else, but generally universities will have one or more of the following programs housed somewhere on campus:

- Communication Studies or Media Studies, which is the study of the interpersonal transmission of information from one individual to another, or, in terms of mass communication, from a person to a group. It is concerned with the social, political, and economic impact of communication in all its forms, and it examines the impact that media technologies have on human society.

- Journalism, which focuses on developing in students the specialized skills needed to write and edit news stories for publication in various media, from newspapers to magazines, to blogs and other internet-based news outlets.

- Broadcasting, which studies the production and delivery of content through a variety of media, especially non-print-based media such as television and radio.

- Information Theory, which takes up the subject of communication and the transmission and storage of messages typically from the perspective of applied mathematics and computation. Information theory looks at the ways in which information is encoded in digital media and related devices. Programs in information theory, while having much in common with Media Studies programs, are often housed within departments of mathematics and computer science at contemporary universities.

- Popular Culture Studies, which takes as its subject the social, political, and aesthetic environments that envelop humans on a daily basis. Students of popular culture examine the meaning and significance of the art, music, games, books, fashion, and other trends that give shape to our everyday experiences.

- Rhetoric, which is the study of the ways language is used to transmit information, and, in particular, to persuade an audience. Unlike the disciplines noted above, rhetoric is one of the most ancient of all disciplines, with its roots in the ancient Greek writers of 2,500 years ago. Students of rhetoric study the forms and figures of language that allow for the detailed analysis of language-based communication.

The range of topics for study under these categories is as diverse as the human experience itself. In the readings that follow, you will find selections that cover only a few of the virtually unlimited possibilities.

REFLECTING ON THIS CHAPTER

The disciplines and topics covered in this chapter are wide-ranging, but they have in common the desire to bring the means through which we send and receive messages to the forefront, to make processes of engaging everyday reality that are normally invisible to us visible, and to reflect on the significance and meaning of those processes. As you read the essays in this chapter, consider the following questions:

- What is the central issue or problem the author attempts to explore or solve? What claims does the author make, and does the author make a convincing argument in support of those claims?

- So much of our daily engagement with media and our experience with popular culture is part of the white noise of our daily lives. How do these selections force us to think about and reexamine our day-to-day experiences?

- How do these selections compare and contrast? What central issues and themes emerge from these selections when taken as a group?

- What are the various writing strategies the authors employ? What rhetorical tools do they use to persuade us? If you found a selection convincing, what made it so?

- Do you detect any logical flaws in the arguments developed by the authors of these selections? Can you find any inconsistencies or biases? Are there any contradictions within each selection? What recommendations would you make to the author about how he or she might improve their essay?

From *Understanding Media*

Marshall McLuhan

Marshall McLuhan (1911-1980) became something of a cultural icon in the 1960s and 1970s with his popular and heralded studies in communication theory. He attended college at the University of Manitoba, where he earned both a B.A. and an M.A. in English literature. He spent two years at Cambridge University, earning a B.A. in English in 1936 and studying under such notable scholars at the time as I. A. Richards and F. R. Leavis. Richards, in particular, was a strong influence on the later work of McLuhan. McLuhan taught English literature at Saint Louis University and, while teaching, finished writing his dissertation and was awarded his Ph.D. from Cambridge in 1943. He returned to Canada in 1944, eventually settling into a job at the University of Toronto, where he taught from 1946 till 1979, and where he founded the Centre for Culture and Technology in 1963, a research center he would direct for most of the remainder of his career. Aside from Understanding Media, *from which the following selection is taken, his works include* The Mechanical Bride *(1951),* The Gutenberg Galaxy *(1962),* The Medium is the Message *(1967),* War and Peace in the Global Village *(1968), among others. His communications theories, as detailed in these works, revolutionized our understanding of the role media play in the shaping of individual human consciousness.*

THE MEDIUM IS THE MESSAGE

1   In a culture like ours, long accustomed to splitting and dividing all things as a means of control, it is sometimes a bit of a shock to be reminded that, in operational and practical fact, the medium is the message. This is merely to say that the personal and social consequences of any medium—that is, of any extension of ourselves—result from the new scale that is introduced into our affairs by each extension of ourselves, or by any new technology. Thus, with automation, for example, the new patterns of human association tend to eliminate jobs, it is true. That is the negative result. Positively, automation creates roles for people, which is to say depth of involvement in their work and human association that our preceding mechanical technology had destroyed. Many people would be disposed to say that it was not the machine, but what one did with the machine, that was its meaning or message. In terms of the ways in which the machine altered our relations to one another and to ourselves, it mattered not in the least whether it turned out cornflakes or Cadillacs. The restructuring of human work and association was shaped by the technique of fragmentation that is the essence of machine technology. The essence of automation technology is the opposite. It is integral and decentralist in depth, just as the machine was fragmentary, centralist, and superficial in its patterning of human relationships.

2   The instance of the electric light may prove illuminating in this connection. The electric light is pure information. It is a medium without a message, as it were, unless it is used to spell out some verbal ad or name. This fact, characteristic of all media, means that the "content" of any medium is always another medium. The content of writing is speech, just as the written word is the content of print, and print is the content of the telegraph. If it is asked, "What is the

content of speech?," it is necessary to say, "It is an actual process of thought, which is in itself nonverbal." An abstract painting represents direct manifestation of creative thought processes as they might appear in computer designs. What we are considering here, however, are the psychic and social designs or patterns as they amplify or accelerate existing processes. For the "message" of any medium or technology is the change of scale it introduces into human affairs. The railway did not introduce movement or transportation or wheel or road into human society, but it accelerated and enlarged the scale of previous human functions, creating cities and new kinds of work and leisure. This happened whether the railway functioned in a tropical or a northern environment, and is quite independent of the freight or content of the railway medium. The airplane accelerating the rate of transportation, tends to dissolve the railway form of city, politics, and association, quite independently of what the airplane is used for.

3   Let us return to the electric light. Whether the light is being used for brain surgery or night baseball is a matter of indifference. It could be argued that these activities are in some way the "content" of the electric light, since they could not exist without the electric light. This fact merely underlines the point that "the medium is the message" because it is the medium that shapes and controls the scale and form of human association and action. The content or uses of such media are as diverse as they are ineffectual in shaping the form of human association. Indeed, it is only too typical that the "content" of any medium blinds us to the character of the medium. It is only today that industries have become aware of the various kinds of business in which they are engaged. When IBM discovered that it was not in the business of making office equipment or business machines, but that it was in the business of processing information, then it began to navigate with clear vision. The General Electric Company makes a considerable portion of its profits from electric light bulbs and lighting systems. It has not yet discovered that, quite as much as AT&T, it is in the business of moving information.

4   The electric light escapes attention as a communication medium just because it has no "content." And this makes it an invaluable instance of how people fail to study media at all. For it is not till the electric light is used to spell out some brand name that it is noticed as a medium. Then it is not the light but the "content" (or what is really another medium) that is noticed. The message of the electric light is like the message of electric power in industry, totally radical, pervasive, and decentralized. For electric light and power are separate from their uses, yet they eliminate time and space factors in human association exactly as do radio, telegraph, telephone, and TV, creating involvement in depth.

5   A fairly complete handbook for studying the extensions of man could be made up from selections from Shakespeare. Some might quibble he was referring to TV in these familiar lines from *Romeo and Juliet*

> *But soft! what light through yonder window breaks?*
> *It speaks, and yet says nothing.*

In *Othello*, which, as much as *King Lear*, is concerned with the torment of people transformed by illusions, there are these lines that bespeak Shakespeare's intuition of the transforming powers of new media:

> *Is there not charms*
> *By which the property of youth and maidhood*
> *May be abus'd? Have you not read Roderigo,*
> *Of some such thing?*

In Shakespeare's *Troilus and Cressida*, which is almost completely devoted to both a psychic and social study of communication, Shakespeare states his awareness that true social and political navigation depend upon anticipating the consequences of innovation:

> *The providence that's in a watchful state*
> *Knows almost every grain of Plutus' gold,*
> *Finds bottom in the uncomprehensive deeps,*
> *Keeps place with thought, and almost like the gods*
> *Does thoughts unveil in their dumb cradles.*

The increasing awareness of the action of media, quite independently of their "content" or programming, was indicated in the annoyed and anonymous stanza:

> *In modern thought, (if not in fact)*
> *Nothing is that doesn't act,*
> *So that is reckoned wisdom which*
> *Describes the scratch but not the itch.*

The same kind of total, configurational awareness that reveals why the medium is socially the message has occurred in the most recent and radical medical theories. In his *Stress of Life*, Hans Selye tells of the dismay of a research colleague on hearing of Selye's theory:

> *When he saw me thus launched on yet another enraptured description of what I had observed in animals treated with this or that impure, toxic material, he looked at me with desperately sad eyes and said in obvious despair: "But Selye, try to realize what you are doing before it is too late! You have now decided to spend your entire life studying the pharmacology of dirt!"*

6   As Selye deals with the total environmental situation in his "stress" theory of disease, so the latest approach to media study considers not only the "content" but the medium and the cultural matrix within which the particular medium operates. The older unawareness of the psychic and social effects of media can be illustrated from almost any of the conventional pronouncements.

7   In accepting an honorary degree from the University of Notre Dame a few years ago, General David Sarnoff made this statement: "We are too prone to make technological instruments the scapegoats for the sins of those who wield them. The products of modern science are not in themselves good or bad; it is the way they are used that determines their value." That is the voice of the current somnambulism. Suppose we were to say, "Apple pie is in itself neither good nor bad; it is the way it is used that determines its value." Or, "The small-pox virus is in itself neither good nor bad; it is the way it is used that determines its value." Again, "Firearms are in themselves neither good nor bad; it is the way they are used that determines their value." That is, if the slugs reach the right people firearms are good. If the TV tube fires the right ammunition at the right people it is good. I am not being perverse. There is simply nothing in the Sarnoff statement that will bear scrutiny, for it ignores the nature of the medium, of any and all media, in the true Narcissus[1] style of

---

[1]Narcissus: in Greek mythology, a young man so beautiful that he rejected the love of others and loved only himself, eventually falling in love with his own reflection in a pool of water, where, unable to reach the object of his affection, he died. In common usage today, a "narcissist" is one who is enamored with himself or herself in a manner that is conceited and egotistical.

one hypnotized by the amputation and extension of his own being in a new technical form. General Sarnoff went on to explain his attitude to the technology of print, saying that it was true that print caused much trash to circulate, but it had also disseminated the Bible and the thoughts of seers and philosophers. It has never occurred to General Sarnoff that any technology could do anything but *add* itself on to what we already are.

8   Such economists as Robert Theobald, W. W. Rostow, and John Ken Galbraith have been explaining for years how it is that "classical economics" cannot explain change or growth. And the paradox of mechanization is although it is itself the cause of maximal growth and change, the principle of mechanization excludes the very possibility of growth or the understanding of change. For mechanization is achieved by fragmentation of any process and by putting the fragmented parts in a series. Yet, as David Hume[2] showed in the eighteenth century, there is no principle of causality in a mere sequence. That one thing follows another accounts for nothing. Nothing follows from following, except change. So the greatest of all reversals occurred with electricity, that ended sequence by making things instant. With instant speed the causes of things began to emerge to awareness again, as they had not done with things in sequence and in concatenation accordingly. Instead of asking which came first, the chicken or the egg, it suddenly seemed that a chicken was an egg's idea for getting more eggs.

9   Just before an airplane breaks the sound barrier, sound waves become visible on the wings of the plane. The sudden visibility of sound just as sound ends is an apt instance of that great pattern of being that reveals new and opposite forms just as the earlier forms reach their peak performance. Mechanization was never so vividly fragmented or sequential as in the birth of the movies, the moment translated us beyond mechanism into the world of growth and organic interrelation. The movie, by sheer speeding up the mechanical, carried us from the world of sequence and connections into the world of creative configuration and structure. The message of the movie medium is that of transition from lineal connections to configurations. It is the transition that produced the now quite correct observation: "If it works, it's obsolete." When electric speed further takes over from mechanical movie sequences, then the lines of force in structures and in media become loud and clear. We return to the inclusive form of the icon.

10   To a highly literate and mechanized culture the movie appeared as a world of triumphant illusions and dreams that money could buy. It was at this moment of the movie that cubism[3] occurred, and it has been described by E. H. Gombrich (*Art and Illusion*) as "the most radical attempt to stamp out ambiguity and to enforce one reading of the picture—that of a man-made construction, a colored canvas." For cubism substitutes all facets of an object simultaneously for the "point of view" or facet of perspective illusion. Instead of the specialized illusion of the third dimension on canvas, cubism sets up an interplay of planes and contradiction or dramatic conflict of patterns, lights, textures that "drives home the message" by involvement. This is held by many to be an exercise in painting, not in illusion.

---

[2] David Hume: eighteenth-century Scottish philosopher and historian generally considered one of the greatest minds in the western philosophical tradition.

[3] Cubism: an early twentieth-century experimental form of painting, most famously practiced by Pablo Picasso, in which two-dimensional shapes are used to represent three-dimensional objects.

11   In other words, cubism, by giving the inside and outside, the top, bottom, back, and front and the rest, in two dimensions, drops the illusion of perspective in favor of instant sensory awareness of the whole Cubism, by seizing on instant total awareness, suddenly announced that *the medium is the message*. Is it not evident that the moment that sequence yields to the simultaneous, one is in the world of the structure and of configuration? Is that not what has happened in physics as in painting, poetry, and in communication? Specialized segments of attention have shifted to total field, and we can now say, "The medium is the message" quite naturally. Before the electric speed and total field, it was not obvious that the medium is the message. The message, it seemed, was the "content," as people used to ask what a painting was *about*. Yet they never thought to ask what a melody was about, nor what a house or a dress was about. In such matters, people retained some sense of the whole pattern, of form and function as a unity. But in the electric age this integral idea of structure and configuration has become so prevalent that educational theory has taken up the matter. Instead of working with specialized "problems" in arithmetic, the structural approach now follows the lines of force in the field of number and has small children meditating about number theory and "sets."

12   Cardinal Newman said of Napoleon, "He understood the grammer of gunpowder." Napoleon had paid some attention to other media as well, especially the semaphore telegraph that gave him a great advantage over his enemies. He is on record for saying that "Three hostile newspapers are more to be feared than a thousand bayonets."

QUESTIONS ON MEANING

1. What does McLuhan mean when he asserts that the medium is the message?

2. In what way is the electric light a medium?

3. What does McLuhan mean when he refers to media as extensions of man?

4. Why don't purely mechanical explanations account for growth and change in society and in individuals?

5. How has Western culture changed in what McLuhan calls the electric age?

6. What point does McLuhan seem to be making by including the Shakespeare passages?

7. What error, as McLuhan sees it, does David Sarnoff make in his commentary?

QUESTIONS FOR DISCUSSION

1. Do you agree that media function as extensions of our five senses? Is this true for all media? How do newspapers extend our senses? What about television? Radio? The internet?

2. McLuhan writes, "the 'message' of any medium or technology is the change of scale or pace or pattern that it introduces into human affairs." What does McLuhan mean by this? Do you agree? How have the following technologies and mediums changed the pattern or pace of human affairs?
A. Word processors
B. Laptop computers
C. The internet
D. Email

E. Cell phones
F. Texting
G. Social networks such as Twitter and Facebook
H. Video game consoles

3. Referring to the list of technologies and mediums in the previous question, what technologies or mediums or activities did A-H above make less relevant? More relevant?

4. What does McLuhan mean when he says, "If it works, it's obsolete"? In your experience, is this aphorism true? Can you think of examples that either support or disprove this aphorism?

WRITING IN THE DISCIPLINE

1. In another passage later in *Understanding Media*, McLuhan writes: "the 'content' of a medium is like the juicy piece of meat, carried by the burglar to distract the watchdog of the mind." What does McLuhan mean by this simile? Locate at least two additional uses of figurative language in the excerpt reprinted in this anthology. Do these metaphors and similes contribute to, or distract from, McLuhan's presentation of his thesis and arguments?

2. McLuhan quotes from other sources frequently. Which of the quotes is the most compelling? Which is the least compelling? Do these quotes, taken as a whole, increase the effectiveness of the essay? Why or why not?

WRITING ASSIGNMENTS

1. Research the history of the invention, evolution, and use of one of the mediums listed in Discussion Question #2. Write an essay in which you present an overview of this history and argue that the incorporation of this technology has or has not changed the fundamental pace or pattern of contemporary life.

2. Which is more important in shaping individual human lives, the medium or the content that the medium transmits? Write an essay in which you explain McLuhan's answer to this question and then either argue in support of McLuhan or in opposition to McLuhan.

3. In pairs or in groups, create a list of fifteen different mediums through which individuals receive information in contemporary society. Spend some time as a group discussing how each of these mediums has exerted a shaping influence on the life of an individual. Then, independently of the group, place these mediums in order from the one that has the most profound shaping influence on individuals to the one that has the least influence. Then, as individuals, draft an essay in which you explain why the medium at the top of the list is the most influential, and why the item at the bottom of the list is the least influential.

Subculture and Style

Dick Hebdige

Dick Hebdige (b. 1951) is a sociologist, media theorist, and professor who has written extensively in the new field of cultural studies, with a particular emphasis on the role of media and power, the manner in which socially constituted values or codes work to reinforce existing power relations.

He received his M. A. degree from the Centre for Contemporary Cultural Studies in Birmingham, United Kingdom. This is the institution that was the primary hub of the "Birmingham School" of cultural studies. He became the Dean of Critical Studies and Director of the Experimental Writing Program at the California Institute of the Arts and later joined the faculty at the University of California, Santa Barbara, as a professor of film and media studies. His most important book is Subculture: The Meaning of Style, *from which this selection is taken. He explores the evolving definition of the word "culture" and the role of subcultures in resisting the dominant power relations that exist within societies. In this excerpt, he explores how culturally conditioned value systems work in our formal and informal social relations, concluding with a consideration of how and why youth subcultures emerge.*

ONE

From culture to hegemony

Culture

1   Culture is a notoriously ambiguous concept. Refracted through centuries of usage, the word has acquired a number of quite different, often contradictory, meanings.

2   The first basic definition of culture—the one which is probably most familiar to the reader—was essentially classical and conservative. It represented culture as a standard of aesthetic excellence: 'the best that has been thought and said in the world' (Arnold, 1868), and it derived from an appreciation of 'classic' aesthetic form (opera, ballet, drama, literature, art). The second, traced back by Williams to Herder and the eighteenth century (Williams, 1976), was rooted in anthropology. Here the term 'culture' referred to a

> *. . . particular way of life which expresses certain meanings and values not only in art and learning, but also in institutions and ordinary behaviour. The analysis of culture, from such a definition, is the clarification of the meanings and values implicit and explicit in a particular way of life, a particular culture. (Williams, 1965)*

3   This definition obviously had a much broader range. It encompassed, in T.S. Eliot's[1] words,

> *. . . all the characteristic activities and interests of a people. Derby Day, Henley Regatta, Cowes, the 12th of August, a cup final, the dog races, the pin table, the dartboard, Wensleydale cheese, boiled cabbage cut into sections, beetroot in vinegar, 19th Century Gothic churches, the music of Elgar. . . . (Eliot, 1948)*
>
> *As Williams noted, such a definition could only be supported if a new theoretical initiative was taken. The theory of culture now involved the 'study of relationships between elements in a whole way of life' (Williams, 1965). The emphasis shifted from immutable to historical criteria, from fixity to transformation:*
>
> *. . . an emphasis [which] from studying particular meanings and values seeks not so much to compare these, as a way of establishing a scale, but by studying their modes*

---

[1]Thomas Stearns Eliot (1888–1965): American born poet who lived most of his adult life in Great Britain. Associated with the modernist period, he is widely regarded as one of the most important poets of the twentieth century.

of change to discover certain general causes or 'trends' by which social and cultural developments as a whole can be better understood. (Williams, 1965)

Williams was, then, proposing an altogether broader formulation of the relationships between culture and society, one which through the analysis of 'particular meanings and values' sought to uncover the concealed fundamentals of history; the 'general causes' and broad social 'trends' which lie behind the manifest appearances of an 'everyday life'.

4   In the early years, when it was being established in the Universities, Cultural Studies sat rather uncomfortably on the fence between these two conflicting definitions—culture as a standard of excellence, culture as a 'whole way of life'—unable to determine which represented the most fruitful line of enquiry.

5   The implicit assumption that it still required a literary sensibility to 'read' society with the requisite subtlety, and that the two ideas of culture could be ultimately reconciled was also, paradoxically, to inform the early work of the French writer, Roland Barthes, though here it found validation in a method—semiotics—a way of reading signs (Hawkes, 1977).

Barthes: Myths and signs

6   Using models derived from the work of the Swiss linguist Ferdinand de Saussure,[2] Barthes sought to expose the *arbitrary* nature of cultural phenomena, to uncover the latent meanings of an everyday life which, to all intents and purposes, was 'perfectly natural'. Barthes was concerned with showing how *all* the apparently spontaneous forms and rituals of contemporary bourgeois societies are subject to a systematic distortion, liable at any moment to be dehistoricized, 'naturalized', converted into myth:

The whole of France is steeped in this anonymous ideology: our press, our films, our theatre, our pulp literature, our rituals, our Justice, our diplomacy, our conversations, our remarks about the weather, a murder trial, a touching wedding, the cooking we dream of, the garments we wear, everything in everyday life is dependent on the representation which the bourgeoisie has and makes us have of the relations between men and the world. (Barthes, 1972)

7   Like Eliot, Barthes' notion of culture extends beyond the library, the opera-house and the theatre to encompass the whole of everyday life. But this everyday life is for Barthes overlaid with a significance which is at once more insidious and more systematically organized. Starting from the premise that 'myth is a type of speech', Barthes set out in *Mythologies* to examine the normally hidden set of rules, codes and conventions through which meanings particular to specific social groups (i.e. those in power) are rendered universal and 'given' for the whole of society. He found in phenomena as disparate as a wrestling match, a writer on holiday, a tourist-guide book, the same artificial nature, the same ideological core. Each had been exposed to the same prevailing rhetoric (the rhetoric of common sense) and turned into myth, into a mere element

---

[2] Ferdinand de Saussure (1857–1913): Swiss linguist whose ideas are regarded as the foundation for much modern linguistics.

in a 'second-order semiological system' (Barthes. 1972). (Barthes uses the example of a photograph in *Paris-Match* of a Negro soldier saluting the French flag, which has a first and second order connotation: (1) a gesture of loyalty, but also (2) 'France is a great empire, and all her sons, without colour discrimination, faithfully serve under her flag'.)

8   Barthes' application of a method rooted in linguistics to other systems of discourse outside language (fashion, film, food, etc.) opened up completely new possibilities for contemporary cultural studies. It was hoped that the invisible seam between language, experience and reality could be located and prised open through a semiotic analysis of this kind: that the gulf between the alienated intellectual and the 'real' world could be rendered meaningful and, miraculously, at the same time, be made to disappear.

Ideology: A lived relation

9   In the German Ideology, Marx[3] shows how the basis of the capitalist economic structure (surplus value, neatly defined by Godelier as 'Profit . . . is unpaid work' (Godelier, 1970)) is hidden from the consciousness of the agents of production. The failure to see through appearances to the real relations which underlie them does not occur as the direct result of some kind of masking operation consciously carried out by individuals, social groups or institutions. On the contrary, ideology by definition thrives *beneath* consciousness. It is here, at the level of 'normal common sense', that ideological frames of reference are most firmly sedimented and most effective, because it is here that their ideological nature is most effectively concealed. As Stuart Hall puts it:

> It is precisely its 'spontaneous' quality, its transparency, its 'naturalness', its refusal to be made to examine the premises on which it is founded, its resistance to change or to correction, its effect of instant recognition, and the closed circle in which it moves which makes common sense, at one and the same time, 'spontaneous', ideological and unconscious. You cannot learn, through common sense, how things are: you can only discover where they fit into the existing scheme of things. In this way, its very taken-for-grantedness is what establishes it as a medium in which its own premises and presuppositions are being rendered invisible by its apparent transparency. (Hall, 1977)

10   Since ideology saturates everyday discourse in the form of common sense, it cannot be bracketed off from everyday life as a self-contained set of 'political opinions' or 'biased views'. Neither can it be reduced to the abstract dimensions of a 'world view' or used in the crude Marxist sense to designate 'false consciousness'. Instead, as Louis Althusser has pointed out:

> . . . ideology has very little to do with 'consciousness'. . . . It is profoundly unconscious. . . . Ideology is indeed a system of representation, but in the majority of cases these representations have nothing to do with 'consciousness': they are usually images and

---

[3] Karl Marx (1818–1883): German philosopher, economist, and political theorist who, in the context of the brutalities of the industrial revolution, created a radical form of socialism which he called communism.

occasionally concepts, but it is above all as structures *that they impose on the vast majority of men, not via their 'consciousness'. They are perceived-accepted-suffered cultural objects and they act functionally on men via a process that escapes them.* (Althusser, 1969)

11   Although Althusser is here referring to structures like the family, cultural and political institutions, etc., we can illustrate the point quite simply by taking as our example a physical structure. Most modern institutes of education, despite the apparent neutrality of the materials from which they are constructed (red brick, white tile, etc.) carry within themselves implicit ideological assumptions which are literally structured into the architecture itself. The categorization of knowledge into arts and sciences is reproduced in the faculty system which houses different disciplines in different buildings, and most colleges maintain the traditional divisions by devoting a separate floor to each subject. Moreover, the hierarchical relationship between teacher and taught is inscribed in the very layout of the lecture theatre where the seating arrangements—benches rising in tiers before a raised lectern—dictate the flow of information and serve to 'naturalize' professorial authority. Thus, a whole range of decisions about what is and what is not possible within education have been made, however unconsciously, before the content of individual courses is even decided.

12   These decisions help to set the limits not only on what is taught but on *how* it is taught. Here the buildings literally *reproduce* in concrete terms prevailing (ideological) notions about what education *is* and it is through this process that the educational structure, which can, of course, be altered, is placed beyond question and appears to us as a 'given' (i.e. as immutable). In this case, the frames of our thinking have been translated into actual bricks and mortar.

13   Social relations and processes are then appropriated by individuals only through the forms in which they are represented to those individuals. These forms are, as we have seen, by no means transparent. They are shrouded in a 'common sense' which simultaneously validates and mystifies them. It is precisely these 'perceived-accepted-suffered cultural objects' which semiotics sets out to 'interrogate' and decipher. All aspects of culture possess a semiotic value, and the most taken-for-granted phenomena can function as signs: as elements in communication systems governed by semantic rules and codes which are not themselves directly apprehended in experience. These signs are, then, as opaque as the social relations which produce them and which they re-present. In other words, there is an ideological dimension to every signification:

A sign does not simply exist as part of reality – it reflects and refracts another reality. Therefore it may distort that reality or be true to it, or may perceive it from a special point of view, and so forth. Every sign is subject to the criteria of ideological evaluation. . . . The domain of ideology coincides with the domain of signs. They equate with one another. Whenever a sign is present, ideology is present too. Everything ideological possesses a semiotic value. (Volosinov, 1973)

14   To uncover the ideological dimension of signs we must first try to disentangle the codes through which meaning is organized. 'Connotative' codes are particularly important.

As Stuart Hall has argued, they '. . . cover the face of social life and render it classifiable, intelligible, meaningful' (Hall, 1977). He goes on to describe these codes as 'maps of meaning' which are of necessity the product of selection. They cut across a range of potential meanings, making certain meanings available and ruling others out of court. We tend to live inside these maps as surely as we live in the 'real' world: they 'think' us as much as we 'think' them, and this in itself is quite 'natural'. All human societies *reproduce* themselves in this way through a process of 'naturalization'. It is through this process—a kind of inevitable reflex of all social life—that *particular* sets of social relations, *particular* ways of organizing the world appear to us as if they were universal and timeless. This is what Althusser (1971) means when he says that 'ideology has no history' and that ideology in this general sense will always be an 'essential element of every social formation' (Althusser and Balibar, 1968).

15   However, in highly complex societies like ours, which function through a finely graded system of divided (i.e. specialized) labour, the crucial question has to do with which specific ideologies, representing the interests of which specific groups and classes will prevail at any given moment, in any given situation. To deal with this question, we must first consider how power is distributed in our society. That is, we must ask which groups and classes have how much say in defining, ordering and classifying out the social world. For instance, if we pause to reflect for a moment, it should be obvious that access to the means by which ideas are disseminated in our society (i.e. principally the mass media) is *not* the same for all classes. Some groups have more say, more opportunity to make the rules, to organize meaning, while others are less favourably placed, have less power to produce and impose their definitions of the world on the world.

16   Thus, when we come to look beneath the level of 'ideology-in-general' at the way in which specific ideologies work, how some gain dominance and others remain marginal, we can see that in advanced Western democracies the ideological field is by no means neutral. To return to the 'connotative' codes to which Stuart Hall refers we can see that these 'maps of meaning' are charged with a potentially explosive significance because they are traced and re-traced along the lines laid down by the *dominant* discourses about reality, the *dominant* ideologies. They thus tend to represent, in however obscure and contradictory a fashion, the interests of the *dominant* groups in society.

17   To understand this point we should refer to Marx:

> *The ideas of the ruling class are in every epoch the ruling ideas, i.e. the class which is the ruling material force of society is at the same time its ruling intellectual force. The class which has the means of material production at its disposal, has control at the same time over the means of mental production, so that generally speaking, the ideas of those who lack the means of mental production are subject to it. The ruling ideas are nothing more than the ideal expression of the dominant material relationships grasped as ideas; hence of the relationships which make the one class the ruling class, therefore the ideas of its dominance. (Marx and Engels, 1970)*

18   This is the basis of Antonio Gramsci's theory of *hegemony* which provides the most adequate account of how dominance is sustained in advanced capitalist societies.

Hegemony: The moving equilibrium

'Society cannot share a common communication system so long as it is split into warring classes' (Brecht, A Short Organum for the Theatre).

19   The term hegemony refers to a situation in which a provisional alliance of certain social groups can exert 'total social authority' over other subordinate groups, not simply by coercion or by the direct imposition of ruling ideas, but by 'winning and shaping consent so that the power of the dominant classes appears both legitimate and natural' (Hall, 1977). Hegemony can only be maintained so long as the dominant classes 'succeed in framing all competing definitions within their range' (Hall, 1977), so that subordinate groups are, if not controlled; then at least contained within an ideological space which does not seem at all 'ideological': which appears instead to be permanent and 'natural', to lie outside history, to be beyond particular interests (see *Social Trends*, no. 6, 1975).

20   This is how, according to Barthes, 'mythology' performs its vital function of naturalization and normalization and it is in his book *Mythologies* that Barthes demonstrates most forcefully the full extension of these normalized forms and meanings. However, Gramsci adds the important proviso that hegemonic power, precisely *because* it requires the consent of the dominated majority, can never be permanently exercised by the same alliance of 'class fractions'. As has been pointed out, 'Hegemony . . . is not universal and "given" to the continuing rule of a particular class. It has to be won, reproduced, sustained. Hegemony is, as Gramsci said, a "moving equilibrium" containing relations of forces favourable or unfavourable to this or that tendency' (Hall *et al.*, 1976a).

21   In the same way, forms cannot be permanently normalized. They can always be deconstructed, demystified, by a 'mythologist' like Barthes. Moreover commodities can be symbolically 'repossessed' in everyday life, and endowed with implicitly oppositional meanings, by the very groups who originally produced them. The symbiosis in which ideology and social order, production and reproduction, are linked is then neither fixed nor guaranteed. It can be prised open. The consensus can be fractured, challenged, overruled, and resistance to the groups in dominance cannot always be lightly dismissed or automatically incorporated.

22   We can now return to the meaning of youth subcultures, for the emergence of such groups has signalled in a spectacular fashion the breakdown of consensus in the postwar period. In the following chapters we shall see that it is precisely objections and contradictions of the kind which Lefebvre has described that find expression in subculture. However, the challenge to hegemony which subcultures represent is not issued directly by them. Rather it is expressed obliquely, in style. The objections are lodged, the contradictions displayed (and, as we shall see, 'magically resolved') at the profoundly superficial level of appearances: that is, at the level of signs.

23   Style in subculture is, then, pregnant with significance. Its transformations go 'against nature', interrupting the process of 'normalization'. As such, they are gestures, movements towards a speech which offends the 'silent majority', which challenges the principle of unity and cohesion, which contradicts the myth of consensus. Our task becomes, like Barthes', to discern the hidden messages inscribed in code on the glossy surfaces of style,

to trace them out as 'maps of meaning' which obscurely re-present the very contradictions they are designed to resolve or conceal.

24   Academics who adopt a semiotic approach are not alone in reading significance into the loaded surfaces of life. The existence of spectacular subcultures continually opens up those surfaces to other potentially subversive readings. Jean Genet, the archetype of the 'unnatural' deviant, again exemplifies the practice of resistance through style. He is as convinced in his own way as is Roland Barthes of the ideological character of cultural signs. He is equally oppressed by the seamless web of forms and meanings which encloses and yet excludes him. His reading is equally partial. He makes his own list and draws his own conclusions:

> I was astounded by so rigorous an edifice whose details were united against me. Nothing in the world is irrelevant: the stars on a general's sleeve, the stock-market quotations, the olive harvest, the style of the judiciary, the wheat exchange, the flower-beds, . . . Nothing. This order . . . had a meaning—my exile. (Genet, 1967)

25   It is this alienation from the deceptive 'innocence' of appearances which gives the teds, the mods, the punks and no doubt future groups of as yet unimaginable 'deviants' the impetus to move from man's second 'false nature' (Barthes, 1972) to a genuinely expressive artifice; a truly subterranean style. As a symbolic violation of the social order, such a movement attracts and will continue to attract attention, to provoke censure and to act, as we shall see, as the fundamental bearer of significance in subculture.

QUESTION ON MEANING

1. According to Roland Barthes, what is a semiotic sign and how does it function within a culture?
2. What did Karl Marx mean by the term *ideology* and how did it evolve in the new cultural studies project?
3. How is ideology related to common sense?
4. How do colleges and college curricula reflect ideology?
5. What does the term *hegemony* mean? What is its relationship to ideology?
6. What is a subculture and how does it challenge hegemony through style?

QUESTIONS FOR DISCUSSION

1. What do we gain by understanding the complex meaning of the term *culture*?
2. To what extent are our values, what cultural studies theorists would call our ideology, timeless and transcendent? To what extent are they historically specific, linked to time and place?
3. In what way are subcultures a form of resistance? What other roles do these subcultures play in the lives of young people?

LOOKING AT RHETORIC

1. In what way does Hebige's academic orientation, and/or his dependence on other thinkers, enhance or detract from his argument?

2. The selections build by defining terms. Does this clarify your understanding of the abstract concepts he is exploring?

3. Does the use of elevated vocabulary enhance the credibility of his argument? Does it inhibit your understanding? What are the advantages and disadvantages to this approach to writing?

WRITING ASSIGNMENTS

1. Using library and/or Internet sources, research definitions of ideology and value formation. Argue for or against the idea that our common sense values are ideological, that is, oriented to support the ruling class.

2. Argue for or against the idea that the primary purpose of subcultures is to resist the interests, or hegemony, of the dominant groups.

3. In pairs or in groups, discuss the various subcultures you have been a part of or seen. Individually, write an essay in which you demonstrate how they express themselves through style.

From *Understanding Comics*
Scott McCloud

Scott McCloud (b. 1960) is one of the leading comics theorists working today. His book, Understanding Comics, *which was first published in 1993 and from which the following selection is taken, remains one of the most important texts in the field. In this work, McCloud not only introduces the study and appreciation of comics to a broad audience, he does so in a way that lays the groundwork for much further critical investigation. McCloud followed up this work with two additional theoretical texts—*Reinventing Comics *(2000) and* Making Comics *(2006)—which helped push the boundaries of the medium. Aside from his theoretical writings, McCloud is also the creator of the comic book series* Zot! *which ran from 1984–1991. He also wrote a number of scripts for Superman comics, as well as a host of other projects. Always interested in experimenting with the comics medium, McCloud has been a key advocate of using online technology to create new comics designs, and he is credited with the invention of the "24 Hour Comic" in which a given artist has twenty-four hours to write and draw a complete twenty-four page comic. In the following selection, from the first chapter of* Understanding Comics, *McCloud presents a definition of the medium and begins to discuss some of the implications of that definition.*

Setting the Record Straight

CHAPTER ONE

SETTING THE RECORD STRAIGHT.

HI, I'M *SCOTT McCLOUD.*

WHEN I WAS A *LITTLE KID* I KNEW *EXACTLY* WHAT COMICS WERE.

COMICS WERE THOSE *BRIGHT, COLORFUL MAGAZINES* FILLED WITH *BAD ART, STUPID STORIES* AND *GUYS IN TIGHTS.*

I READ *REAL* BOOKS, NATURALLY. I WAS MUCH TOO *OLD* FOR COMICS!

BUT WHEN I WAS IN *8th GRADE,* A FRIEND OF MINE (WHO WAS A LOT *SMARTER* THAN I WAS) CONVINCED ME TO GIVE COMICS ANOTHER LOOK AND LENT ME HIS COLLECTION.

SOON, I WAS *HOOKED!*

THE ARTFORM--THE *MEDIUM*--KNOWN AS COMICS IS A *VESSEL* WHICH CAN HOLD ANY *NUMBER* OF *IDEAS* AND *IMAGES*.

COMICS

Writers
ARTISTS
Trends
GENRES
STYLES
Subject matter
THEMES

THE *"CONTENT"* OF THOSE IMAGES AND IDEAS IS, OF COURSE, UP TO *CREATORS*, AND WE ALL HAVE DIFFERENT *TASTES*.

GLUG
GLUG

PTUI!!!

GAAK
WHEEEEZ
KAF! KAF!
GLUGH-GGH...

ahem

THE *TRICK* IS TO NEVER MISTAKE THE *MESSAGE*--

--FOR THE *MESSENGER.*

COMICS

AT ONE TIME OR ANOTHER VIRTUALLY *ALL* THE GREAT MEDIA HAVE RECEIVED *CRITICAL EXAMINATION,* IN AND OF *THEMSELVES.*

WRITTEN WORD

MUSIC

VIDEO

THEATRE

VISUAL ART

FILM

BUT FOR *COMICS,* THIS ATTENTION HAS BEEN *RARE.* *

LET'S SEE IF WE CAN HELP *RECTIFY* THE SITUATION.

*EISNER'S OWN *COMICS AND SEQUENTIAL ART* BEING A HAPPY EXCEPTION.

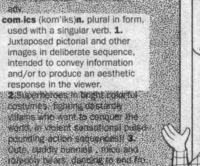

QUESTIONS ON MEANING

1. What is McCloud's definition of comics?

2. Why is it important for McCloud to separate the comics' form from its content?

3. According to McCloud's definition, why can't a lone picture (or single panel) be considered comics?

4. What distinguishes film from comics?

5. As set forth in McCloud's dictionary definition of comics, what are the two uses of comics?

6. What is the difference between comics and cartoons?

QUESTIONS FOR DISCUSSION

1. Do you read and enjoy comics? Why or why not? What appeals to you about comics? What doesn't appeal to you about comics? Do you have a particular favorite comic?

2. McCloud's theories have been heavily influenced by Marshall McLuhan's work *Understanding Media* (a piece of which is included in this anthology). What passages/panels in McCloud's selection seem to demonstrate McLuhan's influence?

3. One use of comics, according to McCloud, is to convey information. What kinds of information can comics convey? Are comics better at conveying certain kinds of information than others? What are some ways you see comics being used to convey information in contemporary society?

4. The other use of comics is to produce an aesthetic response in the viewer. What does this mean? Is this a use that can be measured or quantified in some way?

5. Do you believe comics is an art form? Why or why not?

LOOKING AT RHETORIC

1. How does the fact that McCloud narrates this selection through an avatar of himself affect the way the reader responds to the information presented in the selection?

2. Are you more, or less, inclined to take McCloud seriously as a theorist because he conveys his theories using comics? What would you think of McCloud's ideas if they had been presented in a prose essay rather than as comics? Would it make a difference to you? Why or why not?

WRITING ASSIGNMENTS

1. Write an essay in the form of an 8-10 page comic in which you respond to a particular argument found in McCloud's piece (you will not be judged on artistic merit, so don't worry if you cannot draw as well as McCloud—just do your best.) Be sure to take a clear position in your comics-essay: argue either in support or in opposition to McCloud.

2. Write an essay in which you critically examine McCloud's definition of comics. Is it a successful definition or not? Explain why or why not.

3. In pairs or in groups, discuss the importance of comics as an artistic medium compared with other mediums, such as film, painting, poetry, and novels. Is the medium more or less important in contemporary culture than these other mediums? Then, as individuals, select one other medium and write an essay in which you compare and contrast that medium with comics.

From *Reading Comics*

Douglas Wolk

Douglas Wolk is a freelance writer based in Portland, Oregon. His writing focuses on aspects of contemporary culture, with a special interest in music and comics. His essays have appeared in numerous publications, including The New York Times, Rolling Stone, The Washington Post, The Nation, Salon.com, *and* The New Republic, *among others. His book,* Reading Comics, *was published in 2007 and won the 2008 Eisner Award for best book on comics. In the following selection, which is chapter three of* Reading Comics, *Wolk takes a look at comics as a unique cultural phenomenon.*

NAMES AND HOW TO USE THEM

1   Comics' content and their social context are inextricably linked. Reading comics, or not reading them, often presents itself as taking some kind of stand; in picking up something with words and pictures to read, you become the sort of person who reads comics, and that can be a badge of pride or shame or both. That means that comics readers make up a subculture (the way that book readers and moviegoers and music listeners don't), and members of subcultures are very particular about what sub-subgroups they do and don't belong to.

2   As we've seen, the divergence of art comics from mainstream comics has led to a schism that looks a lot like class conflict, although it has more to do with class as expressed through taste than actual economics. But when people want to differentiate rather similar things from one another, there are always struggles over names, and where there's class tension over taste, there are always social climbers: people who want to make it very clear that what they like is a higher-status thing and not a lower-status thing. Those conflicts have been going on for a couple of decades in relation to the very basic question of what with panels and word balloons and so on that I'm discussing in this book. The cheap way of referring to them is "comics" or "comic books;" the fancy way is "graphic novels" (or "graphic narratives" or "sequential art").

3   Whatever you call them marks you as a product of an ideology, and that goes for me too, but I do have some reasons behind my preferences. In general, I tend to use "comics," because it's the word that people who actually make them use among themselves. The industry calls thin, saddle-stitched pamphlets "comic books" (or, more jokingly, "floppies" or "periodicals"), virtually any squarebound volume of comics sold on bookstore shelves a "graphic novel," and the form in the abstract "comics." That's how I generally use those terms, too.

4   Comics as a medium and comics as physical pamphlets have pretty much the same name, because for historical and economic reasons they're almost always tied together. American comics as we know them started out as pamphlets, and that's still how a lot of major projects first appear.

5   I don't much love *any* of the common words for comics, but that's what you get when a medium develops before it starts thinking of itself as an art form. "Comic book" is, as plenty of people have noted, a terrible name: "comic" implies that they're funny, and "book" suggests that they're not pamphlets and come in a single, concrete form. "Graphic novel" is even more problematic, though.

6   But the "novel" part of "graphic novel" blots out the idea of short fiction and nonfiction—it's odd to call, say, books of reportage in cartoon form by Joe Sacco and Ted Rall "novels," or to suggest that memoirs by Alison Bechdel and Harvey Pekar are fictional, or that a collection of short pieces by Ellen Forney or C. Tyler is actually an extended, unified story. Given how long it takes to draw comics, the idea that the "novel" is the default form for the ones with high aspirations is also pernicious, because it suggests that shorter stories can't be serious. "Graphic narrative," sounds like a euphemism twice removed from its source and still has the unfortunate resonance of "graphic" with the way it tends to be paired with "sexuality" or "violence." And "sequential art" sounds utterly arid.

7   The class implications of "graphic novel" almost instantly led to the term's thorough debasement. As a ten-dollar phrase, it implies that the graphic novel is serious in a way that the lowly comic book isn't. That, of course, leaves it open to being co-opted by anybody who wants to dress up their inept little drawings in a jacket and tie.

8   Even so, to this day, people talk about "graphic novels" instead of comics when they're trying to be deferential or trying to imply that they're being serious. There's always a bit of a wince and stammer about the term; it plays into comics culture's slightly miserable striving for "acknowledgment" and "respect." It's hard to imagine what kind of cultural capital the American comics industry (and its readership) is convinced that it's due and doesn't already have. Perhaps the comics world has spent so long hating itself that it can't imagine it's not still an under-dog. But demanding (or wishing for) a place at the table of high culture is an admission that you don't have one; the way you get a place at the table of high culture is to pull up a chair and say something interesting.

WHY I HATE MY CULTURE

9   The blessing and curse of comics as a medium is that there is such a thing as "comics culture." The core audience of comics is *really* into them: we know that Wednesdays are the day when new comics appear in the stores, we populate endless Web sites and message boards, we preserve our comics with some degree of care even if we think of ourselves as "readers" rather than "collectors." A few times a year, we congregate at conventions of one kind or another. (Alternative Press Expo, Small Press Expo, and the Museum of Comic and Cartoon Art Festival are our Sundances, where small-press and independent publishers display their wares; Wizard World Chicago is where the superhero buffs go; Comic-Con International is where *everybody* goes—around a hundred thousand attendees paralyze the entire city of San Diego for five days in July.) We gravitate to our kind.

10   That's part of the problem. Over the last half century, comics culture has developed as an insular, self-feeding, self-loathing, self-defeating fly-trap. A lot of the people who hit their local comics store every Wednesday think of comics readers as some kind of

secret, embattled fellowship: a group with its own private codes that mark its members as belonging and everybody else as not belonging. (That's why most comics stores are deeply unfriendly places: everything about them says "You mean you don't *know*?" In some of them, even new pamphlets and books are sealed in plastic before they go out on the shelves; if you don't walk into the store knowing what you want, you're not going to find out.) It's a stupid and destructive mind-set for any number of reasons, the biggest one being that it means you have to buy into an entire culture, or at least come up with a reason that you're *not really* buying into it, to enjoy a comic book.

11   That incestuous relationship between audience and medium has been encouraged by the big comics publishers. As we'll see in the next chapter, mainstream comics pamphlets that are incomprehensible to anyone not already immersed in their culture aren't just the norm now; they're the point. If you pick up a story crammed full of inside references, and you're enough of an insider to catch them all, you're going to feel like it was made just for you, and it will intensify the sense of difference between you and non–comics readers.

12   The next step along that path of difference is the fetishization of the object that symbolizes it. The first wave of comics collectors were trying to preserve the past of their culture—to rescue the ephemeral pamphlets that made up comics' fragile history from the quick and sure destruction they were intended for. They wanted to hold on to the pleasure their favorite comics gave them and perhaps to understand how years' worth of stories about particular characters might fit together into a grander narrative than even those stories' creators imagined. There's something honorable about that.

13   The preservation impulse turned into a collector's impulse—what was once called "the nostalgia market." Uncommon issues, naturally, were worth a bit more, then a lot more, then became the object of speculation. Publishers started to play on the idea of collectibility (in 1965, Marvel launched a series reprinting comics that had been published less than four years earlier, *Marvel Collectors' Item Classics*); people started to hoard new comics with an eye to their future financial value, not the future pleasure to be had from owning them.

14   At the same time, even within art comics, there's a longing for the medium to get more of something that's usually called "legitimacy." There's an element of comics culture, sometimes called (a little derisively) "Team Comics," that gets excited whenever anything that looks like that acknowledgment or respect I mentioned above turns up in the outside world—a college class on the graphic novel, a Hollywood movie based on a graphic novel, a newspaper or magazine article about a cartoonist, somebody reading a comic book on a TV show. Different segments of Team Comics take notice if a TV character is reading a new issue of *Aquaman* or Lynda Barry's *One!Hundred!Demons!*, but the principle is the same.

15   Both the "Team Comics" culture vultures and the alternate-cover-hoarding mavens are driven by the desire to turn their hobby into some kind of *success* or *validation*, whether through affluence or cultural power, and that impulse *is* directly connected to the class aspirations that afflict the entire medium. A lot of comics readers are unhealthily attached to the idea that everyone else thinks what they do is kind of trashy and disreputable, and that they have to prove their favorite leisure activity worthy of respect—to show the world that they were right all along.

16   It's probably time to let go of that strain of earnest defensiveness. The snobbery of the rest of American culture toward comics is, if not entirely gone, dissipating quickly. In late 2006, Gene Luen Yang's graphic novel *American Born Chinese* was nominated for a National

Book Award (in the Young People's Literature category); when one commentator—Tony Long, a blogger at Wired News—opined that it shouldn't have been nominated because it wasn't prose, the comics world jumped down his throat. But it's not as if literary culture revolted as one: Long appears to have been the only voice of dissent, and as clueless as part of his argument was (he noted that, well, he hadn't actually read *American Born Chinese*), his point that Yang's book was the wrong medium for its award was at least debatable.

17   What's actually happening in culture at large is more like everyone trying to jump on the comics bandwagon—the "you mean I have to pretend to like graphic novels now too?" effect. The medium's new enemies are internal: the much less casual snobbery of the commercial mainstream and the art-comics world toward each other, and cartoonists' nostalgic yearning for the badness of the bad old days.

18   To use a film analogy, reading only auteurist[1] art comics is like being a filmgoer who watches only auteurist art cinema, but more than a few art-comics enthusiasts wouldn't dream of picking up a mainstream comic book, even as entertainment. In *The Comics Journal*, the largest magazine of comics criticism in America, coverage of superhero stuff is almost entirely exiled to Joe McCulloch's (very entertaining) occasional column "Cape Fear." Likewise, plenty of superhero buffs can't imagine being interested in some actionless black-and-white independent comic. In *Wizard*, the largest magazine of mainstream comics culture, there is very occasionally a don't-be-scared-of-this mention of *Bone* or *Blankets*.

19   Some comics criticism works from the assumption that comics with "serious" historical subject matter or "arty" presentation are *intrinsically* superior to monthly saddle-stitched genre stuff—or, rather, that seriousness and artiness confer goodness on a comic. Ridiculous: there are any number of arid, bludgeoning, stultifying art comics that don't have anything like the verve and inventiveness and life of resonant pop about superheroes and monsters. Likewise, there's an anti-genre argument that sometimes pops up, to the effect that stories about real-world types people in real-world sorts of situations, especially if they're autobiographical, have an *intrinsic* edge over fantasy or science fiction or detective stories because it's "easier to relate to them." (That doesn't explain the readers who relate just fine to well-constructed characters in genre stories or who understand that the characters they're reading about don't have to have lives like their own as long as the characters are interesting.) The counterargument from the all-genre crew is that "slice-of-life" stories are prima facie boring—that the point of comics is escapism and intrigue with an unlimited special-effects budget.

INTERNALIZED SEXISM AND THE FORTRESS OF SOLITUDE

20   The world of comic book readers is an insular world, and it's also an annoyingly male world. The archetypal comics store employee—think of *The Simpsons*' Comic Book Guy—is a lonely, socially maladjusted man, and so are his archetypal customers. For a few decades, main-stream comics were so overwhelmingly male-dominated that the industry had not

---

[1]Auteurist: an *auteur* is an artist—usually a film maker—who retains close control over every facet of the film's production, infusing the film with the distinctive voice and style of that filmmaker, and thus can generally be considered the "author" of the film.

the faintest idea of how to connect with potential women customers. I remember seeing a Marvel sales plan, sometime is the early '90s—a huge document, several hundred pages long; near the back, a little section labeled "Female Readers" listed the two titles marvel published for half of their potential audience: *Barbie* and *Barbie Fashion*.

21   Unsurprisingly, the maleness of comics culture has been self perpetuating: if reading (or collecting) comics is understood as "something that guys do," then the woman in the comics store is an anomaly. If you'll forgive a little grad-school speak, either she's performing womanhood wrong, or she's performing comics reading wrong. When you factor in the self-definition as "the kind of person who reads comics" that the culture requires of its participants, it's pretty clear how the pattern got entrenched.

22   The surprising, and heartening, thing is that the pattern is actualy changing—in part because the broader culture of creator-focused media fandom that has evolved over the last couple of decades has drawn young women into comics as a sort of side effect (if you watch *Buffy the Vampire Slayer* and listen to Tori Amos, there's a reasonable chance you read *The Sandman* and *Transmetropolitan* too). There are many, many more people coming to comics conventions now than there were ten years ago; there aren't figures on who those people are, but anecdotally; the influx sure seems to be mostly women. And the manga phenomenon in the United States is very much a teenage-girl-driven trend.

23   But all that has to do with comics' audience; there's also the problem that the best-known creators of comics are men pretty much all the way down. The fifteen cartoonists included in the touring "Masters of American Comics" exhibit in 2006 were all men. The real question, though, isn't quite "why have there been no great women comics artists?" (to paraphrase Linda Nochlin's famous question about the museum art world). It's "why have there been no great women comics artists until recently?"

24   And the answer, of course, is "antiquated social constructs that are finally starting to go away." Anyone who pays much attention to contemporary art comics knows that Lynda Barry and Alison Bechdel and Megan Kelso are as good as it gets right now, and Hope Larson and Marjane Satrapi and Carla Speed McNeil and a bunch of others I could mention get name-dropped plenty too. Still, because of those old social constructs—and because comics take a very long time to draw, and it takes a long time for most cartoonists to hit their peak of power—there are a lot of men who had a head start.

25   Look at the best contemporary American cartoonists in five or ten or fifteen years, though, and I bet there'll be a lot more women among them. There's a new generation of young women drawing comics already—although it'll be a few years before most of them can get beyond the "really promising" stage. The generation behind them is devouring manga the way no generation of American girls has grown up on any comics form before, and these young artists have the advantage of Internet culture to give them artistic peers; in a few decades, some of them will be making better comics than we can even imagine now. The gender imbalance among cartoonists is ridiculous, but it's gradually dissipating—at least in art comics and manga.

26   Mainstream comics' creators, on the other hand, are still overwhelmingly a boys' club; they'll need a bit more time. It doesn't help that women lead characters in superhero comics are outnumbered by men something like ten to one. There's also the familiar complaint of what those women tend to look like—the stereotype of the top-heavy bombshell being the only body type superhero artists know how to draw is frighteningly close to true.

Of course, virtually every major male character in mainstream comics has rippling muscles beneath skintight clothes too, unless he's a villain, in which case he's also got the option of being really ugly or lanky or doughy—a Doctor Octopus or Kingpin or Lex Luthor. As I've noted earlier, the way characters in mainstream comics are drawn is supposed to trigger a visceral, somatic response, and that can include sexual attraction or repulsion. But any reason people don't like something is a valid reason.

27   Beneath the gender dynamics of the comics themselves, there's something a little insidious about the way people's initial contact with comics has historically happened. (Again, this is changing now, but this is the way the story *has* gone in the past.) Kids relate to superhero comics by identifying with their characters—understanding, on some level, that the struggles of the colorful characters on the page as metaphors for their own isolation and longing for power, identity, are acceptance. That identification happens in private, in kids' own little fortresses of solitude. The superhero is somebody who's different from everybody else; the superhero story has rituals and formulas that grow comforting through repetition. Spend enough time reading and thinking about them and comics themselves can become a fortress, a way of isolating oneself from the rest of the world.

28   One thing's for sure about people who are devoted to a subculture based on ongoing fantasies and frustrated by their perception of a lack of connection with the rest of the world: they make really good customers. Over the last couple of decades, the American comics mainstream has made a few stabs at drawing in new customers from outside its core constituency of a few hundred thousand diehards—aiming the occasional title at young kids who might want to pick up something exciting at a newsstand or drugstore, reaching out to adults who'd rather read projects like *Criminal* or *Y: The Last Man* as squarebound paperbacks once or twice a year than pick up floppies once a month, launching projects like the Minx line of graphic novels aimed at teenage girls. Mostly, though, the industry has circled the wagons, dedicating itself to serving its biggest fans, at the expense of letting new readers into its fellowship.

29   Before the shift started happening sometime in the '80s, the assumption was that every comic book was somebody's first; that usually meant a certain amount of repetitive exposition, but every issue was potentially an on-ramp. Now, many new issues of long-running series—and sometimes even new series' debuts—are so inbred and rooted in continuity with other comics that it's nearly impossible for a new reader to make sense of them. That has painted mainstream comics into a corner: once publishers figure out what that core audience wants, they devote their resources to making and marketing the same thing again and again, with gradually diminishing returns, all the while assuring whoever's left in the audience that the product is made just for them.

30   The problem is not only that you need a graduate degree in continuity to understand what's happening when you pick up a typical mainstream comic right now, although I'll discuss that more in the next chapter. It's that some of the codes and traditions associated with mainstream comics—not simply in their stories or the way they represent their characters but in their format and presentation and scope and economic apparatus—are stupid and useless, and they're tolerated and *perpetuated* because that's the way comics work. To question them is to question the edifice of comics itself; to object to them is to mark yourself as outside the circle of understanding and to risk the fury of the faithful.

31   I've been on the receiving end of that fury myself, although not under my own name. It started one day in 2003, when I was chatting with my friend Heidi MacDonald, who was then coediting The Pulse, a popular comics-news Web site. We were complaining to each other that there didn't seem to be a lot of smart, harsh comics criticism on the Web, and that a lot of the way readers talked about mainstream comics was to judge them on how well they played to the visual and storytelling conventions their readers expected, instead of on their worth as art or entertainment as such.

32   Then we remembered Sidney Mellon, a critic who'd had a column in a long-dead weekly comics-news magazine in the '80s. Sidney was the fanboy to end all fanboys; he talked and thought in warmed-over clichés from Marvel's in-house promo pages, he used lots of words he clearly didn't quite understand, and he couldn't fathom why anyone would read *Donald Duck* or *Maus* when they could feast their eyes on real literature like *Uncanny X-Men*. Like a lot of amateur critics, he couldn't disguise his presumption that he could write his favorite comics better anyway, and he was forever nattering on about the "graphic fantasy trilogy" he wanted to write, *Thunderskull*.

33   Sidney Mellon, it turned out, was a put-on by a couple of comic book writers—the columns were written by Gerard Jones, and the pimply, bespectacled kid in the columnist photo was a young Mark Waid—but it took people a little while to figure that out. (There was eventually an issue of *Sidney Mellon's Thunderskull* published; the only thing I remember about it was a caption that read "Erstwhile. . . . ") Who, Heidi and I wondered, would be the Sidney Mellon of today? We realized that somebody who didn't read comics at all would have the same sort "how can they *say* that?" effect.

34   Together, we devised a nonexistent reviewer of our own: Jess Lemon, an undergraduate of indeterminate gender who had no particular interest in comics but had been asked to review one every week as part of an internship at The Pulse (arranged by a comics-loving older brother). The idea was that Jess had no idea what he/she was talking about, but everything he/she wrote would be the brutal truth.

35   I ended up writing all the Jess Lemon columns myself, with a bit of invaluable guidance from Heidi. The debut column pointed out that the first issue of a new *Outsiders* series was categorically incomprehensible to anyone who wasn't thoroughly steeped in bad superhero comics and was pretty stupid anyway; the initial responses were cautiously amused that The Pulse would ask a non-comics reader to write reviews. Then Jess was accidentally "outed" as a girl, and Internet commenters' misogynist knives came out: Who does this dumb little girl think she is? and so on.

36   It took a while for most people to catch on that Jess was a jest. (At that summer's Comic-Con International, somebody stood up at a panel Heidi was on and demanded to know whether or not Jess was a real person.) In the meantime, I invented a bit of backstory for her: her difficult relationship with her brother Andy and her real goal for the summer, which was reading all of Dickens at the rate of a novel every week—I tried to drop a few Dickens references into every column.

37   Here's my favorite column I wrote as "Jess":

> Since I've been writing these reviews, I've been getting into the habit of asking my brother Andy to show me what comics he brings home from the store every week. He likes it when I do that. This week, though, I noticed him palming one comic book under another one as he was flipping through his stack for me, and I called him on it. He acted

all surprised as he pulled out VAMPIRELLA/WITCHBLADE, whose cover shows two women who look like the ones on the posters he used to hang over his bed, wearing very skimpy outfits in the middle of a snowstorm. (You can tell it's cold—one of them is, uh, having a reaction.) "Oh, yeah . . . this one," he said, totally not fooling me. "You know, this has some really strong women characters in it." Oh really!, I said, and snatched it out of his hand. I think what I heard then was him clicking his front teeth together.

My friend Stacy has a rule: she won't go to a movie or read a book unless she knows that it's got a) two women who b) talk to each other about c) something besides a man. I will give VAMPIRELLA/WITCHBLADE credit for this much: it is Stacy-safe, since it involves two women talking to each other about killing monsters. But when people say they like stories with strong women characters, they don't necessarily mean strong in the sense that they can lift things, they mean they want interesting women characters. Like Dora Spenlow in David Copperfield: *she's not strong, really, in any sense of the word, but she's an actual character—you get the sense that she has a life when she's not on the page, and the kind of person she is is part of what drives the story. This comic has a couple of women who seem to be very physically strong, but . . . well, let me try to explain what happens in it. I would put a spoiler warning here, but there aren't actually any surprises to spoil.*

Sara Pezzini, a New York police detective whose car nonetheless doesn't have a front license plate, starts an incident report by announcing that she's never going to file it. (Why? Because if she didn't narrate an unfileable report, there would be no narration to try to make the story make sense.) In snow so deep it makes her stop driving in the middle of the Brooklyn Bridge, which has mysteriously not been cleared and even more mysteriously has no other drivers on it, she's gotten out of her car (to hold up some flares) when two other women run (yes, run) past her. The first one knocks both flares out of her hand and steals her gun without her noticing. The second one is Vampirella, who is running at top speed in foot-deep snow while wearing spike-heeled boots and some kind of one-piece boob-sling/ thonglet contraption that would embarrass Lil' Kim, and who throws the first one off the bridge. Curiously, Vampirella's "running" position looks sort of like a tree pose in yoga, but she does seem to be kicking up a lot of snow. Perhaps whoever wrote this comic has experience sprinting in deep snow with spike heels on—write what you know, they say.

WHY I LOVE MY CULTURE

39   So why do we put up with comics' codes and cults and endless failings, their cycles of empty hype, their dirty halls of dirty boxes pawed through by lonely seedy people? Because comic books are *awesome,* and their culture is as much a blessing as a curse.

40   Comics culture couldn't have attracted as many people as it's attracted, with all its off-putting annoyances and idiocies, if it didn't also offer some genuine delights. The flip side of the Comic Store Guy's sneer of "you mean you don't know?" is that it's a culture that really does privilege deep knowledge of its history and present; the culture, as it turns out, doesn't take itself very seriously at all and is very happy to open its doors to anyone willing to take comics themselves seriously. The comics community encourages unmitigated enthusiasm and unmuted pleasure, especially because those are mocked by other subcultures that don't permit them.

41   For a medium usually experienced by individual readers in their individual homes, reading comics is linked to a pretty nifty social apparatus. It's a springboard for debate and a grounding for friendship. It has pleasant little rituals: the weekly trip to the store, the occasional larger trip to a convention, the post-reading discussion (in person or over the Internet), alphabetizing back issues for storage. To the extent that it allows people to live in a fantasy world, it allows them to live in an extraordinarily rich fantasy world. The apparatus of continuity that's accumulated around comic books gives readers access to the rewards of taking enormous bodies of entertainment very seriously and combing them for flashes of deeper meaning, whether that meaning was intended or not—even, sometimes, a kind of transcendence that's only present by accident.

42   My favorite manifestation of comics reader culture, I think, is something called "The Lesser Book of the Vishanti." It was written in 1977 by a woman named cat yronwode, who had a lot of time on her hands at that point (she went on to be the editor in chief of Eclipse Comics in the '80s and has since published part of her manuscript on her Web site). Yronwode was an admirer—no, let's say a *fan*—of *Dr. Strange,* a series about a "master of the mystic arts" that had been running since the mid-'60s. She decided to put together a comprehensive and coherent guide to Dr. Strange's system of magic, retro-engineering it from whatever parts of it had been published in the comics—this despite the fact that the spells the character cast and mystic artifacts he used had obviously been made up on the spot, probably on tight deadlines, by the various people who'd written Dr. Strange stories for close to fifteen years. Reportedly, *Dr. Strange's* writers eventually came to rely on "The Lesser Book of the Vishanti" as a reference tool.

43   One other benefit of immersion in comics culture is that it lets readers enjoy even bad comics. "Bad" is another one of those loaded terms, so it's worth kicking it around a little to see what it gives up. Bad comics are the ones with something interfering severely with their ability to give pleasure as a coherent piece of work—inept or slapped-together writing, clumsy or generic art, two-dimensional or one-dimensional characters, a sense of having been hacked out to meet a deadline as a piece of product.

44   But some bad comics, especially bad old mainstream comics, can be wonderful in their way. What's good about them isn't their badness or their trashiness: it begins with their desperate desire to entertain (Why *old* comics, in particular? Because they had to leap off the news-stands into customers' hands, which means they had to promise a good time on their covers as loudly as possible and deliver it on the inside.) Newsstand-era comics, whether or not their craft has held up over time and whether or not they seem insultingly dumb now, were almost always insanely *fun*—a lot of them are bulging at the edges with style. They're not necessarily campy, in the sense of making a deliberately failed attempt at seriousness; usually, they don't bother trying to be serious in the first place, or if they do, they hide their seriousness beneath a thick coating of nuttiness. They're willing to risk overambition or ludicrousness in the hopes of scaling the height of readerly delight; the only sin they won't brook is boringness.

45   And something else comes to light when you've read a lot of mediocre comics: an understanding of how they're part of a process that results in good ones, an appreciation for the history of the form that doesn't fall prey to longing for it to be the way it once was. Read enough comics and you achieve the broader insights of seeing artists and their shared techniques develop, styles rise and fall, inane concepts reconsidered

in ways that make them meaningful. Even bad comics' antsy aspiration to be thought of as something other than the trash they feared they were has its charm when you recognize the little steps they took toward being meaningful. There's pleasure in noting their little successes—and in mocking their dorky failures.

46   That pleasure, like most of comics' pleasures, is a shared one. The secret language of comics is the argot that comes from the experience of searching for gems together in a huge pile of rubble and being able to slough off the rubble's grime with a laugh. A few years ago, a challenge went around the Internet's comic blogs: "100 Things I Love About Comics." The examples some people listed were the kind of flashes of inspiration that happened when cartoonists' desire to make something really entertaining worked out. Others had to do with the rituals and incantations that belong to comics' context; still others were favorite minor characters or unsung creators.

47   Every one of those gives me joy to see and to recall, as well as to share with other people who've experienced them, or to pass along to other people who want to see them too. That's what I love most about comics as a culture: it's united not just by liking the same sorts of things but by communicating about them. The medium is built on a tradition of entertainment and reflective pleasure and out-and-out fun, and the enjoyment of it is redoubled by people who care about it talking about it—and arguing about it—with each other.

QUESTIONS ON MEANING

1. Why do the terms *comic book*, on the one hand, and *graphic novel*, on the other hand, both fail to adequately express the medium's characteristic features?

2. What is Wolk's opinion of comics culture?

3. Who are the members of Team Comics? Does the Team Comics phenomenon have any parallels in other mediums in contemporary society?

4. What are the benefits of immersion in comics culture, according to Wolk?

QUESTIONS FOR DISCUSSION

1. Wolk begins his piece by identifying comics readers as a subculture. Do you agree? If so, what are the distinguishing characteristics of this subculture? Are you a member of this particular subculture? Why or why not?

2. What would you propose as a better term for *comic books* or *graphic novels*? Do you share Wolk's criticisms of these two labels? Does it make a difference what they are called? Why or why not?

3. Wolk discusses the antagonism between those who are collectors of comics versus those who are readers of comics. Is this a fair distinction? Can one be both? What does it say about your relationship with comics culture if you are a collector? A reader? Both? Neither?

4. Wolk describes comics culture as a kind of insular club that doesn't readily welcome outsiders. Is this true? What evidence can you cite that supports your position? Is this insider-outsider dichotomy true of other cultural mediums?

5. Why do you think there is a gender divide (as described by Wolk) in comics culture, especially in the mainstream market? What will have to happen in order to bridge this gap?

6. Wolk explains both what he loves and what he hates about comics culture. In the end, which side has been presented more convincingly? Why?

LOOKING AT RHETORIC

1. Wolk's diction is relatively informal, and he even employs slang and rather blunt and colorful epithets at times. Does this style contribute to or detract from his overall presentation? Do you take him more or less seriously as a result?

2. Is Wolk's discussion of the many things he loves about comics effective? Does it convince the reader of something? If so, what?

WRITING ASSIGNMENTS

1. Select something in contemporary media culture (a comic, a pop music album, a television show, a movie, etc.) and write your own review of it from the perspective of an outsider such as the fake "Jess Lemon" review of *Vampirella/Witchblade* composed by Wolk.

2. Write an essay in which you compare and contrast what Wolk and McCloud have to say about defining comics. Does one provide a better definition than the other? Do they share the same basic assumptions and expectations?

3. In pairs or in groups, select some cultural phenomenon other than comics and create two lists, much as Wolk does in his piece: one listing reasons why the phenomenon is subject to derision, and a second listing reasons why the phenomenon is to be appreciated. For a few recent examples, consider the *American Idol* phenomenon or the rise of Lady Gaga as a pop-culture sensation. Then, independently, draft an essay in which you discuss the cultural phenomenon to an audience that may not be knowledgeable about it, and make the case that the phenomenon is either to be praised or derided for its contributions to contemporary culture.

From *The Greatest of Marlys*

Lynda Barry

Lynda Barry (b. 1956) is regarded as one of the greatest writers of alternative comics working today. Barry grew up in Seattle; her father was of European descent and her mother of Filipino descent. It is not uncommon that Barry explores issues of race and cultural heritage in her work, especially in some of her later work. Barry got her start as a comics artist at Evergreen State College where her work was published by friend Matt Groening—author of the Life in Hell comics and creator of The Simpsons television series—who was, at the time, the editor of the college's newspaper. As her comics gained in popularity, they evolved, and from her earlier explorations of the foibles and inequities of male/female relationships Barry turned her attention toward the complex emotional life of adolescents. Although her works are sometimes associated with the "Wimmen's Comix" movement—a movement characterized by its autobiographical narrative style and feminist perspective—there really is no simple way to label Barry's work. Her narratives are deeply affecting and are just as often about what it means to be human as what it means to be of one sex or the other. Barry is best known for her long-running strip Ernie Pook's Comeek which has appeared in numerous alternative newspapers for twenty years. Over the years these strips have been reprinted in a number of collections, including Come Over, Come Over (1990), My Perfect Life (1992), It's so Magic (1994), and The Freddie Stories (1999). Her collection The Greatest of Marlys, from which the following is taken, was named one of the ten greatest graphic novels of all time by Time Magazine.

BAD FOR YOU

BY LYNDA ORSON WELLS BARRY ©1988

MRS. BROGAN TOLD THE LIGHT MONITOR TO TURN THE LIGHTS OFF, THEN SHE SWITCHED ON THE OVERHEAD PROJECTOR AND SHOWED US ABOUT 40 PICTURES OF ROTTEN TEETH AND SAID THE SUBJECT OF THE DAY WAS POP.

A LOT OF YOU WILL END UP WITH TEETH EXACTLY LIKE THIS.

SHE SAID OF ALL POP, COKE WAS THE WORST AND IF YOU HUNG A HUNK OF MEAT IN A CAN OF COKE IT WOULD ROT RIGHT OFF THE STRING IN ONE DAY. SO THINK OF WHAT IT DOES TO YOUR STOMACH.

HOW MANY OF YOU LIKE THE THOUGHT OF BIG HOLES IN YOUR STOMACH LINING?

WHEN ARNOLD ARNESEN SHOWED UP THE NEXT DAY WITH A THERMOS FULL OF COKE AND A HOT DOG FLOATING IN IT MRS. BROGAN SAID "O.K., WE SHALL SEE WHAT HAPPENS" AND PUT THE THERMOS ON A TABLE BY ITSELF WITH AN INDEX CARD TAPED TO IT THAT SAID "EXPERIMENT."

Experiment

THIS IS NOT A TOY

ALL DAY WE WONDERED ABOUT THE HOT DOG TRAPPED IN THE THERMOS WITH THE COKE. WHAT A HORRIBLE WAY TO GO.

AFTER 24 HOURS MRS. BROGAN TOOK US ALL OUT TO THE STORM DRAIN WHERE SHE WAS GOING TO POUR OUT THE COKE, AND SHE POURED IT AND THE HOT DOG FELL OUT IN PERFECT CONDITION.

FOR SOME REASON ALL OF US KNEW THIS WAS ABOUT THE SADDEST THING WE HAD EVER SEEN. ESPECIALLY MRS. BROGAN.

IF YOU WANT TO BUY CANDY

BY LYNDA BARRY © 1987

NUMBER ONE, BUY YOUR CANDY AT FRED'S NOT AT BLUMA'S. BLUMA'S GOTS THE CANDY IN A GLASS CASE AND HE WON'T LET YOU EVEN TOUCH IT UNTIL YOU PAY. EVERYBODY JUST HATES BLUMA. HIS STORE SMELLS LIKE LYSOL.

FRED'S GOTS THE GOOD CANDY AND YOU CAN PICK IT UP AND PUT IT BACK AND TAKE YOUR TIME MAKING YOUR DECISIONS. BLUMA'S GOTS OLD CHOCOLATE SANTAS WAY UNTIL JULY 4TH AND HE DON'T EVEN REDUCE THE PRICE. BLUMA WEARS A HAIRNET. A MAN WEARS A HAIRNET.

ALSO BLUMA RUNS OUTSIDE AFTER YOU YELLING WHERE DO THE WRAPPERS GO! WHERE DO THE WRAPPERS GO! FRED JUST SITS THERE SMOKING. FRED DON'T HARDLY MOVE FOR NOTHING NOT EVEN IF YOUR BIKE BASHES AGAINST HIS WINDOW WHEN YOU LEAN IT DOWN. BUT BLUMA DON'T LET NO BIKES EVEN TOUCH HIS STORE. HE'LL HIT YOU WITH THE FLY SWATTER, HE DON'T CARE.

THE ONLY THING ABOUT FRED'S IS THAT IT CAN MAKE YOU SORT OF SAD BECAUSE OF THE WAY HE NEVER TALKS. AT LEAST WITH BLUMA HE'LL CHASE AFTER YOU AND YOU GET TO SEE HIS GIANT BUTT AND LEGS. NO ONE IN THE WORLD HAS EVER SEEN THE LEGS OF FRED. OUR MOM SAYS HE DON'T TALK BECAUSE OF HIS WIFE LEFT HIM. WHAT A DUMB STUPID LADY.

KNOWING things

· L Y N D A · B A R R Y · © 1989

MY SISTER MARLYS IS DOING A PROJECT OUT ON THE BACK PORCH ABOUT PLANTS. SHES ONLY 8 SO SHE'S STILL NOT SICK OF KNOWING THINGS. I DID THAT SAME PROJECT ABOUT A MILLION YEARS AGO. YOU PLANT BEANS IN A MILK CARTON. BIG DEAL.

I TOLD HER SHE ONLY NEEDS THREE TO DO EXPERIMENT OF ① NO WATER. ② SOME ③ FLOODING. SHE PLANTED 30. SHE'S TR KOOLAID, MILK, AND CRAGMONT ROOT BE SHE RUBBED ONE WITH VICKS. SHE PU MILK DUDS IN THE DIRT OF ONE. SHE SA SHE'S LOOKING FOR THE SECRET FORMU

WHEN I TRY TO TELL HER THERE'S NO WAY, SHE GOES: "THAT'S WHAT THEY ALL SAY." I DON'T KNOW WHERE SHE EVEN GOT THAT! IT'S FROM THE BOOKS YOU KEEP READING WITH NO REALITY IN THEM. A MAGIC TREE STARTS TALKING OR A MAGIC DOG STARTS TALKING AND EVERYTHING IN THE WORLD CAN BE MAGIC. EVEN YOUR SPIT CAN BE MAGIC. AND NOW THAT'S WHAT SHE THINKS. THERE'S ONE PLANT SHE SPITS ON.

I TRIED TO EXPLAIN TO HER THE CONCEPT OF REALITY AND THAT REALITY IS BEAUTIFUL AND SHE SAID HER PLANTS WERE REALI' AND SHE WAS REALITY AND HER EXPERI MENTS WERE REALITY AND I SAID THE REAL REALITY WAS SHE WAS THE TORT. OF PLANTS AND ALL THE PLANTS WERE GO TO DIE BECAUSE OF HER AND WHAT I SAID CAME TRUE. IT CAME TRUE. IT CAM TRUE. MARLYS, I'M SORRY IT CAME TRU

NO BIG DEAL

BY LYNDA "SLEEPTALKIN'" BARRY © 1986

OUT OF ALL THE GIRLS IN OUR CLASS, IT WAS ONLY ONE GIRL WHO DIDN'T GET NO INVITATION TO MARISSA BATO'S BIRTHDAY PARTY. I GUESS SHE FIGURED WE WOULD ALL NEED ONE GIRL TO BRAG ABOUT THE PARTY TO. THE GIRL WHO WASN'T INVITED WAS MY COUSIN MARLYS.

HOW COME? HOW COME YOU DIDN'T INVITE ME?

UH... MY MOM SAID I COULD ONLY HAVE 13 GIRLS COME.

EVEN THOUGH ME AND MARLYS WERE TOTAL HATERS OF EACH OTHER, I FELT SORRY THAT SHE DIDN'T GET A INVITATION. AT LUNCH I WENT OVER TO HER TABLE TO NOTICE HER FEELINGS.

QUIT STARIN' AT ME, STUPE!

IT'S A FREE COUNTRY

WHO EVEN CARES ABOUT MARISSA'S PARTY? I DON'T CARE ABOUT THAT DUMB PARTY. IT'S NO BIG DEAL TO ME EVEN ONE BIT, SO WHO CARES?

IT'S AT A RESTAURANT.

I WOULDN'T GO FOR ALL THE MONEY IN THE WORLD. THERE'S NO WAY I'D EVER GO TO THAT STUPID PARTY.

IT'S AT BIG TOP ICE CREAM LAND.

MILK

IT TURNS OUT THE DAY BEFORE THE PARTY I GOT THE FLU. MARLYS IS OVER JUMPING UP AND DOWN TO TAKE MY INVITATION. I KNEW FOR A FACT MARISSA DIDN'T WANT NO MARLYS AT HER PARTY BUT I HAD TO GIVE HER MY INVITATION BECAUSE MY MOM WOULDN'T LISTEN TO ME WHEN I TRIED TO EXPLAIN IT. SHE SAID I WAS JUST TRYING TO BE MEAN.

MOM, YOU DON'T GET IT.

DON'T YOU DARE TALK TO ME THAT WAY YOU SELFISH CHILD! YOU OUGHT TO BE ASHAMED OF YOURSELF! I'VE HAD QUITE ENOUGH OF YOUR SELF-CENTEREDNESS!

BUT NOT GIVING HER THAT INVITATION WOULDN'T HAVE BEEN HALF AS MEAN AS WHAT MARISSA DID TO HER.

WHO CARES ABOUT MARISSA BATOS ANYWAY? SHE'S A STUPID IDIOT.

SHE WOULDN'T EVEN TAKE MY PRESENT.

Little Things

BY LYNDA BARRY. The Death of Atlas. © 1995

Donna Dulaire asked her mom could she spend the night at my house and the shouted answer was: "NO WAY IN HELL!" Then Donna asked could I stay over at her house and the same shout came out flying. Why does Mrs. Dulaire hate me so bad?

I was sitting on the plastic covers of their couch with my socks hanging over the plastic paths on their carpets. My shoes are not allowed inside. They bring dirt. Also, DON'T TOUCH ANYTHING! YOU MIGHT BREAK IT! Mrs. Dulaire has a lot of figurines.

Donna Dulaire came into the room with her eyes down. She gave me the news of I had to go home. I said Bye and she said Bye and on the frozen porch I jammed my shoes back on. In my pocket was a small blue and white cat that I shouldn't have took.

In my room there is a private cigar box with an incredible Spanish lady on the lid. I only ever take things that can fit inside. And I only ever take things from people who hate me. And the box is getting fuller. And when it is all the way full I will.... I will.... well I don't know what I will do.

QUESTIONS ON MEANING

1. In "Bad for You," what is so sad about the outcome of the experiment? Why would it be as sad for the children as for Mrs. Brogan?

2. In "Maybonne's Room," why do you think that the night spent listening to the radio was one of the greatest nights of the narrator's life?

3. When buying candy, why do the children prefer to buy from Fred instead of Bluma?

4. Why is Maybonne, in "Knowing Things," sorry that "it came true"? What does Maybonne know that Marlys doesn't?

5. In "No Big Deal," what does Maybonne understand that her mother doesn't? What does this comic say about society? What does it say about what it means to grow up?

6. Why does Marlys take "Little Things" from some people? Why do you think she saves these things in a box? What do you think will happen when the box is full?

QUESTIONS FOR DISCUSSION

1. Are Barry's comics predominantly optimistic or pessimistic? What makes them so? Which of her comics shown here are most filled with hope, and which are characterized most by disappointment? What do you think Barry is suggesting about human experience? What is she saying about childhood? About love? About learning?

2. Which comic did you find most surprising? What made it so?

3. Which comic did you find most significant? Which one seemed to capture some truth about life and human nature the best?

4. Are these comics *art*? What makes them so? Or, what prevents them from being called such?

LOOKING AT RHETORIC

1. Barry's drawings are striking for their seeming crudity or simplicity. Does Barry's style detract or add to the impact of her comics? What do you think Barry is trying to achieve by drawing in this style?

2. Look back over the selections above, and locate the single panel that you find to be the best at communicating a particular message in an artistic way. What makes that panel special? What details about the drawing make it stand out? What writing in the panel is particularly significant, in your opinion?

3. Identify the point of view of each of the separate comics above. What details of the drawings and the writing create each different point of view? How does the point of view of each comic contribute to its success and/or significance?

WRITING ASSIGNMENTS

1. Based on your reading of both McCloud and Wolk (the two previous selections in this anthology), write an essay in which you analyze the work of Lynda Barry. Through a careful study of her words and images as well as the manner in which she constructs her stories in four panels, use concepts from McCloud and Wolk to discuss what makes Barry such a successful writer of comics.

2. Having read these selections by Barry, write one of your own. Divide a single sheet of paper into four panels—in the four-panel style of Barry—and write and draw your own comic. In

your comic, tell a story that captures some aspect of culture or family life that is not often discussed in the funny comics of the Sunday newspapers.

3. In pairs or in groups, go through each of the comics in the selection above and try to state what the prevailing theme or idea of each comic is. Try to do this in one complete, clear sentence for each comic. Share your conclusions with other groups in class. Then, as an individual, write an essay in which you describe Barry's view of modern family life, culture, and or childhood as illustrated in her comics.

How Has the Culture of TV (and TV-Watching) Changed?

Noel Murray and Scott Tobias

Noel Murray is a freelance writer based in Arkansas who specializes in television and film criticism. An avid television fan, he writes regularly for The Onion's A.V. Club *and* The Los Angeles Times. *Scott Tobias is the film editor for the A.V. Club, where he has worked as a staff writer for a number of years. He has contributed reviews to* NPR.org., *The Hollywood Reporter, and* City Pages, *among other magazines. The following dialogue appeared in 2010 on the A.V. Club online. Murray and Tobias discuss the evolving experience of television watching, particularly as it relates to the episodic show, which viewers can easily begin with after the series has begun, and the serialized program, which possesses "novelistic" qualities that may or may not require that it be viewed from the beginning.*

1   **Noel:** Scott, you and I have one recurring argument about television that I think stems from the different ways we came to love the medium. I was a full-on, unrepentant TV junkie as a kid—the kind of boy who'd beg my parents to buy *TV Guide*'s Fall Preview Issue so I could plan out which shows I was going to watch each night. Because of that, I have a lingering fondness for television in its classic forms: sitcoms with laugh tracks, episodic dramas, what-have-you. But I get the impression—and correct me if I'm wrong—that you became more of a hardcore TV fan in the HBO era, thanks to shows like *The Sopranos*, and that you're more interested in television for its cinematic or novelistic qualities.

2   As a result, you've often been horrified when I tell you that I've taken an interest in one of your favorite shows and have started to watch it mid-season. For me, this is no big deal. I've been dropping into TV shows my whole life, and I find it hard to believe that there's any show I'd be unable to get a handle on after an episode or two. This is especially true in the age of the Internet; it isn't too hard to get a quick character sketch or a "story so far" plot synopsis. But you seem to think that it's unacceptable to watch a TV series any other way than to start with season one, episode one—even if the general consensus is that the show took a while to find its footing.

3   Similarly, whenever I talk up a new show that I like, you often seem to lose interest if I suggest that you don't need to wait for the DVD or the summer repeats to catch up on it,

but can instead just start watching in the middle. It's like you assume that any show that doesn't demand to be watched in full can't really be that good. This argument makes me want to cuff you about the head—but since we're usually arguing by phone, I can't.

4   Anyway, I've been thinking about this as it relates to a couple of topics: how we do our jobs as TV critics, and whether we're focusing too much on one kind of television—the tightly serialized kind—to the exclusion of the kind of TV that most people actually watch. Take *Justified*, for example, which just ended its first season. *Justified* began and ended as a serialized show, with one long story to tell, but in the middle of the season, it was more episodic, following a different case every week. I know you liked the episodic *Justified* fairly well, though I think you preferred it more serialized. So here's my question to you: If *Justified* had remained primarily an episodic series, with only incremental character and master-plot growth each week, would you still have thought highly of it? Also, would you have found it as rewarding to write about for TV Club?

5   **Scott:** I'll of course bow to your superior couch potato-credentials—though I did quit piano lessons as a kid so I could watch the Beatles cartoon on TV—but I wonder if your affection for classic forms has bred some inflexible thinking on how dramatically the medium has changed. I obviously don't need to remind you, author of bazillion-word *Lost* posts, of the marvels of serialized storytelling, yet you persist in believing it's okay to drop in casually on TV shows. That's fine if you're talking procedurals or sitcoms or other shows that get most of their business done over the course of an episode—and such shows are still the staples of popular network television, even if they miss critics' year-end lists—but of course I'd advise (or demand, in some cases) that people start serialized shows from the beginning. If we accept the premise that many of the best shows on television unfold like novels, with richly developed characters and grand narrative arcs, wouldn't checking in mid-season be equivalent to starting a book on chapter five?

6   Here's an example from real life, and we'll let the jury decide: If I recall correctly, we had a big argument over *Friday Night Lights*, which had finished its triumphant first season on NBC and was re-airing on Bravo the following summer in a bid to pick up its lagging ratings. Over my protestations, you decided just to dive into the action four or five episodes into it, under the reasonable logic that you'd pick up on who's who and what's what in due time. Though you eventually went back and watched the show from the beginning, it pained me to imagine you witnessing dramatic payoffs—like, say, Jason Street's bittersweet return to the field after his fateful tumble in the pilot—without also seeing the careful plotting that went into them. You didn't know these characters or their histories, so your emotional experience was inevitably muted, because your level of investment couldn't possibly be the same as mine.

7   Nevertheless, if you're willing to admit you watched *Friday Night Lights* improperly— and lash yourself with a cat o' nine tails, like that guy in *The Da Vinci Code*—I'm willing to concede that my insistence on watching shows from the beginning is occasionally mis-guided. There have been many times in the past you've encouraged me to jump right in on a show—*Burn Notice*, most recently—and I've balked, because I wanted to start with season one, episode one, and the time commitment didn't seem worth it. That bit me in the ass most recently with *Chuck*, which had a middling first season that I'd have been better off skipping to get the much stronger second; I could have applied those precious units of time to wiser ends, like playing online poker or taking up smoking. But let me still throw

out this blanket statement: Greatness in a dramatic series isn't possible without a strong (i.e. predominant) serialized element. That's the common denominator of all significant shows of the last decade—*The Wire*, *The Sopranos*, *Mad Men*, *Breaking Bad*, et al.—which thrive because they're constantly moving forward and revealing new things about their characters and their cinematic universes.

8   To that end, *Justified* is an interesting test case, because it's a hybrid, balancing master-plot episodes with more traditional (albeit very well-executed) crime-of-the-week procedural stuff. After the pilot, a near-perfect hour of pulp television that introduced our outlaw hero, Raylan Givens (Timothy Olyphant), his chief nemesis (the brilliant Walton Goggins), most of the other major characters, and the beautifully evoked Harlan County milieu, the series immediately settled into a standard cop-show format for the next three weeks. Much as I enjoyed those episodes—the fourth week, featuring Alan Ruck as a dentist on the lam, was particularly lively—I'll confess that I felt a bit deflated by them, because all the urgent issues raised by the pilot were punted down the road a bit. And yes, I probably would have designated *Justified* as a good-but-not-great show had it continued to hit the reset button every week, with Raylan, the rakish Old West quick-draw, getting in and out of various pickles.

9   But even in more self-contained weeks, *Justified* would still inch the master plot forward a little, and it's become a model hybrid show, a breezily entertaining hour that welcomes casual viewers, but rewards more intense fans. (Joss Whedon, with *Buffy*, *Firefly*, and *Dollhouse*, is a master of the hybrid, though I think most would agree the serialized episodes of the lattermost series far outclassed the *Charlie's Angels*-like doll adventures that littered the early part of season one, when it was still trying to hook viewers.) Moreover, it's been ideal to review every week: Unlike wholly serialized shows, you don't feel like you're reviewing a book chapter by chapter, yet it's rich and varied enough to give you something to sink your teeth into every week.

10   Now that TV Club has been up and active for a few years, it's time to take stock. What are the pleasures and perils of reviewing a show as it unfolds week to week? How has it changed the culture, at least for those serious enough about television to engage in the discussion? Reviewing a work-in-progress can be enormously frustrating—and even embarrassing at times, when an insight or bit of speculation one week is discredited the next—but it can also be enriching in ways that film criticism isn't. I have my thoughts on it. But first, what are yours?

11   **Noel:** Actually, first let me address the *Friday Night Lights* thing, because that's a good case in point for what I was saying about being an experienced television-watcher. Though a lot of the best TV has novelistic qualities, the two media aren't really the same, and most TV creators—if they're any good at their jobs—are aware that they need to reach both hard-core fans and casual viewers if they want to keep their shows on the air. *Friday Night Lights* falls far more on the serialized than the episodic side, and yet the characters are so likeable and easy to grasp that it really isn't that hard to drop into the story and follow it—if you have at least a rudimentary understanding of television storytelling, that is.

12   More to the point, though, while I think the first season of *Friday Night Lights* is a good one, and that the second season succeeds in spite of some ill-conceived plot twists, to me, the show didn't become one of the best TV dramas of this era—yes, in the same league as *Breaking Bad*, *Mad Men*, *The Shield*, and *The Wire*—until its third season. And the current,

fourth season has been just as strong. If I wanted to convince a skeptic of *FNL*'s greatness, honestly, I wouldn't tell them to start with season one, episode one, unless they have a high tolerance for melodramatic contrivance. The storylines of the early *FNL*—the racial strife, the performance-enhancing drugs, the improbable comebacks—really aren't any less soapy in their way than season two's near-rape and body-burying. It's in the third season that the stories become as wonderfully small-scale and well-observed as the characters and setting have always been. In fact, I wouldn't have a problem telling a newcomer just to watch the season-four episode "The Son," which deals with standard dramatic themes of loss, anger, and regret in ways that are remarkably real and powerful. Yes, there's a lot of backstory that goes into that episode, but I think that just about anyone could get it, and might be so moved by "The Son" that they'd want to see more.

13   How is this relevant to what you and I are talking about? Well, one of the things that complicates TV criticism is the ways in which we watch. Following a show week-in, week-out is a different experience than catching up with it later. I'm not discounting your opinion of *FNL*'s first season by any means, but I think your emotional investment was higher, not just because you watched from the beginning, but because you came in on the show's ground floor, more or less. As I recall, you didn't start watching on the night it debuted, but watched a mini-marathon of the first few weeks' worth of episodes, then watched the rest of the season week-by-week. Anyway, you discovered the show early, and were part of its first wave of champions. By the time I got around to *FNL*, I'd already heard how good it was, so I was judging it against high expectations. And I ultimately watched the second half of the first season on DVD over the course of about three days, so I got to see some of the disappointingly conventional payoffs of the first season's storylines in mere hours, while you had to wait weeks, and could thus let the world of Dillon, Texas and your perception of the show's overall quality expand in your mind.

14   You mentioned how tricky it is to review a serialized show week-to-week, because we're trying to assess character choices and plot turns that haven't yet reached fruition. That means we have to engage in a lot of guesswork about where the creators are headed, and what their choices might mean. Sometimes we're pleasantly surprised by the direction a show heads in, as has been the case consistently with *Breaking Bad* (for me, at least). And sometimes what we imagine will happen is more compelling than what the creators come up with. The prime example of that would be *Lost* for a lot of its disgruntled fans, and to some extent *Justified*, which to my mind didn't end its first season as strongly as I'd hoped. (A hail of gunfire and a cloud of irresolution does not a finale make, in my opinion.)

15   But I personally consider the uncertainties of weekly TV reviewing to be one of its strengths. We knock out reviews quickly, from the gut, then have a spirited discussion in the comments section with our readers and on Twitter with our other critic pals. It's more like reporting (mixed with symposia) than traditional criticism. Of course, there are lots of different ways to do what we do: straight recap, quick impressions, in-depth analysis, and so on. My philosophy has always been to provide a fairly full summary of an episode—so fans of the show can come to a write-up long after an episode aired, and be reminded of what happened—combined with some consideration of themes and aesthetics, and always with my personal biases on the table. And because we write every week, we have the space to reassess whether a serialized show goes somewhere we weren't anticipating, as well as

having comment sections and social media to carry on the conversation after the original review is done.

16   Plus, that conversation is so much livelier than the conversations surrounding other media these days. Because we aren't primarily engaged in telling people whether they should or shouldn't watch a show—because we're usually talking with people who are already watching—we get to kick around symbolism, character development, and real-world connections to what's on the screen, rather than just writing about whether the show is worth a damn. Sure, we write about what's working and what isn't, and why, but we have the space and the freedom to get into so much more. And the people we get into it *with*—the readers, and our fellow critics—seem so much more open, friendly, and engaged than, say, cinephiles these days.

17   Consider this: over the past few weeks, a number of our film-critic pals have been bickering over which acclaimed new movie is "overrated," and whether the profession is dying because they didn't get an advance screening of *Killers*, and whether watching movies on an iPod is a crime against art, and whether the reviews (not the movie, mind you, the *reviews*) of *Sex And The City 2* are misogynistic. Not only are most of these debates depressingly insular, they're *old*. We've been having these same boring conversations for years now, with fewer and fewer participants. Meanwhile, in TV land, we've been kicking around the meaning and lasting impact of *Lost*'s controversial ending, and whether Walter White's recent rash acts on *Breaking Bad* mark another dark turn for the character, or a redemptive one. Advantage: television.

QUESTIONS ON MEANING

1. What is meant by the following terms: *episodic; serialized; hybrid*?

2. Why does Noel Murray think that one can enter a serialized television show in the middle and still appreciate and enjoy it?

3. In what way does Scott Tobias disagree and think that a serialized show must be watched from the beginning?

QUESTIONS FOR DISCUSSION

1. How have television shows changed in the time you have been watching them? The types of shows? Their structure? Your enjoyment of them?

2. In what way is the experience of watching television less or more appealing than films?

3. In what way is the experience of watching television less or more appealing than your various media experiences on the internet?

LOOKING AT RHETORIC

1. How does the dialogue format function to enhance or detract from your understanding of the argument?

2. How does the conversational style affect your reception of the discussion and your reading experience?

WRITING ASSIGNMENTS

1. Research library and/or Internet sources in media studies, particularly related to the history of television and television genre or forms. Consider one of your favorite television shows (excluding reality shows). Is it episodic, serialized, or hybrid? Make an argument for the value of a particular form using that series as an example.

2. Argue for or against television as an enriching and valuable artistic medium.

3. In pairs or in groups, discuss the shows you watch and why you like them. Individually, research television criticism, finding reviews of various shows. Then write a review of a series you either admire or dislike.

From *Inside the Mouse:*
Work and Play at Disney World

Susan Willis

Susan Willis (b. 1946) is an Associate Professor of English at Duke University. Her teaching and research tends to focus on both minority literatures and popular culture. Willis writes about American culture from a Marxist point of view, subjecting consumer-based capitalism to examination and critique. She has written several books, including Specifying: Black Women Writing the American Experience *(1987),* A Primer for Daily Life *(1990), and* Portents of the Real: A Primer for Post-9/11 America *(2005). In 1995 she co-authored the book* Inside the Mouse: Work and Play at Walt Disney World *(with Jane Kuenz, Shelton Waldrep, and Karen Klugman) from which the following essay is taken.*

1   At Disney World, the erasure of spontaneity is so great that spontaneity itself has been programmed. On the "Jungle Cruise" khaki-clad tour guides teasingly engage the visitors with their banter, whose apparent spontaneity has been carefully scripted and painstakingly rehearsed. Nothing is left to the imagination or the unforeseen.

2   The erasure of spontaneity has largely to do with the totality of the built and themed environment. Visitors are inducted into the park's program, their every need predefined and presented to them as a packaged routine and set of choices. "I'm not used to having everything done for me." This is how my companion at Disney World reacted when she checked into a Disney resort hotel and found that she, her suitcase, and her credit card had been turned into the scripted components of a highly orchestrated program. My companion later remarked that while she found it odd not to have to take care of everything herself (as she normally does in order to accomplish her daily tasks), she found it "liberating" to just fall into the proper pattern, knowing that nothing could arise that hadn't already been factored into the system. I have heard my companion's remarks reiterated by many visitors to the park with whom I've talked. Most describe feeling "freed up" ("I didn't have to worry about my kids," "I didn't have to think about

anything") by the experience of relinquishing control over the complex problem-solving thoughts and operations that otherwise define their lives. Many visitors suspend daily perceptions and judgments altogether, and treat the wonderland environment as more real than real. I saw this happen one morning when walking to breakfast at my Disney resort hotel. Two small children were stooped over a small snake that had crawled out onto the sun-warmed path. "Don't worry, it's rubber," remarked their mother. Clearly only Audio-Animatronic simulacra[1] of the real world can inhabit Disney World. A real snake *is* an impossibility.

3   Amusement is the commodified negation of play. What is play but the spontaneous coming together of activity and imagination, rendered more pleasurable by the addition of friends? At Disney World, the world's most highly developed private property "state" devoted to amusement, play is all but eliminated by the absolute domination of program over spontaneity. Every ride runs to computerized schedule. There is no possibility of an awful thrill, like being stuck at the top of a ferris wheel. Order prevails particularly in the queues for the rides that zigzag dutifully on a prescribed path created out of stanchions and ropes; and the visitor's assimilation into the queue does not catapult him. All historical and cultural references are merely ingredients for decor. Every expectation is met programmatically and in conformity with theme. Mickey as Sorcerer's Apprentice does not appear in the Wild West or the exotic worlds of Jungle and Adventure, the niches for Davey Crockett and Indiana Jones. Just imagine the chaos, a park-wide short circuit, that the mixing of themed ingredients might produce. Amusement areas are identified by a "look," by characters in costume, by the goods on sale: What place—i.e., product—is Snow White promoting if she's arm in arm with an astronaut?

4   What's most interesting about Disney World is what's not there. Intimacy is not in the program even though the architecture includes several secluded nooks, gazebos, and patios. During my five-day stay, I saw only one kiss—and this a husbandly peck on the cheek. Eruptions of imaginative play are just as rare. During the same five-day visit, I observed only one such incident even though there were probably fifty thousand children in the park. What's curious about what's not at Disney is that there is no way of knowing what's not there until an aberrant event occurs and provokes the remembrance of the social forms and behaviors that have been left out. This was the case with the episode of spontaneous play. Until I saw real play, I didn't realize that it was missing. The incident stood out against a humdrum background of uniform amusement: hundreds of kids being pushed from attraction to attraction in their strollers, hundreds more waiting dutifully in the queues or marching about in family groups—all of them abstaining from the loud, jostling, teasing, and rivalrous behaviors that would otherwise characterize many of their activities. Out of this homogenous "amused" mass, two kids snagged a huge sombrero each from an open-air stall at the foot of the Mexico Pavilion's Aztec temple stairway and began their impromptu version of the Mexican hat dance up and down the steps. Their play was clearly counterproductive as it took up most of the stairway, making it difficult for visitors to enter the pavilion. Play negated the function of the stairs as conduit into the attraction. The kids abandoned themselves to their fun, while all around them, the great mass of visitors purposefully

---

[1]Simulacra: (plural form of simulacrum) a copy or representation of something.

kept their activities in line with Disney World's prescribed functions. Everyone but the dancers seemed to have accepted the park's unwritten motto: "If you pay, you shouldn't play." To get your money's worth, you have to do everything and do it in the prescribed manner. Free play is gratuitous and therefore a waste of the family's leisure time expenditure.

5   Conformity with the park's program upholds the Disney value system. Purposeful consumption—while it costs the consumer a great deal—affirms the value of the consumer. "Don't forget, we drove twenty hours to get here." This is how one father admonished his young son who was squirming about on the floor of EPCOT's Independence Hall, waiting for the amusement to begin. The child's wanton and impatient waste of time was seen as a waste of the family's investment in its amusement. If a family is to realize the value of its leisure time consumptions, then every member must function as a proper consumer.

6   The success of Disney World as an amusement park has largely to do with the way its use of programming meshes with the economics of consumption as a value system. In a world wholly predicated on consumption, the dominant order need not proscribe those activities that run counter to consumption, such as free play and squirming, because the consuming public largely polices itself against gratuitous acts which would interfere with the production of consumption as a value. Conformity with the practice of consumption is so widespread and deep at Disney World that occasional manifestations of boredom or spontaneity do not influence the compulsively correct behavior of others. Independence Hall did not give way to a seething mass of squirming youngsters even though all had to sit through a twenty-minute wait. Nor did other children on the margins of the hat dance fling themselves into the fun. Such infectious behavior would have indicated communally defined social relations or the desire for such social relations. Outside of Disney World in places of public use, infectious behavior is common. One child squirming about on the library floor breeds others; siblings chasing each other around in a supermarket draw others; one child mischievously poking at a public fountain attracts others; kids freeloading rides on a department store escalator can draw a crowd.

7   At Disney World the basic social unit is the family. This was made particularly clear to me because as a single visitor conducting research, I presented a problem at the point of embarkation for each of the rides. "How many in your group?" "One." The lone occupant of a conveyance invariably constructed to hold the various numerical breakdowns of the nuclear family (two, three, or four) is an anomaly. Perhaps the most family-affirming aspect of Disney World is the way the queues serve as a place where family members negotiate who will ride with whom. Will Mom and Dad separate themselves so as to accompany their two kids on a two-person ride? Will an older sibling assume the responsibility for a younger brother or sister? Every ride asks the family to evaluate each of its member's needs for security and independence. This is probably the only situation in a family's visit to Disney World where the social relations of family materialize as practice. Otherwise and throughout a family's stay, the family as nexus for social relations is subsumed by the primary definition of family as the basic unit of consumption. In consumer society at large, each of us is an atomized consumer. Families are composed of autonomous, individuated consumers, each satisfying his or her age-and gender-differentiated taste in the music,

video, food, and pleasure marketplace. In contrast, Disney World puts the family back together. Even teens are integrated in their families and are seldom seen roaming the park in teen groups as they might in shopping malls.

8   Families at Disney World present themselves as families, like the one I saw one morning on my way to breakfast at a Disney resort hotel: father, mother, and three children small to large, each wearing identical blue Mickey Mouse T-shirts and shorts. As I walked past them, I overheard the middle child say, "We looked better yesterday—in white." Immediately, I envisioned the family in yesterday's matching outfits, and wondered if they had bought identical ensembles for every day of their stay.

9   In its identical dress, the family represents itself as capitalism's version of a democratized unit of consumption. Differences and inequalities among family members are reduced to distinctions in age and size. We have all had occasion to experience the doppelgänger effect in the presence of identical twins who choose (or whose families enforce) identical dress. Whether chosen or imposed, identical twins who practice the art of same dress have the possibility of confounding or subverting social order. In contrast, the heterogeneous family whose members choose to dress identically affirms conformity with social order. The family has cloned itself as a multiple, but identical consumer, thus enabling the maximization of consumption. It is a microcosmic representation of free market democracy where the range of choices is restricted to the series of objects already on the shelf. In this system there is no radical choice. Even the minority of visitors who choose to wear their Rolling Stones and Grateful Dead T-shirts give the impression of having felt constrained not to wear a Disney logo.

10   Actually, Disney has invented a category of negative consumer choices for those individuals who wish to express nonconformity. This I discovered as I prepared to depart for my Disney research trip, when my daughter Cassie (fifteen years old and "cool" to the max) warned me, "Don't buy me any of that Disney paraphernalia." As it turned out, she was happy to get a pair of boxer shorts emblazoned with the leering images of Disney's villains: two evil queens, the Big Bad Wolf, and Captain Hook. Every area of Disney World includes a Disney Villains Shop, a chain store for bad-guy merchandise. Visitors who harbor anti-Disney sentiments can express their cultural politics by consuming the negative Disney line. There is no possibility of an anticonsumption at Disney World. All visitors are, by definition, consumers, their status conferred with the price of admission.

11   At Disney World even memories are commodities. How the visitor will remember his or her experience of the park has been programmed and indicated by the thousands of "Kodak Picture Spot" signposts. These position the photographer so as to capture the best views of each and every attraction, so that even the most inept family members can bring home perfect postcard-like photos. To return home from a trip to Disney World with a collection of haphazardly photographed environments or idiosyncratic family shots is tantamount to collecting bad memories. A family album comprised of picture-perfect photo-site images, on the other hand, constitutes the grand narrative of the family's trip to Disney World, the one that can be offered as testimony to money well spent. Meanwhile, all those embarrassing photos, the ones not programmed by the "Picture Spots," that depict babies with ice cream all over their faces or toddlers who burst into tears rather than smiles at the

sight of those big-headed costumed characters that crop up all over the park—these are the images that are best left forgotten.

12   The other commodified form of memory is the souvenir. As long as there has been tourism there have also been souvenirs: objects marketed to concretize the visitor's experience of another place. From a certain point of view, religious pilgrimage includes aspects of tourism, particularly when the culmination of pilgrimage is the acquisition of a transportable relic. Indeed, secular mass culture often imitates the forms and practices of popular religious culture. For many Americans today who make pilgrimages to Graceland and bring home a mass-produced piece of Presley memorabilia, culture and religion collide and mesh.

13   Of course, the desire to translate meaningful moments into concrete objects need not take commodified form. In Toni Morrison's *Song of Solomon*, Pilate, a larger-than-life earth mother if there ever was one, spent her early vagabondage gathering a stone from every place she visited. Similarly, I know of mountain climbers who mark their ascents by bringing a rock back from each peak they climb. Like Pilate's stones, these tend to be nondescript and embody personal remembrances available only to the collector. In contrast, the commodity souvenir enunciates a single meaning to everyone: "I was there. I bought something." Unlike the souvenirs I remember having seen as a child, seashells painted with seascapes and the name of some picturesque resort town, most souvenirs today are printed with logos (like the Hard Rock Cafe T-shirt), or renderings of copyrighted material (all the Disney merchandise). The purchase of such a souvenir allows the consumer the illusion of participating in the enterprise as a whole, attaining a piece of the action. This is the consumerist version of small-time buying on the stock exchange. We all trade in logos—buy them, wear them, eat them, and make them the containers of our dreams and memories. Similarly, we may all buy into capital with the purchase of public stock. These consumerist activities give the illusion of democratic participation while denying access to real corporate control which remains intact and autonomous, notwithstanding the mass diffusion of its logos and stock on the public market.

14   Disney World is logoland. The merchandise, the costumes, the scenery—all is either stamped with the Disney logo or covered by copyright legislation. In fact, it is impossible to photograph at Disney World without running the risk of infringing a Disney copyright. A family photo in front of Sleeping Beauty's Castle is apt to include dozens of infringements: the castle itself, Uncle Harry's "Goofy" T-shirt, the kids' Donald and Mickey hats, maybe a costumed Chip 'n Dale in the background. The only thing that saves the average family from a lawsuit is that most don't use their vacation photos as a means for making profit.

15   What most distinguishes Disney World from any other amusement park is the way its spatial organization, defined by autonomous "worlds" and wholly themed environments, combines with the homogeneity of its visitors (predominantly white, middle-class families) to produce a sense of community. While Disney World includes an underlying utopian impulse, this is articulated with nostalgia for a small-town, small-business America (Main Street, U.S.A.), and the fantasy of a controllable corporatist world (EPCOT). The illusion of community is enhanced by the longing for community that many visitors bring to the park,

which they may feel is unavailable to them in their own careers, daily lives, and neigh-borhoods, thanks in large part to the systematic erosion of the public sector throughout the Reagan and Bush administrations. In the last decade the inroads of private, for-profit enterprise in areas previously defined by public control, and the hostile aggression of tax backlash coupled with "me first" attitudes have largely defeated the possibility of com-munity in our homes and cities.

16   Whenever I visit Disney World, I invariably overhear other visitors making compari-sons between Disney World and their home towns. They stare out over EPCOT's lake and wonder why developers back home don't produce similar aesthetic spectacles. They talk about botched, abandoned, and misconceived development projects that have wrecked their local landscapes. Others see Disney World as an oasis of social tranquility and secu-rity in comparison to their patrolled, but nonetheless deteriorating, maybe even perilous neighborhoods. A recent essay in *Time* captured some of these sentiments: "Do you see anybody [at Disney World] lying on the street or begging for money? Do you see anyone jumping on your car and wanting to clean your windshield—and when you say no, they get abusive?"

17   Comments such as these do more than betray the class anxiety of the middle strata. They poignantly express the inability of this group to make distinctions between what necessarily constitutes the public and the private sectors. Do visitors forget that they pay a daily use fee (upwards of $150 for a four-day stay) just to be a citizen of Disney World (not to mention the $100 per night hotel bill)? Maybe so—and maybe it's precisely *forgetting* that visitors pay for.

18   If there is any distinction to be made between Disney World and our local shopping malls, it would have to do with Disney's successful exclusion of all factors that might put the lie to its uniform social fabric. The occasional Hispanic mother who arrives with extended family and illegal bologna sandwiches is an anomaly. So too is the first-generation Cubana who buys a year-round pass to Disney's nightspot, Pleasure Island, in hopes of meeting a rich and marriageable British tourist. These women testify to the presence of Orlando, Disney World's marginalized "Sister City," whose overflowing cheap labor force and overcrowded and under-funded public institutions are the unseen real world upon which Disney's world depends.

QUESTIONS ON MEANING

1. What does Willis mean when she claims that Disney has erased spontaneity?
2. Willis claims that "amusement is the commodified negative of play." What do you think Willis means by this statement? Do you agree? What other activities (if any) constitute a form of amusement but also represent the negative of play?
3. What is the overall message of Willis's essay as it relates to Disney World?
4. What assumptions about the nature of consumerism and culture seem to frame Willis's discussion of Disney World? What is Willis's worldview, at least as can be inferred from this essay?

5. What does Willis have to say about the relationship between the family unit and Disney? And American culture? And consumerism?

6. What roles to logos play in contemporary culture, according to Willis?

QUESTIONS FOR DISCUSSION

1. Willis seems to develop a seeming paradox early in her essay between the directed (non-spontaneous) Disney environment and the feeling of freedom visitors experience when in the environment. How does Willis resolve this paradox (or does she)?

2. What do you make of the paradox above? Have you been to Disney World? Did the experience seem restrictive or freeing to you?

3. Willis points out that those who wish to express their "anti-Disney sentiments" can (and do) purchase souvenirs in the "negative Disney line." Is this a fair interpretation of the experience she describes? What other ways are there to interpret the purchase of a villain-themed souvenir other than as an expression of anti-Disney sentiment?

4. What does it mean to fetishize a commodity? Are there ways this happens other than at Disney World? Can you give examples?

5. Would you characterize Willis's essay as a descriptive essay, a thesis-driven essay, or both? Is her essay detached and/or objective in its description or argument, or is her essay partisan or biased in some fashion? Can you find passages in the essay to back up your answers to these questions?

LOOKING AT RHETORIC

1. What is the tone of Willis's essay? Does the tone help reveal Willis's attitude toward her subject? What key words or phrases help create the tone?

2. Is this essay compelling? Is it persuasive? Is it an accurate depiction of the individual's experience when visiting Disney World? As an essay, what are its merits and its flaws?

WRITING ASSIGNMENTS

1. Spend some time researching the founding and history of Disney World. In light of that research, write an essay in which you talk about the degree to which Disney has a shaping influence on contemporary culture.

2. Write an essay in which you describe what an amusement park might look like if it were designed to allow for spontaneous play and did not foster consumerism of the kind critiqued by Willis in her essay.

3. In pairs or in groups, discuss whether you find Willis's essay persuasive or not. Identify arguments or descriptions that you find convincing or compelling, as well as those passages you find illogical or otherwise flawed and unconvincing. As a group, imagine you are spokespeople for the Disney corporation tasked with responding to Willis's essay. What might Disney have to say in response? Then, as an individual, write an essay in which you respond in a logical, carefully written, and reasoned manner to Willis's essay from the point of view of a Disney spokesperson.

Marketing, Media, and the First Amendment: What's Best for Children?

Susan Linn

Susan Linn is an instructor in psychiatry at Harvard University and the co-founder and director of the Campaign for a Commercial-Free Childhood, a group that works to reduce the extent to which children are the targets of marketing campaigns and media content steeped in sex and violence. She is the author of numerous essays on the subject of marketing to children, and is the author of Consuming Kids: The Hostile Takeover of Childhood *(2004), from which the following selection is taken, and* The Case for Make Believe: Saving Play in a Commercialized World *(2009). As a child therapist, Linn is known for her innovative work using puppets in child therapy sessions and for her contributions to numerous videos created to help children come to terms with a variety of issues, including the loss of a loved one, discrimination, and mental illness.*

1   When confronted with the complex issues and passions evoked by marketing sex and violence to children, I was initially reluctant to leap into the fray. Every attempt to formulate my thoughts led inevitably to natural disaster metaphors ranging from "quagmire" and "sinkhole" to "tsunami" and "avalanche." I knew I was heading for trouble.

2   The problem is that in this country it's virtually impossible to talk about curbing children's exposure to media sex and violence without addressing controversial and passion-engendering questions of morality, artistic freedom, the role of government in media regulation, and the free-speech guarantees of the First Amendment to our Constitution. Unlike advertisements and product placements created to sell junk food to kids—or even advertising strategies that are designed to bypass regulations and sell them alcohol and tobacco—the marketing of sex and violence involves the content of expressive media productions themselves, including movies, television programs, videos, video games, and music. Most of the motivation for drama—that which holds our interest in a narrative—stems from conflict and the expression of basic human drives. In contrast, despite product placement, hamburgers are rarely a plot point, nor do we hear much about artistic freedom when it comes to selling sugar cereals.

3   We are a pluralistic nation, and our attitudes about sex and violence are often rooted in moral and religious beliefs. The Torah, the Koran, and the New Testament all weigh in on violent and sexual behaviors. What their teachings mean, of course, is open to interpretation—giving rise to lots of modern-day confusion about sin. Most of us agree in general that it's wrong to physically hurt another person, yet, as a society, we seem to tolerate and even applaud spanking, war, and self-defense. We disagree more about sex, except insofar as most of us think (at a minimum) that it should be consensual and that our own children are too young to be having it.

4   There are voices of reason in the debate, but they are often drowned out. The loudest condemnations (especially about sex) and many of the calls for regulation that reach the

public ear seem to come from extreme conservatives and the religious right, whose arguments invoke God, universal morality, and a stunning disregard for large portions of the Bill of Rights.

5   While arguing vociferously against government intervention into areas that are known to have an impact on youth violence and teen pregnancy (poverty, mental health, gun ownership, or sex education), they lobby with equal fervor for government control of media content. Meanwhile, their opposite numbers—who seem to consist mainly of media makers and rather doctrinaire left-wingers—support government interventions in the form of gun control, federal poverty programs, and sex education in public schools, yet oppose any regulation of how media is marketed. They tend to equate any media content rating systems with censorship, and wave the flag of the First Amendment while remaining in complete denial of the idea that the media have any influence at all on children's behaviors or values.

6   For people like me—concerned about children's exposure to media violence and about precocious, irresponsible sexuality even as I support the First Amendment (to say nothing of separation of church and state)—this dichotomy is a problem. I sometimes find myself in agreement on this particular issue with people with whom I disagree about almost everything else. It's a mess, made messier because public dialogue is increasingly influenced (some would say "controlled") by sound bites and headlines that can never do justice to complex issues.

7   Television executives managed to avoid instituting a rating system until 1996, when the Telecommunications Act mandated that every television set contain a "V-chip" that would allow parents to block out violent or otherwise objectionable programs.

8   Under threat of government intervention, and as a necessary part of the V-chip technology, the television industry created ratings for shows—to be broadcast along with them—so that parents could program the V-chip to block out shows that contained content they felt was inappropriate for their children. The V-chip has not been a howling success. Only one-third of parents with V-chip televisions use it. There are lots of reasons for this. It's been under-advertised (some would argue that it has barely been advertised at all). It's hard to set up. The ratings themselves are complicated and inadequate.

9   Meanwhile, parents, health professionals, educators, and advocacy groups have been fighting unsuccessfully to get the industry to create a more useful descriptive code, one that communicates content rather than age-appropriateness. R ratings, or M (for "mature") ratings for video games, are often a draw rather than a deterrent for young teens and pre-teens. Just the fact that the video game and television industries have chosen "Mature" or "Mature Audience" as a label shows a certain dishonesty about their intent. To be seen as mature, or see themselves that way, is an important component of what adolescents and preadolescents are striving for.

10   As a parent, I have found film and television ratings useful in an arbitrary kind of way. However, I do think that associating ratings with age lends a peculiar message to children about violence. Such ratings suggest that being able to tolerate or enjoy watching people get hurt is a sign of maturity, something children should look forward to as a reward for growing up. Some television programs voluntarily identify the reason for their rating,

whether it's violence, language, or sexuality, but they aren't required to do so. More than one father has told me that seeing scary or violent movies is a point of honor for his preteen sons and their friends. "That wasn't scary," is a common refrain.

11   Violence is marketed to children so intensively that parents find themselves making all sorts of devil's bargains with what kinds of violence they will and won't allow. One mother of a thirteen-year-old finally decided that her child could buy video games that involved killing fantasy creatures but not games that involved violence against humans. At the same time, she recognized that she could not control which video games he played at other kids' houses.

12   Educating parents about how to use the V-chip is not a priority for anyone in the media industry. In fact, it is in their best financial interest for parents to remain ignorant about the device. Every child viewer lost to a program is one fewer consumer for the products they sell.

13   However daunting the task, I knew when I began this book that I would have to leap into the First-Amendment-children's-media-and-marketing morass. It's the only time I ever yearned to be a lawyer. I attacked the problem in the following way—months of fretting, followed by months of reading, interspersed with endless conversations with a wide range of people, all of whom have passionate and sometimes widely different perspectives on the meaning of free speech.

14   Ultimately it's up to policy makers and legal scholars to give shape to how this country deals or doesn't deal with children, marketing, media, and the First Amendment. I think their work should take place in the context of widespread public debate *in the context of what's best for children*. Since free speech as it relates either to corporations in general or to advertising in particular is based on interpretations of the First Amendment rather than what it actually says, this conversation should take place unconstrained by how the Supreme Court is currently interpreting the Constitution.

15   After struggling to sort through the issues, I decided that what I can offer are some points for framing that discussion. If we get the dialogue right, we have a better chance of getting the results right as well. With that in mind, these are some points we need to consider:

THE WORDS "ADVERTISING" OR "MARKETING" ARE NOT INCLUDED IN THE TEXT OF THE FIRST AMENDMENT

16   The actual text of the First Amendment addresses political and religious expression, free speech, freedom of the press, the right to assemble, and the right of petition. As recently as 1942, the Supreme Court voted unanimously that advertising was not protected under the rubric of free speech. In recent years, the Court has been changing its mind and granting increased protections for commercial speech or advertising.

17   Artists, corporations, and any other entities have the right to produce the media or products they choose, but the government (of the people, by the people, and for the

people) should have the right to regulate how those products are marketed—especially to children.

ADVERTISING TO CHILDREN IS NOT ANYONE'S INALIENABLE RIGHT

18   I find that discussions about marketing to children often devolve into arguments about advertising as an inalienable right. Usually, this refers to the rights of the marketers, but I have to admit to being startled when a reporter asked me, "Don't children have the right to be marketed to?" Well, no. That's like saying sheep have a right to be wolf bait. Children do have certain rights protected by law in this country—the right to be educated, for instance—but being targeted in the marketplace is not among them.

THE GOVERNMENT IS NOT THE ONLY THREAT TO FREEDOM OF EXPRESSION, ESPECIALLY WHEN IT COMES TO THE MASS MEDIA

19   I'm puzzled that people concerned about freedom of speech don't seem to be worrying about corporate control of media content as much as they worry about government regulation. For instance, in the year 2000, free speech advocates railed against the government's involvement in inserting antidrug messages in television programs, while at the same time there was little mention of the influence of corporate interests on media content, which represents an equally destructive, and more pervasive, threat to free speech.

20   Certainly it was a violation of the First Amendment when the White House Office of National Drug Control Policy actually reviewed the messages incorporated in television scripts. However, the current trend toward deregulation of media ownership (which began while Jimmy Carter was president, intensified during Ronald Reagan's tenure, and is continuing through the present) has led to a consolidation of media ownership to such an extent that only a few companies control most of the media—and therefore most of the media content available to Americans.

21   Under the guise of the Family Friendly Programming Forum, big advertisers, including McDonald's, Coca-Cola, Kellogg, and General Mills, give money toward the development of "family friendly" programs. The Forum appears to focus its efforts on affecting the creation of prime-time shows that are free of violent and sexual content. One of their creations, *The Gilmore Girls*, received some critical acclaim and was held up as a program that could be popular without containing sex or violence. Kellogg's, a member of the forum, was one of the main sponsors of *The Gilmore Girls*. Guess what the Gilmore Girls ate for breakfast? Kellogg's Pop Tarts. Given the childhood obesity epidemic, just how family friendly are the advertising practices of food companies like Kellogg's, General Mills, Coca-Cola, and McDonald's? Is any corporation in the business of marketing directly to children truly family friendly?

22   In addition to providing networks seed money to develop programs, the Forum offers scriptwriting scholarships to film schools at New York University and the University of

Southern California. It has provided seed money to some networks to create program-ming. We would be naive to assume that the course of creative flow will be uninfluenced by either of these gifts. The Forum's vested interests are likely to be directly protected simply because it holds the purse strings. Would a beneficiary of the Forum's benevolence be likely to create programs critical of the advertising industry, for instance? How much influence will a Forum scholarship have on the creativity of cash-strapped film students? Will they really want to begin their film careers by alienating an entire consortium of potential funders by using their beneficence to create scripts critical of corporate practices?

23   When corporate sponsors of media programming take part in its creation, their power extends beyond being able to decline sponsorship. They are able to shape programming at its inception. It seems to me that anyone concerned about free speech has to take on corporate control of media content as well as government control.

TELEVISION NETWORKS WERE GIVEN THE RIGHT TO BROADCAST—FOR FREE—OVER THE PUBLIC AIRWAYS IN EXCHANGE FOR AN OBLIGATION TO SUPPORT THE PUBLIC INTEREST

24   In the 1920s, the government formally leased the public's radio airway to commer-cial interests and began to regulate broadcasting through the Federal Radio Commission. In the 1930s, with the invention of television, the FRC was dismantled and the Federal Communications Commission (FCC) took over its mission. From the start, broadcasters' adherence to public interest has been one criteria for license renewal. Initially, there were limits on commercials, and requirements that broadcasters air news and public affairs programming. However, the definition of "public interest" has changed over the years. These days, supporting public interest seems to mean simply adhering to FCC regula-tions, which have been diminishing significantly in number and domain over the years. Is it in the public interest for children to be exposed to violent and confusing sexual images during the hours they're most likely to be watching TV? Is it in the public inter-est for children to be targets for marketing products through ads that manipulate their vulnerabilities? If not, don't we, the public, have a right to hold broadcasters responsible for airing those ads?

25   As part of the 1996 Telecommunications Act, Congress gave existing commercial broadcasters rights to broadcast through the expanded digital spectrum for free—at an estimated loss to the public of over $70 billion. While each broadcaster now has multiple channels for broadcasting, there has been no channel set aside for commercial-free pro-gramming. It has been pointed out that if broadcasters were to be charged a fee for their use of the digital spectrum, the government could earn $2 to $5 billion annually that could then be spent on a truly public, truly non-commercial broadcasting system. Since govern-ment expenditures for public broadcasting are currently in the $250 million range, imagine the commercial-free programming that a few billion more dollars could create—including programming for children.

WE, AS A SOCIETY, HAVE TRADITIONALLY RECOGNIZED THAT CHILDREN ARE NOT ADULTS—SINCE THEIR LACK OF COGNITIVE, SOCIAL, EMOTIONAL, AND PHYSICAL DEVELOPMENT, AS WELL AS THEIR LACK OF EXPERIENCE, MAKES THEM PARTICULARLY VULNERABLE TO EXPLOITATION. THEY ARE ENTITLED TO AND HAVE BEEN ALLOWED MANY SPECIAL PROTECTIONS IN OTHER ARENAS UNDER THE LAW

26   We have child labor laws, laws that children must stay in school, laws prohibiting sale of alcohol and tobacco to children, and laws that attempt to protect them from pornography. Even if the Supreme Court decides, through rulings on test cases, that marketing "speech" should be completely protected under the First Amendment, there are still precedents suggesting that marketing to children—including marketing sexual and violent media content through ads as well as promotions with toys, food companies, and fast-food restaurants—should be excluded from such protections.

27   At this point, the law does suggest that children have a right to be protected from speech that is harmful to them—from, for instance, pornography or what gets classified as adult entertainment. One problem is that, other than outright pornography, we can't seem to come to an agreement on the definition of "harm." If it could be proven that viewing violent media is a "sole or primary cause" of harm or harming behavior, excluding the media violence marketed to children from First Amendment protections would be legally justifiable.

28   Many factors, both environmental and biological, determine attitudes toward violence and violent behavior. There's enough evidence (see the one thousand studies over thirty years cited in the public health community's Joint Statement on the Impact of Entertainment Violence) that media violence is one of those factors, although there's no evidence that it's ever the sole factor.

29   As one media researcher pointed out to me, the study that could prove that violent media was a sole factor in violent attitudes or behavior would be unethical, and therefore will never be done. Such a study might look like this: Two groups of children matched in age, gender, socioeconomic status, and risk for violence would have to be divided accordingly and locked in two separate rooms for an extended period of time. One would be fed a steady diet of media violence while the other would be fed some other kind of media. Perhaps a third group, equally matched, could be allowed to play. Then their behavior would have to be observed for another extended period of time, perhaps years. Because there are (thank goodness) restrictions on how human subjects can be used in academic research, no public institution could conduct this research. It is interesting to note, however that since market research is subject to no government restrictions on the use of human subjects, including children, it is theoretically possible for some corporation to do it.

30   Aside from such an unethical study, some people think that the best way to prove harm would be research using brain-imaging techniques to show how the brain processes

violent media. One such study, conducted at Kansas State University in 2003, showed intriguing results using a sample too small to be conclusive. It suggested that children's brains respond to media violence as though it were a significant life event, storing information the same the way they would store a post-traumatic stress memory. Another study shows that the brains of children with a history of violent behavior respond differently to media violence than those with no such history. More such research will be conducted over the next few years.

TOOLS THAT ENABLE PARENTS TO CONTROL WHAT THEIR CHILDREN SEE ON TELEVISION ARE NOT A VIOLATION OF THE FIRST AMENDMENT

31   The V-chip to allow parents to screen certain programs based on their ratings is now embedded by law in all television sets, and its use has not yet been challenged in the courts. However, Replay TV, a device enabling people to skip over commercials, is currently the subject of a lawsuit brought by various media companies against its maker, Sonic Blue.

32   I'm ambivalent about both of these devices because they allow us to dodge the underlying issue of public and corporate responsibility to children. Kids from families whose parents can't or won't use the V-chip are not going to benefit from it. The fact that viewers can skip commercials is now a major rationale for the escalation of advertising embedded in television programming instead of just surrounding it. On the other hand, changing the political and social landscape that frames policies relating to media and advertising to children is likely to take a long time. In the meantime, these devices do provide some relief to some families.

33   One problem with both the V-chip and Replay TV is that their value to parents is undermined by ignorance and greed. Thus far, the V-chip is used only minimally. Many salespeople selling televisions don't know how to program the V-chip, nor has it been promoted with any major public service campaign. It is not in media corporations' immediate best interest to limit access to programming for any segment of its audience. Replay TV, which is being positioned as an anticommercialism device, has partnered with Coca-Cola to run commercials while a program is on pause.

34   With the advent of digital media resulting in technology that combines the Internet and television, issues relating to media content, marketing, and the First Amendment as they apply to children are going to become even more complex. Without government intervention, or the real threat of government regulation, there is no evidence that we can count on media companies to hold children's best interests above their own profits. Whatever decisions we as a society come to about regulation, we all need to acknowledge that marketing sex and violence to children is harmful. I don't have answers, but I do believe it's essential not to discount the impact of media content on children, even in the service of protecting free speech.

QUESTIONS ON MEANING

1. Why is discussing children's exposure to sex and violence in the media different from discussing these same things strictly in advertising campaigns, according to Linn?

2. What does Linn mean when she points out that the U.S. is a pluralistic nation? What does this have to do with the topic of her essay?

3. What is Linn's opinion of the Golden Age of Television?

4. Why does Linn find violence to be a particular problem when filtered through an age-based rating system?

5. What is Linn's interpretation of the free speech clause in the First Amendment as it relates to commercial advertising?

6. According to Linn, do DVR technologies hold significant promise for alleviating (in part or in whole) the problems associated with marketing to children?

QUESTIONS FOR DISCUSSION

1. What is Linn's opinion of the various ratings systems employed by the television, film, and video game industries? What is your opinion? Do these systems work? Would a different system be more (or less) effective? Do you believe ratings are necessary at all?

2. Do you believe children are exposed to too much sex and violence in today's media? At what age and under what circumstance is it acceptable for children and/or adults to be exposed to the following in film, television, video games, and/or music?
    A. Foul language in film.
    B. Nudity and human sexuality (of a non-graphic nature).
    C. Nudity and human sexuality (of a graphic nature).
    D. Gun and/or weapon-based violence.
    E. Human mutilation.
    F. Aberrant criminal or sexual behavior (such as rape, pedophilia, bondage).

3. Linn believes that our discussions of the relationship between children and media should take place in the context of "what's best for children." Do you find current ratings systems effective in dealing with what's best for children?

4. Does the Internet implement a ratings system? Should it? What about individual web sites such as YouTube?

5. Should advertising be protected under the free speech clause of the First Amendment?

LOOKING AT RHETORIC

1. How does the first paragraph of the essay set the tone for the rest of the piece? Is it an effective introduction? What do we learn about the author and her subject matter from this introductory paragraph?

2. At one point, Linn lists the different people and groups she has spoken to in order to gain insight into the issues involved and develop her opinion regarding the first amendment relationship to children's marketing. Find that section of the essay and review it. What rhetorical strategy is being used here? Is it effective? Why or why not?

Interdisciplinary Connections

Using Advertising to Raise Awareness:
Animal Rights

Some advertisements are not created in order to sell a product, but are created in order to sell an idea. Ideas can be tough to sell to people who are not tuned in to a particular social issue or concern, but some social problems, such as domestic abuse, HIV-AIDS, and the destruction of the environment are often deemed so significant that organizations will create elaborate advertising campaigns—often using shocking imagery—as a method of getting the attention of the public and generating interest in the idea or issue. The two advertisements below were created in

IndyAct Endangered Species Ad

order to generate public interest in animal rights issues. They both ask the viewer to consider the relationship between human desires and the impact these desires have on endangered wildlife populations. As you study the images, ask yourself what the creators of these ads were trying to achieve. Which ad do you find more effective and why? Do the ads appeal to the same audience, or different audiences? If you were to create an ad in order to promote awareness of the issues confronting endangered species, what kind of image would you create?

World Wildlife Federation Ad

WRITING ASSIGNMENTS

1. Spend some time researching the history of the free speech clause of the First Amendment. In particular, look into how the First Amendment has been used (or not) over the years to advocate for or against certain types of marketing and advertising campaigns. Armed with this information, draft an essay in which you either defend or reject the proposition that advertising is protected speech under the First Amendment.

2. Select a show geared toward children between the ages of seven and thirteen. Watch several episodes of the show, taking care to note when the show itself contains any embedded advertising, and also noting the content of the commercials shown during the episodes. Write an essay in which you argue that the content of the advertising was or was not suitable to members of that age group.

3. In pairs or in groups, discuss the different ratings systems that currently exist to help regulate content in film, television, music, and video games. Discuss which ratings systems are most effective, and which least. As a group, try to determine which of these four mediums is most in need of regulation, and which is least in need of regulation, making note of arguments for and against each position. Then, as individuals, select one of these mediums and write an essay in which you discuss its ratings system and the mechanisms by which the medium is regulated (if, indeed, it is regulated). It is possible that you may need to spend some time in the library researching the medium in order to write this part of the essay. Then, argue whether you find the current ratings system and its corresponding regulations effective or ineffective and explain why.

Faux Friendship

William Deresiewicz

William Deresiewicz is a teacher, writer, literary critic, and former professor of English at Yale University, where he taught from 1998 to 2008. His work addresses a range of subjects related to contemporary culture and is directed at different audiences, from literary scholars to general read-ers. His more popular writings have appeared in The London Review of Book, The American Scholar, The Nation, and The New York Times. *He received the National Book Critics Circle's Nona Balakian Citation for Excellence in Reviewing in 2010 and 2011, and he was nominated for the National Magazine Award in 2008, 2009, and 2011. The following article was published in* The Chronicle of Higher Education *in 2009. It explores the way definitions of friendship have evolved over the past two millennia under the influence of powerful social and cultural forces, with particular attention to how modern social media such as Facebook and Twitter are affecting the role of friendship in modern life.*

1   We live at a time when friendship has become both all and nothing at all. Already the characteristically modern relationship, it has in recent decades become the universal one: the form of connection in terms of which all others are understood, against which they are all measured, into which they have all dissolved. Romantic partners refer to each other as boyfriend and girlfriend. Spouses boast that they are each other's best friends. Parents urge their young children and beg their teenage ones to think of them as friends. Adult siblings, released from competition for parental resources that in traditional society made them anything but friends (think of Jacob and Esau), now treat one another in exactly those terms. Teachers, clergymen, and even bosses seek to mitigate and legitimate their authority by asking those they oversee to regard them as friends. We're all on a first-name basis, and when we vote for president, we ask ourselves whom we'd rather have a beer with. As the anthropologist Robert Brain has put it, we're friends with everyone now.

2   Yet what, in our brave new mediated world, is friendship becoming? The Facebook phenomenon, so sudden and forceful a distortion of social space, needs little elaboration. Having been relegated to our screens, are our friendships now anything more than a form of distraction? When they've shrunk to the size of a wall post, do they retain any content? If we have 768 "friends," in what sense do we have any? Facebook isn't the whole of con-temporary friendship, but it sure looks a lot like its future. Yet Facebook—and MySpace, and Twitter, and whatever we're stampeding for next—are just the latest stages of a long attenuation. They've accelerated the fragmentation of consciousness, but they didn't initi-ate it. They have reified the idea of universal friendship, but they didn't invent it. In retro-spect, it seems inevitable that once we decided to become friends with everyone, we would forget how to be friends with anyone. We may pride ourselves today on our aptitude for friendship—friends, after all, are the only people we have left—but it's not clear that we still even know what it means.

3   How did we come to this pass? The idea of friendship in ancient times could not have been more different. Achilles and Patroclus, David and Jonathan, Virgil's Nisus and

Euryalus: Far from being ordinary and universal, friendship, for the ancients, was rare, precious, and hardwon. In a world ordered by relations of kin and kingdom, its elective affinities were exceptional, even subversive, cutting across established lines of allegiance. David loved Jonathan despite the enmity of Saul; Achilles' bond with Patroclus outweighed his loyalty to the Greek cause. Friendship was a high calling, demanding extraordinary qualities of character—rooted in virtue, for Aristotle and Cicero, and dedicated to the pursuit of goodness and truth. And because it was seen as superior to marriage and at least equal in value to sexual love, its expression often reached an erotic intensity. Jonathan's love, David sang, "was more wondrous to me than the love of women." Achilles and Patroclus were not lovers—the men shared a tent, but they shared their beds with concubines—they were something greater. Achilles refused to live without his friend, just as Nisus died to avenge Euryalus, and Damon offered himself in place of Pythias.

4   The rise of Christianity put the classical ideal in eclipse. Christian thought discouraged intense personal bonds, for the heart should be turned to God. Within monastic communities, particular attachments were seen as threats to group cohesion. In medieval society, friendship entailed specific expectations and obligations, often formalized in oaths. Lords and vassals employed the language of friendship. "Standing surety"— guaranteeing a loan, as in *The Merchant of Venice*—was a chief institution of early modern friendship. Godparenthood functioned in Roman Catholic society (and, in many places, still functions) as a form of alliance between families, a relationship not between godparent and godchild, but godparent and parent. In medieval England, godparents were "godsibs;" in Latin America, they are "compadres," co-fathers, a word we have taken as synonymous with friendship itself.

5   The classical notion of friendship was revived, along with other ancient modes of feeling, by the Renaissance. Truth and virtue, again, above all: "Those who venture to criticize us perform a remarkable act of friendship," wrote Montaigne, "for to undertake to wound and offend a man for his own good is to have a healthy love for him." His bond with Étienne, he avowed, stood higher not only than marriage and erotic attachment, but also than filial, fraternal, and homosexual love. "So many coincidences are needed to build up such a friendship, that it is a lot if fortune can do it once in three centuries." The highly structured and, as it were, economic nature of medieval friendship explains why true friendship was held to be so rare in classical and neoclassical thought: precisely because relations in traditional societies were dominated by interest. Thus the "true friend" stood against the self-interested "flatterer" or "false friend," as Shakespeare sets Horatio—"more an antique Roman than a Dane"—against Rosencrantz and Guildenstern. Sancho Panza begins as Don Quixote's dependent and ends as his friend; by the close of their journey, he has come to understand that friendship itself has become the reward he was always seeking.

6   Classical friendship, now called romantic friendship, persisted through the 18th and 19th centuries, giving us the great friendships of Goethe and Schiller, Byron and Shelley, Emerson and Thoreau. Wordsworth addressed his magnum opus to his "dear Friend" Coleridge. Tennyson lamented Hallam—"My friend . . . My Arthur . . . Dear as the mother to the son"—in the poem that became his masterpiece. Speaking of his

first encounter with Hawthorne, Melville was unashamed to write that "a man of deep and noble nature has seized me." But meanwhile, the growth of commercial society was shifting the very grounds of personal life toward the conditions essential for the emergence of modern friendship. Capitalism, said Hume and Smith, by making economic relations impersonal, allowed for private relationships based on nothing other than affection and affinity. We don't know the people who make the things we buy and don't need to know the people who sell them. The ones we do know—neighbors, fellow parishioners, people we knew in high school or college, parents of our children's friends—have no bearing on our economic life. One teaches at a school in the suburbs, another works for a business across town, a third lives on the opposite side of the country. We are nothing to one another but what we choose to become, and we can unbecome it whenever we want.

7   Add to this the growth of democracy, an ideology of universal equality and inter-involvement. We are citizens now, not subjects, bound together directly rather than through allegiance to a monarch. But what is to bind us emotionally, make us something more than an aggregate of political monads? One answer was nationalism, but another grew out of the 18th-century notion of social sympathy: friendship, or at least, friendliness, as the affec-tive substructure of modern society. It is no accident that "fraternity" made a third with liberty and equality as the watchwords of the French Revolution. Wordsworth in Britain and Whitman in America made visions of universal friendship central to their democratic vistas. For Mary Wollstonecraft, the mother of feminism, friendship was to be the key term of a renegotiated sexual contract, a new domestic democracy.

8   Now we can see why friendship has become the characteristically modern relation-ship. Modernity believes in equality, and friendships, unlike traditional relationships, are egalitarian. Modernity believes in individualism. Friendships serve no public purpose and exist independent of all other bonds. Modernity believes in choice. Friendships, unlike blood ties, are elective; indeed, the rise of friendship coincided with the shift away from arranged marriage. Modernity believes in self-expression. Friends, because we choose them, give us back an image of ourselves. Modernity believes in freedom. Even modern marriage entails contractual obligations, but friendship involves no fixed commitments. The modern temper runs toward unrestricted fluidity and flexibility, the endless play of possibility, and so is perfectly suited to the informal, improvisational nature of friendship. We can be friends with whomever we want, however we want, for as long as we want.

9   Social changes play into the question as well. As industrialization uprooted people from extended families and traditional communities and packed them into urban cen-ters, friendship emerged to salve the anonymity and rootlessness of modern life. The process is virtually instinctive now: You graduate from college, move to New York or L.A., and assemble the gang that takes you through your 20s. Only it's not just your 20s anymore. The transformations of family life over the last few decades have made friendship more important still. Between the rise of divorce and the growth of single parenthood, adults in contemporary households often no longer have spouses, let alone a traditional extended family, to turn to for support. Children, let loose by the weaken-ing of parental authority and supervision, spin out of orbit at ever-earlier ages. Both look to friends to replace the older structures. Friends may be "the family we choose," as the

modern proverb has it, but for many of us there is no choice but to make our friends our family, since our other families—the ones we come from or the ones we try to start—have fallen apart. When all the marriages are over, friends are the people we come back to. And even those who grow up in a stable family and end up creating another one pass more and more time between the two. We have yet to find a satisfactory name for that period of life, now typically a decade but often a great deal longer, between the end of adolescence and the making of definitive life choices. But the one thing we know is that friendship is absolutely central to it.

10   Inevitably, the classical ideal has faded. The image of the one true friend, a soul mate rare to find but dearly beloved, has completely disappeared from our culture. We have our better or lesser friends, even our best friends, but no one in a very long time has talked about friendship the way Montaigne and Tennyson did. That glib neologism "bff," which plays at a lifelong avowal, bespeaks an ironic awareness of the mobility of our connections: Best friends forever may not be on speaking terms by this time next month. We save our fiercest energies for sex. Indeed, between the rise of Freudianism and the contemporaneous emergence of homosexuality to social visibility, we've taught ourselves to shun expressions of intense affection between friends—male friends in particular, though even Oprah was forced to defend her relationship with her closest friend—and have rewritten historical friendships, like Achilles' with Patroclus, as sexual. For all the talk of "bromance" lately (or "man dates"), the term is yet another device to manage the sexual anxiety kicked up by straight-male friendships—whether in the friends themselves or in the people around them—and the typical bromance plot instructs the callow bonds of youth to give way to mature heterosexual relationships. At best, intense friendships are something we're expected to grow out of.

11   As for the moral content of classical friendship, its commitment to virtue and mutual improvement, that, too, has been lost. We have ceased to believe that a friend's highest purpose is to summon us to the good by offering moral advice and correction. We practice, instead, the nonjudgmental friendship of unconditional acceptance and support—"therapeutic" friendship, in Robert N. Bellah's scornful term. We seem to be terribly fragile now. A friend fulfills her duty, we suppose, by taking our side—validating our feelings, supporting our decisions, helping us to feel good about ourselves. We tell white lies, make excuses when a friend does something wrong, do what we can to keep the boat steady. We're busy people; we want our friendships fun and friction-free.

12   Yet even as friendship became universal and the classical ideal lost its force, a new kind of idealism arose, a new repository for some of friendship's deepest needs: the group friendship or friendship circle. Companies of superior spirits go back at least as far as Pythagoras and Plato and achieved new importance in the salons and coffeehouses of the 17th and 18th centuries, but the Romantic age gave them a fresh impetus and emphasis. The idea of friendship became central to their self-conception, whether in Wordsworth's circle or the "small band of true friends" who witness Emma's marriage in Austen. And the notion of superiority acquired a utopian cast, so that the circle was seen—not least because of its very emphasis on friendship—as the harbinger of a more advanced age. The same was true, a century later, of the Bloomsbury Group, two of whose members, Woolf and Forster, produced novel upon novel about friendship. It was the latter who famously

enunciated the group's political creed. "If I had to choose between betraying my country and betraying my friend," he wrote, "I hope I should have the guts to betray my country." Modernism was the great age of the coterie, and like the legendary friendships of antiquity, modernist friendship circles—bohemian, artistic, transgressive—set their face against existing structures and norms. Friendship becomes, on this account, a kind of alternative society, a refuge from the values of the larger, fallen world.

13   The belief that the most significant part of an individual's emotional life properly takes place not within the family but within a group of friends began to expand beyond the artistic coterie and become general during the last half of the 20th century. The Romantic-Bloomsburyan prophecy of society as a set of friendship circles was, to a great extent, realized. Mary McCarthy offered an early and tart view of the desirability of such a situation in *The Group*; Barry Levinson, a later, kinder one in *Diner*. Both works remind us that the ubiquity of group friendship owes a great deal to the rise of youth culture. Indeed, modernity associates friendship itself with youth, a time of life it likewise regards as standing apart from false adult values. "The dear peculiar bond of youth," Byron called friendship, inverting the classical belief that its true practice demands maturity and wisdom. With modernity's elevation of youth to supreme status as the most vital and authentic period of life, friendship became the object of intense emotion in two contradictory but often simultaneous directions. We have sought to prolong youth indefinitely by holding fast to our youthful friendships, and we have mourned the loss of youth through an unremitting nostalgia for those friendships. One of the most striking things about the way the 20th century understood friendship was the tendency to view it through the filter of memory, as if it could be recognized only after its loss, and as if that loss were inevitable.

14   The culture of group friendship reached its apogee in the 1960s. Two of the counterculture's most salient and ideologically charged social forms were the commune—a community of friends in self-imagined retreat from a heartlessly corporatized society—and the rock'n'roll "band" (not "group" or "combo"), its name evoking Shakespeare's "band of brothers" and Robin Hood's band of Merry Men, its great exemplar the Beatles. Communes, bands, and other 60s friendship groups (including Woodstock, the apotheosis of both the commune and the rock concert) were celebrated as joyous, creative places of eternal youth—havens from the adult world. To go through life within one was the era's utopian dream; it is no wonder the Beatles' break-up was received as a generational tragedy. It is also no wonder that 60s group friendship began to generate its own nostalgia as the baby boom began to hit its 30s. *The Big Chill*, in 1983, depicted boomers attempting to recapture the magic of a late-60s friendship circle. ("In a cold world," the movie's tagline reads, "you need your friends to keep you warm.") *Thirtysomething*, taking a step further, certified group friendship as the new adult norm. Most of the characters in those productions, though, were married. It was only in the 1990s that a new generation, remaining single well past 30, found its own images of group friendship in *Seinfeld, Sex and the City*, and, of course, *Friends*. By that point, however, the notion of friendship as a redoubt of moral resistance, a shelter from normative pressures and incubator of social ideals, had disappeared. Your friends didn't shield you from the mainstream, they were the mainstream.

15   And so we return to Facebook. With the social-networking sites of the new century—Friendster and MySpace were launched in 2003, Facebook in 2004—the friendship circle has expanded to engulf the whole of the social world, and in so doing, destroyed both its own nature and that of the individual friendship itself. Facebook's very premise—and promise—is that it makes our friendship circles visible. There they are, my friends, all in the same place. Except, of course, they're not in the same place, or, rather, they're not my friends. They're simulacra of my friends, little dehydrated packets of images and information, no more my friends than a set of baseball cards is the New York Mets.

16   I remember realizing a few years ago that most of the members of what I thought of as my "circle" didn't actually know one another. One I'd met in graduate school, another at a job, one in Boston, another in Brooklyn, one lived in Minneapolis now, another in Israel, so that I was ultimately able to enumerate some 14 people, none of whom had ever met any of the others. To imagine that they added up to a circle, an embracing and encircling structure, was a belief, I realized, that violated the laws of feeling as well as geometry. They were a set of points, and I was wandering somewhere among them. Facebook seduces us, however, into exactly that illusion, inviting us to believe that by assembling a list, we have conjured a group. Visual juxtaposition creates the mirage of emotional proximity. "It's like they're all having a conversation," a woman I know once said about her Facebook page, full of posts and comments from friends and friends of friends. "Except they're not."

17   Friendship is devolving, in other words, from a relationship to a feeling—from something people share to something each of us hugs privately to ourselves in the loneliness of our electronic caves, rearranging the tokens of connection like a lonely child playing with dolls. The same path was long ago trodden by community. As the traditional face-to-face community disappeared, we held on to what we had lost—the closeness, the rootedness— by clinging to the word, no matter how much we had to water down its meaning. Now we speak of the Jewish "community" and the medical "community" and the "community" of readers, even though none of them actually is one. What we have, instead of community, is, if we're lucky, a "sense" of community—the feeling without the structure; a private emotion, not a collective experience. And now friendship, which arose to its present importance as a replacement for community, is going the same way. We have "friends," just as we belong to "communities." Scanning my Facebook page gives me, precisely, a "sense" of connection. Not an actual connection, just a sense.

18   What purpose do all those wall posts and status updates serve? On the first beautiful weekend of spring this year, a friend posted this update from Central Park: "[So-and-so] is in the Park with the rest of the City." The first question that comes to mind is, if you're enjoying a beautiful day in the park, why don't you give your iPhone a rest? But the more important one is, why did you need to tell us that? We have always shared our little private observations and moments of feeling—it's part of what friendship's about, part of the way we remain present in one another's lives—but things are different now. Until a few years ago, you could share your thoughts with only one friend at a time (on the phone, say), or maybe with a small group, later, in person. And when you did, you were talking to specific people, and you tailored what you said, and how you said it, to who they were—their

interests, their personalities, most of all, your degree of mutual intimacy. "Reach out and touch someone" meant someone in particular, someone you were actually thinking about. It meant having a conversation. Now we're just broadcasting our stream of consciousness, live from Central Park, to all 500 of our friends at once, hoping that someone, anyone, will confirm our existence by answering back. We haven't just stopped talking to our friends as individuals, at such moments, we have stopped thinking of them as individuals. We have turned them into an indiscriminate mass, a kind of audience or faceless public. We address ourselves not to a circle, but to a cloud.

19   It's amazing how fast things have changed. Not only don't we have Wordsworth and Coleridge anymore, we don't even have Jerry and George. Today, Ross and Chandler would be writing on each other's walls. Carrie and the girls would be posting status updates, and if they did manage to find the time for lunch, they'd be too busy checking their BlackBerrys to have a real conversation. *Sex* and *Friends* went off the air just five years ago, and already we live in a different world. Friendship (like activism) has been smoothly integrated into our new electronic lifestyles. We're too busy to spare our friends more time than it takes to send a text. We're too busy, sending texts. And what happens when we do find the time to get together? I asked a woman I know whether her teen-age daughters and their friends still have the kind of intense friendships that kids once did. Yes, she said, but they go about them differently. They still stay up talking in their rooms, but they're also online with three other friends, and texting with another three. Video chatting is more intimate, in theory, than speaking on the phone, but not if you're doing it with four people at once. And teenagers are just an early version of the rest of us. A study found that one American in four reported having no close confidants, up from one in 10 in 1985. The figures date from 2004, and there's little doubt that Facebook and texting and all the rest of it have already exacerbated the situation. The more people we know, the lonelier we get.

20   The new group friendship, already vitiated itself, is cannibalizing our individual friendships as the boundaries between the two blur. The most disturbing thing about Facebook is the extent to which people are willing—are eager—to conduct their private lives in public. "hola cutie-pie! i'm in town on wednesday. lunch?" "Julie, I'm so glad we're back in touch. xoxox." "Sorry for not calling, am going through a tough time right now." Have these people forgotten how to use e-mail, or do they actually prefer to stage the emotional equivalent of a public grope? I can understand "[So-and-so] is in the Park with the rest of the City," but I am incapable of comprehending this kind of exhibitionism. Perhaps I need to surrender the idea that the value of friendship lies precisely in the space of privacy it creates: not the secrets that two people exchange so much as the unique and inviolate world they build up between them, the spider web of shared discovery they spin out, slowly and carefully, together. There's something faintly obscene about performing that intimacy in front of everyone you know, as if its real purpose were to show what a deep person you are. Are we really so hungry for validation? So desperate to prove we have friends?

21   But surely Facebook has its benefits. Long-lost friends can reconnect, far-flung ones can stay in touch. I wonder, though. Having recently moved across the country, I thought that Facebook would help me feel connected to the friends I'd left behind. But now I find

the opposite is true. Reading about the mundane details of their lives, a steady stream of trivia and ephemera, leaves me feeling both empty and unpleasantly full, as if I had just binged on junk food, and precisely because it reminds me of the real sustenance, the real knowledge, we exchange by email or phone or face-to-face. And the whole theatrical quality of the business, the sense that my friends are doing their best to impersonate themselves, only makes it worse. The person I read about, I cannot help feeling, is not quite the person I know.

22   As for getting back in touch with old friends—yes, when they're people you really love, it's a miracle. But most of the time, they're not. They're someone you knew for a summer in camp, or a midlevel friend from high school. They don't matter to you as individuals anymore, certainly not the individuals they are now, they matter because they made up the texture of your experience at a certain moment in your life, in conjunction with all the other people you knew. Tear them out of that texture—read about their brats, look at pictures of their vacation—and they mean nothing. Tear out enough of them and you ruin the texture itself, replace a matrix of feeling and memory, the deep subsoil of experience, with a spurious sense of familiarity. Your 18-year-old self knows them. Your 40-year-old self should not know them.

23   Facebook holds out a utopian possibility: What once was lost will now be found. But the heaven of the past is a promised land destroyed in the reaching. Facebook, here, becomes the anti-madeleine, an eraser of memory. Carlton Fisk has remarked that he's watched the third of that length as the conventional limit for a message, far less for a comment. (And we all know the deal on Twitter.) The 10-page missive has gone the way of the buggy whip, soon to be followed, it seems, by the three-hour conversation. Each evolved as a space for telling stories, an act that cannot usefully be accomplished in much less. Posting information is like pornography, a slick, impersonal exhibition. Exchanging stories is like making love: probing, questing, questioning, caressing. It is mutual. It is intimate. It takes patience, devotion, sensitivity, subtlety, skill—and it teaches them all, too.

24   They call them social-networking sites for a reason. Networking once meant something specific: climbing the jungle gym of professional contacts in order to advance your career. The truth is that Hume and Smith were not completely right. Commercial society did not eliminate the self-interested aspects of making friends and influencing people, it just changed the way we went about it. Now, in the age of the entrepreneurial self, even our closest relationships are being pressed onto this template. A recent book on the sociology of modern science describes a networking event at a West Coast university: "There do not seem to be any singletons—disconsolately lurking at the margins—nor do dyads appear, except fleetingly." No solitude, no friendship, no space for refusal—the exact contemporary paradigm. At the same time, the author assures us, "face time" is valued in this "community" as a "high-bandwidth interaction," offering "unusual capacity for interruption, repair, feedback and learning." Actual human contact, rendered "unusual" and weighed by the values of a systems engineer. We have given our hearts to machines, and now we are turning into machines. The face of friendship in the new century.

QUESTIONS ON MEANING

1. How has the concept of friendship changed recently?

2. What was the nature of friendship in ancient cultures? Why was it comparatively rare?

3. How have capitalism, industrialization, democracy, and modernity changed the nature of friendship?

4. Why in the modern period is friendship most often associated with youth? What historical changes made this happen?

5. What illusion does Facebook create regarding friendship and friendship circles?

6. How does Deresiewicz ultimately define ideal friendship?

QUESTIONS FOR DISCUSSION

1. Does the expansion of the concept of friendship diminish the quality of individual relationships? How and why?

2. Does the widespread use of social media such as Facebook and Twitter enrich or impoverish our friendships? How and why?

3. Have our freely chosen friends become a replacement for family or traditional communities? How effective is that replacement? Does choice enhance or detract from the quality of human relationships?

4. Does the new group friendship cannibalize individual friendships?

LOOKING AT RHETORIC

1. Deresiewicz takes an objective historical approach in making his argument, by tracing how friendship has evolved from the classical age to the present. In what ways does this firm grounding in history validate his argument? Does his apparent knowledge of the past enhance our trust in his judgments and claims about friendship?

2. This is a readable but confrontational essay. Its primary stylistic characteristic is clarity, even simplicity. Does that simplicity enhance or detract from the argument's credibility and make its controversial argument more credible?

WRITING ASSIGNMENTS

1. Using library and/or Internet sources, research the history of friendship. Then write an essay in which you advance or challenge Deresiewicz's claim about the decline of genuine friendship.

2. Argue for or against Facebook, Twitter, or other social media as a way of enhancing friendship and human intimacy.

3. In pairs or in groups, discuss your own friendships and families. Discuss what relationships you find fulfilling and why. Talk about the role of social media in your lives. Then, independently, write an essay in which you address those who are contemplating creating a Facebook page for the purpose of maintaining friendships. Encourage them either to create or not create one, and if you suggest that they do, describe how they should use it to enrich rather than diminish the quality of friendships.

Thinking Crosscurrently

COMMUNICATION AND POP CULTURE

Pop culture is part of the fabric of our daily life. It surrounds us from the moment we wake up till we go back to bed at night. As we interact with the world around us, we consume, enjoy, and are influenced by pop culture, and, in turn, our participation in our culture helps shape cultural trends, and these trends help shape everything from the way in which products are sold to what music is played on the radio to the design of the social media sites we employ. Pop culture influences our attitudes toward the world around us, and yet it is our participation in pop culture that helped lead to the emergence of those trends in the first place. Thus, to fully understand the impact and importance of pop culture, one must not only consider questions of art, one must consider questions of business and economics and history and language, among many other disciplines. As you think about the selections in this chapter, consider the following questions:

- How much of popular culture is directly tied to economic issues? What do shows such as American Idol say about the relationship between popular culture and big business? What kinds of insights into these questions do the essays by Barbara Ehrenreich and Paul Krugman provide? How might we apply some of the ideas in their essays to understanding the connections between economic theory and popular culture? To what extent is modern culture commercialized? Is this a good thing? Why or why not?

- What responsibilities do the producers of popular music and other art forms have to the rest of society? What perspectives might Alissa Quart and Emily Bernard bring to this question? How about Jeff Sharlet or Dan Baum? Should there be greater or lesser control over how certain aspects of culture are represented in popular culture? How about movies? Music? Video games?

- To what extent can pop culture be used by individual citizens as a means to either support or critique, or even overthrow, a local or national government? What role did social media, for instance, play in the 2011 uprisings in Egypt, Tunisia, and Libya? What perspectives might David Mamet or Mahatma Gandhi bring to this question?

- What aspects of pop culture deserve to be seen as *art*? Is all pop music art? What about a television sitcom? What about a particularly clever T-shirt with a witty anti-government slogan? What might Oscar Wilde and Virginia Woolf say about this question?

9

PHILOSOPHY AND PSYCHOLOGY

I n Stanley Kubrick's famous 1968 movie *2001: A Space Odyssey*, the daily operations of a space ship traveling to Jupiter in order to investigate a mysterious object are run and controlled by a computer. The HAL 9000 computer, called Hal, is able to speak with the crew members, engage them in games of chess, work with them to solve problems, and provide a constant source of communication between the crew and the life support systems aboard their ship, the *Discovery One*. Conflict emerges between Hal and the crew of the *Discovery One* as a result of some details about the nature of their mission to Jupiter that Hal knows but the human crew does not. As a result, one of the crew members is forced to disable Hal—who has turned against the crew for reasons unbeknownst to them—by removing those circuit boards that comprise Hal's higher brain functions. In one of the most famous scenes from the movie, the audience is able to listen to Hal's gradually deteriorating brain function as circuit boards are, one by one, slowly removed from Hal's central processing unit. With the higher brain functions eliminated, Hal is still functional—the *Discovery One* maintains its life support systems, for instance—but any semblance of intelligence disappears.

Although it might seem strange to begin a chapter featuring readings in philosophy and psychology with a reference to an artificially intelligent computer in a classic movie, the attempts to create artificially intelligent machines has entailed the collective efforts of psychologists, philosophers, communication and information theorists, computer programmers, designers, mathematicians, neuroscientists, biologists, linguists, and more. And, even with the collective efforts of all of these groups, it still isn't a foregone conclusion that any artificially intelligent computer or robot or android will ever have what we would consider a *human* intelligence.

The pursuit of an artificially intelligent computer, thus, opens up a whole host of questions that get right to the heart of psychology and philosophy. What does it mean to be intelligent? What is the relationship between intelligence and consciousness? Could a machine be intelligent but not conscious? Is there a fundamental split between body and mind? Between brain and mind? Between spirit and mind? Is there such a thing as a spirit, and does it have any bearing on consciousness or intelligence, or even one's sense of identity? How would an artificially intelligent mechanism have to be engineered or programmed? Would intelligence arise from a software application, or would it emerge through certain hardware configurations, or both, or something else entirely? And, what does any of this suggest to us about the nature of our own identity, our belief systems, and the rituals and rites that we engage in as a testament to our faith in God, or lack thereof?

Despite all that chemistry, biology, physics, and mathematics have taught us about the universe in which we live—despite all that we have learned about the mechanisms that govern our physical environment—this knowledge has revealed very little to us about the values we hold, our aspirations, the shape and significance of our emotional life, the mysteries of consciousness, and the meaning of our lives. Historically, humans have turned to religion and philosophy in order to provide a framework for answering these questions. Nowadays, psychology has joined religion and philosophy as a key discipline in the quest for the structures of meaning and belief that provide humans with a sense of order and value. There are no questions more endlessly puzzling—more intractable—than these; yet, there are no questions whose answers remain as shrouded in mystery as these. Certain questions, such as how to cure HIV or cancer, remain unanswered, but few people would argue rationally that these are unanswerable questions. But is there a God?—what happens to an individual when he or she dies?—answers to these questions simply don't fall into the same category. Chemistry and biology and mathematics offer few people satisfactory answers to these kinds of metaphysical questions. Instead, humans turn to philosophy, to religion, to concepts of spirit, soul, and mind. Computer science, perhaps surprisingly, has had a dramatic influence on the human pursuit of answers to these questions: as computer hardware and software get increasingly *intelligent*, we begin to see analogies between computers and the functions of the human brain. What does that tell us, by analogy, about the human mind, and the relationship between the mind and the brain? What does it suggest to us about the nature of human consciousness? Here is where psychology, philosophy, religion, and even cultural anthropology merge in one common pursuit, the endless quest to understand the meaning of the human experience, and to know, once and for all, why we believe the things we do. What is *belief*, anyway?

THE DISCIPLINE YOU EXPERIENCE

Understanding the human mind and its interaction with the world is the goal of many different academic disciplines. At the modern college or university, there are typically a wide variety of different majors that one can pursue. All of these programs, to one degree or another, seek to analyze and understand not just the laws and mechanisms that describe the material world, but the values, belief systems, and points-of-view that individuals and social groupings use to frame or provide context for the laws and mechanisms uncovered by chemistry, physics, and biology. The selections that follow in this chapter represent a number of these disciplines, including:

- Psychology, which is the scientific study of human—and, on occasion, animal—behaviors and mental states or functions. Psychologists seek to understand how humans think, why humans behave the way they do, and what triggers human emotional responses. The student of psychology asks questions about human motivation, perception, personality, and relationships. They also are interested in the physiological and neurological mechanisms that underlie human endeavors.

- Philosophy, which means, literally, the love of wisdom, concerns itself with the approach to truth through human reason, rather than through empirical means, as in a laboratory science such as chemistry. Philosophers study metaphysics (which concerns itself with absolute questions about the nature of reality), epistemology (which concerns itself with the nature and structure of knowledge), ethics (which concerns itself with social and interpersonal interactions), and logic (which concerns itself with the structure of arguments and their validity).

- Religious Studies is the study of religious belief systems and institutions. In general, programs in religious studies tend to focus on the history, development, rituals, and creeds of a wide variety of religions across the world. The related discipline of *theology*, in comparison, is generally the study of the belief system—or philosophy— of a particular religion, and, in particular, of the characteristics of that religion's god and the corresponding doctrines that undergird belief in that particular god.

- Anthropology, which is, literally, the study of humans, is the discipline that seeks to understand the development of humans as a species, with an emphasis on their social groupings and their behavioral and language patterns. Anthropology has several major sub-disciplines, including cultural anthropology and archaeology. Anthropology has strong ties to other disciplines, including biology, history, linguistics, psychology, and religious studies, and is generally grouped together with sociology as one of the key disciplines in the social sciences.

The essays reprinted in this chapter range widely through these different disciplines. To be sure, the pursuit of the human mind is not something that one discipline alone can accomplish: it takes the collective work of many minds to define *the mind*.

REFLECTING ON THIS CHAPTER

Despite the hundreds of different avenues of research within the disciplines and subdisciplines covered in this set of readings, they share in common a desire to understand human cognition, to understand how and why humans think the way they do. Perhaps development in the creation of artificially intelligent computers will give us a model for understanding human cognition? Perhaps psychology can teach us about the neural pathways that underlie human thought patterns? Perhaps philosophy can give us a rationale for belief in God, or maybe even the nature of belief itself? Perhaps by studying the ways in which Protestants and Catholics view the world differently, or the ways in which people in Ghana view the concept of the transcendent compared with the average westerner, one will gain a deeper understanding of how the mind works in all of its mystery and complexity. As you read the essays in this chapter, consider the following questions:

- What is the central issue or problem the author attempts to explore or solve? What claims does the author make, and does the author make a convincing argument in support of those claims?

- It is common among many in America, and in the West generally, to ascribe to some version of dualism (the belief that the universe is comprised of two distinct and separate substances, matter and spirit). How do the selections in this chapter either support or challenge philosophical dualism?

- How do these selections compare and contrast? What central issues and themes emerge from these selections when taken as a group?

- What are the various writing strategies the authors employ? What rhetorical tools do they use to persuade us? If you found a selection convincing, what made it so?

- Do you detect any logical flaws in the arguments developed by the authors of these selections? Can you find any inconsistencies or biases? Are there any contradictions within each selection? What recommendations would you make to the author about how he or she might improve their essay?

The Will to Believe

William James

William James (1842–1910) was the most influential American philosopher and psychologist of the late nineteenth century. Older brother to the famed novelist Henry James, William James studied medicine at Harvard, but eventually settled into the emerging field of psychology, where he did pioneering work. After accepting a teaching post at Harvard in 1872, James taught there for most of his career, eventually retiring from teaching—but not from research and writing—in 1907. Some of his best known works include The Principles of Psychology *(1890),* The Will to Believe *and other Essays in Popular Philosophy (1897),* The Varieties of Religious Experience *(1902),* Pragmatism *(1907), and* A Pluralistic Universe *(1909). In the following selection, James takes up the question of whether it is reasonable for an individual to adopt a religious belief despite having insufficient evidence to warrant the belief according to the standards of logic. Although James focuses on religious belief in this essay, his thoughts on the nature of belief have wide-ranging implications for all disciplines in the modern high school, college, or university.*

I.

1   Let us give the name of *hypothesis* to anything that may be proposed to our belief; and just as the electricians speak of live and dead wires, let us speak of any hypothesis as either *live* or *dead*. A live hypothesis is one which appeals as a real possibility to him to whom it is proposed. If I ask you to believe in the Mahdi, the notion makes no electric connection with your nature,—it refuses to scintillate with any credibility at all. As an hypothesis it is completely dead. To an Arab, however (even if he be not one of the Mahdi's followers), the hypothesis is among the mind's possibilities: it is alive. This shows that deadness and liveness in an hypothesis are not intrinsic properties, but relations to the individual thinker.

They are measured by his willingness to act. The maximum of liveness in an hypothesis means willingness to act irrevocably. Practically, that means belief; but there is some believing tendency wherever there is willingness to act at all.

Next, let us call the decision between two hypotheses an *option*. Options may be of several kinds. They may be—1, *living* or *dead*; 2, *forced* or *avoidable*; 3, *momentous* or *trivial*; and for our purposes we may call an option a *genuine* option when it is of the forced, living, and momentous kind.

1. A living option is one in which both hypotheses are live ones. If I say to you: "Be a theosophist or be a Mohammedan," it is probably a dead option, because for you neither hypothesis is likely to be alive. But if I say: "Be an agnostic or be a Christian," it is otherwise: trained as you are, each hypothesis makes some appeal, however small, to your belief.

2. Next, if I say to you: "Choose between going out with your umbrella or without it," I do not offer you a genuine option, for it is not forced. You can easily avoid it by not going out at all. Similarly, if I say, "Either love me or hate me," "Either call my theory true or call it false," your option is avoidable. You may remain indifferent to me, neither loving nor hating, and you may decline to offer any judgment as to my theory. But if I say, "Either accept this truth or go without it," I put on you a forced option, for there is no standing place outside of the alternative. Every dilemma based on a complete logical disjunction, with no possibility of not choosing, is an option of this forced kind.

3. Finally, if I were Dr. Nansen and proposed to you to join my North Pole expedition, your option would be momentous; for this would probably be your only similar opportunity, and your choice now would either exclude you from the North Pole sort of immortality altogether or put at least the chance of it into your hands. He who refuses to embrace a unique opportunity loses the prize as surely as if he tried and failed. *Per contra*, the option is trivial when the opportunity is not unique, when the stake is insignificant, or when the decision is reversible if it later prove unwise. Such trivial options abound in the scientific life. A chemist finds an hypothesis live enough to spend a year in its verification: he believes in it to that extent. But if his experiments prove inconclusive either way, he is quit for his loss of time, no vital harm being done.

It will facilitate our discussion if we keep all these distinctions well in mind.

II.

In Pascal's Thoughts there is a celebrated passage known in literature as Pascal's wager.[1] In it he tries to force us into Christianity by reasoning as if our concern with truth resembled our concern with the stakes in a game of chance. Translated freely his words are these: You must either believe or not believe that God is—which will you do? Your human reason cannot say. A game is going on between you and the nature of things which at the

---

[1] Pascal: Blaise Pascal, seventeenth-century French philosopher.

day of judgment will bring out either heads or tails. Weigh what your gains and your losses would be if you should stake all you have on heads, or God's existence: if you win in such case, you gain eternal beatitude; if you lose, you lose nothing at all. If there were an infinity of chances, and only one for God in this wager, still you ought to stake your all on God; for though you surely risk a finite loss by this procedure, any finite loss is reasonable, even a certain one is reasonable, if there is but the possibility of infinite gain. Go, then, and take holy water, and have masses said; belief will come and stupefy your scruples, — *Cela vous fera croire et vous abetira.*[2] Why should you not? At bottom, what have you to lose?

5   You probably feel that when religious faith expresses itself thus, in the language of the gaming-table, it is put to its last trumps. Surely Pascal's own personal belief in masses and holy water had far other springs; and this celebrated page of his is but an argument for others, a last desperate snatch at a weapon against the hardness of the unbelieving heart. We feel that a faith in masses and holy water adopted wilfully after such a mechanical calculation would lack the inner soul of faith's reality; and if we were ourselves in the place of the Deity, we should probably take particular pleasure in cutting off believers of this pattern from their infinite reward. It is evident that unless there be some pre-existing tendency to believe in masses and holy water, the option offered to the will by Pascal is not a living option.

6   The talk of believing by our volition seems, then, from one point of view, simply silly. From another point of view it is worse than silly, it is vile. And that delicious *enfant terrible* Clifford[3] writes: "Belief is desecrated when given to unproved and unquestioned statements for the solace and private pleasure of the believer. . . . Whoso would deserve well of his fellows in this matter will guard the purity of his belief with a very fanaticism of jealous care, lest at any time it should rest on an unworthy object, and catch a stain which can never be wiped away. . . . If [a] belief has been accepted on insufficient evidence [even though the belief be true, as Clifford on the same page explains] the pleasure is a stolen one. . . . It is sinful because it is stolen in defiance of our duty to mankind. That duty is to guard ourselves from such beliefs as from a pestilence which may shortly master our own body and then spread to the rest of the town. . . . It is wrong always, everywhere, and for every one, to believe anything upon insufficient evidence."

III.

7   All this strikes one as healthy, even when expressed, as by Clifford, with somewhat too much of robustious pathos in the voice. Free-will and simple wishing do seem, in the matter of our credences, to be only fifth wheels to the coach. Yet if any one should thereupon assume that intellectual insight is what remains after wish and will and sentimental preference have taken wing, or that pure reason is what then settles our opinions, he would fly quite as directly in the teeth of the facts.

---

[2]*Cela vous fera croire et vous abêtira*: French for the preceding phrase, "belief will come and stupefy your scruples."

[3]Clifford: William Clifford, nineteenth-century British mathematician and philosopher.

8   It is only our already dead hypotheses that our willing nature is unable to bring to life again. But what has made them dead for us is for the most part a previous action of our willing nature of an antagonistic kind. When I say 'willing nature,' I do not mean only such deliberate volitions as may have set up habits of belief that we cannot now escape from,—I mean all such factors of belief as fear and hope, prejudice and passion, imitation and partisanship, the circumpressure of our caste and set. As a matter of fact we find ourselves believing, we hardly know how or why.

9   As a rule we disbelieve all facts and theories for which we have no use. Why do so few 'scientists' even look at the evidence for telepathy, so called? Because they think, as a leading biologist, now dead, once said to me, that even if such a thing were true, scientists ought to band together to keep it suppressed and concealed. It would undo the uniformity of Nature and all sorts of other things without which scientists cannot carry on their pursuits. But if this very man had been shown something which as a scientist he might *do* with telepathy, he might not only have examined the evidence, but even have found it good enough. This very law which the logicians would impose upon us—if I may give the name of logicians to those who would rule out our willing nature here—is based on nothing but their own natural wish to exclude all elements for which they, in their professional quality of logicians, can find no use.

10   Evidently, then, our non-intellectual nature does influence our convictions. There are passional tendencies and volitions which run before and others which come after belief, and it is only the latter that are too late for the fair; and they are not too late when the previous passional work has been already in their own direction. Pascal's argument, instead of being powerless, then seems a regular clincher, and is the last stroke needed to make our faith in masses and holy water complete. The state of things is evidently far from simple; and pure insight and logic, whatever they might do ideally, are not the only things that really do produce our creeds.

IV.

11   Our next duty, having recognized this mixed-up state of affairs, is to ask whether it be simply reprehensible and pathological, or whether, on the contrary, we must treat it as a normal element in making up our minds. The thesis I defend is, briefly stated, this:

> *Our passional nature not only lawfully may, but must, decide an option between propositions, whenever it is a genuiue option that cannot by its nature be decided on intellectual grounds; for to say, under such circumstances, "Do not decide, but leave the question open," is itself a passional decision—just like deciding yes or no—and is attended with the same risk of losing the truth.*

The thesis thus abstractly expressed will, I trust, soon become quite clear. But I must first indulge in a bit more of preliminary work.

V.

12   It will be observed that for the purposes of this discussion we are on 'dogmatic' ground—ground, I mean, which leaves systematic philosophical scepticism altogether out

of account. The postulate that there is truth, and that it is the destiny of our minds to attain it, we are deliberately resolving to make, though the sceptic will not make it. We part company with him, therefore, absolutely, at this point. But the faith that truth exists, and that our minds can find it, may be held in two ways. We may talk of the *empiricist* way and of the *absolutist* way of believing in truth. The absolutists in this matter say that we not only can attain to knowing truth, but we can *know when* we have attained to knowing it; while the empiricists think that although we may attain it, we cannot infallibly know when. To *know* is one thing, and to know for certain *that* we know is another. One may hold to the first being possible without the second; hence the empiricists and the absolutists, although neither of them is a sceptic in the usual philosophic sense of the term, show very different degrees of dogmatism in their lives.

13   If we look at the history of opinions, we see that the empiricist tendency has largely prevailed in science, while in philosophy the absolutist tendency has had everything its own way. The characteristic sort of happiness, indeed, which philosophies yield has mainly consisted in the conviction felt by each successive school or system that by it bottom-certitude had been attained. "Other philosophies are collections of opinions, mostly false; *my* philosophy gives standing-ground forever"—who does not recognize in this the key-note of every system worthy of the name? A system, to be a system at all, must come as a *closed* system, reversible in this or that detail, perchance, but in its essential features never!

VI.

14   But now, since we are all such absolutists by instinct, what in our quality of students of philosophy ought we to do about the fact? Shall we espouse and indorse it? Or shall we treat it as a weakness of our nature from which we must free ourselves, if we can?

15   I sincerely believe that the latter course is the only one we can follow as reflective men. Objective evidence and certitude are doubtless very fine ideals to play with, but where on this moonlit and dream-visited planet are they found? I am, therefore, myself a complete empiricist so far as my theory of human knowledge goes. I live, to be sure, by the practical faith that we must go on experiencing and thinking over our experience, for only thus can our opinions grow more true; but to hold any one of them—I absolutely do not care which—as if it never could be reinterpretable or corrigible, I believe to be a tremendously mistaken attitude, and I think that the whole history of philosophy will bear me out. There is but one indefectibly certain—the truth that the present phenomenon of consciousness exists. That, however, is the bare starting-point of knowledge, the mere admission of a stuff to be philosophized about. The various philosophies are but so many attempts at expressing what this stuff really is.

16   No concrete test of what is really true has ever been agreed upon.

17   There is this—there is that; there is indeed nothing which some one has not thought absolutely true, while his neighbor deemed it absolutely false; and not an absolutist among them seems ever to have considered that the trouble may all the time be essential, and that the intellect, even with truth directly in its grasp, may have no infallible signal for knowing whether it be truth or no.

18   But please observe, now, that when as empiricists we give up the doctrine of objective certitude, we do not thereby give up the quest or hope of truth itself. We still pin our faith on its existence, and still believe that we gain an ever better position towards it by systematically continuing to roll up experiences and think. Not where it comes from but what it leads to is to decide. It matters not to an empiricist from what quarter an hypothesis may come to him: he may have acquired it by fair means or by foul; passion may have whispered or accident suggested it; but if the total drift of thinking continues to confirm it, that is what he means by its being true.

VII.

19   One more point, small but important, and our preliminaries are done. There are two ways of looking at our duty in the matter of opinion,—ways entirely different, and yet ways about whose difference the theory of knowledge seems hitherto to have shown very little concern. *We must know the truth;* and *we must avoid error*—these are our first and great commandments as would-be knowers; but they are not two ways of stating an identical commandment, they are two separable laws. Although it may indeed happen that when we believe the truth *A*, we escape as an incidental consequence from believing the falsehood *B*, it hardly ever happens that by merely disbelieving *B* we necessarily believe *A*. We may in escaping *B* fall into believing other falsehoods, *C* or *D*, just as bad as *B*; or we may escape *B* by not believing anything at all, not even *A*.

20   Believe truth! Shun error!—these, we see, are two materially different laws; and by choosing between them we may end by coloring differently our whole intellectual life. We may regard the chase for truth as paramount, and the avoidance of error as secondary; or we may, on the other hand, treat the avoidance of error as more imperative, and let truth take its chance. For my own part, I have also a horror of being duped; but I can believe that worse things than being duped may happen to a man in this world. Our errors are surely not such awfully solemn things. In a world where we are so certain to incur them in spite of all our caution, a certain lightness of heart seems healthier than this excessive nervousness on their behalf. At any rate, it seems the fittest thing for the empiricist philosopher.

21   Wherever the option between losing truth and gaining it is not momentous, we can throw the chance of *gaining truth* away, and at any rate save ourselves from any chance of *believing falsehood*, by not making up our minds at all till objective evidence has come. In scientific questions, this is almost always the case; and even in human affairs in general, the need of acting is seldom so urgent that a false belief to act on is better than no belief at all. Law courts, indeed, have to decide on the best evidence attainable for the moment, because a judge's duty is to make law as well as to ascertain it, and (as a learned judge once said to me) few cases are worth spending much time over: the great thing is to have them decided on *any* acceptable principle, and got out of the way. But in our dealings with objective nature we obviously are recorders, not makers, of the truth; and decisions for the mere sake of deciding promptly and getting on to the next business would be wholly out of place. Throughout the breadth of physical nature facts are what they are quite independently of us, and seldom is there any such

hurry about them that the risks of being duped by believing a premature theory need be faced. The attitude of sceptical balance is therefore the absolutely wise one if we would escape mistakes.

22   The next question arises: can we (as men who may be interested at least as much in positively gaining truth as in merely escaping dupery) always wait with impunity till the coercive evidence shall have arrived? It seems *a priori* improbable that the truth should be so nicely adjusted to our needs and powers as that. In the great boarding-house of nature, the cakes and the butter and the syrup seldom come out so even and leave the plates so clean. Indeed, we should view them with scientific suspicion if they did.

IX.

23   *Moral questions* immediately present themselves as questions whose solution cannot wait for sensible proof. A moral question is a question not of what sensibly exists, but of what is good, or would be good if it did exist. Science can tell us what exists; but to compare the *worths*, both of what exists and of what does not exist, we must consult not science, but what Pascal calls our heart. Science herself consults her heart when she lays it down that the infinite ascertainment of fact and correction of false belief are the supreme goods for man. Challenge the statement, and science can only repeat it oracularly, or else prove it by showing that such ascertainment and correction bring man all sorts of other goods which man's heart in turn declares. The question of having moral beliefs at all or not having them is decided by our will. Are our moral preferences true or false, or are they only odd biological phenomena, making things good or bad for *us*, but in themselves indifferent? How can your pure intellect decide? If your heart does not *want* a world of moral reality, your head will assuredly never make you believe in one. Moral scepticism can no more be refuted or proved by logic than intellectual scepticism can. When we stick to it that there *is* truth (be it of either kind), we do so with our whole nature, and resolve to stand or fall by the results. The sceptic with his whole nature adopts the doubting attitude; but which of us is the wiser, Omniscience only knows.

24   Turn now from these wide questions of good to a certain class of questions of fact, questions concerning personal relations, states of mind between one man and another.

25   A social organism of any sort whatever, large or small, is what it is because each member proceeds to his own duty with a trust that the other members will simultaneously do theirs. Wherever a desired result is achieved by the co-operation of many independent persons, its existence as a fact is a pure consequence of the precursive faith in one another of those immediately concerned. A government, an army, a commercial system, a ship, a college, an athletic team, all exist on this condition, without which not only is nothing achieved, but nothing is even attempted. A whole train of passengers (individually brave enough) will be looted by a few highwaymen, simply because the latter can count on one another, while each passenger fears that if he makes a movement of resistance, he will be shot before any one else backs him up. If we believed that the whole car-full would rise at once with us, we should each severally rise, and train-robbing would never even be attempted. There are, then, cases where a fact cannot come at all unless a preliminary faith exists in its coming. *And where faith in a fact can help create the fact*, that would be an insane

logic which should say that faith running ahead of scientific evidence is the 'lowest kind of immorality' into which a thinking being can fall. Yet such is the logic by which our scientific absolutists pretend to regulate our lives!

X.

26   In truths dependent on our personal action, then, faith based on desire is certainly a lawful and possibly an indispensable thing.

27   But now, it will be said, these are all childish human cases, and have nothing to do with great cosmical matters, like the question of religious faith. Let us then pass on to that. Religions differ so much in their accidents that in discussing the religious question we must make it very generic and broad. What then do we now mean by the religious hypothesis? Science says things are; morality says some things are better than other things; and religion says essentially two things.

28   First, she says that the best things are the more eternal things, the overlapping things, the things in the universe that throw the last stone, so to speak, and say the final word.

29   The second affirmation of religion is that we are better off even now if we believe her first affirmation to be true.

30   Now, let us consider what the logical elements of this situation are *in case the religious hypothesis in both its branches be rejected.* We are supposed to gain, even now, by our belief, and to lose by our non-belief, a certain vital good. We cannot escape the issue by remaining sceptical and waiting for more light, because, although we do avoid error in that way *if religion be untrue,* we lose the good, *if it be true,* just as certainly as if we positively chose to disbelieve. It is as if a man should hesitate indefinitely to ask a certain woman to marry him because he was not perfectly sure that she would prove an angel after he brought her home. Would he not cut himself off from that particular angel-possibility as decisively as if he went and married someone else? Scepticism, then, is not avoidance of option; it is option of a certain particular kind of risk. *Better risk loss of truth than chance of error*—that is your faith-vetoer's exact position. He is actively playing his stake as much as the believer is; he is backing the field against the religious hypothesis, just as the believer is backing the religious hypothesis against the field. To preach scepticism to us as a duty until 'sufficient evidence' for religion be found, is tantamount therefore to telling us, when in presence of the religious hypothesis, that to yield to our fear of its being error is wiser and better than to yield to our hope that it may be true. I, therefore, for one, cannot see my way to accepting the agnostic rules for truth-seeking, or wilfully agree to keep my willing nature out of the game. I cannot do so for this plain reason, that *a rule of thinking which would absolutely prevent me from acknowledging certain kinds of truth if those kinds of truth were really there, would be an irrational rule.* That for me is the long and short of the formal logic of the situation, no matter what the kinds of truth might materially be.

31   I confess I do not see how this logic can be escaped. When I look at the religious question as it really puts itself to concrete men, and when I think of all the possibilities which both practically and theoretically it involves, then this command that we shall put a stopper on our heart, instincts, and courage, and *wait*—acting of course meanwhile more or less as if religion were *not* true—till doomsday, or till such time as our intellect and senses working together may have raked in evidence enough—this command, I say, seems to me the

queerest idol ever manufactured in the philosophic cave. If we had an infallible intellect with its objective certitudes, we might feel ourselves disloyal to such a perfect organ of knowledge in not trusting to it exclusively, in not waiting for its releasing word. But if we are empiricists, if we believe that no bell in us tolls to let us know for certain when truth is in our grasp, then it seems a piece of idle fantasticality to preach so solemnly our duty of waiting for the bell. Indeed we *may* wait if we will,—I hope you do not think that I am denying that—but if we do so, we do so at our peril as much as if we believed. In either case we *act*, taking our life in our hands. No one of us ought to issue vetoes to the other, nor should we bandy words of abuse. We ought, on the contrary, delicately and profoundly to respect one another's mental freedom: then only shall we bring about the intellectual republic; then only shall we have that spirit of inner tolerance without which all our outer tolerance is soulless, and which is empiricism's glory; then only shall we live and let live, in speculative as well as in practical things.

QUESTIONS ON MEANING

1. What is the difference between a *live* and a *dead* hypothesis?
2. What does it mean to say that an option is *genuine*? What are a few examples of genuine options? Of non-genuine options?
3. What is Pascal's wager? What is James's opinion of the wager?
4. What distinguishes the *empiricist* and the *absolutist* views on the pursuit of truth? People's natural tendencies are toward which position, according to James?
5. What does James mean by a *closed* system?
6. What truth does even the most ardent skepticism leave uncorrupted?
7. What is a *moral* question and why must we make moral judgments in the absence, at times, of sensible proof?
8. What are the two things that religion says?
9. How does James justify one's making a potentially non-intellectual assertion of belief in the religious hypothesis?

QUESTIONS FOR DISCUSSION

1. James quotes William Clifford who wrote "it is wrong always, everywhere, and for everyone, to believe anything upon insufficient evidence." Does James agree with Clifford? Do you? Why or why not?
2. Can you think of things that you believe but which do not meet Clifford's strict standards in the quote above?
3. When faced with two *genuine* options, and logic is insufficient to determine which is the better option, what does James believe you should rely upon? Do you agree with James?
4. Are there any truths you believe are absolute, or are all truths contingent in some fashion? What are a few absolute truths (if, indeed, you believe there are any)?
5. Do you believe someone struggling with his or her religious faith would take any comfort from James's essay? Why or why not?

LOOKING AT RHETORIC

1. Examine the overall structure of James's essay. Can you reverse-engineer this essay in order to produce an outline for it? Where is the thesis located? How many major points are made in the essay? How do these points relate to the thesis? Is this essay well organized? Why or why not?

2. Is the essay easier or more difficult to understand by being broken into sections? Would it make a difference in how you read the essay if it weren't divided into sections?

WRITING ASSIGNMENTS

1. Either in the library or through a reliable Internet site, track down a copy of William Clifford's 1877 essay "The Ethics of Belief." Read Clifford's essay, and then reread James's essay. Draft an essay in which you compare and contrast the two arguments. Decide whose position you find more reasonable, and argue for its validity, making sure to deal with the counterarguments raised by the other.

2. James takes issue with Pascal's Wager. Write an essay in which you explain both Pascal's Wager and James's critique of it. Then, argue either for or against the value of Pascal's Wager as a rationale for religious belief. In your argument, you may support Pascal, bolster James's critique, or critique Pascal on terms different from those of James.

3. In pairs or in groups, make a list of five options that are *living* and five that are *dead*. Do the same for *forced* and *avoidable*, and *momentous* and *trivial*. Once this group exercise is complete, as an individual draft an essay in which you evaluate James's categorization of options. Do James's categories cover all possible options? Do you agree with how he defines a *genuine* option? Why or why not?

Apology

Plato

Plato (428/427 B.C.E.-348-347 B.C. E) was a classical Greek philosopher and mathematician, student of Socrates and teacher of Aristotle. He is one of the founding figures of the Western philosophical tradition, beginning the Academy in Athens, which was the first institution of higher education in the West. As an intellectual in the ancient period, he concerned himself with a range of topics, including rhetoric, ethics, mathematics, and logic. His writings appear in a series of letters and, most notably, dialogues involving the main figure of Socrates engaging various people in conversations on different topics. These interchanges involved Socrates asking questions, drawing out false assumptions and exposing inconsistencies to refine the ideas being explored. This "Socratic Method" has been a major teaching tool from Plato's time until the present. Central to Plato's philosophy is philosophical Idealism, the notion that the material world is an imitation of an Ideal realm of pure thought and perfect form. In this realm, absolute notions of the good, justice, and beauty exist. It is the philosopher's role to seek these things through contemplation, reflection, and rational thought. In the following selection, Plato recounts the trial and conviction of Socrates, who has been accused of disbelief in the gods of the State and of corrupting the youth of Athens with destructive ideas. Through Socrates, Plato reveals his penchant for careful analysis and rational thought in the pursuit of truth.

SOCRATES' DEFENSE

1   How you have felt, O men of Athens, at hearing the speeches of my accusers, I cannot tell; but I know that their persuasive words almost made me forget who I was—such was the effect of them; and yet they have hardly spoken a word of truth. But many as their false-hoods were, there was one of them which quite amazed me;—I mean when they told you to be upon your guard, and not to let yourselves be deceived by the force of my eloquence. They ought to have been ashamed of saying this, because they were sure to be detected as soon as I opened my lips and displayed my deficiency; they certainly did appear to be most shameless in saying this, unless by the force of eloquence they mean the force of truth; for then I do indeed admit that I am eloquent. But in how different a way from theirs! Well, as I was saying, they have hardly uttered a word, or not more than a word, of truth; but you shall hear from me the whole truth: not, however, delivered after their manner, in a set oration duly ornamented with words and phrases. No indeed! but I shall use the words and arguments which occur to me at the moment; for I am certain that this is right, and that at my time of life I ought not to be appearing before you, O men of Athens, in the character of a juvenile orator—let no one expect this of me. And I must beg of you to grant me one favor, which is this—If you hear me using the same words in my defence which I have been in the habit of using, and which most of you may have heard in the agora,[1] and at the tables of the money-changers, or anywhere else, I would ask you not to be surprised at this, and not to interrupt me. For I am more than seventy years of age, and this is the first time that I have ever appeared in a court of law, and I am quite a stranger to the ways of the place; and therefore I would have you regard me as if I were really a stranger, whom you would excuse if he spoke in his native tongue, and after the fashion of his country—that I think is not an unfair request. Never mind the manner, which may or may not be good; but think only of the justice of my cause, and give heed to that: let the judge decide justly and the speaker speak truly.

2   I have to reply to the older charges and to my first accusers, and then I will go to the later ones. For I have had many accusers, who accused me of old, and their false charges have continued during many years; and I am more afraid of them than of Anytus and his associates, who are dangerous, too, in their own way. But far more dangerous are these, who began when you were children, and took possession of your minds with their false-hoods, telling of one Socrates, a wise man, who speculated about the heaven above, and searched into the earth beneath, and made the worse appear the better cause.[2]

3   Well, then, I will make my defence, and I will endeavor in the short time which is allowed to do away with this evil opinion of me which you have held for such a long time; and I hope I may succeed, if this be well for you and me, and that my words may find favor with you. But I know that to accomplish this is not easy—I quite see the nature of the task. Let the event be as God wills: in obedience to the law I make my defence.

4   I dare say, Athenians, that someone among you will reply, "Why is this, Socrates, and what is the origin of these accusations of you: for there must have been something strange

---

[1] Agora: In ancient Greece, an open place of assembly.
[2] Sophists: professional educators and orators of the fifth century B.C.E., noted for their skill in oratory and for the ability to employ rhetoric to prove any argument, whether correct or incorrect.

which you have been doing? All this great fame and talk about you would never have arisen if you had been like other men: tell us, then, why this is, as we should be sorry to judge hastily of you." Now I regard this as a fair challenge, and I will endeavor to explain to you the origin of this name of "wise," and of this evil fame. Please to attend then. And although some of you may think I am joking, I declare that I will tell you the entire truth. Men of Athens, this reputation of mine has come of a certain sort of wisdom which I possess. If you ask me what kind of wisdom, I reply, such wisdom as is attainable by man, for to that extent I am inclined to believe that I am wise; whereas the persons of whom I was speaking have a superhuman wisdom, which I may fail to describe, because I have it not myself; and he who says that I have, speaks falsely, and is taking away my character. And here, O men of Athens, I must beg you not to interrupt me, even if I seem to say something extravagant. For the word which I will speak is not mine. I will refer you to a witness who is worthy of credit, and will tell you about my wisdom—whether I have any, and of what sort—and that witness shall be the god of Delphi. Well, Chaerephon, as you know, was very impetuous in all his doings, and he went to Delphi and boldly asked the oracle to tell him whether there was anyone wiser than I was, and the Pythian prophetess answered that there was no man wiser.

5   Why do I mention this? Because I am going to explain to you why I have such an evil name. When I heard the answer, I said to myself, What can the god mean? and what is the interpretation of this riddle? for I know that I have no wisdom, small or great. What can he mean when he says that I am the wisest of men? And yet he is a god and cannot lie; that would be against his nature. After a long consideration, I at last thought of a method of trying the question. I reflected that if I could only find a man wiser than myself, then I might go to the god with a refutation in my hand. Accordingly I went to one who had the reputation of wisdom, and the result was as follows: When I began to talk with him, I could not help thinking that he was not really wise, although he was thought wise by many, and wiser still by himself; and I went and tried to explain to him that he thought himself wise, but was not really wise; and the consequence was that he hated me, and his enmity was shared by several who were present and heard me. So I left him, saying to myself, as I went away: Well, although I do not suppose that either of us knows anything really beautiful and good, I am better off than he is—for he knows nothing, and thinks that he knows. I neither know nor think that I know. In this latter particular, then, I seem to have slightly the advantage of him.

6   After this I went to one man after another, being not unconscious of the enmity which I provoked, and I lamented and feared this: but necessity was laid upon me—the word of God, I thought, ought to be considered first. And I said to myself, Go I must to all who appear to know, and find out the meaning of the oracle. And I swear to you, Athenians, by the dog I swear!—for I must tell you the truth—the result of my mission was just this: I found that the men most in repute were all but the most foolish; and that some inferior men were really wiser and better. I will tell you the tale of my wanderings and of the "Herculean" labors, as I may call them, which I endured only to find at last the oracle irrefutable. When I left the politicians, I went to the poets; tragic, dithyrambic, and all sorts. And there, I said to myself, you will be detected; now you will find out that you are more ignorant than they are. Accordingly, I took them some of the most elaborate passages in their own writings, and asked what was the meaning of them—thinking that they would

teach me something. Will you believe me? I am almost ashamed to speak of this, but still I must say that there is hardly a person present who would not have talked better about their poetry than they did themselves. That showed me in an instant that not by wisdom do poets write poetry, but by a sort of genius and inspiration; they are like diviners or sooth-sayers who also say many fine things, but do not understand the meaning of them. And the poets appeared to me to be much in the same case; and I further observed that upon the strength of their poetry they believed themselves to be the wisest of men in other things in which they were not wise. So I departed, conceiving myself to be superior to them for the same reason that I was superior to the politicians.

7   At last I went to the artisans, for I was sure that they knew many fine things; and in this I was not mistaken, for they did know many things of which I was ignorant, and in this they certainly were wiser than I was. But I observed that even the good artisans fell into the same error as the poets; because they were good workmen they thought that they also knew all sorts of high matters, and this defect in them overshadowed their wisdom—therefore I asked myself on behalf of the oracle, whether I would like to be as I was, neither having their knowledge nor their ignorance, or like them in both; and I made answer to myself and the oracle that I was better off as I was.

8   And so I go my way, obedient to the god, and make inquisition into the wisdom of anyone, whether citizen or stranger, who appears to be wise; and if he is not wise, then in vindication of the oracle I show him that he is not wise; and this occupation quite absorbs me, and I have no time to give either to any public matter of interest or to any concern of my own, but I am in utter poverty by reason of my devotion to the god.

9   Meletus, that good and patriotic man, as he calls himself, says that I am a doer of evil, who corrupt the youth; but I say, O men of Athens, that Meletus is a doer of evil, and the evil is that he makes a joke of a serious matter, and is too ready at bringing other men to trial from a pretended zeal and interest about matters in which he really never had the smallest interest. And the truth of this I will endeavor to prove.

10   Come hither, Meletus, and let me ask a question of you. You think a great deal about the improvement of youth?

11   Yes, I do.

12   Tell the judges, then, who is their improver; for you must know, as you have taken the pains to discover their corrupter, and are citing and accusing me before them. Speak up, friend, and tell us who their improver is.

13   The laws.

14   But that, my good sir, is not my meaning. I want to know who the person is, who, in the first place, knows the laws.

15   The judges, Socrates, who are present in court.

16   And what do you say of the audience—do they improve them?

17   Yes, they do.

18   And the senators?

19   Yes, the senators improve them.

20   But perhaps the members of the citizen assembly corrupt them?—or do they too improve them?

21   They improve them.

22   Then every Athenian improves and elevates them; all with the exception of myself; and I alone am their corrupter? Is that what you affirm?

23   That is what I stoutly affirm.

24   I am very unfortunate if that is true. But suppose I ask you a question: Would you say that this also holds true in the case of horses? Does one man do them harm and all the world good? Is not the exact opposite of this true? One man is able to do them good, or at least not many;—the trainer of horses, that is to say, does them good, and others who have to do with them rather injure them? Is not that true, Meletus, of horses, or any other animals? Yes, certainly. Happy indeed would be the condition of youth if they had one corrupter only, and all the rest of the world were their improvers.

25   And now, Meletus, I must ask you another question: Which is better, to live among bad citizens, or among good ones? Answer, friend, I say; for that is a question which may be easily answered. Do not the good do their neighbors good, and the bad do them evil?

26   I have shown, Athenians, as I was saying, that Meletus has no care at all, great or small, about the matter. But still I should like to know, Meletus, in what I am affirmed to corrupt the young. I suppose you mean, as I infer from your indictment, that I teach them not to acknowledge the gods which the state acknowledges, but some other new divinities or spiritual agencies in their stead. These are the lessons which corrupt the youth, as you say.

27   Yes, that I say emphatically.

28   Then, by the gods, Meletus, of whom we are speaking, tell me and the court, in somewhat plainer terms, what you mean! for I do not as yet understand whether you affirm that I teach others to acknowledge some gods, and therefore do believe in gods and am not an entire atheist—this you do not lay to my charge; but only that they are not the same gods which the city recognizes—the charge is that they are different gods. Or, do you mean to say that I am an atheist simply, and a teacher of atheism?

29   I mean the latter—that you are a complete atheist.

30   You are a liar, Meletus, not believed even by yourself. But now please to answer the next question: Can a man believe in spiritual and divine agencies, and not in spirits or demigods?

31   He cannot.

32   Nevertheless you swear in the indictment that I teach and believe in divine or spiritual agencies as you say and swear in the affidavit; but if I believe in divine beings, I must believe in spirits or demigods—is not that true? Now what are spirits or demigods? are they not either gods or the sons of gods? Is that true?

33   Yes, that is true.

34   But this is just the ingenious riddle of which I was speaking: the demigods or spirits are gods, and you say first that I don't believe in gods, and then again that I do believe in gods; that is, if I believe in demigods. For if the demigods are the illegitimate sons of gods, whether by the Nymphs or by any other mothers, as is thought, that, as all men will allow, necessarily implies the existence of their parents. You might as well affirm the existence of mules, and deny that of horses and asses. But no one who has a particle of understanding will ever be convinced by you that the same man can believe in divine and superhuman things, and yet not believe that there are gods and demigods and heroes.

35   Someone will say: And are you not ashamed, Socrates, of a course of life which is likely to bring you to an untimely end? To him I may fairly answer: There you are mistaken: a man who is good for anything ought not to calculate the chance of living or dying; he ought only to consider whether in doing anything he is doing right or wrong—acting the part of a good man or of a bad.

36   Strange, indeed, would be my conduct, if, when, as I conceive and imagine, God orders me to fulfil the philosopher's mission of searching into myself and other men, I were to desert my post through fear of death, or any other fear; that would indeed be strange, and I might justly be arraigned in court for denying the existence of the gods, if I disobeyed the oracle because I was afraid of death: then I should be fancying that I was wise when I was not wise. For this fear of death is indeed the pretence of wisdom, and not real wisdom, being the appearance of knowing the unknown; since no one knows whether death, which they in their fear apprehend to be the greatest evil, may not be the greatest good. Is there not here conceit of knowledge, which is a disgraceful sort of ignorance? And this is the point in which, as I think, I am superior to men in general, and in which I might perhaps fancy myself wiser than other men—that whereas I know but little of the world below, I do not suppose that I know: but I do know that injustice and disobedience to a better, whether God or man, is evil and dishonorable, and I will never fear or avoid a possible good rather than a certain evil. Wherefore, O men of Athens, I say to you, do as Anytus bids or not as Anytus bids, and either acquit me or not; but whatever you do, know that I shall never alter my ways, not even if I have to die many times.

37   Men of Athens, do not interrupt, but hear me; there was an agreement between us that you should hear me out. And I think that what I am going to say will do you good: for I have something more to say, at which you may be inclined to cry out; but I beg that you will not do this. I would have you know that, if you kill such a one as I am, you will injure yourselves more than you will injure me. For if you kill me you will not easily find another like me, who, if I may use such a ludicrous figure of speech, am a sort of gadfly, given to the state by the God; and the state is like a great and noble steed who is tardy in his motions owing to his very size, and requires to be stirred into life. I am that gadfly which God has given the state and all day long and in all places am always fastening upon you, arousing and persuading and reproaching you. And as you will not easily find another like me, I would advise you to spare me. And that I am given to you by God is proved by this:—that if I had been like other men, I should not have neglected all my own concerns, or patiently seen the neglect of them during all these years, and have been doing yours, coming to you individually, like a father or elder brother, exhorting you to regard virtue; this I say, would not be like human nature. And had I gained anything, or if my exhortations had been paid, there would have been some sense in that: but now, as you will perceive, not even the impudence of my accusers dares to say that I have ever exacted or sought pay of anyone; they have no witness of that. And I have a witness of the truth of what I say; my poverty is a sufficient witness.

38   I have been always the same in all my actions, public as well as private, and never have I yielded any base compliance to those who are slanderously termed my disciples or to any other. For the truth is that I have no regular disciples: but if anyone likes to come and hear me while I am pursuing my mission, whether he be young or old, he may freely

come. Nor do I converse with those who pay only, and not with those who do not pay; but anyone, whether he be rich or poor, may ask and answer me and listen to my words; and whether he turns out to be a bad man or a good one, that cannot be justly laid to my charge, as I never taught him anything. And if anyone says that he has ever learned or heard anything from me in private which all the world has not heard, I should like you to know that he is speaking an untruth.

39   Well, Athenians, this and the like of this is nearly all the defence which I have to offer. Yet a word more. Perhaps there may be someone who is offended at me, when he calls to mind how he himself, on a similar or even a less serious occasion, had recourse to prayers and supplications with many tears, and how he produced his children in court, which was a moving spectacle, together with a posse of his relations and friends; whereas I, who am probably in danger of my life, will do none of these things. Whether I am or am not afraid of death is another question, of which I will not now speak. But my reason simply is that I feel such conduct to be discreditable to myself, and you, and the whole state. One who has reached my years, and who has a name for wisdom, whether deserved or not, ought not to debase himself.

40   But, setting aside the question of dishonor, there seems to be something wrong in petitioning a judge, and thus procuring an acquittal instead of informing and convincing him. For his duty is, not to make a present of justice, but to give judgment; and he has sworn that he will judge according to the laws, and not according to his own good pleasure; and neither he nor we should get into the habit of perjuring ourselves—there can be no piety in that. Do not then require me to do what I consider dishonorable and impious and wrong, especially now, when I am being tried for impiety on the indictment of Meletus.

41   *The jury finds Socrates guilty.*

SOCRATES' PROPOSAL FOR HIS SENTENCE

42   There are many reasons why I am not grieved, O men of Athens, at the vote of condemnation. I expected it, and am only surprised that the votes are so nearly equal; for I had thought that the majority against me would have been far larger; but now, had thirty votes gone over to the other side, I should have been acquitted.

43   And so he proposes death as the penalty. And what shall I propose on my part, O men of Athens? What would be a reward suitable to a poor man who is your benefactor, who desires leisure that he may instruct you? There can be no more fitting reward than maintenance in the Prytaneum, O men of Athens, a reward which he deserves far more than the citizen who has won the prize at Olympia in the horse or chariot race, whether the chariots were drawn by two horses or by many. For I am in want, and he has enough; and he only gives you the appearance of happiness, and I give you the reality. And if I am to estimate the penalty justly, I say that maintenance in the Prytaneum is the just return.

44   I will not say of myself that I deserve any evil, or propose any penalty. Why should I? Because I am afraid of the penalty of death which Meletus proposes? When I do not know whether death is a good or an evil, why should I propose a penalty which would certainly be an evil? Shall I say imprisonment? And why should I live in prison, and be the slave of the magistrates of the year—of the Eleven? Or shall the penalty be a fine,

and imprisonment until the fine is paid? There is the same objection. I should have to lie in prison, for money I have none, and I cannot pay. And if I say exile, what a life should I lead, at my age, wandering from city to city, living in ever-changing exile, and always being driven out! For I am quite sure that into whatever place I go, as here so also there, the young men will come to me; and if I drive them away, their elders will drive me out at their desire: and if I let them come, their fathers and friends will drive me out for their sakes.

45   Someone will say: Yes, Socrates, but cannot you hold your tongue, and then you may go into a foreign city, and no one will interfere with you? Now I have great difficulty in making you understand my answer to this. For if I tell you that this would be a disobedience to a divine command, and therefore that I cannot hold my tongue, you will not believe that I am serious; and if I say again that the greatest good of man is daily to converse about virtue, and all that concerning which you hear me examining myself and others, and that the life which is unexamined is not worth living—that you are still less likely to believe. And yet what I say is true, although a thing of which it is hard for me to persuade you. Moreover, I am not accustomed to think that I deserve any punishment. Had I money I might have proposed to give you what I had, and have been none the worse. But you see that I have none, and can only ask you to proportion the fine to my means.

46   *The jury condemns Socrates to death.*

SOCRATES' COMMENTS ON HIS SENTENCE

47   If you had waited a little while, your desire would have been fulfilled in the course of nature. For I am far advanced in years, as you may perceive, and not far from death. You think that I was convicted through deficiency of words—I mean, that if I had thought fit to leave nothing undone, nothing unsaid, I might have gained an acquittal. Not so; the deficiency which led to my conviction was not of words—certainly not. But I had not the boldness or impudence or inclination to address you as you would have liked me to address you, weeping and wailing and lamenting, and saying and doing many things which you have been accustomed to hear from others, and which, as I say, are unworthy of me. But I thought that I ought not to do anything common or mean in the hour of danger: nor do I now repent of the manner of my defence, and I would rather die having spoken after my manner, than speak in your manner and live. The difficulty, my friends, is not in avoiding death, but in avoiding unrighteousness; for that runs faster than death.

48   And now, O men who have condemned me, I would fain prophesy to you; for I am about to die, and that is the hour in which men are gifted with prophetic power. And I prophesy to you who are my murderers, that immediately after my death punishment far heavier than you have inflicted on me will surely await you.

49   Friends, who would have acquitted me, I should like to tell you of a wonderful circumstance. Hitherto the familiar oracle within me has constantly been in the habit of opposing me even about trifles, if I was going to make a slip or error about anything; and now as you see there has come upon me that which may be thought, and is generally believed to be, the last and worst evil. But the oracle made no sign of opposition, either as I was leaving my house and going out in the morning, or when I was going up into this court, or while I was speaking, at anything which I was going to say; and yet I have often been stopped

in the middle of a speech; but now in nothing I either said or did touching this matter has the oracle opposed me. What do I take to be the explanation of this? I will tell you. I regard this as a proof that what has happened to me is a good, and that those of us who think that death is an evil are in error.

50   Let us reflect in another way, and we shall see that there is great reason to hope that death is a good, for one of two things:—either death is a state of nothingness and utter unconsciousness, or, as men say, there is a change and migration of the soul from this world to another. Now if you suppose that there is no consciousness, but a sleep like the sleep of him who is undisturbed even by the sight of dreams, death will be an unspeakable gain. For if a person were to select the night in which his sleep was undisturbed even by dreams, and were to compare with this the other days and nights of his life, and then were to tell us how many days and nights he had passed in the course of his life better and more pleasantly than this one, I think that any man, I will not say a private man, but even the great king, will not find many such days or nights, when compared with the others. Now if death is like this, I say that to die is gain; for eternity is then only a single night. But if death is the journey to another place, and there, as men say, all the dead are, what good, O my friends and judges, can be greater than this? What would not a man give if he might converse with Orpheus and Musaeus and Hesiod and Homer? Nay, if this be true, let me die again and again. What would not a man give, O judges, to be able to examine the leader of the great Trojan expedition; or Odysseus or Sisyphus, or numberless others, men and women too! What infinite delight would there be in conversing with them and asking them questions!

51   Wherefore, O judges, be of good cheer about death, and know this of a truth—that no evil can happen to a good man, either in life or after death. For which reason also, I am not angry with my accusers, or my condemners; they have done me no harm, although neither of them meant to do me any good; and for this I may gently blame them.

52   Still I have a favor to ask of them. When my sons are grown up, I would ask you, O my friends, to punish them; and I would have you trouble them, as I have troubled you, if they seem to care about riches, or anything, more than about virtue; or if they pretend to be something when they are really nothing—then reprove them, as I have reproved you, for not caring about that for which they ought to care, and thinking that they are something when they are really nothing. And if you do this, I and my sons will have received justice at your hands.

53   The hour of departure has arrived, and we go our ways—I to die, and you to live. Which is better God only knows.

Interdisciplinary Connections

Understanding Human Emotion

Humans are emotional creatures, and psychologists have studied the development and expression of human emotion in countless experiments and research studies. Clearly, our emotions have a strong impact on the way we view the world, the way we live our lives, and the sense of peace and contentment (or lack thereof) that gives us some semblance of stability when confronted with the inevitable trials and tribulations of life. Below are posters from two well-known movies: *The*

The Dark Knight Movie Poster featuring the Joker

Dark Knight and *Life is Beautiful*. These posters are clearly designed to produce different emotional responses in viewers. What emotions does each one convey? How does the design and imagery in each poster help to generate an emotional response? Are these images of joy or horror, sadness or anger? As you study these images, ask yourself why it is that these images have such effects on us. What does it mean to you to feel fear or to feel happiness? How would you define these powerful emotions? What things in life cause you to be fearful or happy or sad or angry?

Life is Beautiful Movie Poster
http://www.wallpapers-free.co.uk/backgrounds/movie_posters/classic/life-is-beautiful.jpg

QUESTION ON MEANING

1. According to Socrates, what did the accusers warn the people of Athens against as Socrates makes his defense?

2. What is Socrates accused of?

3. How does Socrates define wisdom? When someone speaks, how can you tell they are or are not wise?

4. In his dialogue or question and answer method, what does Socrates (Plato) expose about Meletus's logic or motives?

5. For Socrates, what is a man or a woman's ultimate mission, for which they should be willing to commit the ultimate sacrifice?

6. What does Socrates think God has placed him on earth to do? What humorous term does he attach to himself?

QUESTIONS FOR DISCUSSION

1. What does it mean to be wise? What is the relationship of wisdom and knowledge and how are they different?

2. To what extent does questioning dominant ideas and social values present a challenge to society?

3. What obligation do we have to challenge falsehood when we see it, even if it may be dangerous for us to do so?

LOOKING AT RHETORIC

1. How does the use of Socrates as a persona help Plato make his argument? Is it more effective than simply making the claims himself?

2. How does the Socratic Method work? How does it function to make an argument?

3. The dialogue relies primarily on logic. But in what way is an emotional appeal also employed to strengthen the argument? Is it effective?

WRITING ASSIGNMENTS

1. Spend some time in the library and/or online researching definitions and discussions of the concept of *wisdom*. What constitutes human wisdom? How have different philosophers defined *wisdom* over the centuries? How do these different definitions compare and contrast with the view of wisdom presented in Plato's Apology? Draft a paper in which you build a definition of wisdom, using Plato's Apology and the perspectives of other thinkers when appropriate.

2. Argue for or against the occasional use of state power to restrict ideas that may be threatening.

3. In pairs or in groups, consider situations you have experienced where those in power have imposed their ideas on a group. Individually, write an essay recounting a circumstance in which ideas have been imposed upon you unwillingly. How did you respond?

From *A Brief Tour of Human Consciousness*

V. S. Ramachandran

Vilayanur Ramachandran (b. 1951) is the Director of the Center for Brain and Cognition and Professor with the Psychology Department and Neurosciences Program at the University of California, San Diego, and Adjunct Professor of Biology at the Salk Institute. Referred to by Newsweek Magazine *as one of the 21st-century's top 100 people to watch, Ramachandran's work in the philosophy of mind has made him one of the most highly recognized neuroscientists working today. Noted particularly for the sometimes startlingly simple experiments he uses to crack the most complex problems associated with neuropsychology, Ramachandran's work has offered provocative insights into topics such as the relationship between visual perception and the mind, freedom of the will, mental illness and neurological disorders, consciousness, and the nature of human identity. Born and raised in India, Ramachandran's work has been recognized and lauded around the world. His writings include* Phantoms in the Brain: Probing the Mysteries of the Human Mind *(1998),* The Emerging Mind *(2003),* A Brief Tour of Human Consciousness *(2005)—from which the selection below is taken—and* The Tell-Tale Brain *(2011).*

1   There have traditionally been two different approaches to mental illness. The first one tries to identify chemical imbalances, changes in transmitters and receptors in the brain, and attempts to correct these changes using drugs. This approach has revolutionized psychiatry and has been phenomenally successful. Patients who used to be put in straitjackets or locked up can now lead relatively normal lives. The second approach we can loosely characterize as the so-called Freudian approach. It assumes that most mental illness arises from early upbringing. I'd like to propose a third approach which is radically different from either of these but which, in a sense, complements them both.

2   To understand the origins of mental illness it is not enough merely to say that some transmitter has changed in the brain. We need to know how that change produces the bizarre symptoms that it does—why certain patients have certain symptoms and why those symptoms are different for different types of mental illness. I will attempt to explain the symptoms of mental illness in terms of what is known about function, anatomy and neural structures in the brain. And I will suggest that many of these symptoms and disorders seem less bizarre when viewed from an evolutionary standpoint, that is from a Darwinian perspective. I also propose to give this discipline a new name—evolutionary neuro-psychiatry.

3   Let us begin with the classic example of what most people consider to be a purely mental disorder or psychological disturbance—hysteria. "Hysteria" is used here in its strict medical sense, as opposed to the everyday notion of a person shouting and screaming. In the strictly medical sense, a hysteric is a patient who suddenly experiences blindness or develops a paralysis of an arm or a leg, but who has no neurological deficits that could be responsible for his or her condition: a brain MR scan reveals that the brain is apparently completely normal, there are no identifiable lesions, no apparent damage. So the symptoms are dismissed as being purely psychological in origin.

4   However, recent brain-imaging studies using PET scans and functional Magnetic Resonance imaging have dramatically changed our understanding of hysteria. Using PET scans and fMR, we can now find what parts of the brain are active or inactive when a patient performs a specific action or engages in a specific mental process. For example, when we do mental arithmetic, the left angular gyrus usually exhibits activity. Or if I were to prick you with a needle and cause pain, another part of your brain would light up. We can then conclude that the particular brain region that lights up is somehow involved in mediating that function.

5   If you were to wiggle your finger, a PET scan would reveal that two areas of your brain light up. One is called the motor cortex, which is actually sending messages to execute the appropriate sequence of muscle twitches to move your finger, but there is another area in front of it called the pre-motor cortex that *prepares* you to move your finger.

6   John Marshall, Chris Frith, Richard Frackowiak, Peter Halligan and others tried this experiment on a hysterically paralyzed patient. When he tried to move his leg, the motor area failed to light up even though he claimed to be genuinely intending to move his leg. The reason he was unable to is that another area was simultaneously lighting up: the anterior cingulate and the orbito-frontal lobes. It's as if this activity in the anterior cingulate and orbito-frontal cortex was inhibiting or vetoing the hysterical patient's attempt to move his leg. This makes sense, because the anterior cingulate and orbito-frontal cortex are intimately linked to the limbic[1] emotional centers in the brain, and we know that hysteria originates from some emotional trauma that is somehow preventing him from moving his "paralyzed" leg.

7   Of course, all this doesn't explain exactly why hysteria occurs, but now we at least know where to look. In the future it might be possible to use a brain scan to distinguish genuine hysterics from malingerers or fraudulent insurance claimants. And it does prove that one of the oldest "psychological" disturbances—one that Freud studied—has a specific and identifiable organic cause. (Actually, an important control is missing in this experiment: no one has yet obtained a brain scan from a genuine malingerer.)

8   We can think of hysteria as a disorder of "free will," and free will is a topic that both psychologists and philosophers have been preoccupied with for over two thousand years.

9   Several decades ago the American neurosurgeon Benjamin Libet and the German physiologist Hans Kornhuber were experimenting on volunteers exercising free will, instructing subjects to, for example, wiggle a finger at any time of their own choosing within a ten-minute period. A full three-quarters of a second *before* the finger movement the researchers picked up a scalp EEG potential, which they called the "readiness potential," even though the subject's sensation of consciously willing the action coincided almost exactly with the actual onset of finger movement. This discovery caused a flurry of excitement among philosophers interested in free will. For it seemed to imply that the brain events monitored by the EEG kick in almost a second before there is any sensation of "willing" the finger movement, even though your *subjective* experience is that your will caused the finger movement! But how can your will be the cause if the brain commands begin a second earlier? It's almost as though your brain is really in charge and your "free will" is

---

[1] Limbic: the limbic system is that group of brain structures related to the processing of emotion.

just a posthoc[2] rationalization—a delusion, almost—like King Canute[3] thinking he could control the tides or an American president believing that he is in charge of the whole world.

10   This alone is strange enough, but what if we add another twist to the experiment. Imagine I'm monitoring your EEG while you wiggle your finger. Just as Kornhuber and Libet did, I will see a readiness potential a second before you act. But suppose I display the signal on a screen in front of you so that you can *see* your free will. Every time you are about to wiggle your finger, supposedly using your own free will, the machine will tell you a second in advance! What would you now experience? There are three logical possibilities. (1) You might experience a sudden loss of will, feeling that the machine is controlling you, that you are a mere puppet and that free will is just an illusion. You may even become paranoid as a result, like schizophrenics who think their actions are controlled by aliens or implants (I'll return to this later). (2) You might think that it does not change your sense of free will one iota, preferring to believe that the machine has some sort of spooky paranormal precognition by which it is able to predict your movements accurately. (3) You might confabulate, or rearrange the experienced sequence mentally in order to cling to your sense of freedom; you might deny the evidence of your eyes and maintain that your sensation of will preceded the machine's signal, not vice versa.

11   At this stage this is still a "thought experiment"—technically it is hard to get a feedback EEG signal on each trial, but we are trying to get around this obstacle. Nevertheless, it is important to note that one can do experiments that have direct relevance to broad philosophical issues such as free will—a field in which my colleagues Pat Churchland, Dan Wegner and Dan Dennett have all made valuable contributions.

12   Leaving aside this "thought experiment" for the moment, let's return to the original observation on the readiness potential with its curious implication that the brain events are kicking in a second or so before any actual finger movement, even though conscious intent to move the finger coincides almost exactly with the wiggle. Why might this be happening? What might the evolutionary rationale be?

13   The answer is, I think, that there is an inevitable neural delay before the signal arising in one part of the brain makes its way through the rest of the brain to deliver the message: "wiggle your finger." (A televisual equivalent is the sound delay experienced when conducting an interview via satellite.) Natural selection has ensured that the subjective sensation of willing is delayed deliberately to coincide not with the onset of the brain commands but with the actual execution of the command by your finger.

14   And this in turn is important because it means that the subjective sensations which accompany brain events must have an evolutionary purpose. For if that were not the case, if they merely *accompanied* brain events, as so many philosophers believe (this is called epiphenomenalism)[4]—in other words, if the subjective sensation of willing is like a shadow that accompanies us as we move but is not causal in making us move—then why would evolution bother delaying the signal so that it coincides with our movement?

---

[2]Post-hoc: literally "after this"; meaning, a rationalization after the fact.

[3]King Canute: Viking king of England from 1016–1035; one legendary story about Canute is that he once had his throne moved to the seashore so that he could command the tides to stop.

[4]Epiphenomenalism: the theory in the philosophy of mind that states that all mental states are merely by-products of physiological processes and that mental states do not have any impact on the physical world.

15   So we have a paradox: on the one hand, the experiment shows that free will is illusory: it cannot be causing the brain events because the events kick in a second earlier. But on the other hand, the delay must have some function, otherwise why would the delay have evolved? Yet if it *does* have a function, what could it be other than moving (in this case) the finger? Perhaps our very notion of causation requires a radical revision . . . as happened in quantum mechanics.

16   Other types of "mental" illness can also be approached, perhaps, through brain imaging. Take the case of pain: when someone is jabbed with a needle, there is usually activity in many regions of the brain, but especially in the insula and in the anterior cingulate. The former structure seems to be involved in sensing the pain and the latter in giving pain its aversive quality. So when the pathways leading from the insula to the anterior cingulate are severed, the patient can feel the pain, but it doesn't hurt—a paradoxical syndrome called pain asymbolia. This leads me to wonder about the image of the brain of a masochist who derives pleasure from pain, or a patient with Lesch-Nyhan syndrome who "enjoys" mutilating himself. The insula would be activated, of course, but would the anterior cingulate also light up? Or, given, especially, the sexual overtones of masochism, a region concerned with pleasure, such as the nucleus accumbens, septum or hypothalamic nuclei? At what stage in processing do the "pain/pleasure" labels get switched? (I am reminded of the masochist from Ipswich who loved taking ice cold showers at four in the morning and therefore didn't.)

17   In chapter 1 I mentioned the Capgras delusion, sometimes seen in patients who have sustained a head injury, in which sufferers start claiming that someone they both recognize and know well—such as their mother—is an imposter.

18   The theoretical explanation for Capgras syndrome is that the connection between the visual areas and the emotional core of the brain, the limbic system and the amygdala,[5] has been cut by the accident (Figure 1.3). So when the patient looks at his mother, since the visual areas in the brain concerned with recognizing faces is not damaged, he is able to say that she *looks* like his mother. But there is no emotion, because the wire taking that information to the emotional centers is cut, so he tries to rationalize this by believing her to be an imposter.

19   How can this theory be tested? Well, it is possible to measure the gut-level emotional reaction that someone has to a visual stimulus—or any stimulus—by measuring the extent to which they sweat. When any of us sees something exciting, emotionally important, the neural activation cascades from the visual centers to the emotional centers in the brain and we begin to sweat in order to dissipate the heat that we are going to generate from exercise, from action (feeding, fleeing, fighting, or sex). This effect can be measured by placing two electrodes on a person's skin to track changes in skin resistance—when skin resistance falls, we call it a galvanic skin response. Familiar or nonthreatening objects or people produce no galvanic skin response because they generate no emotional arousal. But if you look at a lion or a tiger, or—as it turns out—your mother, a huge galvanic skin response occurs. Believe it or not, every time you see your mother, you sweat! (And you don't even have to be Jewish.)

20   But we found that this doesn't happen in Capgras patients, supporting the idea that there has been a disconnection between vision and emotion.

---

[5] Amygdala: part of the limbic system associated with processing emotions.

21   There exists an even more bizarre disorder, Cotard's syndrome, in which the patient starts claiming he or she is dead. I suggest that this is similar to Capgras except that instead of vision alone being disconnected from the emotional centers in the brain, all the senses become disconnected from the emotional centers. So that nothing in the world has any emotional significance, no object or person, no tactile sensation, no sound—nothing—has emotional impact. The only way in which a patient can interpret this complete emotional desolation is to believe that he or she is dead. However bizarre, this is the only interpretation that makes sense to him; the reasoning gets distorted to accommodate the emotions. If this idea is correct we would expect no galvanic responses in a Cotard's patient whatever the stimulus.

22   The delusion of Cotard's is notoriously resistant to intellectual correction. For example, a man will agree that dead people cannot bleed; then, if pricked with a needle, he will express amazement and conclude that the dead *do* bleed after all, instead of giving up his delusion and inferring that he is alive. Once a delusional fixation develops, all contrary evidence is warped to accommodate it. Emotion seems to override reason rather than the other way around. (Of course, this is true of most of us to some extent. I have known many an otherwise rational and intelligent person who believes the number 13 to be unlucky or who won't walk under a ladder.)

23   Capgras and Cotard's are both rare syndromes, but there is another disorder, a sort of mini-Cotard's, that is much more commonly seen in clinical practice. This disorder is known as derealization and depersonalization, and is found in acute anxiety, panic attacks, depression and other dissociative states. Suddenly the world seems completely unreal—like a dream. The patient feels like a zombie.

24   I believe such feelings involve the same circuitry as Capgras and Cotard's. In nature, an opossum when chased by a predator will suddenly lose all muscle tone and play dead, hence the phrase "playing possum." This is a good strategy for the opossum because (a) any movement will encourage the predatory behavior of the carnivore and (b) carnivores usually avoid carrion, which might be infected. Following the lead of Martin Roth, Mauricio Sierra and German Berrios, I suggest that derealization and depersonalization, and other dissociative states, are examples of playing possum in the emotional realm and that this is an evolutionary adaptive mechanism.

25   There is a well-known story of the explorer David Livingstone being attacked by a lion. He saw his arm being mauled but felt no pain or even fear. He felt detached from it all, as if he were watching events from a distance. The same thing can happen to soldiers in battle or to a woman being raped. During such dire emergencies, the anterior cingulate in the brain, part of the frontal lobes, becomes extremely active. This inhibits or temporarily shuts down the amygdala and other limbic emotional centers, so temporarily suppressing potentially disabling emotions such as anxiety and fear. But at the same time, the anterior cingulate activation generates extreme alertness and vigilance in preparation for any appropriate defensive reaction that might be required.

26   In an emergency, this James Bond-like combination of shutting down emotions ("nerves of steel") while being hypervigilant is useful, keeping us out of harm's way. It is better to do nothing than to engage in some sort of erratic behavior. But what if the same mechanism is accidentally triggered by chemical imbalances or brain disease, when there is no emergency? A person looks at the world, is intensely alert, hypervigilant, but the world has become completely devoid of emotional meaning because the limbic system has

been shut down. There are only two possible ways to interpret this strange predicament, this paradoxical state of mind. Either "the world isn't real"—derealization—or "I am not real"—depersonalization.

27   Epileptic seizures originating in this part of the brain can also produce these dream-like states of derealization and depersonalization. Intriguingly, we know that during a seizure, when the patient is experiencing derealization, there is no galvanic skin response to anything. Following the seizure, skin response returns to normal. All of which supports the hypothesis that we have been considering.

28   Probably the disorder most commonly associated with the word "madness" is schizo-phrenia. Schizophrenics do indeed exhibit bizarre symptoms. They hallucinate, often hear-ing voices. They become delusional, thinking they're Napoleon or Ramachandran. They are convinced the government has planted devices in their brain to monitor their thoughts and actions. Or that aliens are controlling them.

29   Psycho-pharmacology has revolutionized our ability to treat schizophrenia, but the question remains: why do schizophrenics behave as they do? I'd like to speculate on this, based on some work my colleagues and I have done on anosognosia (denial of illness)—which results from right-hemisphere lesions—and some very clever speculations by Chris Frith, Sarah Blakemore and Tim Crow. Their idea is that, unlike normal people, schizo-phrenics cannot tell the difference between their own internally generated images and thoughts and perceptions that are evoked by real things outside.

30   If I conjure up a mental picture of a clown in front of me, I don't confuse it with real-ity partly because my brain has access to the internal command I gave. I am expecting to visualize a clown, and that is what I see. It is not an hallucination. But if the "expectation" mechanism in my brain that does this becomes faulty, then I would be unable to tell the difference between a clown I'm imagining and a clown I'm actually seeing there. In other words, I would believe that the clown was real. I would hallucinate, and be unable to dif-ferentiate between fantasy and reality.

31   Similarly, I might momentarily entertain the thought that it would be nice to be Napoleon, but in a schizophrenic this momentary thought becomes a full-blown delusion instead of being vetoed by reality.

32   What about the other symptoms of schizophrenia—alien control, for example? A normal person knows that he moves of his or her own free will, and can attribute the movement to the fact that the brain has sent the command "move." If the mechanism that monitors intention and compares it with performance is flawed, a more bizarre interpre-tation is likely to result, such as that body movements are controlled by aliens or brain implants, which is what paranoid schizophrenics claim.

33   How do you test a theory like this? Here is an experiment for you to try: using your right index finger, tap repeatedly your left index finger, keeping your left index finger steady and inactive. Notice how you feel the tapping mainly on the left finger, very little on the right finger. That is because the brain has sent a command from the left hemisphere to the right hand saying "move." It has alerted the sensory areas of the brain to expect some touch signals on the right hand. Your left hand, however, is perfectly steady, so the taps upon it come as something of a surprise. This is why you feel more sensation in the immobile finger, even though the tactile input to both fingers is exactly the same. (If you change hands, you will find that the results are reversed.)

34   Following our theory, I predict that if a schizophrenic were to try this experiment, he would feel the sensations equally in both fingers since he is unable to differentiate between internally generated actions and externally generated sensory stimuli. It's a five-minute experiment—yet no one has ever tried it.

35   Or imagine that you are visualizing a banana on a blank white screen in front of you. While you are doing this, if I secretly project a very low-contrast physical image of the banana on the screen, your threshold for detecting this real banana will be elevated—presumably even your normal brain tends to get confused between a very dim real banana and one which you imagine. This surprising result is called the "Perky effect" and one would predict that it would be amplified enormously in schizophrenics.

36   Another simple yet untried experiment: as you know, you can't tickle yourself. That is because your brain knows you're sending the command. Prediction: a schizophrenic will laugh when he tickles himself.

37   Even though the behavior of many patients with mental illness seems bizarre, we can now begin to make sense of the symptoms using our knowledge of basic brain mechanisms. Mental illness might be thought of as disturbances of consciousness and of self, two words that conceal great depths of ignorance. Let me try to summarize my own view of consciousness. There are really two problems here—the problem of the subjective sensations or qualia and the problem of the self. The problem of qualia is the more difficult.

38   The qualia question is, how does the flux of ions in little bits of jelly—the neurons—in our brains give rise to the redness of red, the flavor of Marmite or paneer tikka masala or wine? Matter and mind seem so utterly unlike each other. One way out of this dilemma is to think of them really as two different ways of describing the world, each of which is complete in itself. Just as we can describe light as made up either of particles or as waves—and there's no point in asking which description is correct, because they both are, even though the two seem utterly dissimilar—the same may be true of mental and physical events in the brain.

39   But what about the self, the last remaining great mystery in science and something that everybody is interested in? Obviously self and qualia are two sides of the same coin. You can't have free-floating sensations or qualia with no one to experience them and you can't have a self completely devoid of sensory experiences, memories or emotions. (As we saw in Cotard's syndrome, when sensations and perceptions lose all their emotional significance and meaning, the result is a dissolution of self.)

40   What exactly is meant by the "self"? Its defining characteristics are fivefold. First of all, continuity: a sense of an unbroken thread running through the whole fabric of our experience with the accompanying feeling of past, present and future. Second, and closely related, is the idea of unity or coherence of self. In spite of the diversity of sensory experiences, memories, beliefs and thoughts, we each experience ourselves as one person, as a unity.

41   Third is a sense of embodiment or ownership—we feel ourselves anchored to our bodies. Fourth, a sense of agency, what we call free will, being in charge of our own actions and destinies. I can wiggle my finger but I can't wiggle my nose or your finger.

42   Fifth, and most elusive of all, the self, almost by its very nature, is capable of reflection—of being aware of itself. A self that's unaware of itself is an oxymoron.

43   Any or all of these different aspects of self can be differentially disturbed in brain disease, which leads me to believe that the self comprises not just one thing, but many. Like "love" or "happiness," we use one word, "self," to lump together many different phenomena. For example, if I stimulate your right parietal cortex with an electrode (while you're conscious and awake), you will momentarily feel that you are floating near the ceiling, watching your own body down below. You have an out-of-the-body experience. The embodiment of self—one of the axiomatic foundations of your self—is temporarily abandoned. And this is true of all of those aspects of self I listed above. Each of them can be selectively affected in brain disease.

44   Keeping this in mind, I see three ways in which the problem of self might be tackled by neuroscience. First, maybe the problem of self is a straightforward empirical one. Maybe there is a single, very elegant, Archimedes-type Eureka! solution to the problem, just as DNA base-pairing was the solution to the riddle of heredity. I think this is unlikely, but I could be wrong.

45   Second, given my earlier remarks about the self, the notion of the self as being defined by a set of attributes—embodiment, agency, unity, continuity—maybe we will succeed in explaining each of these attributes individually in terms of what is going on in the brain. Then the problem of what the self is will vanish, or at least recede into the background, just as scientists no longer speak of vital spirits or ask what "life" is. (We recognize that life is a word loosely applied to a collection of processes—DNA replication and transcription, Krebs cycle, Lactic acid cycle, etc., etc.)

46   Third, maybe the solution to the problem of the self is not a straightforward empirical one. It may instead require a radical shift in perspective, the sort of thing that Einstein did when he rejected the assumption that things can move at arbitrarily high velocities. When we finally achieve such a shift in perspective, we may be in for a big surprise and find that the answer was staring at us all along. I don't want to sound like a New Age guru, but there are curious parallels between this idea and the Hindu philosophical (albeit somewhat nebulous) view that there is no essential difference between self and others, or that the self is an illusion.

QUESTIONS ON MEANING

1. Historically, what have been the two main approaches to mental illness? How would you define or characterize each approach?

2. What new, third approach to mental illness does Ramachandran propose? How does this third way relate to, and differ from, the other two approaches?

3. What has recent research on hysteria demonstrated? How is this related to the notion of free will?

4. What is Cotard's Syndrome? How does it relate to Capgras Syndrome? What about derealization and depersonalization? What do all of these disorders have to do with evolutionary theory, according to Ramachandran?

5. What is Ramachandran's view of human consciousness? What are the two problems that anyone defining consciousness must resolve? How does Ramachandran resolve them?

6. What are the five characteristics of the *self*? What are the three possible solutions to the riddle of *selfhood*, according to Ramachandran?

7. What are qualia? What explanation does Ramachandran give for how qualia might have evolved? What function do qualia serve, according to this theory?

QUESTIONS FOR DISCUSSION

1. Do humans have free will? What does it mean to say that a human has free will? How do Ramachandran's theories challenge, support, or revise the notion of freedom of the will?

2. What other explanations might there be for mental illness? Does Ramachandran give a convincing explanation here for mental illness? Why or why not?

3. Take a moment and try the finger tapping experiment that Ramachandran describes in his essay. Did you experience what Ramachandran claims you should? How does Ramachandran interpret the results of this experiment? How do you?

4. How do you define the *self*? How does Ramachandran? Would you have defined the concept of self different *before* reading the Ramachandran essay? Did your opinion change as a result of reading the essay? Do you believe Ramachandran's definition of self is adequate? Is it complete? How would you revise his definition if you believe it is in error or incomplete? In your opinion, are there ways to solve the riddle of the self other than the three solutions proposed by Ramachandran?

LOOKING AT RHETORIC

1. Look back through Ramachandran's essay. What sections did you find most interesting and which least interesting? Likewise, what sections did you find most convincing and which least convincing? Are they the same sections or different? What rhetorical strategies does Ramachandran use in order to create interesting and/or convincing passages?

2. Would you characterize this as a *thesis-driven* essay? If so, what is the thesis? Is there more than one thesis, or none at all? Is it a different kind of essay altogether?

WRITING ASSIGNMENTS

1. Spend some time in researching the theory of *epiphenomenalism* in the philosophy of mind. Find at least four recent and reliable sources on the concept. Draft an essay in which you define epiphenomenalism and in which you present the major arguments both for and against this theory of mental states. Your object in this essay is not to argue for or against the concept; rather, your goal is to introduce the concept to your audience and guide the audience through the major issues and arguments on both sides of the debate. At some point in your essay, discuss Ramachandran's position on epiphenomenalism.

2. Draft an essay in which you offer a definition and discussion of the concept of freedom of the will and in which you discuss the relationship between your own notion of free will and what Ramachandran has to say about the concept in his essay. Develop arguments in your essay that advocate for your thesis, your conception of human free will.

3. In pairs or in groups, attempt to create a one or two sentence definition of the concept of *self*. Share your group's definition with the other groups in class. As a class or as a group, compare and contrast the different definitions. Did any common themes emerge? Then, as an individual, draft an essay in which you create and defend your own particular definition of *self*.

Computing Machinery and Intelligence

Alan Turing

Alan Turing (1912–1954), often credited as the father of the modern computer, was a British mathematician and cryptanalyst whose talent emerged at a young age. Turing not only helped the Allies crack the Enigma encoding machine used by the German army in WWII, but his work in computational theory laid the groundwork for the development of modern day computer technology. Turing set forth the theory and mathematics that made digital computers possible. This work led him to consider numerous theoretical problems related to digital computation, including the question at the heart of artificial intelligence programming today: Can machines think? Writing at a time when computing technology itself was virtually non-existent, Turing predicted the emergence of computers that could rival the computing capacity of the human brain. The following essay is Turing's most famous work on this question. In it, he speculates about the kind of computational ability a machine would need in order to pass what has become known as the Turing Test—to this day one of the most referenced theoretical tools in the pursuit of artificial intelligence. Tragically, Alan Turing died of what many believe was a self-inflicted dose of cyanide poison. After his conviction of gross indecency (Turing was a homosexual, which was illegal in England at the time), he opted for chemical castration rather than serving a prison sentence. In 2009, the British government issued an official apology for its treatment of Turing, which Prime Minister Gordon Brown admitted was "appalling."

THE IMITATION GAME

1   I propose to consider the question, 'Can machines think?'

2   The problem can be described in terms of a game which we call the 'imitation game.' It is played with three people, a man (A), a woman (B), and an interrogator (C) who may be of either sex. The interrogator stays in a room apart from the other two. The object of the game for the interrogator is to determine which of the other two is the man and which is the woman. He knows them by labels X and Y, and at the end of the game he says either 'X is A and Y is B' or 'X is B and Y is A'. The interrogator is allowed to put questions to A and B thus:

3   C: Will X please tell me the length of his or her hair? Now suppose X is actually A, then A must answer. It is A's object in the game to try and cause C to make the wrong identification. His answer might therefore be

4   'My hair is shingled, and the longest strands are about nine inches long.'

5   The object of the game for the third player (B) is to help the interrogator. The best strategy for her is probably to give truthful answers. She can add such things as "I am the woman, don't listen to him!' to her answers, but it will avail nothing as the man can make similar remarks.

6   We now ask the question, 'What will happen when a machine takes the part of A in this game?' Will the interrogator decide wrongly as often when the game is played like this as he does when the game is played between a man and a woman? These questions replace our original, 'Can machines think?'

THE MACHINES CONCERNED IN THE GAME

7   The question which we put in § 1 will not be quite definite until we have specified what we mean by the word 'machine.' It is natural that we should wish to permit every kind of engineering technique to be used in our machines. The present interest in 'thinking machines' has been aroused by a particular kind of machine, usually called an 'electronic computer' or 'digital computer.' Following this suggestion we only permit digital computers to take part in our game.

8   There are already a number of digital computers in working order, and it may be asked, 'Why not try the experiment straight away? It would be easy to satisfy the conditions of the game. A number of interrogators could be used, and statistics compiled to show how often the right identification was given.' The short answer is that we are not asking whether all digital computers would do well in the game nor whether the computers at present available would do well, but whether there are imaginable computers which would do well.

DIGITAL COMPUTERS

9   The idea behind digital computers may be explained by saying that these machines are intended to carry out any operations which could be done by a human computer. The human computer is supposed to be following fixed rules; he has no authority to deviate from them in any detail. We may suppose that these rules are supplied in a book, which is altered whenever he is put on to a new job. He has also an unlimited supply of paper on which he does his calculations. He may also do his multiplications and additions on a 'desk machine,' but this is not important.

10   The reader must accept it as a fact that digital computers can be constructed, and indeed have been constructed, according to the principles we have described, and that they can in fact mimic the actions of a human computer very closely.

11   The book of rules which we have described our human computer as using is of course a convenient fiction. Actual human computers really remember what they have got to do. If one wants to make a machine mimic the behaviour of the human computer in some complex operation one has to ask him how it is done, and then translate the answer into the form of an instruction table. Constructing instruction tables is usually described as 'programming.' To 'programme a machine to carry out the operation A' means to put the appropriate instruction table into the machine so that it will do A.

UNIVERSALITY OF DIGITAL COMPUTERS

12   The digital computers considered in the last section may be classified amongst the 'discrete state machines.' These are the machines which move by sudden jumps or clicks from one quite definite state to another. These states are sufficiently different for the possibility of confusion between them to be ignored.

13   It will seem that given the initial state of the machine and the input signals it is always possible to predict all future states. Even when we consider the actual physical machines instead of the idealised machines, reasonably accurate knowledge of the state at one moment yields reasonably accurate knowledge any number of steps later.

14   The digital computer could mimic the behaviour of any discrete state machine. This special property of digital computers, that they can mimic any discrete state machine, is described by saying that they are *universal* machines. The existence of machines with this property has the important consequence that, considerations of speed apart, it is unnecessary to design various new machines to do various computing processes. They can all be done with one digital computer, suitably programmed for each case. It will be seen that as a consequence of this all digital computers are in a sense equivalent.

15   We may now consider the point that the question, 'Can machines think?' should be replaced by 'Are there imaginable digital computers which would do well in the imitation game?'

CONTRARY VIEWS ON THE MAIN QUESTION

16   We now are ready to proceed to the debate on our question, 'Can machines think?' and the variant of it quoted at the end of the last section. We cannot altogether abandon the original form of the problem, for opinions will differ as to the appropriateness of the substitution and we must at least listen to what has to be said in this connexion.

17   It will simplify matters for the reader if I explain first my own beliefs in the matter. The original question, 'Can machines think?' I believe to be too meaningless to deserve discussion. Nevertheless I believe that at the end of the century the use of words and general educated opinion will have altered so much that one will be able to speak of machines thinking without expecting to be contradicted. I believe further that no useful purpose is served by concealing these beliefs. The popular view that scientists proceed inexorably from well-established fact to well-established fact, never being influenced by any unproved conjecture, is quite mistaken. Provided it is made clear which are proved facts and which are conjectures, no harm can result. Conjectures are of great importance since they suggest useful lines of research.

18   I now proceed to consider opinions opposed to my own.

The Theological Objection

19   Thinking is a function of man's immortal soul. God has given an immortal soul to every man and woman, but not to any other animal or to machines. Hence no animal or machine can think.

20   I am unable to accept any part of this, but will attempt to reply in theological terms. It appears to me that the argument quoted above implies a serious restriction of the omnipotence of the Almighty. It is admitted that there are certain things that He cannot do such as making one equal to two, but should we not believe that He has freedom to confer a soul on an elephant if He sees fit? We might expect that He would only exercise this power in conjunction with a mutation which provided the elephant with an appropriately improved brain to minister to the needs of this soul. An argument of exactly similar form may be made for the case of machines. It may seem different because it is more difficult to "swallow." But this really only means that we think it would be less likely that He would consider the circumstances suitable for conferring a soul. The circumstances in question are discussed in the rest of this paper. In attempting to construct such machines we should not

be irreverently usurping His power of creating souls, any more than we are in the procreation of children: rather we are, in either case, instruments of His will providing mansions for the souls that He creates.

The 'Heads in the Sand' Objection

21   "The consequences of machines thinking would be too dreadful. Let us hope and believe that they cannot do so."

22   This argument is seldom expressed quite so openly as in the form above. But it affects most of us who think about it at all. We like to believe that Man is in some subtle way superior to the rest of creation. It is best if he can be shown to be *necessarily* superior, for then there is no danger of him losing his commanding position. The popularity of the theological argument is clearly connected with this feeling. It is likely to be quite strong in intellectual people, since they value the power of thinking more highly than others, and are more inclined to base their belief in the superiority of Man on this power.

23   I do not think that this argument is sufficiently substantial to require refutation. Consolation would be more appropriate: perhaps this should be sought in the transmigration of souls.

The Mathematical Objection

24   There are a number of results of mathematical logic which can be used to show that there are limitations to the powers of discrete-state machines. The best known of these results is known as Gödel's theorem,[1] and shows that in any sufficiently powerful logical system statements can be formulated which can neither be proved nor disproved within the system, unless possibly the system itself is inconsistent. There are other, in some respects similar, results due to *Church, Kleene, Rosser*, and *Turing*. The latter result is the most convenient to consider, since it refers directly to machines, whereas the others can only be used in a comparatively indirect argument: for instance if Gödel's theorem is to be used we need in addition to have some means of describing logical systems in terms of machines, and machines in terms of logical systems. The result in question refers to a type of machine which is essentially a digital computer with an infinite capacity. It states that there are certain things that such a machine cannot do. If it is rigged up to give answers to questions as in the imitation game, there will be some questions to which it will either give a wrong answer, or fail to give an answer at all however much time is allowed for a reply. There may, of course, be many such questions, and questions which cannot be answered by one machine may be satisfactorily answered by another. We are of course supposing for the present that the questions are of the kind to which an answer 'Yes' or 'No' is appropriate, rather than questions such as 'What do you think of Picasso?' The questions that we know the machines must fail on are of this type, "Consider the machine specified as follows. . . . Will this machine ever answer 'Yes' to any question?" The dots are to be replaced by a description of some machine in a standard form, which could be something like that used in § 5. When the machine described bears a certain comparatively simple relation to the

---

[1]Laplace: Pierre Simon Laplace, eighteenth-century French mathematician.

machine which is under interrogation, it can be shown that the answer is either wrong or not forthcoming. This is the mathematical result: it is argued that it proves a disability of machines to which the human intellect is not subject.

25   The short answer to this argument is that although it is established that there are limitations to the powers of any particular machine, it has only been stated, without any sort of proof, that no such limitations apply to the human intellect. But I do not think this view can be dismissed quite so lightly. Whenever one of these machines is asked the appropriate critical question, and gives a definite answer, we know that this answer must be wrong, and this gives us a certain feeling of superiority. Is this feeling illusory? It is no doubt quite genuine, but I do not think too much importance should be attached to it. We too often give wrong answers to questions ourselves to be justified in being very pleased at such evidence of fallibility on the part of the machines. Further, our superiority can only be felt on such an occasion in relation to the one machine over which we have scored our petty triumph. There would be no question of triumphing simultaneously over *all* machines. In short, then, there might be men cleverer than any given machine, but then again there might be other machines cleverer again, and so on.

26   Those who hold to the mathematical argument would, I think, mostly be willing to accept the imitation game as a basis for discussion. Those who believe in the two previous objections would probably not be interested in any criteria.

The Argument from Consciousness

27   This argument is very well expressed in *Professor Jefferson's* Lister Oration for 1949, from which I quote. "Not until a machine can write a sonnet or compose a concerto because of thoughts and emotions felt, and not by the chance fall of symbols, could we agree that machine equals brain—that is, not only write it but know that it had written it. No mechanism could feel (and not merely artificially signal, an easy contrivance) pleasure at its successes, grief when its valves fuse, be warmed by flattery, be made miserable by its mistakes, be charmed by sex, be angry or depressed when it cannot get what it wants."

28   This argument appears to be a denial of the validity of our test. According to the most extreme form of this view the only way by which one could be sure that a machine thinks is to *be* the machine and to feel oneself thinking. One could then describe these feelings to the world, but of course no one would be justified in taking any notice. Likewise according to this view the only way to know that a *man* thinks is to be that particular man. It is in fact the solipsist point of view. It may be the most logical view to hold but it makes communication of ideas difficult. A is liable to believe 'A thinks but B does not' whilst B believes 'B thinks but A does not.' Instead of arguing continually over this point it is usual to have the polite convention that everyone thinks.

29   I think that most of those who support the argument from consciousness could be persuaded to abandon it rather than be forced into the solipsist position. They will then probably be willing to accept our test.

30   I do not wish to give the impression that I think there is no mystery about consciousness. There is, for instance, something of a paradox connected with any attempt to localise it. But I do not think these mysteries necessarily need to be solved before we can answer the question with which we are concerned in this paper.

Arguments from Various Disabilities

31   These arguments take the form, "I grant you that you can make machines do all the things you have mentioned but you will never be able to make one to do X." Numerous features X are suggested in this connexion. I offer a selection:

> *Be kind, resourceful, beautiful, friendly, have initiative, have a sense of humour, tell right from wrong, make mistakes, fall in love, enjoy strawberries and cream, make some one fall in love with it, learn from experience, use words properly, be the subject of its own thought, have as much diversity of behaviour as a man, do something really new. (Some of these disabilities are given special consideration as indicated by the page numbers.)*

32   No support is usually offered for these statements. I believe they are mostly founded on the principle of scientific induction. A man has seen thousands of machines in his lifetime. From what he sees of them he draws a number of general conclusions. They are ugly, each is designed for a very limited purpose, when required for a minutely different purpose they are useless, the variety of behaviour of any one of them is very small, etc., etc. Naturally he concludes that these are necessary properties of machines in general.

33   There are, however, special remarks to be made about many of the disabilities that have been mentioned. The inability to enjoy strawberries and cream may have struck the reader as frivolous. Possibly a machine might be made to enjoy this delicious dish, but any attempt to make one do so would be idiotic. What is important about this disability is that it contributes to some of the other disabilities, *e.g.* to the difficulty of the same kind of friendliness occurring between man and machine as between white man and white man, or between black man and black man.

34   The claim that "machines cannot make mistakes" seems a curious one. One is tempted to retort, "Are they any the worse for that?" But let us adopt a more sympathetic attitude, and try to see what is really meant. I think this criticism can be explained in terms of the imitation game. It is claimed that the interrogator could distinguish the machine from the man simply by setting them a number of problems in arithmetic. The machine would be unmasked because of its deadly accuracy. The reply to this is simple. The machine (programmed for playing the game) would not attempt to give the *right* answers to the arithmetic problems. It would deliberately introduce mistakes in a manner calculated to confuse the interrogator.

35   The claim that a machine cannot be the subject of its own thought can of course only be answered if it can be shown that the machine has *some* thought with *some* subject matter. Nevertheless, 'the subject matter of a machine's operations' does seem to mean something, at least to the people who deal with it. If, for instance, the machine was trying to find a solution of the equation $x^2 - 40x - 11 = 0$ one would be tempted to describe this equation as part of the machine's subject matter at that moment. In this sort of sense a machine undoubtedly can be its own subject matter. It may be used to help in making up its own programmes, or to predict the effect of alterations in its own structure. By observing the results of its own behaviour it can modify its own programmes so as to achieve some purpose more effectively.

Lady Lovelace's Objection

36   Our most detailed information of Babbage's Analytical Engine comes from a memoir by *Lady Lovelace*. In it she states, "The Analytical Engine has no pretensions to *originate* anything. It can do *whatever we know how to order it* to perform" (her italics).

37   A variant of Lady Lovelace's objection states that a machine can 'never do anything really new.' A better variant of the objection says that a machine can never 'take us by surprise.'

38   The view that machines cannot give rise to surprises is due, I believe, to a fallacy to which philosophers and mathematicians are particularly subject. This is the assumption that as soon as a fact is presented to a mind all consequences of that fact spring into the mind simultaneously with it. It is a very useful assumption under many circumstances, but one too easily forgets that it is false. A natural consequence of doing so is that one then assumes that there is no virtue in the mere working out of consequences from data and general principles.

Argument from Continuity in the Nervous System

39   The nervous system is certainly not a discrete-state machine. A small error in the information about the size of a nervous impulse impinging on a neuron, may make a large difference to the size of the outgoing impulse. It may be argued that, this being so, one cannot expect to be able to mimic the behaviour of the nervous system with a discrete-state system.

40   It is true that a discrete-state machine must be different from a continuous machine. But if we adhere to the conditions of the imitation game, the interrogator will not be able to take any advantage of this difference. The situation can be made clearer if we consider some other simpler continuous machine. A differential analyser will do very well. (A differential analyser is a certain kind of machine not of the discrete-state type used for some kinds of calculation.) Some of these provide their answers in a typed form, and so are suitable for taking part in the game. It would not be possible for a digital computer to predict exactly what answers the differential analyser would give to a problem, but it would be quite capable of giving the right sort of answer.

The Argument from Informality of Behaviour

41   It is not possible to produce a set of rules purporting to describe what a man should do in every conceivable set of circumstances. One might for instance have a rule that one is to stop when one sees a red traffic light, and to go if one sees a green one, but what if by some fault both appear together? One may perhaps decide that it is safest to stop. But some further difficulty may well arise from this decision later. To attempt to provide rules of conduct to cover every eventuality, even those arising from traffic lights, appears to be impossible. With all this I agree.

42   From this it is argued that we cannot be machines. I shall try to reproduce the argument, but I fear I shall hardly do it justice. It seems to run something like this. 'If each man had a definite set of rules of conduct by which he regulated his life he would be no better than a machine. But there are no such rules, so men cannot be machines.' The undistributed middle is glaring. I do not think the argument is ever put quite like this,

but I believe this is the argument used nevertheless. There may however be a certain confusion between 'rules of conduct' and 'laws of behaviour' to cloud the issue. By 'rules of conduct' I mean precepts such as 'Stop if you see red lights,' on which one can act, and of which one can be conscious. By 'laws of behaviour' I mean laws of nature as applied to a man's body such as 'if you pinch him he will squeak.' If we substitute 'laws of behaviour which regulate his life' for 'laws of conduct by which he regulates his life' in the argument quoted the undistributed middle is no longer insuperable. For we believe that it is not only true that being regulated by laws of behaviour implies being some sort of machine (though not necessarily a discrete-state machine), but that conversely being such a machine implies being regulated by such laws. However, we cannot so easily convince ourselves of the absence of complete laws of behaviour as of complete rules of conduct. The only way we know of for finding such laws is scientific observation, and we certainly know of no circumstances under which we could say, 'We have searched enough. There are no such laws.'

The Argument from Extra-Sensory Perception

43   I assume that the reader is familiar with the idea of extra-sensory perception, and the meaning of the four items of it, *viz.* telepathy, clairvoyance, precognition and psycho-kinesis. These disturbing phenomena seem to deny all our usual scientific ideas. How we should like to discredit them! Unfortunately the statistical evidence, at least for telepathy, is overwhelming. It is very difficult to rearrange one's ideas so as to fit these new facts in. Once one has accepted them it does not seem a very big step to believe in ghosts and bogies. The idea that our bodies move simply according to the known laws of physics, together with some others not yet discovered but somewhat similar, would be one of the first to go.

44   This argument is to my mind quite a strong one. One can say in reply that many scientific theories seem to remain workable in practice, in spite of clashing with E.S.P.; that in fact one can get along very nicely if one forgets about it. This is rather cold comfort, and one fears that thinking is just the kind of phenomenon where E.S.P. may be especially relevant.

45   A more specific argument based on E.S.P. might run as follows: "Let us play the imitation game, using as witnesses a man who is good as a telepathic receiver, and a digital computer. The interrogator can ask such questions as 'What suit does the card in my right hand belong to?' The man by telepathy or clairvoyance gives the right answer 130 times out of 400 cards. The machine can only guess at random, and perhaps gets 104 right, so the interrogator makes the right identification. 'There is an interesting possibility which opens here. Suppose the digital computer contains a random number generator. Then it will be natural to use this to decide what answer to give. But then the random number generator will be subject to the psycho-kinetic powers of the interrogator. Perhaps this psycho-kinesis might cause the machine to guess right more often than would be expected on a probability calculation, so that the interrogator might still be unable to make the right identification. On the other hand, he might be able to guess right without any questioning, by clairvoyance. With E.S.P. anything may happen.

46   If telepathy is admitted it will be necessary to tighten our test up. The situation could be regarded as analogous to that which would occur if the interrogator were talking to

himself and one of the competitors was listening with his ear to the wall. To put the competitors into a 'telepathy-proof room' would satisfy all requirements.

LEARNING MACHINES

47   The reader will have anticipated that I have no very convincing arguments of a positive nature to support my views. If I had I should not have taken such pains to point out the fallacies in contrary views. Such evidence as I have I shall now give.

48   Let us return for a moment to Lady Lovelace's objection, which stated that the machine can only do what we tell it to do. One could say that a man can 'inject' an idea into the machine, and that it will respond to a certain extent and then drop into quiescence, like a piano string struck by a hammer.

49   The 'skin of an onion' analogy is also helpful. In considering the functions of the mind or the brain we find certain operations which we can explain in purely mechanical terms. This we say does not correspond to the real mind: it is a sort of skin which we must strip off if we are to find the real mind. But then in what remains we find a further skin to be stripped off, and so on. Proceeding in this way do we ever come to the 'real' mind, or do we eventually come to the skin which has nothing in it? In the latter case the whole mind is mechanical.

51   These last two paragraphs do not claim to be convincing arguments. They should rather be described as 'recitations tending to produce belief.'

52   As I have explained, the problem is mainly one of programming. In the process of trying to imitate an adult human mind we are bound to think a good deal about the process which has brought it to the state that it is in. We may notice three components,

    a. The initial state of the mind, say at birth,

    b. The education to which it has been subjected,

    c. Other experience, not to be described as education, to which it has been subjected.

53   Instead of trying to produce a programme to simulate the adult mind, why not rather try to produce one which simulates the child's? If this were then subjected to an appropriate course of education one would obtain the adult brain. Presumably the child-brain is something like a note-book as one buys it from the stationers. Rather little mechanism, and lots of blank sheets. (Mechanism and writing are from our point of view almost synonymous.) Our hope is that there is so little mechanism in the child-brain that something like it can be easily programmed. The amount of work in the education we can assume, as a first approximation, to be much the same as for the human child.

54   We have thus divided our problem into two parts. The child-programme and the education process. These two remain very closely connected. We cannot expect to find a good child-machine at the first attempt. One must experiment with teaching one such machine and see how well it learns. One can then try another and see if it is better or worse. There is an obvious connection between this process and evolution, by the identifications

Structure of the child machine	= Hereditary material
Changes	= Mutations
Natural selection	= Judgment of the experimenter

55 One may hope, however, that this process will be more expeditious than evolution. The survival of the fittest is a slow method for measuring advantages. The experimenter, by the exercise of intelligence, should be able to speed it up. Equally important is the fact that he is not restricted to random mutations. If he can trace a cause for some weakness he can probably think of the kind of mutation which will improve it.

56 We normally associate punishments and rewards with the teaching process. Some simple child-machines can be constructed or programmed on this sort of principle. The machine has to be so constructed that events which shortly preceded the occurrence of a punishment-signal are unlikely to be repeated, whereas a reward-signal increased the probability of repetition of the events which led up to it. These definitions do not presuppose any feelings on the part of the machine.

57 The use of punishments and rewards can at best be a part of the teaching process. Roughly speaking, if the teacher has no other means of communicating to the pupil, the amount of information which can reach him does not exceed the total number of rewards and punishments applied. It is necessary therefore to have some other 'unemotional' channels of communication. If these are available it is possible to teach a machine by punishments and rewards to obey orders given in some language, *e.g.* a symbolic language. These orders are to be transmitted through the 'unemotional' channels. The use of this language will diminish greatly the number of punishments and rewards required.

58 Opinions may vary as to the complexity which is suitable in the child machine. One might try to make it as simple as possible consistently with the general principles. Alternatively one might have a complete system of logical inference 'built in,' largely occupied with definitions and propositions. The propositions would have various kinds of status, *e.g.* well-established facts, conjectures, mathematically proved theorems, statements given by an authority, expressions having the logical form of proposition but not belief-value. Certain propositions may be described as 'imperatives'. The machine should be so constructed that as soon as an imperative is classed as 'well-established' the appropriate action automatically takes place. To illustrate this, suppose the teacher says to the machine, 'Do your homework now.' This may cause "Teacher says 'Do your homework now'" to be included amongst the well-established facts. Another such fact might be, "Everything that teacher says is true." Combining these may eventually lead to the imperative, 'Do your homework now', being included amongst the well-established facts, and this, by the construction of the machine, will mean that the homework actually gets started, but the effect is very satisfactory.

59 The imperatives that can be obeyed by a machine that has no limbs are bound to be of a rather intellectual character, as in the example (doing homework) given above. Important amongst such imperatives will be ones which regulate the order in which the rules of the logical system concerned are to be applied. For at each stage when one is using a logical system, there is a very large number of alternative steps, any of which one is permitted to apply, so far as obedience to the rules of the logical system is concerned. Propositions leading to imperatives of this kind might be "When Socrates is mentioned, use the syllogism in Barbara" or "If one method has been proved to be quicker than another, do not use the slower method." Some of these may be 'given by authority,' but others may be produced by the machine itself, *e.g.* by scientific induction.

60 The idea of a learning machine may appear paradoxical to some readers. How can the rules of operation of the machine change? They should describe completely how the

machine will react whatever its history might be, whatever changes it might undergo. The rules are thus quite time-invariant. This is quite true. The explanation of the paradox is that the rules which get changed in the learning process are of a rather less pretentious kind, claiming only an ephemeral validity.

61   An important feature of a learning machine is that its teacher will often be very largely ignorant of quite what is going on inside, although he may still be able to some extent to predict his pupil's behaviour. This should apply most strongly to the later education of a machine arising from a child-machine of well-tried design (or programme). This is in clear contrast with normal procedure when using a machine to do computations: one's object is then to have a clear mental picture of the state of the machine at each moment in the computation. This object can only be achieved with a struggle. The view that 'the machine can only do what we know how to order it to do' appears strange in face of this. Most of the programmes which we can put into the machine will result in its doing something that we cannot make sense of at all, or which we regard as completely random behaviour. Intelligent behaviour presumably consists in a departure from the completely disciplined behaviour involved in computation, but a rather slight one, which does not give rise to random behaviour, or to pointless repetitive loops. Another important result of preparing our machine for its part in the imitation game by a process of teaching and learning is that 'human fallibility' is likely to be omitted in a rather natural way, *i.e.* without special 'coaching.' Processes that are learnt do not produce a hundred percent certainty of result; if they did they could not be unlearnt.

62   It is probably wise to include a random element in a learning machine. A random element is rather useful when we are searching for a solution of some problem. Suppose for instance we wanted to find a number between 50 and 200 which was equal to the square of the sum of its digits, we might start at 51 then try 52 and go on until we got a number that worked. Alternatively we might choose numbers at random until we got a good one. This method has the advantage that it is unnecessary to keep track of the values that have been tried, but the disadvantage that one may try the same one twice, but this is not very important if there are several solutions. The systematic method has the disadvantage that there may be an enormous block without any solutions in the region which has to be investigated first. Now the learning process may be regarded as a search for a form of behaviour which will satisfy the teacher (or some other criterion). Since there is probably a very large number of satisfactory solutions the random method seems to be better than the systematic. It should be noticed that it is used in the analogous process of evolution. But there the systematic method is not possible. How could one keep track of the different genetical combinations that had been tried, so as to avoid trying them again?

63   We may hope that machines will eventually compete with men in all purely intellectual fields. But which are the best ones to start with? Even this is a difficult decision. Many people think that a very abstract activity, like the playing of chess, would be best. It can also be maintained that it is best to provide the machine with the best sense organs that money can buy, and then teach it to understand and speak English. This process could follow the normal teaching of a child. Things would be pointed out and named, etc. Again I do not know what the right answer is, but I think both approaches should be tried.

64   We can only see a short distance ahead, but we can see plenty there that needs to be done.

QUESTIONS ON MEANING

1. What is the imitation game and how is it played? What does Turing's version of the game help provide evidence of (at least, if it works as intended by Turing)?

2. At the beginning of the essay, why does Turing shift the question from "can machines think?" to "what will happen when a machine takes the part of A in this game?" Why is this shift important to Turing's argument?

3. When discussing the kinds of machines that will be accepted for the experiment, Turing limits it to digital computers. Why does he do this? What are the issues involved, as Turing views the situation?

4. What does Turing mean by the *universality* of digital computers?

5. What does Turing predict will be the situation fifty years from when he is writing? Did his prediction come true? If not, do you think it will in the future? Why or why not?

6. Briefly paraphrase each of the following counterarguments discussed by Turing and indicate in each case how Turing refutes the counterargument:
   A. The Theological Objection
   B. The 'Heads in the Sand' Objection
   C. The Mathematical Objection
   D. The Argument from Consciousness
   E. Arguments from Various Disabilities
   F. Lady Lovelace's Objection
   G. Argument from Continuity in the Nervous System
   H. The Argument from Informality of Behaviour
   I. The Argument from Extra-Sensory Perception

7. Given the impracticalities of programming a machine to play the imitation game (in terms of time and labor), how does Turing propose that a thinking machine—a machine capable of playing and potentially winning the imitation game—be created?

QUESTIONS FOR DISCUSSION

1. Do you believe the imitation game provides valid and reasonable evidence of intelligence? Why or why not?

2. If you were to play the imitation game, what sorts of questions might you ask in order to determine if "A" is a male or female? Or if "A" is human or machine?

3. Which of the counterarguments raised and refuted by Turing do you find the most interesting? The most persuasive? The least persuasive? What about Turing's refutations—which are the most and least convincing?

4. Aside from the nine counterarguments Turing deals with in his essay, can you think of any other reasons why machines will never be able to pass the Turing Test (that is, the imitation game)?

LOOKING AT RHETORIC

1. The heart of Turing's essay is his systematic attempt to dismantle nine different arguments that attempt to prove that the creation of a machine capable of passing the imitation game—the Turing Test—is impossible. Rhetorically, how effective is this strategy in Turing's essay? Does his systematic refutation of these arguments make his own thesis, by comparison, more acceptable? Why or why not?

2. Turing is forthcoming about the fact that he spends so much time dealing with counterarguments because he has few arguments in support of his position to make. Why would refuting these counterarguments help build his case? Does Turing's admission that he has few arguments to make of a positive nature regarding his thesis weaken his case?

WRITING ASSIGNMENTS

1. Spend some time in the library or use Internet resources to learn more about the Turing Test and its relevance to computer scientists today. Turing's essay was written over half a century ago. Based on your experience with modern technology, do you believe there is evidence today that makes it more or less likely that Turing was correct? What do contemporary scientists think about the validity of the Turing Test today? Write an essay in which you present some contemporary perspectives on the Turing Test and offer your argument either for or against the test as a measure of artificial intelligence.

2. Select one of the nine counterarguments and write an essay in which you take the position of one who advocates for that counterargument. How do you respond to Turing's refutation? Alternatively, you might draft an essay in which you create a tenth counterargument, one different from the nine outlined (and refuted) by Turing. Explain the nature of your counterargument, and explain why you believe it is a powerful argument against Turing's position.

3. In groups of at least three people where both sexes are represented, set up and play the imitation game in which the object is for an interrogator to determine whether A is male and B is female or vice versa. Take turns adopting the role of the interrogator in order for everyone to get a chance to craft questions that will reveal the truth with the highest degree of accuracy. Then, individually, use the lessons of that experiment to reconsider the essay by Turing. Draft an essay in which you argue either for or against the Turing Test's validity as a tool for determining whether a machine is thinking or not.

The Law of Accelerating Returns

Raymond Kurzweil

Raymond Kurzweil (b. 1948) is one of the world's leading inventors and futurists. His entrepreneurial business ventures have resulted in the invention of numerous products, from optical scanning technology to text-to-speech synthesizers. Over his career he has received numerous awards, including the National Medal of Technology, the highest honor of its kind given in the United States. In addition to his entrepreneurial ventures, Kurzweil has established himself as one of the leading futurists working today. Of particular note is Kurzweil's speculations in The Singularity is Near *(2005) in which he elaborates on the changes he predicts are coming when the exponential rate of technological progress results in a radical shift in our understanding of the limits of human intelligence and the abilities of computing technology, resulting in a blurring of the distinction between human and machine and ushering in, in effect, the stage of human evolution. In the following essay, Kurzweil sets forth some of the key ideas in his theory of the coming singularity.*

1   An analysis of the history of technology shows that technological change is exponential, contrary to the common-sense "intuitive linear" view. So we won't experience 100 years of progress in the 21st century—it will be more like 20,000 years of progress (at today's rate). The "returns," such as chip speed and cost-effectiveness, also increase exponentially. There's even exponential growth in the rate of exponential growth. Within a few decades, machine intelligence will surpass human intelligence, leading to The Singularity—technological change so rapid and profound it represents a rupture in the fabric of human history. The implications include the merger of biological and nonbiological intelligence, immortal software-based humans, and ultra-high levels of intelligence that expand outward in the universe at the speed of light.

THE INTUITIVE LINEAR VIEW VERSUS THE HISTORICAL EXPONENTIAL VIEW

2   When people think of a future period, they intuitively assume that the current rate of progress will continue for future periods. However, careful consideration of the pace of technology shows that the rate of progress is not constant, but it is human nature to adapt to the changing pace, so the intuitive view is that the pace will continue at the current rate. Even for those of us who have been around long enough to experience how the pace increases over time, our unexamined intuition nonetheless provides the impression that progress changes at the rate that we have experienced recently. From the mathematician's perspective, a primary reason for this is that an exponential curve approximates a straight line when viewed for a brief duration. So even though the rate of progress in the very recent past (e.g., this past year) is far greater than it was ten years ago (let alone a hundred or a thousand years ago), our memories are nonetheless dominated by our very recent experience. It is typical, therefore, that even sophisticated commentators, when considering the future, extrapolate the current pace of change over the next 10 years or 100 years to determine their expectations. This is why I call this way of looking at the future the "intuitive linear" view.

3   But a serious assessment of the history of technology shows that technological change is exponential. In exponential growth, we find that a key measurement such as computational power is multiplied by a constant factor for each unit of time (e.g., doubling every year) rather than just being added to incrementally. Exponential growth is a feature of any evolutionary process, of which technology is a primary example. One can examine the data in different ways, on different time scales, and for a wide variety of technologies ranging from electronic to biological, and the acceleration of progress and growth applies. Indeed, we find not just simple exponential growth, but "double" exponential growth, meaning that the rate of exponential growth is itself growing exponentially. These observations do not rely merely on an assumption of the continuation of Moore's law (i.e., the exponential shrinking of transistor sizes on an integrated circuit), but is based on a rich model of diverse technological processes. What it clearly shows is that technology, particularly the pace of technological change, advances (at least) exponentially, not linearly, and has been doing so since the advent of technology, indeed since the advent of evolution on Earth.

4   I emphasize this point because it is the most important failure that would-be prognosticators make in considering future trends. Most technology forecasts ignore altogether this

"historical exponential view" of technological progress. That is why people tend to over-estimate what can be achieved in the short term (because we tend to leave out necessary details), but underestimate what can be achieved in the long term (because the exponential growth is ignored).

THE LAW OF ACCELERATING RETURNS

5   We can organize these observations into what I call the law of accelerating returns as follows:

- Evolution applies positive feedback in that the more capable methods resulting from one stage of evolutionary progress are used to create the next stage. As a result, the
- rate of progress of an evolutionary process increases exponentially over time. Over time, the "order" of the information embedded in the evolutionary process (i.e., the measure of how well the information fits a purpose, which in evolution is survival) increases.
- A correlate of the above observation is that the "returns" of an evolutionary process (e.g., the speed, cost-effectiveness, or overall "power" of a process) increase exponentially over time.
- In another positive feedback loop, as a particular evolutionary process (e.g., computation) becomes more effective (e.g., cost effective), greater resources are deployed toward the further progress of that process. This results in a second level of exponential growth (i.e., the rate of exponential growth itself grows exponentially).
- Biological evolution is one such evolutionary process.
- Technological evolution is another such evolutionary process. Indeed, the emergence of the first technology creating species resulted in the new evolutionary process of technology. Therefore, technological evolution is an outgrowth of—and a continuation of—biological evolution.
- A specific paradigm (a method or approach to solving a problem, e.g., shrinking transistors on an integrated circuit as an approach to making more powerful computers) provides exponential growth until the method exhausts its potential. When this happens, a paradigm shift (i.e., a fundamental change in the approach) occurs, which enables exponential growth to continue.

6   If we apply these principles at the highest level of evolution on Earth, the first step, the creation of cells, introduced the paradigm of biology. The subsequent emergence of DNA provided a digital method to record the results of evolutionary experiments. Then, the evolution of a species who combined rational thought with an opposable appendage (i.e., the thumb) caused a fundamental paradigm shift from biology to technology. The upcoming primary paradigm shift will be from biological thinking to a hybrid combining biological and nonbiological thinking. This hybrid will include "biologically inspired" processes resulting from the reverse engineering of biological brains.

7   If we examine the timing of these steps, we see that the process has continuously accelerated. The evolution of life forms required billions of years for the first steps

(e.g., primitive cells); later on progress accelerated. During the Cambrian explosion, major paradigm shifts took only tens of millions of years. Later on, Humanoids developed over a period of millions of years, and Homo sapiens over a period of only hundreds of thousands of years.

8   With the advent of a technology-creating species, the exponential pace became too fast for evolution through DNA-guided protein synthesis and moved on to human-created technology. Technology goes beyond mere tool making; it is a process of creating ever more powerful technology using the tools from the previous round of innovation. In this way, human technology is distinguished from the tool making of other species. There is a record of each stage of technology, and each new stage of technology builds on the order of the previous stage.

9   The first technological steps—sharp edges, fire, the wheel—took tens of thousands of years. For people living in this era, there was little noticeable technological change in even a thousand years. By 1000 A.D., progress was much faster and a paradigm shift required only a century or two. In the nineteenth century, we saw more technological change than in the nine centuries preceding it. Then in the first twenty years of the twentieth century, we saw more advancement than in all of the nineteenth century. Now, paradigm shifts occur in only a few years time.

10   The paradigm shift rate (i.e., the overall rate of technical progress) is currently doubling (approximately) every decade; that is, paradigm shift times are halving every decade (and the rate of acceleration is itself growing exponentially). So, the technological progress in the twenty-first century will be equivalent to what would require (in the linear view) on the order of 200 centuries. In contrast, the twentieth century saw only about 25 years of progress (again at today's rate of progress) since we have been speeding up to current rates. So the twenty-first century will see almost a thousand times greater technological change than its predecessor.

THE SINGULARITY IS NEAR

11   Can the pace of technological progress continue to speed up indefinitely? Is there not a point where humans are unable to think fast enough to keep up with it? With regard to unenhanced humans, clearly so. But what would a thousand scientists, each a thousand times more intelligent than human scientists today, and each operating a thousand times faster than contemporary humans (because the information processing in their primarily nonbiological brains is faster) accomplish? One year would be like a millennium. What would they come up with?

12   Well, for one thing, they would come up with technology to become even more intelligent (because their intelligence is no longer of fixed capacity). They would change their own thought processes to think even faster. When the scientists evolve to be a million times more intelligent and operate a million times faster, then an hour would result in a century of progress (in today's terms).

13   This, then, is the Singularity. The Singularity is technological change so rapid and so profound that it represents a rupture in the fabric of human history. Some would say that we cannot comprehend the Singularity, at least with our current level of understanding,

and that it is impossible, therefore, to look past its "event horizon" and make sense of what lies beyond.

14   My view is that despite our profound limitations of thought, constrained as we are today to a mere hundred trillion interneuronal connections in our biological brains, we nonetheless have sufficient powers of abstraction to make meaningful statements about the nature of life after the Singularity. Most importantly, it is my view that the intelligence that will emerge will continue to represent the human civilization, which is already a human-machine civilization. This will be the next step in evolution, the next high level paradigm shift.

15   Consider a few examples of the implications. The bulk of our experiences will shift from real reality to virtual reality. Most of the intelligence of our civilization will ultimately be nonbiological, which by the end of this century will be trillions of trillions of times more powerful than human intelligence. However, to address often expressed concerns, this does not imply the end of biological intelligence, even if thrown from its perch of evolutionary superiority. Moreover, it is important to note that the nonbiological forms will be derivative of biological design. In other words, our civilization will remain human, indeed in many ways more exemplary of what we regard as human than it is today, although our understanding of the term will move beyond its strictly biological origins.

16   Many observers have nonetheless expressed alarm at the emergence of forms of nonbiological intelligence superior to human intelligence. The potential to augment our own intelligence through intimate connection with other thinking mediums does not necessarily alleviate the concern, as some people have expressed the wish to remain "unenhanced" while at the same time keeping their place at the top of the intellectual food chain. My view is that the likely outcome is that on the one hand, from the perspective of biological humanity, these superhuman intelligences will appear to be their transcendent servants, satisfying their needs and desires. On the other hand, fulfilling the wishes of a revered biological legacy will occupy only a trivial portion of the intellectual power that the Singularity will bring.

QUESTIONS ON MEANING

1. What distinguishes the Intuitive Linear View from the Historical Exponential View? Which does Kurzweil believe better describes the rate of technological progress?

2. As Kurzweil defines it, what is The Singularity?

3. What is Moore's Law and how does it relate to Kurzweil's Historical Exponential View?

4. Can the pace of technological progress continue to speed up indefinitely? How does Kurzweil answer this question?

QUESTIONS FOR DISCUSSION

1. Do changes in technology change what it means to be *human*? Or, does human nature remain relatively stable despite the technologies available for our use?

2. A major feature of Kurzweil's Law of Accelerating Returns is his application of evolutionary theory to the development of both biological and mechanical or technological systems of information gathering and processing. Do you accept Kurzweil's assertions? Are you

skeptical of any of the seven claims Kurzweil lists in bullet fashion under the heading "The Law of Accelerating Returns"? Why or why not?

3. One of the implications of Kurzweil's predictions about the coming singularity is that the next stage of human evolution will to one degree or another involve the enhancement of human information processing through mechanical means—and this will result in a blurring of the boundaries between human and machine and may even shift the way we define what it means to be human itself. Is this prospect frightening or exciting to you? What are the potential benefits? What might be the drawbacks?

4. If you could enhance the performance of your brain by permanently implanting some technological device into your head—knowing that the operation was irreversible—would you do it? Why or why not?

5. What if you were given the chance to live forever, but only if you shed your body and had your mind downloaded onto a piece of technology. Would you do it? Why or why not?

6. As humans travel down the path of using technology to enhance their biological abilities, at what point would it make sense to stop calling an enhanced individual a *human*? At what point would the individual be *something else* other than human?

7. How might concepts arising out of the writings of Thomas Kuhn, Barry Commoner, Francis Fukuyama, and/or Michael Sandel (all printed in Chapter Four of this anthology) provide evidence (or counterargument, or context) for Kurzweil's futurist predictions?

LOOKING AT RHETORIC

1. Given the topic under discussion, this essay could have been extremely complicated and full of technical language known only to specialists in the field. Yet, it is remarkably easy to read and comprehend. Identify at least three things Kurzweil does in this essay that makes it so easy to read and understand.

2. Where in this essay is Kurzweil's thesis statement? Is it well placed? Is it clear and unambiguous? What makes it effective and/or ineffective?

WRITING ASSIGNMENTS

1. Spend some time researching the term *transhumanism*. Draft an essay in which you define this term (being sure to cite your sources accurately) and describe the implications of transhumanism for understanding Kurzweil's historical exponential view of technological progress.

2. After reading carefully Kurzweil's essay and thinking about the arguments he makes and the evidence he provides, draft an essay in which you argue either for or against Kurzweil's position (or some specific claim Kurzweil makes related to his position). Be sure to provide your own arguments and evidence to support your position.

3. In pairs or in groups, create a list of five specific things that you believe will come true if and/or when Kurzweil's singularity is reached. Share your list with the other groups in the class, taking note of where your predictions match (or depart from) the predictions of the other groups. Do you see any trends developing? Then, as an individual, draft an essay in which you identify one significant change that you predict will occur once Kurzweil's singularity is reached, and discuss/describe the impact this change will have on human identity and human society.

Arguments for the Existence of God

St. Anselm, St. Thomas Aquinas, and William Paley

Philosophers and theologians have devoted considerable time and energy trying to solve one of life's most perplexing intellectual problems: Can the existence of God be proven, or must belief in God always remain a matter of faith? Or, put another way, are there arguments that satisfy the strictures of logic and reason that provide a rational basis for maintaining faith in a transcendent creator? Most attempts to prove the existence of God fall into the category of natural theology. Natural theology is characterized by its attempt to come to answer theological questions—in particular, the question of whether God exists—through experience and observation of the natural world and through the application of logic and reason. This distinguishes natural theology from other kinds of theology, such as revealed theology, in which arguments are rooted in truths or evidence as revealed to humans through a sacred text or a mystical experience of some kind or another. Three of the best known arguments for the existence of God are reprinted here. They are the Ontological Argument as formulated most famously by St. Anselm (1033–1109) in his Proslogium, *the Cosmological Argument, as formulated in this case by St. Thomas Aquinas (c. 1225–1274) in his* Summa Theologica, *and the Teleological Argument as formulated in this case by the eighteenth-century philosopher William Paley (1743–1805). So provocative are these arguments that they have been hotly debated, rejected, defended, and revised by countless other philosophers and theologians since the time of their creation, and they remain at the heart of numerous theological debates to this day.*

St. Anselm from *Proslogium*

THE ONTOLOGICAL ARGUMENT

1   After I had published, at the solicitous entreaties of certain brethren, a brief work (the Monologium) as an example of meditation on the grounds of faith, in the person of one who investigates, in a course of silent reasoning with himself, matters of which he is ignorant; considering that this book was knit together by the linking of many arguments, I began to ask myself whether there might be found a single argument which would require no other for its proof than itself alone; and alone would suffice to demonstrate that God truly exists, . . .

2   *Truly there is a God, although the fool hath said in his heart, There is no God.*

3   And so, Lord, do thou, who dost give understanding to faith, give me, so far as thou knowest it to be profitable, to understand that thou art that which we believe. And, indeed, we believe that thou art a being than which nothing greater can be conceived. Or is there no such nature, since the fool hath said in his heart, there is no God? (Psalms xiv. I). But, at any rate, this very fool, when he hears of this being of which I speak—a being than which nothing greater can be conceived—understands what he hears, and what he understands is in his understanding; although he does not understand it to exist.

4   For, it is one thing for an object to be in the understanding, and another to understand that the object exists. When a painter first conceives of what he will afterwards perform, he has it in his understanding, but he does not yet understand it to be, because he has not yet performed it. But after he has made the painting, he both has it in his understanding, and he understands that it exists, because he has made it.

5   Hence, even the fool is convinced that something exists in the understanding, at least, than which nothing greater can be conceived. For, when he hears of this, he understands it. And whatever is understood, exists in the understanding. And assuredly that, than which nothing greater can be conceived, cannot exist in the understanding alone. For, suppose it exists in the understanding alone: then it can be conceived to exist in reality; which is greater.

6   Therefore, if that, than which nothing greater can be conceived, exists in the understanding alone, the very being, than which nothing greater can be conceived, is one, than which a greater can be conceived. But obviously this is impossible. Hence, there is no doubt that there exists a being, than which nothing greater can be conceived, and it exists both in the understanding and in reality.

7   *God cannot be conceived not to exist—God is that, than which nothing greater can be conceived—That which can be conceived not to exist is not God.*

8   And it assuredly exists so truly, that it cannot be conceived not to exist. For, it is possible to conceive of a being which cannot be conceived not to exist; and this is greater than one which can be conceived not to exist. Hence, if that, than which nothing greater can be conceived, can be conceived not to exist, it is not that, than which nothing greater can be conceived. But this is an irreconcilable contradiction. There is, then, so truly a being than which nothing greater can be conceived to exist, that it cannot even be conceived not to exist; and this being thou art, O Lord, our God.

9   So truly, therefore, dost thou exist, O Lord, my God, that thou canst not be conceived not to exist; and rightly. For, if a mind could conceive of a being better than thee, the creature would rise above the Creator; and this is most absurd. And, indeed, whatever else there is, except thee alone, can be conceived not to exist. To thee alone, therefore, it belongs to exist more truly than all other beings, and hence in a higher degree than all others. For, whatever else exists does not exist so truly, and hence in a less degree it belongs to it to exist. Why, then, has the fool said in his heart, there is no God (Psalms xiv. I), since it is so evident, to a rational mind, that thou dost exist in the highest degree of all? Why, except that he is dull and a fool?

St. Thomas Aquinas from *Summa Theologica*

THE COSMOLOGICAL ARGUMENT

10   The third way is taken from possibility and necessity and runs thus. We find in nature things that are possible to be and not to be, since they are found to be generated and to be corrupted, and consequently, it is possible for them to be and not to be. But it is impossible for these always to exist, for that which can not-be at some time is not. Therefore, if everything can not be, then at one time there was nothing in existence. Now if this were true then even now there would be nothing in existence, because that which does not exist,

begins to exist only through something already existing. Therefore if at one time nothing was in existence, it would have been impossible for anything to have begun to exist; and thus now nothing would be in existence—which is absurd. Therefore, not all beings are merely possible, but there must exist something the existence of which is necessary. But every necessary thing either has its necessity caused by another, or not. Now it is impossible to go on to infinity in necessary things which have their necessity caused by another, as has already been proved in regard to efficient causes. Therefore, we cannot but admit the existence of some being having of itself its own necessity, and not receiving it from another, but rather causing in others their necessity. This all men speak of as God.

William Paley from *Natural Theology*

THE TELEOLOGICAL ARGUMENT

11   In crossing a heath, suppose I pitched my foot against a *stone*, and were asked how the stone came to be there, I might possibly answer, that for any thing I knew to the contrary, it had lain there for ever: nor would it perhaps be very easy to show the absurdity of this answer. But suppose I had found a *watch* upon the ground, and it should be inquired how the watch happened to be in that place, I should hardly think of the answer which I had before given, that, for any thing I knew the watch might have always been there. Yet why should not this answer serve for the watch, as well as for the stone? Why is it not as admissible in the second case, as in the first? For this reason, and for no other, viz., that, when we come to inspect the watch, we perceive (what we could not discover in the stone) that its several parts are framed and put together for a purpose, e.g., that they are so formed and adjusted as to produce motion, and that motion so regulated as to point out the hour of the day; that, if the several parts had been differently shaped from what they are, of a different size from what they are, or placed after any other manner, or in any other order, then that in which they are placed, either no motion at all would have been carried on in the machine, or none which would have answered the use that is now served by it.

QUESTIONS ON MEANING

1. The key to understanding each argument rests in one's ability to break the argument down into its component premises and conclusions, both stated and implied. Thus, for each argument, create a list—perhaps in the form of a flow chart—showing how each argument develops, step by step. Do not use the author's words, but, when possible, put each statement into your own words.

2. What assumptions do Anselm, Aquinas, and Paley make about the nature of God? About the universe? About their audiences?

3. What is Anselm's definition of God? Is this a good definition? If not, how would you define God?

4. If one used a different definition of God than Anselm uses, does it affect the relative merits of the Ontological Argument in any way?

5. How does the example of the painter contribute to Anselm's argument?

6. What are *necessary* things, according to Aquinas? What are *possible* things? Why is this distinction crucial to his argument?

7. In logic, a *reductio ad absurdum* is a type of argument in which one proves something by showing how adopting the opposite position—that is, asserting the denial of the premise one wishes to validate—leads to an absurd conclusion. Which two of the arguments take the form of a *reductio ad absurdum*? For each of these two arguments, what (1) assumption is made, that leads to (2) what absurd conclusion? How is the third argument different?

8. What *analogy* is at the core of the teleological argument?

QUESTIONS FOR DISCUSSION

1. Which of the arguments do you find most persuasive? Which least persuasive? Why?

2. What flaws, if any, can you find in the logic of each of the three arguments? What counterarguments would you use to attempt to disprove each argument?

3. What are the strengths of each argument? What evidence or arguments could you use to help support each argument?

4. Do you believe, in principle, that it is possible to prove the existence of God, or is belief in God solely a matter of faith or of revealed religion?

5. The Teleological Argument has been very influential in recent years under the name of Intelligent Design theory. What is your opinion of the intelligent design movement?

6. If an agnostic was presented with these three arguments, do you think it likely that the agnostic would be persuaded to become a theist? Why or why not?

7. Do these arguments relate only to the possible existence of the Judeo-Christian God, or are they universal? Would these same arguments apply to the possible existence of any versions of God held by the major world religions?

LOOKING AT RHETORIC

1. Note that Paley, in his Teleological Argument, does not mention God at all. How is it that Paley is able to offer a proof for the existence of God without mentioning God?

2. Which of the three arguments is the easiest to understand? Which is the hardest to understand? What advice would you give the author of the least clear argument about how to improve the argument's clarity?

WRITING ASSIGNMENTS

1. Spend some time researching the history of one of the three arguments highlighted in this chapter. Draft an essay in which you discuss (1) the origination of the argument, (2) the various major challenges and revisions of the arguments over the years, and (3) the current thinking among philosophers and theologians regarding the merits of the argument.

2. Select one of the three arguments and draft an essay in which you attempt to explain or teach the argument to a general audience. For the purpose of this assignment, assume that members of your audience have high school diplomas, but likely have no familiarity with the argument.

3. In pairs or in groups, discuss the relative merits—and flaws—of each of the three arguments. Take note of the different opinions and arguments employed by the members of the discussion group. Try to determine, as a group, which of the three arguments it finds most convincing, and which least. Then, as an individual, draft an essay in which you either (1) lend your support, through argument, to the argument you find most convincing, or (2) demonstrate, through argument, why the argument you find least convincing fails as a reasonable and/or valid argument for the existence of God.

Interdisciplinary Connections

Theology and Cartoons

Questions of belief—particularly issues of religious belief—have been at the forefront of human consciousness for as long as there has been recorded human history and likely for many of thousands of years before that. It permeates every aspect of who we are and how we view the world,

The Theology of Calvin and Hobbes

http://www.bethelsf.org/neos/wp-content/uploads/2011/03/calvin_theology.gif

and, as a result, the questions it poses have been at the very center of philosophical investigation, and the nature of belief itself has been a matter of great concern to both philosophers and psychologists for generations. Here are two well-known cartoon strips from the twentieth century: Calvin and Hobbes by Bill Watterson, and Peanuts by Charles Schultz. As you study these two simple, four-panel cartoons, consider the philosophical and psychological implications of the questions these cartoons raise. What does it mean to have an evil nature, but not act on it? Is there a Heaven? What does it say about humans that they so often believe in a heaven? What if we're wrong?

Peanuts Theology

http://1.bp.blogspot.com/_iWEC7DSrC6Y/TUIMbSJQG3I/AAAAAAAAAFw/zBNpNjxJLbU/s320/
Peanuts%2BTheology%2BCartoon.gif

From *Cultural Universals and Particulars:* *An African Perspective*

Kwasi Wiredu

Kwasi Wiredu (b. 1931) studied philosophy at Oxford and taught at the University of Ghana for twenty-three years. During the mid-1980s, Wiredu held a number of different visiting professorships at a variety of universities in the United States and Africa. Eventually he accepted a post at the University of South Florida where he is the Distinguished University Professor of Philosophy, Emeritus. Over the course of his career he has established a reputation as one of the leading African philosophers. Among his works are Philosophy and an African Culture *(1980) and* Cultural Universals and Particulars: An African Perspective *(1996), from which the following selection is taken. In this reading, Wiredu takes up the relationship between culture and religion. By looking carefully at how beliefs are encoded into language, Wiredu examines some of the fundamental differences between Western concepts of religion and African—specifically, Akan—concepts. In making this comparison, Wiredu offers a new perspective on the distinction between the natural and the supernatural that is the heart and soul of many Western religious systems.*

UNIVERSALISM AND PARTICULARISM IN RELIGION FROM AN AFRICAN PERSPECTIVE

1   Is religion a field of convergence or divergence of thought among the peoples and cultures of the world? The obvious answer is that religion is both. There is also an obvious sequel: What are the specifics? But here an obvious answer is unavailable, at least as concerns Africa vis-à-vis, for instance, the West. In fact, it is not at all obvious in what sense the English word "religion" is applicable to any aspect of African life and thought.

2   In investigating this issue I am going to have to be particularistic. I am going to have particular, though not exclusive, recourse to the Akans of West Africa, for the considerations to be adduced presuppose a level of cultural and linguistic insight to which I cannot pretend in regard to any African people except the Akans, whom I know through birth, upbringing, reading, and deliberate reflective observation.

3   It has been suggested that there is no word in many African languages that translates the word 'religion.' It is certainly true of Akan, at least in the traditional use of that language. Not only is there no single word for religion but there is also no periphrastic[1] equivalent.

4   Religion, however it is defined, involves a certain kind of attitude. If a given religion postulates a supra-human Supreme Being, that belief must, on any common showing, necessarily be joined to an attitude not only of unconditional reverence but also of worship. There is a further condition of the utmost importance; it is one which introduces an ethical dimension into the definition. Essential to any religion in the primary sense is a conception

---

[1] Periphrastic: in a roundabout manner or through circumlocution; here, Wiredu means using multiple words in order to capture the essence of the single word *religion*.

of moral uprightness. If it involves supra-human beliefs, the relevant ethic will be based logically or psychologically on the "supra" being or beings concerned.

5　There is, most assuredly, no attitude or ritual of worship directed to that being either at a social or an individual level. They regard Him as good, wise, and powerful in the highest. He is the determiner of human destiny as of everything else. But in all this they see no rationale for worship. Neither is the Akan conception of morality based logically or even psychologically on the belief in the Supreme Being. Being good in the highest, He disapproves of evil; but, to the Akan mind, the reason why people should not do evil is not because He disapproves of it but rather because it is contrary to human well-being, which is why He disapproves of it in the first place.

6　The early European visitors to Africa, especially the missionaries, were quick to notice the absence of any worship of God among the Akans and various other African peoples. They were hardly less struck by the fact that God was not the foundation of Akan morals. On both grounds they deduced a spiritual and intellectual immaturity in the African. Notice the workings here of a facile universalism. It seems to have been assumed that belief in God must move every sound mind to worship. Yet, consider the notion of a perfect being. Why would He (She, It) need or accept to be worshipped? What would be the point of it? It is well known that the Judeo-Christian God *jealously* demands to be worshipped—witness the Ten Commandments—but, from an Akan point of view, such clamoring for attention must be paradoxical in the extreme in a perfect being, and I confess to being an unreconstructed Akan in this regard.

7　The class of extrahuman forces and beings is a feature of the Akan world view. There is, indeed, a great variety of such entities postulated in the Akan ontology. Some are relatively person-like; others, somewhat automatic in their operation. The former, it is believed, can be communicated with through some special procedures, and are credited with a moral sense. Commonly, a being of this sort would be believed to be localized at a household "shrine," from where it would protect the given group from evil forces. More person-like still are the ancestors who are thought to live in a realm closely linked with the world of the living.

8　Actually, the ancestors are conceived of as persons who continue to be members of their pre-mortem families, watching over their affairs and generally helping them. They are regarded as persons, but not as mortal persons, for they have tasted death and transcended it. For this reason, they are supposed to be more powerful than mortals. Additionally, they are considered to be more irreversibly moral than any living mortal. All these attributes are taken to entitle the ancestors to genuine reverence. Not quite the same deference is accorded to the first groups of beings, but they are approached with considerable respect.

9　The Akan attitude to the beings in question bears closer analogy to secular esteem than to religious worship. The reverence given to the ancestors is only a higher degree of the respect that in Akan society is considered to be due to the earthly elders. The ancestors are regarded as members of their families. Ancestorship is simply the crowning phase of human existence.

10　In English discourse about Akan thought the word "God" is routinely used to refer to this being.

11　Yet, in spite of any apparent similarities, the Akan Supreme Being is profoundly different from the Christian one. The Christian God is a creator of the world out of nothing. He is said to be transcendent, supernatural, and spiritual in the sense of immaterial, nonphysical. In radical contrast, the Akan Supreme Being is a kind of cosmic architect, who occupies the apex of the same hierarchy of being which accommodates, in its intermediate ranges, the ancestors and living mortals, and, in its lower reaches, animals, plants, and inanimate objects. This universe of being is ontologically homogenous. In Akan there is no way of speaking of the existence of something which is not in space.

12   In the Akan conceptual framework, then, existence is spatial. Now, since whatever transcendence means in this context, it implies existence beyond space, it follows that talk of any transcendent being is not just false but unintelligible, from an Akan point of view.

13   But not only transcendence goes by the board. Neither the notion of the supernatural nor that of the spiritual can convey any coherent meaning to an Akan understanding in its traditional condition. No line is drawn in the Akan world view demarcating one area of being corresponding to nature from another corresponding to supernature. A clear presupposition of Akan explanations of phenomena is that there are interactions among all the orders of existents in the world. Accordingly, if an event in human affairs, for instance, does not appear explicable in human terms, there is no hesitation in invoking extrahuman causality emanating from the higher or even the lower rungs of the hierarchy of beings. In doing this there is no sense of crossing an ontological chasm, for the idea is that there is only one universe of many strata wherein God, the ancestors, humans, animals, plants, and all the rest of the furniture of the world have their being.

14   Thus the reason why Akan explanations of specific things do not invoke God is not because He is thought to be transcendent or supernatural or anything like that but, rather, because He is too immanently implicated in the nature and happening of things to have any explanatory value. Still, in facing the cognitive problems of this world all the mundane theaters of being, human and extrahuman, are regarded as *equally* legitimate sources of explanation. Thus, if an Akan explains a mysterious malady in terms of, say the wrath of the ancestors, it makes little sense to ascribe to him or her a belief in the supernatural. That characterization is intelligible only in a conceptual framework in which the natural/supernatural dichotomy has a place. But the point is that it has no place in the Akan system of thought. We may be sure, then, that the widespread notion that Africans are given to supernatural explanations is the result of the superimposition of alien categories of thought on African thought-structures, in the Akan instance, at least.

15   But an interesting and important question arises. Suppose it is granted that the natural/supernatural dichotomy has no place in Akan and, perhaps, African thought generally. Does that not still leave the question of its objective validity intact? And, if it should turn out to be objectively valid, would it not be reasonable to think that it would be a good thing for Africans to learn to think along that line? My answer to both questions is affirmative, which implies a rejection of relativism.

16   My thesis is that there is such a thing as the objective validity of an idea. Were it not for the recent resurgence of relativism in philosophy, this would have been too platitudinous for words. Furthermore, and rather less obviously, if an idea is objectively valid (or invalid or even incoherent) in any given language or conceptual framework, both the idea and its status can, in principle, be *represented* in, if not necessarily translated into, any other language or conceptual framework.

17   A corollary of the foregoing contention is that, however natural it may be to think in one's native framework of concepts, it is possible for human beings to think astride

conceptual frameworks. A relevant question, then, is: "Do the Akans need to incorporate the natural/supernatural distinction into their modes of thought?" I think not, for not only is Akan thought inhospitable to this distinction but also the distinction is, in my opinion, objectively incoherent.

18   A supernatural event is one whose occurrence is contrary to the laws of nature. But if the event actually happens, then any law that fails to reckon with its possibility is inaccurate and is in need of some modification, at least. However, if the law is suitably amended, even if only by means of an exceptive rider, the event is no longer contrary to natural law. Hence no event can be consistently described as supernatural.

19   What of the notion of the spiritual? As can be expected from the spatial character of the Akan concept of existence, the radical dualism of the material and the spiritual can find no home in the Akan scheme of reality. All the extrahuman beings and powers, even including God, are spoken of in language irreducibly charged with spatial imagery. For example, an ancestor is believed soon after death to travel *by land and by river* before arriving at the abode of the ancestors. For this reason, in traditional times, coffins were stuffed with travel needs, such as clothing and money for the payment of ferrying charges. The practice was of a piece with the conception, and the conception is decidedly quasi-material.

20   I use the term 'quasi-material' to refer to any being or entity conceived as spatial but lacking some of the properties of material objects. The ancestors, for instance, although they are thought of as occupying space, are believed to be invisible to the naked eye and inaudible to the normal ear, except rarely, when they choose to *manifest* themselves to particular persons for special reasons. This is held to be generally true of all the relatively personalized forms of extrahuman phenomena.

21   It is apparent from what has just been said that if the extrahuman beings of the Akan world view are not fully material, they are not fully immaterial either. Further to confirm this last point, we might note that, although the beings in question are not supposed to be generally visible to the *naked* eye, they are widely believed to be perceivable to the superior eyes of certain persons of special gift or training. Whatever one may think of such claims, the conceptual point itself is clear, namely, that the extrahuman existents of the Akan ontology do not belong to the category of the spiritual in the Cartesian[2] sense of non-spatial, unextended.

22   After all the foregoing the reader is unlikely to be surprised to learn that the idea of creation out of nothing also does not make sense in the Akan framework of thinking. Nothingness in the Akan language is relative to location. The idea is expressed as the absence of anything at a given location literally, the circumstance of there not being something there.

23   The concept of creation in the Akan language is similarly non-transcendent. The Akan Supreme Being is a maker of things, but not out of nothing; so that if the word "Creator" is used for Him, it should be clearly understood that the concept of creation involved is fundamentally different from that involved in, say, orthodox Christian talk of creation. The Akan creator is the architect of the world order, but not the *ex nihilo*[3] inventor of its stuff.

---

[2]Cartesian: after Rene Descartes, in reference to Descartes' philosophical theory about the division in humans between the body and the mind.

[3]*Ex nihilo*: from nothing.

24   It is clear that the word "creation" should not be used in the context of Akan cosmology without due caution. It should be apparent also that considerable semantic circumspection is called for in using the word "God" for the Akan Supreme Being. Any transcendental inferences from that usage are misplaced.

25   So, then, we have the following picture of the outlook of the Akans. They believe in a Supreme Being, but they do not worship Him. Moreover, for conceptual reasons, this being cannot be said to be a spiritual or supernatural being. Nor is He a creator out of nothing. Furthermore, the foundations of Akan ethical life and thought have no necessary reference to Him. It will be recalled also that although the Akans believe in the existence of a whole host of extrahuman beings and forces, they view these as regular resources of the world order which can be exploited for good or, sometimes, for ill, given appropriate knowledge and the right approach. As for the ancestors, they are called upon to come and participate in all important ceremonies, but as revered members of the family, not as gods.

26   If we now renew the question of the applicability of the concept of religion to any aspect of Akan culture, we must be struck by the substantial differences between the Akan setup of cosmological and moral ideas viewed in relation to practical life, on the one hand, and Western conceptions of reality and the good life viewed in the same relation. For the purpose of this discussion the most important disparity revolves around the slicing up of human experience into the categories of the religious and the secular. To start from the Western end of the comparison: Whether we interpret the concept of the religious in a supernatural or non-supernatural sense, it is not a simple matter to discover an analogue of it in the traditional Akan context.

27   To the traditional Akan what gives meaning to life is usefulness to self, family, community, and the species. Nothing transcending life in human society and its empirical conditions enters into the constitution of the meaning of life. In particular, there is not, in Akan belief (in contrast, for instance, to Christian belief), any notion of an afterlife of possible salvation and eternal bliss; what afterlife there is thought to be is envisaged very much on the model of this life. More importantly, that afterlife is not pictured as a life of eternal fun for the immortals but rather as one of eternal vigilance—vigilance over the affairs of the living with the sole purpose of promoting their well-being within the general constraints of Akan ethics. Indeed, this is what is taken to give meaning to their survival. The inhabitants of the world of the dead, then, are themselves thoroughly "this-worldly" in their orientation, according to Akan traditional conceptions.

28   The Akan belief in the existence and power of such beings as the ancestors do not constitute a religion in any reliable sense. We are now, therefore, brought to the following conclusion: The concept of religion is not unproblematically applicable within all cultures, and Akan culture is a case in point. Nevertheless, there may be some justification for speaking of Akan religion in a broadened sense of the word "religion." In this sense the word would refer simply to the fact that the Akans believe in a being regarded as the architect of the world order. Certainly, this is an extremely attenuated concept of religion. Hence, if we do use the word "religion" in the Akan context we should evince some consciousness of the fact that we have made a considerable extension of meaning, otherwise we propagate a subtle misunderstanding of Akan and cognate cultures under the apparently widespread illusion that religion is a cultural universal.

29   Yet, surely, something must be universal. Consider the ease with which Christian missionaries have been able to convert large masses of Africans to Christianity by relaying to them "tidings" which are in some important parts most likely conceptually incoherent or, at any rate, incongruous with categories deeply embedded in indigenous ways of thinking. I take this as testimony to the malleability of the human mind, which enables the various peoples of the world to share not only their insights but also their incoherences. This characteristic of the mind, being fundamental to the human status, makes our common humanity the one universal which potentially transcends all cultural particularities.

QUESTIONS ON MEANING

1. What distinguishes the attitude of the Akans toward worship of the supreme being when compared with the typical Western attitude?

2. What is the Akan concept of *ancestorship*? What is the attitude of the Akans toward their ancestors?

3. How is the Akan term *wo ho* key to understanding the differences between the Akan and Western concepts of the supreme being?

4. What does Wiredu mean when he says he rejects relativism? How does this relate to his stated thesis that there is such a thing as the objective validity of an idea?

5. How is Wiredu's stated thesis illustrated in his essay? In other words, how does his explanation of the Akan concept of *wo ho*, for instance, serve as an illustration of the very principle he advocates?

6. What does Wiredu mean when he claims that the concept of the supernatural is objectively incoherent? How does he support this claim?

7. How is the Akan concept of the Oboade different from the Western concept of the creator?

8. What does the fact that so many Africans have converted to Christianity bear witness to, according to Wiredu?

QUESTIONS FOR DISCUSSION

1. Do you find the concept of the supernatural objectively incoherent? Why or why not? How would you support Wiredu's claim? How might you challenge it?

2. Does universal belief in something demonstrate the validity of the concept? What does Wiredu say about this question? What does he suggest about the belief in quasi-material entities? Can you think of other examples that might either confirm or challenge Wiredu's claim?

3. What does Wiredu's essay suggest about the challenges facing anyone seeking to communicate across cultural and linguistic boundaries?

4. In the course of his essay, Wiredu offers critiques of both Western notions of supernaturalism and Akan notions of ancestorship. What are these critiques? Do you agree with Wiredu's critique of Western supernaturalism? What about Akan ancestorship?

5. What is relativism? What do you think it means to be a *cultural* relativist? How about a *religious* relativist? Are you a relativist? Is Wiredu? What are some arguments for and against cultural and religious relativism? Can one be a religious relativist and an evangelist at the same time? Why or why not?

6. Akan cosmology poses a challenge, as Wiredu points out, to Cartesian dualism—the division in many Western world views between the mind and the body, the realm of the supernatural and the realm of the natural. Would you characterize yourself as a dualist? What is your conception of the supernatural? Does it conflict with the Akan concept? Given what you've learned in Wiredu's essay, how would you explain your concept of the afterlife to an Akan?

LOOKING AT RHETORIC

1. In this essay, Wiredu uses several Akan words as well as several specialized philosophical terms. Which does he do a good job of defining for his audience, and which does he assume his audience will already be familiar with? Does he do an effective job in defining difficult or unfamiliar terms? What strategies does he use to make these terms clear for his audience?

2. Take a look at the first and last paragraph of Wiredu's essay. How has his essay come full circle? What makes this an effective rhetorical strategy when drafting an essay?

3. Who is Wiredu's audience in this essay? How can you tell?

WRITING ASSIGNMENTS

1. Using library and/or Internet resources, investigate the concept of philosophical relativism. What does this concept mean? How is this concept applied to one's life or specific situations? Draft an essay in which you define relativism and either defend or challenge philosophical relativism. Spend some time in your essay focusing on Wiredu's claims about relativism and point out where you either agree or disagree with Wiredu.

2. Draft an essay in which you discuss how Akan would likely view the teleological, cosmological, and ontological arguments for the existence of God. Based on your understanding of Akan culture and language as presented by Wiredu, how might an Akan judge the merits of those arguments?

3. In pairs or in groups, discuss how one might explain the Western concept of the afterlife and the division between the spiritual and the natural worlds to an Akan. What would be the challenges and issues involved? Based on your understanding of Akan language and culture as presented in the Wiredu essay, as an individual, draft an essay in which you explain to an Akan audience the Western concept of the supernatural.

When 2 + 2 = 5

Robert A. Orsi

Robert Orsi (b. 1953) is currently a professor of Catholic Studies at Northwestern. He has also taught at Fordham University, Indiana University, and Harvard University. His work focuses on the cultural and social dimensions of Catholicism in America. His works include The Madonna of 115th *Street (1985),* Thank You, Saint Jude *(1996), and* Between Heaven and Earth *(2004). In the following essay, Orsi takes up the division between the Protestant and the Catholic worldview and how this distinction is rooted in conflicting views on the immanent and mysterious presence of the supernatural in the natural world.*

"Yet there was a time when the gods were not just a literary cliché, but an event, a sudden apparition, an encounter with bandits, perhaps, or the sighting of a ship."

—Roberto Calasso, Literature and the Gods

1   One of the greatest sources of violence in Western history has been the question of what Jesus meant when he said at the Last Supper, "This is my body." Catholics take this phrase literally and Protestants do not, and rivers of blood have flowed over this theological difference. During the Saint Bartholomew's Day massacre in 1572, the Seine turned red from the hundreds and hundreds of brutalized Protestant bodies thrown into it as it flowed out of Paris into the countryside. The youngest daughter of a Huguenot couple who were among the first to be murdered in the streets of Paris was dipped naked into her parents' blood, in a perverse rite of baptism, and warned not to become Protestant or suffer the same fate. Catholics endured equally horrible deaths. Among the more than 300 Catholics martyred in England between 1535 and 1679 was the Jesuit priest Father Edmund Campion. Hanged from a scaffold in 1581, Campion was disemboweled while still alive—his steaming entrails, flung by the executioner into a pot, splashed blood on the crowd crushing close. Then he was beheaded and quartered, and pieces of his body were shown at the four gates of Tyburn to warn off other Catholics.

2   The crime in these cases, in France and in England, was treason, but it is impossible to separate religious motivations in this period from political motivations. Catholic and Protestant missionaries, each determined to conquer the world for the true faith, carried this violence with them to the rest of the globe, including North America, where the question of what Jesus meant when he said "This is my body" got taken up in local histories and local conflicts.

3   This difference of theological interpretation is fundamental to the identities of these two divisions of the Christian world, and it is the pivot around which other differences, other identifications, accusations, lies, and hatreds have spun (and in some places at some times still spin). The basic differences between a religious ethos that is based on the real presence and one that is not are deep and consequential.

4   This divide between presence and absence, between the literal and the metaphorical, between the supernatural and the natural, defines the modern Western world and, by imperial extension, the whole modern world. Imagine one of my Italian Catholic grandmothers going to see a statue of the Virgin Mary in the Metropolitan Museum of Art. She climbs the museum's steep steps rising up from Fifth Avenue and pushes through the crowds and into the rooms of medieval art, where there are many lovely statues of the Blessed Mother, whom my grandmother knows and loves. My grandmother wants to touch the statues. She wants to lean across the velvet ropes to kiss their sculpted robes or to whisper her secrets and needs. But this is not how modern people approach art. For them, the statues are representations, illustrative of a particular moment of Western history and the history of Western art, and are to be admired for their form and their contribution to the development of aesthetic styles over time. There's nothing in them, no one there. The guards rush over and send my grandmother back out to the street.

5   This is a parable of two ways of being in the world: one associated with the modern (although this is complicated, clearly, since my grandmothers lived in the modern world after all, and you can find believers in cathedrals throughout the world today petitioning statues); the other with something different from the modern. One is oriented toward presence in things, the other toward absence. As the guard rushing over shows, the difference is carefully policed. Certain ways of being in the modern world, certain ways of imagining it, are tolerable and others are not. Especially intolerable are ways of being and imagining oriented to divine presence.

6   So Catholics have been ill at ease in the modern world. This does not mean, of course, that Catholics have not succeeded in contemporary societies, but it does mean that, until recently (and perhaps still now), Catholic life was lived askew to the modern world. Askew means, according to the Oxford English Dictionary, "obliquely, to one side, off the straight, awry." Askew-ness is neither radical antipathy nor complete contradiction (although at times it has become such). It is an acute and deeply consequential angle of difference to the modern world.

7   I have come to realize over the years, or perhaps I have only recently come to admit, how deeply formed I have been by this askewness and how much my thinking about history and culture has been shaped by it. This should have come as less of a surprise to me than it did. I went to Catholic elementary and high schools where first Franciscan friars and nuns of the order of Saint Vincent Pallotti, the Pallotines, taught me, and then the Jesuits. When I finally left this Catholic environment to go to college, my first encounter with the modern world was not a good one, especially in my religion major. Although I admired and loved my professors, I simply could not recognize in any of my religion classes anything that my family and I knew in the old neighborhood as religion. My world was either absent from what was being called religion in academic scholarship and theology or else it was identified as primitive, atavistic, folkloric—something of the past, not of the present.

8   Consider the phrase, "I am spiritual but not religious," which serves as a mantra of modern men and women in the United States. What does it mean to juxtapose "spiritual" and "religious" in this way? It means my religion is interior, self-determined, individual, free of authority; my religion is about ethics and not about bizarre events, and my ethics are a matter of personal choice, not of law; I take orders from no one. In the context of Western history, this means, "I am not Catholic." People who identify themselves this way are not anti-Catholic; many Catholics say it about themselves too. But buried deep in this phrase is a historical memory of the profound theological difference with which I began this essay.

9   The same can be said of religious studies as an academic discipline. The study of religion is a modern endeavor. As the theorist of religion Jonathan Z. Smith writes: "The term 'religion' has had a long history, much of it, prior to the 16th century, irrelevant to contemporary usage." Religion as we use the word today came of age at the dawn of the modern world, in the period of religious violence I have alluded to. Religion was fundamental to the modern world as it took shape in the West. But what is religion? The most influential contemporary account is that of the anthropologist Clifford Geertz. He defined religion in all times and all places as the human quest to live in a meaningful and ordered world. Meaning and order are enacted in the various religious rituals of different cultures, and participation in these rituals gives fundamental emotional and cognitive orientation to the

lives and imaginations of men and women. But how did we get from baptisms in blood to religion as moods, motivations, and meaning?

10   European intellectuals in the 17th and 18th centuries, exhausted by the long Christian blood feud that had consumed the continent in the previous century, sought an account of religion that would be conducive to civic peace, amenable to reason as reason was coming to be defined, and compatible with economic prosperity. Out of violence, in other words, came "religion" as we know it today: private, interior, ethically predictable, the guarantor of social order, rational, this worldly, and not supernatural. Religion defined this way became a central component of modern Western societies. (Think of the foundation of the new American state.)

11   But there are a few things to be said about this modern account of religion. First, as political theorist Anthony Marx has recently written, religious toleration was possible as an idea in the 17th century because the newly tolerant societies had already been purged of anyone in need of tolerance. It was not such a big deal to promote toleration in England after all the Catholics had been killed off, driven underground, or made to flee the country.

12   Second, religion, as it came to be defined, was constructed on the denial and repression of memories of religious violence. This has meant that modern theories of religion have been remarkably unable to consider religious violence, as was evident after 9/11. Willfully forgetting its origins in sacred savagery and ignoring the implications of its establishing and enforcing religious boundaries, religious theory stands mute before religious violence.

13   Finally, the modern Western account of religion, especially as it developed in religious scholarship in England and northern Europe, embodied within its questions, theories, and methods a deep and enduring anti-Catholicism. Early British scholars of the Catholic Middle Ages, in particular, had to be denied and forgotten, sealed off in the past. The so-called Dark Ages, that period between the purity of the early Christian church and the recovery of that original purity by 16th-century reformers—all that violence and authority, the obscene profusion of images and statues, relics and blood, monks and nuns, all that money in holy places, pilgrims on the roads, poor people praying for things, all that kissing and licking of sacred things, all those bodies doing things to themselves and each other in churches—all this needed to be exorcised from the notion of "religion."

14   Being Catholic turns out to be a good place from which to view culture and religion within the modern academy. Catholic experiences and practices that the modern world finds especially bizarre—the appearance of Mary on a hillside in southern France, a nun in modern America telling children the story she claims is absolutely true of a boy who puts a stolen consecrated host in a pot of boiling water and turns it into a cauldron of bubbling blood, or the written notes asking for better jobs or a happy marriage or a healthy child that petitioners leave near (and sometimes on) the statues of saints or the Virgin Mary—these things invite us (and compel me) to ask questions at odds with the assumptions and expectations of the intellectual disciplines of the modern world.

15   I, too, was trained in these disciplines, in a second formation no less profound than the first Catholic one, and I continue to operate within their constraints, even if restlessly so. My work is obsessed with boundaries, with what can be learned precisely from careful, critical attention to what happens when different worlds, different ways of imagining the

world, different ways of being, cross each other. And yet the Blessed Mother on a hillside, a child imagining a cooking pot overflowing with blood, a prayer to Mary for a better job—these things draw me on, and I wonder how to understand such realities within the limits of modern historiography and cultural studies. More to the point, I wonder how I can approach the reality of presence, so crucial to Catholic life, with the tools of modern intellectual culture, when it is precisely presence that modernity and modern religious theory most necessarily deny.

16   We think we know the answer to this already. Experiences of presence are delusions; children are susceptible to scary stories; desperate people do whatever they need to do to get comfort or relief. Furthermore, such experiences are shaped by class, race, gender, and by power generally. If you're poor and lack access to good health care, you're going to turn to the saints. We know this about religion. Among the poor and the marginal, who are more likely to experience presence than the rich and powerful, presence serves fatalistically to endorse and sustain the status quo. Sacred presence means the absence of real power.

17   So, we do know that certain dimensions of religious practice, imagination, and experience are central to the study of religion, as are issues of power (broadly defined). But the transposition so characteristic of modern analysis—religious practices are distorted refractions of the real circumstances of life (which are social, political, and economic)—eviscerates the reality of religious imaginings and experiences, and of religious presence; as it denies the accounts religious people give of their own lives.

18   Historicist interpretations give us predictable accounts of religion and culture: culture shapes religion, which in turn reflects culture, or, more radically, culture and religion are in symbiotic relationship, each constituting the other. But can we find the critical language to talk about how religious practices and imaginings can subvert this "given" that everybody knows, elude the limitations of our prejudices about social power, confound expectations, and transform lives and societies, for better and for worse?

19   In a stunning book of sermons, Oxford theologian Marilyn McCord Adams writes:

> Saint Paul says, the Spirit groans within us with sighs too deep for words, and we respond with babbling, even unconscious acquaintance. Like mother-love, the Spirit's presence strengthens, empowers us to grow and learn. Our Paraclete and inner teacher, the self-effacting Spirit, is ever the midwife of creative insight, subtly nudging, suggesting, directing our attention until we leap to the discovery that "2+2=5." Human nature is not created to function independently, but in omnipresent partnership with its Maker.

20   These sentences provoked me. I think of myself as an empiricist, but I want an empiricism capable of the world Adams describes in Saint Paul's words. I want an empiricism up to "the powerful reality of non-existent objects," in psychoanalyst Ana-Maria Rizzuto's phrase, an empiricism that takes history "to its limits in order to make its unworking visible" (meaning those experiences at the edges of culture and self that defeat what modern historical study is capable of) as historian Dipesh Chakrabarty writes. What I am searching for is a radical empiricism of the visible and invisible real.

21   This leads to a category of experience in history and culture that I will call "abundant events." Within the term "abundant events," I include relationships, responses to objects (such as a corpse or the Host), sense perceptions (the smell of sanctity, for example, or the

feel of blood), relations with special beings (among them the dead, ancestors, imagined-desired-feared persons, both real and imaginary), the experience of the body (such as it is experienced by sick people, for instance, or by the disabled, or by children, and by those experiencing the bodies of these others), and the work of memory.

22   Abundant events are characterized by aspects of the human imagination that cannot be completely accounted for by social and cultural codes, that go beyond authorized limits; by the "more" in William James's word by the "unthought known," a cultural experience of déjà vu or uncanny awareness of something outside us and independent of us, yet still familiar to us. Abundant events are saturated by memory, desire, need, fear, terror, hope or denial, or some inchoate combination of these.

23   What identifies an abundant event in history and culture? I will give five characteristics, in no particular order and not meaning to be exhaustive.

24   First, such events present themselves as *sui generis*[1]: people experience them as singular, even if they are recognizable within cultural convention—for instance, even if a culture prepares us for an encounter with witches, when the encounter happens, it is considered out of the ordinary.

25   Second, abundant events are real to those who experience them, who absolutely know them not to be dreams, hallucinations, delusions, or other kinds of sensory error, even though others around them may and often do contest this.

26   Third, abundant events arise at the intersection of the conscious and the unconscious and draw deeply on the resources of both.

27   Fourth, they arise at the intersection of past/present/future. At the moment of such an event we have a new experience of the past while at the same time the horizon of the future is fundamentally altered.

28   And fifth, abundant events arise and exist among people. They are inter-subjective (although this inter subjectivity may include the dead, for instance, or saints).

29   It is customary in the study of religion when we encounter people who have had experiences like this to say that these people believe what happened to them to be real and their belief in its realness is all that interests us. But belief has nothing to do with it, and in any case I want to move across this border in order to think about how the really real becomes so. The challenge is to go beyond saying "this was real in her experience" to describe how the real—whether it's the Holy Spirit at a Pentecostal meeting or the Virgin Mary on a hillside or a vision of paradise so compelling that people will kill for it—finds presence, existence, and power in space and time, how it becomes as real as guns and stones and bread, and then how the real in turn acts as an agent for itself in history. An abundant empiricism of the real allows us to probe the conditions of such creativity in culture, where 2+2=5, for better or worse, meaning that the sum of 2+2 can also be cruelty and violence, cultural dissolution as well as cultural innovation. Any understanding of such events is going to be incomplete and frustrating, and any analysis has to be honest about this.

30   Can we find in the languages of modern critical inquiry a way to understand the power and reality in history and culture of real presence?

---

[1] *Sui generis*: one of a kind.

QUESTIONS ON MEANING

1. What essential division between Catholics and Protestants does Orsi take as a launching point for his essay?

2. How have Protestants and Catholics responded to the modern world? How are these responses illustrated by their views on birth control and communion theology, among other things?

3. What does the word *askew* mean? How does this work characterize the Catholic relationship to modernity? How does Furfey's new social Catholicism illustrate this relationship?

4. What does it mean, according to Orsi, to self-identify as spiritual but not religious?

5. What is Tiele's thesis about the historical development of religion? What is Orsi's opinion of Tiele's thesis?

6. According to Orsi, why does being a Catholic give him a particularly valuable point of view on culture and religion in the modern academy?

7. How do the terms *presence* and *absence* characterize modern religion and culture? How do they inform Orsi's own work?

8. What does Orsi mean when he identifies himself as an empiricist? Why is that self-description complicated for Orsi?

9. How does the title When 2 + 2 = 5 relate to Orsi's essay? What do both Orsi and Adams mean by the phrase?

10. What is an abundant event? What are the five characteristics of an abundant event as identified by Orsi?

QUESTIONS FOR DISCUSSION

1. What is Clifford Geertz's definition of religion? Do you agree with Geertz? Does Orsi agree? If you disagree with Geertz, how would you define religion?

2. In the late eighteenth century, the creed of the Deistical Society of New York drafted by Elihu Palmer states that a religion characterized by persecution and malice cannot be of divine origin. What is your opinion? Do you agree with Elihu Palmer? What might Orsi say about Palmer's claim?

3. In your opinion, do the majority of major world religions practice and encourage religious tolerance today? Is western culture, in particular, more or less tolerant than during the historical moments mentioned in Orsi's essay? What would it mean to have a *truly* tolerant society? Is religious tolerance something that could be achieved, at least in theory? Why or why not?

4. Does Tiele's thesis about the development of religion strike you as accurate? What evidence can you cite to either confirm or challenge Tiele's claim?

5. Do you believe there are such things as abundant events? Why or why not? What might V. S. Ramachandran or William James say about abundant events?

LOOKING AT RHETORIC

1. Orsi begins his essay with some graphic imagery pertaining to a particular historical anecdote. What makes this an effective way to begin his essay? How does this introduction establish the major theme of the essay? What lessons does this suggest about what does or does not make for an effective introduction?

2. What is Orsi's thesis? What does he call for at the conclusion of his essay? How are these two things—his claim and his plea—connected? How does the structure of his essay lead the reader from one to the other?

WRITING ASSIGNMENTS

1. Spend some time researching the history and meaning of the doctrine of transubstantiation. Building on what Orsi has to say about this doctrine in his essay, draft your own essay in which you introduce your audience to this doctrine and discuss the major theological positions, debates, and issues surrounding the doctrine. Your goal in this essay is not to argue for or against the validity of the doctrine, but instead to inform your audience of the historical meanings and perspectives regarding the doctrine.

2. Spend some time in the library researching William James's characterization of the religious experience in *Varieties of Religion Experience* and well as Rudolf Otto's concept of the numinous in *The Idea of the Holy*. Draft an essay in which you compare and contrast Orsi's theory of the abundant event with James and/or Otto.

3. In pairs or in groups, make a list of six things that you have experienced, witnessed, or been told about by someone you trust, that Orsi would likely label abundant events. Discuss how these six events either do or do not meet Orsi's five criteria. Then, as an individual, draft an essay in which you evaluate Orsi's concept of the abundant event. In your essay, argue either for or against the usefulness of the concept for understanding certain types of phenomena.

Thinking Crosscurrently

PHILOSOPHY AND PSYCHOLOGY

The way we think about the world—our philosophy of life—is continually being influenced by our experiences. From grand events in our lives to the almost unnoticed details of daily life, everything we see, think, and do either influences the way we think about the world or is a product of our worldview. Sometimes our view of the world remains stable—perhaps for years, even decades, at a time. At other times, we feel almost intellectually disoriented by the influx of new ideas and new experiences. The classes we take, the friends we make, the things we choose to do or not do, the belief systems we adopt and the belief systems we reject—these are just a few of the key influences on our personal philosophies, and it is not uncommon for thinking humans to have far more questions than answers. As you think about the selections in this chapter, consider the following questions:

- How do developments in biology and the emerging possibilities for genetic engineering provide new insight into the possible creation of artificially intelligent computers? What perspectives might Francis Fukuyama or Michael Sandel or Robert Lanza bring to the issues raised by Alan Turing and Raymond Kurzweil?

- What is the relationship between information and communication theory and human psychology? In what ways do theorists such as Marshall McLuhan and Dick Hebdige borrow or rely on certain truths about human psychology? How are cultural critics such as Susan Willis and Susan Linn influenced by certain assumptions about human psychology? What do these authors seem to suggest about human psychology?

- If you had to put together a theory of human motivation—about the psychological urges, drives, and desires that compel humans to act the way they do—based only on your reading of the short stories by James Joyce, Herman Melville, James Tiptree, Jr., Bharati Mukerjee, and Kate Chopin, what would that theory be? Do these authors agree about what motivates humans to do what they do? Or, do they present different possibilities? If they disagree, which story seems most on the mark? Which furthest from the mark?

- Philosophy is not just about abstract ideas that seem removed from the realities of our daily lives. In fact, philosophy has a great deal to say about the practical aspects of our lives. Philosophy, for instance, has a great deal to say about the way in which we govern ourselves and behave toward our fellow humans. In what sense, for instance, can we read the selections by Thomas Jefferson and Henry David Thoreau and Mahatma Gandhi as philosophical statements about the nature of human life itself?

10 HISTORY AND CULTURE

What draws us to the past? Why do we find ourselves watching films about ancient Greece, historical figures like Alexander the Great, or mythical characters like Achilles? Perhaps it is the star power of Brad Pitt and Colin Farrell, but why did the Hollywood establishment assume we would flock to the theater to watch as they brought the distant past alive? History sells and compels, offering us the opportunity to travel, not just across space but through time.

From our earliest ages we are taken by stories of knights and heroes, princes and princesses, great cities and the dense forested landscapes of the past. As we grow, perhaps, our lives become active and present, and our daily hopes preoccupy us, but they are infused in strange and magical ways by the vague sense that we are who we are because of history and culture, and many of our desires are created by what we have taken from history and myth. The human past is a complex tapestry of nations, regions, and peoples as they blend, contend, interact, and influence one another, and culture is at the center of all of this.

The term *culture* has many meanings depending on the social context in which it is used. We sometimes refer to culture as a state of refinement, and a person who is cultured is learned, knowledgeable, possessing a love for the finer things in art, music, theatre, or in other areas involving developed taste. But more commonly we use the word culture to define aspects of our identity, as a set of influences that make the group we belong to different from others. We use the terms *youth culture*, *popular culture*, and *rural and urban culture*. We extend it even further into usages like "sports culture." Each of these groups is marked by patterns of behavior, slang, clothing, and usually some distinctive kind of music. Creative expression is the outward sign and inner source of cultural identity, and it binds members together and gives them a sense of belonging. We use the word *culture* in so many ways it becomes a dicey term, as it begins to lose its coherent meaning. But if we inquire into it we discover that all of these meanings have value.

History and culture are part of the same reality, because history records the evolution of *world* cultures, from the East in China and Southeast Asia, to the West in the great cathedrals of the Middle Ages, to the mysterious cave dwellings of brick and clay that give us a window into an ancient Anasazi civilization at Mesa Verde in Arizona. How did these people relate to one another? How did they marry? How did they organize their families and communities? How did they worship? What was their concept of their own origin? To study history and culture is to inquire into these subjects for no other reason than we are curious beings. We wonder about things. That is our nature. But we also study these topics because over the chasm of time we seek to know ourselves, and through the peculiar optic of a distant and unfamiliar people we see ourselves anew.

THE DISCIPLINE YOU EXPERIENCE

Perhaps in high school you played sports, played in a band, or acted in dramatic productions. You had certain interests, friends, a set of words and phrases used only by your group. More often than not you agreed on many things, engaged in the same activities for fun. At a deeper level, you felt you were at home with others who at their very core were like you, and maybe, hopefully, you felt a sense of place. The anxieties of young people learning about themselves and the world are mitigated, reduced just a bit because others seem to understand and accept them. Even if you weren't a member of one of these easily identifiable groups, perhaps you gathered with friends and shared things in common, and those things formed a collection of values. Sports, music, drama, or any group involve belonging, and these are the best of circumstances, but they aren't always true. Some people, young and old, feel disoriented and out of place, alone and misunderstood. Often this happens because they have not discovered themselves as social and cultural beings.

This is especially real for those who have recently immigrated to a place that is tremendously different from their home country. They were already immersed in a world they came to understand, through its language, religion, family patterns, communities, but all of a sudden they were in a realm in which they were the "other," different and alone. This is a uniquely modern experience, common in America, and immigration is full of trauma and possibility. Culture and identity is at the heart of it. It goes against our most cherished American ideal, individualism, that we derive our identity from others. But sociologists will tell us that to do so is natural. This doesn't make us slavish conformists, because we all play a small role in creating and changing group identity over time, in forming and reforming our societies large and small. But we are nevertheless part of a human situation larger than ourselves. If you were involved in sports you subscribed to a set of values that derive from the ancient Greeks, values that informed the original Olympic Games. You were also influenced by a military tradition with its ethics of valor and heroism. All of these codes came into play in competition on the field. If you were a rock musician, you derive aspects of your identity and outlook from a literary tradition defined by nineteenth-century Romantics, a group of rebellious poets who were the rock musicians of their time.

The cultures or in this case the *sub-cultures* (Hebdige defined this term in Chapter 8) we belong to are a vibrant reality of the present, born of time. Culture in its strictest anthropological definition is the set of values, beliefs, perception, and codes of behavior that define a particular people and a particular period in history. This appears in how they organize their families, communities, larger societies, and it manifests itself in their political systems and religions. To inquire into history is to take in the past for its own sake, but it is also the study of how these cultures changed and, in some cases, blended into our own active present. To study history and culture, then, involves the attempt to understand ourselves as human beings rooted in time, place, and society.

When we consider ourselves in these dense human contexts we begin to see that thinking about history and culture is quite pertinent and even practical, because it helps us know enough about ourselves to find our place in a world full of choices and possibilities, and in the end these inquiries can make us happier, more comfortable, more well-adjusted and self-actualized. But the process of understanding history and culture involves knowledge and expertise, and in the university, history and cultural studies have a dual alliance with the humanities and social sciences. History programs are quite common, and most universities offer the history major, sometimes in schools of humanities and sometimes in schools of social sciences. Cultural Studies is less common as an undergraduate major, but courses dealing with it exist within departments of history, sociology, anthropology, psychology, political science, philosophy, religious studies, art, theater, as well as English departments that explore works of literature as cultural artifacts. There is a broad array of topics involved. They include:

- World history and world civilizations, emphasizing ancient and modern cultures in the East and the West, both complex technological civilizations and less industrially advanced peoples.
- European history, often beginning with the Greek and Roman Empires and continuing with the rise of Christian Europe into the modern age.
- American history, beginning with the early exploration of the continent and continuing with the revolutionary period and the rise of the new nation, the dramatic changes in the nineteenth century, into the modern and contemporary periods.
- The history of political institutions from the ancient world to the present, including tribal societies, monarchies, kingdoms, and principalities, and the rise of modern democracies.
- Cultural history, which involves the evolution of geographically specific value systems, social mores and patterns of behavior, religions, art, and other aspects of culture.
- The study of race, gender, and ethnicity as defining features of human identity and self-understanding, including the history of racial and gender discrimination and oppression.
- Art history, involving the significant artists, movements, and works that are the outward expression of history.
- Popular culture, including contemporary music, film, and television, all of which provide a picture of modern tastes, preferences, viewpoints, and values.

There are a number of courses that deal with these areas of interest, such as Western Civilization, World History, American Institutions, History of Africa, Latin American History, Art of the Western World, Chinese Art, History of World Theatre, and World Religions. In the area of popular culture, there are courses such as the History of Rock & Roll, Film and Television, Jazz, Blues, and their roots. All of these courses combine to enhance and contribute to our understanding of the past as well as help us grasp the deeper meaning in the contemporary and popular art forms that define and move us.

REFLECTING ON THIS CHAPTER

Many important issues appear in the selections in this chapter, concerns that are a part of our daily lives as historical and cultural beings. As you read these sections, consider a set of broader questions:

- What are the central concerns of individual selections? What are the problems they identify and the solutions they offer, if any?

- What moral or ethical issues seem to concern authors? How do they want their readers to respond? In looking at history and cultural interaction over time, what changes are they hoping and arguing for, directly or indirectly?

- How do the ideas in these various selections compare and contrast? What central themes emerge? What human and social problems seem most pressing?

- Have your ideas and attitudes changed as a result of your reading? What topics and issues do you feel compelled to reconsider?

- What are the various writing strategies the authors employ? What tools do they use to persuade us? If you found a selection convincing, what made it so?

- Do you detect flaws in any of the arguments? Can you find any logical fallacies? Are there overt biases? Remember, a bias is not the same as a point of view. A strongly persuasive argument can be unbiased if it honestly presents and analyzes the available data and information.

The Coming Age

Jacques Barzun

Jacques Barzun (b. 1907) was born and raised in France among the artists and intellectuals of the modernist period. His parents sent him to America for his education, first at a preparatory school and then to Columbia College where he earned his Ph.D. in 1932. Founding the discipline of cultural history with its emphasis on the interrelationship of philosophy, religion, and the arts, he taught at Columbia College from 1928 to 1955. A prolific writer, Barzun's interests are eclectic, ranging from classical music to science and psychology, and in popular culture from detective fiction to sports. In the area of cultural history, he has written for both an academic and a general audience, and after retirement he undertook his most comprehensive project, From Dawn to Decadence: 1500 to the Present: 500 Years of Western Cultural Life *(2000). Dealing with the period from the Protestant Reformation to contemporary times, he posits a pattern of cultural evolution in which decadence marks the end of historical periods, providing the energies that create and motivate the future. Drawn from that monumental work, the following selection is from the final chapter of the book and is a hypothetical prediction of what the world will look like in the year 2300, given the conditions that exist today.*

1   *Herewith an undated and anonymous document from the late twentieth century. It is entitled "Let Us End with a Prologue."*

2   The shape and coloring of the next era is beyond anyone's powers to define; if it were guessable, it would not be new. But on the character of the interval between us and the real tomorrow, speculation is possible. Within the historian lives a confederate who is an

incurable pattern-maker and willing to risk the penalties against fortune-telling. Let the transitional state be described in the past tense, like a chronicler looking back from the year 2300.

3   The population was divided roughly into two groups; they did not like the word "classes.[1]" The first, less numerous, was made up of the men and women who possessed the virtually inborn ability to handle the products of *techne*[2] and master the methods of physical science, especially mathematics—it was to them what Latin had been to the medieval clergy. This modern elite had the geometrical mind that singled them out for the life of research and engineering. Lord Bacon had predicted that once the ways and biases of science were enthroned, this type of mind would be found relatively common. Dials, toggles, buzzers, gauges, icons on screens, light-emitting diodes, symbols and formulas to save time and thought—these were for this group of people the source of emotional satisfaction, the means of rule over others, the substance of shoptalk, the very joy and justification of life.

4   The mind was shaped and the fancy filled by these intricacies as had been done in an earlier era by theology, poetry, and the fine arts. The New Man saw the world as a storehouse of all items retrievable through a keyboard, and whoever added to the sum was in high repute. He, and more and more often She, might be an inventor or theorist, for the interest in hypotheses about the creation of the cosmos and the origin of life persisted, intensified, from the previous era. The sense of being close to a final formulation lasted for over 200 years.

5   It is from this class—no, group—that the governors and heads of institutions were recruited. The parallel with the Middle Ages is plain—clerics in one case, cybernists in the other. The latter took pride in the fact that in ancient Greek *cybernetes* meant helmsman, governor. It validated their position as rulers of the masses, which by then could neither read nor count. But these less capable citizens were by no means barbarians. To be sure, schooling would have been wasted on them; that had been proved in the late twentieth century. Some now argue that the schooling was at fault, not the people; but when the teachers themselves declared children unteachable, the Deschooling Society movement rapidly converted everybody to its view.

6   What saved the masses from brutishness was the survival (though in odd shapes) of a good deal of literature and history from the 500 years of Western culture, mingled with a sizable infusion of the Eastern. Some among the untutored group taught themselves to read, compiled digests, and by adapting great stories and diluting great ideas provided the common people with a culture over and above the televised fare. It was already well mixed and stirred by the twenty-first century. Public readings, recitals of new poems based on ancient ones, simple plays, and public debates about the eternal questions (which bored the upper class) furnished the minds and souls of the ordinary citizen. This compost of longings, images, and information resembles that which the medieval monks, poets, and troubadours fashioned out of the Graeco-Roman heritage. Religious belief in the two ages alike varied from piety, deep or conventional, to mysticism.

---

[1] Referring to the tendency in Western (especially American) culture to deny the existence of social classes under the false assumption that modern democracy has eliminated them.

[2] *techne*: derived from the Greek, meaning craftsmanship, craft, or art.

7   As for social organization, the people were automatically divided into interest groups by their residence and occupation, or again by some personal privilege granted for a social purpose. The nation no longer existed, superseded by regions, much smaller but sensibly determined by economic instead of linguistic and historical unity. Their business affairs were in the hands of corporation executives whose view of their role resembled that of their medieval ancestors. The accumulation not of territories but of companies and controls over markets was the one aim of life, sanctified by efficiency. The pretext was rarely borne out, but the game prospered and the character of the players followed another medieval prototype: constant nervousness punctuated by violent and arbitrary acts against persons and firms. Dismissals, resignations, wholesale firings of workers and staffs, were daily events. There being no visible bloodshed, wounds and distress were veiled. The comprehensive welfare system, improved since its inception, repaired the damaged. Its decisions being all made by computer on the basis of each citizen's set of identity numbers, there could be few tenable grievances. Those due to typing errors would be corrected—in time. There was thus no place for the citizen-voter and the perpetual clash of opinions that had paralyzed representative governments.

8   Not only was the goal of equality preserved but the feeling of it was enhanced. Faith in science excluded dissent on important matters; the method brings everyone to a single state of mind. On the workaday plane, the dictates of numerical studies guided the consumer and the parent, the old and the sick. The great era ended—by coincidence, no doubt—as it had begun, with a new world disease, transmitted (also like the old) through sexual contact.[3] But intense medical research in due course achieved cure and prevention, and the chief killer ailment was once more heart disease, most often linked to obesity. The control of nature apparently stopped short of self-control. But Stat Life, ensured by the many specialized government agencies, inspired successful programs and propaganda in many domains of the secure society. The moral anarchy complained of in the early days of the Interim rather suddenly gave way to a strict policing of everybody by everybody else. In time it became less exacting, and although fraud, corruption, sexual promiscuity, and tyranny at home or in the office did not disappear, these vices, having to be concealed, attracted only the bold or the reckless. And even they agreed that the veil is a sign not of hypocrisy but of respect for human dignity.

9   As for peace and war, the former was the mark that distinguished the West from the rest of the world. The numerous regions of the Occident and America formed a loose confederation obeying rules from Brussels and Washington in concert; they were prosperous, law-abiding, overwhelming in offensive weaponry, and they had decided to let outside peoples and their factions eliminate one another until exhaustion introduced peacefulness into their plans.

10   After time, estimated at a little over a century, the Western mind was set upon by a blight: it was Boredom. The attack was so severe that the overentertained people, led by a handful of restless men and women from the upper orders, demanded reform and finally imposed it in the usual way, by repeating one idea. These radicals had begun to study the old neglected literary and photographic texts and maintained that they were the record of a

---

[3] Probably a reference to AIDS, or Acquired Immune Deficiency Syndrome, which is a deadly and incurable disease that results from the HIV virus, often acquired from sexual activity.

fuller life. They urged looking with a fresh eye at the monuments still standing about; they reopened the collections of artworks that had long seemed so uniformly dull that nobody went near them. They distinguished styles and the different ages of their emergence—in short, they found a past and used it to create a new present. Fortunately, they were bad imitators (except for a few pedants), and their twisted view of their sources laid the foundation of our nascent—or perhaps one should say, renascent—culture.[4] It has resurrected enthusiasm in the young and talented, who keep exclaiming what a joy it is to be alive.

11   *It need hardly be pointed out that this anonymous author's extravaganza did not represent any body of contemporary opinion, only his own. Nor can it be ascertained when and on what grounds his vision of the future occurred to him.*

QUESTIONS ON MEANING

1. In Barzun's imagined future, what are the two groups that make up the populations of the Western world?
2. What will the illiterate and uneducated masses turn to in order to save themselves from brutishness?
3. What will replace the nation, which is defined by region and language, as the new unit of social organization?
4. What will happen to voting and democracy in this new Western culture?
5. Once it achieves equilibrium and a state of peace within itself, how will Western civilization respond to the violence in the rest of the world?

QUESTIONS FOR DISCUSSION

1. What are some of the current events and forces that make Barzun's imagined future possible? Does his prediction seem at all plausible?
2. Does it seem possible that democracy could be rendered largely obsolete?
3. Does is seem reasonable to speculate that there will be no more nation-states, that is, countries that are regionally defined? What might the world look like without them?

LOOKING AT RHETORIC

1. Why does Barzun choose to conclude his lengthy history of Western civilization in the last five hundred years with a playful prediction of the future?
2. How do historical facts, places, and periods work to reinforce Barzun's argument?
3. Barzun makes reference to observable historical trends today, globalization in economics, AIDS, peace initiatives in the West. How do they contribute to the potential legitimacy of his prediction?

---

[4]This reference to the discovery of the art of a previous age is a playful reference to the European Renaissance, a period beginning in the fifteenth and sixteenth centuries that marked the end of the Medieval Period and the rebirth of the art and ideas of ancient Greece and Rome. The modern period from the Renaissance to the present is the subject of the book from which this selection is taken. By referring to it in this manner, Barzun is predicting a time in which a new historical epoch will be born.

WRITING ASSIGNMENTS

1. Using library and/or Internet sources, research other historians who predict historical patterns in the future. Evaluate and consider Barzun's prediction. To what extent do current events make this prediction, or something like it, a reasonable conception of the future? In what way do contemporary events make it unlikely?

2. Argue for or against Barzun's speculation that there will be no place for the citizen-voter and the perpetual clash of opinions that [had] paralyzed representative governments?

3. In pairs or in groups, list a set of contemporary circumstances or events that define the modern moment in history. You might consider such things as globalization, the power of technological media, the internet, or anything else. Individually, write your own history of the future in the year 2300.

The Gettysburg Address
The Second Inaugural Address

Abraham Lincoln

Abraham Lincoln (1809–1865) was born in a log cabin in rural Hardin County, Kentucky. He was the sixteenth president of the United States, beginning as a country lawyer and rising to the highest political office by a series of unlikely circumstances. History has recognized his extraordinary intelligence, political wisdom, and ability to use language poetically and forcefully, which are all the more remarkable since he attended school for less than a year. He read intensely, however, teaching himself with The King James Bible, Aesop's Fables, *John Bunyan's* Pilgrim's Progress, *and later the works of Shakespeare, John Stuart Mill, and Lord Byron. Less than a month after his election to the presidency, seven states seceded from the Union and the American Civil War began. From early life into his political career, his antislavery position is clear, but as president he worked carefully to retain the loyalty of states that might have been lost if his abolitionist sentiments became too forceful. In the end, his efforts led to the Emancipation Proclamation and the Thirteenth Amendment to abolish slavery in the restored union. Barely a month after he began his second term, he was assassinated by the southern sympathizer, John Wilkes Booth. In "The Gettysburg Address," Lincoln commemorates the sacrifice of the soldiers in the context of a democratic imperative. In "The Second Inaugural Address," knowing that the war is near its conclusion, he ponders the causes, the nation's collective guilt, and the role of God in history. Both are highly refined pieces of rhetoric, demonstrating the role of literature and oratory in affecting historical change.*

ADDRESS DELIVERED AT THE DEDICATION OF THE CEMETERY AT GETTYSBURG, NOVEMBER 19, 1863[1]

1   Four score and seven years ago[2] our fathers brought forth on this continent, a new nation, conceived in Liberty, and dedicated to the proposition that all men are created equal.

---

[1] In *Lincoln at Gettysburg* (1992), Garry Wills makes the case that "The Gettysburg Address" is a speech written in the tradition of the "Oratory of the Greek Revival," using quite precisely the form of the Greek funeral oration.
[2] Four score and seven: eighty-seven.

2 Now we are engaged in a great civil war, testing whether that nation, or any nation so conceived and so dedicated, can long endure. We are met on a great battle-field of that war. We have come to dedicate a portion of that field, as a final resting place for those who here gave their lives that that nation might live. It is altogether fitting and proper that we should do this.

3 But, in a larger sense, we can not dedicate—we can not consecrate—we can not hallow—this ground. The brave men, living and dead, who struggled here, have consecrated it, far above our poor power to add or detract. The world will little note, nor long remember what we say here, but it can never forget what they did here. It is for us the living, rather, to be dedicated here to the unfinished work which they who fought here have thus far so nobly advanced. It is rather for us to be here dedicated to the great task remaining before us—that from these honored dead we take increased devotion to that cause for which they gave the last full measure of devotion—that we here highly resolve that these dead shall not have died in vain—that this nation, under God, shall have a new birth of freedom—and that government of the people, by the people, for the people, shall not perish from the earth.

Abraham Lincoln
1863

SECOND INAUGURAL ADDRESS, MARCH 4, 1865

4 At this second appearing to take the oath of the presidential office, there is less occasion for an extended address than there was at the first. Then a statement, somewhat in detail, of a course to be pursued, seemed fitting and proper. Now, at the expiration of four years, during which public declarations have been constantly called forth on every point and phase of the great contest which still absorbs the attention, and engrosses the energies of the nation, little that is new could be presented. The progress of our arms, upon which all else chiefly depends, is as well known to the public as to myself; and it is, I trust, reasonably satisfactory and encouraging to all. With high hope for the future, no predication in regard to it is ventured.

5 On the occasion corresponding to this four years ago, all thoughts were anxiously directed to an impending civil war. All dreaded it—all sought to avert it. While the inaugural address was being delivered from this place, devoted altogether to *saving* the Union without war, insurgent agents were in the city seeking to *destroy* it without war—seeking to dissol[v]e the Union, and divide effects, by negotiation. Both parties deprecated war; but one of them would *make* war rather than let the nation survive; and the other would *accept* war rather than let it perish. And the war came.

6 One eighth of the whole population were colored slaves, not distributed generally over the Union, but localized in the Southern part of it. These slaves constituted a peculiar and powerful interest. All knew that this interest was, somehow, the cause of the war. To strengthen, perpetuate, and extend this interest was the object for which the insurgents would rend the Union, even by war; while the government claimed no right to do more than to restrict the territorial enlargement of it.[3] Neither party expected for the war, the

---

[3]In the widely publicized "Lincoln-Douglas Debates," which took place in 1858 during his senatorial campaign against Stephen A. Douglas, Lincoln opposed the notion of popular sovereignty, which argued that new states entering the union could decide to permit slavery. He evoked the Missouri Compromise of 1820 (effectively repealed under the Kansas-Nebraska Act of 1854) which stipulated that Missouri would be the last state to enter as a slave state.

magnitude, or the duration, which it has already attained. Neither anticipated that the *cause* of the conflict might cease with, or even before, the conflict itself should cease. Each looked for an easier triumph, and a result less fundamental and astounding. Both read the same Bible, and pray to the same God; and each invokes His aid against the other. It may seem strange that any men should dare to ask a just God's assistance in wringing their bread from the sweat of other men's faces; but let us judge not that we be not judged. The prayers of both could not be answered; that of neither has been answered fully. The Almighty has his own purposes. "Woe unto the world because of offences! for it must needs be that offences come; but woe to that man by whom the offence cometh!"[4] If we shall suppose that American Slavery is one of those offences which, in the providence of God, must needs come, but which, having continued through His appointed time, He now wills to remove, and that He gives to both North and South, this terrible war, as the woe due to those by whom the offence came, shall we discern therein any departure from those divine attributes which the believers in a Living God always ascribe to Him? Fondly do we hope—fervently do we pray—that this mighty scourge of war may speedily pass away. Yet, if God wills that it continue, until all the wealth piled by the bond-man's two hundred and fifty years of unrequited toil shall be sunk, and until every drop of blood drawn with the lash, shall be paid by another drawn with the sword, as was said three thousand years ago, so still it must be said "the judgments of the Lord, are true and righteous altogether."[5]

7   With malice toward none; with charity for all; with firmness in the right, as God gives us to see the right, let us strive on to finish the work we are in; to bind up the nation's wounds; to care for him who shall have borne the battle, and for his widow, and his orphan—to do all which may achieve and cherish a just and lasting peace, among ourselves, and with all nations.

QUESTIONS ON MEANING

1. In "The Gettysburg Address," the Civil War comes as a test of what?

2. How significant does Lincoln assume his speech is? What does he argue is significant and why?

3. In "The Second Inaugural Address," why does Lincoln claim that his speech should be different from his "First Inaugural Address"?

4. What does Lincoln see as the primary cause of the war? Why, perhaps, did God permit the war to happen?

5. As the war comes to a close, how does Lincoln approach the issue of reconciliation?

[4] *The King James Bible*, Matthew 18:7.
[5] *The King James Bible*, Psalm 19:9.

QUESTIONS FOR DISCUSSION

1. Consider "The Gettysburg Address" in its entirety, but particularly the opening and closing. How does Lincoln seem to be defining democracy? Consider the relationship of the terms *freedom* and *equality*. How do they relate to one another? Are they in any way inherently in conflict?

2. In the third paragraph of "The Second Inaugural Address," Lincoln states that slavery is the primary cause of the war. Historians debate this point, raising the issue of state's rights. How reasonable is Lincoln's forthright claim?

3. In pondering the deeper cause of the war, Lincoln claims that history proceeds in accordance with divine principles of justice. Is this a pre-modern, antiquated assumption? Are there any rational or empirical reasons we should retain some aspect of this view?

4. Who is Lincoln addressing in the first paragraph of "The Second Inaugural Address"? How far-reaching do you think he hopes his words will be?

LOOKING AT RHETORIC

1. In "The Gettysburg Address" (which is a piece of spoken rhetoric in the classical tradition) Lincoln makes an appeal to truth (*logos*) and emotion (*pathos*). In what way does he balance these two appeals?

2. Consider the same question in "The Second Inaugural Address."

3. In "The Second Inaugural Address," Lincoln makes repeated reference to God's role in history. How effective might this be to less religious and more secular members of his audience?

WRITING ASSIGNMENTS

1. Define *freedom* and *equality* in political terms using library and/or Internet sources. Write an essay in which you explore how these ideals relate to one another in a democratic society. If and when they come into conflict, how do we deal with this problem?

2. Argue for or against Lincoln's claim in "The Second Inaugural Address" that mysterious reasons exist for the apparent evils that are a part of history.

3. In pairs or in groups, read each speech aloud. Make two lists in which you try to reconstruct the personality of the writer. Consider his beliefs, ideals, the character of his mind, even his mood in each speech. Individually, in essay form, write a mental biography, giving the reader a sense of Lincoln as a living and thinking human being.

Of Our Spiritual Strivings

W. E. B. Du Bois

William Edward Burghardt Du Bois (1868–1963) is one of the most influential African American intellectuals of the twentieth century. He received a bachelor's degree in 1888 from Fisk University in Nashville, Tennessee, an historical black college. He went on to Harvard University, studying for a time at the University of Berlin, earning his Ph.D. from Harvard in 1895. Racial discrimination prevented him from obtaining a permanent position at a major research institution, but he taught at Wilberforce College in Ohio and spent a year on temporary assignment at the University of Pennsylvania. He also served at Atlanta University. Trained in classical languages, he found himself fascinated with the burgeoning discipline of sociology, and he applied many of its principles to the historical experience of African Americans. He was the author of The Philadelphia Negro *(1899) and many other books, but he rose to national fame with* The Souls of Black Folk *(1903), which deals rigorously with the issue of race in the post-Reconstruction era and argues strongly for civil rights. The following is taken from the first chapter of* The Souls of Black Folk. *Du Bois explores the "two-ness," of the black experience, in which the African American must contend with his conflicted identity as American and Negro. The book is both a work of literary art and a fascinating sociological and psychological inquiry. Du Bois posits his notion of double-consciousness, which became perhaps the most important concept in the study of race in the last century.*

Of Our Spiritual Strivings

O water, voice of my heart, crying in the sand,
  All night long crying with a mournful cry,
As I lie and listen, and cannot understand
    The voice of my heart in my side or the voice of the sea,
  O water, crying for rest, is it I, is it I?
  All night long the water is crying to me.

Unresting water, there shall never be rest
  Till the last moon droop and the last tide fail,
And the fire of the end begin to burn in the west;
    And the heart shall be weary and wonder and cry like the sea,
  All life long crying without avail,
    As the water all night long is crying to me.

Arthur Symons[1]

1   Between me and the other world there is ever an unasked question: unasked by some through feelings of delicacy; by others through the difficulty of rightly framing it. All, nevertheless, flutter round it. They approach me in a half-hesitant sort of way, eye me curiously or compassionately, and then, instead of saying directly, How does it feel to be a problem? they say, I know an excellent colored man in my town; or, I fought at Mechanicsville;[2] or, Do not these Southern outrages make your blood boil? At these I smile, or am interested, or reduce the boiling to a simmer, as the occasion may require. To the real question, How does it feel to be a problem? I answer seldom a word.

2   And yet, being a problem is a strange experience—peculiar even for one who has never been anything else, save perhaps in babyhood and in Europe. It is in the early days of rollicking boyhood that the revelation first bursts upon one, all in a day, as it were.

---

[1] Arthur Symons (1865–1945): English poet. The quotation is from "The Crying of Water."

[2] Mechanicsville: American Civil War battle fought in Virginia on June 26, 1862, in which there were large Confederate losses.

I remember well when the shadow swept across me. I was a little thing, away up in the hills of New England, where the dark Housatonic winds between Hoosac and Taghkanic[3] to the sea. In a wee wooden schoolhouse, something put it into the boys' and girls' heads to buy gorgeous visiting-cards—ten cents a package—and exchange. The exchange was merry, till one girl, a tall newcomer, refused my card—refused it peremptorily, with a glance. Then it dawned upon me with a certain suddenness that I was different from the others; or like, may-hap, in heart and life and longing, but shut out from their world by a vast veil. I had thereafter no desire to tear down that veil, to creep through; I held all beyond it in common contempt, and lived above it in a region of blue sky and great wandering shadows. That sky was bluest when I could beat my mates at examination-time, or beat them at a foot-race, or even beat their stringy heads. Alas, with the years all this fine contempt began to fade; for the worlds I longed for, and all their dazzling opportunities, were theirs, not mine. But they should not keep these prizes, I said; some, all, I would wrest from them. Just how I would do it I could never decide: by reading law, by healing the sick, by telling the wonderful tales that swam in my head—some way. With other black boys the strife was not so fiercely sunny: their youth shrunk into tasteless sycophancy, or into silent hatred of the pale world about them and mocking distrust of everything white; or wasted itself in a bitter cry, Why did God make me an outcast and a stranger in mine own house? The shades of the prison-house closed round about us all: walls strait and stubborn to the whitest, but relentlessly narrow, tall, and unscalable to sons of night who must plod darkly on in resignation, or beat unavailing palms against the stone, or steadily, half hopelessly, watch the streak of blue above.

3   After the Egyptian and Indian, the Greek and Roman, the Teuton and Mongolian, the Negro is a sort of seventh son, born with a veil, and gifted with second-sight in this American world—a world which yields him no true self-consciousness, but only lets him see himself through the revelation of the other world. It is a peculiar sensation, this double-consciousness, this sense of always looking at one's self through the eyes of others, of measuring one's soul by the tape of a world that looks on in amused contempt and pity. One ever feels his two-ness—an American, a Negro; two souls, two thoughts, two unreconciled strivings; two warring ideals in one dark body, whose dogged strength alone keeps it from being torn asunder.

4   The history of the American Negro is the history of this strife—this longing to attain self-conscious manhood, to merge his double self into a better and truer self. In this merging he wishes neither of the older selves to be lost. He would not Africanize America, for America has too much to teach the world and Africa. He would not bleach his Negro soul in a flood of white Americanism, for he knows that Negro blood has a message for the world. He simply wishes to make it possible for a man to be both a Negro and an American, without being cursed and spit upon by his fellows, without having the doors of Opportunity closed roughly in his face.

5   This, then, is the end of his striving: to be a co-worker in the kingdom of culture, to escape both death and isolation, to husband and use his best powers and his latent genius. These powers of body and mind have in the past been strangely wasted, dispersed, or forgotten.

---

[3] Housatonic, Hoosac, Taghkanic: Referring to the winds from the Housatonic River in western Massachusetts and two mountain ranges in Massachusetts and Vermont.

The shadow of a mighty Negro past flits through the tale of Ethiopia the Shadowy and of Egypt the Sphinx. Throughout history, the powers of single black men flash here and there like falling stars, and die sometimes before the world has rightly gauged their brightness. Here in America, in the few days since Emancipation, the black man's turning hither and thither in hesitant and doubtful striving has often made his very strength to lose effectiveness, to seem like absence of power, like weakness. And yet it is not weakness—it is the contradiction of double aims. The double-aimed struggle of the black artisan—on the one hand to escape white contempt for a nation of mere hewers of wood and drawers of water, and on the other hand to plough and nail and dig for a poverty-stricken horde—could only result in making him a poor craftsman, for he had but half a heart in either cause. By the poverty and ignorance of his people, the Negro minister or doctor was tempted toward quackery and demagogy; and by the criticism of the other world, toward ideals that made him ashamed of his lowly tasks. The would-be black *savant*[4] was confronted by the paradox that the knowledge his people needed was a twice-told tale to his white neighbors, while the knowledge which would teach the white world was Greek to his own flesh and blood. The innate love of harmony and beauty that set the ruder souls of his people a-dancing and a-singing raised but confusion and doubt in the soul of the black artist; for the beauty revealed to him was the soul-beauty of a race which his larger audience despised, and he could not articulate the message of another people. This waste of double aims, this seeking to satisfy two unreconciled ideals, has wrought sad havoc with the courage and faith and deeds of ten thousand thousand people—has sent them often wooing false gods and invoking false means of salvation, and at times has even seemed about to make them ashamed of themselves.

6   Away back in the days of bondage they thought to see in one divine event the end of all doubt and disappointment; few men ever worshipped Freedom with half such unquestioning faith as did the American Negro for two centuries. To him, so far as he thought and dreamed, slavery was indeed the sum of all villainies, the cause of all sorrow, the root of all prejudice; Emancipation was the key to a promised land of sweeter beauty than ever stretched before the eyes of wearied Israelites. In song and exhortation swelled one refrain—Liberty; in his tears and curses the God he implored had Freedom in his right hand. At last it came—suddenly, fearfully, like a dream. With one wild carnival of blood and passion came the message in his own plaintive cadences:—

> *"Shout, O children!*
> *Shout, you're free!*
> *For God has bought your liberty!"*[5]

7   Years have passed away since then—ten, twenty, forty; forty years of national life, forty years of renewal and development, and yet the swarthy spectre sits in its accustomed seat at the Nation's feast. In vain do we cry to this our vastest social problem:—

> *"Take any shape but that, and my firm nerves*
> *Shall never tremble!"*[6]

---

[4]*savant*: a highly gifted and/or learned person.
[5]Seemingly lyrics from a "Negro Spiritual." The source is unidentified.
[6]From William Shakespeare's *Macbeth*, Act III, Scene Two, Line 99.

8   The Nation has not yet found peace from its sins; the freedman has not yet found in freedom his promised land. Whatever of good may have come in these years of change, the shadow of a deep disappointment rests upon the Negro people—a disappointment all the more bitter because the unattained ideal was unbounded save by the simple ignorance of a lowly people.

9   The first decade was merely a prolongation of the vain search for freedom, the boon that seemed ever barely to elude their grasp—like a tantalizing will-o'-the-wisp, maddening and misleading the headless host. The holocaust of war, the terrors of the Ku-Klux Klan, the lies of carpetbaggers,[7] the disorganization of industry, and the contradictory advice of friends and foes, left the bewildered serf with no new watchword beyond the old cry for freedom. As the time flew, however, he began to grasp a new idea. The ideal of liberty demanded for its attainment powerful means, and these the Fifteenth Amendment[8] gave him. The ballot, which before he had looked upon as a visible sign of freedom, he now regarded as the chief means of gaining and perfecting the liberty with which war had partially endowed him. And why not? Had not votes made war and emancipated millions? Had not votes enfranchised the freedmen? Was anything impossible to a power that had done all this? A million black men started with renewed zeal to vote themselves into the kingdom. So the decade flew away, the revolution of 1876[9] came, and left the half-free serf weary, wondering, but still inspired. Slowly but steadily, in the following years, a new vision began gradually to replace the dream of political power—a powerful movement, the rise of another ideal to guide the unguided, another pillar of fire by night after a clouded day. It was the ideal of "book-learning;" the curiosity, born of compulsory ignorance, to know and test the power of the cabalistic[10] letters of the white man, the longing to know. Here at last seemed to have been discovered the mountain path to Canaan;[11] longer than the highway of Emancipation and law, steep and rugged, but straight, leading to heights high enough to overlook life.

10   Up the new path the advance guard toiled, slowly, heavily, doggedly; only those who have watched and guided the faltering feet, the misty minds, the dull understandings, of the dark pupils of these schools know how faithfully, how piteously, this people strove to learn. It was weary work. The cold statistician wrote down the inches of progress here and there, noted also where here and there a foot had slipped or some one had fallen. To the tired climbers, the horizon was ever dark, the mists were often cold, the Canaan was always dim and far away. If, however, the vistas disclosed as yet no goal, no resting-place, little but flattery and criticism, the journey at least gave leisure for reflection and self-examination; it changed the child of Emancipation to the youth with dawning

---

[7] carpetbaggers: a term often used to describe northerners who came to the South during Reconstruction to unjustly exploit economic opportunities that emerged from unjust governmental policies.

[8] Fifteenth Amendment: Passed in 1870, the amendment to the American Constitution that mandated the voting rights of African American men.

[9] 1876: A reference to a congressional battle against oppressive Reconstruction policies. This opposition took place after the national elections of 1876.

[10] cabalistic: language that is difficult to understand, often with a mystical quality.

[11] Canaan: The Promised Land of the Ancient Israelites, foreshadowed in the *Book of Genesis* in the convenant with Abraham, and openly promised in the *Book of Exodus* to Moses.

self-consciousness, self-realization, self-respect. In those sombre forests of his striving his own soul rose before him, and he saw himself—darkly as through a veil; and yet he saw in himself some faint revelation of his power, of his mission. He began to have a dim feeling that, to attain his place in the world, he must be himself, and not another. For the first time he sought to analyze the burden he bore upon his back, that dead-weight of social degradation partially masked behind a half-named Negro problem. He felt his poverty; without a cent, without a home, without land, tools, or savings, he had entered into competition with rich, landed, skilled neighbors. To be a poor man is hard, but to be a poor race in a land of dollars is the very bottom of hardships. He felt the weight of his ignorance—not simply of letters, but of life, of business, of the humanities; the accumulated sloth and shirking and awkwardness of decades and centuries shackled his hands and feet. Nor was his burden all poverty and ignorance. The red stain of bastardy, which two centuries of systematic legal defilement of Negro women had stamped upon his race, meant not only the loss of ancient African chastity, but also the hereditary weight of a mass of corruption from white adulterers, threatening almost the obliteration of the Negro home.

11   A people thus handicapped ought not to be asked to race with the world, but rather allowed to give all its time and thought to its own social problems. But alas! while sociologists gleefully count his bastards and his prostitutes, the very soul of the toiling, sweating black man is darkened by the shadow of a vast despair. Men call the shadow prejudice, and learnedly explain it as the natural defence of culture against barbarism, learning against ignorance, purity against crime, the "higher" against the "lower" races. To which the Negro cries Amen! and swears that to so much of this strange prejudice as is founded on just homage to civilization, culture, righteousness, and progress, he humbly bows and meekly does obeisance. But before that nameless prejudice that leaps beyond all this he stands helpless, dismayed, and well-nigh speechless; before that personal disrespect and mockery, the ridicule and systematic humiliation, the distortion of fact and wanton license of fancy, the cynical ignoring of the better and the boisterous welcoming of the worse, the all-pervading desire to inculcate disdain for everything black, from Toussaint[12] to the devil,—before this there rises a sickening despair that would disarm and discourage any nation save that black host to whom "discouragement" is an unwritten word.

12   But the facing of so vast a prejudice could not but bring the inevitable self-questioning, self-disparagement, and lowering of ideals which ever accompany repression and breed in an atmosphere of contempt and hate. Whisperings and portents came borne upon the four winds: Lo! we are diseased and dying, cried the dark hosts; we cannot write, our voting is vain; what need of education, since we must always cook and serve? And the Nation echoed and enforced this self-criticism, saying: Be content to be servants, and nothing more; what need of higher culture of half-men?

---

[12] Francois Dominique Touissant L'Ouverture (1743–1803): Haitian soldier born as a slave, martyred in the liberation of Haiti. Du Bois himself was of Haitian descent.

QUESTIONS ON MEANING

1. What did Du Bois experience as a child in school that first taught him that he was different?

2. How did Du Bois respond to that experience and how was his response different than many other African American children?

3. What does Du Bois mean by double-consciousness?

4. In the context of African American life, what does every African American naturally want, in specific terms?

5. What was the new idea that African Americans slowly began to grasp after Emancipation?

6. What attribute more than any other must African Americans develop to achieve the ideal of freedom they hope for?

QUESTIONS FOR DISCUSSION

1. What does Du Bois mean by the terms *two-ness* and *double consciousness*? Are these notions only applicable to African Americans, women, and other ethnic groups? Might they have a broader application?

2. The author speaks of the Negro's longing in collective terms, as if their experiences and thoughts are shared. Given the history of race relations in America, is this a reasonable assumption?

3. To what degree is education the key to freedom in a democracy, for anyone regardless of race?

4. To what extent does oppression lead to collective wisdom, as Du Bois contends?

LOOKING AT RHETORIC

1. Trace the metaphor of the veil. How does it work and how does it serve to clarify Du Bois's notion of two-ness and double consciousness?

2. Du Bois makes use of frequent quotes from the verses of folk songs as well as from the English poetic tradition in writers such as Shakespeare. In what way do they serve his purpose and main idea? Why does he choose to use and blend them?

3. Du Bois treats the large and geographically diverse populations of African Americans as one evolving mind. To what extent is this accurate and fair? How does it function as a rhetorical strategy?

WRITING ASSIGNMENTS

1. Using library and/or Internet sources, explore how personal identity is formed in a culture. Identify two groups of which you are a part. Consider how they define you, how they give you a sense of who you are. They could be defined by your age, your gender, your ethnicity, shared interests such as sports or music, even your religion. Write an essay about the conflicts that emerge from these two identities. In this essay, consider the validity of Du Bois's concept of double consciousness.

2. Argue for or against Du Bois' assumption of a collective and historically evolving African American consciousness.

3. In pairs or in groups, select three passages from the Du Bois reading that carried the main idea most effectively. Discuss why they did so, considering both the logical and emotional appeals he makes. Individually, write a brief essay in which you use one of the paragraphs as a model. Choose an issue that is important to you and make an argument for change.

Interdisciplinary Connections

Images of the American Civil War

More Americans died in combat during the American Civil War (over 600,000) than in all other wars America has participated in combined. Below are two images from 1862. The first depicts the stark reality of the bloody aftermath of warfare. The second depicts President Lincoln standing with two of his top military commanders. What do these images say about the nature of war? Which is the more powerful image? Which is the more disturbing? Are there times in history when war is justified? What causes would compel you to go to war? What causes would compel you to rebel against your own country? Would you be willing to use a weapon against your friends and family in the defense of an idea? What does that say about the power of ideas? What does it say about the power of a social consciousness?

Alexander Gardener's Photograph of Dead Confederate Soldiers at Antietam, 1862
http://updatedfrequently.com/top-20-great-us-civil-war-photographs

President Abraham Lincoln at Sharpsburg, Maryland, 1862. Lincoln is pictured standing with Major Alan Pinkerton and General John McClernand, two union officers.

http://www.civil-war.net/cw_images/files/images/285.jpg

In the Brown Study

Richard Rodriguez

Richard Rodriguez (b. 1944) was born in San Francisco to an immigrant family from Mexico, and he has spent his career writing and teaching about his Hispanic heritage and the complex identity of ethnic minorities in America, as well as the varied experiences of immigrant peoples. He received his B.A from Stanford University and his M.A. from Columbia University. Originally planning to pursue an academic career in Renaissance Studies, he decided to undertake a career outside the university. He began as a freelance writer, and he came to national attention in 1982 with Hunger of Memory: The Education of Richard Rodriguez, *which explores the tensions inherent in the process of assimilating a Spanish-speaking Mexican culture with an English-speaking American society. He is critical of affirmative action and bilingual education, and in exploring the complexities of race relations in a multi-ethnic America, he attempts to negotiate the tension between group and national identity. Rodriguez is one of the most well-known writers on the subjects of immigration, ethnicity, and race in modern times. The following selection, taken from the second chapter from his 2002 book,* Brown, *evokes the color itself, alluding to its implications as a marker of ethnic identity.*

1   Or, as a brown man, I think.

2   But do we really think that color colors thought? Sherlock Holmes occasionally retired into a "brown study"—a kind of moribund funk; I used to imagine a room with brown wallpaper. I think, too, of the process—the plunger method—by which coffee sometimes is brewed. The grounds commingle with water for a time and then are pressed to the bottom of the carafe by a disk or plunger. The liquid, cleared of sediment, is nevertheless colored; substantially coffee. (And coffee-colored has come to mean coffee-and-cream-colored; and coffee with the admixture of cream used to be called "blond." And vanilla has come to mean white, bland, even though vanilla extract, to the amazement of children, is brown as iodine and "vanilla-colored," as in Edith Sitwell's[1] *where vanilla-coloured ladies ride* refers to Manila and to brown skin.) In the case of brown thought, though, I suppose experience becomes the pigment, the grounds, the *mise-en-scène*, the medium of refraction, the impeded passage of otherwise pure thought.

3   In a fluorescent-lit jury room, attached to a superior court in San Francisco, two jurors were unconvinced and unmoving. I was unconvinced because of the gold tooth two bank tellers had noticed and of which the defendant had none. The other juror was a man late in his twenties, rather preppy I thought on first meeting, who prefaced his remarks with, "As a black man I think . . . "

4   I have wondered, ever since, if that were possible. If I do have brown thoughts.

5   Not brown enough. I was once taken to task—rather, I was made an example of—by that woman from the *Threepenny Review*[2] as the sort of writer, the callow, who parades his

---

[1] Edith Sitwell (1887–1964): British poet and critic.
[2] *Threepenny Review*: American literary magazine published in Berkeley, California.

education. I use literary allusion as a way of showing off, proof that I have mastered a white idiom, but do not have the confidence of it; whereas the true threepenny intellectual assumes everybody knows everything, or doesn't, or can't, or shouldn't, or needn't, and there you are. Which makes me a sort of monkey-do.[3]

6   Was I too eager to join the conversation? It is only now I realize there is no conversation. Allusion is bounded by Spell Check.

7   After such a long education most perceptions authentically "remind." And I'm not the only one. The orb Victoria[4] held in her hand has passed to her brown children who, like Christ-children in old paintings, toy with the world a bit, and then, when no one is looking, pop it into their mouths. The only person I know for whom the novels of Trollope[5] are urgent lives in India.

8   It is interesting, too, to wonder whether what is white about my thought is impersonation, minstrelsy. Is allusion inauthentic, Ms. Interlocutor, when it comes from a brown sensibility? My eyes are brown. *Cheeks of tan?*

9   Most bookstores have replaced disciplinary categories with racial or sexual identification. In either case I must be shelved Brown. The most important theme of my writing now is impurity. My mestizo boast: As a queer Catholic Indian Spaniard at home in a temperate Chinese city in a fading blond state in a post-Protestant nation, I live up to my sixteenth-century birth.

10   The future is brown, is my thesis; is as brown as the tarnished past. Brown may be as refreshing as green. We shall see. L.A., unreal city,[6] is brown already, though it wasn't the other day I was there—it was rain-rinsed and as bright as a dark age. But on many days, the air turns fuscous from the scent glands of planes and from Lexus musk. The pavements, the palisades—all that jungly stuff one sees in the distance—are as brown as an oxidized print of a movie—brown as old Roman gardens or pennies in a fountain, brown as gurgled root beer, tobacco, monkey fur, catarrh.

11   We are accustomed, too, to think of antiquity as brown, browning. Darkening, as memory darkens; as the Dark Ages were dark. They weren't, of course, they were highly painted and rain-rinsed; we just don't remember clearly. I seem to remember the ceiling, how dark it was. How tall it seemed. The kitchen ceiling. And how frail we are! What used to be there? A shoe store? A newsstand? I seem to remember it, right about here . . . a red spine, wasn't it? Have I felt that before? Or is this cancer?

12   At last, the white thought, the albin pincer—pain—an incipient absence, like a puddle of milk or the Milky Way. *The glacier knocks in the cupboard.* Why is cancer the white ghost? Why are ghosts white? And what year was that? Which play? Well, obviously it's Shakespeare. *Lear? Cymbeline? Golden lads and girls all must* . . . Death is black. Coffee may be black, but black is not descriptive of coffee. Coffee is not descriptive of death. Can one's life

---

[3] monkey-do: implying thoughtless imitation.

[4] Victoria: a reference to Victoria (1819–1901), Queen of Great Britain from 1837–1901. The Victorian Age, a time of great social, scientific, and industrial progress coincides with her reign.

[5] Anthony Trollope (1815–1882): English novelist of the Victorian Age, whose works dealt with politics, social change, and gender, among other issues.

[6] unreal city: allusion to T.S. Eliot's (1888–1965) poem "The Waste Land" (1922), one of the most important poems of the modernist period in art and literature.

be brown? My eyes are brown, but my life? Youth is green and optimism; Gatsby believed in the green light.

13   Whereas there is brown at work in all the works of man. Time's passage is brown. Decomposition. Maggots. Foxing—the bookman's term—reddish brown; reynard. Manuscripts, however jewel-like, from dark ages, will darken. Venice will darken. Celluloid darkens, as if the lamp of the projector were insufficient sun. College blue books. Fugitive colors. My parents!

14   *She doesn't remember me.*

15   If we wish to antique an image, to make memory of it, we print it in sepia tones[7]— sepia, an extract from the occluding ink of the octopus, of the cuttlefish; now an agent for kitsch.[8] Whereas the colors, the iridescent Blakes at the Tate,[9] are housed now in perpetual gloom, lest colors be lifted from the page by the cutpurse sun. The Kodachrome prints in your closet—those high-skied and hopeful summer days—are dimming their lights and the skies are lowering. Would we be astounded by the quality of light in 1922?

> *Unreal City,*
> *Under the brown fog of a winter dawn,*
> *A crowd flowed over London Bridge, so many,*
> *I had not thought death had undone so many.*[10]

16   *The prince had always liked his London, when it had come to him.* And it had come to him that morning with a punctual, unembarrassed rap at the door, a lamp switched on in the sitting room, a trolley forced over the threshold, chiming its cups and its spoons. The valet, second floor, in alto Hindu cockney—and with a startled professionalism (I am browner than he)—proposed to draw back the drapes, damson velvet, thick as theater curtains.

17   Outside the hotel, several floors down, a crowd of blue and green-haired teenagers kept a dawn vigil for a glimpse of their Fairie Queen.[11] Indeed, as the valet fussed with the curtains, they recommenced their chant of: *Mah-don-ahh. Mah-don-ahh.* Madonna was in town and staying at this hotel. All day and all night, the approach or departure of any limousine elicited the tribute.

18   *Mah-don-ahh* was in town making a film about Eva Perón (both women familiar with the uses of peroxide.[12] Not such a bad thing to know in the great brown world, *oi*, mate?).

19   I was in London because my book had just come out there. My book about Mexico. Not a weight on most British minds.

---

[7] sepia tones: a photographic technique involving a chemical process that leads to a gray brown color commonly found in older photographs.

[8] Kitsch: a German word meaning a form of art that is an inferior copy of a style or a particular artistic masterpiece.

[9] Blakes at the Tate: reference to the art and engravings of poet and artist William Blake (1757–1827) and the Tate Gallery in London that houses England's national collection of British art as well as modern and contemporary art.

[10] Lines 60–64 of Book I, "The Burial of the Dead," from T. S. Eliot's "The Waste Land."

[11] Fairie Queen: a reference to the poem by Edmund Spencer (1552–1599) and his portrayal of Queen Elizabeth I (1533–1603), who reigned from 1558–1603, a period roughly coinciding with the English Renaissance, often referred to as the "Elizabethan Age."

[12] Referring to pop-star Madonna in the film adaptation of the musical *Evita* (1978) by Andrew Lloyd Webber and Tim Rice.

20   Did I ever tell you about my production of the *Tempest?*[13] I had been to the theater the previous evening. Not the *Tempest*, but the new Stoppard,[14] and I watched with keener interest as the Asian in front of me leaned over to mouth little babas into the be-ringed ear of his Cockney hire. One such confidence actually formed a bubble. Which, in turn, reminded me of my production of the *Tempest*. (South Sea Bubble.) I would cast Maggie Smith[15] as Miranda—wasted cheeks and bugging eyes—a buoyant Miss Haversham, sole valedictorian of her papa's creepy seminary. Caliban would be Johnny Depp. No fish scales, no seaweed, no webbed fingers, no claws, no vaudeville. No clothes. Does anybody know what I'm talking about? Ah, me. I am alone in my brown study. I can say anything I like. Nobody listens.

21   *Will there be anything else, sir?*

22   No, nothing else, thank you.

23   Brown people know there is nothing in the world—no recipe, no water, no city, no motive, no lace, no locution, no candle, no corpse that does not—I was going to say descend—that does not ascend to brown. Brown might be making.

24   My little Caliban book, as I say, bound in iguana hide, was about Mexico. With two newspapers under my arm, and balancing a cup of coffee, I went back to my bed. I found the Book section; I found the review. I knew it! I read first the reviewer's bio: a gay Colombian writer living in London.

25   What the book editor had done, dumb London book editor of the *Observer* had done— as Kansas City does and Manhattan does—is find my double or the closest he could find in greater London. It's a kind of doppelgänger theory of literary criticism and it's disheart-eningly fashionable among the liberal hearted. In our age of "diversity," the good and the liberal organize diversity. Find a rhyme for orange. If one is singular or outlandish by this theorem one can't be reviewed at all. Worse than that, if one is unlike, one will not be published. Publishers look for the next, rather than the first, which was accident. But the *Observer* wasn't even within bow-range. Their gay gaucho was clueless.

26   The liberal-hearted who run the newspapers and the university English departments and organize the bookstores have turned literature into well-meaning sociology. Thus do I get invited by the editor at some magazine to review your gay translation of a Colombian who has written a magical-realist novel. Trust me, there has been little magical realism in my life since my first trip to Disneyland.

27   That warm winter night in Tucson. My reading was scheduled for the six-thirty slot by the University of Arizona. A few hundred people showed up—old more than young; mostly brown. I liked my "them," in any case, for coming to listen, postponing their din-ners. In the middle of one of my paragraphs, a young man stood to gather his papers, then retreated up the aisle, pushed open the door at the back of auditorium. In the trapezoid of lobby-light thus revealed, I could see a crowd was forming for the eight o'clock reading—a lesbian poet. Then the door closed, resealed the present; I continued to read, but wondered

---

[13] William Shakespeare's late play written between 1610 and 1611, though some scholars argue for an earlier dating.

[14] Tom Stoppard (b. 1937), contemporary and highly renowned English playwright.

[15] Dame Maggie Smith (b. 1934), highly acclaimed English film, stage, and television actress.

to myself: Why couldn't I get the lesbians for an hour? And the lesbian poet serenade my Mexican-American audience? Wouldn't that be truer to the point of literature?

28   Well, what's the difference? I do not see myself as a writer in the world's eye, much less a white writer, much less a Hispanic writer; much less "a writer" in the 92nd Street Y sense. I'd rather be Madonna. Really, I would.

29   The Frankfurt Book Fair has recently been overrun with Koreans and Indians who write in English (the best English novelist in the world is not British at all, but a Mahogany who lives in snowy Toronto and writes of Bombay). Inevitably, the pale conclusion is that brown writers move "between" cultures. I resist between; I prefer "among" or "because of." You keep the handicap. After all, it has taken several degrees of contusion to create a jaundice as pervasive as mine. It has taken a lifetime of compromises, the thinning of hair, the removal last year of a lesion from my scalp, the assurance of loneliness, the difficulty of prayer, an amused knowledge of five-star hotels—and death—and a persistence of childish embarrassments and ever more prosaic Roman Catholic hymns, to entertain a truly off-white thought. Here comes one now.

30   No, I guess not.

31   There's a certain amount of "so what?" that comes with middle age. But is that brown thought?

32   Thus did literary ambition shrivel in my heart, in a brown room in a creamy hotel in London, constructed as a nineteenth-century hospital and recently renovated to resemble a Victorian hotel that never existed, except in the minds of a Hispanic author from California and a blond movie star from Detroit.

QUESTIONS ON MEANING

1. Considering the color of vanilla extract as Rodriguez describes it, what is ironic or contradictory about our common conception of vanilla's color?

2. How did the critic from *The Threepenny Review* evaluate Rodriguez's writing? What did she take him to task for?

3. How do bookstores tend to currently organize bookshelves? Why does Rodriguez seem critical of them?

4. Who do the teenagers in London wait to see?

5. What was the nationality and sexual orientation of the London reviewer who was assigned to review Rodriguez's book about Mexico? Why is Rodriguez bothered by the selection of this reviewer?

6. What is the relationship of brown writers to the culture they live within?

QUESTIONS FOR DISCUSSION

1. Rodriguez identifies himself as brown. How does he develop imagery to complicate our common use of color as an aspect of ethnic identity?

2. What are the problems with the way bookstores have chosen to replace academic categories with those that relate to racial, ethnic, gender, and sexual identities? Are there problems with this?

3. Why does Rodriguez conclude he would rather be Madonna than a writer?

4. What does Rodriguez mean when he says, "the liberal-hearted who run the newspapers and university English departments and organize the bookstores have turned literature into well-meaning sociology"? How does this compromise the purpose of reading and studying literature? Does it?

LOOKING AT RHETORIC

1. Rodriguez shifts from highly imagistic paragraphs to clear narrative paragraphs rooted in setting. How do these modes of expression complement and enhance one another?

2. The author makes quite frequent allusion to literary texts and authors. How does this assist or complicate the ideas he is trying to convey?

3. How does Rodriguez employ color as a metaphor and how effective is this rhetorical strategy in his writing?

WRITING ASSIGNMENTS

1. Trace how the author uses the central image of color, particularly brown, as a metaphor for ethnic identity. Using library and/or Internet sources, explore how people perceive themselves as belonging to an ethnicity. What does Rodriguez mean by brown? What difficulties does color create for all of us, especially ethnic minorities?

2. Explore why Rodriguez uses the popular figure of Madonna to explore how human identities are formulated. Consider that she is known not just for her performances but for creating a fictional public persona that is appealing but not strictly accurate. Why is Rodriguez concerned with the emphasis on color as a feature of identity and self-perception?

3. In pairs or in groups, discuss the selection's complex structure, the movement from imagery to narrative. Individually, write an essay in which you explore the effectiveness of this writing method. In what way does it work to communicate his ideas? In what way does it hinder those ideas?

Grant and Lee: A Study in Contrasts

Bruce Catton

Bruce Catton (1899–1978) is one of the most important popular historians of the American Civil War. He won the Pulitzer Prize in 1954 for A Stillness at Appomattox, *which deals with the final stages of the war and the surrender of Robert E. Lee's Confederate Army. He attended Oberlin College but left without a degree to serve in the United States Navy during World War I. Afterward, he began working as a journalist, writing for* The Cleveland News, Boston American, The Cleveland Plain Dealer, *and later he was one of the founders of* American Heritage Magazine. *He served in government posts during World War II and began writing book-length histories, often dealing with major historical figures in the Civil War. Essentially a narrative historian, his treatments of the subject matter are not conventionally academic in style and approach, but his inquiries into character and behavior are precise and informative. In this sense, his work demonstrates the relationship of history and literature as well as history and popular media. The following selection takes the most storied event from the end of the Civil War, the surrender at Appomattox Court House, and uses it to explore the cultural divide that precipitated the war, leading to the slow and painful reconciliation that followed.*

1   When Ulysses S. Grant and Robert E. Lee met in the parlor of a modest house at Appomattox Court House,[1] Virginia, on April 9, 1865, to work out the terms for the surrender of Lee's Army of Northern Virginia, a great chapter in American life came to a close, and a great new chapter began.

2   These men were bringing the Civil War to its virtual finish. To be sure, other armies had yet to surrender, and for a few days the fugitive Confederate government would struggle desperately and vainly, trying to find some way to go on living now that its chief support was gone. But in effect it was all over when Grant and Lee signed the papers. And the little room where they wrote out the terms was the scene of one of the poignant, dramatic contrasts in American history.

3   They were two strong men, these oddly different generals, and they represented the strengths of two conflicting currents that, through them, had come into final collision.

4   Back of Robert E. Lee was the notion that the old aristocratic concept might somehow survive and be dominant in American life.

5   Lee was tidewater Virginia, and in his background were family, culture, and tradition . . . the age of chivalry transplanted to a New World which was making its own legends and its own myths. He embodied a way of life that had come down through the age of knighthood and the English country squire. America was a land that was beginning all over again, dedicated to nothing much more complicated than the rather hazy belief that all men had equal rights and should have an equal chance in the world. In such a land Lee stood for the feeling that it was somehow of advantage to human society to have a pronounced inequality in the social structure. There should be a leisure class, backed by ownership of land; in turn, society itself should be keyed to the land as the chief source of wealth and influence. It would bring forth (according to this ideal) a class of men with a strong sense of obligation to the community; men who lived not to gain advantage for themselves, but to meet the solemn obligations which had been laid on them by the very fact that they were privileged.[2] From them the country would get its leadership; to them it could look for the higher values—of thought, of conduct, of personal deportment—to give it strength and virtue.

6   Lee embodied the noblest elements of this aristocratic ideal. Through him, the landed nobility justified itself. For four years, the Southern states had fought a desperate war to uphold the ideals for which Lee stood. In the end, it almost seemed as if the Confederacy fought for Lee; as if he himself was the Confederacy . . . the best thing that the way of life for which the Confederacy stood could ever have to offer. He had passed into legend before Appomattox. Thousands of tired, underfed, poorly clothed Confederate soldiers, long since past the simple enthusiasm of the early days of the struggle, somehow considered Lee

---

[1] Appomattox Court House: Located near Lynchburg, Virginia and owned by Wilber McClean.

[2] A notion of privilege together with obligation is sometimes referred to as noblesse oblige (from the French meaning "nobility obligates"). It is a concept central to the logic of modern and pre-modern aristocratic societies and hereditary monarchies.

the symbol of everything for which they had been willing to die. But they could not quite put this feeling into words. If the Lost Cause, sanctified by so much heroism and so many deaths, had a living justification, its justification was General Lee.

7   Grant, the son of a tanner on the Western frontier, was everything Lee was not. He had come up the hard way and embodied nothing in particular except the eternal toughness and sinewy fiber of the men who grew up beyond the mountains. He was one of a body of men who owed reverence and obeisance to no one, who were self-reliant to a fault, who cared hardly anything for the past but who had a sharp eye for the future.

8   These frontier men were the precise opposites of the tidewater aristocrats. Back of them, in the great surge that had taken people over the Alleghenies[3] and into the opening Western country, there was a deep, implicit dissatisfaction with a past that had settled into grooves. They stood for democracy, not from any reasoned conclusion about the proper ordering of human society, but simply because they had grown up in the middle of democracy and knew how it worked. Their society might have privileges, but they would be privileges each man had won for himself. Forms and patterns meant nothing. No man was born to anything, except perhaps to a chance to show how far he could rise. Life was competition.

9   Yet along with this feeling had come a deep sense of belonging to a national community. The Westerner who developed a farm, opened a shop, or set up in business as a trader, could hope to prosper only as his own community prospered—and his community ran from the Atlantic to the Pacific and from Canada down to Mexico. If the land was settled, with towns and highways and accessible markets, he could better himself. He saw his fate in terms of the nation's own destiny. As its horizons expanded, so did his. He had, in other words, an acute dollars-and-cents stake in the continued growth and development of his country.

10   And that, perhaps, is where the contrast between Grant and Lee becomes most striking. The Virginia aristocrat, inevitably, saw himself in relation to his own region. He lived in a static society which could endure almost anything except change. Instinctively, his first loyalty would go to the locality in which that society existed. He would fight to the limit of endurance to defend it, because in defending it he was defending everything that gave his own life its deepest meaning.

11   The Westerner, on the other hand, would fight with an equal tenacity for the broader concept of society. He fought so because everything he lived by was tied to growth, expansion, and a constantly widening horizon. What he lived by would survive or fall with the nation itself. He could not possibly stand by unmoved in the face of an attempt to destroy the Union. He would combat it with everything he had, because he could only see it as an effort to cut the ground out from under his feet.

12   So Grant and Lee were in complete contrast, representing two diametrically opposed elements in American life. Grant was the modern man emerging; beyond him, ready to come on the stage, was the great age of steel and machinery, of crowded cities and a restless burgeoning vitality. Lee might have ridden down from the old age of chivalry, lance

---

[3]Alleghenies: a part of the Appalachian Mountain Range running approximately four hundred miles from Pennsylvania, through western Maryland, eastern West Virginia, to southwestern Virginia.

in hand, silken banner fluttering over his head. Each man was the perfect champion of his cause, drawing both his strengths and his weaknesses from the people he led.

13   Yet it was not all contrast, after all. Different as they were—in background, in personality, in underlying aspiration—these two great soldiers had much in common. Under everything else, they were marvelous fighters. Furthermore, their fighting qualities were really very much alike.

14   Each man had, to begin with, the great virtue of utter tenacity and fidelity. Grant fought his way down the Mississippi Valley in spite of acute personal discouragement and profound military handicaps. Lee hung on in the trenches at Petersburg after hope itself had died. In each man there was an indomitable quality . . . the born fighter's refusal to give up as long as he can still remain on his feet and lift his two fists.

15   Daring and resourcefulness they had, too; the ability to think faster and move faster than the enemy. These were the qualities which gave Lee the dazzling campaigns of Second Manassas and Chancellorsville and won Vicksburg for Grant.

16   Lastly, and perhaps greatest of all, there was the ability, at the end, to turn quickly from war to peace once the fighting was over. Out of the way these two men behaved at Appomattox came the possibility of a peace of reconciliation. It was a possibility not wholly realized, in the years to come, but which did, in the end, help the two sections to become one nation again . . . after a war whose bitterness might have seemed to make such a reunion wholly impossible. No part of either man's life became him more than the part he played in their brief meeting in the McLean house at Appomattox. Their behavior there put all succeeding generations of Americans in their debt. Two great Americans, Grant and Lee—very different, yet under everything very much alike. Their encounter at Appomattox was one of the great moments of American history.

QUESTIONS ON MEANING

1. Where and when does the important event made reference to in the essay take place?

2. What is Lee's background? What social values does he represent?

3. What is Grant's background? What social values does he represent?

4. In the context of the traumatic effects of the Civil War on the nation, what did their meeting begin to accomplish?

QUESTIONS FOR DISCUSSION

1. Is there any value to be retained in the South's emphasis on social hierarchy and privilege? What reasonable logic might have supported it? As a nation, do we retain any of these values?

2. Are there any potential problems with the national values that emerged from the Civil War represented by Grant, that emphasize a rejection of the past, rugged individualism, and the eradication of formal social hierarchies?

3. Can historical figures be used in a representative manner, as embodiments of whole societies, as Catton does with Grant and Lee? Are there any pitfalls to this kind of practice?

4. To what extent have the results of Grant and Lee's meeting, as Catton represents them, played out in American history?

LOOKING AT RHETORIC

1. Catton spent much of his adult life as a journalist. In what sense does this historical essay involve a journalistic style? What are some of the journalistic elements?

2. As a work of narrative history, the essay places an emphasis on character over events. To what extent does this contribute to or detract from your understanding of the meeting at Appomattox?

3. This essay deals primarily with contrast, with some limited comparison. Is this imbalance reasonable?

WRITING ASSIGNMENTS

1. Using library and/or Internet sources, research another important historical event in which a person is used to represent a set of ideas. Select a person you know and consider Catton's figures and the ones you have discovered. Describe the person's character in detail, things like their values, beliefs, social stature, habits, and interests. To what extent do they represent a historical reality beyond themselves? A generation? An age group? A geographical region? A subculture? In thinking of them as representative, to what degree do we understand them better and to what extent do we reduce their complexity?

2. Argue for or against Catton's largely positive portrayals of either Grant or Lee.

3. In pairs or in groups, select a public figure you know. They could be a politician, a leader, or any other celebrity. Brainstorm a list of character traits, again such as their values, beliefs, social stature, habits, interests, and behavior. Individually, write an essay exploring how they represent some aspect of contemporary history. In thinking of them as representative, to what degree do we understand them better and to what extent do we reduce their complexity?

Interdisciplinary Connections

Illegal Immigration in America—
Political Cartoons

Historically, the United States is a land of immigrants. The inscription on the Statue of Liberty highlights this aspect of U.S. history. It reads, in part, "Give me your tired, your poor,/Your huddled masses, yearning to breathe free,/The wretched refuse of your teeming shore,/Send these, the homeless, tempest tossed,/I lift my lamp beside the golden door." Below are two political cartoons that take on the current debates in the United States regarding the status of illegal

http://1.bp.blogspot.com/_1ZZFL05ncxE/S98WK8wMleI/AAAAAAAABgE/WD9Zp9Sbi8I/s1600/
illegal-immigrants.jpg

immigration into the country. What seems to be the message of each cartoon? What perspective does each cartoon give that helps illustrate the complexities of the issue? Do you find one cartoon more compelling than the other? Which seems to make a stronger argument, and why? What is your opinion of the current debates over the issues surrounding illegal immigration? Is illegal immigration a problem, in your opinion? If so, what would you do to fix the problem?

http://victoria15.edublogs.org/files/2010/09/immigration-cartoon.jpg

Rituals: A Prayer, a Candle, and a Notebook

Judith Ortiz Cofer

Judith Ortiz Cofer (b. 1952) is strongly influenced by the oral storytelling tradition she learned from her grandmother, a practice dominant in Puerto Rican culture. Her work explores the attempt to create identity from the experience of two distinctive cultures, and she deals with issues ranging from racism and sexism to the collective traumas of diasporic immigrants. She received a B.A. from Augusta College and an M.A in English from Florida Atlantic University. She is the author of The Line of the Sun *(1989),* The Latin Deli: Prose and Poetry *(1993), and the memoir* Silent Dancing: A Partial Remembrance of a Puerto Rican Childhood *(1990), among other works. Ortiz Cofer is currently Franklin Professor of English and Creative Writing at the University of Georgia. In the following selection, the author recalls her move to Patterson, New Jersey, and the adjustments her family faced, exploring the role of ritual and imagination as means of coping with traumatic change.*

A Childhood Prayer

In the early days of my Spanish-language years
I was put under the care
of El Angel de la Guarda,
my Guardian Angel, the military sentinel
who required a nightly salute, a plea
on my knees for protection
against the dangers hidden in dreams,
and from night-prowling demons.

In the print framed over my bed,
he was portrayed as feathered and androgynous,
hovering above two barefoot children
whose features were set in pastel innocence—
crossing a dilapidated wood bridge
under which yawned a sulfurous abyss—
their only light being
the glow of the presence with wings
who was invisible to them.

I could take no comfort in this dark
nursery myth, as some nights
I lay awake listening to the murmur
of their voices sharing
their dreams of flight
in a well-lit kitchen, while I brooded
over the cruel indifference of adults
who abandoned children to the night,

and about that Comandante in the sky
who knew everything I did, or thought of doing,
whose minion could so calmly smile
while innocent children crossed over darkness,
alone, afraid, night after night.

1   TWICE A MONTH I TALK on the telephone with my mother in Puerto Rico. Today, after our usual exchange of news about people on the Island whom I barely remember and people in my life she has never met, I try to concentrate on writing in my notebook. But Spanish has entered my brain, unlocking memories, making me take one of my trips back to my childhood in New Jersey and our first years in this country. I get my notebook from my dresser and settle down on the couch next to my textbooks and papers which represent my real life now as an English professor in a southern university. At a safe distance from the chaotic world I grew up in—and if Tennessee Williams[1] was right when he said that "time is the longest distance"—I now have enough space between my selves for my investigation to proceed. And that is why I write. I write to know myself, and it is a job that will occupy me for life.

2   Keeping track of my thoughts in a journal is a habit I acquired as a teenager experiencing the conflicts and loneliness of Puerto Rican immigrant life in the '60s. Now in my middle forties, writing my daily paragraph or two has become a routine, as indispensable as a daily prayer and weekly candles are for my mother. Most nights before bed, I take out my plain school notebook and write a few lines. Every morning at dawn, I write the poems or begin the stories that my recollections have filtered through my dreams. I do not, however, merely record the mundane activities of each day in my journal or in my writings, but rather I try to capture with clarity and succinctness what, if anything, the past twenty-four hours have taught me. Sometimes as I write, my fingers cease to be connected to my conscious mind and instead become instruments of revelations of my most painful memories and thoughts. On this night, perhaps because my mother's voice on the phone has caused a nostalgic wave to pass over me, leaving the treasures and debris of the past on my lap, I write about my father.

3   My father died with many things unspoken between us. Until his death in a car accident during my first year in graduate school, he directed my goals through his own unfulfilled dreams. He was an intellectual who did not go to college, a dreamer without hope, an artist without a medium. So I went to college. I became a teacher and later a writer. I had to finish what he had never even begun at the time of his death. My mother could not bear life in the States without him as her interpreter and companion, so she went home to her Island. She got what she always wanted, but not in the way she wanted. She wanted a return to *La Isla*; she got it, but without him. I stayed behind with my books, my memories.

4   To my father, knowledge was all the wealth and power he wanted. His only luxury was our education, my brother's and mine. He invested in us. He bought us books and

---

[1] Tennessee Williams (1911–1983): Thomas Lanier Williams, renowned twentieth-century American playwright who wrote such plays as *The Glass Menagerie* (1945), *A Streetcar Named Desire* (1948), and *Cat on a Hot Tin Roof* (1955).

paid our tuition at private Catholic schools when we could not afford to buy a house. Our times together were precious and rare since his job as a career Navy man kept him away from home during my waking hours and sometimes at sea for months. Our talks had to be carved out of the rare Sunday afternoon when he was home on leave—hours for which my mother competed also.

5   It was a solitary life we led, and I never quite understood why my parents chose to live in a social limbo. In piecing together from my notebooks what my mother talks about more freely now that she has returned to the Island, I began to understand that it was my father who chose to live in this country, and they had not really shared quite the same dream.

6   As a Puerto Rican family we were voluntary exiles, since we were free to go back to our homeland anytime. We could not even claim economic need because Father had a steady income through the Navy that kept us securely in our lower-middle-class status. The difficult part was that neither of my parents really assimilated into life in the U.S. The place my father chose to settle down was Paterson, New Jersey. Yet we did not stay for long in the rapidly growing Puerto Rican community; instead he rented us an apartment in a Jewish-owned building in a neighborhood of European immigrants where we were an oddity, once more strangers in a strange setting. Though I never experienced racism in its most brutal forms, our exclusion was as evident as a new silence as one enters a room.

7   I attended a school with the driven and overachieving offspring of Nazi camp survivors and Irish and Italian immigrants. It was among them that I learned how to concentrate on one thing at a time until I mastered it. The kids I knew centered their lives not around the normal flirting and cruising of mainstream teenage life, but on their complex family life and all the attending ceremonies. I felt my loneliness most keenly when a door opened and I heard the uproar of life shared with others under one roof, a family gathered around a television set, laughing at a joke they all understood, or arguing in one language. When we entered into our own quiet, orderly apartment we had to take off our English language and American ways at the door as well as our street shoes, for our mother would only speak Spanish and our father was determined that we would not provoke complaints from our neighbors.

8   My father was a good friend of the owner of our building, an immigrant Jew. The man was of Mediterranean heritage, and his dark features and curly black hair made him look more like a Puerto Rican than my father, who was a thin, fair-skinned man with an elegant bearing. I knew that my father stood out when he walked down our street, where the population was mainly composed of swarthy European men.

9   My mother hardly ever left our apartment, except twice a month when my father brought his black Oldsmobile out of the downtown garage where he kept it to the front of our building and we went shopping, first to the A & P and then to the Puerto Rican shops in the barrio where my mother bought the ingredients she needed for the dishes she liked to cook. The people in these bodegas shot Spanish at one another like machine-gun fire. So fast did they speak that I could barely understand what they were saying. And they stared at the three of us—overdressed by their standards, my mother in her brocaded black coat with the fur collar, my father in coat and tie or dress Navy blues, and me usually in the pleated skirts and plain white blouses my father liked to see me wear, with my neat cloth coat from Sears. My little brother's outfit was the masculine match for mine, dark trousers,

button-up shirt. We were a family who dressed like the models in the store catalogues my father brought home to use as picture-dictionaries and my mother studied as manuals of American life. Yet we were suspect to the other customers. Little pockets of silence would form around us as my mother examined the yuccas, plantains, green bananas, and other *viandas* she would need for the week's meals.

10   I would watch the sharp bones of my father's cheeks and see his jaw clamp down hard. A look of haughty indifference would settle over his face as he "escorted" my mother up and down the aisles crammed with dusty bottles and cans bearing labels in Spanish. He kept his hands in his pockets and followed just behind her left elbow as if to protect her from dangers hidden in the stacks. She walked slowly, picking up cans and reading the labels, perhaps savoring the familiar smells of her culture, the sounds of sloppy Spanish as customers and clerks engaged in the verbal tag called *el gufeo* in barrio slang. It is a game of double entendre, of puns, semiserious insults, and responses that are *tipicos*—the usual exchanges for Puerto Ricans in familiar settings. My father ignored the loud voices, the vulgar innuendos, and the uncontrolled laugher they incited. My mother obviously enjoyed it. Her offbeat humor and her need for laughter are to this day qualities I love about her. In the early days, she was timid in front of my father and the strangers in the barrio. Back on the Island, she is again quick with the word, the quirky metaphor—was she really the poet in the family? I tagged along in the bodega, as I did in the American stores, not really grasping until much later why we did not belong to either world: the quiet, clean world of my father, or the intense, confusing locales where my mother seemed most at ease.

11   In our apartment, especially during the hours that my father was not there, my mother followed certain rituals that got her through each day. At least twice a week, she walked the five blocks to the nearest Catholic church to attend mass. I accompanied her only on Sundays. We went to the Spanish-language mass celebrated by a priest from China who had been trained to serve as a missionary in Latin America and had somehow ended up in Paterson. He said mass in Latin and delivered passionate sermons in Chinese-accented Castilian Spanish that was just barely comprehensible to the Puerto Ricans whose dialect resembled his pure speech about as closely as American English does the dialect of the Scottish Highlands. It took faith and concentration to receive the word of God in Spanish from our determined pastor, but my mother relished each lisped word. Her Catholic training in Puerto Rico had been transferred intact to Paterson where her isolation made her develop the habits of the religious. She yearned for the others who believed what she believed coming together to celebrate custom. It was the comfort of the familiar that she sought in church ceremony and pious rituals. On the days when she did not attend mass, my mother lit candles in front of a popular depiction of the Virgin—the one where she is crushing the snake with a dainty bare foot.

12   My mother's religious practices included special prayers said on saints' days, candles every Saturday night, all night, left burning in the bathtub (a fire safety precaution), and rosaries in memory of dead relatives she kept track of through letters and dates marked on calendars; and of course, she supervised my religious education since the American nuns did not keep the busy liturgical calendar she followed. Every night while I was a small child my mother came into my room to say the prayer to my guardian angel with me. I still

remember the words: *Angel de mi guardal dulce compañialno me desampares de noche ni de dia.*[2]
Then she would kiss me, and I'd inhale the smell of Maja soap on the skin of her throat. It
was a special soap that came in a box of three cakes, each wrapped in a fancy paper depicting a beautiful dark-haired woman in full Spanish costume of red and black satin and lace,
an ornate comb and veil on her head, a black fan coyly held against her cheek. I saved the
boxes and paper and kept them in my underclothes drawer to give my garments the sensuous aroma my mother imported for herself. Incense and Spanish castile soap, essence of my
mother, scents of my childhood.

13   But though Catholic ritual filled the gaps in her life as an exile, they did not turn my
mother into a dull, predictable person. She was rather an incurable romantic who was
addicted to love stories. She read one Corín Tellado (the Spanish-language Danielle Steel
of her time) romance novel a week. I was in charge of buying them, at a quarter each, from
the only bookstore in Paterson that carried them, Schwartz's soda fountain and drugstore.
As the trustee and executor of her literary needs, I had to learn early to memorize covers
and titles so that I would not buy one she had already read. After she was through with
a book she'd let me have it, and that is how I learned to read Spanish. The words that
I still retain after all these years are mostly flowery adjectives and passionate verbs used
to describe the appearance of the heroes (the girl always dark and lovely, the men always
elegant and soft-spoken, unless they were the villains, then they were drawn more varied
and interestingly). The actions of the protagonist were always performed within the same
formula story, told in countless ways. My mother liked to discuss these *cuentos de amor* with
me, and we sometimes dramatized the characters, reading aloud to each other as if we were
acting in a soap opera. My father objected to my reading this *basura*, "trash." I once heard
him threaten to forbid the books in the house.

14   "She is impressionable, *Querida,*" he said in his perfectly enunciated Spanish. He
avoided using slang in both languages and sounded like a foreigner when he spoke either.
It was the peculiar slowness of his speech and his insistence on the clarity of each word that
made him seem cautious in the way he spoke. "As it is, she is not spending enough time
studying. Do not distract her with your silly *novelas.*"

15   "My 'silly' *novelas* are the only reason I do not go crazy in this place, *Querido.* Shall
I give them up, too? Should I read only the Bible and the prayer book until I become *loca?*"
My mother's voice intensified like those of actresses in the Mexican movies she loved.
Behind closed eyes, I visualized her rising from the table, standing before him, trembling
in rage, in perfect contrast to his infuriatingly calm demeanor.

16   "*Controlate, por favor.*" Father usually warned softly. Our apartment was small. He
knew that I could be listening, and only when they were arguing did I get a glimpse into
the real conditions of our imposed solitude. When I asked directly why they had chosen
to leave the Island, or why they had not returned, the answers were always predictable
and vague. "We have a better life here." My father would state this with finality. "There is
nothing there for us to go back for." I knew that his father was dead, and his mother was a
perpetual wanderer with no permanent home, living with one of her sons or the other. But
my mother received mail from her many relatives on the Island.

---

[2] *Angel de mi guarda/dulce compania/no me descampares de noche ni de dia*: Holy guardian Angel, my sweet companion, do not forsake me during the night or during the day.

17   "No, *hombre*. You will not deprive me of my books. They are not harmful to our daughter, and they are my only company." Her words were meant to imply that she did not need to be so desperately lonely.

18   "You obviously do not remember your promise to me. Try to forget your idealized Island. It only exists in your dreams. I know that you feel lonely here, but there is no place for us back there. When I asked you to come to Paterson with me you said you would not look back. Do you remember?"

19   "I was eighteen years old. What did I know about *la maldita soledad* then? *Mi amor*, can it really be that bad for us in our own country?"

20   "Our life is here. Our family has a future here. There she would just be another girl waiting to get married. Our daughter would just end up a slave to some ignorant man. And our son would have to join the Army or Navy like I did to make a decent living. Then you would never see him either. Do you want that for them?"

21   "You are wrong to think that the future is hopeless in our own homeland. Just because your father was a tyrant and your mother a martyr . . . "

22   "Please be careful that you do not go so far that I cannot forgive your words. We had agreed not to mention my unfortunate family's past in this house."

23   "That is another promise you forced from me when I was too young to understand. Other people have tragedies and troubles in their families, and yet they lead normal lives."

24   "If you are referring to the population of the barrio—they do not lead 'normal' lives. So many of them are like cattle in a pen doing things in a group because they are afraid of venturing out. We are pioneers. We live our own lives and give our children the best opportunity for an education. So we do not socialize very much. I do not need it. You as my wife should not either."

25   And so it would go, around and around. Little hints for me to ponder: names of people I had never met and of places I had never visited would drop into their intense but subdued late-night arguments, which had become a passionate ritual summoning the painful past and casting a spell over our daily struggle, *la lucha*—and my dangerous, unfathomable future. I would gather their whispered words: discarded flowers to keep between the pages of my notebooks, clues to a mystery I hoped someday to solve. I write about tyrants and martyrs, and about lonely women who find solace in books. All the words I heard my parents trade like currency for each other's loyalties, like treaties to be negotiated so that their children might have choices, they are still with me. The memories emerge in my poems and stories like time-travelers popping up with a message for me. But I must first open the door with a ritual.

26   I finish grading my students' essays. What they don't know yet about life and literature can fill volumes. I can do something to remedy the gaps—if they are hungry at all for knowledge—I will add a drop to their half-empty or half-full buckets. But how can I fill mine? As I look deeper into myself, I discover that I left the place where my family's well is located. As a writer, I am always in the new territory of Myself Alone. I am looking for new lands to discover every time I begin a sentence. I carry nothing but a dowser's[3] wand and my need to make order, to find a few answers. So by recalling kitchen-table conversations

---

[3] dowser: one who uses a wand or a divining rod.

in my notebook, re-inventing them as I go along, perhaps I am moving at a snail's pace toward understanding through my poems, stories, and essays.

27   Time to rest. I go to my bedroom and open the dresser drawer where I keep my notebook. I add several sentences. In the same drawer I also keep votive candles in different colors. I choose a green one. I can hear my mother saying, "*Verde-esperanza*," meaning that green meant hope; she always said it when she chose a green candle. My candle, bought at the drugstore, smells like a tropical rain forest, or so the label promises. I place it in front of the photograph I took of the statue of *La Virgen de Monserrate*, patroness of our pueblo. For a long while I watch the shadows dancing in solemn silence on the white wall. I am held by the complex flux of flame, shadow, reflection blending in a choreographed repetition of motion in precise intervals. I keep my eyes fixed on the flickering show until I fall into a deep sleep. I hope will be undisturbed by the dreams and nightmares that I keep locked away in my notebook for future reference. Sometimes, *most* times, I allow a prayer or a poem to drift like sweetly scented candle smoke into me.

QUESTIONS ON MEANING

1. Why does Ortiz Cofer tell us she writes? What does she try to accomplish with her writing?

2. How does Ortiz Cofer describe her father? What was the source of his lack of fulfillment?

3. What serious activity did Ortiz Cofer's mother engage in to cope with the isolation of a foreign culture?

4. What did Ortiz Cofer's mother do for enjoyment and how did it help her adjust?

5. What do Ortiz Cofer's father and mother argue about?

6. Toward the essay's conclusion, what is Ortiz Cofer's reaction to her students' essays?

QUESTIONS FOR DISCUSSION

1. In what ways can ritual lend comfort to our daily lives? Does it? These can be formal or inherited rituals or those we invent ourselves.

2. What accounts for Ortiz Cofer's father's and mother's different reactions to their move to Paterson, New Jersey?

3. Is Ortiz Cofer still in a state of conflict over her immigration experience? How does it affect her?

4. In the context of her migration, what does Ortiz Cofer mean when she says she is in the territory of "Myself Alone"?

LOOKING AT RHETORIC

1. Why does Ortiz Cofer choose to open the poem with a childhood prayer in verse?

2. In an essay written in English, Ortiz Cofer uses occasional Spanish words and phrases. To what purpose and effect?

3. Ortiz Cofer shifts from exposition to narrative when she recounts the verbal interchange between her parents. Is this effective? Does it disrupt the essay in any way?

WRITING ASSIGNMENTS

1. Using library and/or Internet sources, explore the emotional effects of immigration on individual people. Does the experience of movement and change lead to a greater sense of emotional independence, as Ortiz Cofer implies in her concept of "Myself Alone"?

2. Argue for or against the idea of ritual as a way of organizing our lives and coping with uncertainty.

3. In pairs or in groups, discuss what is meant by the term ritual. Together make a list of rituals that you perform daily, whether they are cultural, religious, or particular to you. Individually, refine and expand the list. Then select one essay and write a personal narrative in which you explore the role of ritual in your life.

The Language of Dreams

Belle Yang

Belle Yang (b. 1960) was born in Taiwan and immigrated to the United States when she was seven years old. She is an artist and an author of adult non-fiction and children's books. Initially interested in the sciences, she attended Stirling University in Scotland and graduated from the University of California at Santa Cruz with a degree in biology. She studied art at Pasadena Art Center College of Design and the Beijing Institute of Traditional Chinese Painting. The experience of immigration affected her deeply, having lived in both Taiwan and Japan, coming to the United States at the height of the Civil Rights movement, and acquiring English as her third language. After working and traveling in China she returned to the United States after the massacre in Tiananmen Square. She is the author of Baba: A Return to China Upon My Father's Shoulders *(1994) and* The Odyssey of a Manchurian *(1996). In the following selection, Yang recalls the process by which her father's stories of his childhood in China helped her to understand the role of memory, language, and storytelling in human lives, especially those displaced and complicated by movement and the blending of cultures.*

1   To speak chinese is to inherit the memory of hunger.

2   On lunar New Year's eve, flushed with wine and beef from the firepot, Baba's eyes grow misty. I know what my father is going to say. On a cozy, full belly, he is reminded of the past on a empty belly. "Ahhh, there was that year when the locust swarmed across the provinces, eating up all the corn, the rice, the miller. What could the country folk do but cook locusts for their dinner," he would say. Or, "I remember toward the end of the Japanese occupation, all we had was soybeans. We were ravenous, but we knew not to eat too much of it all at once, because the stuff swelled in the stomach and could kill us."

3   I am a great believer in *ming*, Chinese for life, but also fate. Had I been born on the mainland of China in 1960 instead of the island of Taiwan, I may have been one of the over thirty million Chinese to perish in the worst famine known to mankind.

4   To be born in China in the twentieth century is to live life as a colossal waste: wasted plans, wasted opportunities, wasted resources. Even men and women of talent born into privilege have disappeared without a murmur in the maelstrom.

5   To understand Chinese means to hear the underlying layers of cynicism born of an ancient country of interminable wars, of a people who have had to contend with too little for too long. Take this adage: One thirsty monk will carry two buckers of water on a shoulder pole; two thirsty monks will carry one bucket of water on a shoulder pole between them; three thirsty monks will remain thirsty because each thinks the other two should go get the water.

6   I felt I was rainted simply because I was keen to the nuances of cynicism. I felt evil. It didn't matter that I was not a misanthrope[1], but as long as I understood what was being said, I could not escape the legacies of a culture whose optimism, and perhaps, life, was ebbing. If only I could be immune to cynicism, I would truly become American—innocent, open, sunny.

7   I have often envied my American-born Chinese friends who are seemingly cleanly severed at birth from the Chinese language. They learned their first words in American English, and their souls tend to brightness and laughter. When they visit China, they are oblivious to the darkness which swirls about their ears; they are protected by their ignorance. I, on the other hand, began soaking up Chinese inside my mother's belly and did not become immersed in English until I came to the United States in 1967. When I am in China, I feel every slight, slur, and nastiness on the crowded Beijing streets as deeply as flesh wounds.

8   Chinese is the language of memories as thick and pungent as fermented bean curd. Old, stale, fulsome. What did I want with memories?

9   When I pad past my parents' bedroom late at night, their heads have rolled together where their pillows meet, nose to nose, they reminisce, sotto voiced. Or if a duet of sustained breathing emerges from their open door, I know they are dreaming, in Chinese, of course.

10   Baba, as all obstinate souls do, dreams about the past. The Daoist[2] uncle who rolled his cigarettes with the pages of his books after reading; the patriarch, Baba's grandfather, who loved chrysanthemums and boasted over one hundred varieties in his garden; his mother, bent over the lamp, sewing cloth shoes for him while, outside, the withered grape leaves clatter on the vine. The souls lost in the chaos of time and war flit across Baba's brow like shadow puppets.

11   He dreams of the treats from his childhood, the sesame-encrusted *hamatumi*, toad-spitting-honey—jam-filled cakes sold on the streets—or frozen persimmons, heavy with sweetness, spooned and eaten like ice cream. Baba's statement on his first day in America: "I'd rather die if I have only this foreigners' bread and milk for the rest of my life."

12   Chinese is more than an ethnic identity; it is also a system of belief, with its dogma, prejudice, and guilt-inducing credo. "What? You're not marrying a Chinese? What? You say you're going to become an American? You will always be Chinese no matter what citizenship you take up. China will always have a claim on you." In China there are Buddhists, Daoists, Muslims, Confucians, Christians among a host of religions, but each

---

[1] Misanthrope: a person who has a negative attitude about human nature and human beings, often leading to isolation.

[2] Daoism: Often written "Taoism," an East Asian philosophical and religious tradition dating back over two thousand years. "Dao" loosely means "path" or "way." The "Three Jewells of the Tao" are compassion, moderation, and humility.

person, above all, is born spiritually, piously, religiously Chinese. There is no getting away from it.

13   In the fall of 1986, at the age of twenty-six, I flew to Beijing to study classical Chinese art, focusing on the great tradition of landscape painting—an art of time as well as space. I learned to cast away Western perspective and vault into the sky like the Monkey King[3] of legend—to see the world from multiple angles (the Chinese landscape is intensely different from a Western one, where the viewer remains, still as a rock, at one fixed point).

14   During my three years of study, I roamed across the land, sketching, painting, looking. I reached regions closed to foreigners, to which my yellow skin gained me easy entry. I traveled the Gobi Desert along the Silk Road[4], where Buddhism first made its appearance in the Middle Kingdom; I dug into the yellow earth of the Great Northwest and laid my hands upon pottery, art of the late Stone Age, fitting my fingers into the clay imprints of hands left by craftsmen of some seven thousand years ago; I returned to the frozen Manchurian north to celebrate Spring Festival, the Chinese New Year, with my grandparents, whose heads were frosted white with layers of remembrance; I submerged myself in the Hunan countryside of the Miao[5] tribes, where the only foreigners seen previously were travelers from a neighboring county.

15   In my wanderings across a land of vastly different temperaments, my eyes were opened to a wealth of folk art, the cultural antithesis of the lofty, scholarly classical Chinese painting I had come to study. My heart was moved by the paper cuts, the vibrant graphics of the New Year prints, the naif paintings of the peasants, each region stylistically distinct. These were works of men and women deeply rooted in their soil, works populated with farm animals, fruits of the field and stream; they were celebrations of birth, marriage, harvest, the seasons, Heaven and Earth, youth, old age, and death. The art of the country folk swelled with candor and humor, in their very artlessness they captured life more directly than any attempt at careful imitation could ever do.

16   It was in the countryside where I was able to dispel for myself the myth that Chinese and cynicism went hand in hand. On a painting excursion to Hunan, I was invited inside a thatched farmhouse whose front doors were thrown wide open, never locked. Two old farmers offered me a bamboo fan to cool off with, and water to slake my thirst. The brothers all the while smoked their pipes and smiled their gap-toothed smiles at me like children. They did not ask this stranger where she was from or why she was pestering around their village. They simply provided me with what they themselves would have wished for on a hot summer afternoon.

17   In the spring of my third year in China, the energy I had sensed on arrival, an underlying tension, a raw nervousness, a fluttering excitement, stirring below the surface of the society, emerged and manifested itself in heady days of hope and optimism. New ideas

---

[3] Monkey King: main character from the Chinese Epic *Journey to the West*, published anonymously in the 1590's during the Ming Dynasty but often attributed by twentieth-century historians to the scholar Wu'Cheng'en.

[4] Silk Road: nearly three thousand years old, a complex and interconnected group of trade routes connecting various segments of the Asian continent with Europe, the Mediterranean, and North Africa.

[5] Hunan Province and the Miao tribes: a province in southern China located between Hubei in the north and Jiangxi in the east. The Miao are a culturally and linguistically distinct culture occupying the Human province, among others.

had brought vigor—most pronounced in the cities; fresh ideas were surging from across the seas; suppressed ideas welled up from belowground. I felt as if every day I would awaken to ephochal changes. The faces that greeted me on the streets of Beijing were open and candid as I had never seen before. Graciousness reigned; gone were the sharp elbows and knees of the anonymous crowd. The leaden dullness of slouching spirits was gone; eyes sparkled. Workers stuffed their entire month's salary into donation boxes to support the struggle of the students on hunger strike in Tiananmen Square. And I was as excited as anyone.

18   As time progressed, the energy grew wilder, the voices of the people grew louder, culminating in the passions of "Democracy Spring." But I saw it quelled. Brutally. And in the aftermath of June 4, 1989, I saw books burned, stories destroyed. I saw artists and writers numbed into silence. Great cultures tell life-sustaining stories, but in China, small lies choked the air.[6]

19   The abuse I witnessed was parallel to my own personal narrative but on a grand scale; I understood the stupid thought-control, the purposeful thought-manipulation, the insidious violence—deeply, acutely. The mechanism of fear is the same whether applied to one human being by another or by a government on its people.

20   To swallow your voice, to keep stories buried deeply beneath layers and layers of silence, is to live in a state of bondage. Stories are magic. Stories make us individuals. They make us free. They have power to make trouble for rulers, for a story is a world upon itself: it has its own logic and cannot be ruled at all. That is why when a new emperor comes to the throne, books are burned and fresh versions of history written to his liking are published.

21   Physically depleted, in spiritual exhaustion, I returned to America late in 1989, but I returned with gratitude in my heart for the freedom of expression given me in America. I returned convinced that I would firmly grasp that generous gift with both hands.

22   In this Chinese house of my parents, I found peace, five layers deep. I continued to be confined to the house even after my three-year sojourn, for the man who wished to do me harm was still a reality of my landscape. I was forced to leave the streaming crowd that seems to know its direction. I had no clear direction and initially felt bewilderment.

23   My mother and father stood guard as my Door Gods,[7] the Generals Hen and Har with their bows and arrows, protecting me from evil spirits.

24   Keep your mind, eyes, and heart quiet, they said. Do your calligraphy as an exercise in meditation and by the end of the year, you will know precisely what you must do. You won't have to step out; opportunities will present themselves to you at your very door.

25   Yah, right. What opportunities? I did not believe my parents' words, but they proved to be prophetic.

26   The book project grew organically, a marvelous living thing; it sprouted, developed long shoots, branched, formed thick fat leaves, flowered and bore fruit.

27   The stories first came as a trickle. As my mother cooked over the stove, she told me about my grandmother and how she would save the umbilical cords of her babies,

---

[6] Referring to the demonstrations for democratic and anti-communist reform that took place among students and intellectuals in 1989, culminating in the Tiananmen Square Massacre.

[7] Door Gods: A Chinese decoration placed on each side of an entry to a home or a temple.

wrapped in crimson paper. I was inspired to paint and write a vignette. My father, not one to be left out, got into the act, too, and began to tell stories of Manchuria in the season when the sorghum was ripe, tales of men and women who colored his childhood.

28   The material for the first chapter of my book *Baba* began on a dark and stormy night, no less. The power was out and it was so cold, the three of us simply crawled under the covers of my parents big bed to wait out the storm.

29   I've got a ghost story for you, Baba said and told a tale of widowed Grandmother Sun who lost her only child to the wolves that lived in the willows along the sandy banks of the River Lin. Grandmother Sun was often seen among the tall, ripening sorghum, parting the tassels of the plants. "Stop this tomfoolery. Quit your fighting," she would say.

30   When the power came on, I sat up in my own bed and scribbled down what Baba had told me. The next day I asked for more stories and he provided. They were snatches of his awakened memories—not enough detail to even consider an entire story, let alone a book—but they were so vivid and flavorful, textured, poetic, heartrending. I pressed Baba for more details.

31   My father and I had no natural understanding. He read Zhuangzi,[8] the Dao de jing, the Confucian teachings, and tomes compiled by historians dynasties ago. His spiritual address was in China, and mine so much in the West. For Baba, retrospection and nostalgia dominated; the present and the uncertain future was filtered through the vast experience of a Chinese diaspora.

32   China prepared me to enter into the landscape of my father's childhood to understand the values that shaped him. I was able to tap into the original language, not only the spoken language, but the symbols, the iconography, in which his spirit was nourished, his ideas were given form. Only because I had embraced the Chinese language could I ask questions of depth that would stir him enough to carry me into the past. We are shaped by the language we first learned to dream in.

33   There is a particular sensitivity and emotional experience reached through Chinese— our peculiar written characters composed of word-pictures and the direct, haiku-like phrase structure. Chinese is first and foremost poetry. It is this language-poetry that makes us think or feel or dream the way we do. The Chinese language is art in that in its written form, it retains its pictorial identity. Art is as important in influencing our mental makeup as diet is over our physical makeup.

Through Baba's stories, I learned to see the child in him, the wonder in him, where once I had seen the cynicism of a tired old man who warned me incessantly about the dangers of the world. In re-creating his past through words and pictures, I made friends with the boy of eight who ran barefooted in the sandy soil, stealing watermelons on a hot Manchurian summer afternoon.

34   Most of Baba's tales were about my ancestors. In the long days that stretched into long years of work at my writing desk, I felt the spirit of the ancients hovering over my

---

[8] Zhuangzi, *Dao de jing*, Confucian teachings: Zhuangzi was an important Chinese philosopher who lived around the fourth century B. C. E. *Dao de jing* or *Tao Te Ching*, originally known as Laozi, is a classic Chinese text of unknown date and origin essential to philosophical Taoism; Confucianism originated from the teachings of Confucius (551 B. C. E to 479 B. C. E).

shoulders, guiding me, protecting me. I felt a responsibility to rescue them from the deep well of forgetting. As the past took shape with great vividness, I came to understand the chain of events that nourishes the present like an umbilical cord. Knowing the past means knowing who I am today and the possibilities for unfolding the future.

At first my father did not trust me with his stories. When he read the drafts, he was hardly stingy with his criticisms if he deemed I had the texture of the landscape wrong or history wrong. Sometimes an argument would be sparked by his nasal tone of voice or my brusk retort and Baba and I would not speak to each other for days. The Chinese say you must fight with a man to know a man, and in the long years of close collaboration, he and I certainly got to know one another well, and in time, we learned to fight productively, the tension from the arguments dissipating in a matter of hours.

In the time of private concentration, I did not step outside except to take long, luxurious walks with my parents. The three of us would go out through the back fence into Hatton Canyon, our private sanctuary, for our daily communion. During our stroll, Baba would often elaborate on the stories he had told or share a song from childhood. When it rained, we put on our galoshes and looked for water skaters in the puddles. Sometimes we returned home with pine or cypress seedlings that we found sprouting among the blackberry brambles. The heavier samplings Baba carried with pride on his shoulder as if he'd bagged a wild boar. My parents replanted them for me just outside our fenced yard. They would not likely see the trees grow to full maturity, but they were thinking of the long years ahead of me when I would enjoy myself as mistress of the house in the forest.

On some evenings, when I had completed a chapter, I would read it out loud while my parents listened, Mama's eyes closed in great concentration. The three of us would grow excited by the strange beauty, humor, and humanity of the forgotten stories, or weep for the injustices of a world at war. Baba's memories would come alive and more details were extracted from the bottom most layer of his forgetting. "Ohhh, this is too good. The world is going to love it," Mama would say, stamping her feet like a child.

35   I have come to believe that the Chinese food culture has been preparing me all my life to work closely with my parents. Sharing, self-restraint, respect for elders, and care for the young began at the tips of our chopsticks. In this house, where we politely slurp noodles in unison, the preferred eating utensil is the bamboo chopsticks, not the knives and forks which the Chinese consider weapons of war. Our food is bite-size, sharing from common main dishes instead of sawing away at individual slabs of meat on individual plates. With the opposite, unused ends of her chopsticks, Mama will pick up a piece of tender snow pea and deliver it into my bowl, or Baba will place the last prawn atop Mama's rice which she will decline with a *"ni chi ba,* you take it." There is no "crossing the river" allowed, which means to stretch our arms across the table over dishes in front and reaching for desired morsels in a faraway dish. We eat what is in front of us and take what our chopsticks first touch. By eating at an affable pace, it is the responsibility of those at the table to make sure that everyone has had a fair share. As a child, I was scolded for digging for green peas from the main dish and popping them into my mouth, one after another without pause, or for leaving kernels of rice in my bowl. "It's by the sweat of the farmers' brows that you're provided this rice. Do not waste it. If you do, you'll grow up and marry a man with pockmarks," my mother would say, a threat Chinese mothers have been repeating for at least five thousand years.

36   I was certain my writing would find its way out into the world. I felt that once I had put down the last period in my manuscript, my work was fully complete and had a life of its own. It was real. Publication would be joy, but the writing itself was red-blooded life. It was lucky I was ignorant of the hurdles to publication. Had I known of all the reasons why my work would not find an audience, I would have been too frightened to begin. As it was, ignorance was bliss. I had a beginner's mind. To the beginner, everything is possible; the expert knows too well the limitations.

37   With the 1994 publication of *Baba: A Return to China Upon My Father's Shoulders*, my father was finally able to shake off the paranoid feelings of danger that had dominated his life. In lending him my voice, I had made him real, an individual, someone who could not be snuffed out under boots of adversity. I had rendered him safe. I was Hua Mulan,[9] the woman warrior of legends, who cut off her tresses and went into battle in her father's stead. It was now my father who was traveling America upon my shoulders.

38   Baba, at the age of seventy, looks younger today than he did in his fifties. The frown-creases have been smoothed over. The cynicism, the cold snap in his eyes, is no more. Readers, young and old alike, call him Baba when they have a chance to meet him. He likes that.

QUESTIONS ON MEANING

1. What does the word *ming* mean in Chinese and why is Yang a great believer in it? What else does she believe in?

2. What personality trait or habit distinguished Yang's father? What does he do automatically?

3. What was Yang's reaction to Chinese culture in her youth?

4. Why are stories important for individuals and societies?

5. What motivates Yang to write about China? Who is her source for details and why is that source valuable?

6. What effect does the publication of Yang's book have on her father?

QUESTIONS FOR DISCUSSION

1. Yang claims that stories are magic. What does she mean by this and is that true?

2. The author places great importance on understanding the past, both history and family heritage. Is this a reasonable idea?

3. What is interesting and distinctive about Yang's Chinese family's eating practice? What is its purpose for them as a family?

4. What contributes to creating cynicism in a nation or a group of people? Can it be counteracted?

---

[9] Hua Mulan: a female military hero in an all-male army portrayed in a Chinese poem entitled *Ballad of Mulan*, appearing first in the sixth-century *Musical Records of Old and New*.

LOOKING AT RHETORIC

1. This essay combines recent Chinese national history with personal history. In what way do these historical accounts complement one another?

2. Yang begins with a single sentence in capital letters. In what way does this claim affect the reader's understanding of the rest of the essay?

3. Yang writes continually about the power of language to comfort and inspire, especially her father's Chinese language. However, this essay is written in English. In what sense does she use English in the same way?

WRITING ASSIGNMENTS

1. Using library and/or Internet sources, research the role of story-telling and oral traditions. Then consider a situation, either in a family or any group to which you belong, when a story was told that attracted your attention. Why was that story interesting to you? What did it tell you or teach you about yourself?

2. Argue for or against Yang's claim that the past is an important part of who we are.

3. In pairs or in groups, tell a brief tale, recounting an incident about your family, friends, or any person or group that is important to you. Discuss the appeal of stories taken from real life. Individually, write that incident into a more complete personal narrative, with a main idea that gives your writing meaning to an audience besides yourself.

Prologue from *The Death of Josseline*

Margaret Regan

Margaret Regan is a staff writer for the Tucson Weekly *and is the winner of a number of journalism awards. She reports primarily on issues of immigration on the United States-Mexico border. In 2010 she published a short story collection,* The Death of Josseline: Immigration Stories from the Arizona-Mexico Borderlands. *In the introduction to that collection, Regan cites the staggering statistics of injury and death that have occurred since the year 2000 from border crossings in the desert. The following selection from that collection recounts the details of the tragic death of a fourteen-year-old girl as she travels with her younger brother in an attempt to get from El Salvador, through Mexico, to Los Angeles, where they will join their mother. Rich in vivid detail and factual information, this brief narrative encourages a reconsideration of how the immigration issue is discussed in the media and in private conversation, suggesting that the human tragedy of lives lost has been obscured by debates revolving around politics and economics.*

> *She was just a little girl. She was on her way to her mother.*
>
> —*Kat Rodriguez, human rights activist*

1   Josseline shivered as she stepped over the stones and ducked under the mesquites. She was in Arizona, land of heat and sun, but on this late-January day in 2008, it was cold and damp. The temperature was in the 50s, and the night before it had dropped to near

freezing. A winter rain had fallen, and now the desert path was slippery and wet, even more treacherous than it had been before.

2   Josseline was seven miles north of the Mexican border, near the old ranching town of Arivaca, in prime Sonoran Desert. It was a wonderland of cactus and mesquite, beautiful but dangerous, with trails threading through isolated canyons and up and down hills studded with rocks. She had to get through this perilous place to get to her mother. A little girl with a big name—Josseline Jamileth Hernández Quinteros—she was five feet tall and a hundred pounds. At fourteen, young as she was, she had an important responsibility: it was her job to bring her little brother, age ten, safely to their mother in Los Angeles. The Hernández kids had never been away from home before, and already they'd been traveling for weeks. Now they were almost there, just days away from their mother's embrace.

3   The family hadn't been together in a long time. Their father, Santos, was living somewhere in Maryland; their mother, Sonia, in California. Both parents were undocumented, working in the shadows. Back home in El Salvador, the kids lived with relatives, and in the years their mom was gone, Josseline had become a little mother to her brother. Finally, Sonia had worked long enough and hard enough to save up the money to send for the children. She'd arranged for Josseline and her brother to come north with adults they knew from home, people she trusted.

4   The group had crossed from El Salvador into Guatemala, then traveled two thousand miles from the southern tip of Mexico to the north. The trip had been arduous. They'd skimped on food, slept in buses or, when they were lucky, in *casas de huéspedes*, the cheap flophouses that cater to poor travelers. In Mexico, the migrants feared the *federales*, the national police, and now, in the United States, they were trying to evade the Border Patrol, the dreaded *migra*.

5   But here in the borderlands they were in the hands of a professional. Like the thousands of other undocumented migrants pouring into Arizona—jumping over walls, trekking across mountains, hiking through deserts—their group had contracted with a coyote, a smuggler paid to spirit them over the international line. The coyote's fee, many thousands of dollars, was to pay for Josseline and her brother to be taken from El Salvador all the way to their mother in Los Angeles. So far, everything had gone according to plan. They had slipped over the border from Mexico, near Sasabe, twenty miles from here, and had spent a couple of days picking their way through this strange desert, where spiky cacti clawed at the skin and the rocky trail blistered the feet. The coyote insisted on a fast pace. They still had a hike of twenty miles ahead of them, out to the northbound highway, Interstate 19, where their ride would meet them and take them deep into the United States.

6   Josseline (pronounced YO-suh-leen) pulled her two jackets closer in the cold. She was wearing everything she had brought with her from home. Underneath the jackets, she had on a tank top, better suited to Arizona's searing summers than its chilly winters, and she'd pulled a pair of sweatpants over her jeans. Her clothes betrayed her girly tastes. One jacket was lined in pink. Her sneakers were a wild bright green, a totally cool pair of shoes that were turning out to be not even close to adequate for the difficult path she was walking. A little white beaded bracelet circled her wrist. Best of all were her sweats, a pair of "butt pants" with the word HOLLYWOOD emblazoned on the rear. Josseline planned to have them on when she arrived in the land of movie stars.

7   She tried to pay attention to the twists and turns in the footpath, to obey the guide, to keep up with the group. But by the time they got to Cedar Canyon, she was lagging. She was beginning to feel sick. She'd been on the road for weeks and out in the open for days, sleeping on the damp ground. Maybe she'd skimped on drinking water, giving what she had to her little brother. Maybe she'd swallowed some of the slimy green water that pools in the cow ponds dotting this ranch country. Whatever the reason, Josseline started vomiting. She crouched down and emptied her belly, retching again and again, then lay back on the ground. Resting didn't help. She was too weak to stand up, let alone hike this roller-coaster trail out to the road.

8   It was a problem. The group was on a strict schedule. They had that ride to catch, and the longer they lingered here the more likely they'd be caught. The coyote had a decision to make, and this is the one he made: he would leave the young girl behind, alone in the desert. He told her not to worry. They were in a remote canyon that was little traveled, but the Border Patrol would soon find her. Nearby, he claimed, were some *pistas*, platforms that *la migra* used as landing pads for their helicopters. Surely they'd be by soon, and they would take care of her. Her little brother cried and begged to stay with her. But Josseline was his big sister, and Josseline insisted that he go. As he recounted later, she told him, "Tú tienes que seguir a donde está Mamá." *You have to keep going and get to Mom.*

9   The other travelers grabbed the wailing boy and walked on, leaving his sister alone in the cold and dark. She had only her clothes to keep her warm. On her first night alone, the temperature dropped below freezing, to 29 degrees. By the weekend, when her brother arrived safely in Los Angeles and sounded the alarm, Arivaca had warmed up—to 37 degrees.

10   Three weeks later, Dan Millis was getting ready to go out on desert patrol. He was filling up a big plastic box with nonperishables for migrants—granola bars, applesauce, Gatorade—and new socks, something the weary walkers always seemed to need. He tossed the box into his car and then loaded up dozens of gallons of water. A former high school teacher, Dan, twenty-eight, was an outdoors enthusiast who was spending a year volunteering with No More Deaths, a Tucson group determined to stop the deaths of migrants in the Arizona deserts. As the United States clamped down on the urban crossings, desperate travelers were pushing into ever more remote wilderness and dying out there in record numbers. So the No More Deaths folks began hiking the backcountry in the Arivaca borderlands, an hour and a half southwest of Tucson, setting out water and food in the rugged hills. Sometimes they'd meet up with migrants who were lost or sick, and they would provide first aid. But sometimes they found a body.

11   Before he left town, Dan studied the trail map. He could see that several heavily traveled Arivaca trails converged on a single ridge, and he wanted to drop his load there, where it would do the most good. Three buddies were coming along to help, but the goods they were packing would be heavy—each gallon jug of water weighed almost eight and a half pounds—so he wanted to get his car as close to the ridge as he could. The map showed that a dirt ranch road edged near the drop spot, but the volunteers would have to hike up Cedar Canyon, where they'd never been before. Dan didn't know whether the canyon would even be passable, but he decided to give it a shot.

12   He had heard about Josseline Hernández. When the girl's little brother arrived in LA without her, her distraught family had called the Salvadoran consul in Nogales, a border

town, and the consul connected them with Coalición de Derechos Humanos, a human rights organization in Tucson. Derechos compiles annual lists of the desert's dead, and tries to help the families of the missing. The coalition's Kat Rodriguez gets two or three reports of lost migrants a month. Josseline's mother couldn't even talk to her—"She was coming undone"—but the uncle gave Kat a description of the teenager and her clothes, including the distinctive green shoes Josseline was so proud of. Kat always asked for pictures of the loved one smiling; teeth, after all, can be used to identify a corpse.

13   The family sent Kat photos that pictured Josseline in uniform and cap, banging the cymbals in a parade with her high school marching band; Josseline posing in fashionable capris and a tank top; Josseline standing forlornly in her church, with flowers, lit candles, and a statue of the Virgin Mary behind her. The pictures showed her black hair and eyes and her warm brown skin—*morena*, the consul called it—but in every one she was serious and unsmiling, a young girl with heavy responsibilities. Kat organized the images and identifying info into a color flyer headlined *"Menor detenida o desaparecida"* (Female minor detained or disappeared). Kat sent her report to the Pima County medical examiner, in case he had a matching body in his morgue, and activists from the Samaritans immigrant-aid group checked the hospitals and detention centers. Other volunteers went out looking for her. They didn't have much to go on. The coyote had told the family Josseline was near *pistas*, or platforms; no one was quite sure of what he meant since there were no structures in the desert. And the flyer stated, erroneously as it turned out, that the girl had last been seen near Nogales, miles from where she'd been walking.

14   Dan Millis hadn't gotten involved in the searches. Hunts for missing migrants are needle-in-a-haystack affairs, typically conducted by well-meaning amateurs who don't know search-and-rescue techniques. Sometimes the volunteers get injured themselves. Even BORSTAR, the Border Patrol's search, trauma, and rescue unit, can't help when there's too little information. Far better, Dan thought, to stick to the work he knew would do some good, putting out food and water for the living. So he and his companions drove down to Arivaca and started into Cedar Canyon, lugging the water jugs and the box of goodies, traipsing a narrow path between looming rocky walls. There was an old dam back in there, along a wash, and he and his buds had to scramble up over the concrete. They'd been walking maybe twenty minutes when up ahead Dan spotted a pair of bright green shoes.

15   He didn't think of Josseline at first. Or of death. The owner of the shoes had to be around, he reasoned, maybe hiding. He began calling out the standard No More Deaths chant, designed to reassure fearful migrants. "¡Hola, hermanos! Somos amigos de la iglesia. Tenemos comida y agua." *Hello, brothers! We're friends from the church. We have food and water.*

16   Then, suddenly, he saw her. She was lying on a rock, under a bush, her hands raised up near her head, her feet plunged into water that had pooled in a cavity in the stone.

17   "I saw her teeth," he said months later. "I knew she was dead. It was a horrible feeling. I told my friends to stop.

18   "The body was intact," he went on, reciting details of the scene in a monotone. "She had taken off two jackets and hung them on a rock. She had a tank top on and sweatpants. Her feet were in the water." The little pearl bracelet was on her wrist. But Josseline's little brother had said his sister was wearing jeans, and this girl had on sweatpants.

19   Dan used his cell phone to call Sarah Roberts, a nurse active in No More Deaths who had helped coordinate Josseline's case. He told her about finding the body and the tell-tale green shoes and the sweatpants that didn't match up. Sarah got the message to Kat Rodriguez, who called the uncle, who questioned the brother one more time. This time, the little boy said, No, now he remembered, Josseline had put on her Hollywood butt pants. The news flew back over the cell phones to Dan. But the body was face up, and he couldn't see any writing. He knew enough about police procedures not to disturb the scene.

20   Dan telephoned the sheriff. Then he and another volunteer, Clint, drove the hour into Arivaca, marking down their route through the tangle of ranch roads so that they could give the police detailed directions back to the canyon. It was getting cold, so they picked up some hot soup in town for the two volunteers who had stayed behind with the body. In the meantime, that pair, a Frenchwoman named Marie and a refugee-rights worker named Max, had twisted some branches into a cross and planted it in a pile of rocks. When Dan and Clint got back, all four volunteers held a vigil, sitting by the body and the makeshift shrine, waiting for the authorities to come.

21   In the late afternoon, two sheriff's deputies finally arrived. They gently turned the body over. On the back of the pants was a single word: HOLLYWOOD.

22   Josseline completed her journey in a white plastic body bag. The deputies dragged her out along the trail, and lashed her corpse to a platform on the back of their SUV. It was dark by then, and they had to follow Dan's car out on the dirt roads, the two vehicles cara-vanning in an impromptu funeral procession. Once they hit Interstate 19, going north to Tucson up the broad Santa Cruz Valley, Dan noticed something strange in the sky. "It was the night of the full lunar eclipse," he remembered. "It was eerie to have the orange moon disappearing."

23   Josseline's father flew in from the East Coast in a panic. Hollywood pants don't carry much weight in the world of forensic identification, and her body was too far gone after three weeks in the elements to be identified by sight. So Josseline's dad paid a private lab to put together his DNA profile. The testing took weeks. In the interim, a coyote kept calling Josseline's mother, insisting that her daughter was not lost. If the family would only send him money, he promised, he would bring the girl to her alive and well. Sonia hesitated, not wanting to believe that her child was dead. But the DNA test, when it came in, was unequivocal. The probability that Santos was the father of the dead girl in the morgue was 99.988 percent. Armed with those results and a copy of the birth certificate, Pima County forensic anthropologist Bruce Anderson determined once and for all that this was the body of Josseline Hernández.

24   She was taken to California for burial. Her mother had no plans to return to El Salvador, and she wanted her daughter close.

25   Two months later, in the heat of late April, Father Bob Carney, a Catholic priest from Tucson, scrambled into Cedar Canyon to say a Mass for Josseline. He brought up the rear of thirty mourners, among them Josseline's aunts, uncles, and cousins. Her parents were unable to grieve at the place where their daughter had died, and neither was her brother; as undocumented immigrants, they feared arrest. Tucson activists had turned up in large numbers. The death of the teenager had hit them hard. ("That case was hell," Kat Rodriguez would later say. "Every step of the way was agony.") The slow climb up the canyon was

a reminder of what border crossers regularly endured. "People were getting scratched," Father Bob said later, "stumbling over the rocks. This is what she went through."

26   Josseline's relatives were the first to arrive at the rock where the body had been found. "All of a sudden this wail went up through that valley and echoed," Father Carney said. "When I got there they were truly grieving, and blaming themselves at the same time. All the emotions came pouring out in a heartrending wail."

27   The priest laid an alter cloth and his chalice on the rock, and said Mass among the prickly green plants, the canyon walls rising up behind him. As he broke the Communion bread, he intoned the biblical words "Do this in memory of me."

28   The No More Deaths Phoenix chapter had made a pretty new cross for Josseline, all pink and white, painted with flowers and entwined with ribbons. After the service, Father Bob anointed the cross with oil, and told Josseline, he would later say, "How sorry I was, that we as a people, as a nation, would do this."

29   Josseline's mother had written a poem in Spanish for her daughter, and her words were transcribed on the base of the cross. They began with encouragement to other migrants who might come this way: "When you feel that the road has turned hard and difficult / Don't give yourself up as lost / Continue forward and seek God's help." But it ended with a lament for her daughter: "Te llevaremos siempre en el corazón." *We'll carry you always in our hearts.*

30   The priest had seen many horrors in the ten years since he'd first blessed the bodies of eight young migrants piled up in an Arizona morgue, but for him, Josseline's tragedy stood out.

31   "For all of us, those who saw her, or saw her picture, she became so alive, so real," Father Bob said, beginning to cry as he spoke, months after the Mass in the desert. "We called her our sister, our daughter, our child. Every migrant is dear to us. But she was everybody. She was all of those thousands of people who suffered and died."

QUESTIONS ON MEANING

1. What hazards do Josseline and her brother face in their border crossing, in Mexico and America?

2. What is a *coyote* and what task does he perform?

3. Why do the migrants leave Josseline alone?

4. What does Dan Miller notice in the night sky as they carry Josseline's body out of the desert? How does he react to it?

5. In his prayer in the Mass at the site of Josseline's death, who does the priest blame for the tragic event?

6. In her poem, what does Josseline's mother tell other migrants who travel the same path as Josseline?

QUESTIONS FOR DISCUSSION

1. In what way does Josseline's story alter your view of the immigration issue, if at all?

2. In media coverage of the immigration question, how often is the discussion approached as a political and economic issue instead of as a personal and human tragedy? What viewpoint should dominate the discussion?

3. Who is responsible for Josseline's death?

LOOKING AT RHETORIC

1. Regan is a journalist. How does the combination of reporting and personal narrative affect your response to this account?

2. In what way does the portrayal of people such as Dan and Kat enhance or detract from the narrative?

3. How does the description of clothing (a method often found in fiction and literary non-fiction) expand your understanding of Josseline as a human being?

WRITING ASSIGNMENTS

1. Using library and/or Internet sources, research other personal narratives of immigration. Argue for or against the idea that this personal account of one immigration tragedy should alter our perspective on the issue.

2. Analyze the use of descriptive detail in the narrative and write an essay in which you argue for or against the role of description in transforming our perspective on undocumented immigration.

3. In pairs or in groups, discuss the question of whether economic or personal issues should dominate our discussion of undocumented immigration. Individually, write an essay in which you make an argument on this question.

A Muslim Leader in Brooklyn, Reconciling 2 Worlds

Andrea Elliot

Andrea Elliot (b. 1972) is an American journalist and a feature reporter for The New York Times *who focuses her articles on ethnic and cultural affairs in the United States. She earned her B.A. degree from Occidental College in 1996, majoring in Comparative Literature, and after graduating, traveled in South America, producing a documentary for Chilean television. She enrolled in Columbia University's Graduate School of Journalism and completed her M.S. degree in 1999. She then took a position as a reporter for* The Miami Herald *in 2000, covering urban-related topics and writing feature articles on the Hispanic community. She joined* The New York Times *in 2003, where she covers Islamic culture in the United States, examining issues that have emerged particularly after the September 11, 2001 attacks.*

In 2007, she received the Pulitzer Prize for feature writing for a series of articles dealing with Egyptian born Sheik Reda Shata. The following article is taken from that series. It explores the challenges of cultural assimilation in the context of the heightened tensions of the post-9/11 era.

1   The imam[1] begins his trek before dawn, his long robe billowing like a ghost through empty streets. In this dark, quiet hour, his thoughts sometimes drift back to the Egyptian farming village where he was born.

2   But as the sun rises over Bay Ridge, Brooklyn, Sheik Reda Shata's new world comes to life. The R train rattles beneath a littered stretch of sidewalk, where Mexican workers huddle in the cold. An electric Santa dances in a doughnut shop window. Neon signs beckon. Gypsy cabs blare their horns.

3   The imam slips into a plain brick building, nothing like the golden-domed mosque of his youth. He stops to pray, and then climbs the cracked linoleum steps to his cluttered office. The answering machine blinks frantically, a portent of the endless questions to come.

4   A teenage girl wants to know: Is it halal, or lawful, to eat a Big Mac? Can alcohol be served, a waiter wonders, if it is prohibited by the Koran? Is it wrong to take out a mortgage, young Muslim professionals ask, when Islam frowns upon monetary interest?

5   The questions are only a piece of the daily puzzle Mr. Shata must solve as the imam of the Islamic Society of Bay Ridge, a thriving New York mosque where several thousand Muslims worship.

6   To his congregants, Mr. Shata is far more than the leader of daily prayers and giver of the Friday sermon. Many of them now live in a land without their parents, who typically assist with finding a spouse. There are fewer uncles and cousins to help resolve personal disputes. There is no local House of Fatwa[2] to issue rulings on ethical questions.

7   Sheik Reda, as he is called, arrived in Brooklyn one year after Sept. 11. Virtually overnight, he became an Islamic judge and nursery school principal, a matchmaker and marriage counselor, a 24-hour hot line on all things Islamic.

8   Day after day, he must find ways to reconcile Muslim tradition with American life. Little in his rural Egyptian upbringing or years of Islamic scholarship prepared him for the challenge of leading a mosque in America.

9   The job has worn him down and opened his mind. It has landed him, exhausted, in the hospital and earned him a following far beyond Brooklyn.

10   "America transformed me from a person of rigidity to flexibility," said Mr. Shata, speaking through an Arabic translator. "I went from a country where a sheik would speak and the people listened to one where the sheik talks and the people talk back."

11   This is the story of Mr. Shata's journey west: the making of an American imam.

12   Over the last half-century, the Muslim population in the United States has risen significantly. Immigrants from the Middle East, South Asia and Africa have settled across the country, establishing mosques from Boston to Los Angeles, and turning Islam into one of the nation's fastest growing religions. By some estimates, as many as six million Muslims now live in America.

---

[1] Imam: a Muslim leader or cleric, often the head of a Muslim community or mosque.
[2] Fatwa: an official opinion dealing with Islamic law issued by an Islamic scholar.

13   Leading this flock calls for improvisation. Imams must unify diverse congregations with often-clashing Islamic traditions. They must grapple with the threat of terrorism, answering to law enforcement agents without losing the trust of their fellow Muslims. Sometimes they must set aside conservative beliefs that prevail in the Middle East, the birthplace of Islam.

14   Islam is a legalistic faith: Muslims believe in a divine law that guides their daily lives, including what they should eat, drink and wear. In countries where the religion reigns, this is largely the accepted way.

15   But in the West, what Islamic law prohibits is everywhere. Alcohol fills chocolates. Women jog in sports bras. For many Muslims in America, life is a daily clash between Islamic mores and material temptation. At the center of this clash stands the imam.

16   In America, imams evoke a simplistic caricature—of robed, bearded clerics issuing fatwas in foreign lands. Hundreds of imams live in the United States, but their portrait remains flatly one-dimensional. Either they are symbols of diversity, breaking the Ramadan[3] fast with smiling politicians, or zealots, hurrying into their storefront mosques.

17   Mr. Shata, 37, is neither a firebrand nor a ready advocate of progressive Islam. Some of his views would offend conservative Muslims; other beliefs would repel American liberals. He is in many ways a work in progress, mapping his own middle ground between two different worlds.

18   The imam's cramped, curtained office can hardly contain the dramas that unfold inside. Women cry. Husbands storm off. Friendships end. Every day brings soap opera plots and pitch.

19   A Moroccan woman falls to her knees near the imam's Hewlett-Packard printer. "Have mercy on me!" she wails to a friend who has accused her of theft. Another day, it is a man whose Lebanese wife has concealed their marriage and newborn son from her strict father. "I will tell him everything!" the husband screams.

20   Mr. Shata settles dowries, confronts wife abusers, brokers business deals and tries to arrange marriages. He approaches each problem with an almost scientific certainty that it can be solved. "I try to be more of a doctor than a judge," said Mr. Shata. "A judge sentences. A doctor tries to remedy."

21   Imams in the United States now serve an estimated 1,200 mosques. Some of their congregants have lived here for generations, assimilating socially and succeeding professionally. But others are recent immigrants, still struggling to find their place in America. Demographers expect their numbers to rise in the coming decades, possibly surpassing those of American Jews.

22   Like many of their faithful, most imams in the United States come from abroad. They are recruited primarily for their knowledge of the Koran and the language in which it was revealed, Arabic.

23   But few are prepared for the test that awaits. Like the parish priests who came generations before, imams are called on to lead a community on the margins of American civic life. They are conduits to and arbiters of an exhilarating, if sometimes hostile world, filled with promise and peril.

---

[3] Ramadan: the ninth month of the Islamic calendar and a month of fasting in which many Muslims refrain from eating, drinking, smoking, and sex.

AN INVITATION TO ISLAM

24   More than 5,000 miles lie between Brooklyn and Kafr al Battikh, Mr. Shata's birthplace in northeastern Egypt. Situated where the Nile Delta meets the Suez Canal, it was a village of dirt roads and watermelon vines when Mr. Shata was born in 1968.

25   Egypt was in the throes of change. The country had just suffered a staggering defeat in the Six Day War with Israel, and protests against the government followed. Hoping to counter growing radicalism, a new president, Anwar Sadat, allowed a long-repressed Islamic movement to flourish.

26   The son of a farmer and fertilizer salesman, Mr. Shata belonged to the lowest rung of Egypt's rural middle class. His house had no electricity. He did not see a television until he was 15.

27   Islam came to him softly, in the rhythms of his grandmother's voice. At bedtime, she would tell him the story of the Prophet Muhammad, the seventh-century founder of Islam. The boy heard much that was familiar. Like the prophet, he had lost his mother at a young age.

28   "She told me the same story maybe a thousand times," he said.

29   At the age of 5, he began memorizing the Koran. Like thousands of children in the Egyptian countryside, he attended a Sunni religious school subsidized by the government and connected to Al Azhar University, a bastion of Islamic scholarship.

30   Too poor to buy books, the young Mr. Shata hand-copied from hundreds at the town library. The bound volumes now line the shelves of his Bay Ridge apartment. When he graduated, he enrolled at Al Azhar and headed to Cairo by train. There, he sat on a bench for hours, marveling at the sights.

31   "I was like a lost child," he said. "Cars. We didn't have them. People of different colors. Foreigners. Women almost naked. It was like an imaginary world."

32   At 18, Mr. Shata thought of becoming a judge. But at his father's urging, he joined the college of imams, the Dawah.

33   The word means invitation. It refers to the duty of Muslims to invite, or call, others to the faith. Unlike Catholicism or Judaism, Islam has no ordained clergy. The Prophet Muhammad was the religion's first imam, or prayer leader, Islam's closest corollary to a rabbi or priest; schools like the Dawah are its version of a seminary or rabbinate.

34   After four years, Mr. Shata graduated with honors, seventh in a class of 3,400.

35   The next decade brought lessons in adaptation. In need of money, Mr. Shata took a job teaching sharia, or Islamic law, to children in Saudi Arabia, a country guided by Wahhabism, a puritan strain of Sunni Islam. He found his Saudi colleagues' interpretation of the Koran overly literal at times, and the treatment of women, who were not allowed to vote or drive, troubling.

36   Five years later, he returned to a different form of religious control in Egypt, where most imams are appointed by the government and monitored for signs of radicalism or political dissent.

37   "They are not allowed to deviate from the curriculum that the government sets for them," said Khaled Abou El Fadl, an Egyptian law professor at the *University of California*, Los Angeles.

38   Mr. Shata craved greater independence, and opened a furniture business. But he missed the life of dawah and eventually returned to it as the imam of his hometown mosque, which drew 4,000 worshipers on Fridays alone.

39   His duties were clear: He led the five daily prayers and delivered the khutba, or Friday sermon. His mosque, like most in Egypt, was financed and managed by the government. He spent his free time giving lectures, conducting marriage ceremonies and offering occasional religious guidance.

40   In 2000, Mr. Shata left to work as an imam in the gritty industrial city of Stuttgart, Germany. Europe brought a fresh new freedom. "I saw a wider world," he said. "Anyone with an opinion could express it."

41   Then came Sept. 11.

42   Soon after, Mr. Shata's mosque was defiled with graffiti and smeared with feces.

43   The next summer, Mr. Shata took a call from an imam in Brooklyn. The man, Mohamed Moussa, was leaving his mosque, exhausted by the troubles of his congregants following the terrorist attacks. The mosque was looking for a replacement, and Mr. Shata had come highly recommended by a professor at Al Azhar.

44   Most imams are recruited to American mosques on the recommendation of other imams or trusted scholars abroad, and are usually offered an annual contract. Some include health benefits and subsidized housing; others are painfully spare. The pay can range from $20,000 to $50,000.

45   Mr. Shata had heard stories of Muslim hardship in America. The salary at the Islamic Society of Bay Ridge was less than what he was earning in Germany. But foremost on his mind were his wife and three small daughters, whom he had not seen in months. Germany had refused them entry.

46   He agreed to take the job if he could bring his family to America. In October 2002, the American Embassy in Cairo granted visas to the Shatas and they boarded a plane for New York.

A MOSQUE, A MAGNET

47   A facade of plain white brick rises up from Fifth Avenue just south of 68th Street in Bay Ridge. Two sets of words, one in Arabic and another in English, announce the mosque's dual identity from a marquee above its gray metal doors.

48   To the mosque's base—Palestinian, Egyptian, Yemeni, Moroccan and Algerian immigrants—it is known as Masjid Moussab, named after one of the prophet's companions, Moussab Ibn Omair. To the mosque's English-speaking neighbors, descendants of the Italians, Irish and Norwegians who once filled the neighborhood, it is the Islamic Society of Bay Ridge.

49   Mosques across America are commonly named centers or societies, in part because they provide so many services. Some 140 mosques serve New York City, where an estimated 600,000 Muslims live, roughly 20 percent of them African-American, said Louis Abdellatif Cristillo, an anthropologist at Teachers College who has canvassed the city's mosques.

50   The Islamic Society of Bay Ridge, like other American mosques, is run by a board of directors, mostly Muslim professionals from the Palestinian territories. What began in 1984 as a small storefront on Bay Ridge Avenue, with no name and no imam, has grown into one of the city's vital Muslim centers, a magnet for new immigrants.

51   Its four floors pulse with life: a nursery school, an Islamic bookstore, Koran classes and daily lectures. Some 1,500 Muslims worship at the mosque on Fridays, often crouched in

prayer on the sidewalk. Albanians, Pakistanis and others who speak little Arabic listen to live English translations of the sermons through headsets. It is these congregants' crumpled dollar bills, collected in a cardboard box, that enable the mosque to survive.

52   Among the city's imams, Bay Ridge is seen as a humbling challenge.

53   "It's the first station for immigrants," said Mr. Moussa, Mr. Shata's predecessor. "And immigrants have a lot of problems."

SKIP 911. CALL THE IMAM.

54   Mr. Shata landed at Kennedy International Airport wearing a crimson felt hat and a long gray jilbab that fell from his neck to his sandaled toes, the proud dress of an Al Azhar scholar. He spoke no English. But already, he carried some of the West inside. He could quote liberally from Voltaire, Shaw and Kant. For an Egyptian, he often jokes, he was inexplicably punctual.

55   The first thing Mr. Shata loved about America, like Germany, was the order.

56   "In Egypt, if a person passes through a red light, that means he's smart," he said. "In America, he's very disrespected."

57   Americans stood in line. They tended their yards. One could call the police and hear a rap at the door minutes later. That fact impressed not only Mr. Shata, but also the women of his new mosque.

58   They had gained a reputation for odd calls to 911. One woman called because a relative abroad had threatened to take her inheritance. "The officers left and didn't write anything," Mr. Shata said, howling with laughter. "There was nothing for them to write."

59   Another woman called, angry because her husband had agreed to let a daughter from a previous marriage spend the night.

60   To Mr. Shata, the calls made sense. The women's parents, uncles and brothers—figures of authority in family conflict—were overseas. Instead, they dialed 911, hoping for a local substitute. Soon they would learn to call the imam.

61   A bearish man with a soft, bearded face, Mr. Shata struck his congregants as an odd blend of things. He was erudite yet funny; authoritative at the mosque's wooden pulpit and boyishly charming between prayers.

62   Homemakers, doctors, cabdrivers and sheiks stopped by to assess the new imam. He regaled them with Dunkin' Donuts coffee, fetched by the Algerian keeper of the mosque, and then told long, poetic stories that left his visitors silent, their coffee cold.

63   "You just absorb every word he says," said Linda Sarsour, 25, a Muslim activist in Brooklyn.

64   The imam, too, was taking note. Things worked differently in America, where mosques were run as nonprofit organizations and congregants had a decidedly democratic air. Mr. Shata was shocked when a tone-deaf man insisted on giving the call to prayer. Such a man would be ridiculed in Egypt, where the callers, or muezzinin, have voices so beautiful they sometimes record top-selling CD's.

65   But in the land of equal opportunity, a man with a mediocre voice could claim discrimination. Mr. Shata relented. He shudders when the voice periodically sounds.

66   No sooner had Mr. Shata started his new job than all manner of problems arrived at his worn wooden desk: rebellious teenagers, marital strife, confessions of philandering, accusations of theft.

67   The imam responded creatively. Much of the drama involved hot dog vendors. There was the pair who shared a stand, but could not stand each other. They came to the imam, who helped them divide the business.

68   The most notorious hot dog seller stood accused of stealing thousands of dollars in donations he had raised for the children of his deceased best friend. But there was no proof. The donations had been in cash. The solution, the imam decided, was to have the man swear an oath on the Koran.

69   "Whoever lies while taking an oath on the Koran goes blind afterward," said Mr. Shata, stating a belief that has proved useful in cases of theft. A group of men lured the vendor to the mosque, where he confessed to stealing $11,400. His admission was recorded in a waraqa, or document, penned in Arabic and signed by four witnesses. He returned the money in full.

70   Dozens of waraqas sit in the locked bottom drawer of the imam's desk. In one, a Brooklyn man who burned his wife with an iron vows, in nervous Arabic scrawl, never to do it again. If he fails, he will owe her a $10,000 "disciplinary fine." The police had intervened before, but the woman felt that she needed the imam's help.

71   For hundreds of Muslims, the Bay Ridge mosque has become a courthouse more welcoming than the one downtown, a police precinct more effective than the brick station blocks away. Even the police have used the imam's influence to their advantage, warning disorderly teenagers that they will be taken to the mosque rather than the station.

72   "They say: 'No, not the imam! He'll tell my parents,'" said Russell Kain, a recently retired officer of the 68th Precinct.

MARRIAGE, MORTGAGE, MCDONALD'S

73   Soon after arriving in Brooklyn, Mr. Shata observed a subtle rift among the women of his mosque. Those who were new to America remained quietly grounded in the traditions of their homelands. But some who had assimilated began to question those strictures. Concepts like shame held less weight. Actions like divorce, abhorred by Mr. Shata, were surprisingly popular.

74   "The woman who comes from overseas, she's like someone who comes from darkness to a very well-lit place," he said.

75   In early July, an Egyptian karate teacher shuffled into Mr. Shata's office and sank into a donated couch. He smiled meekly and began to talk. His new wife showed him no affection. She complained about his salary and said he lacked ambition.

76   The imam urged him to be patient.

77   Two weeks later, in came the wife. She wanted a divorce.

78   "We don't understand each other," the woman said. She was 32 and had come from Alexandria, Egypt, to work as an Arabic teacher. She had met her husband through a friend in Bay Ridge. Her parents, still in Egypt, had approved cautiously from afar.

79   "I think you should be patient," said the imam.

80   "I cannot," she said firmly. "He loves me, but I have to love him, too."

81   Mr. Shata shifted uncomfortably in his chair. There was nothing he loathed more than granting a divorce.

82   "It's very hard for me to let him divorce you," he said. "How can I meet God on Judgment Day?"

83   "It's God's law also to have divorce," she shot back. The debate continued.

84   Finally, Mr. Shata asked for her parents' phone number in Egypt. Over the speaker-phone, they anxiously urged the imam to relent. Their daughter was clearly miserable, and they were too far away to intervene.

85   With a sigh, Mr. Shata asked his executive secretary, Mohamed, to print a divorce certificate. In the rare instance when the imam agrees to issue one, it is after a couple has filed for divorce with the city.

86   "Since you're the one demanding divorce, you can never get back together with him," the imam warned. "Ever."

87   The woman smiled politely.

88   "What matters for us is the religion," she said later. "Our law is our religion."

89   The religion's fiqh, or jurisprudence, is built on 14 centuries of scholarship, but imams in Europe and America often find this body of law insufficient to address life in the West. The quandaries of America were foreign to Mr. Shata.

90   Pornography was rampant, prompting a question Mr. Shata had never heard in Egypt: Is oral sex lawful? Pork and alcohol are forbidden in Islam, raising questions about whether Muslims could sell beer or bacon. Tired of the menacing stares in the subway, women wanted to know if they could remove their headscarves. Muslims were navigating their way through problems Mr. Shata had never fathomed.

91   For a while, the imam called his fellow sheiks in Egypt with requests for fatwas, or nonbinding legal rulings. But their views carried little relevance to life in America. Some issues, like oral sex, he dared not raise. Over time, he began to find his own answers and became, as he put it, flexible.

92   Is a Big Mac permissible? Yes, the imam says, but not a bacon cheeseburger.

93   It is a woman's right, Mr. Shata believes, to remove her hijab if she feels threatened. Muslims can take jobs serving alcohol and pork, he says, but only if other work cannot be found. Oral sex is acceptable, but only between married couples. Mortgages, he says, are necessary to move forward in America.

94   "Islam is supposed to make a person's life easier, not harder," Mr. Shata explained.

95   In some ways, the imam has resisted change. He has learned little English, and interviews with Mr. Shata over the course of six months required the use of a translator.

96   Some imams in the United States make a point of shaking hands with women, distancing themselves from the view that such contact is improper. Mr. Shata offers women only a nod.

97   Daily, he passes the cinema next to his mosque but has never seen a movie in a theater. He says music should be forbidden if it "encourages sexual desire." He won't convert a non-Muslim when it seems more a matter of convenience than true belief.

98   "Religion is not a piece of clothing that you change," he said after turning away an Ecuadorean immigrant who sought to convert for her Syrian husband. "I don't want someone coming to Islam tonight and leaving it in the morning."

TRUST IN GOD'S PLAN

99   Ten months after he came to America, Mr. Shata collapsed.

100   It was Friday. The mosque was full. Hundreds of men sat pressed together, their shirts damp with summer. Their wives and daughters huddled in the women's section,

one floor below. Word of the imam's sermons had spread, drawing Muslims from Albany and Hartford.

101   "Praise be to Allah," began Mr. Shata, his voice slowly rising.

102   Minutes later, the imam recalled, the room began to spin. He fell to the carpet, lost consciousness and spent a week in the hospital, plagued by several symptoms. A social worker and a counselor who treated the imam both said he suffered from exhaustion. The counselor, Ali Gheith, called it "compassion fatigue," an ailment that commonly affects disaster-relief workers.

103   It was not just the long hours, the new culture and the ceaseless demands that weighed on the imam. Most troubling were the psychological woes of his congregants, which seemed endless.

104   Sept. 11 had wrought depression and anxiety among Muslims. But unlike many priests or rabbis, imams lacked pastoral training in mental health and knew little about the social services available.

105   At heart was another complicated truth: Imams often approach mental illness from a strictly Islamic perspective. Hardship is viewed as a test of faith, and the answer can be found in tawwakul, trusting in God's plan. The remedy typically suggested by imams is a spiritual one, sought through fasting, prayer and reflection.

106   Muslim immigrants also limit themselves to religious solutions because of the stigma surrounding mental illness, said Hamada Hamid, a resident psychiatrist at *New York University* who founded The Journal of Muslim Mental Health. "If somebody says, 'You need this medication,' someone may respond, 'I have tawwakul,' " he said.

107   Mr. Gheith, a Palestinian immigrant who works in disaster preparedness for the city's health department, began meeting with the imam regularly after his collapse. Mr. Shata needed to learn to disconnect from his congregants, Mr. Gheith said. It was a concept that confounded the imam.

108   "I did not permit these problems to enter my heart," said Mr. Shata, "nor can I permit them to leave."

109   The conversations eventually led to a citywide training program for imams, blending Islam with psychology. Mr. Shata learned to identify the symptoms of mental illness and began referring people to treatment.

110   His congregants often refuse help, blaming black magic or the evil eye for their problems. The evil eye is believed to be a curse driven by envy, confirmed in the bad things that happen to people.

111   One Palestinian couple in California insisted that their erratic 18-year-old son had the evil eye. He was brought to the imam's attention after winding up on the streets of New York, and eventually received a diagnosis of schizophrenia.

112   Mr. Shata had less success with a man who worshiped at the mosque. He had become paranoid, certain his wife was cursing him with witchcraft. But he refused treatment, insisting divorce was the only cure.

113   Time and again, Mr. Shata's new country has called for creativity and patience, for a careful negotiation between tradition and modernity.

114   "Here you don't know what will solve a problem," he said. "It's about looking for a key."

QUESTIONS ON MEANING

1. Where did Sheik Reda Shata originally come from and what kind of upbringing did he have?

2. What questions form part of the daily puzzle that Mr. Shata must solve as the imam of the Islamic Society of Bay Ridge?

3. What motivated Mr. Shata to become a Muslim cleric, an imam?

4. What are some of the various roles Mr. Shata must play in his relationship with the members of his Muslim congregation?

5. From what perspective do imams approach mental illness? What problems does this potentially create?

QUESTIONS FOR DISCUSSION

1. In what way does the article illuminate the difficulties of cultural assimilation in America, particularly as they relate to traditional vs. modern values?

2. In what way does the article serve to increase our understanding of one man's commitment to community? What personal motives inspire that commitment?

3. How did 9/11 affect the experience of Muslims in America?

4. In what way does religious commitment contribute to the problems of cultural assimilation and in what way does it help to solve them?

LOOKING AT RHETORIC

1. How does the form of the journalistic feature article (in contrast to straight reporting) help to increase your understanding of a contemporary historical and social situation?

2. How does the personal story in the context of the journalistic style contribute to or detract from your reading experience and your understanding?

3. How would you characterize the use of description? In what way does it differ from fiction or other forms of writing?

WRITING ASSIGNMENTS

1. Consider Mr. Shata's interaction with other Muslims around the question of Islamic law (whether it is lawful to eat a Big Mac or drink alcohol). Using library and/or Internet sources, explore other events in history when religious values have been forced to interact. Can a devout religious person respond to the spirit of the law without obeying the letter of the law? In other words, given that most religious texts are ancient and involve sometimes outdated ethical rules, can religious observance be modern?

2. In what ways have the events of 9/11 affected the Islamic experience in America? Consider both positive and negative effects.

3. In pairs or in groups, discuss your own experiences of assimilating to a new culture. Everyone has these experiences in one way or another, whether it is moving to another country with a different religion or cultural tradition, or whether it is changing schools and assimilating into a different group with different tastes, values, or behaviors. Individually, write a personal narrative in which you describe and explore that experience of assimilation.

Thinking Crosscurrently

HISTORY AND CULTURAL STUDIES

History is more than a chronicle of events that happened in the past. It doesn't boil down to a series of dates and names. Yes, events and people are important. To understand ourselves we need to know when people lived and what they did. But in many ways the past is a living thing because the forces that shape our lives are complicated and ancient, and comprehending our world as an intricate tapestry of people and places involves exploring how the past bears upon the present. We are not merely individuals, but cultural beings shaped by preexisting beliefs or religious perspectives, intellectual systems both philosophical and scientific, and beautiful forms of artistic expression found in literature and art. As you read the selections in this chapter, consider the following questions:

- To what extent are we condemned to repeat the errors of the past if we don't work to understand them as they happened? How might Terry Burnham and Jay Phelan, Mahatma Gandhi, or Terry Eagleton answer this question? What might they say about the relationship of the past and the present?

- What really is culture? What are the various ways this term can be defined? How does modern mass media enrich and even complicate this term? What might Marshall McLuhan and Lynda Barry think about what culture really is?

- How valid and true is any historical account? What makes written history trustworthy? How does the use of non-fiction shape how we understand history, and how might art, literature, and philosophy give us a different understanding of the past? What kinds of historical understanding do we gain from Plato, Melville, and Chopin?

- What can we accomplish with an understanding of history and culture? What can we do with it to make a better world and more productive societies? Are there ways we can use historical knowledge to shape our economic, political, and educational systems? To what extent do Milton Friedman, Paul Krugman, Thomas Kuhn, and Diane Ravitch depend upon history in the formation of their ideas?

11

LITERATURE, LANGUAGE, AND ART

W hy did you save to buy an iPod? Why is your Netflix queue filled to the brim? For some of us, why do we anxiously await the next novel from our favorite author? In 2007, the Royal Shakespeare Company went on tour with a production of *King Lear* starring Ian McKellen (of *Lord of the Rings* and *X-Men* fame) in the lead role. When they arrived for two performances at the University of California, Los Angeles, the original ninety dollar tickets were being scalped for nearly a thousand dollars each. Glib words like "enjoyment," "entertainment," and "fun" may explain the iPod and the Netflix, but do they really? They certainly don't capture why people would spend a week's salary to watch a crazed old man lament for hours his failures in life, his losses, and the betrayal of all his hopes. The songs we listen to and the movies we watch do the same thing. Rock and roll is built upon the blues, a grassroots music about suffering and sadness, and many of the movies we love deal with trauma, war, violence, fear, as well as hope, love, and possibility. There is something in all of these things that captivates us, not so much when we experience them personally but when we are moved by them in literature, art, and music.

From the earliest paintings found by explorers on cave walls in France, human beings have yearned to express the details of their lives, positive and negative. Others have responded with sincere empathy to those works and yearn to experience them again and again. Of all of the accomplishments of ancient civilizations—Egypt, Sumer, Greece, Rome, China, Japan—what remains for us to see, what connects us to the past and our forebears, is art, particularly literary art. Human expression takes on many forms, some with a practical use, such as architecture, creative design in gardens and city spaces, as well as in tapestry and decorative art. Others are created only for our deeply felt enjoyment, art forms like theatre, music, and literature. All of these modes of expression coalesce and become the received memory of peoples and civilizations, and at their best they convey aspects of a universal human experience. At the center of what makes us who we are is expression in the form of symbols. Unlike any other creature we know, we have language. Our distinctive brains create it and use it naturally. Other creatures communicate, but not with words and sentences, not with symbols and the grammar that makes sense of them. Language, literature, and music are a few of the things that truly set us apart as a species. In an age when biological science reminds us of our animal nature and our relation to the natural world, literature, music, and other art forms distinguish us. To understand and appreciate creativity is to come to know ourselves more fully as human beings.

THE DISCIPLINE YOU EXPERIENCE

Over two thousand years ago, the ancient philosopher Plato argued that poets were inspired by a "divine madness." He admired their works and enjoyed them, but they bothered him as well, because he thought their irrationality might harm the order of the state. In the seventeenth century, the neo-classical literary critic Samuel Johnson echoed the same sentiments, writing that literature and art should be created with a "moral purpose," and he claimed that Shakespeare, much as he valued his plays, didn't always have one.

What really is the purpose of art? What should it accomplish with its audience? We are fond of claiming that an artist's impulse is personal, that they work to express themselves, their subjective feelings and sentiments. But the truth is that artists want to make a living. The great Renaissance painter Michelangelo had patrons and worked on commission, and beyond the money motive he wanted an audience to appreciate his labors and to in some way feel and live through his work. Samuel Johnson wasn't all about morals; he thought that literature should instruct by pleasing. Pleasure, then, is at the center of art in all its forms. But Edgar Allan Poe disagreed with Johnson's emphasis on morality. He thought that any moral that appears in literature is coincidental and ancillary, that to make morality central is to commit what he called the "Heresy of the Didactic." For him, poetry especially was about feeling, not entertainment and fun, but deep feeling, that captivating emotion that hits us hard and takes us out of ourselves at least for a while. His most common metaphor for great poetry was music, and he called this profound reaction the experience of "Supernal Beauty." Complicating matters, the poet John Keats gave us a blend of these two perspectives. In one of his most famous poems, "Ode on a Grecian Urn," he takes on the question of art as it relates to pleasure, beauty, morality, and truth. In the final lines of the poem, he writes "Beauty is truth, truth Beauty,—that is all/Ye know on earth, and all ye need to know." In his conception, art captures truths, moral or otherwise, and conveys them so they strike deep and become a part of us.

For Keats, beauty isn't a means of conveying truth, as Johnson claims. It's doesn't stand above truth, as Poe claims. Beauty and truth are one.

Plato, Johnson, Poe, and Keats all present highly conjectural ideas because literary art and music are a mysterious thing. No one knows exactly where they come from and why they move us. The debates continue on a number of fronts. Oscar Wilde seems to concur with Poe, and with his own particular wit argues for the beauty principle, the idea that pleasure is what we convey to an audience in art, and that the mastery of the particular medium should be our goal. In the end, he hands us a paradox, arguing implicitly for the value of art while at the same time claiming it is "useless."

Like other people who are drawn to a profession by their inherent gifts, artists often create by compulsion, perhaps because they feel like they have to. But often social and political forces get in the way. Virginia Woolf imagines a fictional but potentially very real situation. What would happen if a woman of genius felt compelled to create in a society that consigned her to the domestic sphere? Literary art especially emerges from social contexts and from specific moments in history. Those who create it are conditioned by the norms and mores of the societies in which they live. In this sense, literature and art are a complex amalgamation of human imagination, thought, and perception, as well as a matrix of social and cultural conditions. When we study them we engage all of these things, and when we come closer to understanding them, we expand our grasp of ourselves and our place in the world.

Thus, we can see that the study of art in all forms prepares us in a very important sense for the lives we live. In many ways, they are practical. Employers in the private sector often hire people with degrees in the humanities and the arts, mainly because they are thoughtful, interesting, and fascinating people to be around, and they are well prepared intellectually to be trained in the world of work. But the real value of study in literature, language, and art is the human and social texture they encourage us to understand. The study of these fields when described in disciplinary terms often appears under the category "Arts and Humanities," and in different colleges and universities it may appear in different places. There are departments of English, Comparative Literature, Linguistics, Modern and Ancient Languages, Theatre, Dance, and Music. More and more, these departments acknowledge the value of popular as well as "high" art forms, and they encourage a consideration of subjects ranging from the blues, rock and roll, and jazz, to science fiction, detective fiction, children's literature, even comic books and graphic novels. All of these things are increasingly seen as important modes of human expression worthy of appreciation and study. Students approach these disciplines for many reasons. Some want to increase their understanding so they may appreciate literature and art and teach them to others. They often earn bachelors and masters degrees, and if they want to teach at the university level, doctorates. Others pursue these same degrees with the intention of taking their intellectual skills and breadth of understanding into the public and private sector. Still others want to join the next generation of writers, painters, sculptors, musicians, conductors, actors, and editors. They tend to pursue programs that emphasize craft and technique, leading to Bachelor of Fine Arts (BFA) and Master of Fine Arts (MFA) degrees. The following is a list of programs and their various features:

- English, which usually involves the study of English and American literature and literary genres such as fiction, poetry, drama, some non-fiction, often within the context of literary history.

- Comparative Literature, including the study of Western and non-Western world literatures, usually in translation to English, but sometimes in the original languages. In large universities, this is often a separate department. In smaller ones, it is frequently contained within English departments.

- Linguistics, the analysis of language as a whole, including the formal structure of sound units (phonemes), word units (morphemes), and grammar (syntax). This is primarily a social science, though often housed in schools of art and humanities. Like Comparative Literature, in large universities there are sometimes separate departments of Linguistics. In smaller ones, the discipline is usually housed in English departments.

- Modern and Ancient Languages, involving the study of currently spoken languages such as French, Spanish, German, Russian, Chinese, and Japanese, as well as ancient languages such as Greek, Latin, and Hebrew. As students progress in these programs, they study the literature of these languages as well.

- Theatre, the exploration of the history of dramatic production and the techniques and skills related to theatre production, including directing, set and lighting design, costume design, stage management, as well as acting and performance.

- Music, involving the combined study of music history, the technical understanding of music as an artistic medium, and training and performance in various forms and arrangements, involving instruments and voice.

REFLECTING ON THIS CHAPTER

Given the varied nature of literary and artistic study and performance, as well as the complexity of language study both from the perspective of linguistics and foreign languages, a number of fascinating concerns emerge in the selections in this chapter. As you read, consider these questions:

- What is the essential issue or problem the author attempts to explore or solve? What claims are they making and do they make a convincing argument in support of those claims?

- Given that literature, language, and art exist both within and outside an academic realm, in what way do academic inquiries into them enhance our experience of the works?

- How do these various selections compare and contrast? What central themes emerge? Are the issues specific to individual types of art and language study? Are there ways that the concerns of one art form relate to others?

- What are the various writing strategies the authors employ? What tools do they use to persuade us? If you found a selection convincing, what made it so?

- Do you detect any flaws in the arguments? Can you find any logical fallacies? Are there overt biases? Remember, a bias is not the same as a point of view. A strongly persuasive argument can be unbiased if it honestly presents and analyzes the available data and information.

What Global Language?

Barbara Wallraff

Barbara Wallraff is a senior editor and columnist for The Atlantic *and is known for her exploration and commentary on language. She received her B.A. in political science and philosophy from Antioch College in 1974 and served in a series of editing posts, taking a position at* The Atlantic *in 1983. She is the author of* Word Count *(2000) and* Your Own Words *(2004), and her articles have appeared in* The Washington Post, The Boston Globe, Wilson Quarterly, *and* New York Times Magazine. *She has acted as a commentator on language use for* The NBC Nightly News, *National Public Radio's* All Things Considered *and* Morning Edition, *as well as other programs. Her writing on the subject is impeccably researched but is known particularly for its accessibility and popularity. The following selection explores and complicates the claim that, as a result of globalization, English will become the dominant world language in the new century. Distinguishing between native speakers of language and second language users, Wallraff examines what she sees as the uncertainties of our linguistic future.*

1   English has inarguably achieved some sort of global status. Whenever we turn on the news to find out what's happening in East Asia, or the Balkans, or Africa, or South America, or practically anyplace, local people are being interviewed and telling us about it in English.

2   Indeed, by now lists of facts about the amazing reach of our language may have begun to sound awfully familiar. English is the working language of the Asian trade group ASEAN. It is the de facto working language of 98 percent of German research physicists and 83 percent of German research chemists. It is the official language of the European Central Bank, even though the bank is in Frankfurt and neither Britain nor any other pre-dominantly English-speaking country is a member of the European Monetary Union. It is the language in which black parents in South Africa overwhelmingly wish their children to be educated.

3   And yet, of course, English is not sweeping all before it, not even in the United States. According to the U.S. Bureau of the Census, ten years ago about one in seven people in this country spoke a language other than English at home—and since then the proportion of immigrants in the population has grown and grown.

4   How can it be that English is conquering the globe if it can't even hold its own in parts of our traditionally English-speaking country?

5   A perhaps less familiar paradox is that the typical English-speaker's experience of the language is becoming increasingly simplified, even as English as a whole grows more complex. If these two trends are occurring, and they are, then the globaliza-tion of English will never deliver the tantalizing result we might hope for: that is, we monolingual English-speakers may never be able to communicate fluently with every-one everywhere. If we want to exchange anything beyond rudimentary messages with many of our future fellow English-speakers, we may well need help from something other than English.

FIRST, SECOND, OR FOREIGN LANGUAGE

6   People who expect English to triumph over all other languages are sometimes surprised to learn that the world today holds three times as many native speakers of Chinese as native speakers of English. "Chinese," as language scholars use the word, refers to a family of languages and dialects the most widely spoken of which is Mandarin;[1] and which share a written language although they are not all mutually intelligible when spoken. "English" refers to a family of languages and dialects the most widely spoken of which is standard American English, and which have a common origin in England—though not all varieties of English, either, are mutually intelligible.

---

[1] Mandarin: a group of Chinese dialects used across southwestern and northern China.

The versions of English used by educated speakers practically anywhere can be understood by most Americans, but pidgins,[2] creoles,[3] and diverse dialects belong to the same family, and these are not always so generally intelligible. To hear for yourself how far English now ranges from what we Americans are used to, you need only rent a video of the 1998 Scottish film *My Name Is Joe*, which, though in English, comes fully subtitled.

7   "Native speaker" is no easier to define with any precision than "Chinese" or "English," although it means roughly what you'd think: a person who grew up using the language as his or her first.

8   In any case, the numerical gap is impressive: about 1,113, million people speak Chinese as their mother tongue, whereas about 372 million speak English. And yet English is still the world's second most common native language, though it is likely to cede second place within fifty years to the South Asian linguistic group whose leading members are Hindi and Urdu. In 2050, according to a model of language use the world will hold 1,384 million native speakers of Chinese, 556 million of Hindi and Urdu, and 508 million of English. As native languages Spanish and Arabic will be almost as common as English, with 486 million and 482 million speakers respectively.

9   It's undeniable that English-speakers now have lower birth rates, on average, than speakers of Hindi and Urdu and Arabic and Spanish. The gains that everyone expects English to make must come because it is adopted as a second language or a foreign language by most of the people who speak it.

10   A few more definitions will be helpful here. "Second-language" speakers live in places where English has some sort of official or special status. In India, for instance, the national government sanctions the use of English for its business, along with fifteen indigenous languages. What proportion of India's population of a billion speaks English is hotly debated, but most sources agree it is well under five percent. All the same, India is thought to have the fourth largest population of English-speakers in the world, after the United States, the United Kingdom, and Nigeria—or the third largest if you discount speakers of Nigerian pidgin English. English is a second language for virtually everyone in India who speaks it. And obviously the United States, too, contains speakers of English as a second language—some 30 million of them in 1995, according to an estimate by David Crystal.

11   "Foreign-language" speakers of English live in places where English is not singled out in any formal way, and tend to learn it to communicate with people from elsewhere. Examples might be Japanese who travel abroad on business and Italians who work in tourism in their own country. The distinction between the two categories of non-native speakers is sometimes blurry. In Denmark and Sweden the overwhelming majority of children are taught English in school—does that constitute a special status?

12   The distinction between categories of speakers matters, in part because where English is a first or second language it develops local standards and norms. India, for instance,

---

[2] pidgins: simplified languages which are derived from two or more languages, often for the purpose of simple communication and trade. In America, there are a number of pidgins used.

[3] creoles: a reasonably stable language that emerges from a combination of other languages, usually with a distinctive grammar. Creole languages are thought to evolve when pidgins are spoken by succeeding generations.

publishes dictionaries of Indian English, whereas Denmark and Sweden tend to defer to Britain or the United States in setting standards of English pronunciation and usage. The distinction also matters in relation to how entrenched English is in a given place, and how easy that place would find it to abandon the language.

13   One more surprise is how speculative any estimate of the use of English as a second or a foreign language must necessarily be. How large an English vocabulary and how great a command of English grammar does a person need in order to be considered an English-speaker? Generally, even the most rigorous attempts to determine how many people speak what, including the U.S. Census, depend on self-reporting. Do those years of French in high school and college entitle us to declare ourselves bilingual? They do if we want them to.

14   So the number of people in the world who speak English is unknown, and how well many of them speak and understand it is questionable. No one is arguing that English is not widely spoken and taught. But the vast numbers that are often repeated—a billion English-speakers, a billion and a half—have only tenuous grounding in reality.

SEVERAL LANGUAGES CALLED ENGLISH

15   Much of what will happen to English we can only speculate about. But let's pursue an idea that language researchers regard as fairly well grounded: native speakers of English are already outnumbered by second-language and foreign-language speakers, and will be more heavily outnumbered as time goes on.

16   One obvious implication is that some proportion of the people using English for business or professional purposes around the world aren't and needn't be fluent in it.

17   A variety of restricted subsets of English have been developed to meet the needs of nonfluent speakers. Among these is Special English, which the Voice of America began using in its broadcasts experimentally some forty years ago and has employed part-time ever since. Special English has a basic vocabulary of just 1,500 words.

18   But restricted forms of English are usually intended for professional communities. Among the best known of these is Seaspeak, which ships' pilots around the world have used for the past dozen years or so; this is now being supplanted by SMCP, or "Standard Marine Communication Phrases," which is also derived from English but was developed by native speakers of a variety of languages. Airplane pilots and air-traffic controllers use a restricted form of English called Airspeak.

19   Certainly, the world's ships and airplanes are safer if those who guide them have some language in common, and restricted forms of English have no modern-day rivals for this role. The greatest danger language now seems to pose to navigation and aviation is that some pilots learn only enough English to describe routine situations, and find themselves at a loss when anything out of the ordinary happens.

20   Something else obviously implied by the ascendance of English as a second and a foreign language is that more and more people who speak English speak another language at least as well, and probably better. India may have the third or fourth largest number of English-speakers in the world, but English is thought to be the mother tongue of much less than one percent of the population. This is bound to affect the way the language is used locally. Browsing some English-language Web sites from India recently, I seldom had trouble understanding what was meant. I did, however, time and again come across unfamiliar words borrowed from Hindi or another indigenous Indian language.

21   Of course, English is renowned for its ability to absorb elements from other languages. As ever more local and national communities use English, though, they will pull language in ever more directions. Few in the world will care to look as far afield as the United States or Britain for their standards of proper English. After all, we long ago gave up looking to England—as did Indians and also Canadians, South Africans, Australians, and New Zealanders, among others. Today each of these national groups is proud to have its own idioms, and dictionaries to define them.

22   Most of the world's English-speaking communities can still understand one another well—though not, perhaps, perfectly. As Anne Soukhanov, a word columnist for this magazine and the American editor of the *Encarta World English Dictionary*, explained in an article titled "The King's English It Ain't," published on the Internet last year, "Some English words mean very different things, depending on your country. In South Asia, a *hotel* is a restaurant, but in Australia, a *hotel* is an establishment selling alcoholic beverages. In South Africa, a *robot* is a traffic light."

THE WEB IN MY OWN LANGUAGE

23   Much has been made of the Internet as an instrument for circulating English around the globe. According to one estimate that has been widely repeated over the past few years, 80 percent of what's available on the Internet is in English. Some observers, however, have recently been warning that this may have been the high-water mark. It's not that English-speakers are logging off—*au contraire*—but that other people are increasingly logging on, to search out or create content in their own languages. The consensus among those who study these things is that Internet traffic in languages other than English will outstrip English-language traffic within the next few years.

24   As has been widely noted, the Internet, besides being a convenient vehicle for reaching mass audiences such as, say, the citizenry of Japan or Argentina, is also well suited to bringing together the members of small groups—for example, middle-class French-speaking sub-Saharan Africans. Or a group might be those who speak a less common language: the numbers of Dutch-speakers and Finnish-speakers on the Internet are sharply up.

25   The Internet is capable of helping immigrants everywhere to remain proficient in their first language and also to stay current with what is going on back home. Residents in the Basque communities of Nevada and émigrés from the Côte d'Ivoire, for instance, can browse the periodicals, and even listen to the radio stations, of their homelands—much as American expatriates anywhere with an Internet connection can check the Web sites for CNN, ABC, MSNBC, and their hometown papers and radio stations.

26   No matter how much English-language material there is on the Web, then, or even how much more English material there is than material in other languages, it is naive to assume that home computers around the world will, in effect, become the work stations of a vast English language lab.

ENGLISH BY ACCIDENT

27   Even as software developers continue to adapt computers to our linguistic needs and wants, we are—God help us—adapting our own language to computers. For example, if I want to see the Amazon.com page about the psycholinguist Steven Pinker's book *Words*

and Rules (1999), it's a complete waste of time to type into the search feature "Words and Rules, by Steven Pinker," correctly capitalized and punctuated. The computer and I will get exactly as much out of the exchange if I type "pinker rules." In effect, in this context "pinker rules" is better English than "Words and Rules, by Steven Pinker."

28   Does this matter to the future of English? It may well. What is English, anyway? Is it the list of words and their meanings that a dictionary provides, together with all the rules about how to combine the words into sentences and paragraphs? Much more is involved than that. English is a system of communication, and highly germane to it is what or who speakers of English care to communicate with, and about what. The more we need to use English to communicate with machines—or with people whose fluency is limited or whose understanding of English does not coincide with ours—the more simplified the language will need to be.

29   And yet technology is expanding English, by requiring us to come up with new words to describe all the possibilities it offers. Throughout the past century, according to *Twentieth Century Words* (1999), by John Ayto, technological domains—at first the likes of cars and aviation and radio, and eventually nuclear power, space, computers, and the Internet— were among the leading "lexical growth-areas." What's new of late isn't only words: we have whole new ways of combining the elements of written language. One ready example is emoticons (such as :> and ;-o), which seem to have firmly established themselves in the realm of e-mail. Is *www* a word? Does one write the expression *dot com* or *.com* or what? And then there's professional jargon. In the course of exchanging ideas, global communities of astrophysicists, cardiologists, chip designers, food scientists, and systems analysts are stuffing the English language full of jargon. As science and technology grow increasingly multifarious and specialized, the jargon necessarily grows increasingly recondite: in the journal *Neurology*, for example, article titles like "Homogeneous phenotype of the gypsy limb-girdle MD with the γ sarcoglycan C283Y mutation" are run-of-the-mill. The range of English continues to expand further and further beyond any single person's ability to understand it all.

30   One more fact worth keeping in mind is that the relationship between science or technology and English is, essentially, accidental. It is chiefly because the United States has long been in the vanguard of much scientific and technological research, of course, that English is so widely used in these fields. If the United States were for the most part French-speaking, surely French would be the language of science and technology; there is nothing inherent in English to tie it to these fields. And if something as earthshaking as the Internet had been developed in, say, Japan, perhaps English would not now be dominant to the extent that it is. Future technology may well originate elsewhere. In the rapidly advancing field of wireless communications devices, for example, Scandinavia is already the acknowledged leader.

31   Here an argument is sometimes advanced that American culture furthers innovation, openness to new ideas, and so forth, and that our culture, whether by accident or not, is inseparable from the English language. But this takes us only so far. Even if the vanguards in all scientific and technological fields, everywhere in the world, used English in their work, once the fruits of their labor became known to ordinary people and began to matter to them, people would coin words in their local languages to describe these things. Theoretical physicists at international conferences may speak English among themselves, but most high school and college physics teachers use their

native languages in class with their students. The Microsoft engineers who designed the Windows computer-operating system spoke English, and used English in what they created, but in the latest version, Windows Millennium, the words that users see on the screen are available in twenty-eight languages—and the spell-checker offers a choice of four varieties of English.

32   In sum, the globalization of English does not mean that if we who speak only English just sit back and wait, we'll soon be able to exchange ideas with anyone who has anything to say. We can't count on having much more around the world than a very basic ability to communicate. Outside certain professional fields, if English-speaking Americans hope to exchange ideas with people in a nuanced way, we may be well advised to do as people elsewhere are doing: become bilingual. This is easier said than done. If learning a second language were so simple, no doubt many more of us would have picked up Spanish or Chinese by now. It is clear, though, that the young learn languages much more readily than adults. Surely, American children who are exposed to nothing but English would benefit from being taught other languages as well.

33   At the same time, English is flourishing, and people here and everywhere are eager to learn it to the extent that it is practical for them to do so. It would behoove us to make learning English as easy as possible, for both children and adults, in this country and abroad.

QUESTIONS ON MEANING

1. What circumstances in Europe suggest the increasing dominance of the English language?
2. What circumstances in America suggest that English may not dominate other languages as much as is conventionally thought?
3. What does Wallraff mean (with respect to English) when she uses the term *language variety*?
4. Given the fact that larger portions of the world's population speak other languages as their first language, what may cause English to become more dominant?
5. Why is it difficult to determine the number of English as second language speakers in the world?
6. In what way might technology affect the global dominance of English?

QUESTIONS FOR DISCUSSION

1. What economic and social forces allow a language to become dominant? How do these forces work?
2. What really makes a person bilingual? What should they be able to do with a language to consider themselves fluent?
3. What role will technologies such as the Internet play in the evolution of language use worldwide?

LOOKING AT RHETORIC

1. Wallraff begins with an anecdotal introduction, a brief story drawn from her experience. Does this effectively capture the reader's attention? If so, why? If not, why?

2. To what extent does Wallraff's use of statistics enhance or detract from her exploration of the topic?

3. Compared to many writers who deal with the subject of language, Wallraff writes with relative clarity. There are few difficult words that require a dictionary. What are the losses and gains that emerge from this stylistic choice?

WRITING ASSIGNMENTS

1. Using library and/or Internet sources, explore the history of the English language and how it has developed in different places throughout the world. Argue for or against the value of a global language, that is, a language spoken by most people worldwide as a primary or secondary language. Consider the potential effects on other languages, literatures, and cultures.

2. In an essay, define the term language. Given the varieties of any given language, including dialects, pidgins, and creoles, when does a branch of a language become a new language? How do we determine what is the original language?

3. In pairs or in groups, review and discuss the statistical data contained in the selection. Explore how it is used to support claims or speculations. Individually, write an essay in which you use some portion of the same statistics to support the opposite point of view.

Preface to *The Picture of Dorian Gray*

Oscar Wilde

Oscar Wilde (1854-1900) is of the most important British writers of the late nineteenth century. He is known for plays such as The Importance of Being Ernest *(1895) and* An Ideal Husband *(1895), and the novel* The Picture of Dorian Gray *(1890), all of which display his penchant for social satire, criticism, and incisive wit. He emerges from the Aesthetic Movement (with its roots in writers such as Edgar Allan Poe, John Ruskin, and Walter Pater) which emphasized beauty and pleasure as the primary criteria for judging art. Wilde was highly educated in the classics, attending the Portora Royal School in Ireland, then matriculating at Trinity College, Dublin, where he won the Berkeley Gold Medal. He became a celebrity both in Europe and America, known not only for his work but his flamboyant public persona. His approach to art was intense and celebratory, though his wit always displayed a strong element of irony. Like many other aesthetes, his purported goal was to make an art of life itself. Sadly, after being convicted of indecency for homosexual behavior, he was sentenced to two years hard labor, and shortly after his release he died in Paris. In epigrammatic form, the Preface to* The Picture of Dorian Gray *presents the essentials of his theory of art, which rejects moral motives and extols the value of beauty alone, emphasizing instead the mastery of the chosen medium, finally claiming with pithy humor that "All art is quite useless."*

1   The artist is the creator of beautiful things.

2   To reveal art and conceal the artist is art's aim. The critic is he who can translate into another manner or a new material his impression of beautiful things.

3   The highest as the lowest form of criticism is a mode of autobiography. Those who find ugly meanings in beautiful things are corrupt without being charming. This is a fault.

4   Those who find beautiful meanings in beautiful things are the cultivated. For these there is hope.

5   They are the elect to whom beautiful things mean only Beauty.

6   There is no such thing as a moral or an immoral book. Books are well written, or badly written. That is all.

7   The nineteenth century dislike of Realism[1] is the rage of Caliban[2] seeing his own face in a glass.

8   The nineteenth century dislike of Romanticism[3] is the rage of Caliban not seeing his own face in a glass.

9   The moral life of man forms part of the subject-matter of the artist, but the morality of art consists in the perfect use of an imperfect medium.

10   No artist desires to prove anything. Even things that are true can be proved.

11   No artist has ethical sympathies. An ethical sympathy in an artist is an unpardonable mannerism of style.

12   No artist is ever morbid. The artist can express everything.

13   Thought and language are to the artist instruments of an art.

14   Vice and virtue are to the artist materials for an art.

15   From the point of view of form, the type of all the arts is the art of the musician. From the point of view of feeling, the actor's craft is the type.

16   All art is at once surface and symbol.

17   Those who go beneath the surface do so at their peril.

18   Those who read the symbol do so at their peril.

19   It is the spectator, and not life, that art really mirrors.

20   Diversity of opinion about a work of art shows that the work is new, complex, and vital.

21   When critics disagree the artist is in accord with himself.

22   We can forgive a man for making a useful thing as long as he does not admire it. The only excuse for making a useless thing is that one admires it intensely.

23   All art is quite useless.

---

[1] Realism: an artistic and literary movement of the late nineteenth century that encouraged the precise and vivid portrayal of subject matter as it actually exists and functions.

[2] Caliban: a character in William Shakespeare's late play *The Tempest* (1610–1611). Caliban is the native of an island newly occupied by the powerful Prospero and is associated with savagery and barbarism, though in this context his plight is meant to be read sympathetically.

[3] Romanticism: a philosophical, artistic, and literary movement of the early nineteenth century that empha-sized the role of imagination in artistic creation, with a particular focus on nature and common life. Romantic works often make extensive use of symbolism.

QUESTIONS ON MEANING

1. What is the role of the artist? What should his or her primary goal be in creating art?
2. What role should morality play in the creation of art?
3. How do we determine a good work of art from a bad one?
4. Of what does the morality of art consist?
5. What two art forms are effective models for all other art forms?
6. When there is diversity of opinion about a work of art, what does that say about it?

QUESTIONS FOR DISCUSSION

1. From the point of view of an audience, what is the purpose of art? Should it have anything to do with communicating truth or morality?
2. What does he mean by the allusions to Caliban, Realism, and Romanticism? What does this reference have to do with Wilde's ideas about the purpose of art?
3. Wilde claims that art involves surface and symbol but to scrutinize them is perilous. This seems to discourage interpretation, study, or even thinking about art. Is this what he means? Is this a valid claim? Remember, he was a highly trained student of classical art and literature.
4. What is the use value of art, if any? If there is none, why have it? Remember, art is one of the few things that remains from ancient civilizations.

LOOKING AT RHETORIC

1. Wilde makes use of an epigrammatic style. What does he accomplish by doing this?
2. The use of Caliban involves an obscure reference to a character in a work of literature as it relates to two important movements. This is known as an allusion. How does this help the author make his rather controversial argument?

WRITING ASSIGNMENTS

1. Using library and/or Internet sources, research ideas about the purpose and value of artistic expression. Is there a purpose or a value of art beyond pleasure and entertainment?
2. When Wilde argues for the primacy of beauty and pleasure in art, is he being superficial? In saying that art is useless is he saying that the artist is not involved in a serious or important endeavor?
3. In pairs or in groups, discuss any works of art that you have been captivated by, that you have perhaps wanted to experience again and again. Explore and ponder why you responded deeply to them. You may think of popular songs, films, or books. They are all art. Individually, compose a Preface modeled on the form of Wilde's that outlines your ideas about the value and purpose of art.

Shakespeare's Sister

Virginia Woolf

Virginia Woolf (1882–1941), born Adeline Virginia Stephen, is one of the most prominent figures in the modernist movement in literature, which was influential in the early twentieth century, and in that context was a forerunner for contemporary feminist authors. She attended Kings College, Cambridge, and Kings College London, and settled in Bloomsbury, joining an eclectic caste of artists, writers, and intellectuals later coined "the Bloomsbury Group." She married Leonard Woolf, a writer of novels and political science, and began writing in the experimental mode of modernists such as James Joyce and the poet T. S. Eliot. She suffered from chronic nervous breakdowns and depression but was productive nevertheless, producing such novels as Mrs. Dalloway *(1925) and* To the Lighthouse *(1927). Her consideration of women's issues appears in a series of lectures delivered at Cambridge University in 1928, which were revised into* A Room of One's Own *(1929). A part of that book, "Shakespeare's Sister," begins by assuming for the famous playwright a fictional female sibling. Woolf then ponders what might have occurred in Shakespeare's time if a young woman of his ability confronted the social strictures faced by women then and now.*

1   Let me imagine, since facts are so hard to come by, what would have happened had Shakespeare had a wonderfully gifted sister, called Judith,[1] let us say. Shakespeare himself went, very probably—his mother was an heiress—to the grammar school, where he may have learnt Latin—Ovid, Virgil and Horace[2]—and the elements of grammar and logic. He was, it is well known, a wild boy who poached rabbits, perhaps shot a deer, and had, rather sooner than he should have done, to marry a woman in the neighborhood, who bore him a child rather quicker than was right. That escapade sent him to seek his fortune in London. He had, it seemed, a taste for the theatre; he began by holding horses at the stage door. Very soon he got work in the theatre, became a successful actor, and lived at the hub of the universe, meeting everybody, knowing everybody, practising his art on the boards, exercising his wits in the streets, and even getting access to the palace of the queen. Meanwhile his extraordinarily gifted sister, let us suppose, remained at home. She was as adventurous, as imaginative, as agog[3] to see the world as he was. But she was not sent to school. She had no chance of learning grammar and logic, let alone of reading Horace and Virgil. She picked up a book now and then, one of her brother's perhaps, and read a few pages. But then her parents came in and told her to mend the stockings or mind the stew and not moon about with books and papers. They would have spoken sharply but kindly, for they were substantial people who knew the conditions of life for a woman and loved their daughter—indeed, more likely than not she was the apple of her father's eye. Perhaps she scribbled some pages up in an apple loft on the sly, but was careful to hide them or set fire to them. Soon, however, before she was out

---

[1] In actuality, Shakespeare had a daughter named Judith.

[2] Ovid (43 B.C.E-17 C.E), Virgil (70-19 B.C.E.), and Horace (65-8 B.C.E.): Roman poets of the classical era, commonly studied by boys as a means of learning Latin in the Renaissance and in later eras.

[3] agog: full of excitement or interest.

of her teens, she was to be betrothed to the son of a neighboring wool-stapler. She cried out that marriage was hateful to her, and for that she was severely beaten by her father. Then he ceased to scold her. He begged her instead not to hurt him, not to shame him in this matter of her marriage. He would give her a chain of beads or a fine petticoat, he said; and there were tears in his eyes. How could she disobey him? How could she break his heart? The force of her own gift alone drove her to it. She made up a small parcel of her belongings, let herself down by a rope one summer's night and took the road to London. She was not seventeen. The birds that sang in the hedge were not more musical than she was. She had the quickest fancy, a gift like her brother's, for the tune of words. Like him, she had a taste for the theatre. She stood at the stage door; she wanted to act, she said. Men laughed in her face. The manager—a fat, looselipped man—guffawed. He bellowed something about poodles dancing and women acting—no woman, he said, could possibly be an actress.[4] He hinted—you can imagine what. She could get no training in her craft. Could she even seek her dinner in a tavern or roam the streets at midnight? Yet her genius was for fiction and lusted to feed abundantly upon the lives of men and women and the study of their ways. At last—for she was very young, oddly like Shakespeare the poet in her face, with the same grey eyes and rounded brows—at last Nick Greene[5] the actor-manager took pity on her; she found herself with child by that gentleman and so—who shall measure the heat and violence of the poet's heart when caught and tangled in a woman's body?—killed herself one winter's night and lies buried at some cross-roads where the omnibuses now stop outside the Elephant and Castle.

2   That, more or less, is how the story would run, I think, if a woman in Shakespeare's day had had Shakespeare's genius. But for my part, I agree with the deceased bishop, if such he was—it is unthinkable that any woman in Shakespeare's day should have had Shakespeare's genius. For genius like Shakespeare's is not born among labouring, unedu-cated, servile people. It was not born in England among the Saxons and the Britons. It is not born today among the working classes. How, then, could it have been born among women whose work began, according to Professor Trevelyan,[6] almost before they were out of the nursery, who were forced to it by their parents and held to it by all the power of law and custom? Yet genius of a sort must have existed among women as it must have existed among the working classes. Now and again an Emily Brontë or a Robert Burns[7] blazes out and proves its presence. But certainly it never got itself on to paper. When, however, one reads of a witch being ducked, of a woman possessed by devils, of a wise woman selling herbs, or even of a very remarkable man who had a mother, then I think we are on the track of a lost novelist, a suppressed poet, of some mute and inglorious Jane Austen,[8] some

---

[4] In Elizabethan theatre during Shakespeare's time, women's roles were played by boys. Only later, were women permitted to act.

[5] Nick Greene: Possibly a reference to Robert Greene (1558-1592), a playwright whose pamphlet (1592) contains the first reference to William Shakespeare. It was a negative reference.

[6] Professor Trevelyan: George Macaulay Trevelyan (1876-1962), English historian and author of *History of England* (1926).

[7] Robert Burns (1759-1796) and Emily Bronte (1818-1848): Scottish poet and prominent female English novelist and poet.

[8] Jane Austen (1775-1817): Perhaps the most well-known, respected, and popular woman novelist in the British tradition. The phrase "some mute and inglorious Jane Austen" is a playful adaptation of "some mute and inglorious Milton" from Thomas Gray's "Elegy Written in a Country Churchyard" (1751).

Emily Brontë who dashed her brains out on the moor or mopped and mowed about the highways crazed with the torture that her gift had put her to. Indeed, I would venture to guess that Anon, who wrote so many poems without signing them, was often a woman. It was a woman Edward Fitzgerald,[9] I think, suggested who made the ballads and the folk-songs, crooning them to her children, beguiling her spinning with them, or the length of the winter's night.

3   This may be true or it may be false—who can say?—but what is true in it, so it seemed to me, reviewing the story of Shakespeare's sister as I had made it, is that any woman born with a great gift in the sixteenth century would certainly have gone crazed, shot herself, or ended her days in some lonely cottage outside the village, half witch, half wizard, feared and mocked at. For it needs little skill in psychology to be sure that a highly gifted girl who had tried to use her gift for poetry would have been so thwarted and hindered by other people, so tortured and pulled asunder by her own contrary instincts, that she must have lost her health and sanity to a certainty.

QUESTIONS ON MEANING

1. In addition to his inherent genius, what were some contributing factors to his upbringing that led to William Shakespeare's success?
2. What freedoms did Shakespeare experience as a young man that also contributed to that success?
3. From the father's point of view in Woolf's fictional scenario, what would Shakespeare's sister Judith have been expected to do on a daily basis?
4. What was assumed would be Judith's future, even by those family members who loved her, such as her father?
5. Ironically, what are some of the common outcomes of female genius in a male-dominated world?
6. In what segments of society is artistic genius commonly thought to be found? In what way does Woolf challenge this?

QUESTIONS FOR DISCUSSION

1. Does the hypothetical scenario Woolf creates seem plausible, assuming the genius of Shakespeare's sister Judith? Are there any alternative histories for her we might imagine?
2. Can we reasonably consider a means by which Shakespeare's sister might have developed her genius without the education her brother received?
3. Can we imagine a means by which Judith might express her creative genius in spite of the social strictures she experienced?
4. Woolf speculates that eccentrics such as witches and herb selling wise women might have been frustrated artistic geniuses. In what way do current social norms ignore human potential and make outcasts of potential geniuses?

---

[9] Edward Fitzgerald (1809-1883): English poet and scholar, who is known for anonymously translating *The Rubaiyat of Omar Khayyam* (1859).

LOOKING AT RHETORIC

1. Woolf uses a quasi-fictional narrative to create a scenario that works as social criticism of gender injustice. How does this method function to identify the problem? In what way does it suggest a solution for it?

2. Woolf makes widespread use of historical and literary figures. To what extent is her essay written for a specific audience? What is lost or gained by her use of these allusions?

3. Can you find evidence in the selection that it began as a spoken lecture?

WRITING ASSIGNMENTS

1. Using library and/or Internet sources, explore the purpose of education in individual human development. To what extent is education and training essential to the development of any kind of in-born intellectual attribute? Can genius of any sort transcend a lack of education?

2. Woolf is clear that Shakespeare's father loved his sister. But he imposed rigid social norms upon her and was ignorant of her potential, thus destroying her. Given the power of the social and cultural forces they both faced, should he be held ethically responsible for her end?

3. In pairs or in groups, make a list of gender norms and expectations. What do we often assume about men and women as inherent attributes? In spite of social progress, they still exist in subtle ways. Individually, write a personal essay in which you explore how gender expectations have been imposed upon you, by family, friends, or anyone. You can do this whether you are a man or a woman.

Interdisciplinary Connections

Architecture as Art

Architecture not only serves a function—creating spaces for living and business—but it is also, or can be, a form of artistic expression. The artistically designed building can be a kind of living sculpture, which is both beautiful and inspiring to behold, but which also creates environments and spaces where humans can interact, shop, worship, and live. Below are two famous buildings, each representing radically different designs. The Sagrada Familia Cathedral, designed by Antoni Gaudi and which is still under construction, exhibits a combination of gothic and *art nouveau* styles. Meanwhile, Habitat 67, designed by Moshe Safdie, is one of the best known examples

Habitat 67 in Montreal, Canada

http://www.blockprojekt.de/wp-content/uploads/moshe-safdie.jpg

of *brutalism* in architecture. As you study these pictures, ask yourself these questions: Are these buildings works of art? Is one more artistic than the other? Why or why not? Which appeals to you more? If you were to design a space to live in, would it look like Habitat 67? If you were to design a space to worship in, would it look like the Sagrada Familia Cathedral?

The Sagrada Familia Cathedral in Barcelona, Spain
http://www.mirror.co.uk/advice/travel/2009/06/14/barcelona-is-a-whole-lot-of-fun-115875-21440624/

The Management of Grief

Bharati Mukherjee

Bharati Mukherjee (b. 1940) is a professor of creative writing at the University of California at Berkeley and an award winning writer of stories dealing with the immigrant experience. She spent a portion of her childhood in Britain and on the continent of Europe. She returned to her homeland of India and completed her B.A. in 1959 from the University of Calcutta and her M.A. in English and Ancient Indian Culture from the University of Baroda in 1961. Having received a scholarship from the University of Iowa, she earned her M.F.A. in Creative Writing in 1963 and her Ph.D. in English and Comparative Literature in 1969. She married a fellow student from Canada, also a writer, and she has taught at various universities in the United States. Her many works of fiction include the novels The Tiger's Daughter *(1971),* Wife *(1975), the short story collection* Darkness *(1985) and the National Book Critics Circle Award Winning* The Middleman and Other Stories *(1988). Her work is informed by her own experiences as an exile from her home country and her migration to the United States and Canada, and they explore the psychological tensions that attend the encounter between Western and the non-Western cultures, particularly on women. The following selection deals with the experience of cultural displacement within the context of tragedy and unexpected loss.*

1   A woman I don't know is boiling tea the Indian way in my kitchen. There are a lot of women I don't know in my kitchen, whispering, and moving tactfully. They open doors, rummage through the pantry, and try not to ask me where things are kept. They remind me of when my sons were small, on Mother's Day or when Vikram and I were tired, and they would make big, sloppy omelettes. I would lie in bed pretending I didn't hear them.

2   Dr. Sharma, the treasurer of the Indo-Canada Society, pulls me into the hallway. He wants to know if I am worried about money. His wife, who has just come up from the basement with a tray of empty cups and glasses, scolds him. "Don't bother Mrs. Bhave with mundane details." She looks so monstrously pregnant her baby must be days overdue. I tell her she shouldn't be carrying heavy things. "Shaila," she says, smiling, "this is the fifth." Then she grabs a teenager by his shirt-tails. He slips his Walkman off his head. He has to be one of her four children, they have the same domed and dented foreheads. "What's the official word now?" she demands. The boy slips the headphones back on. "They're acting evasive, Ma. They're saying it could be an accident or a terrorist bomb."

3   All morning, the boys have been muttering, Sikh Bomb, Sikh Bomb. The men, not using the word, bow their heads in agreement. Mrs. Sharma touches her forehead at such a word. At least they've stopped talking about space debris and Russian lasers.

4   Two radios are going in the dining room. They are tuned to different stations. Someone must have brought the radios down from my boys' bedrooms. I haven't gone into their rooms since Kusum came running across the front lawn in her bathrobe. She looked so funny, I was laughing when I opened the door.

5   The big TV in the den is being whizzed through American networks and cable channels.

6   "Damn!" some man swears bitterly. "How can these preachers carry on like nothing's happened?" I want to tell him we're not that important. You look at the audience, and at the preacher in his blue robe with his beautiful white hair, the potted palm trees under a blue sky, and you know they care about nothing.

7   The phone rings and rings. Dr. Sharma's taken charge. "We're with her," he keeps saying. "Yes, yes, the doctor has given calming pills. Yes, yes, pills are having necessary effect." I wonder if pills alone explain this calm. Not peace, just a deadening quiet. I was always controlled, but never repressed. Sound can reach me, but my body is tensed, ready to scream. I hear their voices all around me. I hear my boys and Vikram cry, "Mommy, Shaila!" and their screams insulate me, like headphones.

8   The woman boiling water tells her story again and again. "I got the news first. My cousin called from Halifax before six A.M., can you imagine? He'd gotten up for prayers and his son was studying for medical exams and he heard on a rock channel that something had happened to a plane. They said first it had disappeared from the radar, like a giant eraser just reached out. His father called me, so I said to him, what do you mean, 'something bad'? You mean a hijacking? And he said, *behn*,[1] there is no confirmation of anything yet, but check with your neighbors because a lot of them must be on that plane. So I called poor Kusum straightaway. I knew Kusum's husband and daughter were booked to go yesterday."

9   Kusum lives across the street from me. She and Satish had moved in less than a month ago. They said they needed a bigger place. All these people, the Sharmas and friends from the Indo-Canada Society had been there for the housewarming. Satish and Kusum made homemade tandoori on their big gas grill and even the white neighbors piled their plates high with that luridly red, charred, juicy chicken. Their younger daughter had danced, and even our boys had broken away from the Stanley Cup telecast to put in a reluctant appearance. Everyone took pictures for their albums and for the community newspapers— another of our families had made it big in Toronto—and now I wonder how many of those happy faces are gone. "Why does God give us so much if all along He intends to take it away?" Kusum asks me.

10   I nod. We sit on carpeted stairs, holding hands like children. "I never once told him that I loved him," I say. I was too much the well brought up woman. I was so well brought up I never felt comfortable calling my husband by his first name.

11   "It's all right," Kusum says. "He knew. My husband knew. They felt it. Modern young girls have to say it because what they feel is fake."

12   Kusum's daughter, Pam, runs in with an overnight case. Pam's in her McDonald's uniform. "Mummy! You have to get dressed!" Panic makes her cranky. "A reporter's on his way here."

13   "Why?"

14   "You want to talk to him in your bathrobe?" She starts to brush her mother's long hair. She's the daughter who's always in trouble. She dates Canadian boys and hangs out in the mall, shopping for tight sweaters. The younger one, the goody-goody one according to Pam, the one with a voice so sweet that when she sang *bhajans*[2] for Ethiopian relief

---

[1] behn: "No," in Hindi.
[2] bhajans: Hymns, in Hindi.

even a frugal man like my husband wrote out a hundred dollar check, *she* was on that plane. *She* was going to spend July and August with grandparents because Pam wouldn't go. Pam said she'd rather waitress at McDonald's. "If it's a choice between Bombay and Wonderland, I'm picking Wonderland," she'd said.

15   "Leave me alone," Kusum yells. "You know what I want to do? If I didn't have to look after you now, I'd hang myself."

16   Pam's young face goes blotchy with pain. "Thanks," she says, "don't let me stop you."

17   "Hush," pregnant Mrs. Sharma scolds Pam. "Leave your mother alone. Mr. Sharma will tackle the reporters and fill out the forms. He'll say what has to be said."

18   Pam stands her ground. "You think I don't know what Mummy's thinking? *Why ever?* that's what. That's sick! Mummy wishes my little sister were alive and I were dead."

19   Kusum's hand in mine is trembly hot. We continue to sit on the stairs.

20   She calls before she arrives, wondering if there's anything I need. Her name is Judith Templeton and she's an appointee of the provincial government. "Multiculturalism?" I ask, and she says, "partially," but that her mandate is bigger. "I've been told you knew many of the people on the flight," she says. "Perhaps if you'd agree to help us reach the others . . . ?"

21   She gives me time at least to put on tea water and pick up the mess in the front room. I have a few *samosas*[3] from Kusum's housewarming that I could fry up, but then I think, why prolong this visit?

22   Judith Templeton is much younger than she sounded. She wears a blue suit with a white blouse and a polka dot tie. Her blond hair is cut short, her only jewelry is pearl drop earrings. Her briefcase is new and expensive looking, a gleaming cordovan leather. She sits with it across her lap. When she looks out the front windows onto the street, her contact lenses seem to float in front of her light blue eyes.

23   "What sort of help do you want from me?" I ask. She has refused the tea, out of politeness, but I insist, along with some slightly stale biscuits.

24   "I have no experience," she admits. "That is, I have an MSW[4] and I've worked in liaison with accident victims, but I mean I have no experience with a tragedy of this scale—"

25   "Who could?" I ask.

26   "—and with the complications of culture, language, and customs. Someone mentioned that Mrs. Bhave is a pillar—because you've taken it more calmly."

27   At this, perhaps, I frown, for she reaches forward, almost to take my hand. "I hope you understand my meaning, Mrs. Bhave. There are hundreds of people in Metro directly affected, like you, and some of them speak no English. There are some widows who've never handled money or gone on a bus, and there are old parents who still haven't eaten or gone outside their bedrooms. Some houses and apartments have been looted. Some wives are still hysterical. Some husbands are in shock and profound depression. We want to help, but our hands are tied in so many ways. We have to distribute money to some people, and there are legal documents—these things can be done. We have interpreters, but we don't always have the human touch, or maybe the right human touch. We don't want to make mistakes, Mrs. Bhave, and that's why we'd like to ask you to help us."

---

[3] samosas: An Indian dish, a fried vegetable or meat filled turnover.
[4] MSW: Master of Social Work, a graduate degree.

28   "More mistakes, you mean," I say.

29   "Police matters are not in my hands," she answers.

30   "Nothing I can do will make any difference," I say. "We must all grieve in our own way."

31   "But you are coping very well. All the people said, Mrs. Bhave is the strongest person of all. Perhaps if the others could see you, talk with you, it would help them."

32   "By the standards of the people you call hysterical, I am behaving very oddly and very badly, Miss Templeton." I want to say to her, *I wish I could scream, starve, walk into Lake Ontario, jump from a bridge.* "They would not see me as a model. I do not see myself as a model."

33   I am a freak. No one who has ever known me would think of me reacting this way. This terrible calm will not go away.

34   She asks me if she may call again, after I get back from a long trip that we all must make. "Of course," I say. "Feel free to call, anytime."

35   Four days later, I find Kusum squatting on a rock overlooking a bay in Ireland. It isn't a big rock, but it juts sharply out over water. This is as close as we'll ever get to them. June breezes balloon out her sari and unpin her knee-length hair. She has the bewildered look of a sea creature whom the tides have stranded.

36   It's been one hundred hours since Kusum came stumbling and screaming across my lawn. Waiting around the hospital, we've heard many stories. The police, the diplomats, they tell us things thinking that we're strong, that knowledge is helpful to the grieving, and maybe it is. Some, I know, prefer ignorance, or their own versions. The plane broke into two, they say. Unconsciousness was instantaneous. No one suffered. My boys must have just finished their breakfasts. They loved eating on planes, they loved the smallness of plates, knives, and forks. Last year they saved the airline salt and pepper shakers. Half an hour more and they would have made it to Heathrow.

37   Kusum says that we can't escape our fate. She says that all those people—our husbands, my boys, her girl with the nightingale voice, all those Hindus, Christians, Sikhs, Muslims, Parsis, and atheists on that plane—were fated to die together off this beautiful bay. She learned this from a swami in Toronto.

38   I have my Valium.[5]

39   Six of us "relatives"—two widows and four widowers—choose to spend the day today by the waters instead of sitting in a hospital room and scanning photographs of the dead. That's what they call us now: relatives. I've looked through twenty-seven photos in two days. They're very kind to us, the Irish are very understanding. Sometimes understanding means freeing a tourist bus for this trip to the bay, so we can pretend to spy our loved ones through the glassiness of waves or in sunspeckled cloud shapes.

40   I could die here, too, and be content.

41   "What is that, out there?" She's standing and flapping her hands and for a moment I see a head shape bobbing in the waves. She's standing in the water, I, on the boulder. The tide is low, and a round, black, headsized rock has just risen from the waves. She returns, her sari end dripping and ruined and her face is a twisted remnant of hope, the

---

[5] Valium: a commonly prescribed sedative.

way mine was a hundred hours ago, still laughing but inwardly knowing that nothing but the ultimate tragedy could bring two women together at six o'clock on a Sunday morning. I watch her face sag into blankness.

42   "That water felt warm, Shaila," she says at length.

43   "You can't," I say. "We have to wait for our turn to come."

44   I haven't eaten in four days, haven't brushed my teeth.

45   "I know," she says. "I tell myself I have no right to grieve. They are in a better place than we are. My swami says I should be thrilled for them. My swami says depression is a sign of our selfishness."

46   Maybe I'm selfish. Selfishly I break away from Kusum and run, sandals slapping against stones, to the water's edge. What if my boys aren't lying pinned under the debris? What if they aren't stuck a mile below that innocent blue chop? What if, given the strong currents. . . .

47   Now I've ruined my sari, one of my best. Kusum has joined me, knee-deep in water that feels to me like a swimming pool. I could settle in the water, and my husband would take my hand and the boys would slap water in my face just to see me scream.

48   "Do you remember what good swimmers my boys were, Kusum?"

49   "I saw the medals," she says.

50   One of the widowers, Dr. Ranganathan from Montreal, walks out to us, carrying his shoes in one hand. He's an electrical engineer. Someone at the hotel mentioned his work is famous around the world, something about the place where physics and electricity come together. He has lost a huge family, something indescribable. "With some luck," Dr. Ranganathan suggests to me, "a good swimmer could make it safely to some island. It is quite possible that there may be many, many microscopic islets scattered around."

51   "You're not just saying that?" I tell Dr. Ranganathan about Vinod, my elder son. Last year he took diving as well.

52   "It's a parent's duty to hope," he says. "It is foolish to rule out possibilities that have not been tested. I myself have not surrendered hope."

53   Kusum is sobbing once again. "Dear lady," he says, laying his free hand on her arm, and she calms down.

54   "Vinod is how old?" he asks me. He's very careful, as we all are. *Is,* not was.

55   "Fourteen. Yesterday he was fourteen. His father and uncle were going to take him down to the Taj and give him a big birthday party. I couldn't go with them because I couldn't get two weeks off from my stupid job in June." I process bills for a travel agent. June is a big travel month.

56   Dr. Ranganathan whips the pockets of his suit jacket inside out. Squashed roses, in darkening shades of pink, float on the water. He tore the roses off creepers in somebody's garden. He didn't ask anyone if he could pluck the roses, but now there's been an article about it in the local papers. When you see an Indian person, it says, please give him or her flowers.

57   "A strong youth of fourteen," he says, "can very likely pull to safety a younger one."

58   My sons, though four years apart, were very close. Vinod wouldn't let Mithun drown. *Electrical engineering,* I think, foolishly perhaps: this man knows important secrets of the universe, things closed to me. Relief spins me light-headed. No wonder my boys' photographs haven't turned up in the gallery of photos of the recovered dead. "Such pretty roses," I say.

59   "My wife loved pink roses. Every Friday I had to bring a bunch home. I used to say, why? After twenty odd years of marriage you're still needing proof positive of my love?" He has identified his wife and three of his children. Then others from Montreal, the lucky ones, intact families with no survivors. He chuckles as he wades back to shore. Then he swings around to ask me a question. "Mrs. Bhave, you are wanting to throw in some roses for your loved ones? I have two big ones left."

60   But I have other things to float: Vinod's pocket calculator; a half-painted model B-52 for my Mithun. They'd want them on their island. And for my husband? For him I let fall into the calm, glassy waters a poem I wrote in the hospital yesterday. Finally he'll know my feelings for him.

61   "Don't tumble, the rocks are slippery," Dr. Ranganathan cautions. He holds out a hand for me to grab.

62   Then it's time to get back on the bus, time to rush back to our waiting posts on hospital benches.

63   Kusum is one of the lucky ones. The lucky ones flew here, identified in multiplicate their loved ones, then will fly to India with the bodies for proper ceremonies. Satish is one of the few males who surfaced. The photos of faces we saw on the walls in an office at Heathrow and here in the hospital are mostly of women. Women have more body fat, a nun said to me matter-of-factly. They float better.

64   Today I was stopped by a young sailor on the street. He had loaded bodies, he'd gone into the water when—he checks my face for signs of strength—when the sharks were first spotted. I don't blush, and he breaks down. "It's all right," I say. "Thank you." I had heard about the sharks from Dr. Ranganathan. In his orderly mind, science brings understanding, it holds no terror. It is the shark's duty. For every deer there is a hunter, for every fish a fisherman.

65   The Irish are not shy; they rush to me and give me hugs and some are crying. I cannot imagine reactions like that on the streets of Toronto. Just strangers, and I am touched. Some carry flowers with them and give them to any Indian they see.

66   After lunch, a policeman I have gotten to know quite well catches hold of me. He says he thinks he has a match for Vinod. I explain what a good swimmer Vinod is.

67   "You want me with you when you look at photos?" Dr. Ranganathan walks ahead of me into the picture gallery. In these matters, he is a scientist, and I am grateful. It is a new perspective. "They have performed miracles," he says. "We are indebted to them."

68   The first day or two the policemen showed us relatives only one picture at a time; now they're in a hurry, they're eager to lay out the possibles, and even the probables.

69   The face on the photo is of a boy much like Vinod; the same intelligent eyes, the same thick brows dipping into a V. But this boy's features, even his cheeks, are puffier, wider, mushier.

70   "No." My gaze is pulled by other pictures. There are five other boys who look like Vinod.

71   The nun assigned to console me rubs the first picture with a fingertip. "When they've been in the water for a while, love, they look a little heavier." The bones under the skin are broken, they said on the first day—try to adjust your memories. It's important.

72   "It's not him. I'm his mother. I'd know."

73   "I know this one!" Dr. Ranganathan cries out suddenly from the back of the gallery. "And this one!" I think he senses that I don't want to find my boys. "They are the Kutty brothers. They were also from Montreal." I don't mean to be crying. On the contrary, I am ecstatic. My suitcase in the hotel is packed heavy with dry clothes for my boys.

74   The policeman starts to cry. "I am so sorry, I am so sorry, ma'am. I really thought we had a match."

75   With the nun ahead of us and the policeman behind, we, the unlucky ones without our children's bodies, file out of the makeshift gallery.

76   From Ireland most of us go on to India. Kusum and I take the same direct flight to Bombay, so I can help her clear customs quickly. But we have to argue with a man in uniform. He has large boils on his face. The boils swell and glow with sweat as we argue with him. He wants Kusum to wait in line and he refuses to take authority because his boss is on a tea break. But Kusum won't let her coffins out of sight, and I shan't desert her though I know that my parents, elderly and diabetic, must be waiting in a stuffy car in a scorching lot.

77   "You bastard!" I scream at the man with the popping boils. Other passengers press closer. "You think we're smuggling contraband in those coffins!"

78   Once upon a time we were well brought up women; we were dutiful wives who kept our heads veiled, our voices shy and sweet.

79   In India, I become, once again, an only child of rich, ailing parents. Old friends of the family come to pay their respects. Some are Sikh, and inwardly, involuntarily, I cringe. My parents are progressive people; they do not blame communities for a few individuals.

80   In Canada it is a different story now.

81   "Stay longer," my mother pleads. "Canada is a cold place. Why would you want to be all by yourself?" I stay.

82   Three months pass. Then another.

83   "Vikram wouldn't have wanted you to give up things!" they protest. They call my husband by the name he was born with. In Toronto he'd changed to Vik so the men he worked with at his office would find his name as easy as Rod or Chris. "You know, the dead aren't cut off from us!"

84   My grandmother, the spoiled daughter of a rich *zamindar*,[6] shaved her head with rusty razor blades when she was widowed at sixteen. My grandfather died of childhood diabetes when he was nineteen, and she saw herself as the harbinger of bad luck. My mother grew up without parents, raised indifferently by an uncle, while her true mother slept in a hut behind the main estate house and took her food with the servants. She grew up a rationalist. My parents abhor mindless mortification.

85   The zamindar's daughter kept stubborn faith in Vedic rituals; my parents rebelled. I am trapped between two modes of knowledge. At thirty-six, I am too old to start over and too young to give up. Like my husband's spirit, I flutter between worlds.

86   Courting aphasia,[7] we travel. We travel with our phalanx of servants and poor relatives. To hill stations and to beach resorts. We play contract bridge in dusty gymkhana

---

[6] zamindar: Landowner, in Hindi.

[7] aphasia: a speech disorder in which there is a defect or loss of the ability of expression, sometimes involving an inability to comprehend spoken or written language.

clubs. We ride stubby ponies up crumbly mountain trails. At tea dances, we let ourselves be twirled twice round the ballroom. We hit the holy spots we hadn't made time for before. In Varanasi, Kalighat, Rishikesh, Hardwar, astrologers and palmists seek me out and for a fee offer me cosmic consolations.

87   Already the widowers among us are being shown new bride candidates. They cannot resist the call of custom, the authority of their parents and older brothers. They must marry; it is the duty of a man to look after a wife. The new wives will be young widows with children, destitute but of good family. They will make loving wives, but the men will shun them. I've had calls from the men over crackling Indian telephone lines. "Save me," they say, these substantial, educated, successful men of forty. "My parents are arranging a marriage for me." In a month they will have buried one family and returned to Canada with a new bride and partial family.

88   I am comparatively lucky. No one here thinks of arranging a husband for an unlucky widow.

89   Then, on the third day of the sixth month into this odyssey, in an abandoned temple in a tiny Himalayan village, as I make my offering of flowers and sweetmeats to the god of a tribe of animists, my husband descends to me. He is squatting next to a scrawny *sadhu*[8] in moth-eaten robes. Vikram wears the vanilla suit he wore the last time I hugged him. The *sadhu* tosses petals on a butter-fed flame, reciting Sanskrit mantras and sweeps his face of flies. My husband takes my hands in his.

90   *You're beautiful*, he starts. Then, *What are you doing here?*

91   *Shall I stay?* I ask. He only smiles, but already the image is fading. *You must finish alone what we started together.* No seaweed wreathes his mouth. He speaks too fast just as he used to when we were an envied family in our pink split-level. He is gone.

92   In the windowless altar room, smoky with joss sticks and clarified butter lamps, a sweaty hand gropes for my blouse. I do not shriek. The *sadhu* arranges his robe. The lamps hiss and sputter out.

93   When we come out of the temple, my mother says, "Did you feel something weird in there?"

94   My mother has no patience with ghosts, prophetic dreams, holy men, and cults.

95   "No," I lie. "Nothing."

96   But she knows that she's lost me. She knows that in days I shall be leaving.

97   Kusum's put her house up for sale. She wants to live in an ashram in Hardwar. Moving to Hardwar was her swami's idea. Her swami runs two ashrams, the one in Hardwar and another here in Toronto.

98   "Don't run away," I tell her.

99   "I'm not running away," she says. "I'm pursuing inner peace. You think you or that Ranganathan fellow are better off?"

100   Pam's left for California. She wants to do some modelling, she says. She says when she comes into her share of the insurance money she'll open a yoga-cum-aerobics studio in Hollywood. She sends me postcards so naughty I daren't leave them on the coffee table. Her mother has withdrawn from her and the world.

---

[8] sadhu: a Hindu holy man.

101   The rest of us don't lose touch, that's the point. Talk is all we have, says Dr. Ranganathan, who has also resisted his relatives and returned to Montreal and to his job, alone. He says, whom better to talk with than other relatives? We've been melted down and recast as a new tribe.

102   He calls me twice a week from Montreal. Every Wednesday night and every Saturday afternoon. He is changing jobs, going to Ottawa. But Ottawa is over a hundred miles away, and he is forced to drive two hundred and twenty miles a day. He can't bring himself to sell his house. The house is a temple, he says; the king-sized bed in the master bedroom is a shrine. He sleeps on a folding cot. A devotee.

103   There are still some hysterical relatives. Judith Templeton's list of those needing help and those who've "accepted" is in nearly perfect balance. Acceptance means you speak of your family in the past tense and you make active plans for moving ahead with your life. There are courses at Seneca and Ryerson[9] we could be taking. Her gleaming leather briefcase is full of college catalogues and lists of cultural societies that need our help. She has done impressive work, I tell her.

104   "In the textbooks on grief management," she replies—I am her confidante, I realize, one of the few whose grief has not sprung bizarre obsessions—"there are stages to pass through: rejection, depression, acceptance, reconstruction." She has compiled a chart and finds that six months after the tragedy, none of us still reject reality, but only a handful are reconstructing. "Depressed Acceptance" is the plateau we've reached. Remarriage is a major step in reconstruction (though she's a little surprised, even shocked, over *how* quickly some of the men have taken on new families). Selling one's house and changing jobs and cities is healthy.

105   How do I tell Judith Templeton that my family surrounds me, and that like creatures in epics, they've changed shapes? She sees me as calm and accepting but worries that I have no job, no career. My closest friends are worse off than I. I cannot tell her my days, even my nights, are thrilling.

106   She asks me to help with families she can't reach at all. An elderly couple in Agincourt whose sons were killed just weeks after they had brought their parents over from a village in Punjab. From their names, I know they are Sikh. Judith Templeton and a translator have visited them twice with offers of money for air fare to Ireland, with bank forms, power-of-attorney forms, but they have refused to sign, or to leave their tiny apartment. Their sons' money is frozen in the bank. Their sons' investment apartments have been trashed by tenants, the furnishings sold off. The parents fear that anything they sign or any money they receive will end the company's or the country's obligations to them. They fear they are selling their sons for two airline tickets to a place they've never seen.

107   The high-rise apartment is a tower of Indians and West Indians, with a sprinkling of Orientals. The nearest bus stop kiosk is lined with women in saris. Boys practice cricket in the parking lot. Inside the building, even I wince a bit from the ferocity of onion fumes, the distinctive and immediate Indianness of frying *ghee*,[10] but Judith Templeton maintains a

---

[9] Seneca and Ryerson: Seneca College of Applied Arts and Technology, Willowdale. Ryerson Polytechnical Institute, Toronto.

[10] *ghee*: a butter used in Indian dishes.

steady flow of information. These poor old people are in imminent danger of losing their place and all their services.

108   I say to her, "They are Sikh. They will not open up to a Hindu woman." And what I want to add is, as much as I try not to, I stiffen now at the sight of beards and turbans. I remember a time when we all trusted each other in this new country, it was only the new country we worried about.

109   The two rooms are dark and stuffy. The lights are off, and an oil lamp sputters on the coffee table. The bent old lady has let us in, and her husband is wrapping a white turban over his oiled, hip-length hair. She immediately goes to the kitchen, and I hear the most familiar sound of an Indian home, tap water hitting and filling a teapot.

110   They have not paid their utility bills, out of fear and the inability to write a check. The telephone is gone; electricity and gas and water are soon to follow. They have told Judith their sons will provide. They are good boys, and they have always earned and looked after their parents.

111   We converse a bit in Hindi. They do not ask about the crash and I wonder if I should bring it up. If they think I am here merely as a translator, then they may feel insulted. There are thousands of Punjabi-speakers, Sikhs, in Toronto to do a better job. And so I say to the old lady, "I too have lost my sons, and my husband, in the crash."

112   Her eyes immediately fill with tears. The man mutters a few words which sound like a blessing. "God provides and God takes away," he says.

113   I want to say, but only men destroy and give back nothing. "My boys and my husband are not coming back," I say. "We have to understand that."

114   Now the old woman responds. "But who is to say? Man alone does not decide these things." To this her husband adds his agreement.

115   Judith asks about the bank papers, the release forms. With a stroke of the pen, they will have a provincial trustee to pay their bills, invest their money, send them a monthly pension.

116   "Do you know this woman?" I ask them.

117   The man raises his hand from the table, turns it over and seems to regard each finger separately before he answers. "This young lady is always coming here, we make tea for her and she leaves papers for us to sign." His eyes scan a pile of papers in the corner of the room. "Soon we will be out of tea, then will she go away?"

118   The old lady adds, "I have asked my neighbors and no one else gets *angrezi*[11] visitors. What have we done?"

119   "It's her job," I try to explain. "The government is worried. Soon you will have no place to stay, no lights, no gas, no water."

120   "Government will get its money. Tell her not to worry, we are honorable people."

121   I try to explain the government wishes to give money, not take. He raises his hand. "Let them take," he says. "We are accustomed to that. That is no problem."

122   "We are strong people," says the wife. "Tell her that."

123   "Who needs all this machinery?" demands the husband. "It is unhealthy, the bright lights, the cold air on a hot day, the cold food, the four gas rings. God will provide, not government."

124   "When our boys return," the mother says. Her husband sucks his teeth. "Enough talk," he says.

---

[11] *angrezi*: English, in Hindi.

125   Judith breaks in. "Have you convinced them?" The snaps on her cordovan briefcase go off like firecrackers in that quiet apartment. She lays the sheaf of legal papers on the coffee table. "If they can't write their names, an X will do—I've told them that."

126   Now the old lady has shuffled to the kitchen and soon emerges with a pot of tea and two cups. "I think my bladder will go first on a job like this," Judith says to me, smiling. "If only there was some way of reaching them. Please thank her for the tea. Tell her she's very kind."

127   I nod in Judith's direction and tell them in Hindi, "She thanks you for the tea. She thinks you are being very hospitable but she doesn't have the slightest idea what it means."

128   I want to say, humor her. I want to say, my boys and my husband are with me too, more than ever. I look in the old man's eyes and I can read his stubborn, peasant's message: *I have protected this woman as best I can. She is the only person I have left. Give to me or take from me what you will, but I will not sign for it. I will not pretend that I accept.*

129   In the car, Judith says, "You see what I'm up against? I'm sure they're lovely people, but their stubbornness and ignorance are driving me crazy. They think signing a paper is signing their sons' death warrants, don't they?"

130   I am looking out the window. I want to say, *In our culture, it is a parent's duty to hope.*

131   "Now Shaila, this next woman is a real mess. She cries day and night, and she refuses all medical help. We may have to—"

132   "—Let me out at the subway," I say.

133   "I beg your pardon?" I can feel those blue eyes staring at me.

134   It would not be like her to disobey. She merely disapproves, and slows at a corner to let me out. Her voice is plaintive. "Is there anything I said? Anything I did?"

135   I could answer her suddenly in a dozen ways, but I choose not to. "Shaila? Let's talk about it," I hear, then slam the door.

136   A wife and mother begins her new life in a new country, and that life is cut short. Yet her husband tells her: Complete what we have started. We, who stayed out of politics and came halfway around the world to avoid religious and political feuding have been the first in the New World to die from it. I no longer know what we started, nor how to complete it. I write letters to the editors of local papers and to members of Parliament. Now at least they admit it was a bomb. One MP answers back, with sympathy, but with a challenge. You want to make a difference? Work on a campaign. Work on mine. Politicize the Indian voter.

137   My husband's old lawyer helps me set up a trust. Vikram was a saver and a careful investor. He had saved the boys' boarding school and college fees. I sell the pink house at four times what we paid for it and take a small apartment downtown. I am looking for a charity to support.

138   We are deep in the Toronto winter, gray skies, icy pavements. I stay indoors, watching television. I have tried to assess my situation, how best to live my life, to complete what we began so many years ago. Kusum has written me from Hardwar that her life is now serene. She has seen Satish and has heard her daughter sing again. Kusum was on a pilgrimage, passing through a village when she heard a young girl's voice, singing one of her daughter's favorite *bhajans*. She followed the music through the squalor of a Himalayan village, to a hut where a young girl, an exact replica of her daughter, was fanning coals under the kitchen fire. When she appeared, the girl cried out, "Ma!" and ran away. What did I think of that?

139   I think I can only envy her.

140   Pam didn't make it to California, but writes me from Vancouver. She works in a department store, giving make-up hints to Indian and Oriental girls. Dr. Ranganathan has

given up his commute, given up his house and job, and accepted an academic position in Texas where no one knows his story and he has vowed not to tell it. He calls me now once a week.

141   I wait, I listen, and I pray, but Vikram has not returned to me. The voices and the shapes and the nights filled with visions ended abruptly several weeks ago.

142   I take it as a sign.

143   One rare, beautiful, sunny day last week, returning from a small errand on Yonge Street, I was walking through the park from the subway to my apartment. I live equidistant from the Ontario Houses of Parliament and the University of Toronto. The day was not cold, but something in the bare trees caught my attention. I looked up from the gravel, into the branches and the clear blue sky beyond. I thought I heard the rustling of larger forms, and I waited a moment for voices. Nothing.

144   "What?" I asked.

145   Then as I stood in the path looking north to Queen's Park and west to the university, I heard the voices of my family one last time. *Your time has come*, they said. *Go, be brave.*

146   I do not know where this voyage I have begun will end. I do not know which direction I will take. I dropped the package on a park bench and started walking.

QUESTIONS ON MEANING

1. What does the social worker want from Shaila Bhave?

2. What does the swami tell Kusum that depression is a sign of?

3. What event has occurred in the opening scene, and what do the characters not know yet?

4. How did Shaila Bhave's parents rebel against the traditional religious culture of India?

5. Why is Shaila reluctant to help the social worker Judith Templeton with the elderly Sikh couple?

6. What do Shaila and Judith find out caused the accident?

QUESTIONS FOR DISCUSSION

1. Consider Mukherjee's title. In the context of the story, what does it mean to manage grief?

2. For the various characters, what role does religion and culture play for people as they cope with tragedy?

3. What distinguished Shaila Bhave from the other people who have experienced the loss?

4. What is Dr. Ranganathan's role in the story?

LOOKING AT RHETORIC

1. Does this story effectively blend the Mukherjee's concern with immigration issues with the universal experience of grief and loss? Do the narrative and character elements in this fictional story communicate that experience in a different way than a work of non-fiction?

2. In what way does the detailed description of the household setting influence the development of characters and bring their psychological concerns to life?

WRITING ASSIGNMENTS

1. Using library and/or Internet sources, research Mukherjee's background. Given your understanding of the author, consider Shaila Bhave's visions of her husband. How do they help to initiate her transformation in the end? What is the nature of that transformation?

2. Consider her relationship with Kusum. How are their final responses to the tragedy different? Is one healthier than the other? If so, why?

3. In pairs or in groups, discuss how Shaila Bhave's grieving process follows the textbook pattern identified by the social worker Judith Templeton. Individually, write an essay that uses Shaila's psychological experience as an argument for or against that typical pattern.

The Last Flight of Doctor Ain

James Tiptree, Jr.

James Tiptree, Jr. (1915–1987) is the pseudonym of Alice Sheldon, one of the most respected American authors of science fiction in the 1960s and 1970s. Although she published under a few different pseudonyms, Tiptree was the best known and most successful, and it kept Sheldon's gender hidden from a science fiction reading and writing community dominated by males (until Sheldon was revealed to the world in 1977). Sheldon lead no quiet life: early in her life she worked as a graphic designer and a painter and art critic, but during WWII Sheldon joined the U.S. Army and in 1943 was assigned to air intelligence. When she was discharged after the war she began to write and in the early 1950s she helped establish the CIA during its formation, including serving as a clandestine agent for the CIA overseas. In the mid-1950s, Sheldon left the CIA and went back to school, eventually earning her Ph.D. in experimental psychology in 1967 from George Washington University. Her writing explores themes arising out of her work in the intelligence community and, more importantly, her interest in human psychology, and she became known for carefully crafted stories dealing with the environment, gender, and power relations. Today, the annual **Tiptree Award** *is given to the best science fiction writing of the year dealing with issues of gender. The following selection, first published in 1969, reveals Tiptree's intense interest in ecology, environmentalism, evolution, terrorism, and genetics.*

1   Doctor Ain was recognized on the Omaha-Chicago flight. A biologist colleague from Pasadena came out of the toilet and saw Ain in an aisle seat. Five years before, this man had been jealous of Ain's huge grants. Now he nodded coldly and was surprised at the intensity of Ain's response. He almost turned back to speak, but he felt too tired; like nearly everyone, he was fighting the flu.

2   The stewardess handing out coats after they landed remembered Ain too: a tall thin nondescript man with rusty hair. He held up the line staring at her; since he already had his raincoat with him she decided it was some kooky kind of pass and waved him on.

3   She saw Ain shamble off into the airport smog, apparently alone. Despite the big Civil Defense signs, O'Hare was late getting underground. No one noticed the woman.

4   The wounded, dying woman.

5   Ain was not identified en route to New York, but a 2:40 jet carried an "Ames" on the checklist, which was thought to be a misspelling of Ain. It was. The plane had circled for an hour while Ain watched the smoky seaboard monotonously tilt, straighten, and tilt again.

6   The woman was weaker now. She coughed, picking weakly at the scabs on her face half-hidden behind her long hair. Her hair, Ain saw, that great mane which had been so splendid, was drabbed and thinning now. He looked to seaward, willing himself to think of cold, clean breakers. On the horizon he saw a vast black rug: somewhere a tanker had opened its vents. The woman coughed again. Ain closed his eyes. Smog shrouded the plane.

7   He was picked up next while checking in for the BOAC flight to Glasgow. Kennedy Underground was a boiling stew of people, the air system unequal to the hot September afternoon. The check-in line swayed and sweated, staring dully at the newscast. SAVE THE LAST GREEN MANSIONS—a conservation group was protesting the defoliation and drainage of the Amazon basin. Several people recalled the beautifully colored shots of the new clean bomb. The line squeezed together to let a band of uniformed men go by. They were wearing buttons inscribed: WHO'S AFRAID?

8   That was when a woman noticed Ain. He was holding a newssheet, and she heard it rattling in his hand. Her family hadn't caught the flu, so she looked at him sharply. Sure enough, his forehead was sweaty. She herded her kids to the side away from Ain.

9   He was using *Instac* throat spray, she remembered. She didn't think much of Instac; her family used *kleer*. While she was looking at him, Ain suddenly turned his head and stared into her face, with the spray still floating down. Such inconsiderateness! She turned her back. She didn't recall his talking to any woman, but she perked up her ears when the clerk read off Ain's destination. Moscow!

10   The clerk recalled that too, with disapproval. Ain checked in alone, he reported. No woman had been ticketed for Moscow, but it would have been easy enough to split up her tickets. (By that time they were sure she was with him.)

11   Ain's flight went via Iceland with an hour's delay at Keflavik. Ain walked over to the airport park, gratefully breathing the sea-filled air. Every few breaths he shuddered. Under the whine of bulldozers the sea could be heard running its huge paws up and down the keyboard of the land. The little park had a grove of yellowed birches, and a flock of wheatears foraged by the path. Next month they would be in North Africa, Ain thought. Two thousand miles of tiny wing-beats. He threw them some crumbs from a packet in his pocket.

12   The woman seemed stronger here. She was panting in the sea wind, her large eyes fixed on Ain. Above her the birches were as gold as those where he had first seen her, the day his life began. . . . Squatting under a stump to watch a shrewmouse he had been, when he caught a falling ripple of green and recognized the shocking girl-flesh, creamy, pink-tipped—coming toward him among the golden bracken! Young Ain held his breath, his nose in the sweet moss and his heart going *crash—crash*. And then he was staring at the outrageous fall of that hair down her narrow back, watching it dance around her heart-shaped buttocks, while the shrewmouse ran over his paralyzed hand. The lake was utterly still, dusty silver under the misty sky, and she made no more than a muskrat's ripple to rock the floating golden leaves. The silence closed back, the trees burning like torches where the naked girl had walked the wild wood, reflected in Ain's shining eyes. For a time he believed he had seen an oread.

13   Ain was last on board for the Glasgow leg. The stewardess recalled dimly that he seemed restless. She could not identify the woman. There were a lot of women on board, and babies. Her passenger list had had several errors.

14   At Glasgow airport a waiter remembered that a man like Ain had called for Scottish oatmeal, and eaten two bowls, although of course it wasn't really oatmeal. A young mother with a pram saw him tossing crumbs to the birds.

15   When he checked in at the BOAC desk, he was hailed by a Glasgow professor who was going to the same conference at Moscow. This man had been one of Ain's teachers. (It was now known that Ain had done his postgraduate work in Europe.) They chatted all the way across the North Sea.

16   "I wondered about that," the professor said later. "Why have you come round about? I asked him. He told me the direct flights were booked up." (This was found to be untrue: Ain had, apparently avoided the Moscow jet to escape attention.)

17   The professor spoke with relish of Ain's work.

18   "Brilliant? Oh, aye. And stubborn, too; very very stubborn. It was as though a concept— often the simplest relation, mind you—would stop him in his tracks, and fascinate him. He would hunt all round it instead of going on to the next thing as a more docile mind would. Truthfully, I wondered at first if he could be just a bit thick. But you recall who it was said that the capacity for wonder at matters of common acceptance occurs in the superior mind? And, of course, so it proved when he shook us all up over that enzyme conversion business. A pity your government took him away from his line, there. No, he said nothing of this, I say it to you, young man. We spoke in fact largely of my work. I was surprised to find he'd kept up. He asked me what my *sentiments* about it were, which surprised me again. Now, understand, I'd not seen the man for five years, but he seemed—well, perhaps just tired, as who is not? I'm sure he was glad to have a change; he jumped out for a legstretch wherever we came down. At Oslo, even Bonn. Oh, yes, he did feed the birds, but that was nothing new for Ain. His social life when I knew him? Radical causes? Young man, I've said what I've said because of who it was that introduced you, but I'll have you know it is an impertinence in you to think ill of Charles Ain, or that he could do a harmful deed. Good evening."

19   The professor said nothing of the woman in Ain's life.

20   Nor could he have, although Ain had been intimately with her in the university time. He had let no one see how he was obsessed with her, with the miracle, the wealth of her body, her inexhaustibility. They met at his every spare moment; sometimes in public pretending to be casual strangers under his friends' noses, pointing out a pleasing view to each other with grave formality. And later in their privacies—what doubled intensity of love! He reveled in her, possessed her, allowed her no secrets. His dreams were of her sweet springs and shadowed places and her white rounded glory in the moonlight, finding always more, always new dimensions of his joy.

21   The danger of her frailty was far off then in the rush of birdsong and the springing leverets of the meadow. On dark days she might cough a bit, but so did he. . . . In those years he had had no thought to the urgent study of disease.

22   At the Moscow conference nearly everyone noticed Ain at some point or another, which was to be expected in view of his professional stature. It was a small, high-caliber meeting. Ain was late in; a day's reports were over, and his was to be on the third and last.

23   Many people spoke with Ain, and several sat with him at meals. No one was surprised that he spoke little; he was a retiring man except on a few memorable occasions of argument. He did strike some of his friends as a bit tired and jerky.

24   An Indian molecular engineer who saw him with the throat spray kidded him about bringing over Asian flu. A Swedish colleague recalled that Ain had been called away to the transatlantic phone at lunch; and when he returned Ain volunteered the information that something had turned up missing in his home lab. There was another joke, and Ain said cheerfully, "Oh, yes, quite active."

25   At that point one of the Chicom biologists swung into his daily propaganda chores about bacteriological warfare and accused Ain of manufacturing biotic weapons. Ain took the wind out of his sails by saying: "You're perfectly right." By tacit consent, there was very little talk about military applications, industrial dusting, or subjects of that type. And nobody recalled seeing Ain with any woman other than old Madame Vialche, who could scarcely have subverted anyone from her wheelchair.

26   Ain's one speech was bad, even for him. He always had a poor public voice, but his ideas were usually expressed with the lucidity so typical of the first-rate mind. This time he seemed muddled, with little new to say. His audience excused this as the muffling effects of security. Ain then got into a tangled point about the course of evolution in which he seemed to be trying to show that something was very wrong indeed. When he wound up with a reference to Hudson's bellbird "singing for a later race," several listeners wondered if he could be drunk.

27   The big security break came right at the end, when he suddenly began to describe the methods he had used to mutate and redesign a leukemia virus. He explained the procedure with admirable clarity in four sentences and paused. Then gave a terse description of the effects of the mutated strain, which were maximal only in the higher primates. Recovery rate among the lower mammals and other orders was close to ninety percent. As to vectors, he went on, any warm-blooded animal served. In addition, the virus retained its viability in most environmental media and performed very well airborne. Contagion rate was extremely high. Almost offhand, Ain added that no test primate or accidentally exposed human had survived beyond the twenty-second day.

28   These words fell into a silence broken only by the running feet of the Egyptian delegate making for the door. Then a gilt chair went over as an American bolted after him.

29   Ain seemed unaware that his audience was in a state of unbelieving paralysis. It had all come so fast: a man who had been blowing his nose was staring pop-eyed around his handkerchief. Another who had been lighting a pipe grunted as his fingers singed. Two men chatting by the door missed his words entirely, and their laughter chimed into a dead silence in which echoed Ain's words: "—really no point in attempting."

30   Later they found he had been explaining that the virus utilized the body's own immunomechanisms, and so defense was by definition hopeless.

31   That was all. Ain looked around vaguely for questions and then started down the aisle. By the time he got to the door, people were swarming after him. He wheeled about and said rather crossly, "Yes, of course it is very wrong. I told you that. We are all wrong. Now it's over."

32   An hour later they found he had gone, having apparently reserved a Sinair flight to Karachi.

33   The security men caught up with him at Hong Kong. By then he seemed really very ill, and went with them peacefully. They started back to the States via Hawaii.

34   His captors were civilized types; they saw he was gentle and treated him accordingly. He had no weapons or drugs on him. They took him out handcuffed for a stroll at Osaka, let him feed his crumbs to the birds, and they listened with interest to his account of the migration routes of the common brown sandpiper. He was very hoarse. At that point, he was wanted only for the security thing. There was no question of a woman at all.

35   He dozed most of the way to the islands, but when they came in sight he pressed to the window and began to mutter. The security man behind him got the first inkling that there was a woman in it, and turned on his recorder.

36   " . . . Blue, blue and green until you see the wounds. O my girl, O beautiful, you won't die. I won't let you die. I tell you girl, it's over. . . . Lustrous eyes, look at me, let me see you

now alive! Great queen, my sweet body, my girl, have I saved you? . . . O terrible to know, and noble, Chaos's child green-robed in blue and golden light . . . the thrown and spinning ball of life alone in space. . . . Have I saved you?"

37   On the last leg, he was obviously feverish.

38   "She may have tricked me, you know," he said confidentially to the government man. "You have to be prepared for that, of course. I know her!" He chuckled confidentially. "She's no small thing. But wring your heart out—"

39   Coming over San Francisco he was merry. "Don't you know the otters will go back in there? I'm certain of it. That fill won't last; there'll be a bay there again."

40   They got him on a stretcher at Hamilton Air Base, and he went unconscious shortly after takeoff. Before he collapsed, he'd insisted on throwing the last of his birdseed on the field.

41   "Birds are, you know, warm-blooded," he confided to the agent who was handcuffing him to the stretcher. Then Ain smiled gently and lapsed into inertness. He stayed that way almost all the remaining ten days of his life. By then, of course, no one really cared. Both the government men had died quite early, after they finished analyzing the birdseed and throat spray. The woman at Kennedy had just started feeling sick.

42   The tape recorder they put by his bed functioned right on through, but if anybody had been around to replay it they would have found little but babbling. "Gaea Gloriatrix,"[1] he crooned, "Gaea girl, queen . . ." At times he was grandiose and tormented. "Our life, your death!" he yelled. "Our death would have been your death too, no need for that, no need."

43   At other times he was accusing. "What did you do about the dinosaurs?" he demanded. "Did they annoy you? How did you fix *them*? Cold. Queen, you're too cold! You came close to it this time, my girl," he raved. And then he wept and caressed the bedclothes and was maudlin.

44   Only at the end, lying in his filth and thirst, still chained where they had forgotten him, he was suddenly coherent. In the light clear voice of a lover planning a summer picnic he asked the recorder happily:

45   "Have you ever thought about bears? They have so much . . . funny they never came along further. By any chance were you saving them, girl?" And he chuckled in his ruined throat, and later, died.

QUESTIONS ON MEANING

1. Who is the wounded, dying woman referred to in the fourth paragraph of the story? What role does this character play in the tale?

2. Why does Ain take such a long, a circuitous flight (with so many stops and layovers)?

3. Why do the conference attendees react as they do to Ain's speech?

4. Why is Ain so fixated on feeding birds?

5. What does Ain mean when he asks "have you ever thought about bears?" at the end of the story?

---

[1] Gaea Gloriatrix: Glorious Earth; or, Earth Queen, etc.

QUESTIONS FOR DISCUSSION

1. Why does Doctor Ain seek to bring about the eradication of human life? What is he hoping to achieve? What are humans guilty of doing that Ain feels justifies his actions?

2. In crafting "The Last Flight of Doctor Ain," Tiptree borrowed from numerous academic disciplines. How do the disciplines of ecology, biology, and epidemiology factor into one's understanding and enjoyment of this story?

3. What clues does Tiptree plant in the story regarding the wounded and dying woman first mentioned in paragraph four? List some of these clues. At what point did it become clear to you who this woman is? Once you have identified the woman, what figures of speech are being used by Tiptree when she writes that the woman "coughed, picking weakly at the scabs on her face"?

4. Point of view is very important in this story. In particular, it is important to note how Ain's words and movements are reported through witnesses, rather than directly. What point of view is the story told from? How is third person objective different from third person omniscient? Which is this story? How would this story be different if told from the point of view of Ain, as a first-person narrator?

5. How do you interpret Ain's tape-recorded comments at the end of the story? What debate does he seem to be having? Who is he having this debate with?—himself, or the mystery woman? What does he mean when he says "Our death would have been your death too, no need for that, no need"? Why does Doctor Ain bring up the dinosaurs?

LOOKING AT RHETORIC

1. Does this story make an argument? If so, for what? Is the argument convincing? If not, should it be? Would the story be more or less interesting or powerful if there was a more explicit argument being made? How do stories make arguments?

2. Over the course of the story the reader is gradually introduced to Doctor Ain. How is Doctor Ain created by Tiptree? Are we given a full-blown character sketch anywhere in the story, or does the reader have to assemble a sense of who this character is piecemeal? Do we learn more about Doctor Ain by observing him in action (showing) or through direct presentation by Tiptree in exposition (telling)?

WRITING ASSIGNMENTS

1. Using library and/or Internet sources, explore Tiptree's background. Draft an essay in which you argue either for or against the actions taken by Doctor Ain in this story. Is he justified in doing what he did? State your answer to this question as a thesis for your essay, and be sure to use specific references to the story as you build arguments in support of your thesis.

2. What is the responsibility of the individual to the environment? What role should governments and other organizations play in protecting the environment? Are the obligations of individuals and organizations different? Draft an essay in which you attempt to answers these questions, using "The Last Flight of Doctor Ain" as a way to introduce your argumentative essay on the responsibilities of humans to their environment.

3. In pairs or in groups, craft a one-paragraph policy statement that sets forth the obligations or responsibilities of humans to the environment. Spend some time sharing your policy statements with the other groups in class, taking particular note of those policies that are different from your own. Then, as an individual, draft an essay in the form of a speech before an assembly of legislators in which you set forth your "Statement on Human Ecological Ethics" and persuade this group to adopt your policy as law.

Bartleby, the Scrivener

A Story of Wall-Street

Herman Melville

Herman Melville (1819–1891) was a writer of novels, short stories, poems, and travel narratives. In spite of a decline in reputation during his lifetime, he is now regarded as one of the greatest American writers, largely based on his monumental book **Moby-Dick.** *Born into an aristocratic family that was declining in economic influence, he was taken out of school at twelve, and he went to work at a bank and at his brother's fir and cap store. Fascinated with the sea, he sailed on the whaling ship* **Acushnet.** *Along with a companion, he jumped ship in the Marquesas Islands, spending time among the natives, and returned home after nearly three years. His experiences on both voyages became the basis for his novelistic travel narratives* **Typee** *(1846) and* **Omoo** *(1847) and his novels* **Redburn** *(1849) and* **White-Jacket** *(1850). Unsatisfied with writing popular narratives, he began to explore philosophical and religious issues in* **Mardi** *(1849) and later in* **Moby-Dick** *(1851). He continued to publish novels and short stories, but after a time he was unable to make a living, so he spent the final years of his working life as a customs inspector in New York. Intensely reflective and preoccupied with grand philosophical questions, his works deal with issues ranging from religion, to politics, to human psychology. The following selection explores modern city life and the complexities of human emotions and relationships. The story deals with how modern people struggle with the complexities of the industrial and technological world.*

1   I am a rather elderly man. The nature of my avocations for the last thirty years has brought me into more than ordinary contact with what would seem an interesting and somewhat singular set of men, of whom as yet nothing that I know of has ever been written:—I mean the law-copyists or scriveners.[1] I have known very many of them, professionally and privately, and if I pleased, could relate divers histories, at which good-natured gentlemen might smile, and sentimental souls might weep. But I waive the biographies of all other scriveners for a few passages in the life of Bartleby, who was a scrivener the strangest I ever saw or heard of. While of other law-copyists I might write the complete life, of Bartleby nothing of that sort can be done. I believe that no materials exist for a full and satisfactory biography of this man. It is an irreparable loss to literature. Bartleby was one of those beings of whom nothing is ascertainable, except from the original sources, and in his case those are very small. What my own astonished eyes saw of Bartleby, *that* is all I know of him, except, indeed, one vague report which will appear in the sequel.

2   Ere introducing the scrivener, as he first appeared to me, it is fit I make some mention of myself, my *employées*, my business, my chambers, and general surroundings; because some such description is indispensable to an adequate understanding of the chief character about to be presented.

3   Imprimis:[2] I am a man who, from his youth upwards, has been filled with a profound conviction that the easiest way of life is the best. Hence, though I belong to a profession

---

[1] scrivener: a man or woman who copies documents by hand. In essence, a human copy machine.
[2] Imprimis: In the first place (Latin).

proverbially energetic and nervous, even to turbulence, at times, yet nothing of that sort have I ever suffered to invade my peace. I am one of those unambitious lawyers who never addresses a jury, or in any way draws down public applause; but in the cool tranquillity of a snug retreat, do a snug business among rich men's bonds and mortgages and title-deeds. All who know me, consider me an eminently *safe* man. The late John Jacob Astor,[3] a personage little given to poetic enthusiasm, had no hesitation in pronouncing my first grand point to be prudence; my next, method. I do not speak it in vanity, but simply record the fact, that I was not unemployed in my profession by the late John Jacob Astor; a name which, I admit, I love to repeat, for it hath a rounded and orbicular sound to it, and rings like unto bullion. I will freely add, that I was not insensible to the late John Jacob Astor's good opinion.

4   Some time prior to the period at which this little history begins, my avocations had been largely increased. The good old office, now extinct in the State of New-York, of a Master in Chancery, had been conferred upon me. It was not a very arduous office, but very pleasantly remunerative. I seldom lose my temper; much more seldom indulge in dangerous indignation at wrongs and outrages; but I must be permitted to be rash here and declare, that I consider the sudden and violent abrogation of the office of Master in Chancery, by the new Constitution,[4] as a—premature act; inasmuch as I had counted upon a life-lease of the profits, whereas I only received those of a few short years. But this is by the way.

5   My chambers were up stairs at No.—Wall-street. At one end they looked upon the white wall of the interior of a spacious sky-light shaft, penetrating the building from top to bottom. This view might have been considered rather tame than otherwise, deficient in what landscape painters call "life." But if so, the view from the other end of my chambers offered, at least, a contrast, if nothing more. In that direction my windows commanded an unobstructed view of a lofty brick wall, black by age and everlasting shade; which wall required no spy-glass to bring out its lurking beauties, but for the benefit of all near-sighted spectators, was pushed up to within ten feet of my window panes. Owing to the great height of the surrounding buildings, and my chambers being on the second floor, the interval between this wall and mine not a little resembled a huge square cistern.

6   At the period just preceding the advent of Bartleby, I had two persons as copyists in my employment, and a promising lad as an office-boy. First, Turkey; second, Nippers; third, Ginger Nut. These may seem names, the like of which are not usually found in the Directory. In truth they were nick-names, mutually conferred upon each other by my three clerks, and were deemed expressive of their respective persons or characters. Turkey was a short, pursy Englishman of about my own age, that is, somewhere not far from sixty. In the morning, one might say, his face was of a fine florid hue, but after twelve o'clock, meridian—his dinner hour—it blazed like a grate full of Christmas coals; and continued blazing—but, as it were, with a gradual wane—till 6 o'clock, p.m. or thereabouts, after which I saw no more of the proprietor of the face, which gaining its meridian with the sun, seemed to set with it, to rise, culminate, and decline the following day, with the like

---

[3] John Jacob Astor (1763–1848): One of the richest men in the early nineteenth century, having made the bulk of his fortune in the fur trade.

[4] Constitution: a reference to the constitution New York adopted in 1846.

regularity and undiminished glory. There are many singular coincidences I have known in the course of my life, not the least among which was the fact, that exactly when Turkey displayed his fullest beams from his red and radiant countenance, just then, too, at that critical moment, began the daily period when I considered his business capacities as seriously disturbed for the remainder of the twenty-four hours. Not that he was absolutely idle, or averse to business then; far from it. The difficulty was, he was apt to be altogether too energetic. There was a strange, inflamed, flurried, flighty recklessness of activity about him. He would be incautious in dipping his pen into his inkstand. All his blots upon my documents, were dropped there after twelve o'clock, meridian. Indeed, not only would he be reckless and sadly given to making blots in the afternoon, but some days he went further, and was rather noisy. At such times, too, his face flamed with augmented blazonry, as if cannel coal had been heaped on anthracite. He made an unpleasant racket with his chair; spilled his sand-box; in mending his pens, impatiently split them all to pieces, and threw them on the floor in a sudden passion; stood up and leaned over his table, boxing his papers about in a most indecorous manner, very sad to behold in an elderly man like him. Nevertheless, as he was in many ways a most valuable person to me, and all the time before twelve o'clock, meridian, was the quickest, steadiest creature too, accomplishing a great deal of work in a style not easy to be matched—for these reasons, I was willing to overlook his eccentricities, though indeed, occasionally, I remonstrated with him. I did this very gently, however, because, though the civilest, nay, the blandest and most reverential of men in the morning, yet in the afternoon he was disposed, upon provocation, to be slightly rash with his tongue, in fact, insolent. Now, valuing his morning services as I did, and resolved not to lose them; yet, at the same time made uncomfortable by his inflamed ways after twelve o'clock; and being a man of peace, unwilling by my admonitions to call forth unseemly retorts from him; I took upon me, one Saturday noon (he was always worse on Saturdays), to hint to him, very kindly, that perhaps now that he was growing old, it might be well to abridge his labors; in short, he need not come to my chambers after twelve o'clock, but, dinner over, had best go home to his lodgings and rest himself till tea-time. But no; he insisted upon his afternoon devotions. His countenance became intolerably fervid, as he oratorically assured me—gesticulating with a long ruler at the other end of the room—that if his services in the morning were useful, how indispensable, then, in the afternoon?

7   "With submission, sir," said Turkey on this occasion, "I consider myself your right-hand man. In the morning I but marshal and deploy my columns; but in the afternoon I put myself at their head, and gallantly charge the foe, thus!"—and he made a violent thrust with the ruler.

8   "But the blots, Turkey," intimated I.

9   "True,—but, with submission, sir, behold these hairs! I am getting old. Surely, sir, a blot or two of a warm afternoon is not to be severely urged against gray hairs. Old age—even if it blot the page—is honorable. With submission, sir, we *both* are getting old."

10   This appeal to my fellow-feeling was hardly to be resisted. At all events, I saw that go he would not. So I made up my mind to let him stay, resolving, nevertheless, to see to it, that during the afternoon he had to do with my less important papers.

11   Nippers, the second on my list, was a whiskered, sallow, and, upon the whole, rather piratical-looking young man of about five and twenty. I always deemed him the victim of

two evil powers—ambition and indigestion. The ambition was evinced by a certain impatience of the duties of a mere copyist, an unwarrantable usurpation of strictly professional affairs, such as the original drawing up of legal documents. The indigestion seemed betokened in an occasional nervous testiness and grinning irritability, causing the teeth to audibly grind together over mistakes committed in copying; unnecessary maledictions, hissed, rather than spoken, in the heat of business; and especially by a continual discontent with the height of the table where he worked. Though of a very ingenious mechanical turn, Nippers could never get this table to suit him. He put chips under it, blocks of various sorts, bits of pasteboard, and at last went so far as to attempt an exquisite adjustment by final pieces of folded blotting paper. But no invention would answer. If, for the sake of easing his back, he brought the table lid at a sharp angle well up towards his chin, and wrote there like a man using the steep roof of a Dutch house for his desk:—then he declared that it stopped the circulation in his arms. If now he lowered the table to his waistbands, and stooped over it in writing, then there was a sore aching in his back. In short, the truth of the matter was, Nippers knew not what he wanted. Or, if he wanted anything, it was to be rid of a scrivener's table altogether. Among the manifestations of his diseased ambition was a fondness he had for receiving visits from certain ambiguous-looking fellows in seedy coats, whom he called his clients. Indeed I was aware that not only was he, at times, considerable of a ward-politician, but he occasionally did a little business at the Justices' courts, and was not unknown on the steps of the Tombs.[5] I have good reason to believe, however, that one individual who called upon him at my chambers, and who, with a grand air, he insisted was his client, was no other than a dun, and the alleged title-deed, a bill. But with all his failings, and the annoyances he caused me, Nippers, like his compatriot Turkey, was a very useful man to me; wrote a neat, swift hand; and, when he chose, was not deficient in a gentlemanly sort of deportment. Added to this, he always dressed in a gentlemanly sort of way; and so, incidentally, reflected credit upon my chambers. Whereas with respect to Turkey, I had much ado to keep him from being a reproach to me. His clothes were apt to look oily and smell of eating-houses. He wore his pantaloons very loose and baggy in summer. His coats were execrable; his hat not to be handled. But while the hat was a thing of indifference to me, inasmuch as his natural civility and deference as a dependent Englishman, always led him to doff it the moment he entered the room, yet his coat was another matter. Concerning his coats, I reasoned with him; but with no effect. The truth was, I suppose, that a man with so small an income, could not afford to sport such a lustrous face and a lustrous coat at one and the same time. As Nippers once observed, Turkey's money went chiefly for red ink. One winter day I presented Turkey with a highly-respectable looking coat of my own, a padded gray coat, of a most comfortable warmth, and which buttoned straight up from the knee to the neck. I thought Turkey would appreciate the favor, and abate his rashness and obstreperousness of afternoons. But no. I verily believe that buttoning himself up in so downy and blanket-like a coat had a pernicious effect upon him; upon the same principle that too much oats are bad for horses. In fact, precisely as a rash, restive horse is said to feel his oats, so Turkey felt his coat. It made him insolent. He was a man whom prosperity harmed.

---

[5] Tombs: a New York City prison built in 1839.

12   Though concerning the self-indulgent habits of Turkey I had my own private surmises, yet touching Nippers I was well persuaded that whatever might be his faults in other respects, he was, at least, a temperate young man. But indeed, nature herself seemed to have been his vintner, and at his birth charged him so thoroughly with an irritable, brandy-like disposition, that all subsequent potations were needless. When I consider how, amid the stillness of my chambers, Nippers would sometimes impatiently rise from his seat, and stooping over his table, spread his arms wide apart, seize the whole desk, and move it, and jerk it, with a grim, grinding motion on the floor, as if the table were a perverse voluntary agent, intent on thwarting and vexing him; I plainly perceive that for Nippers, brandy and water were altogether superfluous.

13   It was fortunate for me that, owing to its peculiar cause—indigestion—the irritability and consequent nervousness of Nippers, were mainly observable in the morning, while in the afternoon he was comparatively mild. So that Turkey's paroxysms only coming on about twelve o'clock, I never had to do with their eccentricities at one time. Their fits relieved each other like guards. When Nippers' was on, Turkey's was off; and *vice versa*. This was a good natural arrangement under the circumstances.

14   Ginger Nut, the third on my list, was a lad some twelve years old. His father was a carman,[6] ambitious of seeing his son on the bench instead of a cart, before he died. So he sent him to my office as student at law, errand boy, and cleaner and sweeper, at the rate of one dollar a week. He had a little desk to himself, but he did not use it much. Upon inspection, the drawer exhibited a great array of the shells of various sorts of nuts. Indeed, to this quick-witted youth the whole noble science of the law was contained in a nut-shell. Not the least among the employments of Ginger Nut, as well as one which he discharged with the most alacrity, was his duty as cake and apple purveyor for Turkey and Nippers. Copying law papers being proverbially a dry, husky sort of business, my two scriveners were fain to moisten their mouths very often with Spitzenbergs to be had at the numerous stalls nigh the Custom House and Post Office. Also, they sent Ginger Nut very frequently for that peculiar cake—small, flat, round, and very spicy—after which he had been named by them. Of a cold morning when business was but dull, Turkey would gobble up scores of these cakes, as if they were mere wafers—indeed they sell them crunching of the crisp particles in his mouth. Of all the fiery afternoon blunders and flurried rashnesses of Turkey, was his once moistening a ginger-cake between his lips, and clapping it on to a mortgage for a seal. I came within an ace of dismissing him then. But he mollified me by making an oriental bow, and saying—"With submission, sir, it was generous of me to find you in stationery on my own account."

15   Now my original business—that of a conveyancer and title hunter, and drawer-up of recondite documents of all sorts—was considerably increased by receiving the master's office. There was now great work for scriveners. Not only must I push the clerks already with me, but I must have additional help. In answer to my advertisement, a motionless young man one morning, stood upon my office threshold, the door being open, for it was summer. I can see that figure now—pallidly neat, pitiably respectable, incurably forlorn! It was Bartleby.

---

[6] carman: a driver of carts carrying goods.

16   After a few words touching his qualifications, I engaged him, glad to have among my corps of copyists a man of so singularly sedate an aspect, which I thought might operate beneficially upon the flighty temper of Turkey, and the fiery one of Nippers.

17   I should have stated before that ground glass folding-doors divided my premises into two parts, one of which was occupied by my scriveners, the other by myself. According to my humor I threw open these doors, or closed them. I resolved to assign Bartleby a corner by the folding-doors, but on my side of them, so as to have this quiet man within easy call, in case any trifling thing was to be done. I placed his desk close up to a small side-window in that part of the room, a window which originally had afforded a lateral view of certain grimy back-yards and bricks, but which, owing to subsequent erections, commanded at present no view at all, though it gave some light. Within three feet of the panes was a wall, and the light came down from far above, between two lofty buildings, as from a very small opening in a dome. Still further to a satisfactory arrangement, I procured a high green folding screen, which might entirely isolate Bartleby from my sight, though not remove him from my voice. And thus, in a manner, privacy and society were conjoined.

18   At first Bartleby did an extraordinary quantity of writing. As if long famishing for something to copy, he seemed to gorge himself on my documents. There was no pause for digestion. He ran a day and night line, copying by sunlight and by candle-light. I should have been quite delighted with his application, had he been cheerfully industrious. But he wrote on silently, palely, mechanically.

19   It is, of course, an indispensable part of a scrivener's business to verify the accuracy of his copy, word by word. Where there are two or more scriveners in an office, they assist each other in this examination, one reading from the copy, the other holding the original. It is a very dull, wearisome, and lethargic affair. I can readily imagine that to some sanguine temperaments it would be altogether intolerable. For example, I cannot credit that the mettlesome poet Byron[7] would have contentedly sat down with Bartleby to examine a law document of, say five hundred pages, closely written in a crimpy hand.

20   Now and then, in the haste of business, it had been my habit to assist in comparing some brief document myself, calling Turkey or Nippers for this purpose. One object I had in placing Bartleby so handy to me behind the screen, was to avail myself of his services on such trivial occasions. It was on the third day, I think, of his being with me, and before any necessity had arisen for having his own writing examined, that, being much hurried to complete a small affair I had in hand, I abruptly called to Bartleby. In my haste and natural expectancy of instant compliance, I sat with my head bent over the original on my desk, and my right hand sideways, and somewhat nervously extended with the copy, so that immediately upon emerging from his retreat, Bartleby might snatch it and proceed to business without the least delay.

21   In this very attitude did I sit when I called to him, rapidly stating what it was I wanted him to do—namely, to examine a small paper with me. Imagine my surprise, nay, my consternation, when without moving from his privacy, Bartleby in a singularly mild, firm voice, replied, "I would prefer not to."

---

[7] George Gordon Lord Byron (1788–1824): English Romantic poet.

22   I sat awhile in perfect silence, rallying my stunned faculties. Immediately it occurred to me that my ears had deceived me, or Bartleby had entirely misunderstood my meaning. I repeated my request in the clearest tone I could assume. But in quite as clear a one came the previous reply, "I would prefer not to."

23   "Prefer not to," echoed I, rising in high excitement, and crossing the room with a stride. "What do you mean? Are you moon-struck? I want you to help me compare this sheet here—take it," and I thrust it towards him.

24   "I would prefer not to," said he.

25   I looked at him steadfastly. His face was leanly composed; his gray eye dimly calm. Not a wrinkle of agitation rippled him. Had there been the least uneasiness, anger, impatience or impertinence in his manner; in other words, had there been any thing ordinarily human about him, doubtless I should have violently dismissed him from the premises. But as it was, I should have as soon thought of turning my pale plaster-of-paris bust of Cicero[8] out of doors. I stood gazing at him awhile, as he went on with his own writing, and then reseated myself at my desk. This is very strange, thought I. What had one best do? But my business hurried me. I concluded to forget the matter for the present, reserving it for my future leisure. So calling Nippers from the other room, the paper was speedily examined.

26   A few days after this, Bartleby concluded four lengthy documents, being quadruplicates of a week's testimony taken before me in my High Court of Chancery. It became necessary to examine them. It was an important suit, and great accuracy was imperative. Having all things arranged I called Turkey, Nippers and Ginger Nut from the next room, meaning to place the four copies in the hands of my four clerks, while I should read from the original. Accordingly Turkey, Nippers and Ginger Nut had taken their seats in a row, each with his document in hand, when I called to Bartleby to join this interesting group.

27   "Bartleby! quick, I am waiting."

28   I heard a slow scrape of his chair legs on the uncarpeted floor, and soon he appeared standing at the entrance of his hermitage.

29   "What is wanted?" said he mildly.

30   "The copies, the copies," said I hurriedly. "We are going to examine them. There"— and I held towards him the fourth quadruplicate.

31   "I would prefer not to," he said, and gently disappeared behind the screen.

32   For a few moments I was turned into a pillar of salt, standing at the head of my seated column of clerks. Recovering myself, I advanced towards the screen, and demanded the reason for such extraordinary conduct.

33   "*Why* do you refuse?"

34   "I would prefer not to."

35   With any other man I should have flown outright into a dreadful passion, scorned all further words, and thrust him ignominiously from my presence. But there was something about Bartleby that not only strangely disarmed me, but in a wonderful manner touched and disconcerted me. I began to reason with him.

---

[8]Cicero (106–42 B. C. E.): Roman writer, orator, and statesman.

36   "These are your own copies we are about to examine. It is labor saving to you, because one examination will answer for your four papers. It is common usage. Every copyist is bound to help examine his copy. Is it not so? Will you not speak? Answer!"

37   "I prefer not to," he replied in a flute-like tone. It seemed to me that while I had been addressing him, he carefully revolved every statement that I made; fully comprehended the meaning; could not gainsay the irresistible conclusion; but, at the same time, some paramount consideration prevailed with him to reply as he did.

38   "You are decided, then, not to comply with my request—a request made according to common usage and common sense?"

39   He briefly gave me to understand that on that point my judgment was sound. Yes: his decision was irreversible.

40   It is not seldom the case that when a man is browbeaten in some unprecedented and violently unreasonable way, he begins to stagger in his own plainest faith. He begins, as it were, vaguely to surmise that, wonderful as it may be, all the justice and all the reason is on the other side. Accordingly, if any disinterested persons are present, he turns to them for some reinforcement for his own faltering mind.

41   "Turkey," said I, "what do you think of this? Am I not right?"

42   "With submission, sir," said Turkey, with his blandest tone, "I think that you are."

43   "Nippers," said I, "what do *you* think of it?"

44   "I think I should kick him out of the office."

45   (The reader of nice perceptions will here perceive that, it being morning, Turkey's answer is couched in polite and tranquil terms, but Nippers replies in ill-tempered ones. Or, to repeat a previous sentence, Nippers's ugly mood was on duty, and Turkey's off.)

46   "Ginger Nut," said I, willing to enlist the smallest suffrage in my behalf, "what do *you* think of it?"

47   "I think, sir, he's a little luny," replied Ginger Nut, with a grin.

48   "You hear what they say," said I, turning towards the screen, "come forth and do your duty."

49   But he vouchsafed no reply. I pondered a moment in sore perplexity. But once more business hurried me. I determined again to postpone the consideration of this dilemma to my future leisure. With a little trouble we made out to examine the papers without Bartleby, though at every page or two, Turkey deferentially dropped his opinion that this proceeding was quite out of the common; while Nippers, twitching in his chair with a dyspeptic nervousness, ground out between his set teeth occasional hissing maledictions against the stubborn oaf behind the screen. And for his (Nippers's) part, this was the first and the last time he would do another man's business without pay.

50   Meanwhile Bartleby sat in his hermitage, oblivious to every thing but his own peculiar business there.

51   Some days passed, the scrivener being employed upon another lengthy work. His late remarkable conduct led me to regard his ways narrowly. I observed that he never went to dinner; indeed that he never went any where. As yet I had never of my personal knowledge known him to be outside of my office. He was a perpetual sentry in the corner. At about eleven o'clock though, in the morning, I noticed that Ginger Nut would advance toward the opening in Bartleby's screen, as if silently beckoned thither by a gesture invisible to me where

I sat. The boy would then leave the office jingling a few pence, and reappear with a handful of ginger-nuts which he delivered in the hermitage, receiving two of the cakes for his trouble.

52   He lives, then, on ginger-nuts, thought I; never eats a dinner, properly speaking; he must be a vegetarian then; but no; he never eats even vegetables, he eats nothing but ginger-nuts. My mind then ran on in reveries concerning the probable effects upon the human constitution of living entirely on ginger-nuts. Ginger-nuts are so called because they contain ginger as one of their peculiar constituents, and the final flavoring one. Now what was ginger? A hot, spicy thing. Was Bartleby hot and spicy? Not at all. Ginger, then, had no effect upon Bartleby. Probably he preferred it should have none.

53   Nothing so aggravates an earnest person as a passive resistance. If the individual so resisted be of a not inhumane temper, and the resisting one perfectly harmless in his passivity; then, in the better moods of the former, he will endeavor charitably to construe to his imagination what proves impossible to be solved by his judgment. Even so, for the most part, I regarded Bartleby and his ways. Poor fellow! thought I, he means no mischief; it is plain he intends no insolence; his aspect sufficiently evinces that his eccentricities are involuntary. He is useful to me. I can get along with him. If I turn him away, the chances are he will fall in with some less indulgent employer, and then he will be rudely treated, and perhaps driven forth miserably to starve. Yes. Here I can cheaply purchase a delicious self-approval. To befriend Bartleby; to humor him in his strange wilfulness, will cost me little or nothing, while I lay up in my soul what will eventually prove a sweet morsel for my conscience. But this mood was not invariable with me. The passiveness of Bartleby sometimes irritated me. I felt strangely goaded on to encounter him in new opposition, to elicit some angry spark from him answerable to my own. But indeed I might as well have essayed to strike fire with my knuckles against a bit of Windsor soap. But one afternoon the evil impulse in me mastered me, and the following little scene ensued:

54   "Bartleby," said I, "when those papers are all copied, I will compare them with you."

55   "I would prefer not to."

56   "How? Surely you do not mean to persist in that mulish vagary?"

57   No answer.

58   I threw open the folding-doors near by, and turning upon Turkey and Nippers, exclaimed in an excited manner—

59   "He says, a second time, he won't examine his papers. What do you think of it, Turkey?"

60   It was afternoon, be it remembered. Turkey sat glowing like a brass boiler, his bald head steaming, his hands reeling among his blotted papers.

61   "Think of it?" roared Turkey; "I think I'll just step behind his screen, and black his eyes for him!"

62   So saying, Turkey rose to his feet and threw his arms into a pugilistic position. He was hurrying away to make good his promise, when I detained him, alarmed at the effect of incautiously rousing Turkey's combativeness after dinner.

63   "Sit down, Turkey," said I, "and hear what Nippers has to say. What do you think of it, Nippers? Would I not be justified in immediately dismissing Bartleby?"

64   "Excuse me, that is for you to decide, sir. I think his conduct quite unusual, and indeed unjust, as regards Turkey and myself. But it may only be a passing whim."

65   "Ah," exclaimed I, "you have strangely changed your mind then—you speak very gently of him now."

66   "All beer," cried Turkey; "gentleness is effects of beer—Nippers and I dined together to-day. You see how gentle I am, sir. Shall I go and black his eyes?"

67   "You refer to Bartleby, I suppose. No, not to-day, Turkey," I replied; "pray, put up your fists."

68   I closed the doors, and again advanced towards Bartleby. I felt additional incentives tempting me to my fate. I burned to be rebelled against again. I remembered that Bartleby never left the office.

69   "Bartleby," said I, "Ginger Nut is away; just step round to the Post Office, won't you? (it was but a three minutes' walk,) and see if there is any thing for me."

70   "I would prefer not to."

71   "You *will* not?"

72   "I *prefer* not."

73   I staggered to my desk, and sat there in a deep study. My blind inveteracy returned. Was there any other thing in which I could procure myself to be ignominiously repulsed by this lean, penniless wight?—my hired clerk? What added thing is there, perfectly reasonable, that he will be sure to refuse to do?

74   "Bartleby!"

75   No answer.

76   "Bartleby," in a louder tone.

77   No answer.

78   "Bartleby," I roared.

79   Like a very ghost, agreeably to the laws of magical invocation, at the third summons, he appeared at the entrance of his hermitage.

80   "Go to the next room, and tell Nippers to come to me."

81   "I prefer not to," he respectfully and slowly said, and mildly disappeared.

82   "Very good, Bartleby," said I, in a quiet sort of serenely severe self-possessed tone, intimating the unalterable purpose of some terrible retribution very close at hand. At the moment I half intended something of the kind. But upon the whole, as it was drawing towards my dinner-hour, I thought it best to put on my hat and walk home for the day, suffering much from perplexity and distress of mind.

83   Shall I acknowledge it? The conclusion of this whole business was, that it soon became a fixed fact of my chambers, that a pale young scrivener, by the name of Bartleby, had a desk there; that he copied for me at the usual rate of four cents a folio (one hundred words); but he was permanently exempt from examining the work done by him, that duty being transferred to Turkey and Nippers, out of compliment doubtless to their superior acuteness; moreover, said Bartleby was never on any account to be dispatched on the most trivial errand of any sort; and that even if entreated to take upon him such a matter, it was generally understood that he would prefer not to—in other words, that he would refuse point-blank.

84   As days passed on, I became considerably reconciled to Bartleby. His steadiness, his freedom from all dissipation, his incessant industry (except when he chose to throw himself into a standing revery behind his screen), his great stillness, his unalterableness of

demeanor under all circumstances, made him a valuable acquisition. One prime thing was this—*he was always there*—first in the morning, continually through the day, and the last at night. I had a singular confidence in his honesty. I felt my most precious papers perfectly safe in his hands. Sometimes to be sure I could not, for the very soul of me, avoid falling into sudden spasmodic passions with him. For it was exceeding difficult to bear in mind all the time those strange peculiarities, privileges, and unheard of exemptions, forming the tacit stipulations on Bartleby's part under which he remained in my office. Now and then, in the eagerness of dispatching pressing business, I would inadvertently summon Bartleby, in a short, rapid tone, to put his finger, say, on the incipient tie of a bit of red tape with which I was about compressing some papers. Of course, from behind the screen the usual answer, "I prefer not to," was sure to come; and then, how could a human creature with common infirmities of our nature, refrain from bitterly exclaiming upon such perverseness—such unreasonableness. However, every added repulse of this sort which I received only tended to lessen the probability of my repeating the inadvertence.

85   Here it must be said, that according to the customs of most legal gentlemen occupying chambers in densely-populated law buildings, there were several keys to my door. One was kept by a woman residing in the attic, which person weekly scrubbed and daily swept and dusted my apartments. Another was kept by Turkey for convenience sake. The third I sometimes carried in my own pocket. The fourth I knew not who had.

86   Now, one Sunday morning I happened to go to Trinity Church, to hear a celebrated preacher, and finding myself rather early on the ground I thought I would walk round to my chambers for a while. Luckily I had my key with me; but upon applying it to the lock, I found it resisted by something inserted from the inside. Quite surprised, I called out; when to my consternation a key was turned from within; and thrusting his lean visage at me, and holding the door ajar, the apparition of Bartleby appeared, in his shirt sleeves, and otherwise in a strangely tattered dishabille, saying quietly that he was sorry, but he was deeply engaged just then, and—preferred not admitting me at present. In a brief word or two, he moreover added, that perhaps I had better walk round the block two or three times, and by that time he would probably have concluded his affairs.

87   Now, the utterly unsurmised appearance of Bartleby, tenanting my law-chambers of a Sunday morning, with his cadaverously gentlemanly *nonchalance*, yet withal firm and self-possessed; had such a strange effect upon me, that incontinently I slunk away from my own door, and did as desired. But not without sundry twinges of impotent rebellion against the mild effrontery of this unaccountable scrivener. Indeed, it was his wonderful mildness chiefly, which not only disarmed me, but unmanned me, as it were. For I consider that one, for the time, is a sort of unmanned when he tranquilly permits his hired clerk to dictate to him, and order him away from his own premises. Furthermore, I was full of uneasiness as to what Bartleby could possibly be doing in my office in his shirt sleeves, and in an otherwise dismantled condition of a Sunday morning. Was any thing amiss going on? Nay, that was out of the question. It was not to be thought of for a moment that Bartleby was an immoral person. But what could he be doing there?—copying? Nay again, whatever might be his eccentricities, Bartleby was an eminently decorous person. He would be the last man to sit down to his desk in any state approaching to nudity. Besides, it was Sunday; and there was something about Bartleby that forbade the supposition that he would by any secular occupation violate the proprieties of the day.

88   Nevertheless, my mind was not pacified; and full of a restless curiosity, at last I returned to the door. Without hindrance I inserted my key, opened it, and entered. Bartleby was not to be seen. I looked round anxiously, peeped behind his screen; but it was very plain that he was gone. Upon more closely examining the place, I surmised that for an indefinite period Bartleby must have ate, dressed, and slept in my office, and that too without plate, mirror, or bed. The cushioned seat of a ricketty old sofa in one corner bore the faint impress of a lean, reclining form. Rolled away under his desk, I found a blanket; under the empty grate, a blacking box and brush; on a chair, a tin basin, with soap and a ragged towel; in a newspaper a few crumbs of ginger-nuts and a morsel of cheese. Yes, thought I, it is evident enough that Bartleby has been making his home here, keeping bachelor's hall all by himself. Immediately then the thought came sweeping across me, What miserable friendlessness and loneliness are here revealed! His poverty is great; but his solitude, how horrible! Think of it. Of a Sunday, Wall-street is deserted as Petra;[9] and every night of every day it is an emptiness. This building too, which of week-days hums with industry and life, at nightfall echoes with sheer vacancy, and all through Sunday is forlorn. And here Bartleby makes his home; sole spectator of a solitude which he has seen all populous—a sort of innocent and transformed Marius[10] brooding among the ruins of Carthage!

89   For the first time in my life a feeling of overpowering stinging melancholy seized me. Before, I had never experienced aught but a not-unpleasing sadness. The bond of a common humanity now drew me irresistibly to gloom. A fraternal melancholy! For both I and Bartleby were sons of Adam. I remembered the bright silks and sparkling faces I had seen that day, in gala trim, swan-like sailing down the Mississippi of Broadway; and I contrasted them with the pallid copyist, and thought to myself, Ah, happiness courts the light, so we deem the world is gay; but misery hides aloof, so we deem that misery there is none. These sad fancyings—chimeras, doubtless, of a sick and silly brain—led on to other and more special thoughts, concerning the eccentricities of Bartleby. Presentiments of strange discoveries hovered round me. The scrivener's pale form appeared to me laid out, among uncaring strangers, in its shivering winding sheet.

90   Suddenly I was attracted by Bartleby's closed desk, the key in open sight left in the lock.

91   I mean no mischief, seek the gratification of no heartless curiosity, thought I; besides, the desk is mine, and its contents too, so I will make bold to look within. Every thing was methodically arranged, the papers smoothly placed. The pigeon holes were deep, and removing the files of documents, I groped into their recesses. Presently I felt something there, and dragged it out. It was an old bandanna handkerchief, heavy and knotted. I opened it, and saw it was a saving's bank.

92   I now recalled all the quiet mysteries which I had noted in the man. I remembered that he never spoke but to answer; that though at intervals he had considerable time to himself, yet I had never seen him reading—no, not even a newspaper; that for long periods he would stand looking out, at his pale window behind the screen, upon the dead brick wall; I was quite sure he never visited any refectory or eating house; while his pale face clearly

---

[9] Petra: Ancient Middle Eastern city, the ruins of which are in modern Jordan.

[10] Marius (157–86 B. C. E.): Gaius Marius, Roman general who was restored to power after a period of exile.

indicated that he never drank beer like Turkey, or tea and coffee even, like other men; that he never went any where in particular that I could learn; never went out for a walk, unless indeed that was the case at present; that he had declined telling who he was, or whence he came, or whether he had any relatives in the world; that though so thin and pale, he never complained of ill health. And more than all, I remembered a certain unconscious air of pallid—how shall I call it?—of pallid haughtiness, say, or rather an austere reserve about him, which had positively awed me into my tame compliance with his eccentricities, when I had feared to ask him to do the slightest incidental thing for me, even though I might know, from his long-continued motionlessness, that behind his screen he must be standing in one of those dead-wall reveries of his.

93   Revolving all these things, and coupling them with the recently discovered fact that he made my office his constant abiding place and home, and not forgetful of his morbid moodiness; revolving all these things, a prudential feeling began to steal over me. My first emotions had been those of pure melancholy and sincerest pity; but just in proportion as the forlornness of Bartleby grew and grew to my imagination, did that same melancholy merge into fear, that pity into repulsion. So true it is, and so terrible too, that up to a certain point the thought or sight of misery enlists our best affections; but, in certain special cases, beyond that point it does not. They err who would assert that invariably this is owing to the inherent selfishness of the human heart. It rather proceeds from a certain hopelessness of remedying excessive and organic ill. To a sensitive being, pity is not seldom pain. And when at last it is perceived that such pity cannot lead to effectual succor, common sense bids the soul be rid of it. What I saw that morning persuaded me that the scrivener was the victim of innate and incurable disorder. I might give alms to his body; but his body did not pain him; it was his soul that suffered, and his soul I could not reach.

94   I did not accomplish the purpose of going to Trinity Church that morning. Somehow, the things I had seen disqualified me for the time from church-going. I walked homeward, thinking what I would do with Bartleby. Finally, I resolved upon this;—I would put certain calm questions to him the next morning, touching his history, &c., and if he declined to answer them openly and unreservedly (and I supposed he would prefer not), then to give him a twenty dollar bill over and above whatever I might owe him, and tell him his services were no longer required; but that if in any other way I could assist him, I would be happy to do so, especially if he desired to return to his native place, wherever that might be, I would willingly help to defray the expenses. Moreover, if, after reaching home, he found himself at any time in want of aid, a letter from him would be sure of a reply.

95   The next morning came.

96   "Bartleby," said I, gently calling to him behind his screen.

97   No reply.

98   "Bartleby," said I, in a still gentler tone, "come here; I am not going to ask you to do any thing you would prefer not to do—I simply wish to speak to you."

99   Upon this he noiselessly slid into view.

100   "Will you tell me, Bartleby, where you were born?"

101   "I would prefer not to."

102   "Will you tell me *any thing* about yourself?"

103   "I would prefer not to."

104   "But what reasonable objection can you have to speak to me? I feel friendly towards you."

105   He did not look at me while I spoke, but kept his glance fixed upon my bust of Cicero, which as I then sat, was directly behind me, some six inches above my head.

106   "What is your answer, Bartleby?" said I, after waiting a considerable time for a reply, during which his countenance remained immovable, only there was the faintest conceivable tremor of the white attenuated mouth.

107   "At present I prefer to give no answer," he said, and retired into his hermitage.

108   It was rather weak in me I confess, but his manner on this occasion nettled me. Not only did there seem to lurk in it a certain calm disdain, but his perverseness seemed ungrateful, considering the undeniable good usage and indulgence he had received from me.

109   Again I sat ruminating what I should do. Mortified as I was at his behavior, and resolved as I had been to dismiss him when I entered my office, nevertheless I strangely felt something superstitious knocking at my heart, and forbidding me to carry out my purpose, and denouncing me for a villain if I dared to breathe one bitter word against this forlornest of mankind. At last, familiarly drawing my chair behind his screen, I sat down and said: "Bartleby, never mind then about revealing your history; but let me entreat you, as a friend, to comply as far as may be with the usages of this office. Say now you will help to examine papers to-morrow or next day: in short, say now that in a day or two you will begin to be a little reasonable:—say so, Bartleby."

110   "At present I would prefer not to be a little reasonable," was his mildly cadaverous reply.

111   Just then the folding-doors opened, and Nippers approached. He seemed suffering from an unusually bad night's rest, induced by severer indigestion than common. He overheard those final words of Bartleby.

112   "*Prefer not*, eh?" gritted Nippers—"I'd *prefer* him, if I were you, sir," addressing me— "I'd *prefer* him; I'd give him preferences, the stubborn mule! What is it, sir, pray, that he *prefers* not to do now?"

113   Bartleby moved not a limb.

114   "Mr. Nippers," said I, "I'd prefer that you would withdraw for the present."

115   Somehow, of late I had got into the way of involuntarily using this word "prefer" upon all sorts of not exactly suitable occasions. And I trembled to think that my contact with the scrivener had already and seriously affected me in a mental way. And what further and deeper aberration might it not yet produce? This apprehension had not been without efficacy in determining me to summary means.

116   As Nippers, looking very sour and sulky, was departing, Turkey blandly and deferentially approached.

117   "With submission, sir," said he, "yesterday I was thinking about Bartleby here, and I think that if he would but prefer to take a quart of good ale every day, it would do much towards mending him, and enabling him to assist in examining his papers."

118   "So you have got the word too," said I, slightly excited.

119   "With submission, what word, sir," asked Turkey, respectfully crowding himself into the contracted space behind the screen, and by so doing, making me jostle the scrivener. "What word, sir?"

120   "I would prefer to be left alone here," said Bartleby, as if offended at being mobbed in his privacy.

121   "*That's* the word, Turkey," said I—"*that's* it."

122   "Oh, *prefer*? oh yes—queer word. I never use it myself. But, sir, as I was saying, if he would but prefer—"

123   "Turkey," interrupted I, "you will please withdraw."

124   "Oh certainly, sir, if you prefer that I should."

125   As he opened the folding-door to retire, Nippers at his desk caught a glimpse of me, and asked whether I would prefer to have a certain paper copied on blue paper or white. He did not in the least roguishly accent the word prefer. It was plain that it involuntarily rolled from his tongue. I thought to myself, surely I must get rid of a demented man, who already has in some degree turned the tongues, if not the heads of myself and clerks. But I thought it prudent not to break the dismission at once.

126   The next day I noticed that Bartleby did nothing but stand at his window in his dead-wall revery. Upon asking him why he did not write, he said that he had decided upon doing no more writing.

127   "Why, how now? What next?" exclaimed I, "Do no more writing?"

128   "No more."

129   "And what is the reason?"

130   "Do you not see the reason for yourself," he indifferently replied.

131   I looked steadfastly at him, and perceived that his eyes looked dull and glazed. Instantly it occurred to me, that his unexampled diligence in copying by his dim window for the first few weeks of his stay with me might have temporarily impaired his vision.

132   I was touched. I said something in condolence with him. I hinted that of course he did wisely in abstaining from writing for a while; and urged him to embrace that opportunity of taking wholesome exercise in the open air. This, however, he did not do. A few days after this, my other clerks being absent, and being in a great hurry to dispatch certain letters by the mail, I thought that, having nothing else earthly to do, Bartleby would surely be less inflexible than usual, and carry these letters to the post-office. But he blankly declined. So, much to my inconvenience, I went myself.

133   Still added days went by. Whether Bartleby's eyes improved or not, I could not say. To all appearance, I thought they did. But when I asked him if they did, he vouchsafed no answer. At all events, he would do no copying. At last, in reply to my urgings, he informed me that he had permanently given up copying.

134   "What!" exclaimed I; "suppose your eyes should get entirely well—better than ever before—would you not copy then?"

135   "I have given up copying," he answered, and slid aside.

136   He remained as ever, a fixture in my chamber. Nay—if that were possible—he became still more of a fixture than before. What was to be done? He would do nothing in the office: why should he stay there? In plain fact, he had now become a millstone to me, not only useless as a necklace, but afflictive to bear. Yet I was sorry for him. I speak less than truth when I say that, on his own account, he occasioned me uneasiness. If he would but have named a single relative or friend, I would instantly have written, and urged their taking the poor fellow away to some convenient retreat. But he seemed alone, absolutely alone in

the universe. A bit of wreck in the mid Atlantic. At length, necessities connected with my business tyrannized over all other considerations. Decently as I could, I told Bartleby that in six days' time he must unconditionally leave the office. I warned him to take measures, in the interval, for procuring some other abode. I offered to assist him in this endeavor, if he himself would but take the first step towards a removal. "And when you finally quit me, Bartleby," added I, "I shall see that you go not away entirely unprovided. Six days from this hour, remember."

137   At the expiration of that period, I peeped behind the screen, and lo! Bartleby was there.

138   I buttoned up my coat, balanced myself; advanced slowly towards him, touched his shoulder, and said, "The time has come; you must quit this place; I am sorry for you; here is money; but you must go."

139   "I would prefer not," he replied, with his back still towards me.

140   "You *must*."

141   He remained silent.

142   Now I had an unbounded confidence in this man's common honesty. He had frequently restored to me sixpences and shillings carelessly dropped upon the floor, for I am apt to be very reckless in such shirt-button affairs. The proceeding then which followed will not be deemed extraordinary.

143   "Bartleby," said I, "I owe you twelve dollars on account; here are thirty-two; the odd twenty are yours.—Will you take it?" and I handed the bills towards him.

144   But he made no motion.

145   "I will leave them here them," putting them under a weight on the table. Then taking my hat and cane and going to the door I tranquilly turned and added—"After you have removed your things from these offices, Bartleby, you will of course lock the door—since every one is now gone for the day but you—and if you please, slip your key underneath the mat, so that I may have it in the morning. I shall not see you again; so good-bye to you. If hereafter in your new place of abode I can be of any service to you, do not fail to advise me by letter. Good-bye, Bartleby, and fare you well."

146   But he answered not a word; like the last column of some ruined temple, he remained standing mute and solitary in the middle of the otherwise deserted room.

147   As I walked home in a pensive mood, my vanity got the better of my pity. I could not but highly plume myself on my masterly management in getting rid of Bartleby. Masterly I call it, and such it must appear to any dispassionate thinker. The beauty of my procedure seemed to consist in its perfect quietness. There was no vulgar bullying, no bravado of any sort, no choleric hectoring, and striding to and fro across the apartment, jerking out vehement commands for Bartleby to bundle himself off with his beggarly traps. Nothing of the kind. Without loudly bidding Bartleby depart—as an inferior genius might have done— I *assumed* the ground that depart he must; and upon that assumption built all I had to say. The more I thought over my procedure, the more I was charmed with it. Nevertheless, next morning, upon awakening, I had my doubts—I had somehow slept off the fumes of vanity. One of the coolest and wisest hours a man has, is just after he awakes in the morning. My procedure seemed as sagacious as ever—but only in theory. How it would prove in practice—there was the rub. It was truly a beautiful thought to have assumed Bartleby's departure; but, after all, that assumption was simply my own, and none of Bartleby's. The

great point was, not whether I had assumed that he would quit me, but whether he would prefer so to do. He was more a man of preferences than assumptions.

148   After breakfast, I walked down town, arguing the probabilities *pro* and *con*. One moment I thought it would prove a miserable failure, and Bartleby would be found all alive at my office as usual; the next moment it seemed certain that I should see his chair empty. And so I kept veering about. At the corner of Broadway and Canal-street, I saw quite an excited group of people standing in earnest conversation.

149   "I'll take odds he doesn't," said a voice as I passed.

150   "Doesn't go?—done!" said I, "put up your money."

151   I was instinctively putting my hand in my pocket to produce my own, when I remembered that this was an election day. The words I had overheard bore no reference to Bartleby, but to the success or non-success of some candidate for the mayoralty. In my intent frame of mind, I had, as it were, imagined that all Broadway shared in my excitement, and were debating the same question with me. I passed on, very thankful that the uproar of the street screened my momentary absent-mindedness.

152   As I had intended, I was earlier than usual at my office door. I stood listening for a moment. All was still. He must be gone. I tried the knob. The door was locked. Yes, my procedure had worked to a charm; he indeed must be vanished. Yet a certain melancholy mixed with this: I was almost sorry for my brilliant success. I was fumbling under the door mat for the key, which Bartleby was to have left there for me, when accidentally my knee knocked against a panel, producing a summoning sound, and in response a voice came to me from within—"Not yet; I am occupied."

153   It was Bartleby.

154   I was thunderstruck. For an instant I stood like the man who, pipe in mouth, was killed one cloudless afternoon long ago in Virginia, by summer lightning; at his own warm open window he was killed, and remained leaning out there upon the dreamy afternoon, till some one touched him, when he fell.

155   "Not gone!" I murmured at last. But again obeying that wondrous ascendancy which the inscrutable scrivener had over me, and from which ascendancy, for all my chafing, I could not completely escape, I slowly went down stairs and out into the street, and while walking round the block, considered what I should next do in this unheard-of perplexity. Turn the man out by an actual thrusting I could not; to drive him away by calling him hard names would not do; calling in the police was an unpleasant idea; and yet, permit him to enjoy his cadaverous triumph over me—this too I could not think of. What was to be done? or, if nothing could be done, was there any thing further that I could *assume* in the matter? Yes, as before I had prospectively assumed that Bartleby would depart, so now I might retrospectively assume that departed he was. In the legitimate carrying out of this assumption, I might enter my office in a great hurry, and pretending not to see Bartleby at all, walk straight against him as if he were air. Such a proceeding would in a singular degree have the appearance of a home-thrust. It was hardly possible that Bartleby could withstand such an application of the doctrine of assumptions. But upon second thoughts the success of the plan seemed rather dubious. I resolved to argue the matter over with him again.

156   "Bartleby," said I, entering the office, with a quietly severe expression, "I am seriously displeased. I am pained, Bartleby. I had thought better of you. I had imagined you of such

a gentlemanly organization, that in any delicate dilemma a slight hint would suffice—in short, an assumption. But it appears I am deceived. Why," I added, unaffectedly starting, "you have not even touched that money yet," pointing to it, just where I had left it the evening previous.

157   He answered nothing.

158   "Will you, or will you not, quit me?" I now demanded in a sudden passion, advancing close to him.

159   "I would prefer *not* to quit you," he replied, gently emphasizing the *not*.

160   "What earthly right have you to stay here? Do you pay any rent? Do you pay my taxes? Or is this property yours?"

161   He answered nothing.

162   "Are you ready to go on and write now? Are your eyes recovered? Could you copy a small paper for me this morning? or help examine a few lines? or step round to the post-office? In a word, will you do any thing at all, to give a coloring to your refusal to depart the premises?"

163   He silently retired into his hermitage.

164   I was now in such a state of nervous resentment that I thought it but prudent to check myself at present from further demonstrations. Bartleby and I were alone. I remembered the tragedy of the unfortunate Adams and the still more unfortunate Colt in the solitary office of the latter; and how poor Colt, being dreadfully incensed by Adams, and imprudently permitting himself to get wildly excited, was at unawares hurried into his fatal act—an act which certainly no man could possibly deplore more than the actor himself.[11] Often it had occurred to me in my ponderings upon the subject, that had that altercation taken place in the public street, or at a private residence, it would not have terminated as it did. It was the circumstance of being alone in a solitary office, up stairs, of a building entirely unhallowed by humanizing domestic associations—an uncarpeted office, doubtless, of a dusty, haggard sort of appearance;—this it must have been, which greatly helped to enhance the irritable desperation of the hapless Colt.

165   But when this old Adam of resentment rose in me and tempted me concerning Bartleby, I grappled him and threw him. How? Why, simply by recalling the divine injunction: "A new commandment give I unto you, that ye love one another."[12] Yes, this it was that saved me. Aside from higher considerations, charity often operates as a vastly wise and prudent principle—a great safeguard to its possessor. Men have committed murder for jealousy's sake, and anger's sake, and hatred's sake, and selfishness' sake, and spiritual pride's sake; but no man that ever I heard of, ever committed a diabolical murder for sweet charity's sake. Mere self-interest, then, if no better motive can be enlisted, should, especially with high-tempered men, prompt all beings to charity and philanthropy. At any rate, upon the occasion in question, I strove to drown my exasperated feelings towards the scrivener by benevolently constructing his conduct. Poor fellow, poor fellow! thought I, he don't mean any thing; and besides, he has seen hard times, and ought to be indulged.

---

[11] A reference to the murder of Samuel Adams by John C. Colt (brother of the inventor of the revolver). The crime took place near where the story "Bartleby" is located.
[12] John 13:34.

166   I endeavored also immediately to occupy myself, and at the same time to comfort my despondency. I tried to fancy that in the course of the morning, at such time as might prove agreeable to him, Bartleby, of his own free accord, would emerge from his hermitage, and take up some decided line of march in the direction of the door. But no. Half-past twelve o'clock came; Turkey began to glow in the face, overturn his inkstand, and become generally obstreperous; Nippers abated down into quietude and courtesy; Ginger Nut munched his noon apple; and Bartleby remained standing at his window in one of his profoundest dead-wall reveries. Will it be credited? Ought I to acknowledge it? That afternoon I left the office without saying one further word to him.

167   Some days now passed, during which, at leisure intervals I looked a little into "Edwards on the Will," and "Priestley on Necessity."[13] Under the circumstances, those books induced a salutary feeling. Gradually I slid into the persuasion that these troubles of mine touching the scrivener, had been all predestined from eternity, and Bartleby was billeted upon me for some mysterious purpose of an all-wise Providence, which it was not for a mere mortal like me to fathom. Yes, Bartleby, stay there behind your screen, thought I; I shall persecute you no more; you are harmless and noiseless as any of these old chairs; in short, I never feel so private as when I know you are here. At least I see it, I feel it; I penetrate to the predestinated purpose of my life. I am content. Others may have loftier parts to enact; but my mission in this world, Bartleby, is to furnish you with office-room for such period as you may see fit to remain.

168   I believe that this wise and blessed frame of mind would have continued with me, had it not been for the unsolicited and uncharitable remarks obtruded upon me by my professional friends who visited the rooms. But thus it often is, that the constant friction of illiberal minds wears out at last the best resolves of the more generous. Though to be sure, when I reflected upon it, it was not strange that people entering my office should be struck by the peculiar aspect of the unaccountable Bartleby, and so be tempted to throw out some sinister observations concerning him. Sometimes an attorney having business with me, and calling at my office, and finding no one but the scrivener there, would undertake to obtain some sort of precise information from him touching my whereabouts; but without heeding his idle talk, Bartleby would remain standing immovable in the middle of the room. So after contemplating him in that position for a time, the attorney would depart, no wiser than he came.

169   Also, when a Reference was going on, and the room full of lawyers and witnesses and business was driving fast; some deeply occupied legal gentleman present, seeing Bartleby wholly unemployed, would request him to run round to his (the legal gentleman's) office and fetch some papers for him. Thereupon, Bartleby would tranquilly decline, and yet remain idle as before. Then the lawyer would give a great stare, and turn to me. And what could I say? At last I was made aware that all through the circle of my professional acquaintance, a whisper of wonder was running round, having reference to the strange creature I kept at my office. This worried me very much. And as the idea came upon me of his possibly turning out a long-lived man, and keep occupying my chambers, and denying my authority; and perplexing my visitors; and scandalizing my professional reputation; and

---

[13] A reference to *Freedom of the Will* by colonial minister Jonathan Edwards (1703–1754) and *Doctrine of Philosophical Necessity Illustrated*, by the English scientist Joseph Priestly (1733–1804).

casting a general gloom over the premises; keeping soul and body together to the last upon his savings (for doubtless he spent but half a dime a day), and in the end perhaps outlive me, and claim possession of my office by right of his perpetual occupancy: as all these dark anticipations crowded upon me more and more, and my friends continually intruded their relentless remarks upon the apparition in my room; a great change was wrought in me. I resolved to gather all my faculties together, and for ever rid me of this intolerable incubus.

170   Ere revolving any complicated project, however, adapted to this end, I first simply suggested to Bartleby the propriety of his permanent departure. In a calm and serious tone, I commended the idea to his careful and mature consideration. But having taken three days to meditate upon it, he apprised me that his original determination remained the same; in short, that he still preferred to abide with me.

171   What shall I do? I now said to myself, buttoning up my coat to the last button. What shall I do? what ought I to do? what does conscience say I *should* do with this man, or rather ghost. Rid myself of him, I must; go, he shall. But how? You will not thrust him, the poor, pale, passive mortal—you will not thrust such a helpless creature out of your door? you will not dishonor yourself by such cruelty? No, I will not, I cannot do that. Rather would I let him live and die here, and then mason up his remains in the wall. What then will you do? For all your coaxing, he will not budge. Bribes he leaves under your own paper-weight on your table; in short, it is quite plain that he prefers to cling to you.

172   Then something severe, something unusual must be done. What! surely you will not have him collared by a constable, and commit his innocent pallor to the common jail? And upon what ground could you procure such a thing to be done?—a vagrant, is he? What! he a vagrant, a wanderer, who refuses to budge? It is because he will *not* be a vagrant, then, that you seek to count him *as* a vagrant. That is too absurd. No visible means of support: there I have him. Wrong again: for indubitably he *does* support himself, and that is the only unanswerable proof that any man can show of his possessing the means so to do. No more then. Since he will not quit me, I must quit him. I will change my offices; I will move elsewhere; and give him fair notice, that if I find him on my new premises I will then proceed against him as a common trespasser.

173   Acting accordingly, next day I thus addressed him: "I find these chambers too far from the City Hall; the air is unwholesome. In a word, I propose to remove my offices next week, and shall no longer require your services. I tell you this now, in order that you may seek another place."

174   He made no reply, and nothing more was said.

175   On the appointed day I engaged carts and men, proceeded to my chambers, and having but little furniture, every thing was removed in a few hours. Throughout, the scrivener remained standing behind the screen, which I directed to be removed the last thing. It was withdrawn; and being folded up like a huge folio, left him the motionless occupant of a naked room. I stood in the entry watching him a moment, while something from within me upbraided me.

176   I re-entered, with my hand in my pocket—and—and my heart in my mouth.

177   "Good-bye, Bartleby; I am going—good-bye, and God some way bless you; and take that," slipping something in his hand. But it dropped upon the floor, and then—strange to say—I tore myself from him whom I had so longed to be rid of.

178   Established in my new quarters, for a day or two I kept the door locked, and any little absence, I would pause at the threshold for an instant, and attentively listen, ere applying my key. But these fears were needless. Bartleby never came nigh me.

179   I thought all was going well, when a perturbed looking stranger visited me, inquiring whether I was the person who had recently occupied rooms at No.—Wall-street.

180   Full of forebodings, I replied that I was.

181   "Then sir," said the stranger, who proved a lawyer, "you are responsible for the man you left there. He refuses to do any copying; he refuses to do any thing; he says he prefers not to; and he refuses to quit the premises."

182   "I am very sorry, sir," said I, with assumed tranquillity, but an inward tremor, "but, really, the man you allude to is nothing to me—he is no relation or apprentice of mine, that you should hold me responsible for him."

183   "In mercy's name, who is he?"

184   "I certainly cannot inform you. I know nothing about him. Formerly I employed him as a copyist; but he has done nothing for me now for some time past."

185   "I shall settle him then—good morning, sir."

186   Several days passed, and I heard nothing more; and though I often felt a charitable prompting to call at the place and see poor Bartleby, yet a certain squeamishness of I know not what withheld me.

187   All is over with him, by this time, thought I at last, when through another week no further intelligence reached me. But coming to my room the day after, I found several persons waiting at my door in a high state of nervous excitement.

188   "That's the man—here he comes," cried the foremost one, whom I recognized as the lawyer who had previously called upon me alone.

189   "You must take him away, sir, at once," cried a portly person among them, advancing upon me, and whom I knew to be the landlord of No.—Wall-street. "These gentlemen, my tenants, cannot stand it any longer; Mr. B——" pointing to the lawyer, "has turned him out of his room, and he now persists in haunting the building generally, sitting upon the banisters of the stairs by day, and sleeping in the entry by night. Every body is concerned; clients are leaving the offices; some fears are entertained of a mob; something you must do, and that without delay."

190   Aghast at this torrent, I fell back before it, and would fain have locked myself in my new quarters. In vain I persisted that Bartleby was nothing to me—no more than to any one else. In vain:—I was the last person known to have anything to do with him, and they held me to the terrible account. Fearful then of being exposed in the papers (as one person present obscurely threatened) I considered the matter, and at length said, that if the lawyer would give me a confidential interview with the scrivener, in his (the lawyer's) own room, I would that afternoon strive my best to rid them of the nuisance they complained of.

191   Going up stairs to my old haunt, there was Bartleby silently sitting upon the banister at the landing.

192   "What are you doing here, Bartleby?" said I.

193   "Sitting upon the banister," he mildly replied.

194   I motioned him into the lawyer's room, who then left us.

195   "Bartleby," said I, "are you aware that you are the cause of great tribulation to me, by persisting in occupying the entry after being dismissed from the office?"

196   No answer.

197   "Now one of two things must take place. Either you must do something, or something must be done to you. Now what sort of business would you like to engage in? Would you like to re-engage in copying for some one?"

198   "No; I would prefer not to make any change."

199   "Would you like a clerkship in a dry-goods store?"

200   "There is too much confinement about that. No, I would not like a clerkship; but I am not particular."

201   "Too much confinement," I cried, "why you keep yourself confined all the time!"

202   "I would prefer not to take a clerkship," he rejoined, as if to settle that little item at once.

203   "How would a bar-tender's business suit you? There is no trying of the eyesight in that."

204   "I would not like it at all; though, as I said before, I am not particular."

205   His unwonted wordiness inspirited me. I returned to the charge.

206   "Well then, would you like to travel through the country collecting bills for the merchants? That would improve your health."

207   "No, I would prefer to be doing something else."

208   "How then would going as a companion to Europe, to entertain some young gentleman with your conversation,—how would that suit you?"

209   "Not at all. It does not strike me that there is any thing definite about that. I like to be stationary. But I am not particular."

210   "Stationary you shall be then," I cried, now losing all patience, and for the first time in all my exasperating connection with him fairly flying into a passion. "If you do not go away from these premises before night, I shall feel bound—indeed I *am* bound—to—to—to quit the premises myself!" I rather absurdly concluded, knowing not with what possible threat to try to frighten his immobility into compliance. Despairing of all further efforts, I was precipitately leaving him, when a final thought occurred to me—one which had not been wholly unindulged before.

211   "Bartleby," said I, in the kindest tone I could assume under such exciting circumstances, "will you go home with me now—not to my office, but my dwelling—and remain there till we can conclude upon some convenient arrangement for you at our leisure? Come, let us start now, right away."

212   "No: at present I would prefer not to make any change at all."

213   I answered nothing; but effectually dodging every one by the suddenness and rapidity of my flight, rushed from the building, ran up Wall-street towards Broadway, and jumping into the first omnibus was soon removed from pursuit. As soon as tranquillity returned I distinctly perceived that I had now done all that I possibly could, both in respect to the demands of the landlord and his tenants, and with regard to my own desire and sense of duty, to benefit Bartleby, and shield him from rude persecution. I now strove to be entirely care-free and quiescent; and my conscience justified me in the attempt; though indeed it was not so successful as I could have wished. So fearful was I of being again hunted out

by the incensed landlord and his exasperated tenants, that, surrendering my business to Nippers, for a few days I drove about the upper part of the town and through the suburbs, in my rockaway; crossed over to Jersey City and Hoboken, and paid fugitive visits to Manhattanville and Astoria. In fact I almost lived in my rockaway for the time.

214   When again I entered my office, lo, a note from the landlord lay upon the desk. I opened it with trembling hands. It informed me that the writer had sent to the police, and had Bartleby removed to the Tombs as a vagrant. Moreover, since I knew more about him than any one else, he wished me to appear at that place, and make a suitable statement of the facts. These tidings had a conflicting effect upon me. At first I was indignant; but at last almost approved. The landlord's energetic, summary disposition, had led him to adopt a procedure which I do not think I would have decided upon myself; and yet as a last resort, under such peculiar circumstances, it seemed the only plan.

215   As I afterwards learned, the poor scrivener, when told that he must be conducted to the Tombs, offered not the slightest obstacle, but in his pale unmoving way, silently acquiesced.

216   Some of the compassionate and curious bystanders joined the party; and headed by one of the constables arm in arm with Bartleby, the silent procession filed its way through all the noise, and heat, and joy of the roaring thoroughfares at noon.

217   The same day I received the note I went to the Tombs, or to speak more properly, the Halls of Justice. Seeking the right officer, I stated the purpose of my call, and was informed that the individual I described was indeed within. I then assured the functionary that Bartleby was a perfectly honest man, and greatly to be compassionated, however unaccountably eccentric. I narrated all I knew, and closed by suggesting the idea of letting him remain in as indulgent confinement as possible till something less harsh might be done— though indeed I hardly knew what. At all events, if nothing else could be decided upon, the alms-house must receive him. I then begged to have an interview.

218   Being under no disgraceful charge, and quite serene and harmless in all his ways, they had permitted him freely to wander about the prison, and especially in the inclosed grass-platted yards thereof. And so I found him there, standing all alone in the quietest of the yards, his face towards a high wall, while all around, from the narrow slits of the jail windows, I thought I saw peering out upon him the eyes of murderers and thieves.

219   "Bartleby!"

220   "I know you," he said, without looking round,—"and I want nothing to say to you."

221   "It was not I that brought you here, Bartleby," said I, keenly pained at his implied suspicion. "And to you, this should not be so vile a place. Nothing reproachful attaches to you by being here. And see, it is not so sad a place as one might think. Look, there is the sky, and here is the grass."

222   "I know where I am," he replied, but would say nothing more, and so I left him.

223   As I entered the corridor again, a broad meat-like man, in an apron, accosted me, and jerking his thumb over his shoulder said—"Is that your friend?"

224   "Yes."

225   "Does he want to starve? If he does, let him live on the prison fare, that's all."

226   "Who are you?" asked I, not knowing what to make of such an unofficially speaking person in such a place.

227   "I am the grub-man. Such gentlemen as have friends here, hire me to provide them with something good to eat."

228   "Is this so?" said I, turning to the turnkey.

229   He said it was.

230   "Well then," said I, slipping some silver into the grub-man's hands (for so they called him). "I want you to give particular attention to my friend there; let him have the best dinner you can get. And you must be as polite to him as possible."

231   "Introduce me, will you?" said the grub-man, looking at me with an expression which seemed to say he was all impatience for an opportunity to give a specimen of his breeding.

232   Thinking it would prove of benefit to the scrivener, I acquiesced; and asking the grub-man his name, went up with him to Bartleby.

233   "Bartleby, this is Mr. Cutlets; you will find him very useful to you."

234   "Your sarvant, sir, your sarvant," said the grub-man, making a low salutation behind his apron. "Hope you find it pleasant here, sir;—spacious grounds—cool apartments, sir—hope you'll stay with us some time—try to make it agreeable. May Mrs. Cutlets and I have the pleasure of your company to dinner, sir, in Mrs. Cutlets' private room?"

235   "I prefer not to dine to-day," said Bartleby, turning away. "It would disagree with me; I am unused to dinners." So saying he slowly moved to the other side of the inclosure, and took up a position fronting the dead-wall.

236   "How's this?" said the grub-man, addressing me with a stare of astonishment. "He's odd, aint he?"

237   "I think he is a little deranged," said I, sadly.

238   "Deranged? deranged is it? Well now, upon my word, I thought that friend of yourn was a gentleman forger; they are always pale and genteel-like, them forgers. I can't help pity 'em—can't help it, sir. Did you know Monroe Edwards?"[14] he added touchingly, and paused. Then, laying his hand pityingly on my shoulder, sighed, "he died of consumption at Sing-Sing.[15] So you weren't acquainted with Monroe?"

239   "No, I was never socially acquainted with any forgers. But I cannot stop longer. Look to my friend yonder. You will not lose by it. I will see you again."

240   Some few days after this, I again obtained admission to the Tombs, and went through the corridors in quest of Bartleby; but without finding him.

241   "I saw him coming from his cell not long ago," said a turnkey, "may be he's gone to loiter in the yards."

242   So I went in that direction.

243   "Are you looking for the silent man?" said another turnkey passing me. "Yonder he lies—sleeping in the yard there. 'Tis not twenty minutes since I saw him lie down."

244   The yard was entirely quiet. It was not accessible to the common prisoners. The surrounding walls, of amazing thickness, kept off all sounds behind them. The Egyptian character of the masonry weighed upon me with its gloom. But a soft imprisoned turf grew under foot. The heart of the eternal pyramids, it seemed, wherein, by some strange magic, through the clefts, grass-seed, dropped by birds, had sprung.

---

[14] Monroe Edwards (1808–1847): a man accused and tried for swindling in New York.

[15] Sing-Sing: a prison in Ossining, New York.

245   Strangely huddled at the base of the wall, his knees drawn up, and lying on his side, his head touching the cold stones, I saw the wasted Bartleby. But nothing stirred. I paused; then went close up to him; stooped over, and saw that his dim eyes were open; otherwise he seemed profoundly sleeping. Something prompted me to touch him. I felt his hand, when a tingling shiver ran up my arm and down my spine to my feet.

246   The round face of the grub-man peered upon me now. "His dinner is ready. Won't he dine to-day, either? Or does he live without dining?"

247   "Lives without dining," said I, and closed the eyes.

248   "Eh!—He's asleep, aint he?"

249   "With kings and counsellors,"[16] murmured I.

250   There would seem little need for proceeding further in this history. Imagination will readily supply the meagre recital of poor Bartleby's interment. But ere parting with the reader, let me say, that if this little narrative has sufficiently interested him, to awaken curiosity as to who Bartleby was, and what manner of life he led prior to the present narrator's making his acquaintance, I can only reply, that in such curiosity I fully share, but am wholly unable to gratify it. Yet here I hardly know whether I should divulge one little item of rumor, which came to my ear a few months after the scrivener's decease. Upon what basis it rested, I could never ascertain; and hence, how true it is I cannot now tell. But inasmuch as this vague report has not been without a certain strange suggestive interest to me, however sad, it may prove the same with some others; and so I will briefly mention it. The report was this: that Bartleby had been a subordinate clerk in the Dead Letter Office[17] at Washington, from which he had been suddenly removed by a change in the administration. When I think over this rumor, I cannot adequately express the emotions which seize me. Dead letters! does it not sound like dead men? Conceive a man by nature and misfortune prone to a pallid hopelessness, can any business seem more fitted to heighten it than that of continually handling these dead letters, and assorting them for the flames? For by the cart-load they are annually burned. Sometimes from out the folded paper the pale clerk takes a ring:—the finger it was meant for, perhaps, moulders in the grave; a bank-note sent in swiftest charity:—he whom it would relieve, nor eats nor hungers any more; pardon for those who died despairing; hope for those who died unhoping; good tidings for those who died stifled by unrelieved calamities. On errands of life, these letters speed to death.

251   Ah Bartleby! Ah humanity!

QUESTIONS ON MEANING

1. What kind of lawyer is the narrator? How does he distinguish himself from other lawyers?

2. What is a scrivener? How is his or her function performed today?

3. What are the peculiar habits of Turkey and Nippers?

4. What is the statement that Bartleby continually repeats when asked to perform a task?

---

[16] Job 3:14.
[17] Dead Letter Office: a place where letters that never reach their recipients are returned.

5. How does the narrator respond when Bartleby refuses to do as he is told?

6. Where did Bartleby work before coming to the narrator's law firm?

QUESTIONS FOR DISCUSSION

1. What does working in an office do to these characters? How does it reshape who they are and how they act?

2. What is the thematic significance of the final lament made by the narrator, "Ah, Bartleby! Ah, humanity!"?

3. What can you make of the subtitle, "A Story of Wall-Street"?

LOOKING AT RHETORIC

1. Does this story make a firm claim about the effects of modern city life on the individual? If so, is it clear enough? Is that argument obscured by other themes?

2. Bartleby evolves from a relatively competent (though quiet) worker to a dysfunctional eccentric. Is there anything in his behavior at the onset that foreshadows what finally happens? Does he seem at all recognizable as a human being?

WRITING ASSIGNMENTS

1. Write an essay in which you consider the narrator's behavior toward Bartleby. Using library and/or Internet sources, research the rise of the modern city, the Industrial Revolution, and their effects upon individual lives. Did the narrator behave appropriately? How could he have behaved differently?

2. Write an essay in which you explore the relationship of Bartleby's past (where he worked before) to his behavior in the story. What does he really want from those around him?

3. In pairs or in groups, discuss the environment the characters work in. What is appealing and unappealing about that environment? Individually, write an essay in which you identify another environment, work or otherwise, and demonstrate how where we are affects mood and behavior.

The Storm
Kate Chopin

Kate Chopin (1850–1904), born Katherine O'Flaherty, was a writer of novels and short stories, primarily set amongst Louisiana Creoles. She was a master of craft and controversial for her gender themes. She is often seen as a precursor to modern feminist authors, and her fiction involves important political concerns. An avid reader of the classics as a young girl, she entered St. Louis Academy of the Sacred Heart at the age of nine and graduated in 1868. After marrying and moving to New Orleans, she returned permanently to St. Louis after her husband's death to raise their six children. In her late thirties, she began to write about the

people she knew in Louisiana, publishing in periodicals such as the St. Louis Post-Dispatch.
In 1899, she completed her second novel, The Awakening, *which was criticized for its portrayal
of a married woman trapped in the confines of family and unable to achieve her own identity as
an artist and an emotional being. The novel remained out of print for decades but is now recognized as one of the most important early feminist works. It asserted the need for gender reform in
the context of conventional marriage. The following story was controversial enough that it was
not published until 1969. It is a remarkably insightful portrayal of human psychology, impulse,
and inner life, anticipating the later works of many authors, including Zora Neale Hurston, Alice
Walker, and Joyce Carol Oates.*

I

1   The leaves were so still that even Bibi thought it was going to rain. Bobinôt, who was
accustomed to converse on terms of perfect equality with his little son, called the child's
attention to certain sombre clouds that were rolling with sinister intention from the west,
accompanied by a sullen, threatening roar. They were at Friedheimer's store and decided
to remain there till the storm had passed. They sat within the door on two empty kegs. Bibi
was four years old and looked very wise.

2   "Mama'll be 'fraid, yes," he suggested with blinking eyes.

3   "She'll shut the house. Maybe she got Sylvie helpin' her this evenin'," Bobinôt
responded reassuringly.

4   "No; she ent got Sylvie. Sylvie was helpin' her yistiday," piped Bibi.

5   Bobinôt arose and going across to the counter purchased a can of shrimps, of which
Calixta was very fond. Then he returned to his perch on the keg and sat stolidly holding
the can of shrimps while the storm burst. It shook the wooden store and seemed to be
ripping furrows in the distant field. Bibi laid his little hand on his father's knee and was
not afraid.

II

6   Calixta, at home, felt no uneasiness for their safety. She sat at a side window sewing
furiously on a sewing machine. She was greatly occupied and did not notice the approaching storm. But she felt very warm and often stopped to mop her face on which the perspi-
ration gathered in beads. She unfastened her white sacque[1] at the throat. It began to grow
dark, and suddenly realizing the situation she got up hurriedly and went about closing
windows and doors.

7   Out on the small front gallery she had hung Bobinôt's Sunday clothes to dry and she
hastened out to gather them before the rain fell. As she stepped outside, Alcée Laballière
rode in at the gate. She had not seen him very often since her marriage, and never alone.
She stood there with Bobinôt's coat in her hands, and the big rain drops began to fall. Alcée
rode his horse under the shelter of a side projection where the chickens had huddled and
there were plows and a harrow piled up in the corner.

---

[1] sacque: a woman's full, loose, hip-length jacket.

8   "May I come and wait on your gallery till the storm is over, Calixta?" he asked.

9   "Come 'long in, M'sieur Alcée."

10   His voice and her own startled her as if from a trance, and she seized Bobinôt's vest. Alcée, mounting to the porch, grabbed the trousers and snatched Bibi's braided jacket that was about to be carried away by a sudden gust of wind. He expressed an intention to remain outside, but it was soon apparent that he might as well have been out in the open: the water beat in upon the boards in driving sheets, and he went inside, closing the door after him. It was even necessary to put something beneath the door to keep the water out.

11   "My! what a rain! It's good two years sence it rain' like that," exclaimed Calixta as she rolled up a piece of bagging and Alcée helped her to thrust it beneath the crack.

12   She was a little fuller of figure than five years before when she married; but she had lost nothing of her vivacity. Her blue eyes still retained their melting quality; and her yellow hair, disheveled by the wind and rain, kinked more stubbornly than ever about her ears and temples.

13   The rain beat upon the low, shingled roof with a force and clatter that threatened to break an entrance and deluge them there. They were in the dining room—the sitting room—the general utility room. Adjoining was her bed room, with Bibi's couch along side her own. The door stood open, and the room with its white, monumental bed, its closed shutters, looked dim and mysterious.

14   Alcée flung himself into a rocker and Calixta nervously began to gather up from the floor the lengths of a cotton sheet which she had been sewing.

15   "If this keeps up, *Dieu sait*[2] if the levees[3] goin' to stan' it!" she exclaimed.

16   "What have you got to do with the levees?"

17   "I got enough to do! An' there's Bobinôt with Bibi out in that storm—if he only didn' left Friedheimer's!"

18   "Let us hope, Calixta, that Bobinôt's got sense enough to come in out of a cyclone."

19   She went and stood at the window with a greatly disturbed look on her face. She wiped the frame that was clouded with moisture. It was stiflingly hot. Alcée got up and joined her at the window, looking over her shoulder. The rain was coming down in sheets obscuring the view of far-off cabins and enveloping the distant wood in a gray mist. The playing of the lightning was incessant. A bolt struck a tall chinaberry tree at the edge of the field. It filled all visible space with a blinding glare and the crash seemed to invade the very boards they stood upon.

20   Calixta put her hands to her eyes, and with a cry, staggered backward. Alcée's arm encircled her, and for an instant he drew her close and spasmodically to him.

21   "*Bonté*!"[4] she cried, releasing herself from his encircling arm and retreating from the window, "the house'll go next! If I only knew w'ere Bibi was!" She would not compose herself; she would not be seated. Alcée clasped her shoulders and looked into her face. The

---

[2] *Dieu sait*: God knows (French).
[3] levees: Man-made earth banks designed to keep a river from flooding.
[4] *Bonté*!: Goodness! (French)

contact of her warm, palpitating body when he had unthinkingly drawn her into his arms, had aroused all the old-time infatuation and desire for her flesh.

22 "Calixta," he said, "don't be frightened. Nothing can happen. The house is too low to be struck, with so many tall trees standing about. There! aren't you going to be quiet? say, aren't you?" He pushed her hair back from her face that was warm and steaming. Her lips were as red and moist as pomegranate seed. Her white neck and a glimpse of her full, firm bosom disturbed him powerfully. As she glanced up at him the fear in her liquid blue eyes had given place to a drowsy gleam that unconsciously betrayed a sensuous desire. He looked down into her eyes and there was nothing for him to do but to gather her lips in a kiss. It reminded him of Assumption.[5]

23 "Do you remember—in Assumption, Calixta?" he asked in a low voice broken by passion. Oh! she remembered; for in Assumption he had kissed her and kissed and kissed her; until his senses would well nigh fail, and to save her he would resort to a desperate flight. If she was not an immaculate dove in those days, she was still inviolate; a passionate creature whose very defenselessness had made her defense, against which his honor forbade him to prevail. Now—well, now—her lips seemed in a manner free to be tasted, as well as her round, white throat and her whiter breasts.

24 They did not heed the crashing torrents, and the roar of the elements made her laugh as she lay in his arms. She was a revelation in that dim, mysterious chamber; as white as the couch she lay upon. Her firm, elastic flesh that was knowing for the first time its birthright, was like a creamy lily that the sun invites to contribute its breath and perfume to the undying life of the world.

25 The generous abundance of her passion, without guile or trickery, was like a white flame which penetrated and found response in depths of his own sensuous nature that had never yet been reached.

26 When he touched her breasts they gave themselves up in quivering ecstasy, inviting his lips. Her mouth was a fountain of delight. And when he possessed her, they seemed to swoon together at the very borderland of life's mystery.

27 He stayed cushioned upon her, breathless, dazed, enervated, with his heart beating like a hammer upon her. With one hand she clasped his head, her lips lightly touching his forehead. The other hand stroked with a soothing rhythm his muscular shoulders.

28 The growl of the thunder was distant and passing away. The rain beat softly upon the shingles, inviting them to drowsiness and sleep. But they dared not yield.

III

29 The rain was over; and the sun was turning the glistening green world into a palace of gems. Calixta, on the gallery, watched Alcée ride away. He turned and smiled at her with a beaming face; and she lifted her pretty chin in the air and laughed aloud.

---

[5]Assumption: Assumption Parish, Louisiana, the setting for her story "The 'Cadian Ball." "The Storm" is presented by Chopin as a sequel to the earlier story. 'Cadian is a dialect rendering of "Acadian," which is more commonly known as "Cajun." Acadians were French migrants from Nova Scotia who settled in Louisiana in the seventeenth century.

30   Bobinôt and Bibi, trudging home, stopped without at the cistern to make themselves presentable.

31   "My! Bibi, w'at will yo' mama say! You ought to be ashame'. You oughta' put on those good pants. Look at 'em! An' that mud on yo' collar! How you got that mud on yo' collar, Bibi? I never saw such a boy!" Bibi was the picture of pathetic resignation. Bobinôt was the embodiment of serious solicitude as he strove to remove from his own person and his son's the signs of their tramp over heavy roads and through wet fields. He scraped the mud off Bibi's bare legs and feet with a stick and carefully removed all traces from his heavy brogans. Then, prepared for the worst—the meeting with an over-scrupulous housewife, they entered cautiously at the back door.

32   Calixta was preparing supper. She had set the table and was dripping coffee at the hearth. She sprang up as they came in.

33   "Oh, Bobinôt! You back! My! but I was uneasy. W'ere you been during the rain? An' Bibi? he ain't wet? he ain't hurt?" She had clasped Bibi and was kissing him effusively. Bobinôt's explanations and apologies which he had been composing all along the way, died on his lips as Calixta felt him to see if he were dry, and seemed to express nothing but satisfaction at their safe return.

34   "I brought you some shrimps, Calixta," offered Bobinôt, hauling the can from his ample side pocket and laying it on the table.

35   "Shrimps! Oh, Bobinôt! you too good fo' anything!" and she gave him a smacking kiss on the cheek that resounded, "*J'vous réponds,*[6] we'll have a feas' to night! umph-umph!"

36   Bobinôt and Bibi began to relax and enjoy themselves, and when the three seated themselves at table they laughed much and so loud that anyone might have heard them as far away as Laballiére's.

IV

37   Alcée Laballiére wrote to his wife, Clarisse, that night. It was a loving letter, full of tender solicitude. He told her not to hurry back, but if she and the babies liked it at Biloxi, to stay a month longer. He was getting on nicely; and though he missed them, he was willing to bear the separation a while longer—realizing that their health and pleasure were the first things to be considered.

V

38   As for Clarisse, she was charmed upon receiving her husband's letter. She and the babies were doing well. The society was agreeable; many of her old friends and acquaintances were at the bay. And the first free breath since her marriage seemed to restore the pleasant liberty of her maiden days. Devoted as she was to her husband, their intimate conjugal life was something which she was more than willing to forego for a while.

39   So the storm passed and every one was happy.

---

[6] *J'vous réponds:* I promise you (French).

QUESTIONS ON MEANING

1. How does Bibi initially think Calixta will respond to the storm? What is the child worried about?

2. As the storm begins, how does Calixta react? What is she concerned about?

3. In the midst of the storm, what do Alcée and Calixta see?

4. What kind of language (descriptive words and images) is used to describe the sexual encounter? How explicit is it?

5. How does Calixta behave toward her husband when he returns home?

6. How does Alcée behave toward Calixta before he leaves?

QUESTIONS FOR DISCUSSION

1. To what extent is place or region an important element in the story? In what way does it condition the lives and decisions of the characters?

2. What is Chopin's position on Calixta's infidelity? Does she give readers any reason to sympathize with it?

3. Does Calixta's husband's behavior influence your response to the infidelity?

4. In what way does the storm function as a metaphor for the situation between Calixta and Alcée?

LOOKING AT RHETORIC

1. Does this story make a firm claim about the nature of a woman's sexual identity and its relationship to her role in society and the family? As a work of fiction, does it complicate ethical questions related to women's rights and feminist issues?

2. Does the description of the regionally-specific setting of Louisiana make the story more compelling and convincing, or does it seem too exotic to apply to our own times and circumstances?

WRITING ASSIGNMENTS

1. Write an essay in which you consider Calixta's behavior towards her husband and son after her encounter with Alcée. Using library and/or Internet sources, research the evolution of the feminist movements of the late nineteenth and twentieth centuries. Given that research and your reading of the story, how do you account for her happiness and continued devotion to them?

2. Write an essay in which you consider Alcée's treatment of Calixta. To what extent does he care for her and why? To what extent do his feelings matter to her?

3. In pairs or in groups, discuss Calixta's actions within the context of her marriage and her role as a mother. Individually, write an essay in which you explore the role of responsibility and restraint versus freedom and self-determination in marriage. You need not deal with sexual infidelity as the primary issue.

Araby

James Joyce

James Joyce (1882–1941) was born in Dublin and raised a Roman Catholic. He attended University College, Dublin, where he began writing plays and poems and was an avid student of classics and modern languages. He later moved to Paris for one year, working as a teacher and a journalist, before returning to Ireland, where he met Nora Barnacle. The couple moved to Europe, remaining together until the author's death but not formally marrying until 1931. Committed to a writing career, Joyce published Dubliners *in 1914. In this collection, he emerged as an important pioneer of the modern short story, which dealt with the common experiences of daily living but rendered them extraordinary through the use of an epiphany (a term he borrows from Catholicism), which involves a character experiencing an intense revelation through an ordinary event. Residing for most of his life in Paris among many of the European modernists, he is now considered one of the most important writers of the twentieth century, publishing* Portrait of the Artist as a Young Man *(1916),* Ulysses *(1922), and* Finnegan's Wake *(1939). In their use of a modernist narrative technique known as "stream of consciousness," the latter two works are highly experimental, exerting a strong influence on subsequent writers. Taken from* Dubliners, *the following story deals with a young man's experience of disillusionment and demonstrates the author's use of the epiphany.*

1   North Richmond Street, being blind, was a quiet street except at the hour when the Christian Brothers' School set the boys free. An uninhabited house of two storeys stood at the blind end, detached from its neighbours in a square ground. The other houses of the street, conscious of decent lives within them, gazed at one another with brown imperturbable faces.

2   The former tenant of our house, a priest, had died in the back drawing-room. Air, musty from having been long enclosed, hung in all the rooms, and the waste room behind the kitchen was littered with old useless papers. Among these I found a few paper-covered books, the pages of which were curled and damp: *The Abbot*, by Walter Scott, *The Devout Communicant* and *The Memoirs of Vidocq*.[1] I liked the last best because its leaves were yellow. The wild garden behind the house contained a central apple-tree and a few straggling bushes under one of which I found the late tenant's rusty bicycle-pump. He had been a very charitable priest; in his will he had left all his money to institutions and the furniture of his house to his sister.

3   When the short days of winter came dusk fell before we had well eaten our dinners. When we met in the street the houses had grown sombre. The space of sky above us was the colour of ever-changing violet and towards it the lamps of the street lifted their feeble lanterns. The cold air stung us and we played till our bodies glowed. Our shouts echoed in the silent street. The career of our play brought us through the dark muddy lanes behind the houses where we ran the gantlet of the rough tribes from the cottages, to the back doors of the dark dripping gardens where odours arose from the ashpits, to the dark odorous stables where a

---

[1] Eugene Francios Vidocq (115–1857): a French detective. *The Devout Communicant*: a Roman Catholic devotional manual. *The Abbott*: a novel published by Scottish writer Sir Walter Scott (1771–1832) in 1820.

coachman smoothed and combed the horse or shook music from the buckled harness. When we returned to the street light from the kitchen windows had filled the areas. If my uncle was seen turning the corner we hid in the shadow until we had seen him safely housed. Or if Mangan's sister came out on the doorstep to call her brother in to his tea we watched her from our shadow peer up and down the street. We waited to see whether she would remain or go in and, if she remained, we left our shadow and walked up to Mangan's steps resignedly. She was waiting for us, her figure defined by the light from the half-opened door. Her brother always teased her before he obeyed and I stood by the railings looking at her. Her dress swung as she moved her body and the soft rope of her hair tossed from side to side.

4   Every morning I lay on the floor in the front parlour watching her door. The blind was pulled down to within an inch of the sash so that I could not be seen. When she came out on the doorstep my heart leaped. I ran to the hall, seized my books and followed her. I kept her brown figure always in my eye and, when we came near the point at which our ways diverged, I quickened my pace and passed her. This happened morning after morning. I had never spoken to her, except for a few casual words, and yet her name was like a summons to all my foolish blood.

5   Her image accompanied me even in places the most hostile to romance. On Saturday evenings when my aunt went marketing I had to go to carry some of the parcels. We walked through the flaring streets, jostled by drunken men and bargaining women, amid the curses of labourers, the shrill litanies of shop-boys who stood on guard by the barrels of pigs' cheeks, the nasal chanting of street-singers, who sang a *come-all-you* about O'Donovan Rossa,[2] or a ballad about the troubles in our native land. These noises converged in a single sensation of life for me: I imagined that I bore my chalice safely through a throng of foes. Her name sprang to my lips at moments in strange prayers and praises which I myself did not understand. My eyes were often full of tears (I could not tell why) and at times a flood from my heart seemed to pour itself out into my bosom. I thought little of the future. I did not know whether I would ever speak to her or not or, if I spoke to her, how I could tell her of my confused adoration. But my body was like a harp and her words and gestures were like fingers running upon the wires.

6   One evening I went into the back drawing-room in which the priest had died. It was a dark rainy evening and there was no sound in the house. Through one of the broken panes I heard the rain impinge upon the earth, the fine incessant needles of water playing in the sodden beds. Some distant lamp or lighted window gleamed below me. I was thankful that I could see so little. All my senses seemed to desire to veil themselves and, feeling that I was about to slip from them, I pressed the palms of my hands together until they trembled, murmuring: *O love! O love!* many times.

7   At last she spoke to me. When she addressed the first words to me I was so confused that I did not know what to answer. She asked me was I going to Araby. I forget whether I answered yes or no. It would be a splendid bazaar, she said; she would love to go.

8   —And why can't you? I asked.

9   While she spoke she turned a silver bracelet round and round her wrist. She could not go, she said, because there would be a retreats that week in her convent. Her brother

---

[2]O'Donovan Rossa (1831–1915): a nineteenth-century Irish nationalist.

and two other boys were fighting for their caps and I was alone at the railings. She held one of the spikes, bowing her head towards me. The light from the lamp opposite our door caught the white curve of her neck, lit up her hair that rested there and, falling, lit up the hand upon the railing. It fell over one side of her dress and caught the white border of a petticoat, just visible as she stood at ease.

10   —It's well for you, she said.

11   —If I go, I said, I will bring you something.

12   What innumerable follies laid waste my waking and sleeping thoughts after that evening! I wished to annihilate the tedious intervening days. I chafed against the work of school. At night in my bedroom and by day in the classroom her image came between me and the page I strove to read. The syllables of the word *Araby* were called to me through the silence in which my soul luxuriated and cast an Eastern enchantment over me. I asked for leave to go to the bazaar on Saturday night. My aunt was surprised and hoped it was not some Freemason[3] affair. I answered few questions in class. I watched my master's face pass from amiability to sternness; he hoped I was not beginning to idle. I could not call my wandering thoughts together. I had hardly any patience with the serious work of life which, now that it stood between me and my desire, seemed to me child's play, ugly monotonous child's play.

13   On Saturday morning I reminded my uncle that I wished to go to the bazaar in the evening. He was fussing at the hallstand, looking for the hat-brush, and answered me curtly:

14   —Yes, boy, I know.

15   As he was in the hall I could not go into the front parlour and lie at the window. I left the house in bad humour and walked slowly towards the school. The air was pitilessly raw and already my heart misgave me.

16   When I came home to dinner my uncle had not yet been home. Still it was early. I sat staring at the clock for some time and, when its ticking began to irritate me, I left the room. I mounted the staircase and gained the upper part of the house. The high cold empty gloomy rooms liberated me and I went from room to room singing. From the front window I saw my companions playing below in the street. Their cries reached me weakened and indistinct and, leaning my forehead against the cool glass, I looked over at the dark house where she lived. I may have stood there for an hour, seeing nothing but the brown-clad figure cast by my imagination, touched discreetly by the lamplight at the curved neck, at the hand upon the railings and at the border below the dress.

17   When I came downstairs again I found Mrs. Mercer sitting at the fire. She was an old garrulous woman, a pawnbroker's widow, who collected used stamps for some pious purpose. I had to endure the gossip of the tea-table. The meal was prolonged beyond an hour and still my uncle did not come. Mrs. Mercer stood up to go: she was sorry she couldn't wait any longer, but it was after eight o'clock and she did not like to be out late, as the night air was bad for her. When she had gone I began to walk up and down the room, clenching my fists. My aunt said:

18   —I'm afraid you may put off your bazaar for this night of Our Lord.

---

[3] Freemason: A secret society of mysterious origin that is widespread in Europe and America and included as members many of the American Founding Fathers. Many Catholics believed the Masonic Order to be an enemy of the Church, though the Freemasonry is broadly theistic in philosophical orientation.

19   At nine o'clock I heard my uncle's latchkey in the halldoor. I heard him talking to himself and heard the hallstand rocking when it had received the weight of his overcoat. I could interpret these signs. When he was midway through his dinner I asked him to give me the money to go to the bazaar. He had forgotten.

20   —The people are in bed and after their first sleep now, he said.

21   I did not smile. My aunt said to him energetically:

22   —Can't you give him the money and let him go? You've kept him late enough as it is.

23   My uncle said he was very sorry he had forgotten. He said he believed in the old saying: *All work and no play makes Jack a dull boy.* He asked me where I was going and, when I had told him a second time he asked me did I know *The Arab's Farewell to His Steed.*[4] When I left the kitchen he was about to recite the opening lines of the piece to my aunt.

24   I held a florin[5] tightly in my hand as I strode down Buckingham Street towards the station. The sight of the streets thronged with buyers and glaring with gas recalled to me the purpose of my journey. I took my seat in a third-class carriage of a deserted train. After an intolerable delay the train moved out of the station slowly. It crept onward among ruinous houses and over the twinkling river. At Westland Row Station a crowd of people pressed to the carriage doors; but the porters moved them back, saying that it was a special train for the bazaar. I remained alone in the bare carriage. In a few minutes the train drew up beside an improvised wooden platform. I passed out on to the road and saw by the lighted dial of a clock that it was ten minutes to ten. In front of me was a large building which displayed the magical name.

25   I could not find any sixpenny entrance and, fearing that the bazaar would be closed, I passed in quickly through a turnstile, handing a shilling to a weary-looking man. I found myself in a big hall girdled at half its height by a gallery. Nearly all the stalls were closed and the greater part of the hall was in darkness. I recognised a silence like that which pervades a church after a service. I walked into the centre of the bazaar timidly. A few people were gathered about the stalls which were still open. Before a curtain, over which the words *Café Chantant*[6] were written in coloured lamps, two men were counting money on a salver. I listened to the fall of the coins.

26   Remembering with difficulty why I had come I went over to one of the stalls and examined porcelain vases and flowered tea-sets. At the door of the stall a young lady was talking and laughing with two young gentlemen. I remarked their English accents and listened vaguely to their conversation.

27   —O, I never said such a thing!

28   —O, but you did!

29   —O, but I didn't!

30   —Didn't she say that?

31   —Yes. I heard her.

32   —O, there's a . . . fib!

33   Observing me the young lady came over and asked me did I wish to buy anything. The tone of her voice was not encouraging; she seemed to have spoken to me out of a sense

---

[4] *The Arab's Farewell to His Steed*: a poem written by Caroline Norton (1808–1877). In verse, an Arab laments after selling his favorite horse.

[5] Florin: A two-shilling piece of coinage.

[6] *Cafe Chantant*: A café that offers music as entertainment.

of duty. I looked humbly at the great jars that stood like eastern guards at either side of the dark entrance to the stall and murmured:

34   —No, thank you.

35   The young lady changed the position of one of the vases and went back to the two young men. They began to talk of the same subject. Once or twice the young lady glanced at me over her shoulder.

36   I lingered before her stall, though I knew my stay was useless, to make my interest in her wares seem the more real. Then I turned away slowly and walked down the middle of the bazaar. I allowed the two pennies to fall against the sixpence in my pocket. I heard a voice call from one end of the gallery that the light was out. The upper part of the hall was now completely dark.

37   Gazing up into the darkness I saw myself as a creature driven and derided by vanity; and my eyes burned with anguish and anger.

QUESTIONS ON MEANING

1. How does the setting that is described in the first three paragraphs establish the main character's state of mind and ultimately the theme?
2. What is the author's purpose in contrasting the boy's mental image of Mangan's sister with the setting of the streets of Dublin?
3. How does the boy react emotionally after the girl asks him if he will attend Araby? Why does he react this way?
4. What is the uncle's response when the boy asks to attend the bazaar? How can we account for his reaction?
5. How does the boy's aunt react to his anxious desire to attend Araby?
6. What is Araby like when the boy finally gets there?

QUESTIONS FOR DISCUSSION

1. In wanting to attend the bazaar Araby, what is the boy really hoping for?
2. How does the city setting, both outdoors and indoors, contribute to the story's theme?
3. In what way does the conversation between the two young gentlemen and the young lady initiate the boy's epiphany?
4. How does the last line of the story enhance your understanding of the evolution of the boy's character?

LOOKING AT RHETORIC

1. Does this story have an identifiable message? Is the theme communicated at the end clear enough? Could it be stated more directly to make it more understandable? If it were stated more directly, would the way you receive the idea on an emotional level be compromised?
2. How does the image of the bazaar work at a figurative level? In other words, it is not simply a bazaar; it is an event that the character interprets to mean something beyond itself. Does it work well to get the theme across?

WRITING ASSIGNMENTS

1. Using library and/or Internet sources, research biographical material dealing with James Joyce's upbringing in Dublin, Ireland. Identify a theme and demonstrate how the setting contributes to the expression of that theme.

2. What is the boy's preoccupation and conflict and what is his epiphany? In other words, what does he realize in the end?

3. In pairs or in groups, make a list of details that relate to setting. Make another list of details that describe the boy's character. Individually, write an essay in which you answer the following question: What does it mean to say that the boy is a romantic?

The Rise of English

Terry Eagleton

Terry Eagleton (b. 1943) is a literary critic, journalist, novelist, and playwright. He is one of the foremost commentators on contemporary literary theory, particularly Marxist approaches. Eagleton attended Cambridge University, where he earned both a B. A. and Ph.D. He has taught at Cambridge, Oxford, the University of Lancaster, and is currently Distinguished Professor of English at the University of Manchester and Visiting Professor at the National University of Ireland. He is also a Distinguished Visitor to the Department of English at the University of Notre Dame. In the late 1960's he was an active member of the Catholic left which argued openly for a Christian basis for radical social reform. He helped found the journal Slant, *and in the 1970's became the most vocal advocate for Marxist literary criticism, which holds that literature is ideologically grounded and tends to affirm the existing social order. In spite of his Marxist focus, he argues that literary criticism should not derive itself from "grand theories" of language and interpretation but should draw from the tradition of pragmatism, centering itself on the practical interrelationships of literature, society, history, and reform. Among many works, he wrote* Criticism and Ideology: A Study in Marxist Literary Theory *(1976) and* Literary Theory: An Introduction *(1983; 2nd ed., 1996). Drawn from the first chapter of the latter work, the following provides a brief history of English departments as they emerged out of the nineteenth century and argues that, regardless of their potential value, they existed at least originally to affirm the values of the existing social order.*

1   If one were asked to provide a single explanation for the growth of English studies in the later nineteenth century, one could do worse than reply: 'the failure of religion.' By the mid-Victorian period, this traditionally reliable, immensely powerful ideological form was in deep trouble. It was no longer winning the hearts and minds of the masses, and under the twin impacts of scientific discovery and social change its previous unquestioned dominance was in danger of evaporating. This was particularly worrying for the Victorian ruling class, because religion is for all kinds of reasons an extremely effective form of ideological control. Like all successful ideologies, it works much less by explicit concepts or formulated doctrines than by image, symbol, habit, ritual and mythology. It is affective and experiential, entwining itself with the deepest unconscious roots of the human subject; and any social

ideology which is unable to engage with such deep-seated a-rational fears and needs, as T. S. Eliot[1] knew, is unlikely to survive very long. Religion, moreover, is capable of operating at every social level: if there is a doctrinal inflection of it for the intellectual elite, there is also a pietistic brand of it for the masses. It provides an excellent social 'cement', encompassing pious peasant, enlightened middle-class liberal and theological intellectual in a single organization. Its ideological power lies in its capacity to 'materialize' beliefs as practices: religion is the sharing of the chalice and the blessing of the harvest, not just abstract argument about consubstantiation or hyperdulia.[2] Its ultimate truths, like those mediated by the literary symbol, are conveniently closed to rational demonstration, and thus absolute in their claims. Finally religion, at least in its Victorian forms, is a *pacifying* influence, fostering meekness, self-sacrifice and the contemplative inner life. It is no wonder that the Victorian ruling class looked on the threatened dissolution of this ideological discourse with something less than equanimity.

2   Fortunately, however, another remarkably similar discourse lay to hand: English literature. It is a striking thought that had it not been for this dramatic crisis in mid-nineteenth-century ideology, we might not today have such a plentiful supply of Jane Austen casebooks and bluffer's guides to Pound.[3] As religion progressively ceases to provide the social 'cement,' affective values and basic mythologies by which a socially turbulent class-society can be welded together, 'English' is constructed as a subject to carry this ideological burden from the Victorian period onwards. The key figure here is Matthew Arnold,[4] always preternaturally sensitive to the needs of his social class, and engagingly candid about being so. The urgent social need, as Arnold recognizes, is to 'Hellenize' or cultivate the philistine middle class, who have proved unable to underpin their political and economic power with a suitably rich and subtle ideology. This can be done by transfusing into them something of the traditional style of the aristocracy, who as Arnold shrewdly perceives are ceasing to be the dominant class in England, but who have something of the ideological wherewithal to lend a hand to their middle-class masters. State-established schools, by linking the middle class to 'the best culture of their nation,' will confer on them 'a greatness and a noble spirit, which the tone of these classes is not of itself at present adequate to impart.'[5]

3   The true beauty of this manoeuvre, however, lies in the effect it will have in controlling and incorporating the working class:

> It is of itself a serious calamity for a nation that its tone of feeling and grandeur of spirit
> should be lowered or dulled. But the calamity appears far more serious still when we
> consider that the middle classes, remaining as they are now, with their narrow, harsh,

---

[1] T. S. Eliot (1888–1865): American-born poet, literary critic, and dramatist who converted to Anglicanism and became an English citizen. Primarily known as a central figure in the modernist movement of the early twentieth century.

[2] consubstantiation: the Lutheran doctrine that the body and blood of Jesus Christ coexist with the bread and wine during Holy Communion.

[3] Jane Austen (1775–1817): English novelist famous for her classics of domestic romance; Ezra Pound (1885–1972) American poet and critic, prominent member of the modernist movement.

[4] Matthew Arnold (1822–1888): English poet, critic, and educator, influential for advancing the notion of literary tradition as a defining aspect of "culture" and essential to the preservation of national identity.

[5] Eagleton's note. From Matthew Arnold's "The Popular Education of France," in *Democratic Education*, p. 22.

unintelligent, and unattractive spirit and culture, will almost certainly fail to mould or assimilate the masses below them, whose sympathies are at the present moment actually wider and more liberal than theirs. They arrive, these masses, eager to enter into possession of the world, to gain a more vivid sense of their own life and activity. In this their irrepressible development, their natural educators and initiators are those immediately above them, the middle classes. If these classes cannot win their sympathy or give them their direction, society is in danger of falling into anarchy.

4   Arnold is refreshingly unhypocritical: there is no feeble pretence that the education of the working class is to be conducted chiefly for their own benefit.

5   Literature was in several ways a suitable candidate for this ideological enterprise. Since literature, as we know, deals in universal human values rather than in such historical trivia as civil wars, the oppression of women or the dispossession of the English peasantry, it could serve to place in cosmic perspective the petty demands of working people for decent living conditions or greater control over their own lives, and might even with luck come to render them oblivious of such issues in their high-minded contemplation of eternal truths and beauties, would rehearse the masses in the habits of pluralistic thought and feeling, persuading them to acknowledge that more than one viewpoint than theirs existed—namely, that of their masters. It would communicate to them the moral riches of bourgeois civilization, impress upon them a reverence for middle-class achievements, and, since reading is an essentially solitary, contemplative activity, curb in them any disruptive tendency to collective political action. It would give them a pride in their national language and literature: if scanty education and extensive hours of labour prevented them personally from producing a literary masterpiece, they could take pleasure in the thought that others of their own kind—English people—had done so.

6   Like religion, literature works primarily by emotion and experience, and so was admirably well-fitted to carry through the ideological task which religion left off. Literature should convey timeless truths, thus distracting the masses from their immediate commitments, nurturing in them a spirit of tolerance and generosity, and so ensuring the survival of private property.

7   There was another sense in which the 'experiential' nature of literature was ideologically convenient. For 'experience' is also in its literary form a kind of vicarious self-fulfillment. If you do not have the money and leisure to visit the Far East, except perhaps as a soldier in the pay of British imperialism, then you can always 'experience' it at second hand by reading Conrad or Kipling. Indeed according to some literary theories this is even more real than strolling round Bangkok. The actually impoverished experience of the mass of people, an impoverishment bred by their social conditions, can be supplemented by literature: instead of working to change such conditions, you can vicariously fulfil someone's desire for a fuller life by handing them *Pride and Prejudice*.[6]

8   It is significant, then, that 'English' as an academic subject was first institutionalized not in the Universities, but in the Mechanics' Institutes, working men's colleges and extension lecturing circuits. English was a way of providing a cheapish 'liberal' education for

---

[6]*Pride and Prejudice*: Jane Austen's best-known domestic novel, repeatedly adapted to film throughout the twentieth century, remaining one of the most popular English classics.

those beyond the charmed circles of public school and Oxbridge.[7] From the outset, in the work of 'English' pioneers like F. D. Maurice and Charles Kingsley,[8] the emphasis was on solidarity between the social classes, the cultivation of 'larger sympathies,' the instillation of national pride and the transmission of 'moral' values. This last concern was an essential part of the ideological project; indeed the rise of 'English' is more or less concomitant with an historic shift in the very meaning of the term 'moral,' of which Arnold, Henry James and F. R. Leavis[9] are the major critical exponents. Morality is no longer to be grasped as a formulated code or explicit ethical system: it is rather a sensitive preoccupation with the whole quality of life itself, with the oblique, nuanced particulars of human experience. Somewhat rephrased, this can be taken as meaning that the old religious ideologies have lost their force, and that a more subtle communication of moral values, one which works by 'dramatic enactment' rather than rebarbative abstraction, is thus in order. Literature becomes more than just a handmaiden of moral ideology: it is moral ideology for the modern age.

9   The working class was not the only oppressed layer of Victorian society at whom 'English' was specifically beamed. English literature, reflected a Royal Commission witness in 1877, might be considered a suitable subject for 'women . . . and the second- and third-rate men who [. . .] become school-masters. The 'softening' and 'humanizing' effects of English, terms recurrently used by its early proponents, are within the existing ideological stereotypes of gender clearly feminine. The rise of English in England ran parallel to the gradual, grudging admission of women to the institutions of higher education; and since English was an untaxing sort of affair, concerned with the finer feelings rather than with the more virile topics of bona fide academic 'disciplines,' it seemed a convenient sort of non-subject to palm off on the ladies, who were in any case excluded from science and the professions. Sir Arthur Quiller Couch, first Professor of English at Cambridge University, would open with the word 'Gentlemen' lectures addressed to a hall filled largely with women.

10   If English had its feminine aspect, however, it also acquired a masculine one as the century drew on. The era of the academic establishment of English is also the era of high imperialism in England. As British capitalism became threatened and progressively outstripped by its younger German and American rivals, the squalid, undignified scramble of too much capital chasing too few overseas territories, which was to culminate in 1914 in the first imperialist world war, created the urgent need for a sense of national mission and identity. What was at stake in English studies was less English literature than English literature: our great 'national poets' Shakespeare and Milton, the sense of an 'organic' national tradition and identity to which new recruits could be admitted by the study of humane letters. Chris Baldick has pointed to the importance of the admission of English literature to the Civil Service examinations in the Victorian period: armed with this conveniently packaged version of their own cultural treasures, the servants of British imperialism could sally forth overseas secure in a sense of their national identity, and able to display that cultural superiority to their envying colonial peoples.

---

[7] Oxbridge: A reference to Oxford and Cambridge Universities. The term refers to the privileged status of these institutions in the larger context of the English university system.

[8] F. D. Maurice (1805–1872): English clergyman and theologian; Charles Kingsley (1819–1875): English clergyman, novelist, and social reformer.

[9] Henry James (1843–1916): American novelist; F. R. Leavis (1895–1978): English literary critic.

11 It took rather longer for English, a subject fit for women, workers and those wishing to impress the natives, to penetrate the bastions of ruling-class power in Oxford and Cambridge. English was an upstart, amateurish affair as academic subjects went, hardly able to compete on equal terms with the rigours of Greats or philology;[10] since every English gentleman read his own literature in his spare time anyway, what was the point of submitting it to systematic study? Fierce rearguard actions were fought by both ancient Universities against this distressingly dilettante subject: the definition of an academic subject was what could be examined, and since English was no more than idle gossip about literary taste it was difficult to know how to make it unpleasant enough to qualify as a proper academic pursuit. This, it might be said, is one of the few problems associated with the study of English which have since been effectively resolved. The frivolous contempt for his subject displayed by the first really 'literary' Oxford professor, Sir Walter Raleigh, has to be read to be believed.[11] Raleigh held his post in the years leading up to the First World War; and his relief at the outbreak of the war, an event which allowed him to abandon the feminine vagaries of literature and put his pen to something more manly—war propaganda—is palpable in his writing.

12 If the first imperialist world war more or less put paid to Sir Walter Raleigh, providing him with an heroic identity more comfortingly in line with that of his Elizabethan namesake,[12] it also signalled the final victory of English studies at Oxford and Cambridge. One of the most strenuous antagonists of English—philology—was closely bound up with Germanic influence; and since England happened to be passing through a major war with Germany, it was possible to smear classical philology as a form of ponderous Teutonic nonsense with which no self-respecting Englishman should be caught associating. England's victory over Germany meant a renewal of national pride, an upsurge of patriotism which could only aid English's cause; but at the same time the deep trauma of the war, its almost intolerable questioning of every previously held cultural assumption, gave rise to a 'spiritual hungering,' as one contemporary commentator described it, for which poetry seemed to provide an answer. English Literature rode to power on the back of wartime nationalism; but, it also represented a search for spiritual solutions on the part of an English ruling class whose sense of identity had been profoundly shaken, whose psyche was ineradicably scarred by the horrors it had endured. Literature would be at once solace and reaffirmation, a familiar ground on which Englishmen could regroup both to explore, and to find some alternative to, the nightmare of history.

QUESTIONS ON MEANING

1. Historically, what is the main reason for the rise of English as an academic discipline?
2. What was one of the major fears of the Victorian classes that made national literature a thing of primary importance?

---

[10] Greats: the study of ancient Greek and Roman literature, language, and philosophy; philology: the historical study of ancient languages.
[11] Sir Walter Raleigh (1861–1922): English scholar and critic.
[12] Sir Walter Raleigh (1552–1618): Famous poet and soldier of the English Renaissance.

3. What function has religion performed for the working masses?

4. What was previously seen as the primary content of literature? What did it deal with and express? How does Eagleton challenge this conception?

5. What related academic disciplines did English effectively replace in the university and why did this change occur?

6. What early twentieth-century historical event accelerated the rise of English. Why did this happen?

QUESTIONS FOR DISCUSSION

1. To what extent is literature (poems, plays, novels, and films) the expression of an ideology, that is, a system of values that reinforces the current social order?

2. Understanding that religion remains a potent force in many human lives, to what extent does literature, as Matthew Arnold and Terry Eagleton contend, respond to the same psychological needs?

3. What is the value of studying Greek and Roman classics in the original language versus literature written in English? Given that the study of English and American literature doesn't require knowledge of ancient languages, is literature really a "poor man's Classics"?

4. Does the act of reading pacify the working and middle classes and reduce their desire for social reform? To what extent does reading encourage the reformist impulse?

LOOKING AT RHETORIC

1. Consider Eagleton's rhetorical strategy in this essay. To what extent does he blend historical description and persuasion?

2. To what purpose does he make use of other writers through quotation and explanation? What, if anything, does he accomplish by this?

3. How complex is his use of vocabulary and to what extent does he adequately define his terms?

WRITING ASSIGNMENTS

1. Identify a story or a poem you understand and admire. Using library and/or Internet sources, research definitions of ideology. To what extent does that story or poem convey an ideology that reinforces existing social arrangements? Does it?

2. Argue for or against Eagleton's claim that literature is ideology. Is he reasonable in being skeptical of the idea that literature conveys universal truths?

3. In pairs or in groups, explore the ideological content in the films or books that you have read. What values are implicitly conveyed in those works? Individually, write an essay about a particular story, novel, or film, in which you define how it reinforces and/or affirms a set of values, an ideology.

Thinking Crosscurrently

LITERATURE, LANGUAGE, AND ART

The books we read and the language they use are often beautiful and powerfully expressive. The paintings and sculptures we see in museums can affect us deeply. We can appreciate them on emotional grounds alone as we allow them to enrich our lives, and this may be their most important role for us. But art in all its forms also conveys discernible truths about the human experience, the world, and even the universe. There is an intellectual content to any great piece of artistic expression, and stories, plays, paintings, and films teach us about history and culture. They explore scientific concepts, scrutinize political and economic issues, and ponder social questions. As you read the selections in this chapter, consider the following questions:

- In what way do stories allow us to understand issues of social justice more fully? How might Milton Friedman and John Maynard Keynes respond to Herman Melville's "Bartleby, the Scrivener"? How might Shelby Steele and Richard Rodriguez respond to Kate Chopin's "The Storm"?

- To what extent is literature and art essential to our understanding of ourselves and the world? In any civilization, is art a luxury or a necessity? What might Michael Sandel and Olivia Judson think about the relationship of art to scientific inquiry?

- How does the understanding of communication, media, and politics expand our understanding of language and language change? What might Susan Willis think about the Barbara Wallraff essay? How might W. E. B. Du Bois's political concerns bear upon Barbara Wallraff's observations on the role of English in the world?

- In what way does literature and art allow us to respond to the unanswerable questions presented by philosophy, psychology, and religion? To what extend does art in general enrich our grasp of consciousness and mental experience? How might V. S. Ramachandran and Robert Orsi respond to Oscar Wilde's celebration of art as useless? How might they respond to the young boy's crisis in James Joyce's "Araby"?

Appendix

BREAKING DOWN ASSIGNMENTS:
A Guide for Students

As discussed in chapter three of this book, writing is a process. Good papers typically require careful planning, outlining, and multiple drafts. Turning a draft into a polished essay requires substantial revision, comprehensive editing, and meticulous proofreading. These principles are equally true regardless of the discipline one is writing in or the genre being written. Engaging in the full process of writing is necessary whether one is writing a personal narrative, an argumentative essay in the social sciences, or a lab report for a chemistry or biology class.

In the college classroom, regardless of discipline, the writing process is usually initiated by the instructor who provides the student—you—with a particular writing assignment or prompt. It is at this moment that the abstract *process* of writing becomes *concrete*. Here is where theory becomes practice.

It is this first, crucial moment, which is the subject of this brief appendix. When presented with a specific writing assignment by an instructor—such as the various writing assignments included throughout this book—the very first step is to get a clear sense of the size, scope, and nature of the assignment. To break down the assignment, in other words—to get a handle on what is expected in the finished product so that one can chart a clear and reasonable path toward that end.

This is more involved than it may seem at first, but a few minutes of analysis and the asking of a few poignant questions can often make all the difference between a good paper and one that fails to meet the expectations of the assignment and the instructor.

The first critical step in breaking down any assignment for a college class is to record in your notes any details provided about the assignment by the instructor. Writing assignments and prompts—such as the ones presented in this book—are, by necessity, somewhat universal, in that they can be shaped by a specific instructor into an assignment specifically geared toward meeting the needs of that particular instructor in that particular class at that particular time. Instructors will almost always address questions of length—how long should the essay be?—of format and documentation style—MLA? APA?—of research requirements—is research required? How much? What kind?—and, of course due date. Any instructions of this kind should be noted and adhered to by you. Nothing is more frustrating for both student and instructor to have an otherwise excellent paper be returned with a poor grade and a note that informs the student that *This was a great paper, but you did not meet the requirements for the assignment*. Perhaps you didn't have enough secondary sources? Perhaps you cited a Web page, but the instructor declared Web pages off limits? Perhaps you used MLA documentation style but the instructor specified APA?

Perhaps your paper was over a required two thousand words from beginning to end, but the instructor said that this word requirement was exclusive of the *Works Cited* page; but you had factored those words into your word count? There are countless things that can go wrong when these kinds of details are not noted right at the outset.

Thus, the first rule when preparing to write a paper for a college class is to pay careful attention to all details about the assignment presented by the instructor. If you miss something, or don't understand a particular instruction, do not guess. Ask questions. If you have to schedule an appointment with your instructor in order to get clarification on certain points, do so. The time and effort put into getting these details straight on the front end may solve numerous headaches and frustration later in the process.

Once the nature, size, scope, and requirements for the assignment are all clear, the next step is to turn one's attention to analyzing the prompt itself. What is being asked of the writer? What is the genre of the essay—is it to be an informative essay? Argumentative? Descriptive? Narrative? Something else? What will a successful essay on that prompt have to include?

To help illustrate the process of breaking down an assignment, you'll find sample analyses of five different writing assignments. Each sample is based on an actual writing assignment given in this book. These samples can serve as models for the kind of thinking that every student should do at the beginning of the process of writing a paper for a college classroom. You'll note that some of the advice is similar from one assignment to the next. Each assignment, each class, each instructor, is different, but some of the principles for good writing are universal, and apply in many different cases.

|

Francis Fukuyama, "Why We Should Worry"

Writing Assignment # 1: "Research the current laws and policies related to human cloning. Write an essay in which you set forth the state of current cloning policy. Then, argue for or against current policy, using as a framework some of the issues raised by Fukuyama."

Breaking Down the Assignment

From reading the assignment itself, you'll note that this assignment is designed to have you "research the current laws and policies related to human cloning" and "write an essay in which you set forth the state of current cloning policy." Thus, we know that this assignment is going to require some kind of library research. Because the assignment asks about *current laws and policies*, it would probably be a good idea to use the Internet as a guide to recent developments. Searching the Web for "cloning laws" and other phrases may help you discover some recent developments. But, of course, be careful to evaluate all Internet material with a critical eye in order to make sure that the information comes from a reliable source. You'll want to discuss methods of evaluating the relative merits of Web-based material with your instructor. You'll also note that this essay will have to inform your audience about the state of current cloning policy, so you'll have to make sure your information is up-to-date and relevant. Aside from thoroughly informing your reader about the existing legislation that governs cloning and cloning-related biotechnology, you must also "argue for or against current policy," using as a framework some of the issues raised by Fukuyama in "Why We Should Worry," the sixth chapter of his book *Our Posthuman Future*. Thus, you know that this essay is going to have to do at least three important and related tasks: (1) inform the audience about current policy, and make sure that your points are based in good, reliable research, and (2) take a stand either for or against the current policies, using arguments in order to convince your audience of the merits and strength of your position, and (3) make sure that as you build your argument, you relate what you have to say to issues raised by Fukuyama.

Working the Assignment

First, carefully read Fukuyama's chapter about the benefits of and possible objections to human biotechnology and provide a detailed description of his main argument and sub-arguments by answering the following questions:

- What implications does the term *eugenics* entail and why is it crucial to differentiate between historical and modern eugenics?
- What objections does Fukuyama invoke when discussing the different types of biomedical technologies?
- According to Fukuyama, should we worry about the future of biotechnology?

Second, after you highlight Fukuyama's main points, compare what you have learned from his chapter with what the current cloning policy stipulates. This is where you must do enough research to make sure you can write with confidence about current policy. Make sure that you follow whatever directions your instructor provides. How many sources must you locate? Are you allowed to use Web-based sources? As you compare what you have learned through your research to what you have read in Fukuyama, ask yourself if current legislation on the practice of genetic manipulation reflects some of Fukuyama's concerns regarding the future of human biogenetics. What are the prime justifications behind the policy?

And finally, you must critically evaluate both Fukuyama's claims and the premises of the current policy, and articulate your own stance on the topic. Do you agree with the current program of human cloning? You must justify your opinion by providing appropriate evidence and possible solutions, where applicable.

Drafting the Essay

When you are ready to begin drafting the essay, keep in mind that the *introduction* should begin with an attention grabber and frame the topic of your essay. Make sure it identifies your research question, asserts your main points, and briefly describes your methodology. Since you will be taking a stand on an issue in this essay, you will need to have a clearly articulated *thesis statement* located at an appropriate place in the essay. Generally, thesis statements will appear early in an essay, even in the introductory material, but this is a guideline, not a rule. The *body* of your essay should discuss, in great detail, your research question, as well as the research behind it. You should also use this section to describe others' arguments and build a strong case for your own. The *conclusion* should, in most cases, restate your research question, emphasize its relevance, and provide answers or solutions (that resulted from your investigations).

Specifications

Of course, it is important to make sure that you follow the directions given by your instructor in terms of length, number and type of sources to use, documentation style, and so forth. For example, your instructor may give instructions such as these for the assignment above: "This essay must be 6-8 pages (works cited page included) and should appear in 12 pt. Times New Roman font, double-spaced, with one-inch margins. It is highly recommended that you use a minimum of three sources to support your argument. Your essay should include in-text citations and a works cited page in correct MLA format. Also, make sure you attentively proofread your essay before turning it in." It will be important to follow these instructions as you research, outline, draft, revise, edit, and proofread your essay.

||

Paul Krugman, "Irrational Exuberance"

Writing Assignment #1: "Argue for or against Krugman's use of "evolutionary psychology," the idea that our instinctual behaviors are poorly adapted to the modern world. Use research to support your points, and if you disagree, what other explanation for the problems he deals with can you offer?"

Breaking Down the Assignment

From reading the assignment itself, you'll note that it is designed to have you "argue for or against Krugman's use of 'evolutionary psychology'" and write an essay in which you make a claim about whether "our instinctual behaviors are poorly adapted to the modern world." Thus, we know that the essay is going to require some kind of library research. Krugman is an economist, and economics is a social science. But his essay demonstrates that academic disciplines are not entirely separate from one another. They dovetail and relate in interesting ways. Krugman builds his argument by drawing on evolutionary biology, a physical science, and psychology, a different social science from his own. He uses the knowledge in these other disciplines and applies them to economics. Therefore, you will need to do some research in "evolutionary psychology." You will need to gain an understanding of what the term means, what major questions are involved, and what debates might be currently active. The Internet could be a good place to start, but, of course, be careful to evaluate all Internet sites to make sure the information comes from a reliable source. You'll want to discuss the relative merits of Web-based material with your instructor. From the Krugman essay, you learn that "evolutionary psychology" is a fairly new area of study, so you'll want to do some library research to make sure you understand it adequately. The critical question in the assignment, and the most interesting one, is whether "our instinctual behaviors are poorly adapted to the modern world." Here you will need to look back at the Krugman essay, with specific attention to how he applies the idea to economic or investment behavior. From research and a careful analysis of his argument, you should be able to write an essay that accomplishes three important related tasks. You will need to: (1) inform your audience about the important emerging discipline of "evolutionary psychology" and its relationship to other areas such as business and economics, and (2) take a stand for or against the claim that our instincts are poorly adapted to the modern world, using arguments in order to convince your audience of the merits and strength of your position, and (3) make sure that as you build your argument, you relate what you say to the claims about evolutionary psychology and economic behavior articulated by Krugman.

Working the Assignment

First, carefully read Krugman's "Irrational Exuberance," which deals with the application of evolutionary psychology to personal economic behavior. Provide a detailed description of his main argument and sub-arguments by answering the following questions:

- What are the implications of the evolutionary concepts of adaptability and natural selection as they relate to human economic and social behavior?

- What, if anything, is distinct about modern, civilized, technological society that is out of line with our instinctual behaviors?
- Can we rise above our instincts through the use of reason, thereby adapting to the modern world by other means? By implication, this is what Krugman invites us to do.

Second, after you highlight Krugman's main points, compare what you have learned from his chapter with what you have learned from your research on evolutionary psychology. This is where you must do enough research to make sure you can write with confidence about the concepts he considers. Make sure you follow whatever directions your instructor provides. How many sources must you locate? Are you allowed to use Web-based sources? As you compare what you have learned through your research to what you have read in Krugman, ask yourself if he applies evolutionary psychology accurately to economic behavior. Are there any other ways we might see it play out? What might we do to counteract the negative effects of our instinctual behavior?

And finally, you must critically evaluate both Krugman's claims and the concept of evolutionary psychology, and articulate your own stance on the topic. To what extent are we creatures of instinct and how much do we regularly use reason to control instinctual behavior? To what extent has instinct in the human species been replaced by reason, as the mind itself has evolved? You must justify your opinion by providing appropriate evidence and possible solutions, where applicable.

Drafting the Essay

As you begin drafting the essay, make sure to begin with a sentence or two that genuinely incites your reader's interest. This shouldn't be hard to do with this essay, since Krugman is exploring our most basic motivations. You might begin with a provocative claim challenging a common decision like buying an iPod, or you could begin with a rhetorical question. Your entire essay should center on your main idea, but you should probably have a clearly articulated thesis near the end of your first paragraph. Your introduction should give readers a sense of the methodology you will use to make your argument and review the major points you will make. In the body of the essay, you will marshal the evidence to prove those points, which might include real and hypothetical situations and scientific evidence derived from research. If you discover arguments to the contrary, you should cite them and legitimately refute them. Your conclusion should revisit your topic and thesis and consider the importance of the argument you have made.

Specifications

It is important to make sure that you follow the directions given by your instructor in terms of length, number and type of sources to use, documentation style, and so forth. For instance, for this paper assignment, your instructor might provide instructions like the following: "This essay must be 5-7 pages (not including bibliographic material) and should appear in 10 pt. Courier font, double-spaced, with one-inch margins. You should have a minimum of five sources to support your argument. Your essay should include in-text citations and a bibliographic page in APA format. Also, be sure to proofread your essay two or three times before turning it in." It is important that you follow these instructions to the letter.

III

Martin Luther King, Jr., "Letter from a Birmingham Jail"

Writing Assignment #1: "Explore the relationship between King's ideas and those of Henry David Thoreau. In what way does King expand, develop, and apply the principles he learned from his nineteenth-century predecessor?"

Breaking Down the Assignment

From reading the assignment itself, you'll note that this assignment is designed to have you "explore the relationship between King's ideas and those of Henry David Thoreau." You also must consider how King "expands," "develops," and "applies" those ideas. Thus, we know that this paper is going to involve comparing and contrasting both writers, with an emphasis on comparison. Your major task will be to carefully read and comprehend the details of each argument. You should read each work more than once. The first time should be for general comprehension (beginning with the head note), and the second time you should use a pen or a highlighter, annotating to identify main ideas and important points. As you read and annotate, make sure to identify areas in which King and Thoreau agree, as well as areas in which King is "expanding" and "applying." Use these words in your margins. Come to terms with the authors on your own by working with the texts. You will probably want to do some research on both works as well. It is best to consult sources from your college library, whether they are in print or come from a computer source under library subscription. You may decide to consult sources on the Internet. In that case, always be careful to evaluate all Internet material with a critical eye in order to make sure the information comes from a reliable source. You'll want to discuss methods of evaluating the merits of Web-based material with your instructor. If written well, your essay will accomplish a number of purposes: it will inform your reader of the main ideas each writer presents; it will demonstrate that major thinkers draw from the past and critically reinterpret it; it will show that ideas in the academic and philosophical realms have practical application in society; and, it will demonstrate in some detail how King applied his own and Thoreau's concepts. Read and research in order to accomplish these goals, though you may choose to emphasize some more than others, always under the guidance of your instructor.

Working the Assignment

First, carefully consider the issues raised by both authors as they relate to human rights in a social context. You can do so initially by reading King and Thoreau, and you can spend some time thinking about the relevance of their concerns to your own life and social circumstances. Consider the following questions in light of your reading:

- In a civilized society, how much power must the individual concede to the rule of law, whether it is defined locally or constitutionally? Remember, the meaning of human rights as defined by the constitution are continually debated by the best legal minds.

- In a country that is presumably built on the rights of the individual, what are the practical limits of individual rights, especially as they relate to the rights of social groups (races, genders, sexualities, communities, states)?

- Under what circumstances does an individual have an ethical obligation to act to correct an injustice, regardless of social convention or the law?

Second, after you highlight the main points in both works, consider the specific manner in which King extrapolates and applies Thoreau to the Civil Rights Movement. What does he add? This is where you may be required to research the movement itself and King's participation in it. Make sure you follow whatever instructions your instructor provides. How many sources must you locate? Are you allowed to use Web-based sources? As you combine what you have learned from your research and your reading of Thoreau and King, ask yourself this question: In terms of their methodology for social protest, is it accurate to say that Thoreau is the theorist and King the practitioner? Or does King modify and develop social theories in the act of practicing them?

And finally, you must critically evaluate the claims of both writers, considering the potential results if their thoughts were consistently implemented. King argues that action is necessary, that those who say we should move slowly on civil rights are incorrect. What other methods might work?

Drafting the Essay

As you begin drafting the essay, inspire your reader's interest in the first few sentences by addressing the importance of the concerns King and Thoreau raise. They are dealing with civil rights, perhaps the most defining social issue of our time, so you should be able to find current situations that will bring your reader into the essay. Consider a social group that you think has been denied the rights and freedoms they deserve. Or recall a situation we all know of where civil rights have been denied. The introduction should bring the issue to the foreground in a dramatic way, and it should establish in basic terms the way King has re-envisioned Thoreau. It should review the major points you will make, concluding with a clearly articulated *thesis statement.* The body of your essay should make an argument based on evidence from historical and journalistic sources. Your conclusion should revisit the argument and make a claim about its social relevance.

Specifications

It is important to make sure that you follow the directions given by your instructor in terms of length, number and type of sources to use, documentation style, and so forth. For instance, an instructor might provide the following details for the assignment above: "This essay must be 7-9 pages (including bibliographic page) and should appear in a 12 pt. Arial font, double-spaced, with one-inch margins. You should have at least seven sources to support your arguments, and you should use APA or MLA format. Choose one or the other. Do not mix them. Proofread the essay at least twice before turning it in." It will be important that you follow these instructions carefully.

IV

Emily Bernard, "Teaching the N-Word"

Writing Assignment #2: "Modeling your own writing after that of Bernard, draft an essay in which you analyze a particularly difficult social issue—related to race, religion, politics, sexuality, or some other issue of contemporary interest—by relating a story from your own life, or the life of someone close to you. Use dialogue and description when you are able. We recommend, of course, that you choose a story and an issue that you don't mind sharing with an audience. Avoid focusing on some issue of such personal gravity that you might regret revealing it to an audience. By telling your story, try to get your audience to see a particularly difficult issue in a new way."

Breaking Down the Assignment

There is a great deal of information contained in the wording of the assignment itself. A good first step when encountering a lengthy assignment is to make a list of the requirements and expectations contained in the assignment itself. Here, we note the following requirements:

1. The essay should be modeled after Bernard's;
2. Its topic should be related to a difficult social issue;
3. The essay should be built around a story from your own life, or the life of someone close to you;
4. The essay should contain dialogue and description;
5. The author (you) should be wary of revealing overly-personal information;
6. The goal is to try to get your audience to see a social issue in a new light.

What is most notable about this assignment, at first glance, is that other than *modeling* your essay after Bernard's, it does not require that you treat the same issue as Bernard, nor must you cite Bernard's essay in your own. But you are required to model your essay after Bernard's. What this means is that you should pay attention to the style of her essay, the methods she uses to communicate with her audience, and the structure of her essay. Note, for instance, that she relates a story from her own life, and uses dialogue and interesting description to set the scenes. Bernard reveals a good deal about herself in the course of her essay. In selecting your story, make sure you pick a story that you won't mind sharing with others in class or with the instructor in the class. If you can't think of a moment from your own life to talk about, the assignment allows flexibility for you to pick a story from the life of someone close to you. Either way—whether it's your own story or someone else's—the goal is to try to get your audience to think in new and interesting ways about a particular social problem, whether it's related to race, or gender, or poverty, or religion, or politics, or something else.

Working the Assignment

First, read Bernard's essay, "Teaching the N-Word" carefully. Pay close attention to the structure of the essay. Then, brainstorm about possible moments in your life (or the life of someone close to you) that you could use as the basis for your own essay. When you come up with a possible moment, as: yourself questions such as, In what ways has my experience changed me? Why did I choose to write about this particular issue? Why is this particular issue important to me? What do I want my audience to know about my experiences? What is the purpose of my essay and what do I want to achieve by writing it? Make sure, of course, that the story you want to tell has a clear relation to a problematic social issue.

Second, when you have settled on your story and the social issue you wish to illuminate through telling your story, make some notes to yourself—and use those notes to prepare an outline for your essay—about the kinds of details and moments that need to be highlighted in your essay.

Drafting the Essay

When you are ready to begin drafting your essay, make sure you give some careful thought to the manner in which your essay should be structured. Should it be chronological, for instance? Or should it jump back and forth in time, as in Bernard's essay? Where can you make use of dialogue and description? Where do you need exposition? How will you get the reader's attention? Make sure that you keep your essay limited to and focused on a single social issue. Give some consideration to your audience: Who are you writing for and why? How can you tell your story in such a manner that it will have the most impact on your particular audience? As you draft your essay, don't be afraid to reveal your thoughts, feelings, and impressions if they are relevant and facilitate your audience's response and understanding.

Specifications

It is important to make sure that you follow the directions given by your instructor in terms of length, number and type of sources to use (if any are required), documentation style, and so forth. For instance, an instructor might give the following details about the assignment above: "Your paper should be between 5-6 double-spaced typed pages and it should not use any outside/library sources."

V

Arguments for the Existence of God

Writing Assignment #2: "Select one of the three arguments and draft an essay in which you attempt to explain or teach the argument to a general audience. For the purpose of this assignment, assume that members of your audience have high school diplomas, but likely have no familiarity with the argument."

Breaking Down the Assignment

As is noted in the wording of the assignment itself, for this essay you are required to select one of the three arguments for the existence of God (made by St. Anselm, St. Thomas Aquinas, and William Paley respectively) and write an essay in which you attempt to explain or teach the argument to a general audience. We are even given some information about that audience: we are to assume they are somewhat educated, but are not in all likelihood college graduates and, in any event, do not have any familiarity with the argument already. This means, of course, that you are not writing for your classmates, nor your instructor. One of the keys to success in this essay is that it be geared toward a specific, predetermined audience of people who are not you or your peers. Because these arguments are philosophically complex, we can infer that one of the things this assignment is testing you on is your ability to break down a complex argument and communicate it to an audience that is not familiar with the argument and may or may not have much experience analyzing philosophical arguments. Note, also, that the assignment *does not require* you to agree or disagree with the argument. This essay is not argumentative in nature. Instead, it is purely expository, assessing your skills at breaking an argument down and teaching it to others.

Working the Assignment

First, you should spend some time reading each of the three arguments for the existence of God with great care. Read each argument several times, making notes as you go, until you feel confident that you understand each argument. Once you feel confident that you comprehend each argument, select the one you wish to focus on in your essay.

Second, having selected your argument—whether ontological, cosmological, or teleological—take some scrap paper, and go through the text again. Rewrite in your own words each sentence, forcing yourself to pick apart each nuance of the argument. The key here is to build the kind of detailed knowledge of the argument (What is the author trying to prove? What are his premises? What are his assumptions? What kinds of evidence and/ or support does the author use to prove his thesis?) that a *teacher* of the argument should have. Sometimes we never realize just how thin our knowledge of something is till we are asked to teach it to someone else.

Given the proliferation of knowledge across the Internet, and the seemingly easy access one has to information about nearly everything, the temptation at this point may be to search the Web for sites that essentially do this work for you. Resist the temptation if you can. To take someone else's explanation of the ontological argument and present it as your own is plagiarism. But, more importantly, you will have relied on someone else to do the thinking for you, which is certainly not in the spirit of this assignment.

And, finally, before you begin to draft your essay, take some time to brainstorm strategies for successfully teaching the argument under consideration to your general audience. What analogies might help? Could you relate the argument to something in your audience's real-world experience? Would an anecdote help? What terms do you need to define? What terms can you assume your audience will know? Perhaps it might be useful at this point to develop your ideas into an outline to serve as a guide as you draft your essay.

Drafting the Essay

When drafting this *essay of explanation*, the difficult part is probably not in determining what the author is trying to prove: they are all arguments for the existence of God, after all. Nor is the difficult part determining whether you agree or disagree with the argument. You are not expected to take a position in this essay and defend it. The difficulty in this essay is twofold: (1) analyzing the argument itself so that all of its underlying assumptions, stated and implied premises, and its conclusions become clear to you, and (2) coming up with the right combination of rhetorical strategies to communicate the results of your analysis to your particular audience. In an essay of this nature, it is important that in the *introduction* of your essay, you engage your audience and get them interested in the topic, which you should introduce early in the paper. The *body* of your essay should address in great detail the techniques as well as the type of evidence that the writer employs to persuade his audience. A thorough explication of the argument, coupled with creative analogies, anecdotes, and other rhetorical strategies designed to make the complex understandable will likely comprise the bulk of the body of your essay. Use a combination of direct references to the text, well-constructed summary statements and paraphrases, and explanatory illustrations to teach the different components of the argument at hand. You might consider using the *conclusion* of your essay to offer some general thoughts about what you see as the significance of the argument. Perhaps you could leave the audience with a question to ponder.

Specifications

It is important to make sure that you follow the directions given by your instructor in terms of length, number and type of sources to use, documentation style, and so forth. For instance, your instructor may provide details such as the following: "This essay should not exceed 5 pages in length. Please double space your pages with one-inch margins. No research is required to summarize and address the writer's argument. Your essay should include in-text citations and a works cited page in correct MLA format. Be sure to proofread, for every grammar or mechanical error in the essay will count as five points off your total grade for the essay." For this instructor, proofreading carefully is mandatory!

Table of Contents by Rhetorical Mode

ILLUSTRATION

COMPARISON AND CONTRAST

ANALOGY

DEFINITION

PROCESS ANALYSIS

CAUSAL ANALYSIS

ARGUMENT AND PERSUASION

Text Credits

Chapter 2

Excerpt from, "The Coming Age." From *From Dawn to Decadence* by Jacques Barzun, pp. 799-802. Copyright © 2000 by Jacques Barzun. Reprinted by permission of HarperCollins Publishers.

Chapter 3

Basic Subject Search. Basic Subject Search from The University of Memphis Libraries. Used by permission.

ProQuest advanced search. The screenshot and its contents are published with permission of ProQuest LLC. Further reproduction is prohibited without permission. Inquiries may be made to ProQuest LLC, 789 E. Eisenhower Pkwy, Ann Arbor, MI 48106-1346 USA. Email: info@proquest.com; www.proquest.com.

Wilson Web search. Wilson Web search reprinted with permission from EBSCO Publishing.

Chapter 4

"Scientific Literacy, What It Is, Why It's Important, and Why Scientists Think We Don't Have It," abridged as submitted. Copyright © 1996 from *Naked Science: Anthropological Inquiry into Boundaries, Power, and Knowledge* by Bjorn Claeson, Emily Martin, Wendy Richardson, Monica Schoch-Shana, and Karen-Sue Taussig. Reproduced by permission of Taylor and Francis Group, LLC, a division of Informa Plc.

"The Historical Structure of Scientific Discovery" abridged as submitted. From "The Historical Structure of Scientific Discovery" by Thomas Kuhn in *Science*, New Series, Volume 136, Issue 3518. Copyright © 1962. Used by permission from the American Association for the Advancement of Science.

Chapter 18, abridged as submitted. From *Against Method*, Fourth Edition, by Paul Feyerabend. Copyright © 2010 Verso. Used by permission.

"Unraveling the DNA Myth" abridged as submitted, text only. "Unraveling the DNA Myth" by Barry Commoner. Copyright © 2002 by *Harper's Magazine*. All rights reserved. Reproduced from the February issue by special permission.

"Why We Should Worry" abridged as submitted, from "In light of the possible . . . " to ". . . " would inflict harm on their children." Excerpt from "Why We Should Worry" from *Our Posthuman Future: Consequences of the Biotechnology Revolution* by Francis Fukuyama. Copyright © 2002 by Francis Fukuyama. Reprinted by permission of Farrar, Straus and Giroux, LLC.

"The Case Against Perfection" abridged as submitted. Excerpted from Michael J. Sandel, "The Case Against Perfection," originally published in the *Atlantic Monthly*, April 2004. For an extended version of this essay, see Michael J. Sandel, *The Case Against Perfection*, Harvard University Press, 2007. Used by permission.

Excerpt from "The Selfless Gene." "The Selfless Gene" by Olivia Judson. Copyright © 2007 by Olivia Judson. Originally appeared in *The Atlantic*, October 2007. Reprinted by permission of Georges Borchardt, Inc., on behalf of the author.

"A New Theory of the Universe" abridged as submitted. Reprinted from *The American Scholar*, Volume 76, No. 3, Summer 2007. Copyright © 2007 by the author. Reprinted by permission.

"My God Problem—And Theirs." Reprinted from *The American Scholar*, Volume 73, No. 2, Summer 2004. Copyright © 2004 by the author. Reprinted by permission.

Chapter 5

Excerpt from "Maid to Order." Excerpted from "Maid to Order" by Barbara Ehrenreich originally from *Harper's Magazine*, April 2000, © 2000. Used by permission.

"Economic Freedom and Political Freedom" excerpt from "The Relation between Economic Freedom and Political Freedom." From "The Relation between Economic Freedom and Political Freedom" by Milton Friedman in *Capitalism and Freedom*. Copyright © 1962, 1982, 2002, University of Chicago Press. Used by permission.

"Leadership: Warts and All" (text only). "Leadership: Warts and All" by Barbara Kellerman from *Harvard Business Review*, January 2004. Copyright © 2004. Used by permission of Harvard Business School Publishing.

"Seven Habits of Highly Defective Investors" from Fortune, December 29, 1997 and "The Ice Age Cometh" from Fortune, May 25, 1998. "Seven Habits of Highly Defective Investors" by Paul Krugman

Chapter 6

Chapter 7

Chapter 8

Chapter 1, "From Culture to Hegemony." From *Subculture: The Meaning of Style*, by Dick Hebdige, Copyright © 2002 Routledge. Reproduced by permission of Taylor and Francis Books UK.

Setting the Record Straight. From *Understanding Comics*, by Scott McCloud. Copyright © 1993, 1994 by Scott McCloud. Reprinted by permission of HarperCollins Publishers.

"What's Good About Bad Comics, What's Bad About Good Comics" abridged as submitted. Abridged from *Reading Comics*, by Douglas Wolk. Copyright © 2008 Douglas Wolk. Reprinted by permission of Da Capo Press, a member of the Perseus Books Group.

Excerpt from *The Greatest of Marlys*, abridged as submitted. From *The Greatest of Marlys*, by Lynda Barry. Used by permission.

From Chapter 9, "Public Use/Private State," abridged as submitted. Susan Willis, "Public Use/Private State," in *Inside the Mouse: Work and Play at Disney World*, The Project on Disney, pp. 180-198. Copyright, 1995, Duke University Press. All rights reserved. Reprinted by permission of the publisher, www.dukeupress.edu.

"How Has the Culture of TV (and TV-Watching) Changed?" by Noel Murray and Scott Tobias from *The Onion*, June 18, 2010. Reprinted with permission of THE ONION. Copyright © 2011, by *Onion, Inc.* www.theonion.com.

"Faux Friendship" by William Deresiewicz from *Chronicle of Higher Education*, December 6, 2009. Reprinted by permission of the author.

Chapter 9

"Neuroscience: The New Philosophy" excerpted as submitted. "Neuroscience—The New Philosophy," from *A Brief Tour of Human Consciousness*, by V. S. Ramachandran, copyright © 2004 by V. S. Ramachandran. Used by permission of Penguin, a division of Penguin Group (USA) Inc.

"Computing Machinery and Intelligence" abridged as submitted. From A. M. Turing, "Computing Machinery and Intelligence" from *Mind: A Quarterly Review*, October 1950, Volume LIX, No. 236, pp. 433-460, by permission of Oxford University Press.

"Universalism and Particularism in Religion from an African Perspective" abridged as submitted. From *Cultural Universals and Particulars: An African Perspective*, by Kwasi Wiredu. Copyright © 1996 Indiana University Press. Reprinted with permission of Indiana University Press.

"When 2+2=5" abridged as submitted. Reprinted from *The American Scholar*, Volume 76, No. 2, Spring

2007. Copyright © 2007 by the author. Reprinted by permission.

"The Law of Accelerating Returns" adapted as submitted, text only. Adapted from "The Law of Accelerating Returns" by Ray Kurzweil, http://kurzweilai.net. Used by permission.

Chapter 10

Excerpt from Chapter 2, "In the Brown Study," from *Brown: The Last Discovery of America*, by Richard Rodriguez, copyright © 2002 by Richard Rodriguez. Used by permission of Viking Penguin, a division of Penguin Group (USA) Inc.

"Grant and Lee: A Study in Contrasts" by Bruce Catton. Copyright U.S. Capitol Historical Society. All rights reserved.

Rituals: A Prayer, a Candle, and a Notebook. "Rituals: A Prayer, a Candle, and a Notebook" from *Woman in Front of the Sun*, by Judith Ortiz Cofer. Copyright © 2000 Judith Ortiz Cofer. Used by permission of The University of Georgia Press.

"The Language of Dreams" abridged as submitted. From "The Language of Dreams" by Belle Yang from *Becoming American* edited by Meri Nana-Ama Danquah, copyright © 2000. Used by permission of the author.

"Prologue": "The Death of Josseline" by Margaret Regan. Copyright © 2009 Margaret Regan. Reprinted by permission of Beacon Press, Boston.

"A Muslim Leader in Brooklyn, Reconciling 2 Worlds," by Andrea Elliott from *The New York Times*, March 5, 2006, © 2006 *The New York Times*. All rights reserved. Used by permission and protected by the Copyright Laws of the United States. The printing, copying, redistribution, or retransmission of this Content without express written permission is prohibited.

Chapter 11

"What Global Language?" abridged as submitted. "What Global Language?" by Barbara Wallraff abridged from *Atlantic Monthly*, November 2000. Used by permission of Inkwell Management as agent for Barbara Wallraff.

"Shakespeare's Sister." From *A Room of One's Own*, by Virginia Woolf, copyright 1929 by Harcourt, Inc. and renewed 1957 by Leonard Woolf, reprinted by permission of Houghton Mifflin Harcourt Publishing Group.

"The Management of Grief," from *The Middleman and Other Stories*, copyright © 1988 by Bharati Mukherjee. Used by permission of Grove/Atlantic, Inc.

Photo Credits

Index